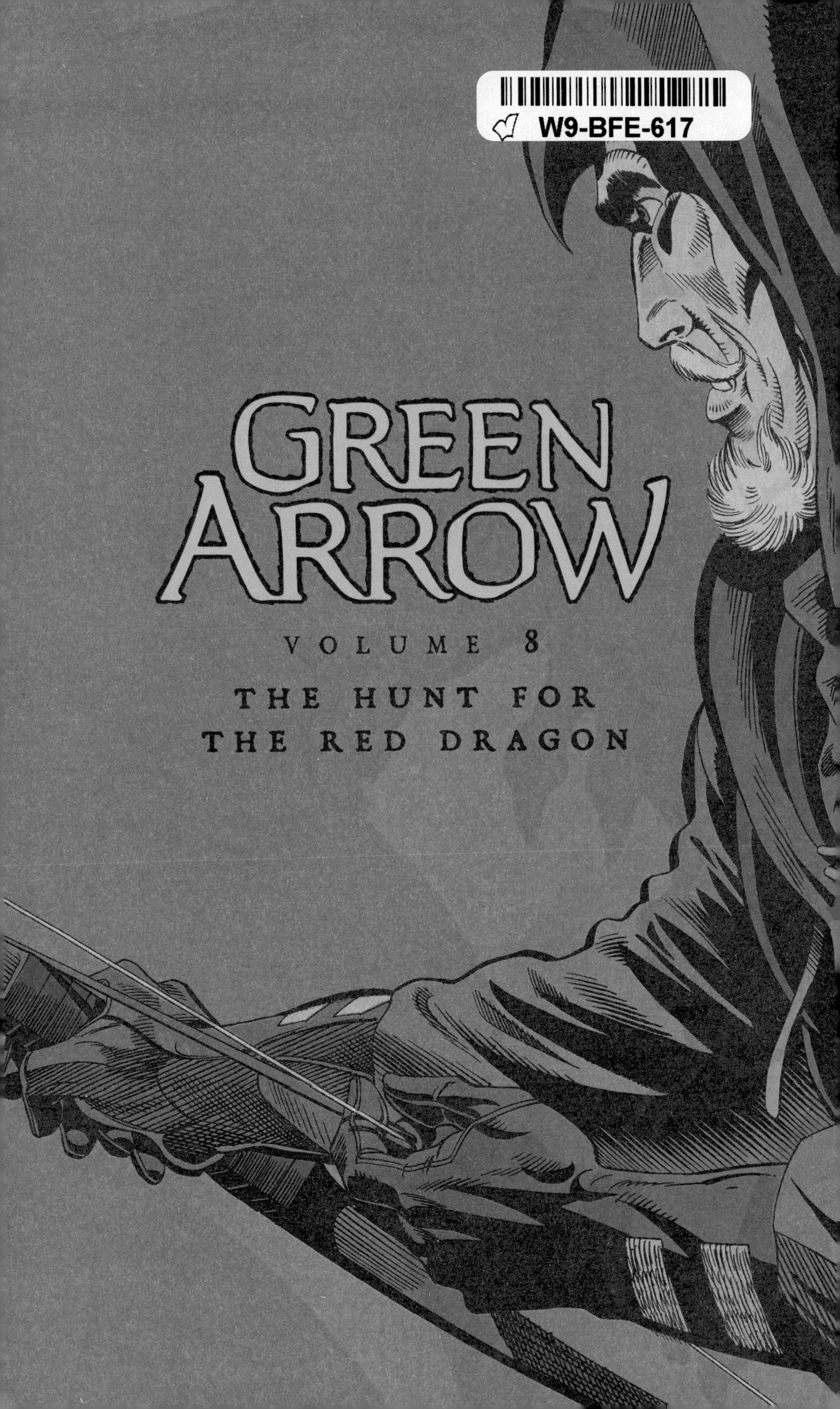

GREEN ARROW

VOLUME 8

THE HUNT FOR THE RED DRAGON

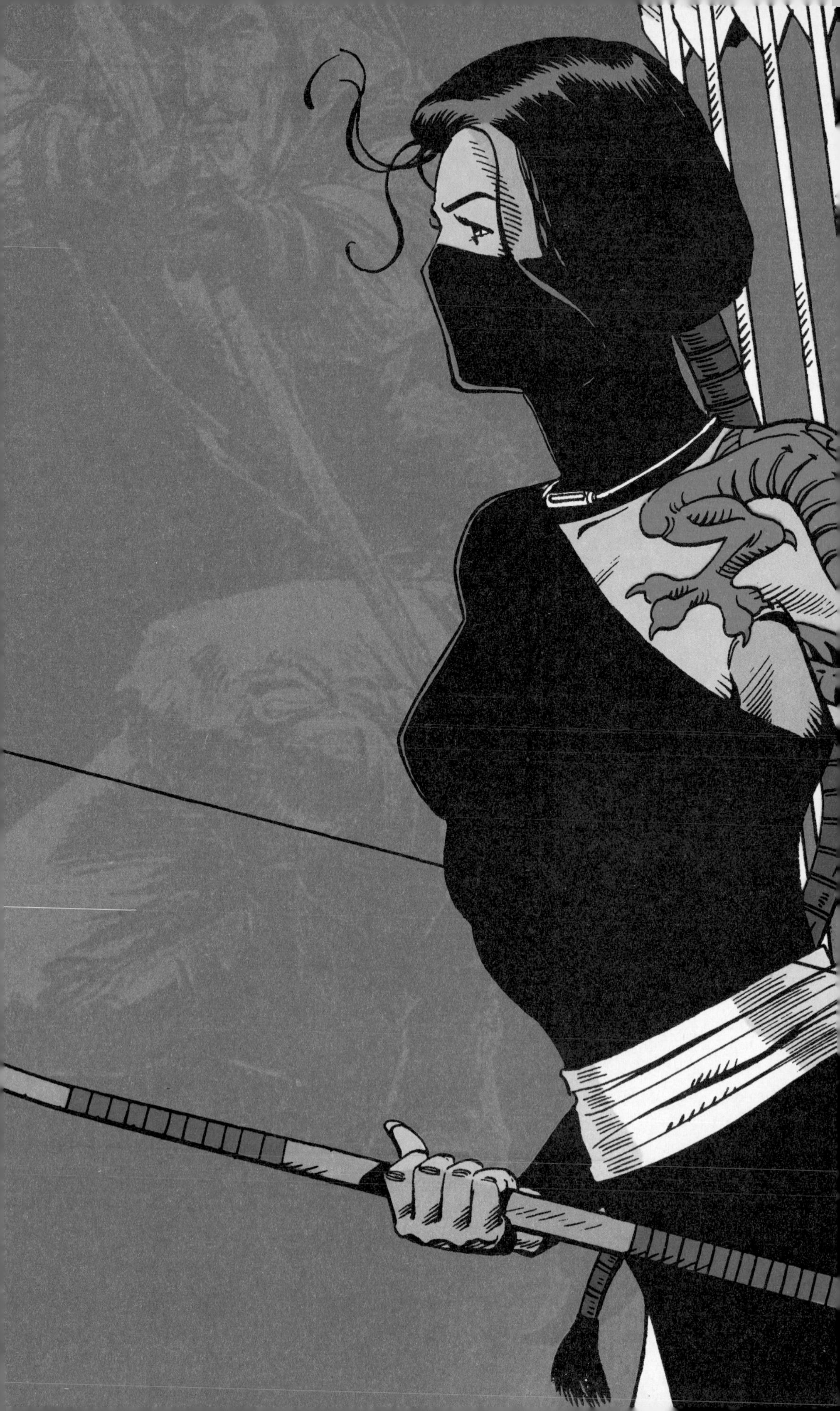

GREEN ARROW

VOLUME 8
THE HUNT FOR
THE RED DRAGON

MIKE GRELL
Writer

RICK HOBERG
FRANK SPRINGER
Pencillers

JOHN NYBERG
PABLO MARCOS
Inkers

JULIA LACQUEMENT
Colorist

STEVE HAYNIE
Letterer

MIKE GRELL
Collection and Series Cover Art

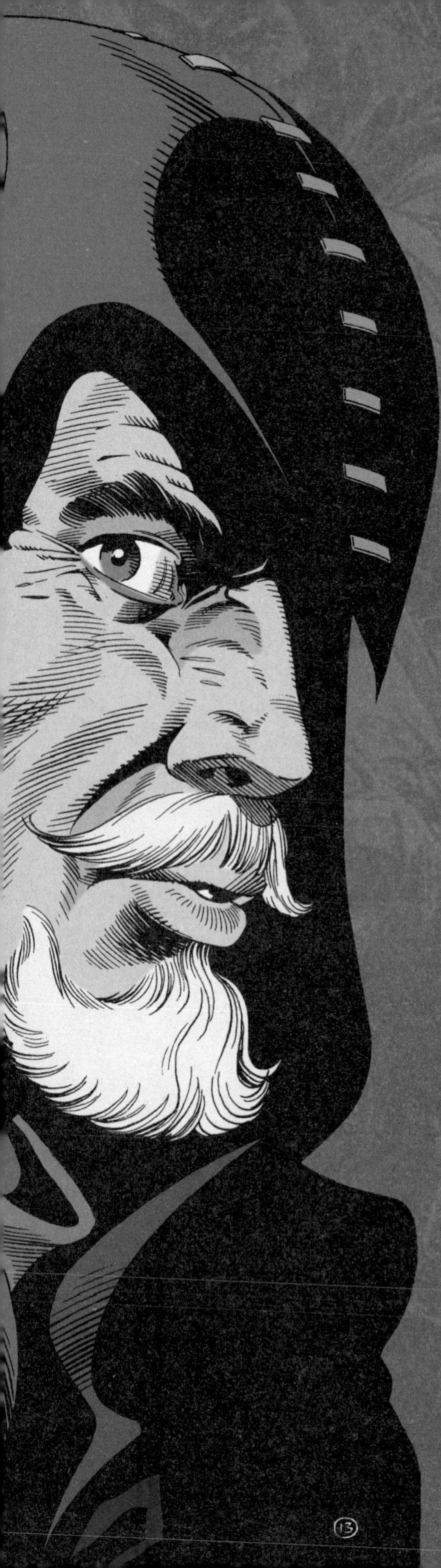

Mike Gold Editor – Original Series
Katie Main Associate Editor – Original Series
Jeb Woodard Group Editor – Collected Editions
Suzannah Rowntree Editor – Collected Edition
Steve Cook Design Director – Books
Damian Ryland Publication Design

Bob Harras Senior VP – Editor-in-Chief, DC Comics

Diane Nelson President
Dan DiDio Publisher
Jim Lee Publisher
Geoff Johns President & Chief Creative Officer
Amit Desai Executive VP – Business & Marketing Strategy, Direct to Consumer & Global Franchise Management
Sam Ades Senior VP – Direct to Consumer
Bobbie Chase VP – Talent Development
Mark Chiarello Senior VP – Art, Design & Collected Editions
John Cunningham Senior VP – Sales & Trade Marketing
Anne DePies Senior VP – Business Strategy, Finance & Administration
Don Falletti VP – Manufacturing Operations
Lawrence Ganem VP – Editorial Administration & Talent Relations
Alison Gill Senior VP – Manufacturing & Operations
Hank Kanalz Senior VP – Editorial Strategy & Administration
Jay Kogan VP – Legal Affairs
Thomas Loftus VP – Business Affairs
Jack Mahan VP – Business Affairs
Nick J. Napolitano VP – Manufacturing Administration
Eddie Scannell VP – Consumer Marketing
Courtney Simmons Senior VP – Publicity & Communications
Jim (Ski) Sokolowski VP – Comic Book Specialty Sales & Trade Marketing
Nancy Spears VP – Mass, Book, Digital Sales & Trade Marketing

GREEN ARROW VOLUME 8: THE HUNT FOR THE RED DRAGON

DC Comics 2900 West Alameda Ave. Burbank, CA 91505

Printed by LSC Communications, Owensville, MO, USA. 4/14/17.
First Printing. ISBN: 978-1-4012-6903-6

Library of Congress Cataloging-in-Publication Data is available.

PEFC
PEFC/29-31-337
PEFC Certified
Printed on paper from sustainably managed forests, controlled sources
www.pefc.org

TABLE OF CONTENTS

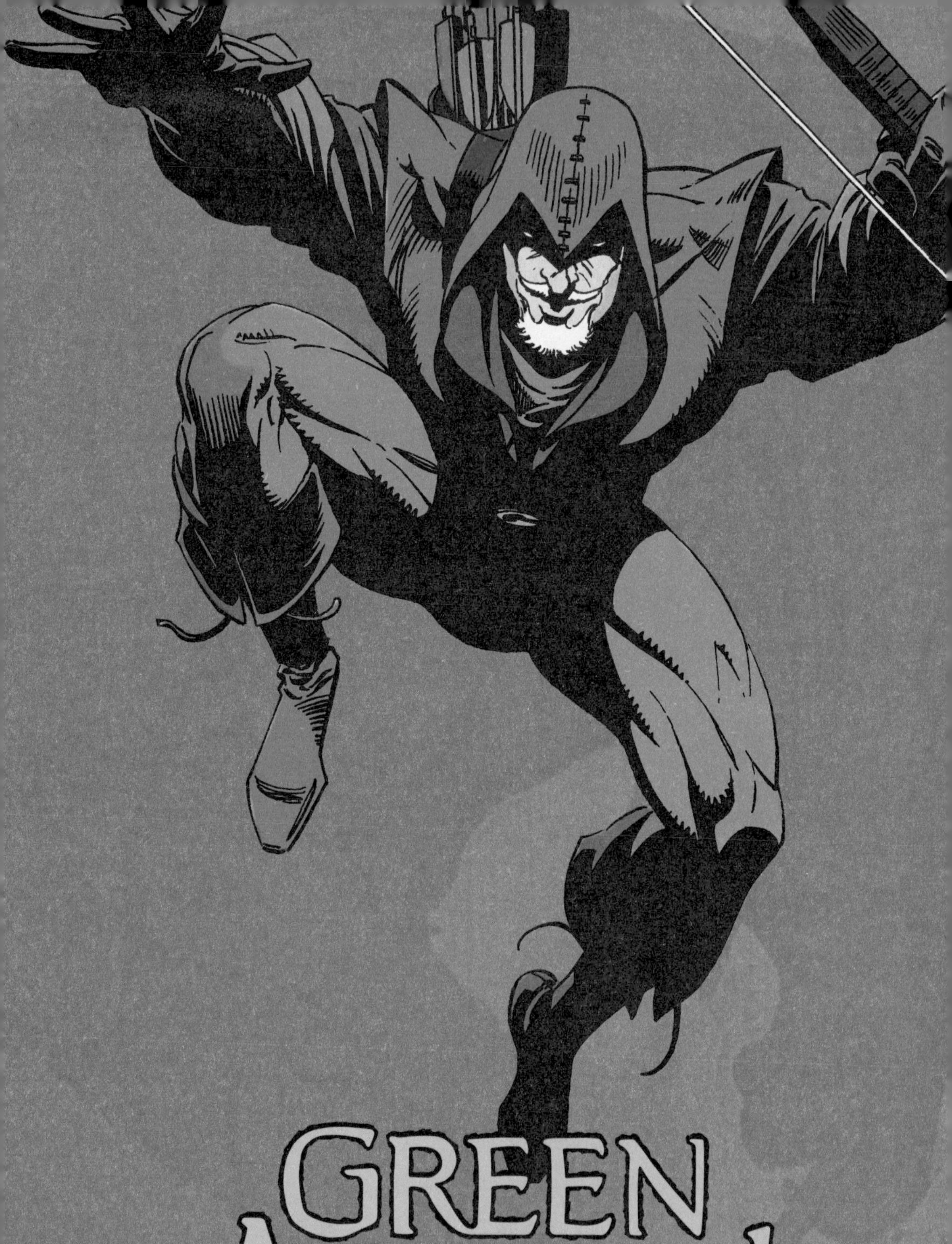

GREEN ARROW

HOMECOMING

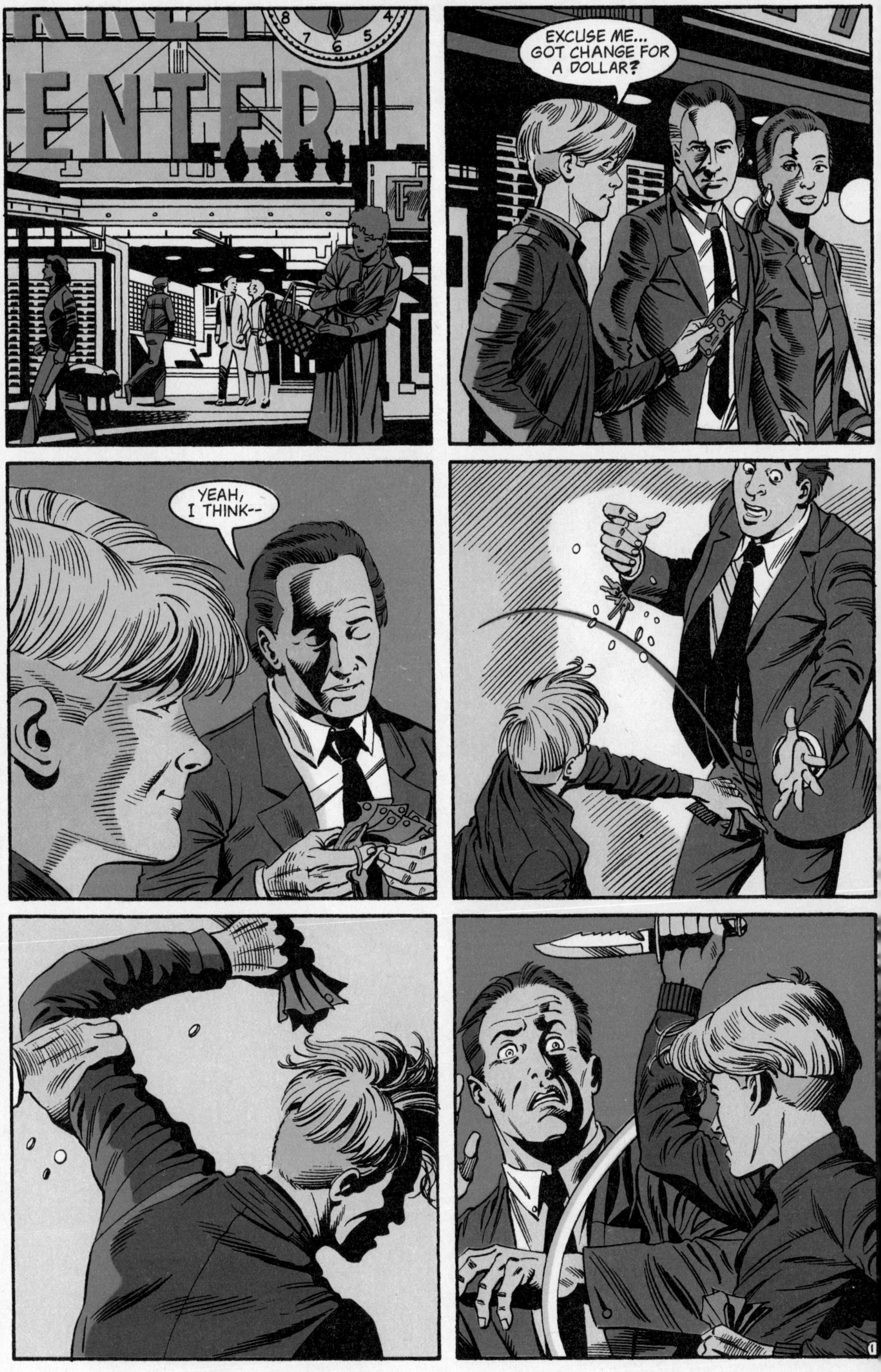
ENTER
EXCUSE ME... GOT CHANGE FOR A DOLLAR?
YEAH, I THINK--

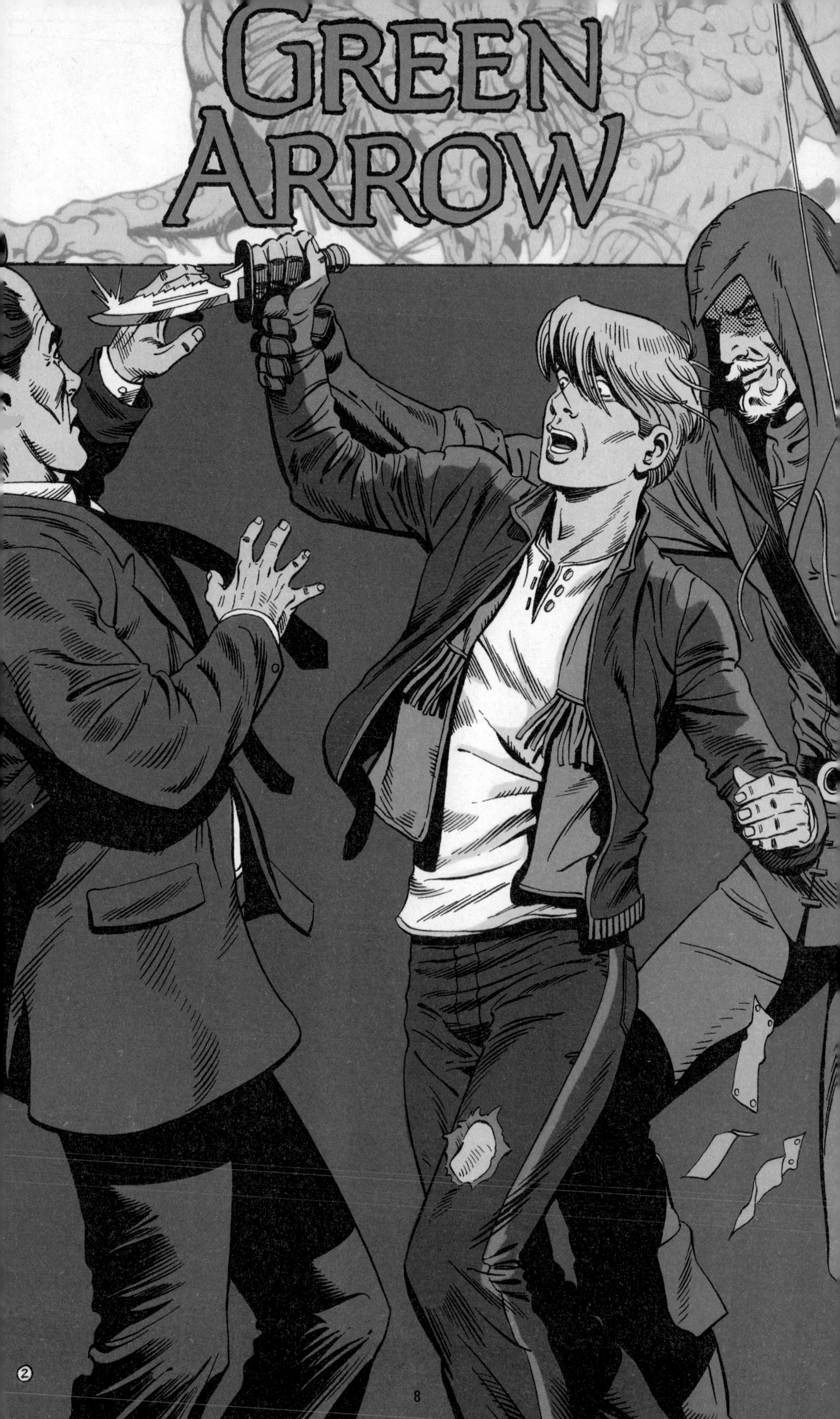
GREEN ARROW

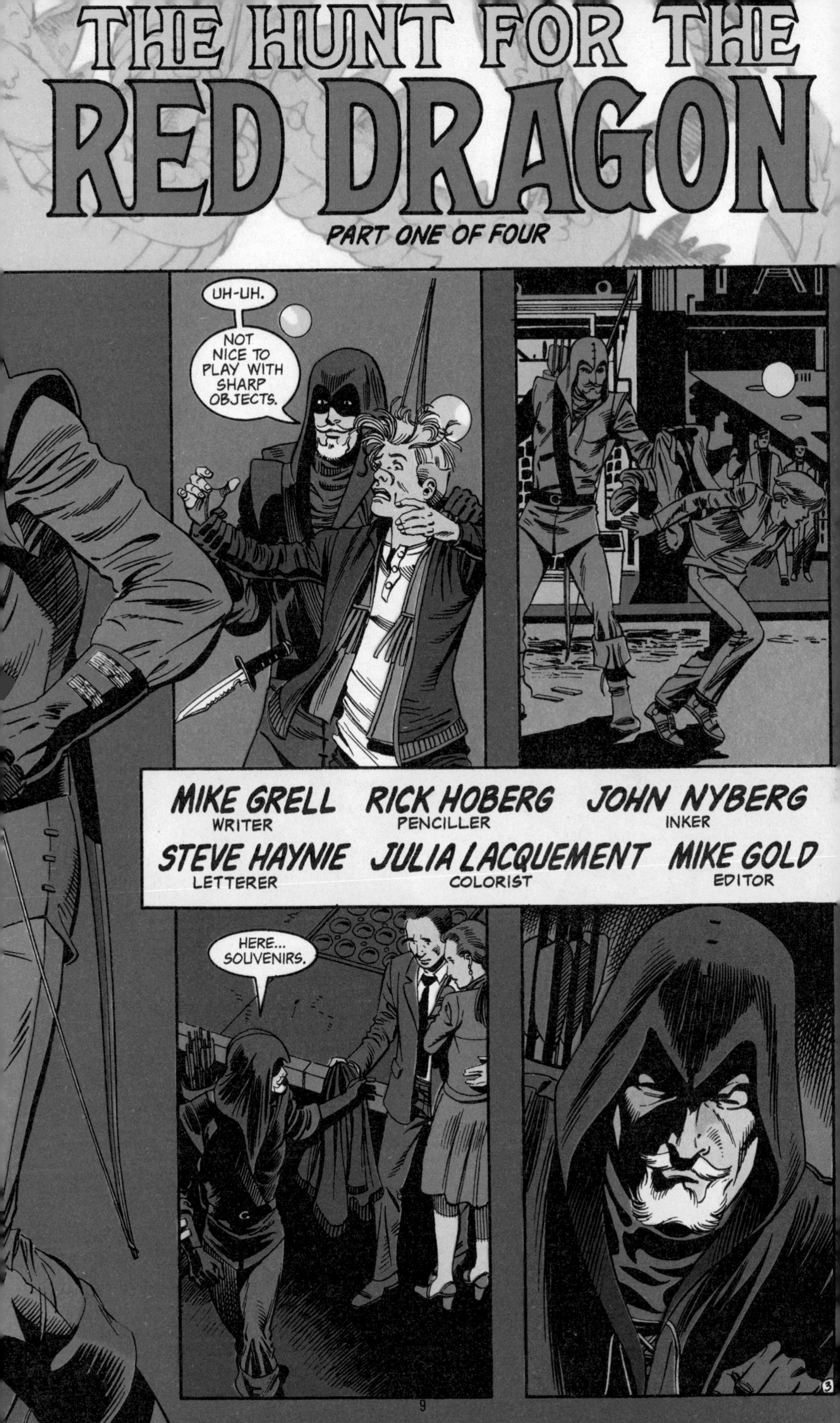
THE HUNT FOR THE
RED DRAGON
PART ONE OF FOUR
UH-UH.
NOT NICE TO PLAY WITH SHARP OBJECTS.
MIKE GRELL WRITER
RICK HOBERG PENCILLER
JOHN NYBERG INKER
STEVE HAYNIE LETTERER
JULIA LACQUEMENT COLORIST
MIKE GOLD EDITOR
HERE... SOUVENIRS.
3

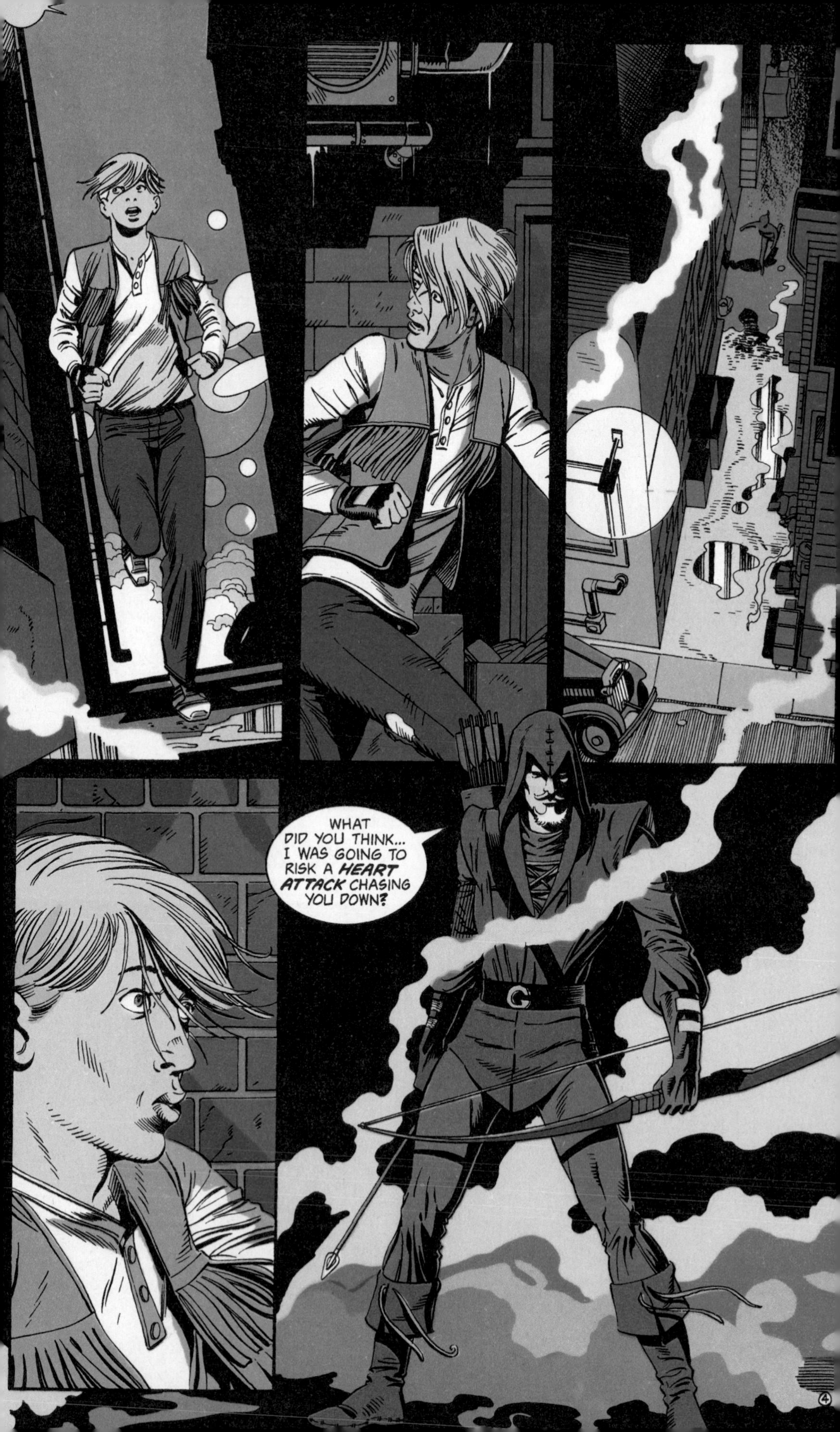
WHAT DID YOU THINK... I WAS GOING TO RISK A HEART ATTACK CHASING YOU DOWN?

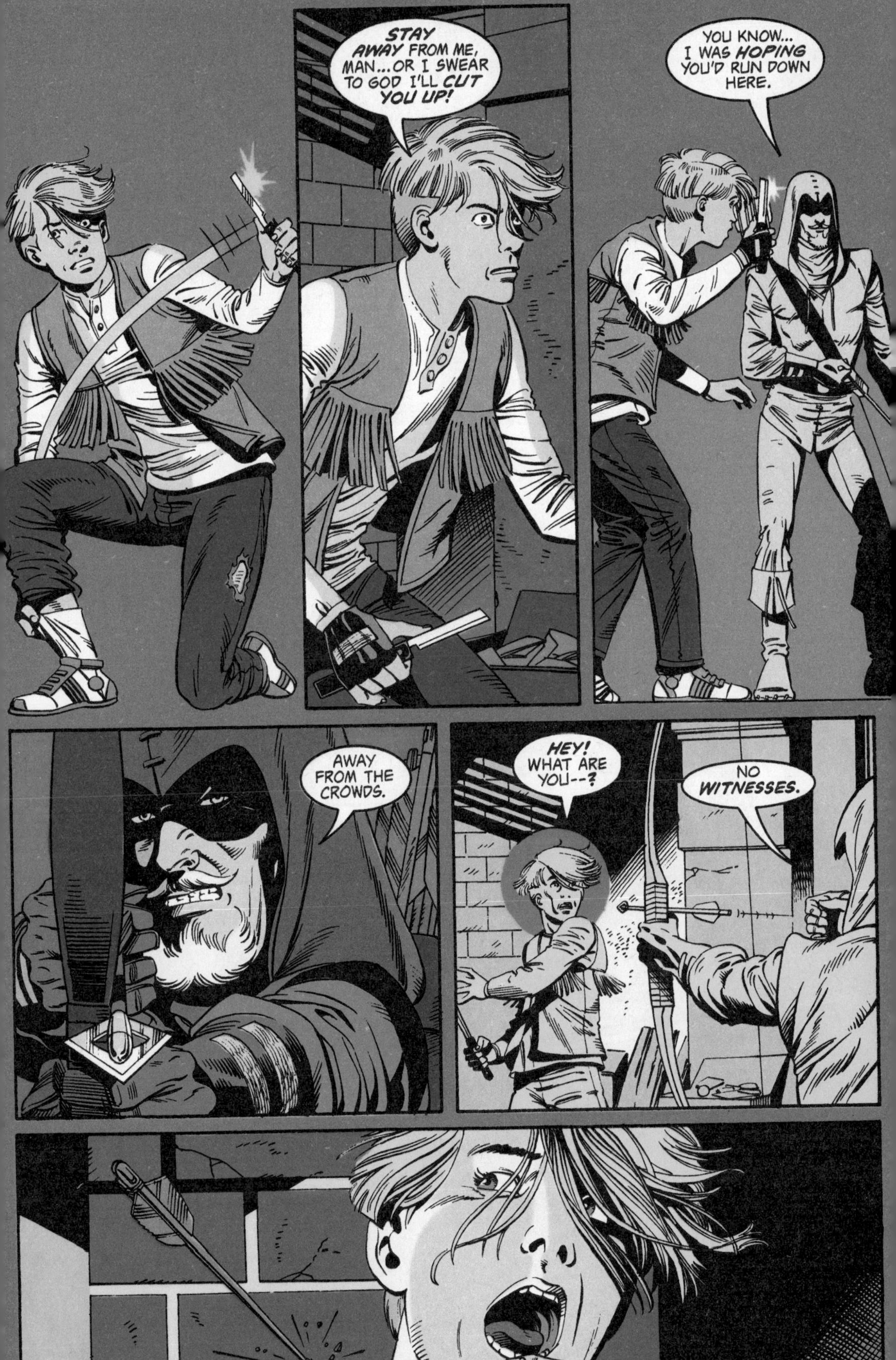
STAY AWAY FROM ME, MAN...OR I SWEAR TO GOD I'LL CUT YOU UP!
YOU KNOW... I WAS HOPING YOU'D RUN DOWN HERE.
AWAY FROM THE CROWDS.
HEY! WHAT ARE YOU--?
NO WITNESSES.
5

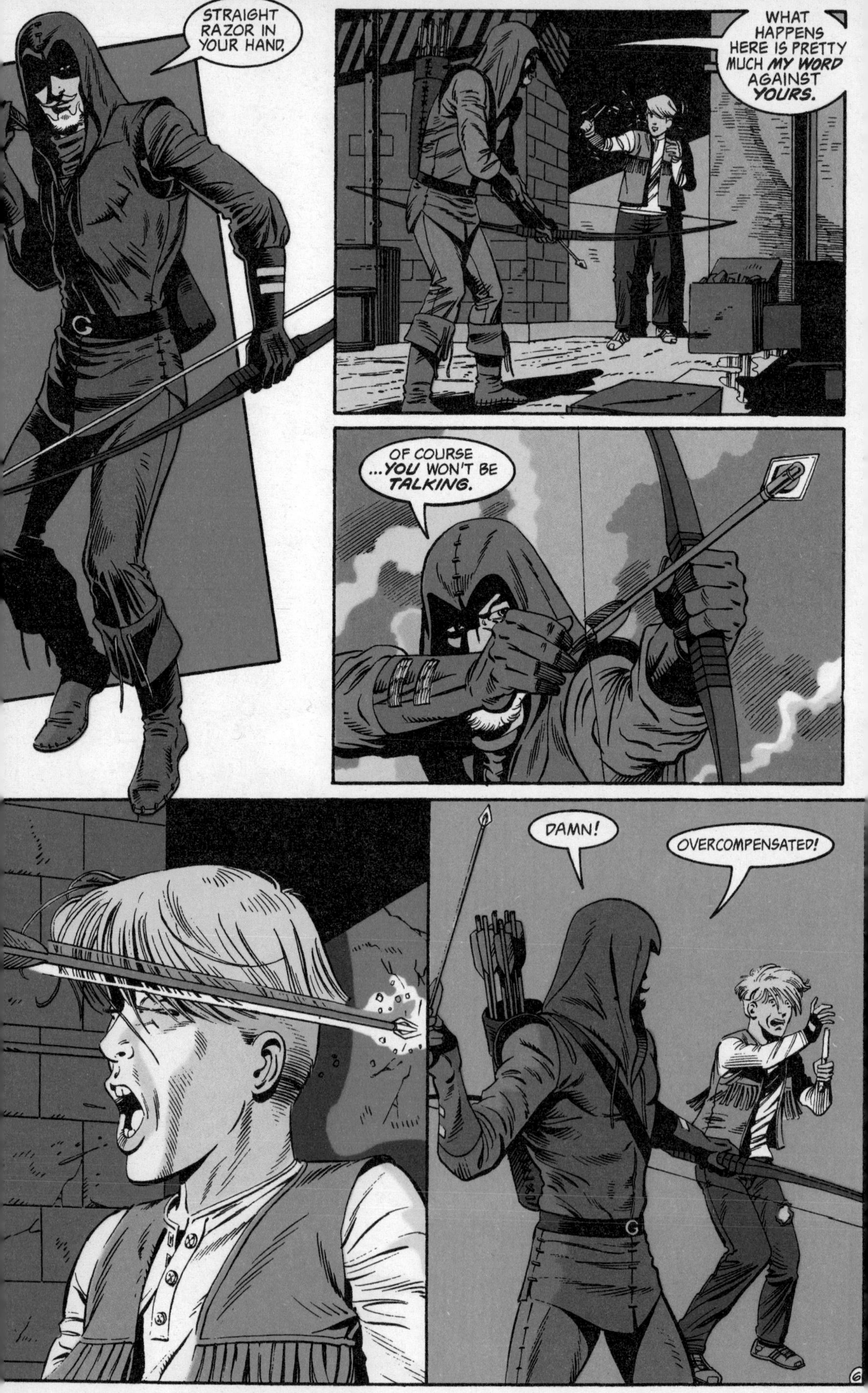
STRAIGHT RAZOR IN YOUR HAND,
WHAT HAPPENS HERE IS PRETTY MUCH MY WORD AGAINST YOURS.
OF COURSE ...YOU WON'T BE TALKING.
DAMN!
OVERCOMPENSATED!
6

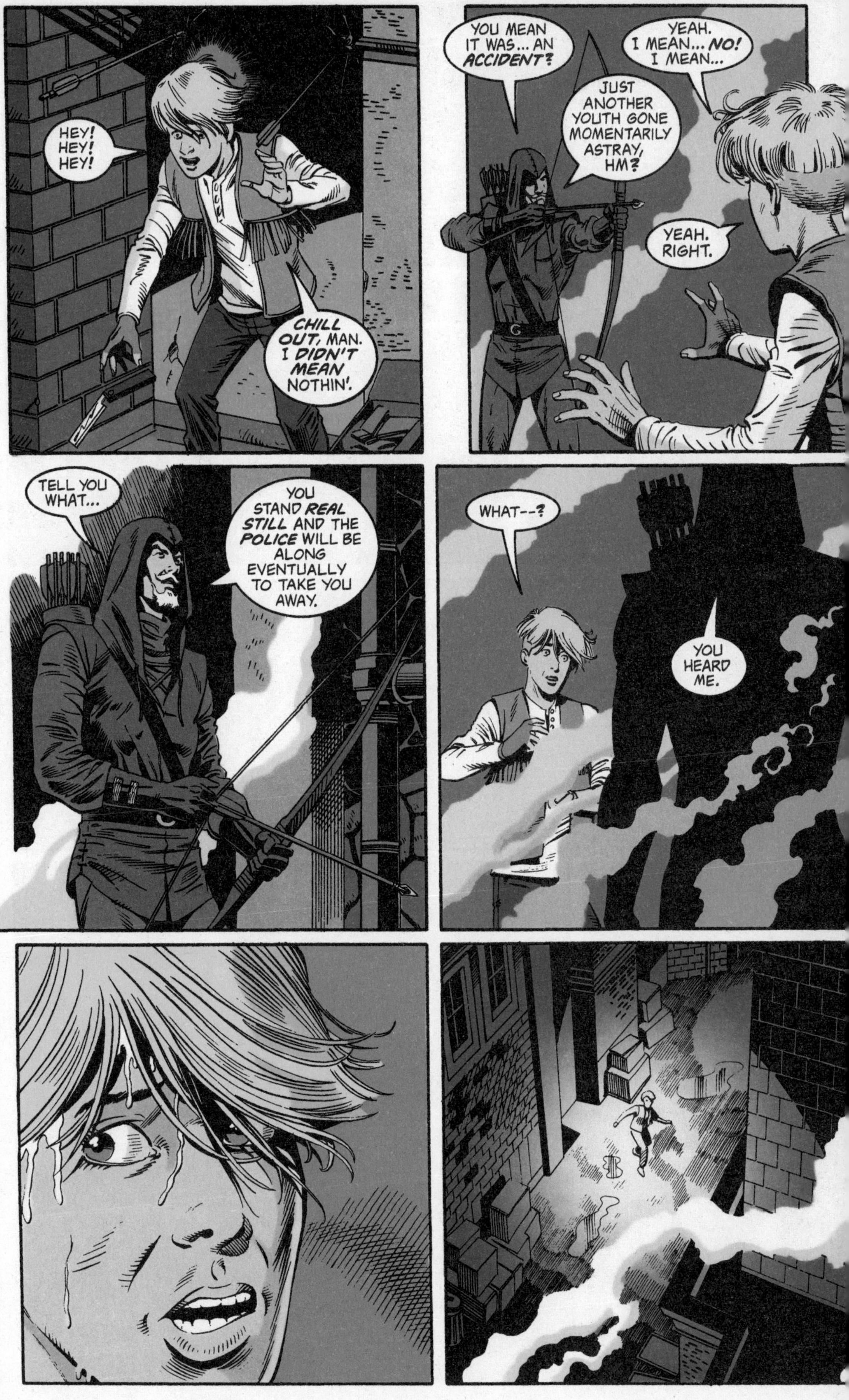
HEY! HEY! HEY!
CHILL OUT, MAN. I DIDN'T MEAN NOTHIN'.
YOU MEAN IT WAS... AN ACCIDENT?
JUST ANOTHER YOUTH GONE MOMENTARILY ASTRAY, HM?
YEAH. I MEAN... NO! I MEAN...
YEAH. RIGHT.
TELL YOU WHAT...
YOU STAND REAL STILL AND THE POLICE WILL BE ALONG EVENTUALLY TO TAKE YOU AWAY.
WHAT--?
YOU HEARD ME.

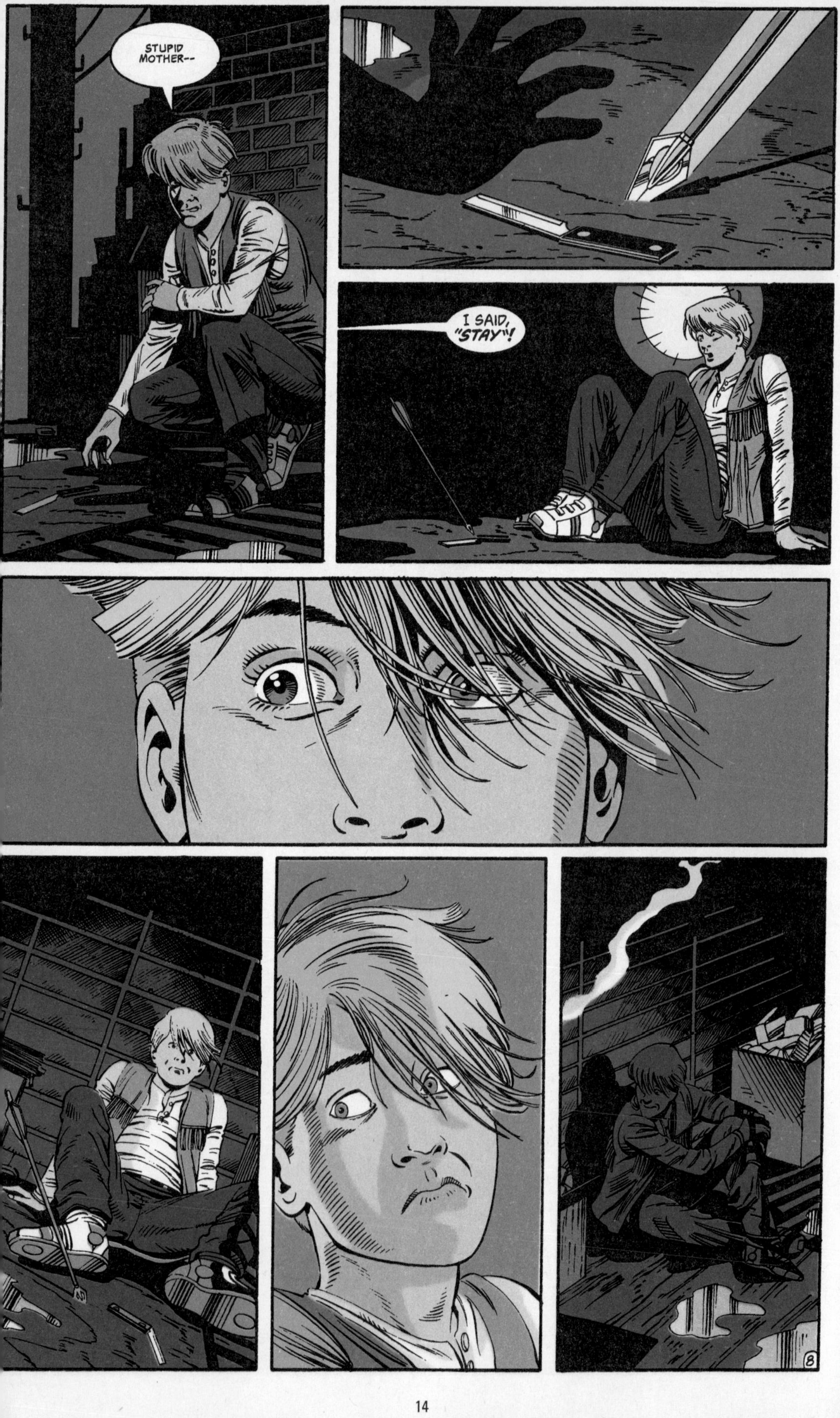
STUPID MOTHER--
I SAID, "STAY"!
8

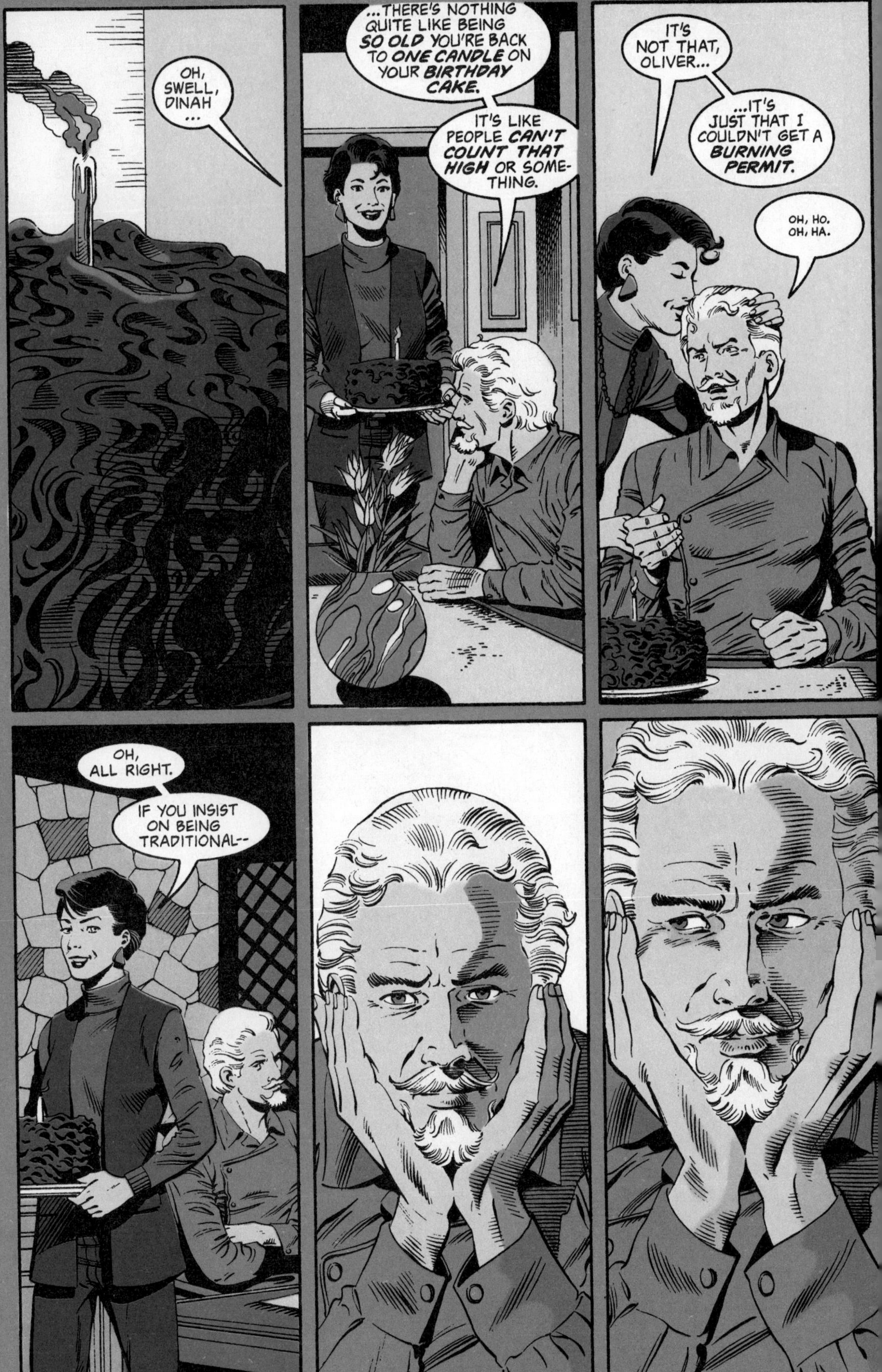
OH, SWELL, DINAH ...
...THERE'S NOTHING QUITE LIKE BEING SO OLD YOU'RE BACK TO ONE CANDLE ON YOUR BIRTHDAY CAKE.
IT'S LIKE PEOPLE CAN'T COUNT THAT HIGH OR SOMETHING.
IT'S NOT THAT, OLIVER...
...IT'S JUST THAT I COULDN'T GET A BURNING PERMIT.
OH, HO. OH, HA.
OH, ALL RIGHT.
IF YOU INSIST ON BEING TRADITIONAL--

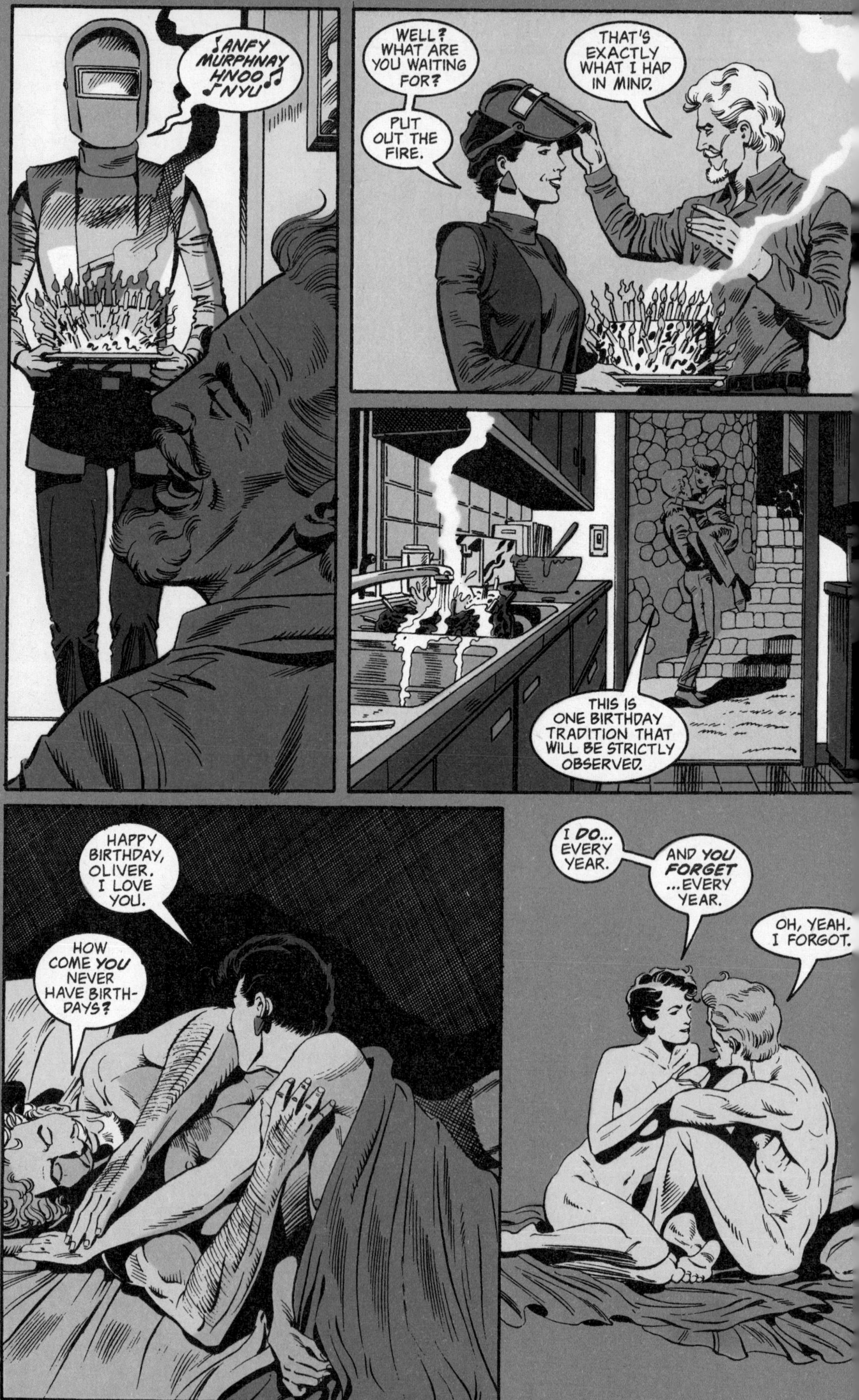
♪ANFY MURPHNAY HNOO♪♫ ♪NYU
WELL? WHAT ARE YOU WAITING FOR?
PUT OUT THE FIRE.
THAT'S EXACTLY WHAT I HAD IN MIND.
THIS IS ONE BIRTHDAY TRADITION THAT WILL BE STRICTLY OBSERVED.
HAPPY BIRTHDAY, OLIVER. I LOVE YOU.
HOW COME YOU NEVER HAVE BIRTH-DAYS?
I DO... EVERY YEAR.
AND YOU FORGET ...EVERY YEAR.
OH, YEAH. I FORGOT.

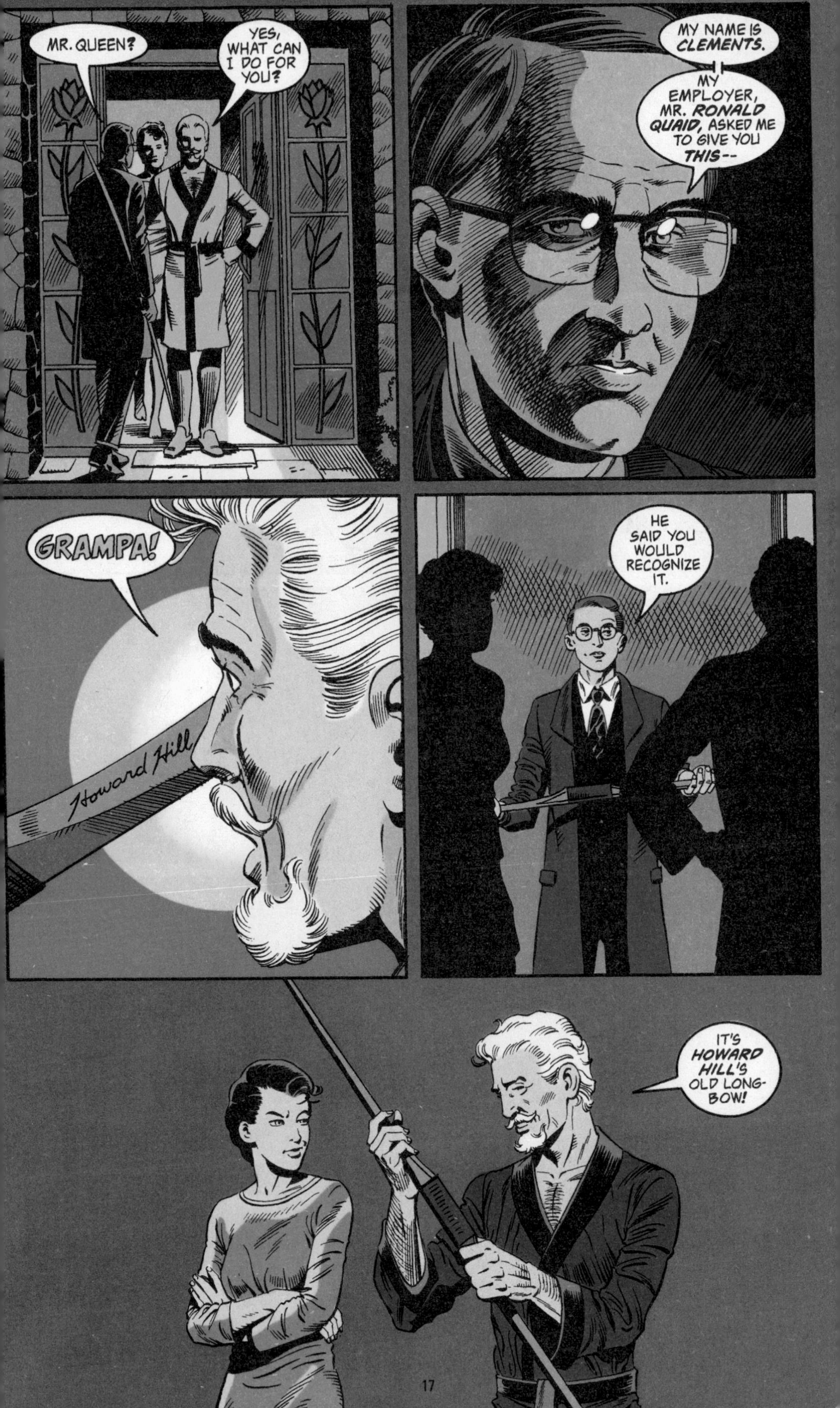
MR. QUEEN?
YES, WHAT CAN I DO FOR YOU?
MY NAME IS CLEMENTS.
MY EMPLOYER, MR. RONALD QUAID, ASKED ME TO GIVE YOU THIS--
GRAMPA!
Howard Hill
HE SAID YOU WOULD RECOGNIZE IT.
IT'S HOWARD HILL'S OLD LONG-BOW!

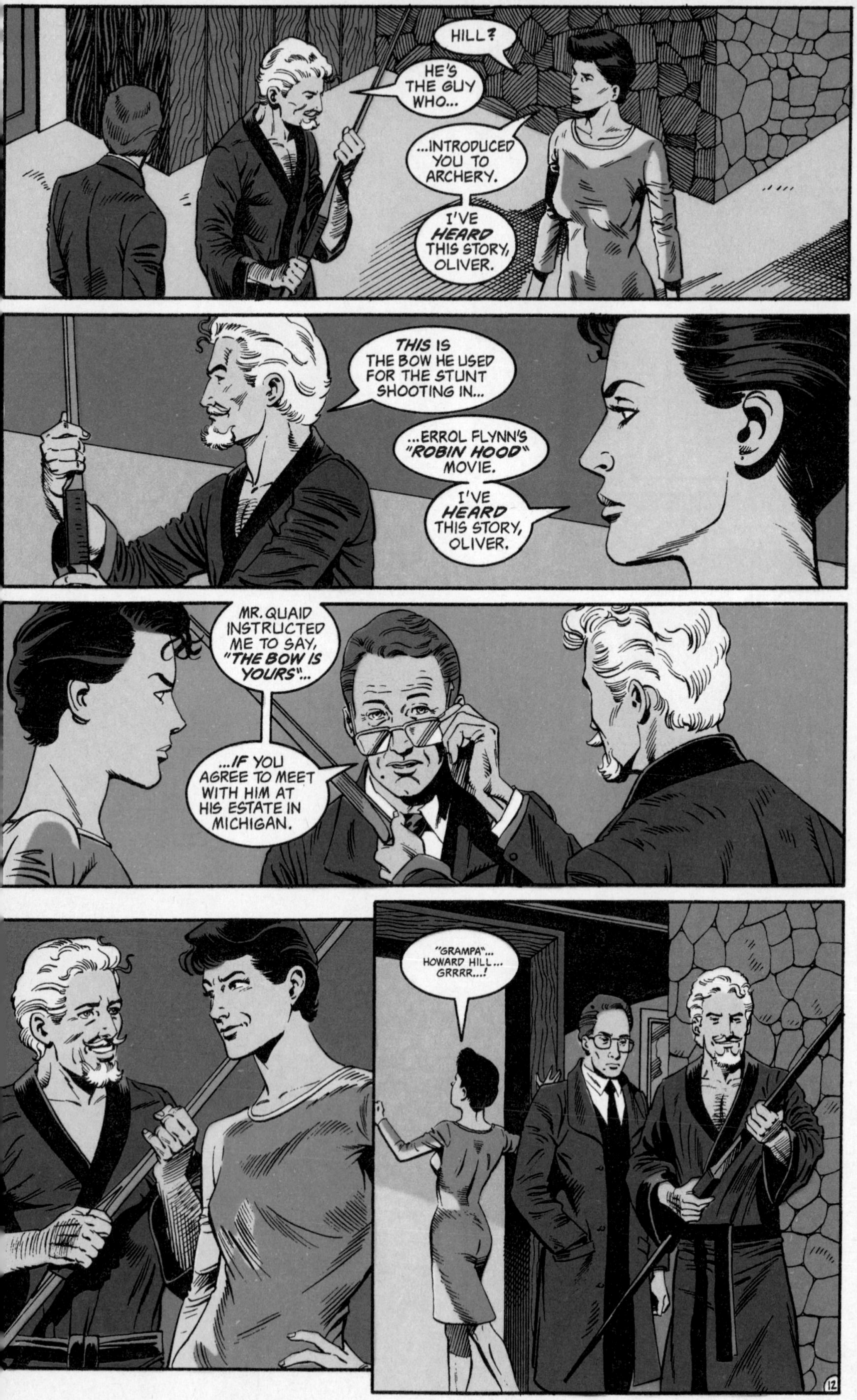
HILL?
HE'S THE GUY WHO...
...INTRODUCED YOU TO ARCHERY.
I'VE HEARD THIS STORY, OLIVER.
THIS IS THE BOW HE USED FOR THE STUNT SHOOTING IN...
...ERROL FLYNN'S "ROBIN HOOD" MOVIE.
I'VE HEARD THIS STORY, OLIVER.
MR. QUAID INSTRUCTED ME TO SAY, "THE BOW IS YOURS"...
...IF YOU AGREE TO MEET WITH HIM AT HIS ESTATE IN MICHIGAN.
"GRAMPA"... HOWARD HILL... GRRRR...!
12

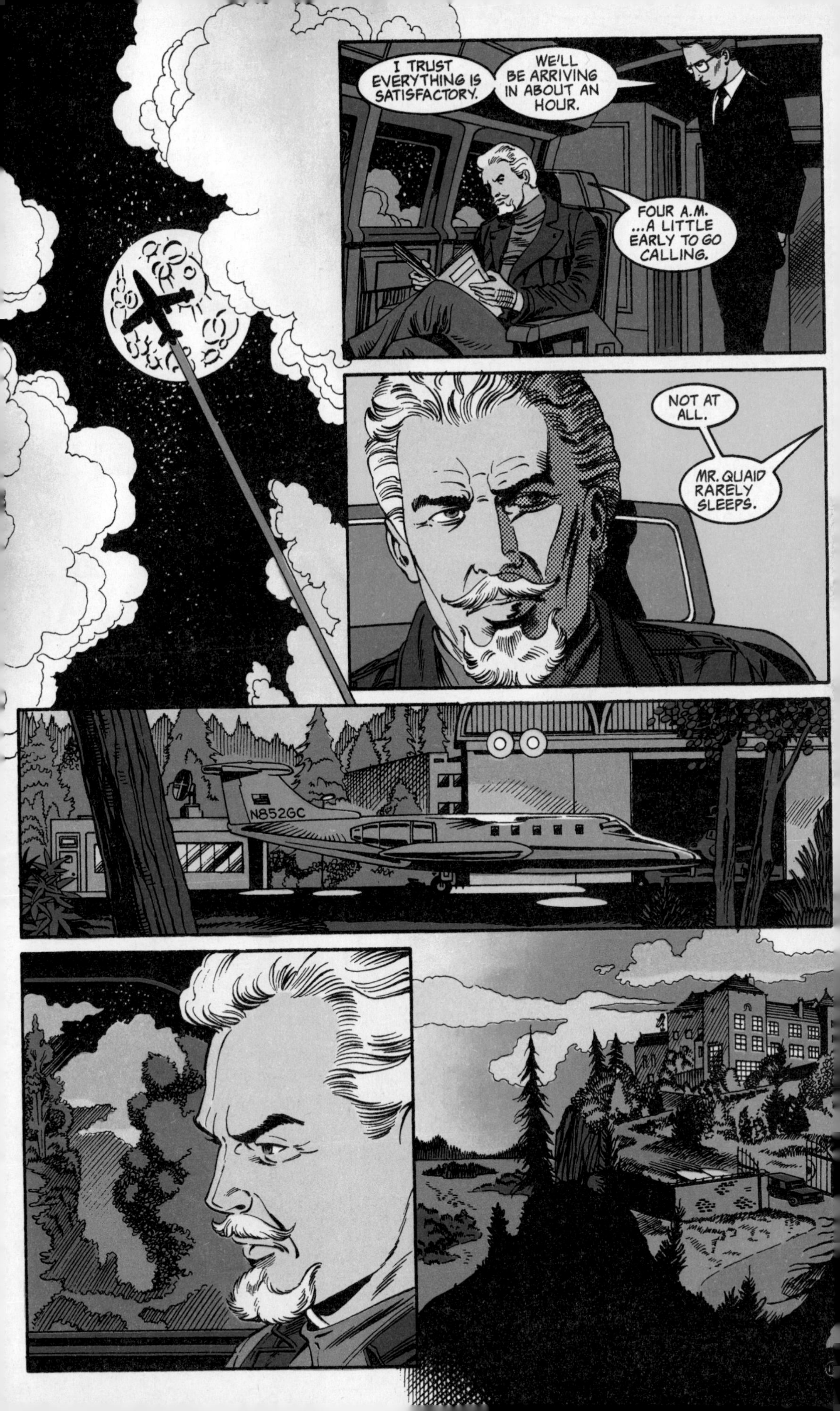

I TRUST EVERYTHING IS SATISFACTORY.
WE'LL BE ARRIVING IN ABOUT AN HOUR.
FOUR A.M. ...A LITTLE EARLY TO GO CALLING.
NOT AT ALL.
MR. QUAID RARELY SLEEPS.
N852GC

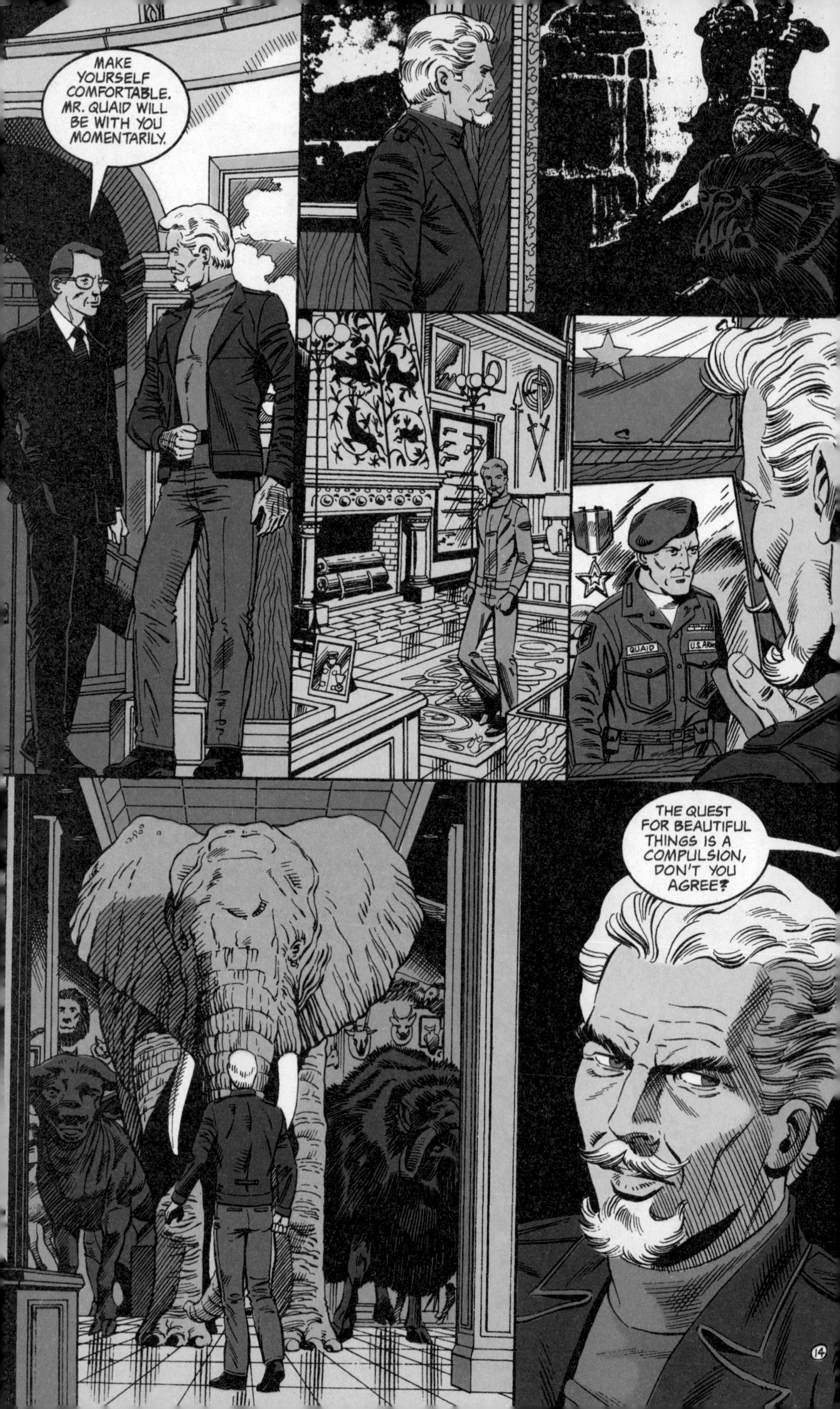
MAKE YOURSELF COMFORTABLE. MR. QUAID WILL BE WITH YOU MOMENTARILY.
QUAID
U.S. ARMY
THE QUEST FOR BEAUTIFUL THINGS IS A COMPULSION, DON'T YOU AGREE?
14

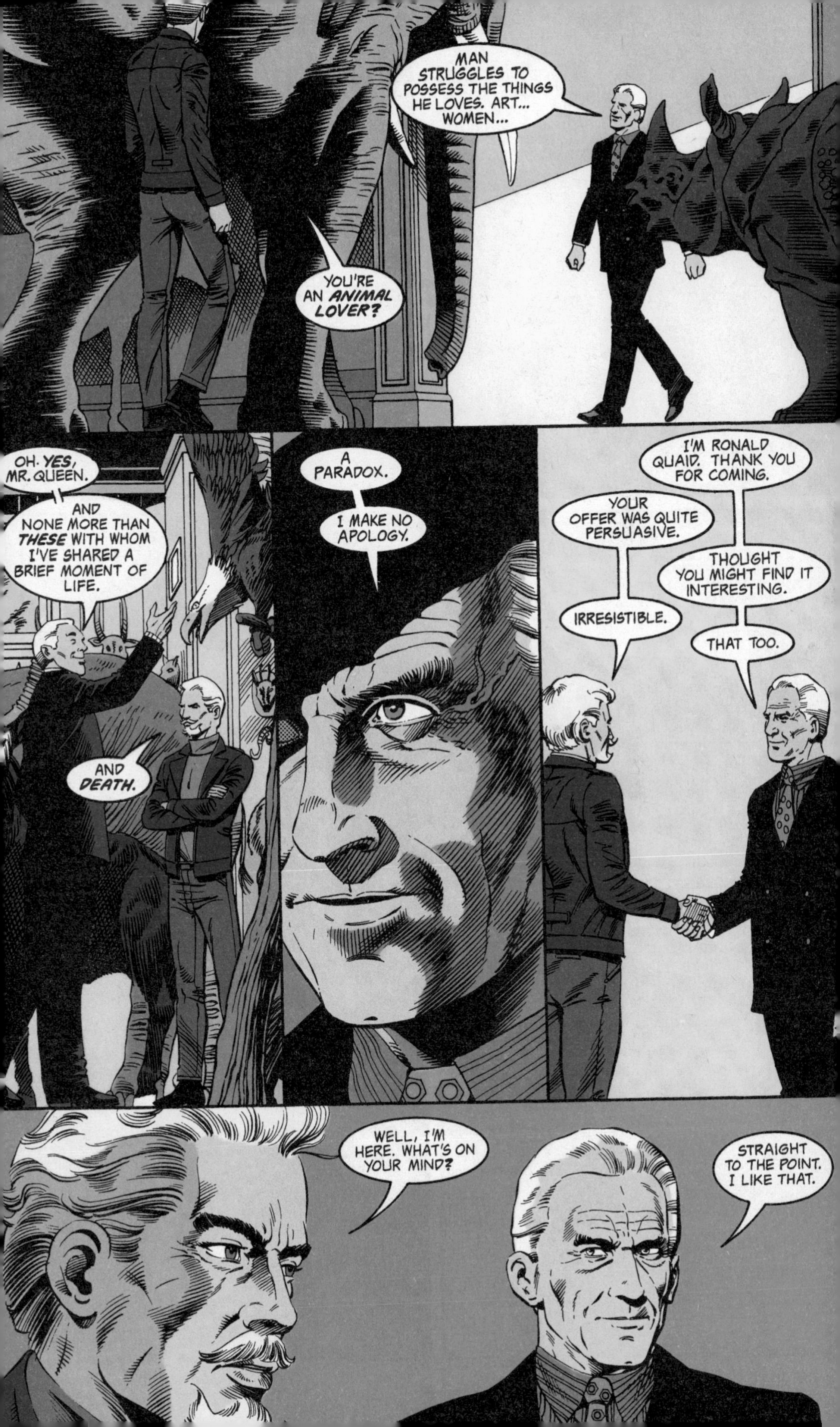
MAN STRUGGLES TO POSSESS THE THINGS HE LOVES. ART... WOMEN...
YOU'RE AN ANIMAL LOVER?
OH. YES, MR. QUEEN.
AND NONE MORE THAN THESE WITH WHOM I'VE SHARED A BRIEF MOMENT OF LIFE.
AND DEATH.
A PARADOX.
I MAKE NO APOLOGY.
I'M RONALD QUAID. THANK YOU FOR COMING.
YOUR OFFER WAS QUITE PERSUASIVE.
THOUGHT YOU MIGHT FIND IT INTERESTING.
IRRESISTIBLE.
THAT TOO.
WELL, I'M HERE. WHAT'S ON YOUR MIND?
STRAIGHT TO THE POINT. I LIKE THAT.

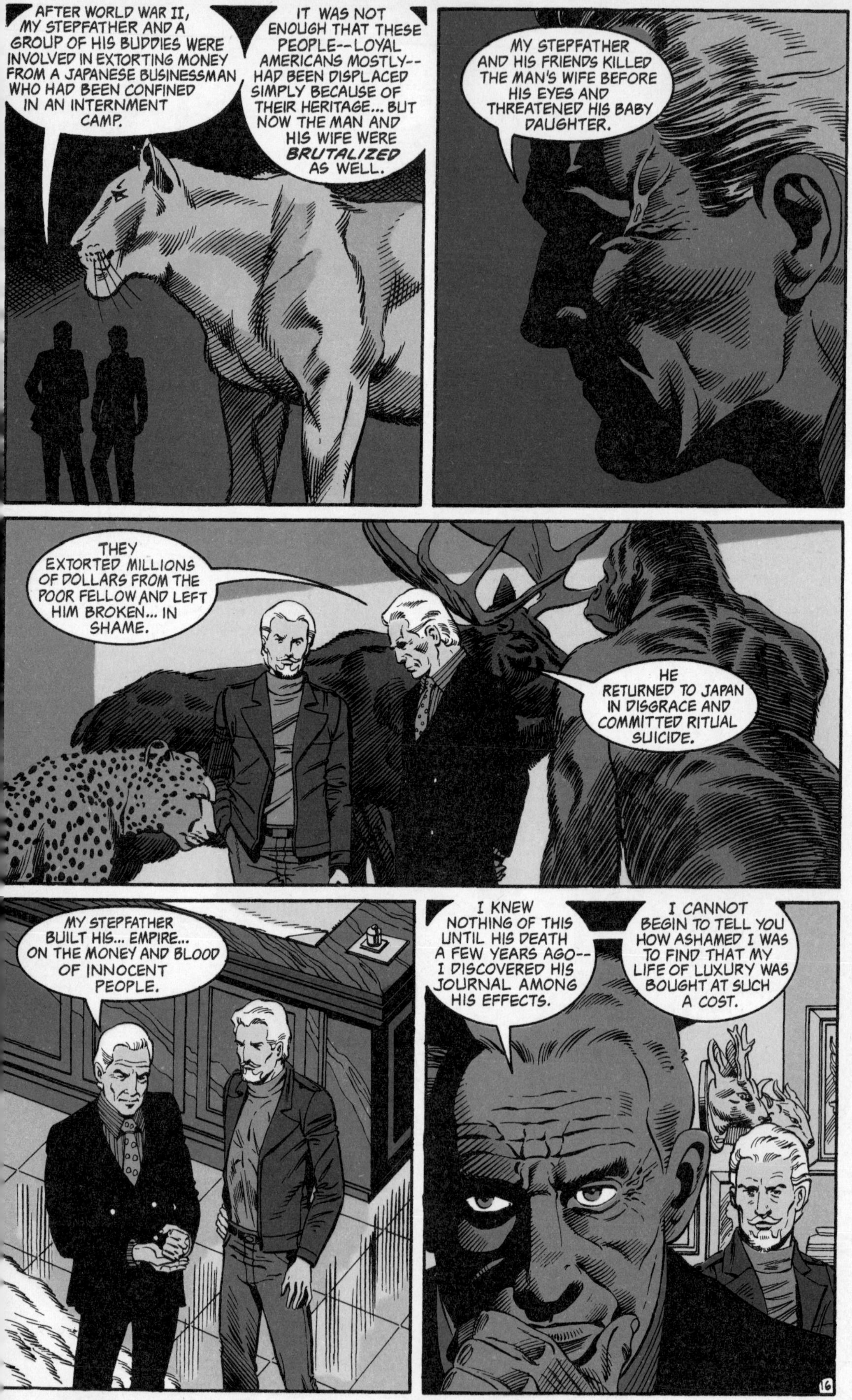
AFTER WORLD WAR II, MY STEPFATHER AND A GROUP OF HIS BUDDIES WERE INVOLVED IN EXTORTING MONEY FROM A JAPANESE BUSINESSMAN WHO HAD BEEN CONFINED IN AN INTERNMENT CAMP.
IT WAS NOT ENOUGH THAT THESE PEOPLE--LOYAL AMERICANS MOSTLY--HAD BEEN DISPLACED SIMPLY BECAUSE OF THEIR HERITAGE... BUT NOW THE MAN AND HIS WIFE WERE BRUTALIZED AS WELL.
MY STEPFATHER AND HIS FRIENDS KILLED THE MAN'S WIFE BEFORE HIS EYES AND THREATENED HIS BABY DAUGHTER.
THEY EXTORTED MILLIONS OF DOLLARS FROM THE POOR FELLOW AND LEFT HIM BROKEN... IN SHAME.
HE RETURNED TO JAPAN IN DISGRACE AND COMMITTED RITUAL SUICIDE.
MY STEPFATHER BUILT HIS... EMPIRE... ON THE MONEY AND BLOOD OF INNOCENT PEOPLE.
I KNEW NOTHING OF THIS UNTIL HIS DEATH A FEW YEARS AGO--I DISCOVERED HIS JOURNAL AMONG HIS EFFECTS.
I CANNOT BEGIN TO TELL YOU HOW ASHAMED I WAS TO FIND THAT MY LIFE OF LUXURY WAS BOUGHT AT SUCH A COST.
16

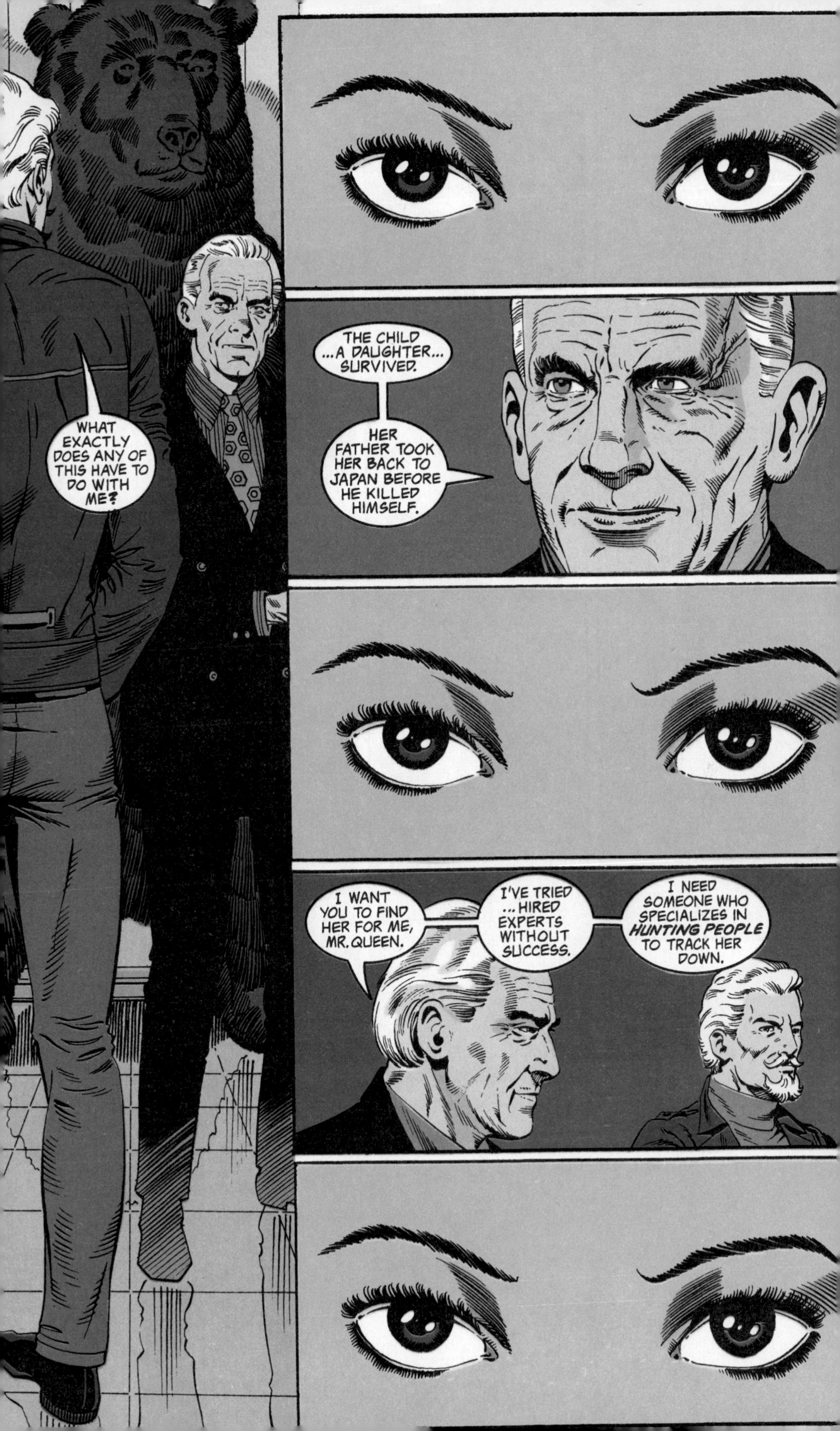
THE CHILD ...A DAUGHTER... SURVIVED.
HER FATHER TOOK HER BACK TO JAPAN BEFORE HE KILLED HIMSELF.
WHAT EXACTLY DOES ANY OF THIS HAVE TO DO WITH ME?
I WANT YOU TO FIND HER FOR ME, MR. QUEEN.
I'VE TRIED ...HIRED EXPERTS WITHOUT SUCCESS.
I NEED SOMEONE WHO SPECIALIZES IN HUNTING PEOPLE TO TRACK HER DOWN.

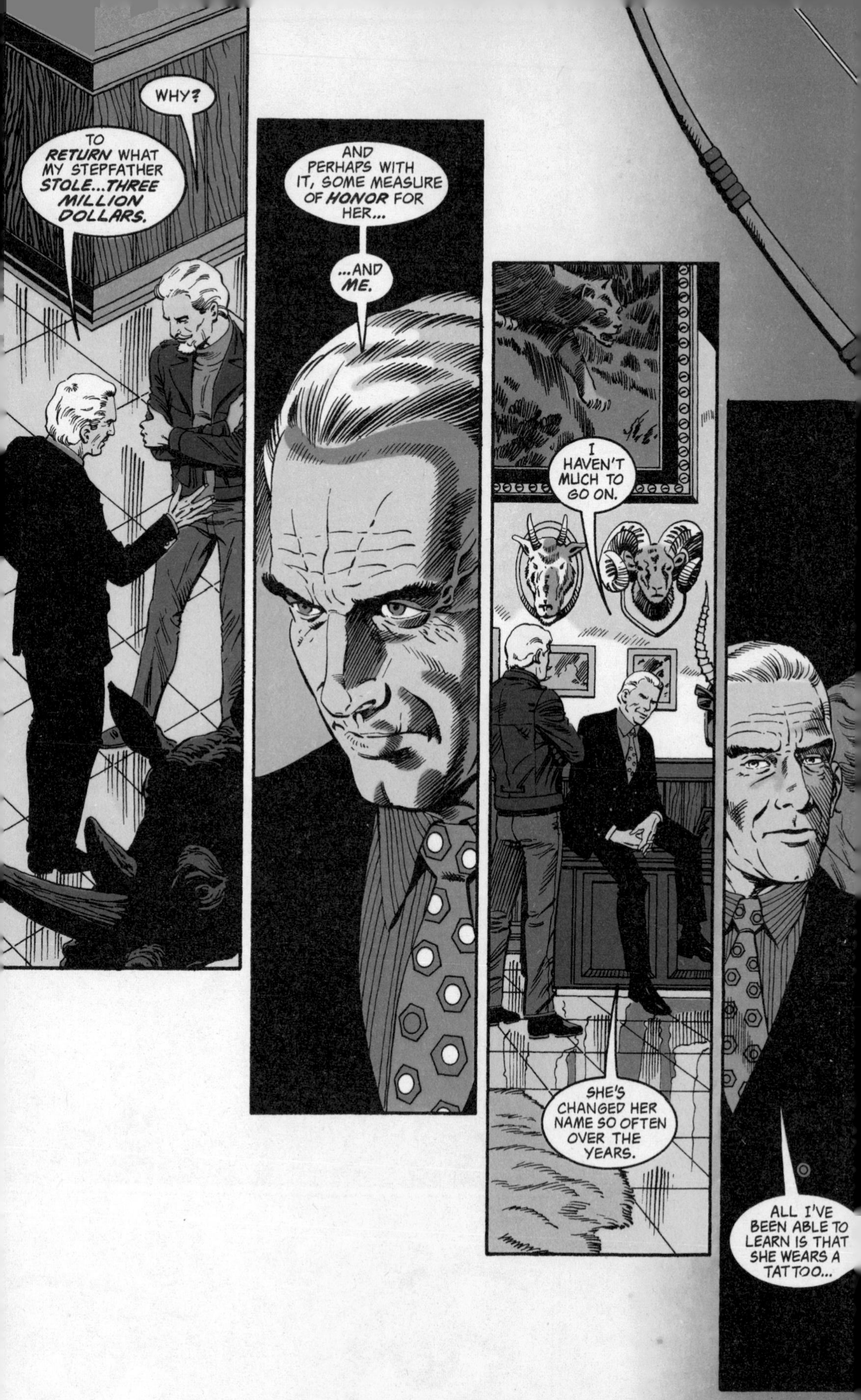
WHY?
TO *RETURN* WHAT MY STEPFATHER *STOLE...THREE MILLION DOLLARS.*
AND PERHAPS WITH IT, SOME MEASURE OF *HONOR* FOR HER...
...AND *ME.*
I HAVEN'T MUCH TO GO ON.
SHE'S CHANGED HER NAME SO OFTEN OVER THE YEARS.
ALL I'VE BEEN ABLE TO LEARN IS THAT SHE WEARS A TATTOO...

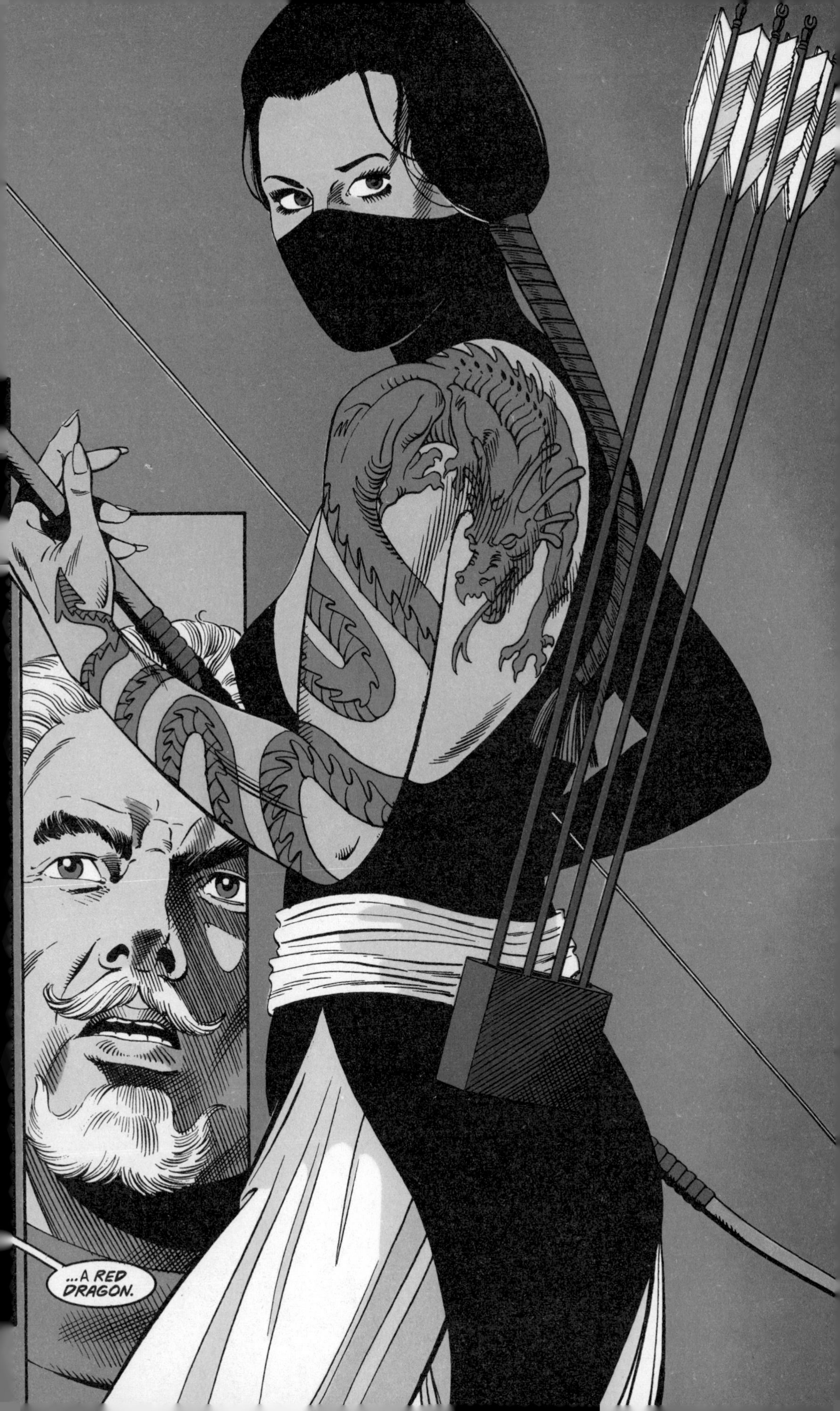
...A RED DRAGON.

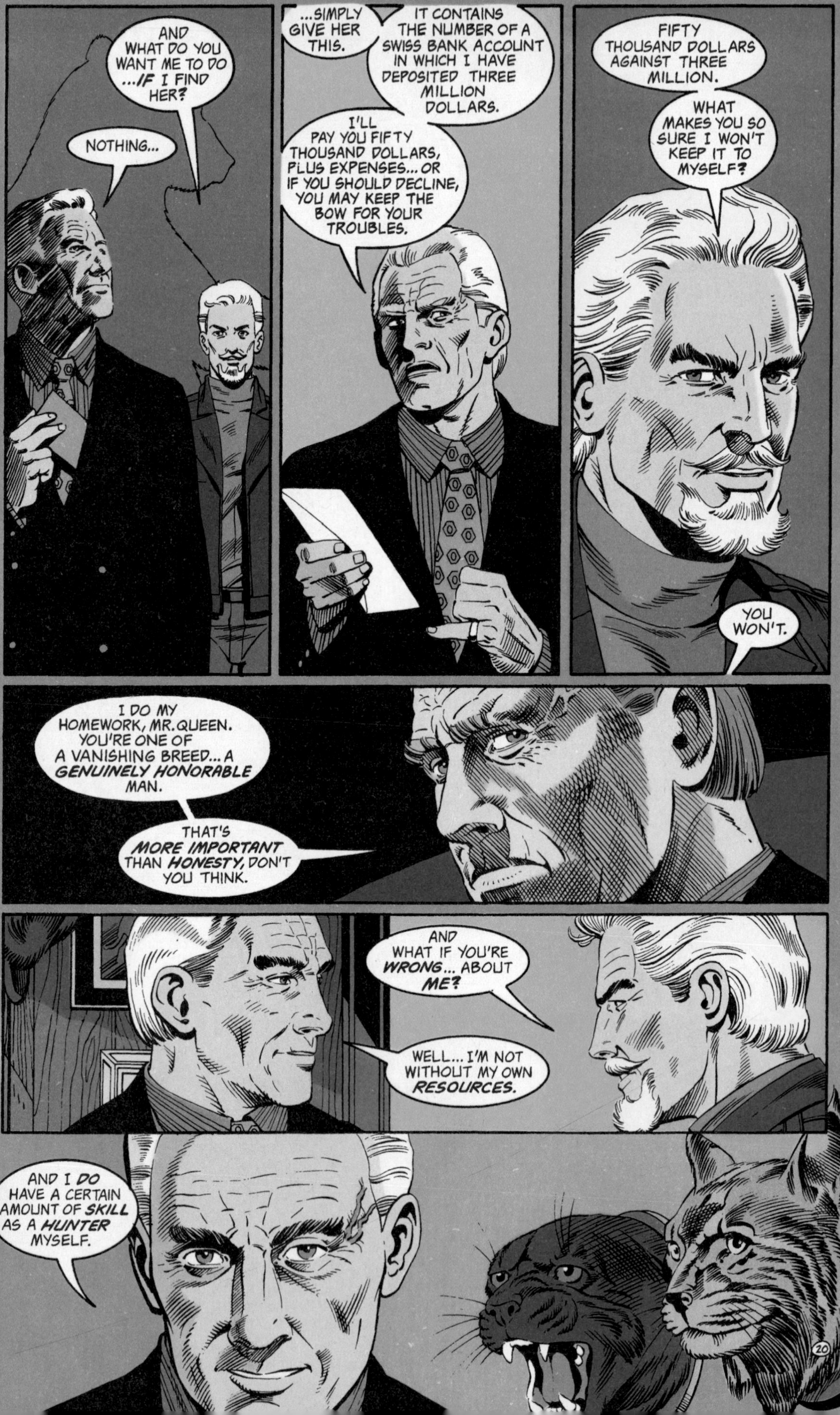

AND WHAT DO YOU WANT ME TO DO ...*IF* I FIND HER?
NOTHING...
...SIMPLY GIVE HER THIS.
IT CONTAINS THE NUMBER OF A SWISS BANK ACCOUNT IN WHICH I HAVE DEPOSITED THREE MILLION DOLLARS.
I'LL PAY YOU FIFTY THOUSAND DOLLARS, PLUS EXPENSES... OR IF YOU SHOULD DECLINE, YOU MAY KEEP THE BOW FOR YOUR TROUBLES.
FIFTY THOUSAND DOLLARS AGAINST THREE MILLION.
WHAT MAKES YOU SO SURE I WON'T KEEP IT TO MYSELF?
YOU WON'T.
I DO MY HOMEWORK, MR. QUEEN. YOU'RE ONE OF A VANISHING BREED... A *GENUINELY HONORABLE* MAN.
THAT'S *MORE IMPORTANT* THAN *HONESTY,* DON'T YOU THINK.
AND WHAT IF YOU'RE *WRONG*... ABOUT *ME?*
WELL... I'M NOT WITHOUT MY OWN *RESOURCES*.
AND I *DO* HAVE A CERTAIN AMOUNT OF *SKILL* AS A *HUNTER* MYSELF.
20

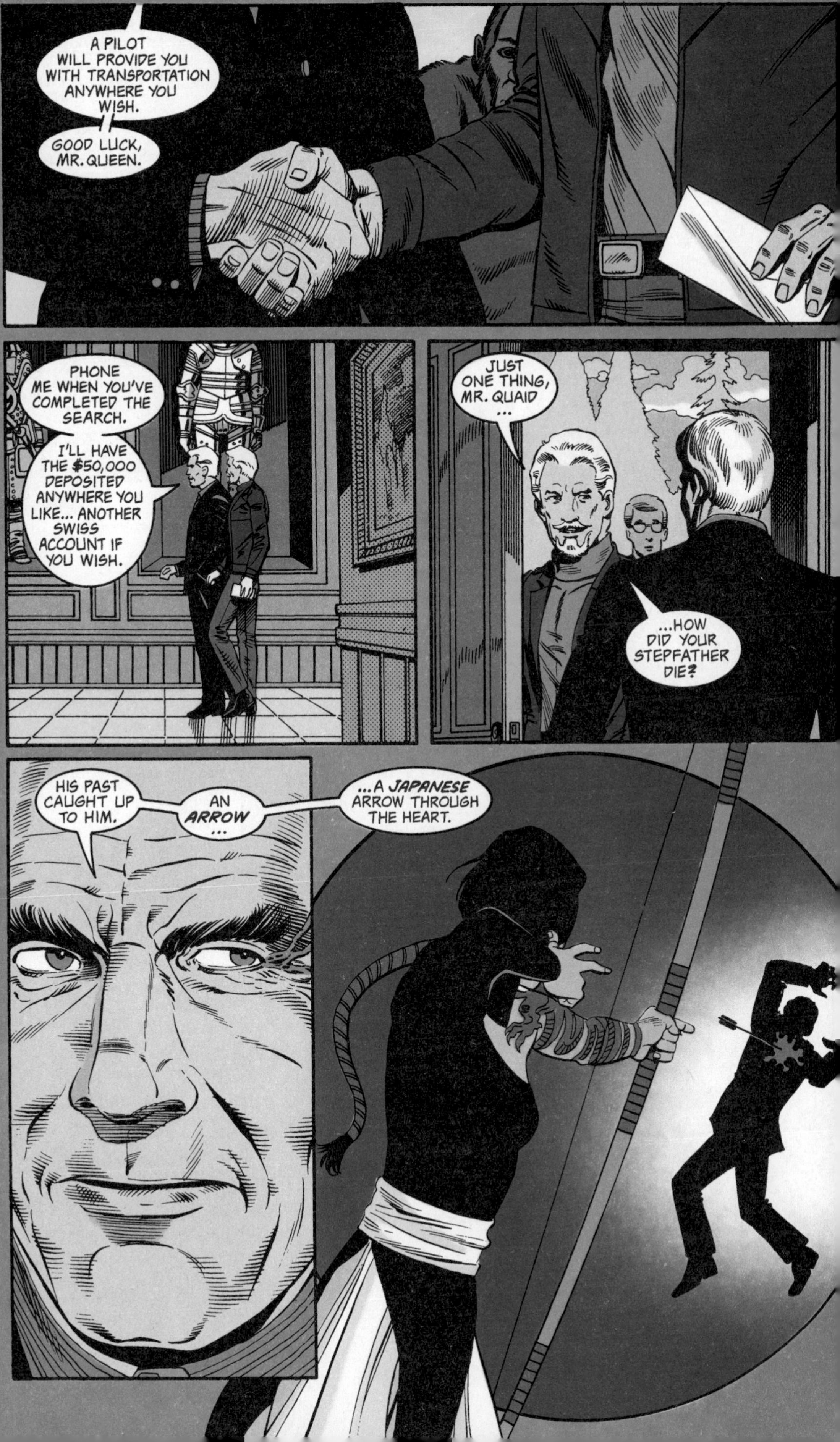
A PILOT WILL PROVIDE YOU WITH TRANSPORTATION ANYWHERE YOU WISH.
GOOD LUCK, MR. QUEEN.
PHONE ME WHEN YOU'VE COMPLETED THE SEARCH.
I'LL HAVE THE $50,000 DEPOSITED ANYWHERE YOU LIKE... ANOTHER SWISS ACCOUNT IF YOU WISH.
JUST ONE THING, MR. QUAID ...
...HOW DID YOUR STEPFATHER DIE?
HIS PAST CAUGHT UP TO HIM.
AN *ARROW* ...
...A *JAPANESE* ARROW THROUGH THE HEART.

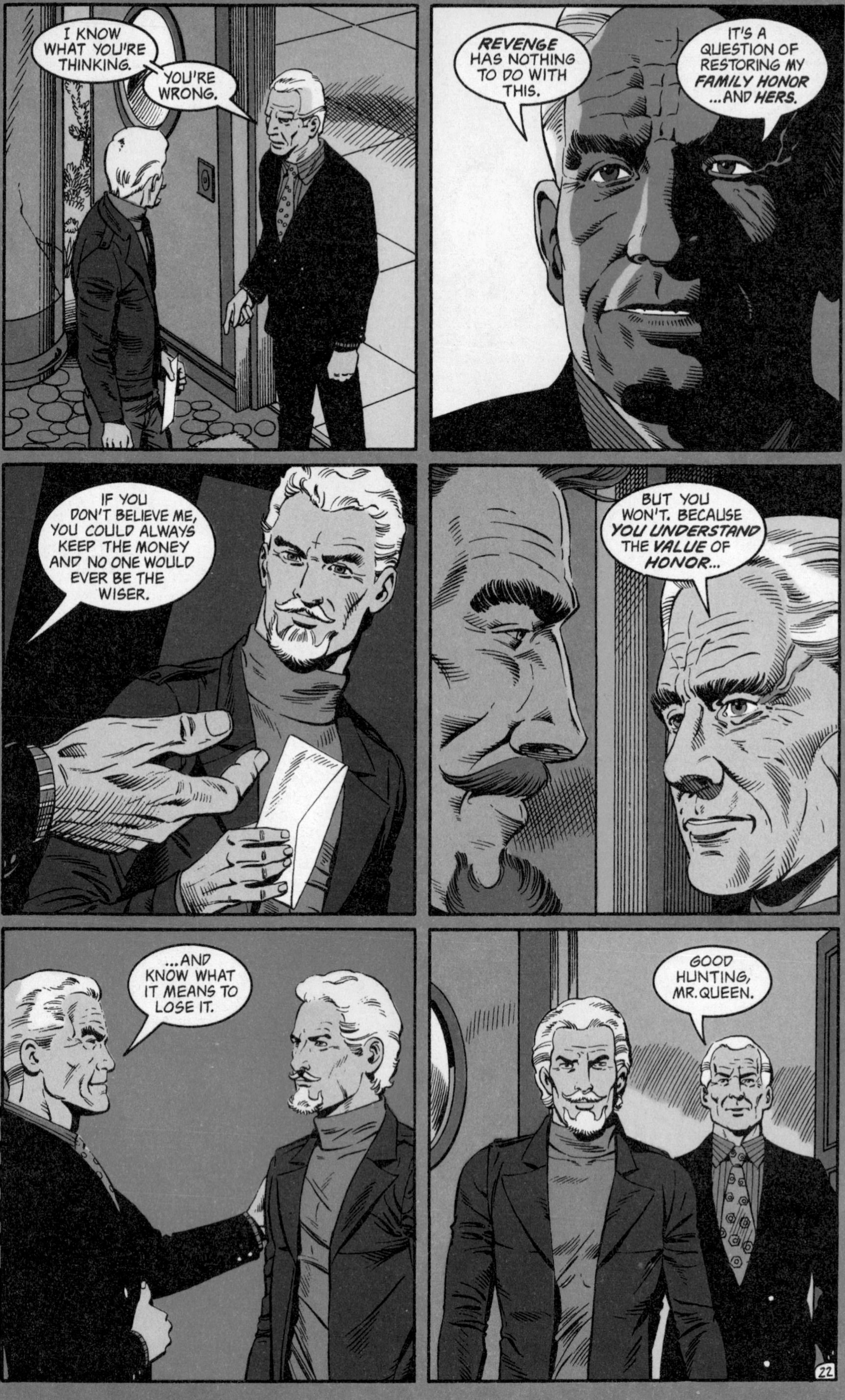
I KNOW WHAT YOU'RE THINKING.
YOU'RE WRONG.
REVENGE HAS NOTHING TO DO WITH THIS.
IT'S A QUESTION OF RESTORING MY FAMILY HONOR ...AND HERS.
IF YOU DON'T BELIEVE ME, YOU COULD ALWAYS KEEP THE MONEY AND NO ONE WOULD EVER BE THE WISER.
BUT YOU WON'T. BECAUSE YOU UNDERSTAND THE VALUE OF HONOR...
...AND KNOW WHAT IT MEANS TO LOSE IT.
GOOD HUNTING, MR. QUEEN.
22

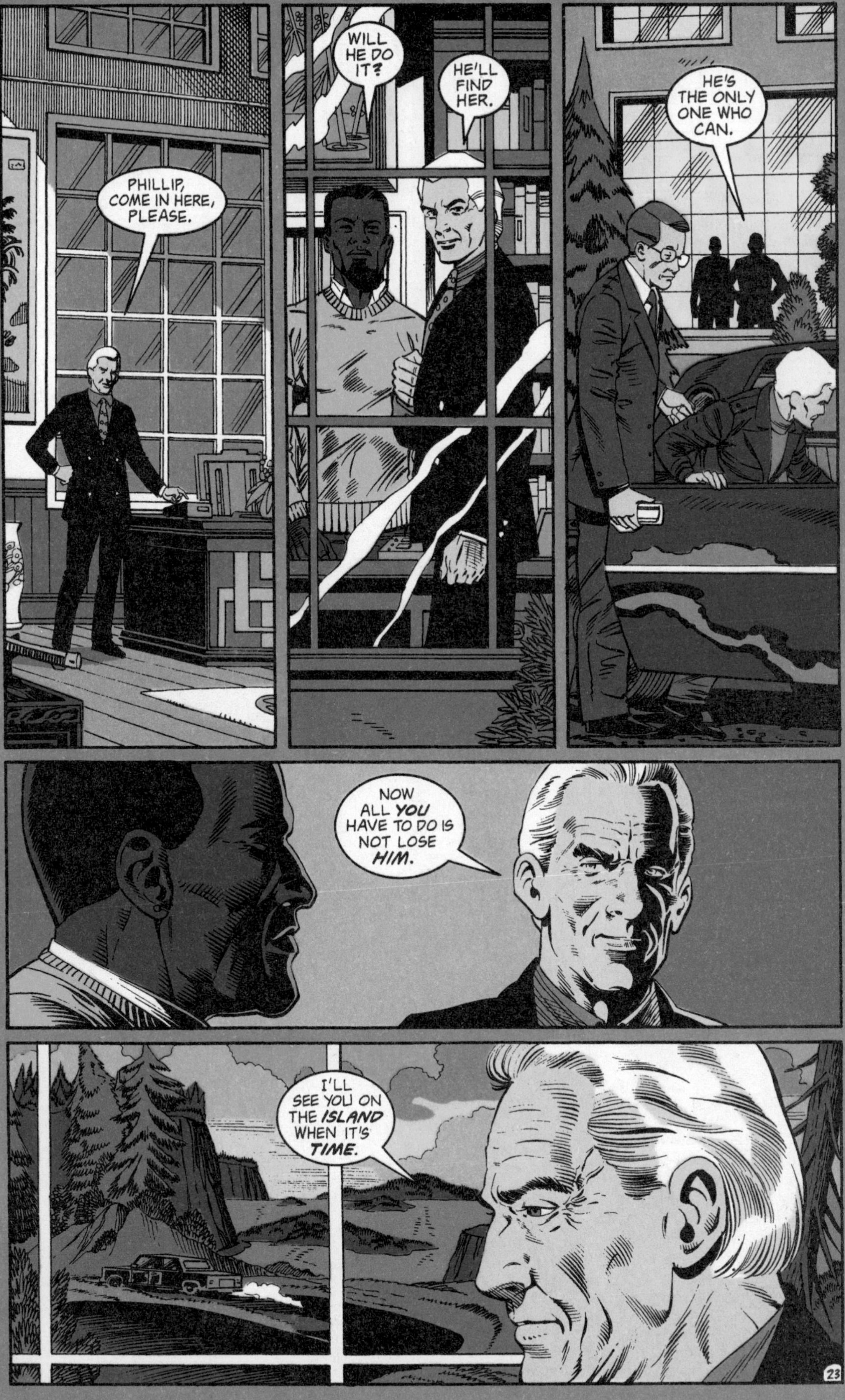
PHILLIP, COME IN HERE, PLEASE.
WILL HE DO IT?
HE'LL FIND HER.
HE'S THE ONLY ONE WHO CAN.
NOW ALL YOU HAVE TO DO IS NOT LOSE HIM.
I'LL SEE YOU ON THE ISLAND WHEN IT'S TIME.
23

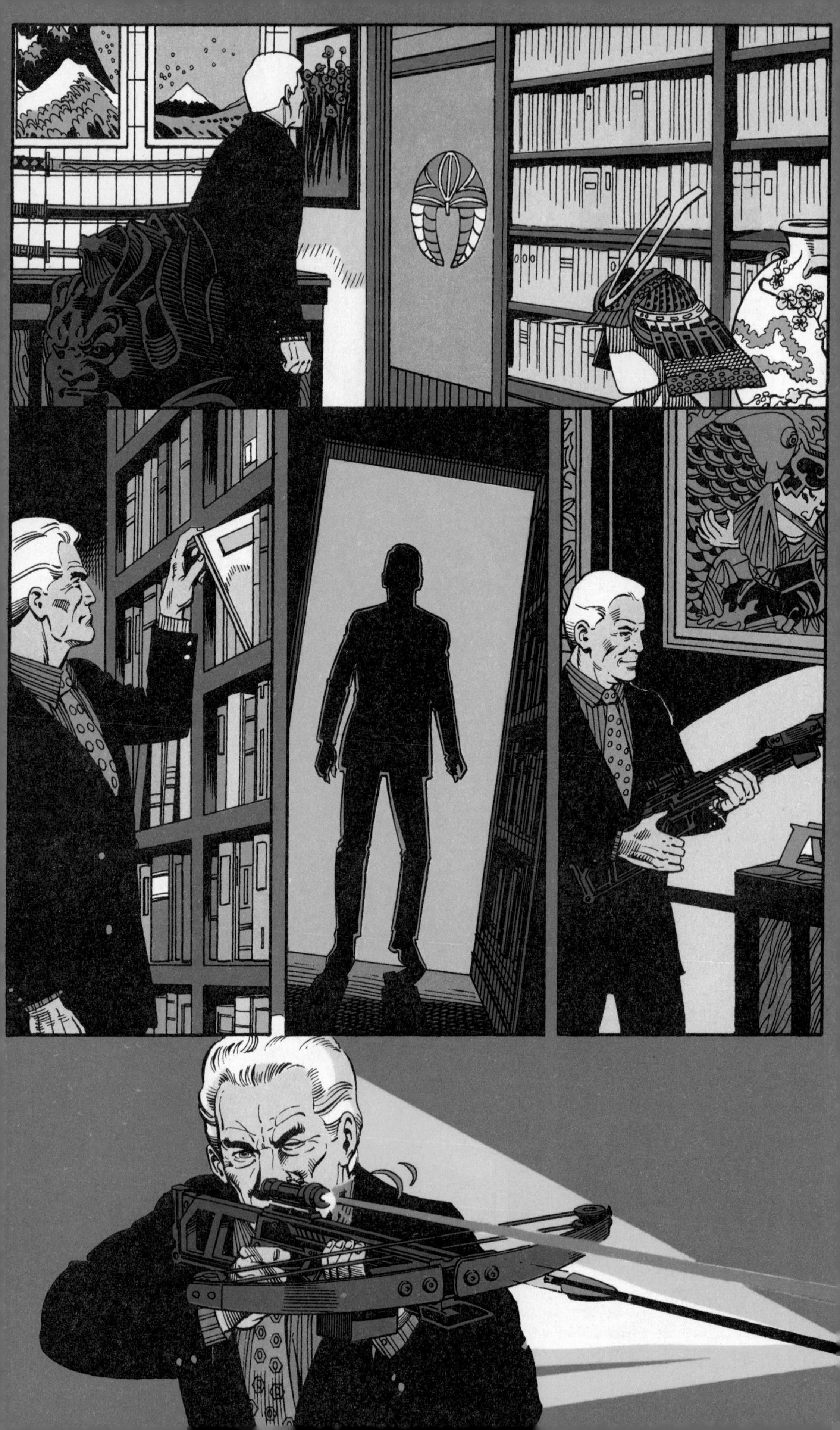

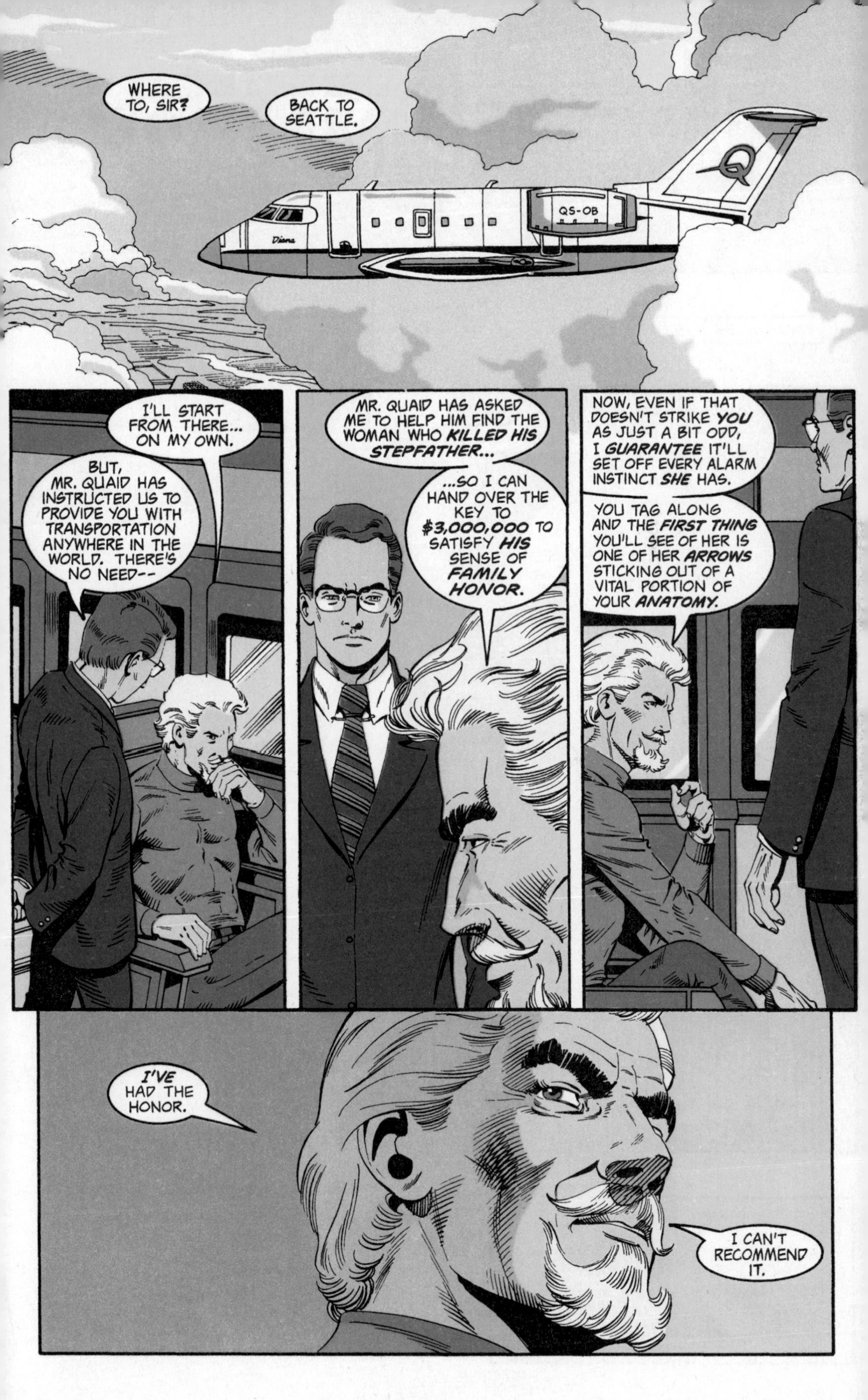
WHERE TO, SIR?
BACK TO SEATTLE.
QS-OB
Diana
I'LL START FROM THERE... ON MY OWN.
BUT, MR. QUAID HAS INSTRUCTED US TO PROVIDE YOU WITH TRANSPORTATION ANYWHERE IN THE WORLD. THERE'S NO NEED--
MR. QUAID HAS ASKED ME TO HELP HIM FIND THE WOMAN WHO KILLED HIS STEPFATHER...
...SO I CAN HAND OVER THE KEY TO $3,000,000 TO SATISFY HIS SENSE OF FAMILY HONOR.
NOW, EVEN IF THAT DOESN'T STRIKE YOU AS JUST A BIT ODD, I GUARANTEE IT'LL SET OFF EVERY ALARM INSTINCT SHE HAS.
YOU TAG ALONG AND THE FIRST THING YOU'LL SEE OF HER IS ONE OF HER ARROWS STICKING OUT OF A VITAL PORTION OF YOUR ANATOMY.
I'VE HAD THE HONOR.
I CAN'T RECOMMEND IT.

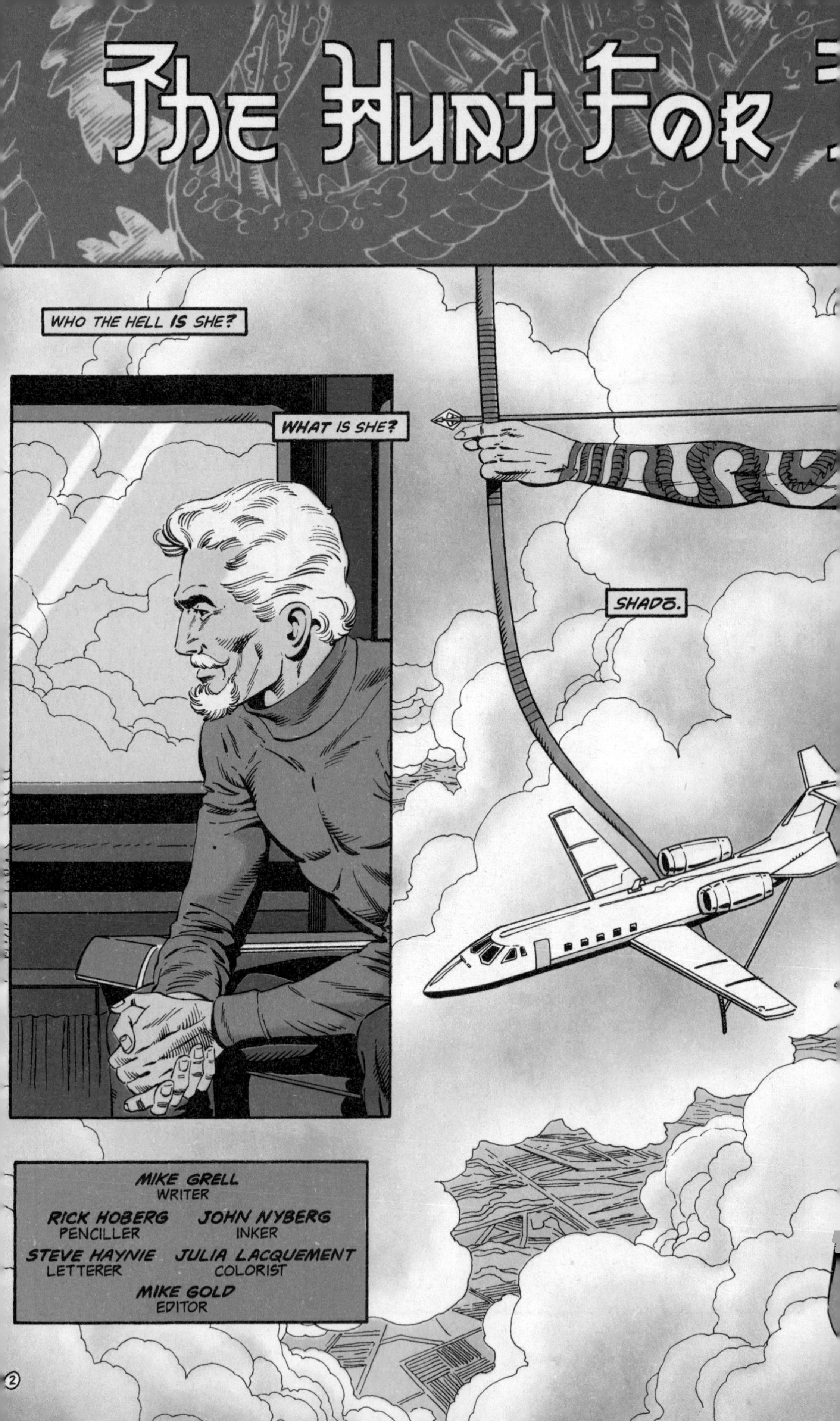
THE HUNT FOR
WHO THE HELL IS SHE?
WHAT IS SHE?
SHADŌ.
MIKE GRELL
WRITER
RICK HOBERG
PENCILLER
JOHN NYBERG
INKER
STEVE HAYNIE
LETTERER
JULIA LACQUEMENT
COLORIST
MIKE GOLD
EDITOR

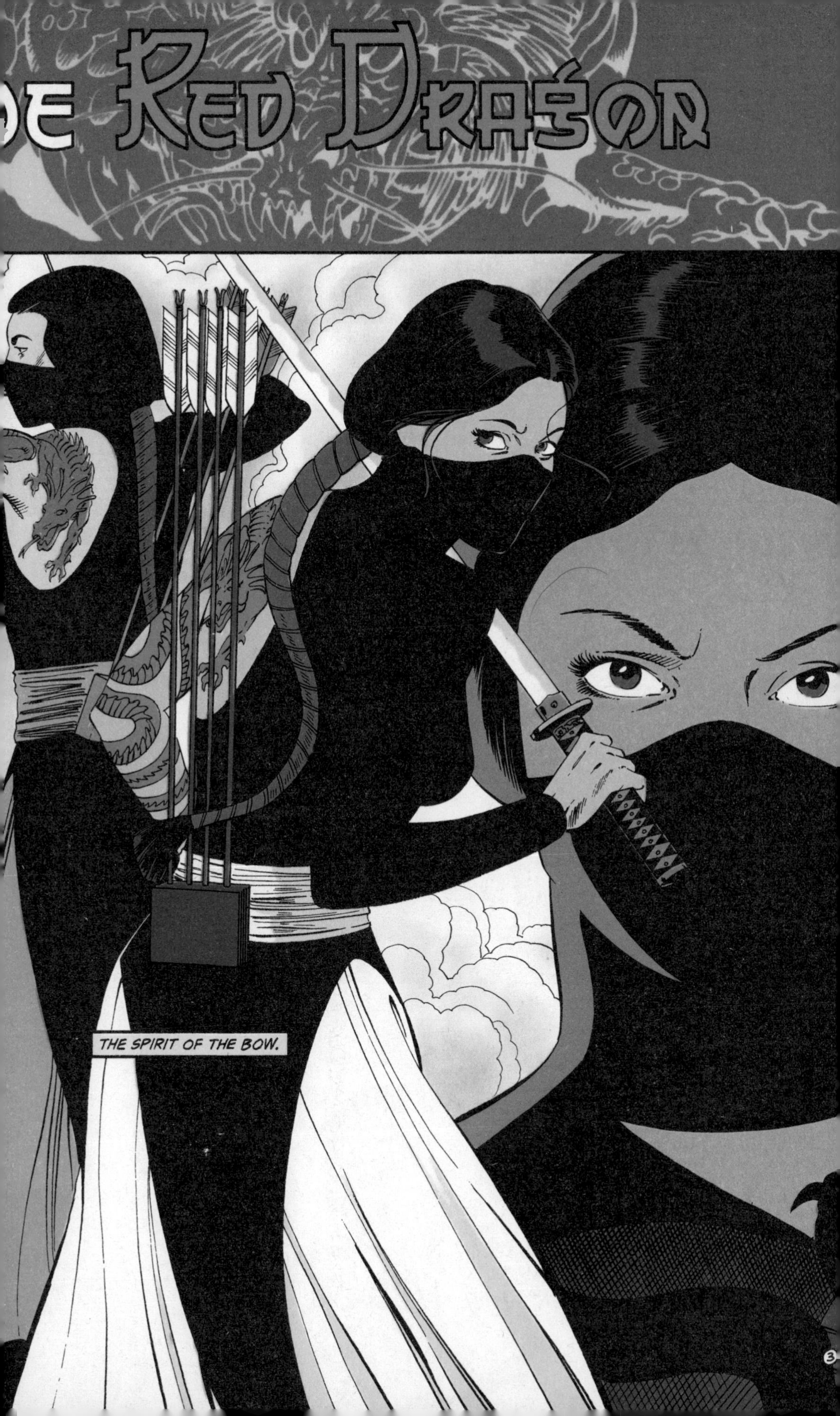
THE RED DRAGON
THE SPIRIT OF THE BOW.

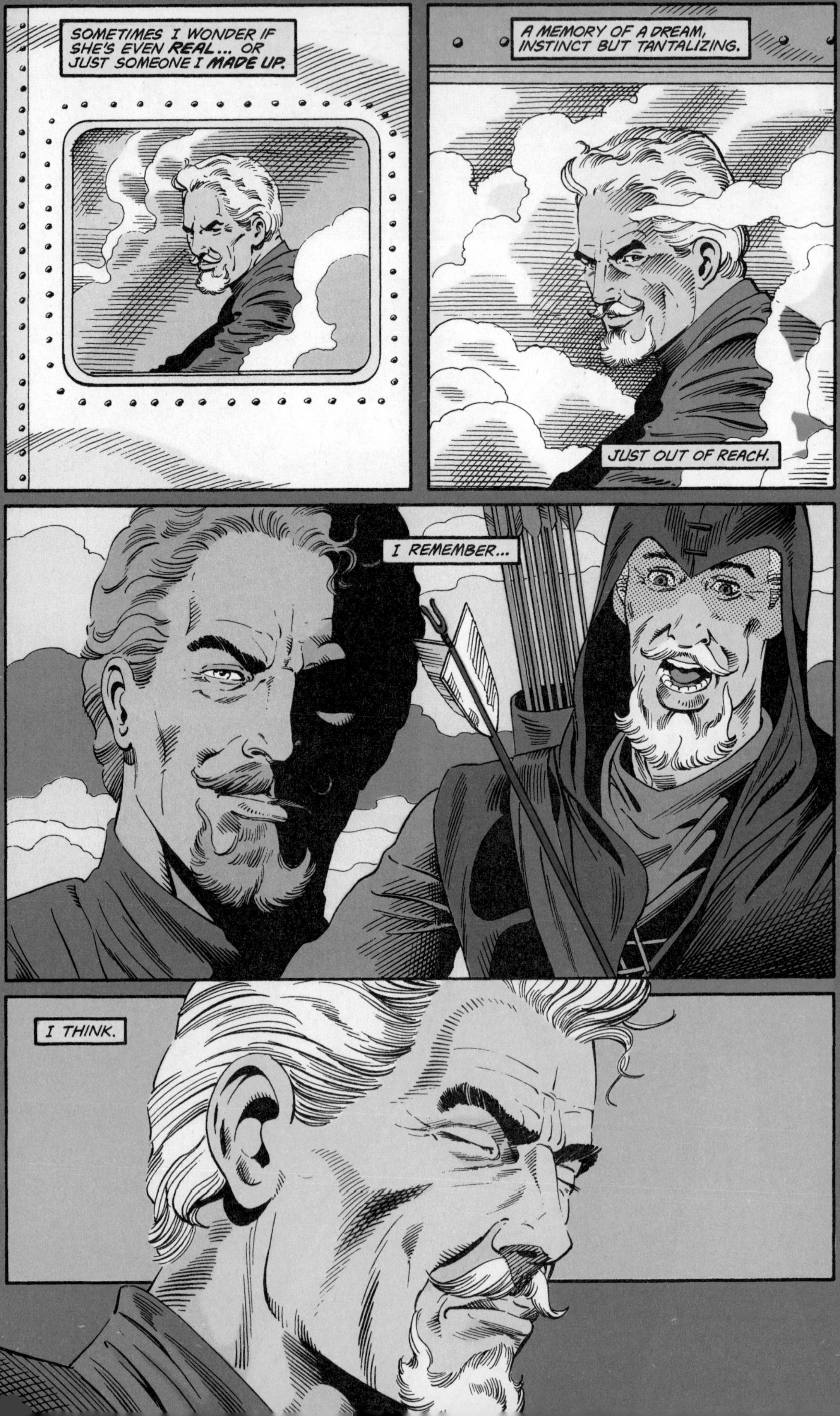
SOMETIMES I WONDER IF SHE'S EVEN REAL... OR JUST SOMEONE I MADE UP.
A MEMORY OF A DREAM, INSTINCT BUT TANTALIZING.
JUST OUT OF REACH.
I REMEMBER...
I THINK.

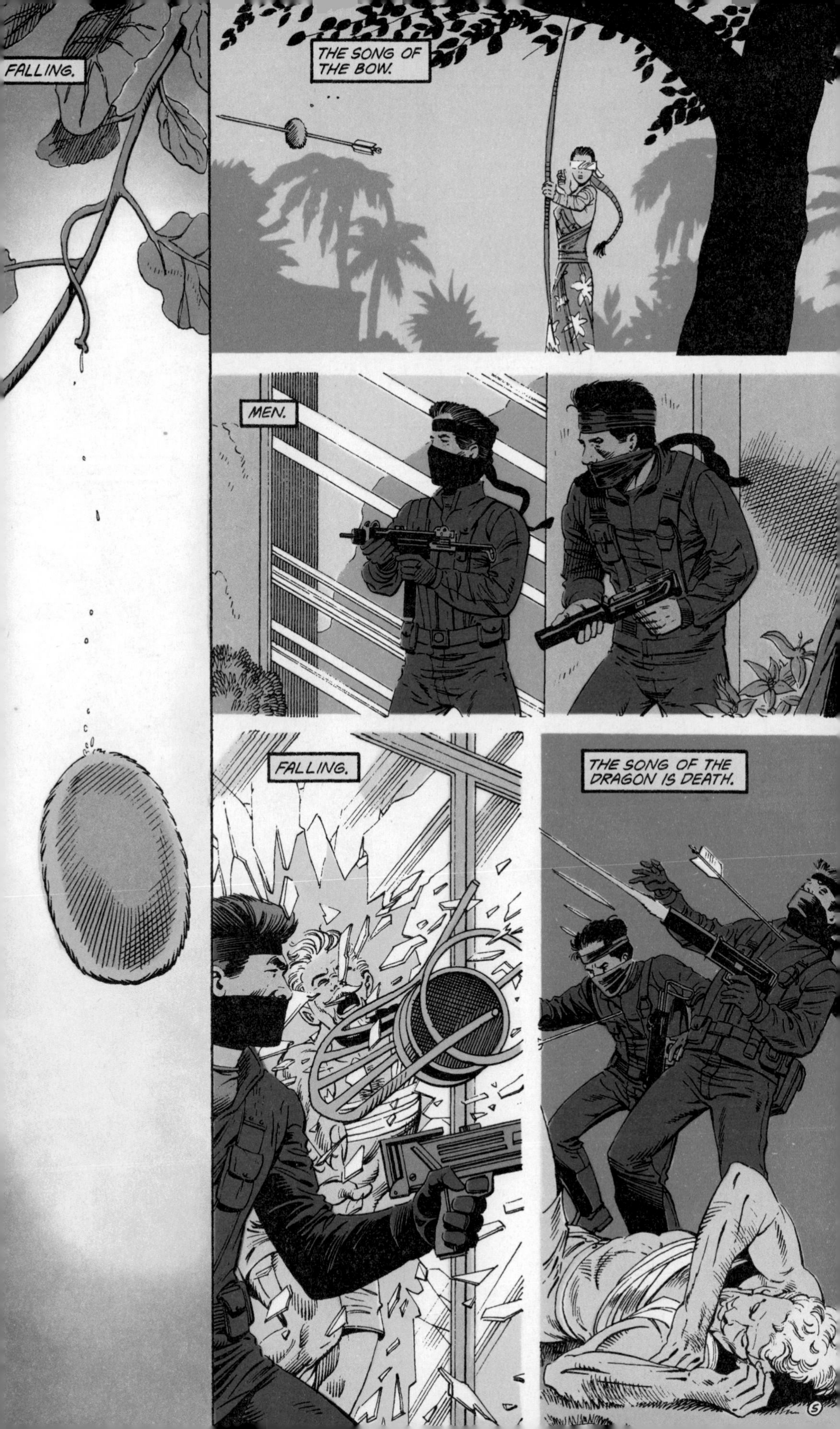
FALLING.
THE SONG OF THE BOW.
MEN.
FALLING.
THE SONG OF THE DRAGON IS DEATH.
5

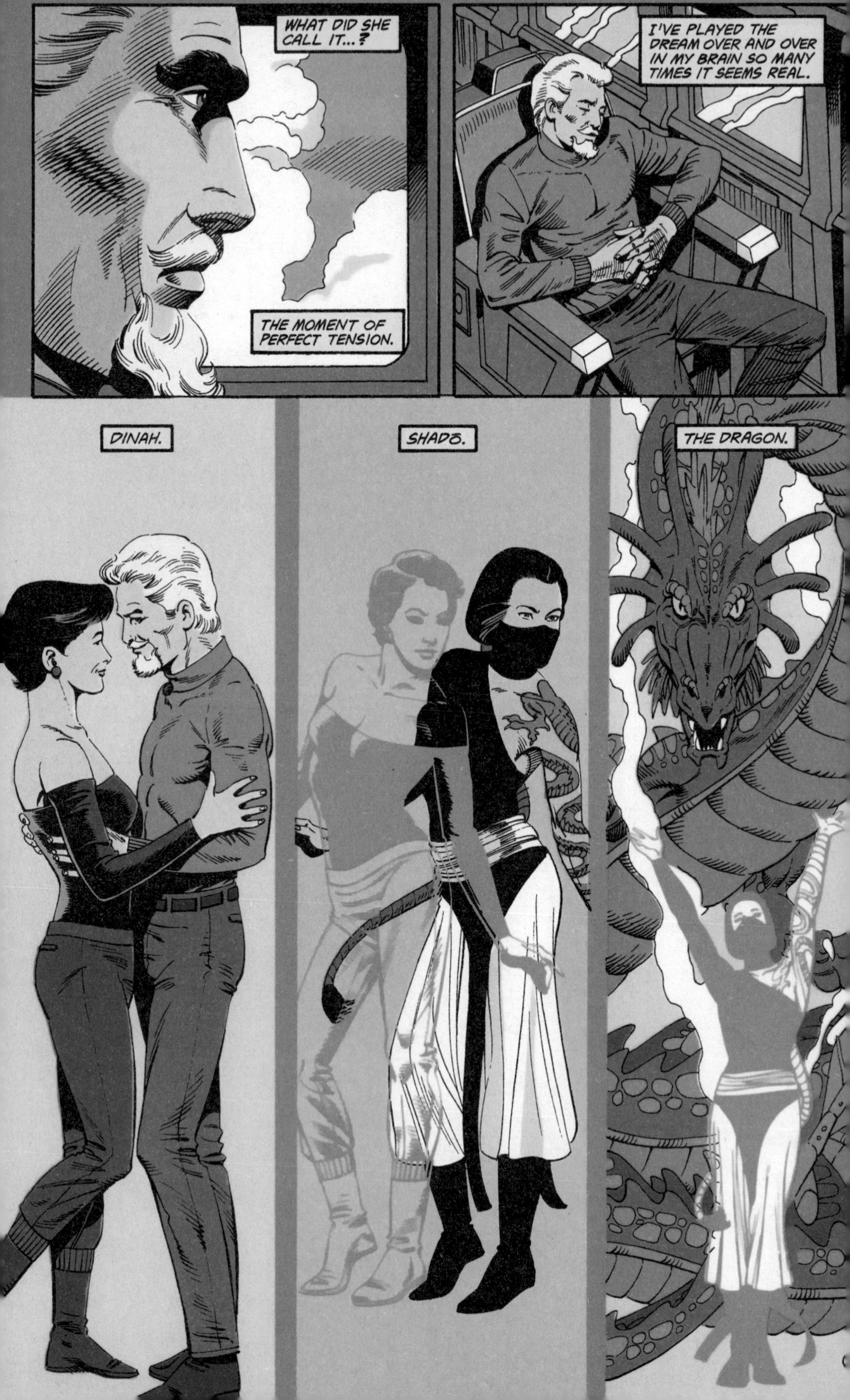
WHAT DID SHE CALL IT...?
THE MOMENT OF PERFECT TENSION.
I'VE PLAYED THE DREAM OVER AND OVER IN MY BRAIN SO MANY TIMES IT SEEMS REAL.
DINAH.
SHADO.
THE DRAGON.

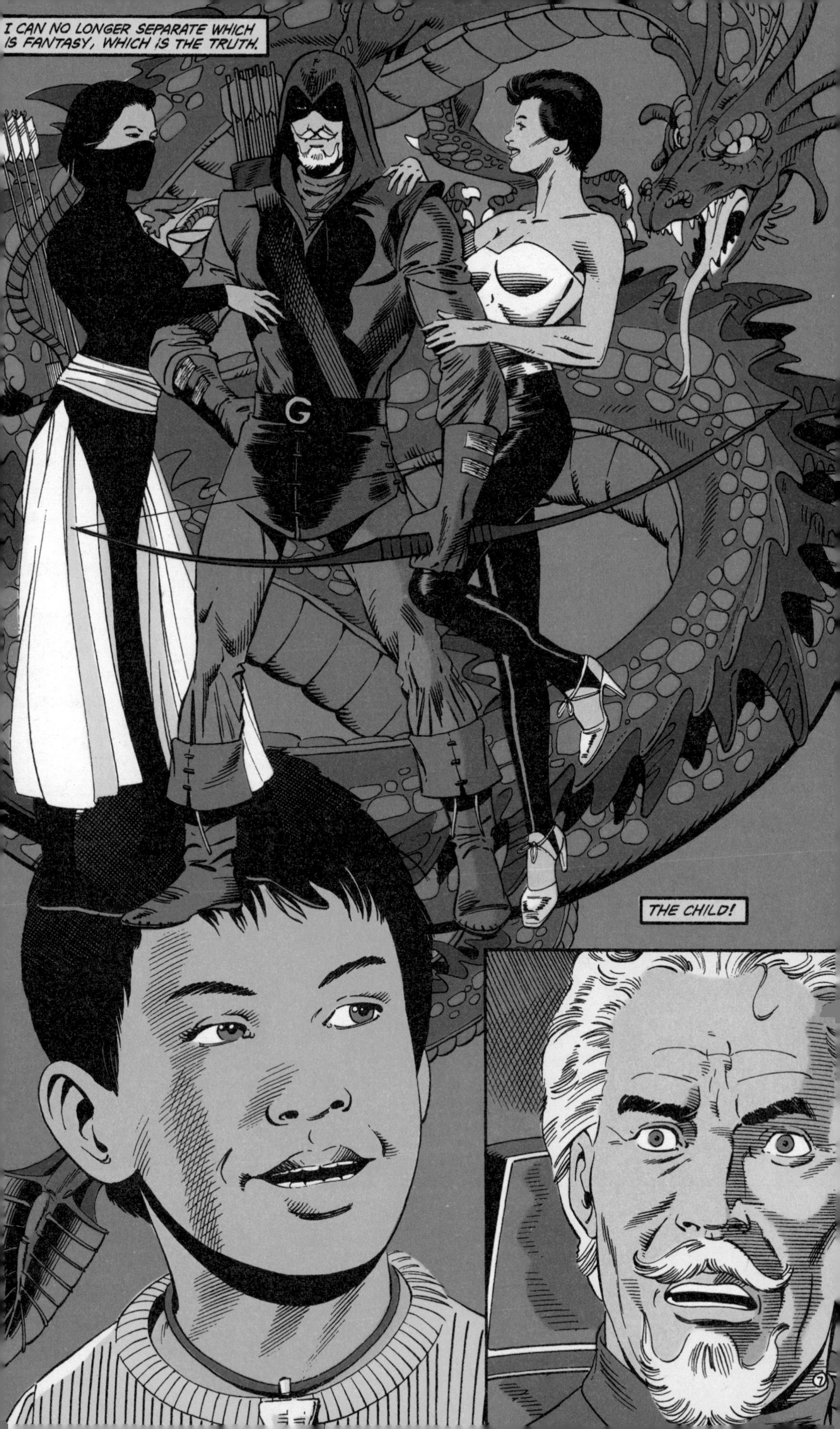
I CAN NO LONGER SEPARATE WHICH IS FANTASY, WHICH IS THE TRUTH.
THE CHILD!

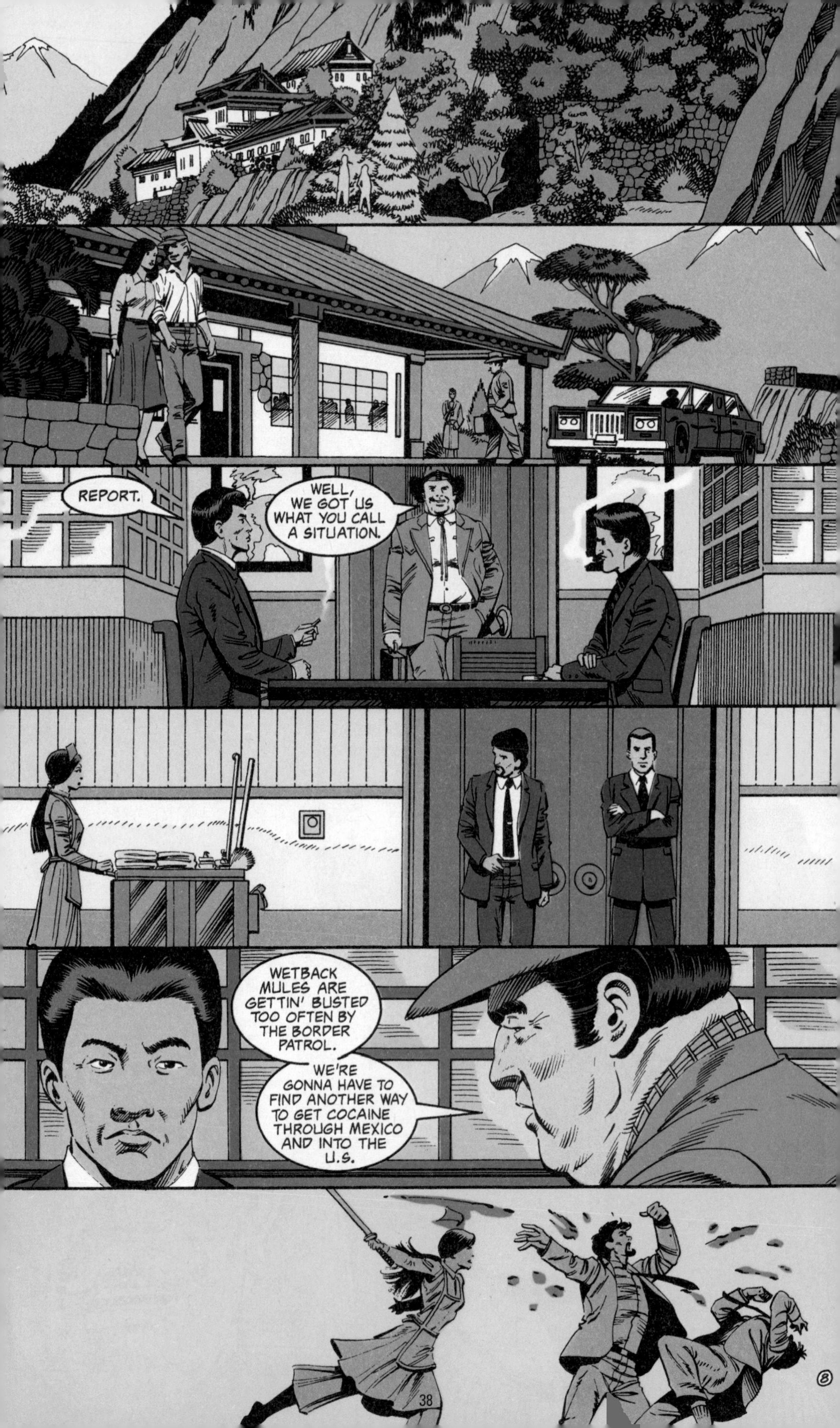
REPORT.
WELL, WE GOT US WHAT YOU CALL A SITUATION.
WETBACK MULES ARE GETTIN' BUSTED TOO OFTEN BY THE BORDER PATROL.
WE'RE GONNA HAVE TO FIND ANOTHER WAY TO GET COCAINE THROUGH MEXICO AND INTO THE U.S.
8

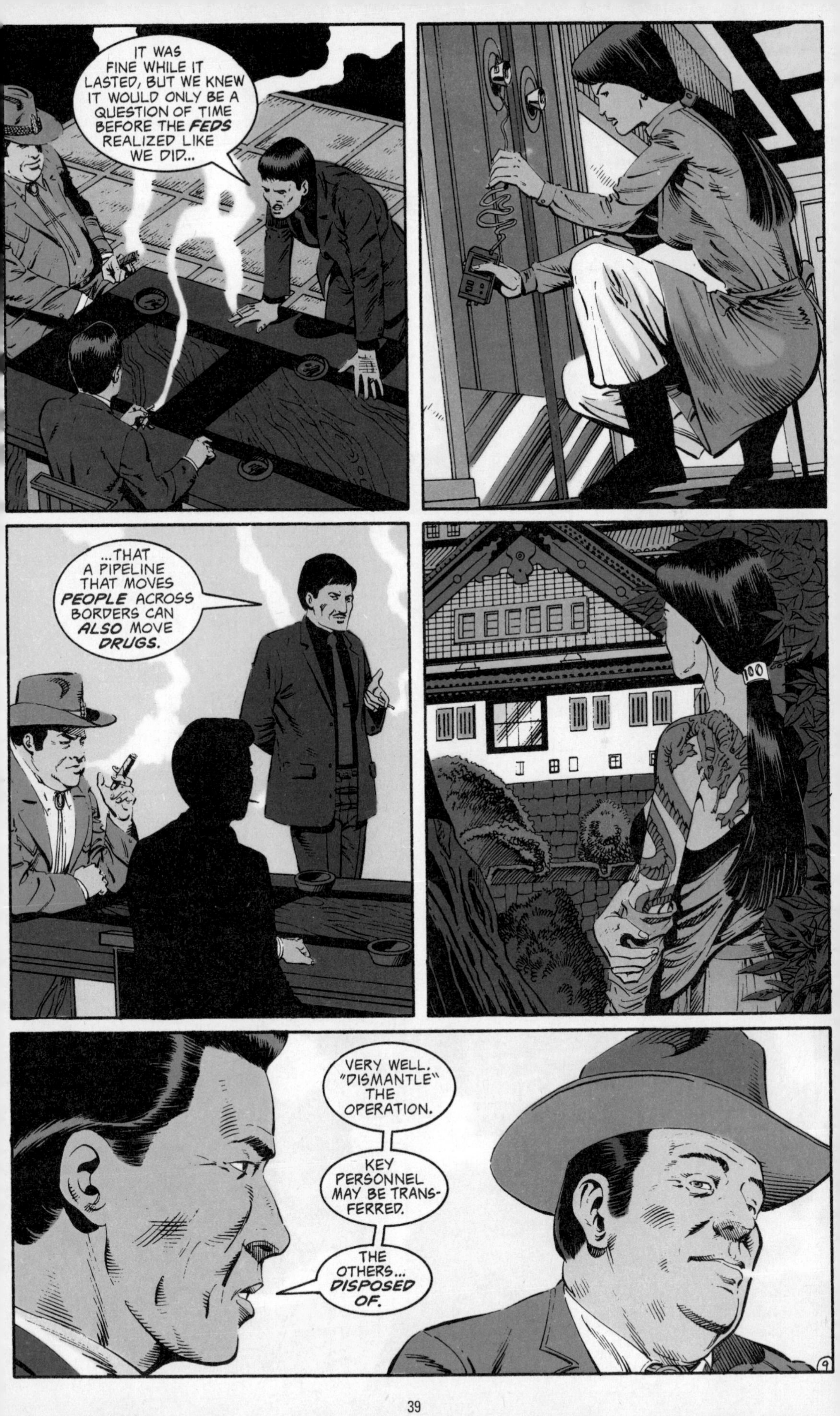
IT WAS FINE WHILE IT LASTED, BUT WE KNEW IT WOULD ONLY BE A QUESTION OF TIME BEFORE THE FEDS REALIZED LIKE WE DID...
...THAT A PIPELINE THAT MOVES PEOPLE ACROSS BORDERS CAN ALSO MOVE DRUGS.
100
VERY WELL. "DISMANTLE" THE OPERATION.
KEY PERSONNEL MAY BE TRANS-FERRED.
THE OTHERS... DISPOSED OF.
9

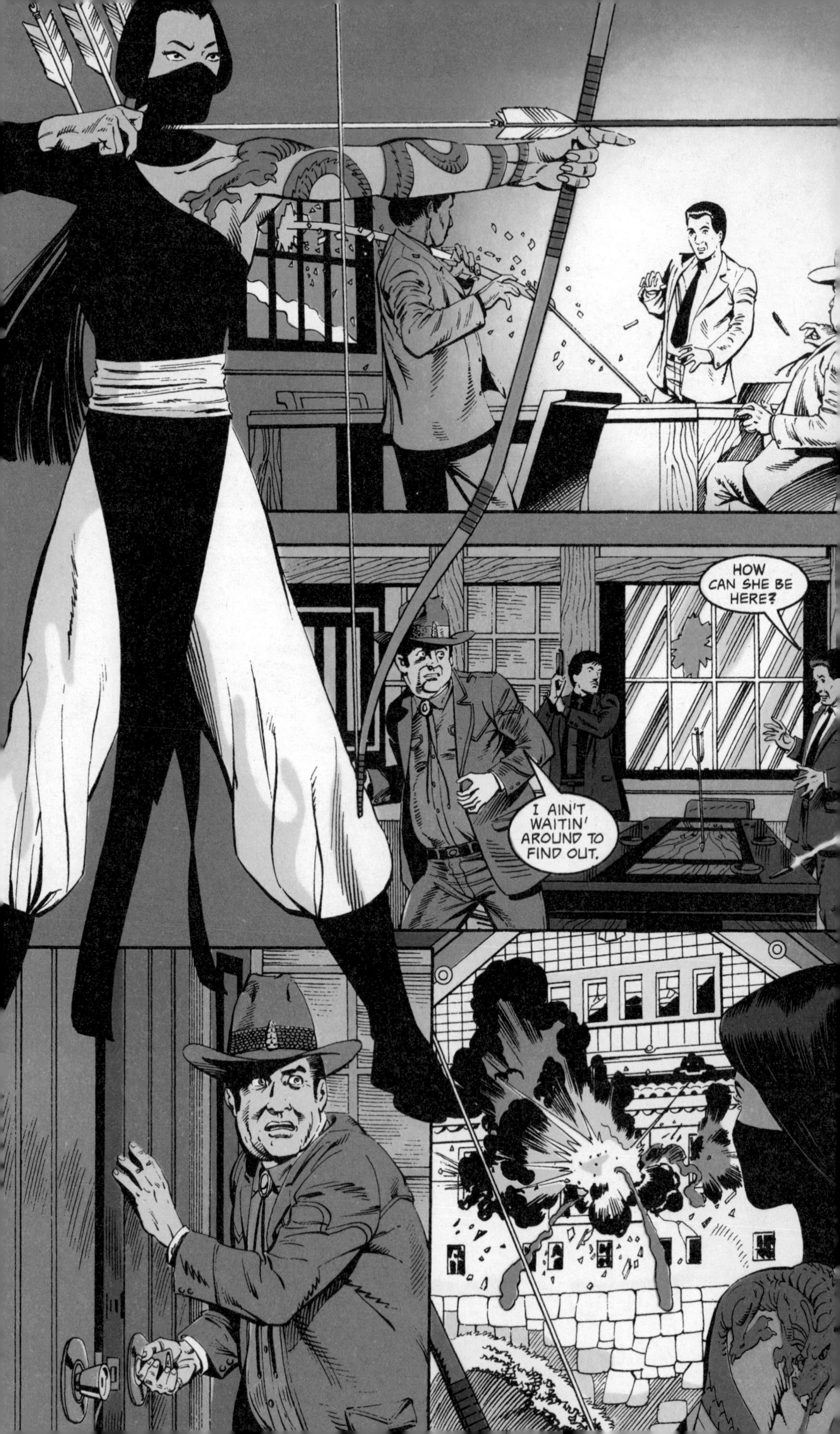
HOW CAN SHE BE HERE?
I AIN'T WAITIN' AROUND TO FIND OUT.

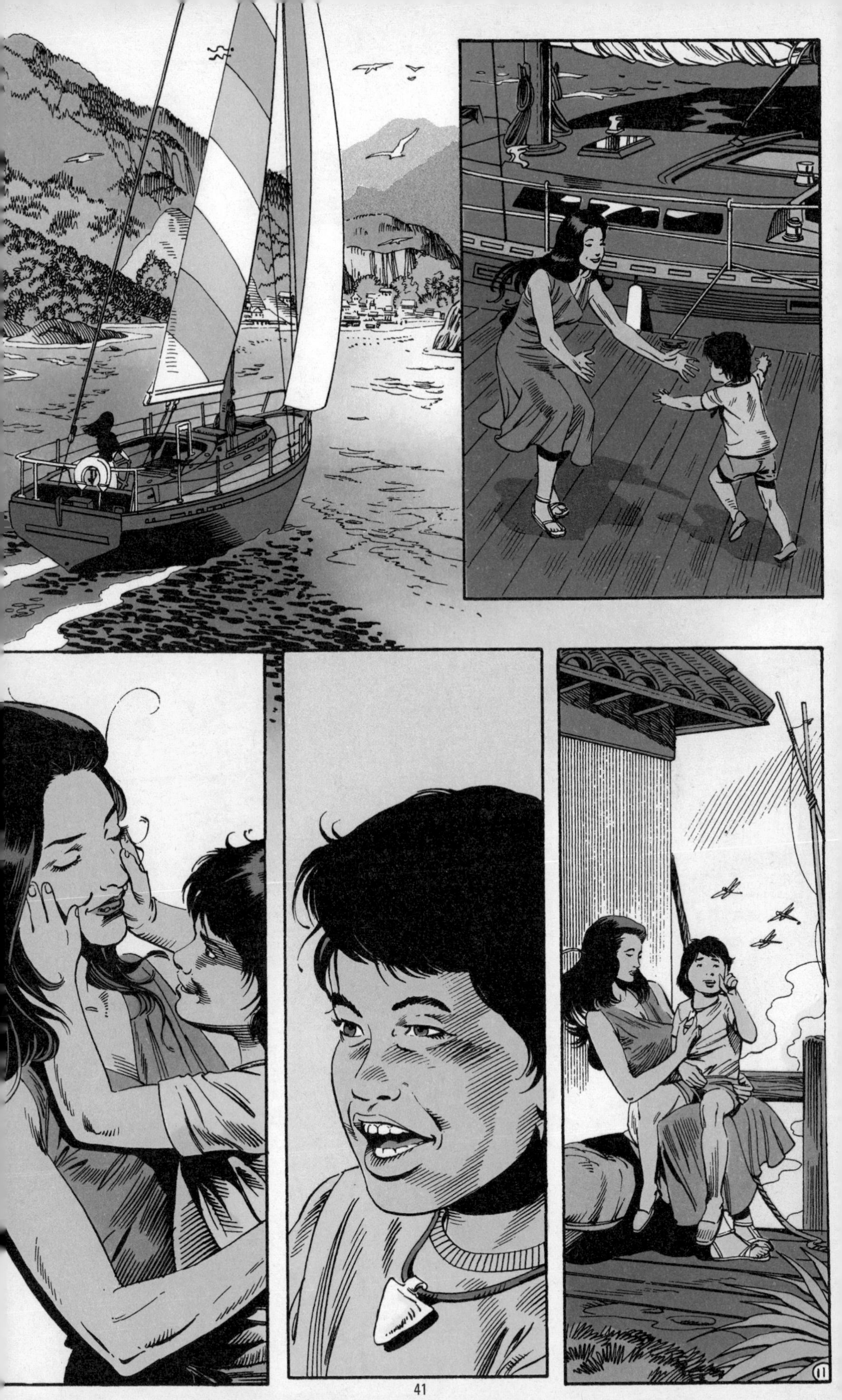
11

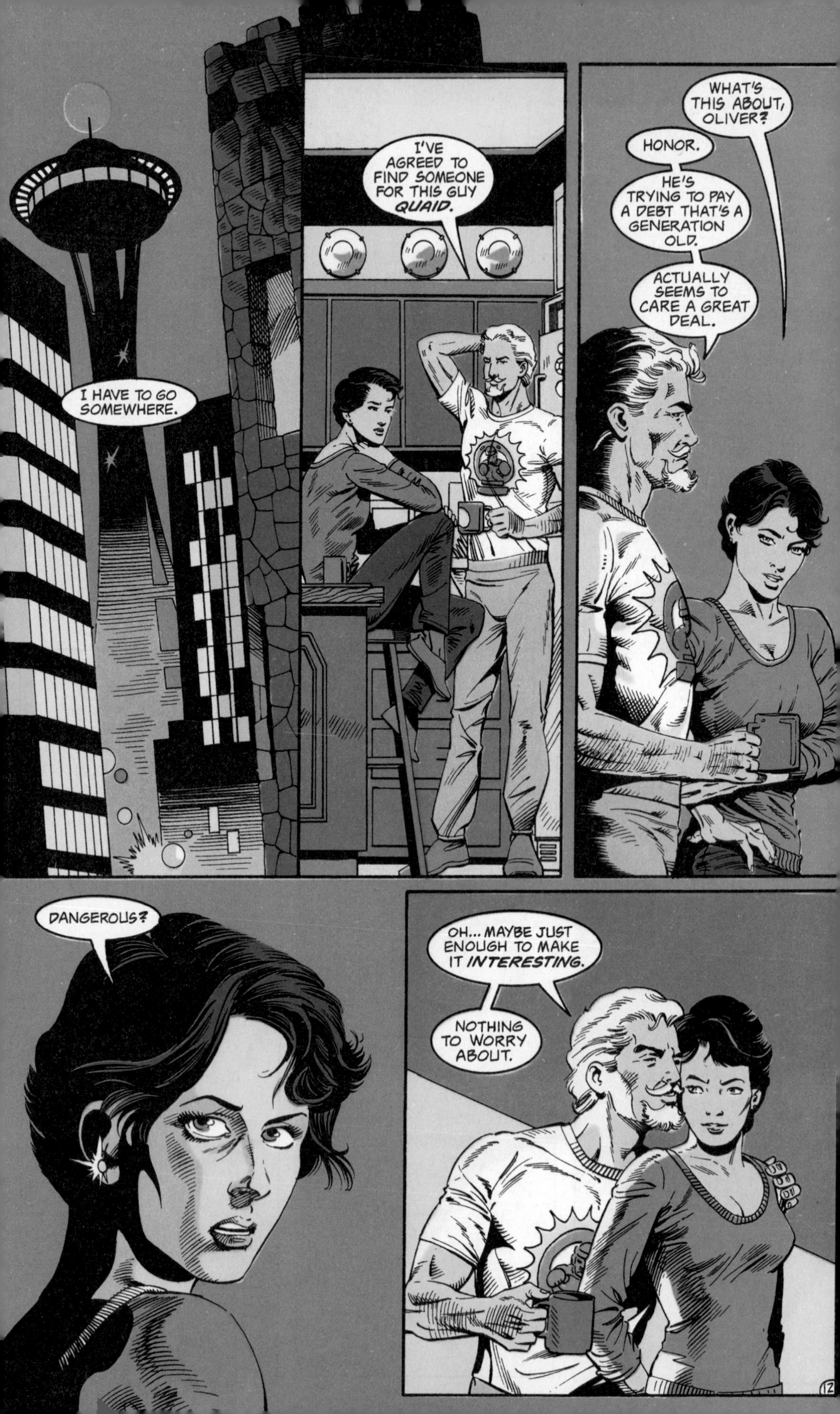
I HAVE TO GO SOMEWHERE.
I'VE AGREED TO FIND SOMEONE FOR THIS GUY QUAID.
WHAT'S THIS ABOUT, OLIVER?
HONOR.
HE'S TRYING TO PAY A DEBT THAT'S A GENERATION OLD.
ACTUALLY SEEMS TO CARE A GREAT DEAL.
DANGEROUS?
OH... MAYBE JUST ENOUGH TO MAKE IT INTERESTING.
NOTHING TO WORRY ABOUT.
12

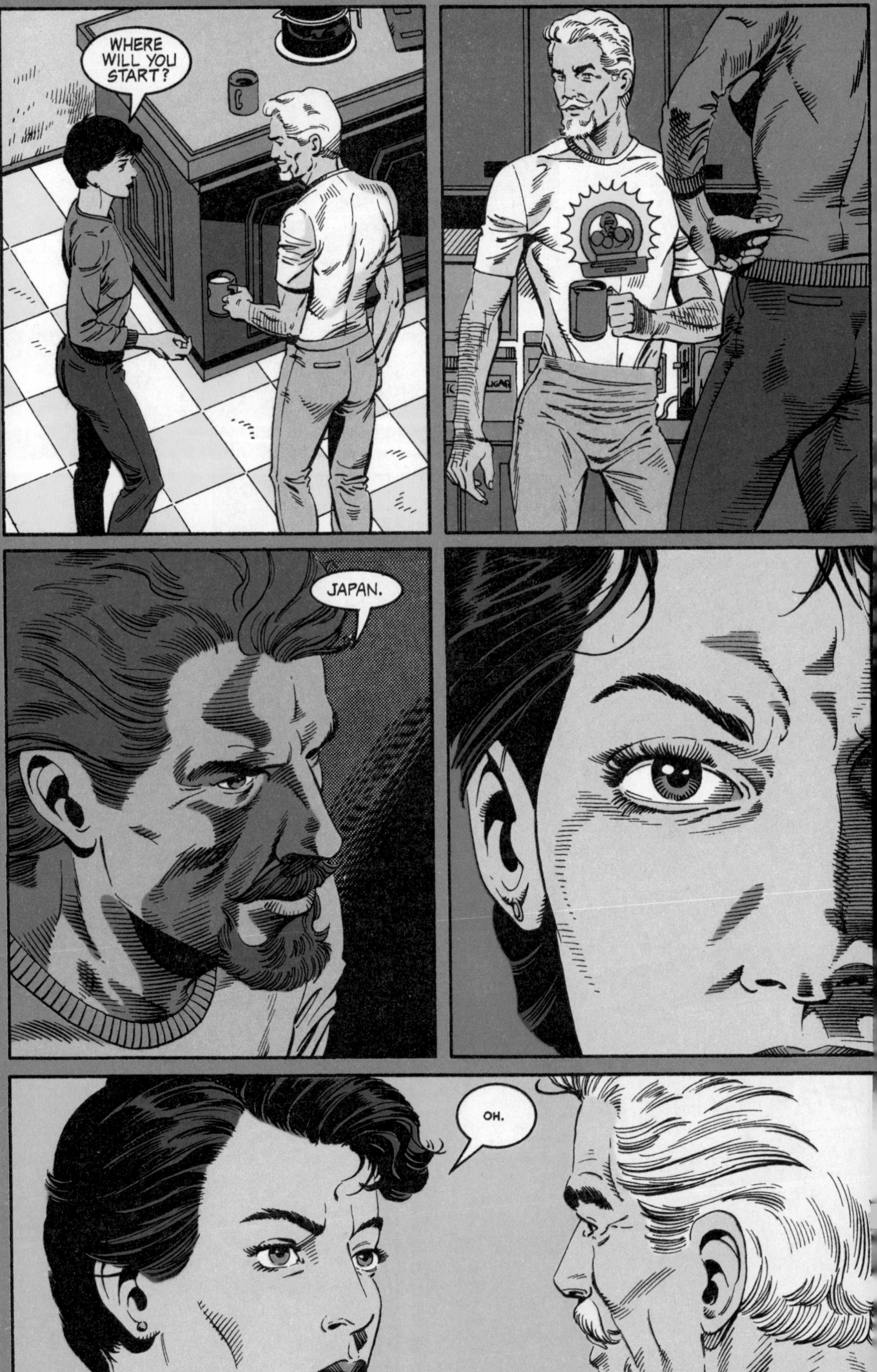
WHERE WILL YOU START?
JAPAN.
OH.
"HER"

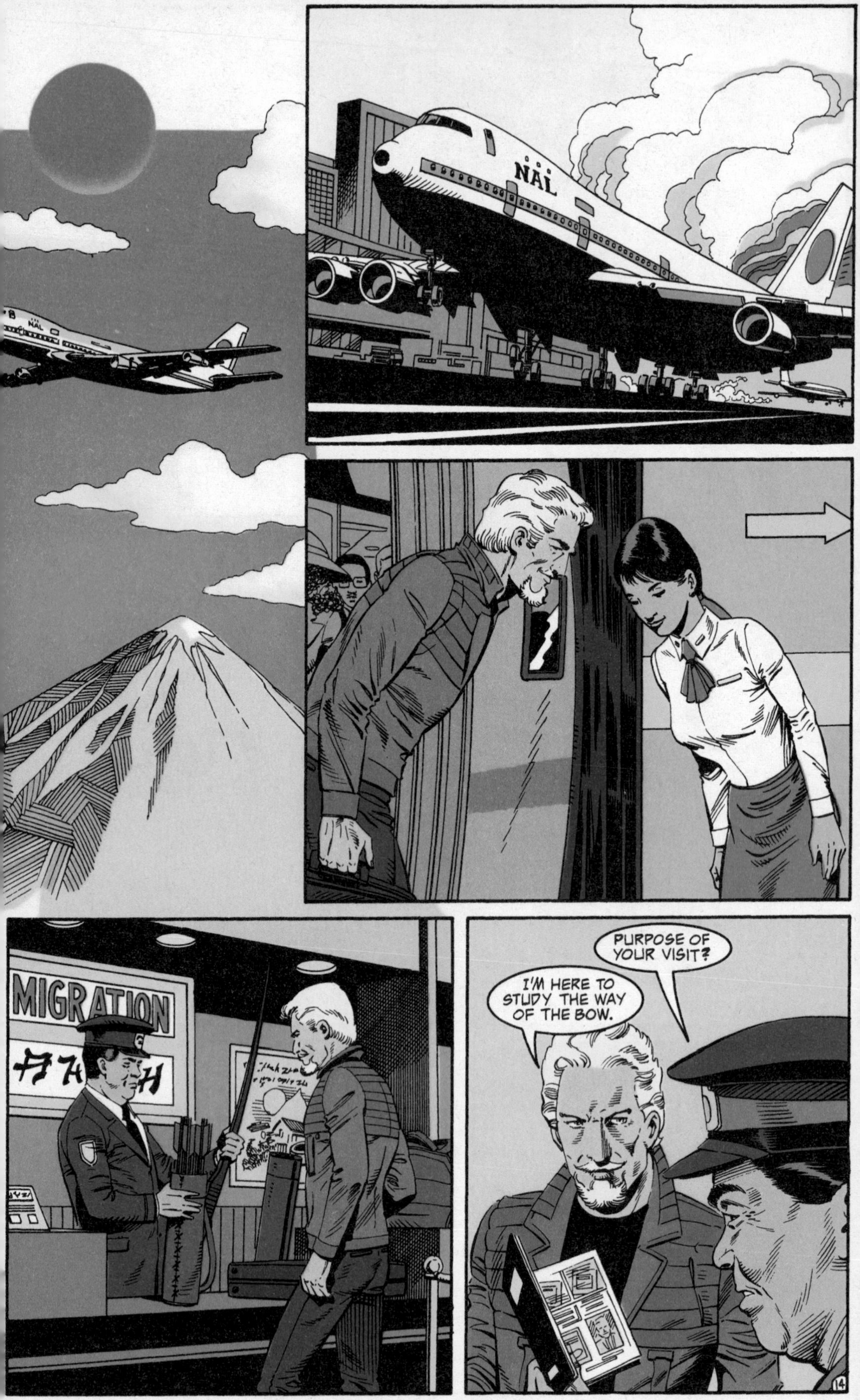
NAL
MIGRATION
PURPOSE OF YOUR VISIT?
I'M HERE TO STUDY THE WAY OF THE BOW.
14

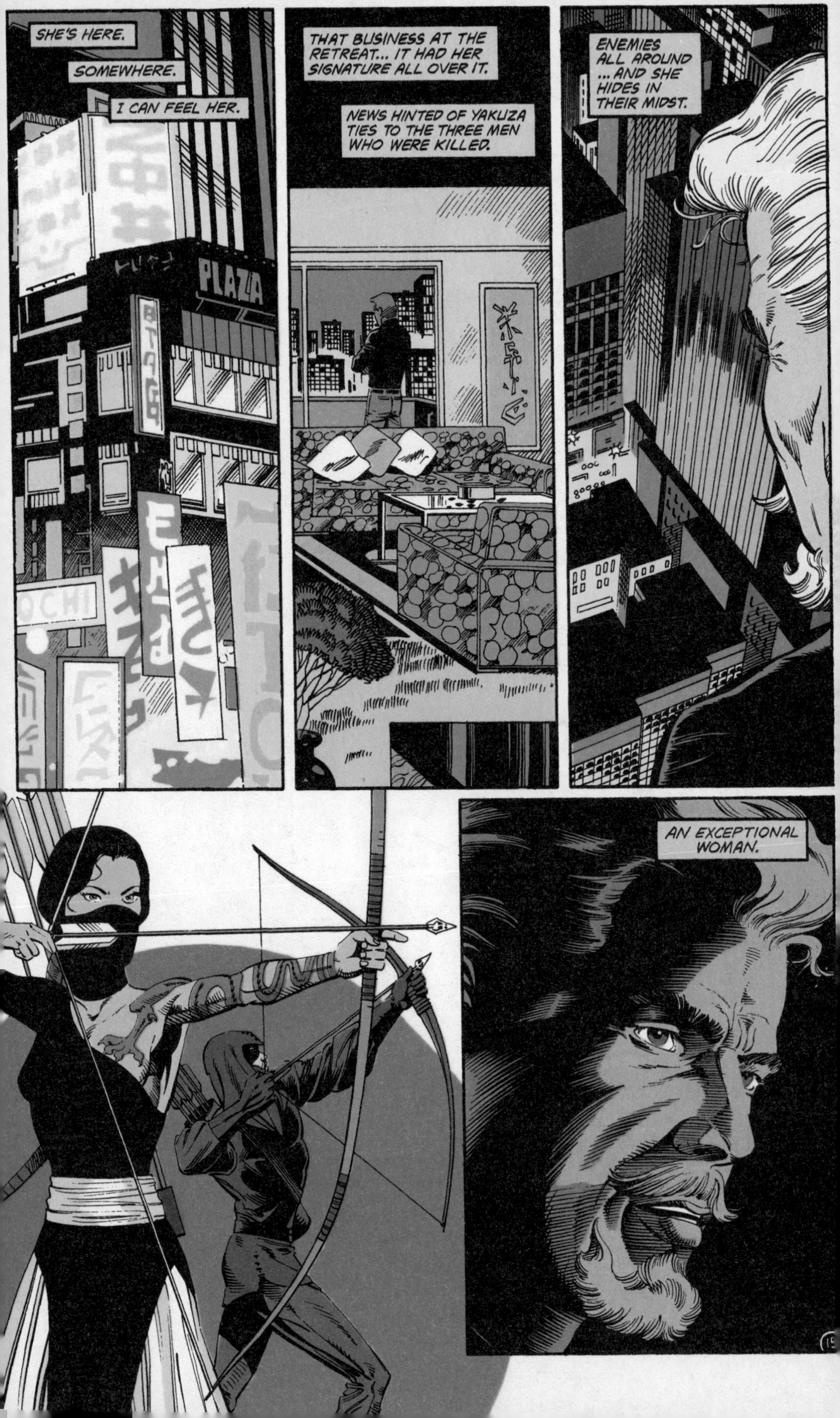
SHE'S HERE.
SOMEWHERE.
I CAN FEEL HER.
PLAZA
THAT BUSINESS AT THE RETREAT... IT HAD HER SIGNATURE ALL OVER IT.
NEWS HINTED OF YAKUZA TIES TO THE THREE MEN WHO WERE KILLED.
ENEMIES ALL AROUND ...AND SHE HIDES IN THEIR MIDST.
AN EXCEPTIONAL WOMAN.

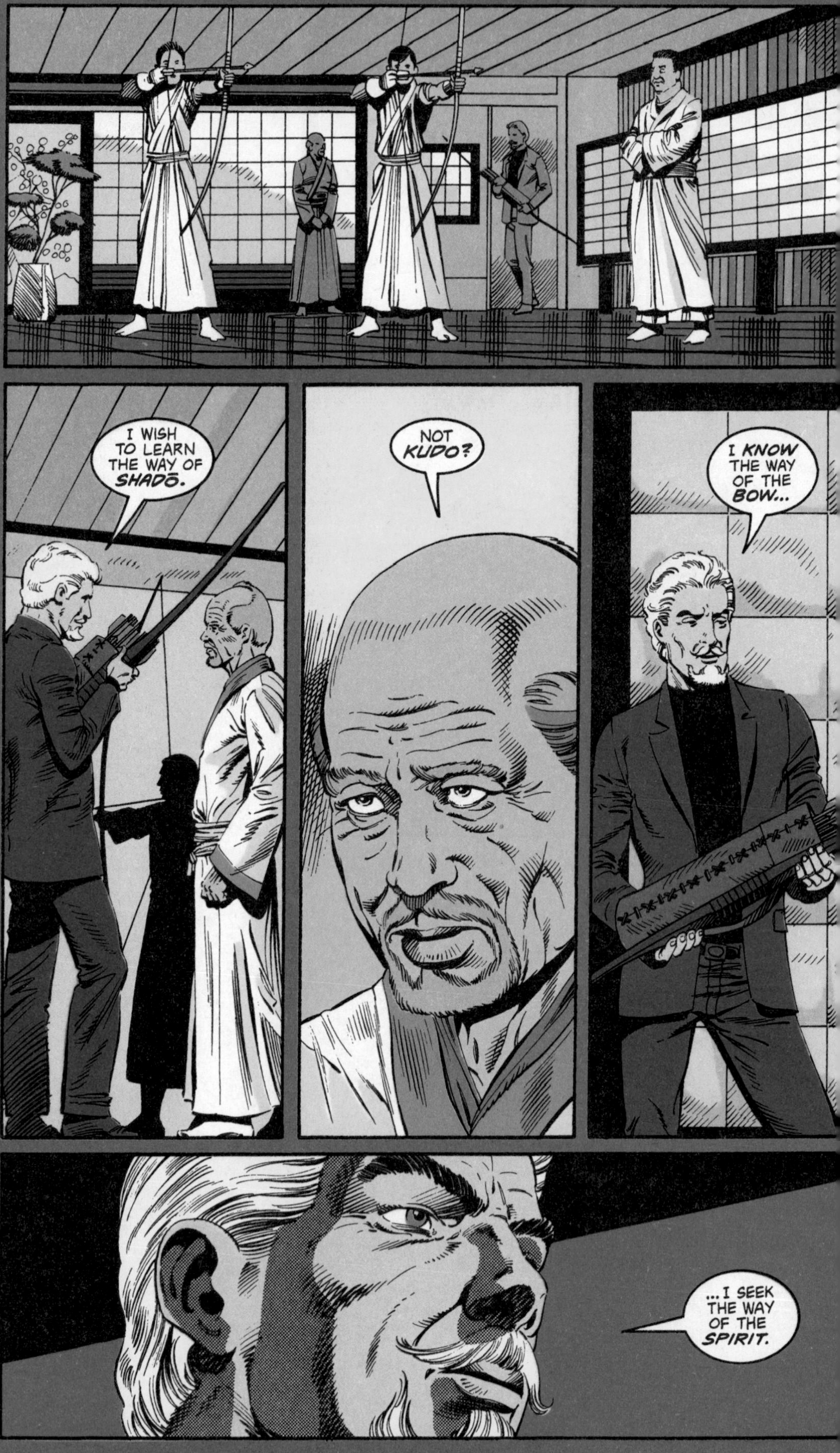
I WISH TO LEARN THE WAY OF SHADŌ.
NOT KUDO?
I KNOW THE WAY OF THE BOW...
...I SEEK THE WAY OF THE SPIRIT.

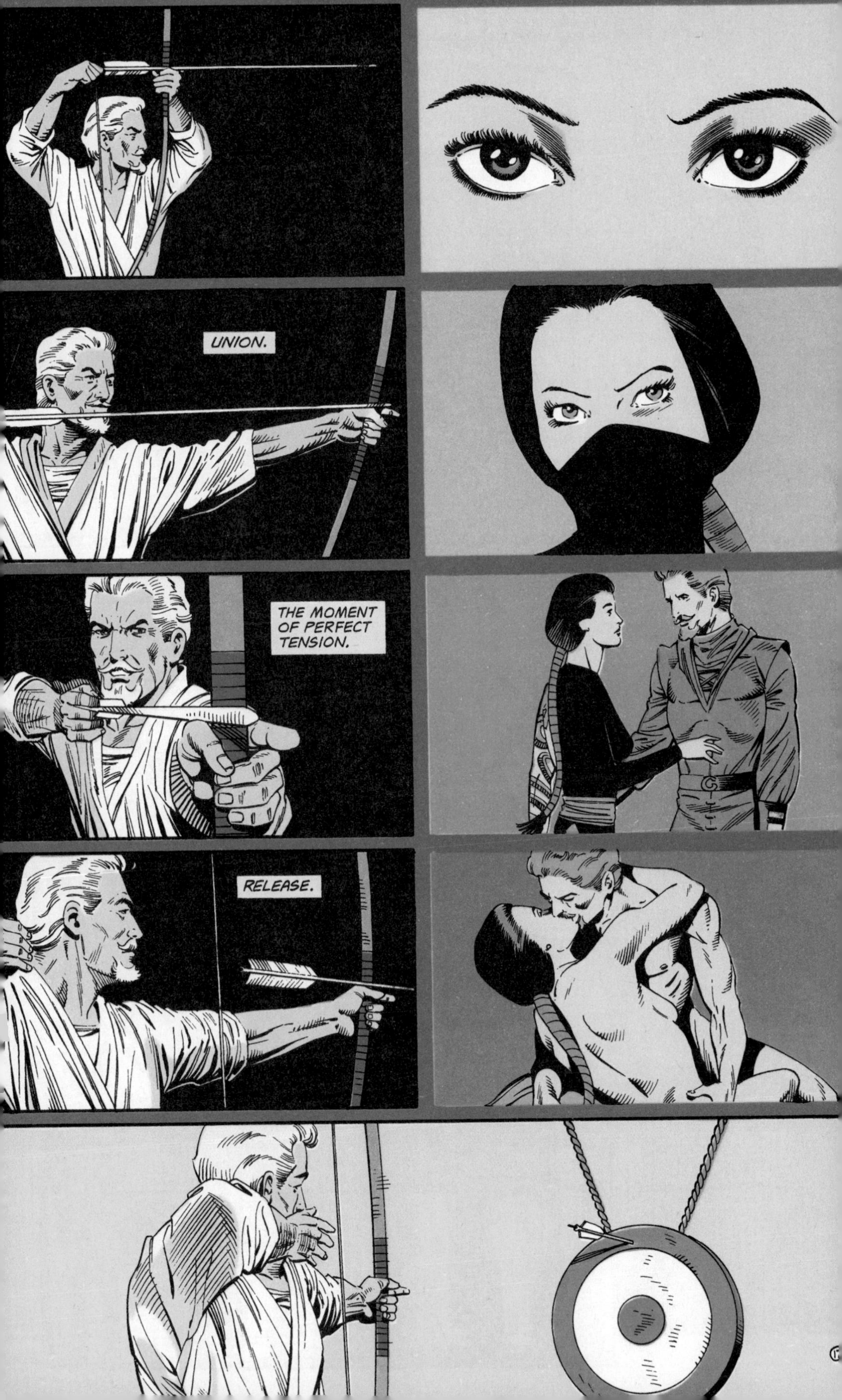
UNION.
THE MOMENT OF PERFECT TENSION.
RELEASE.

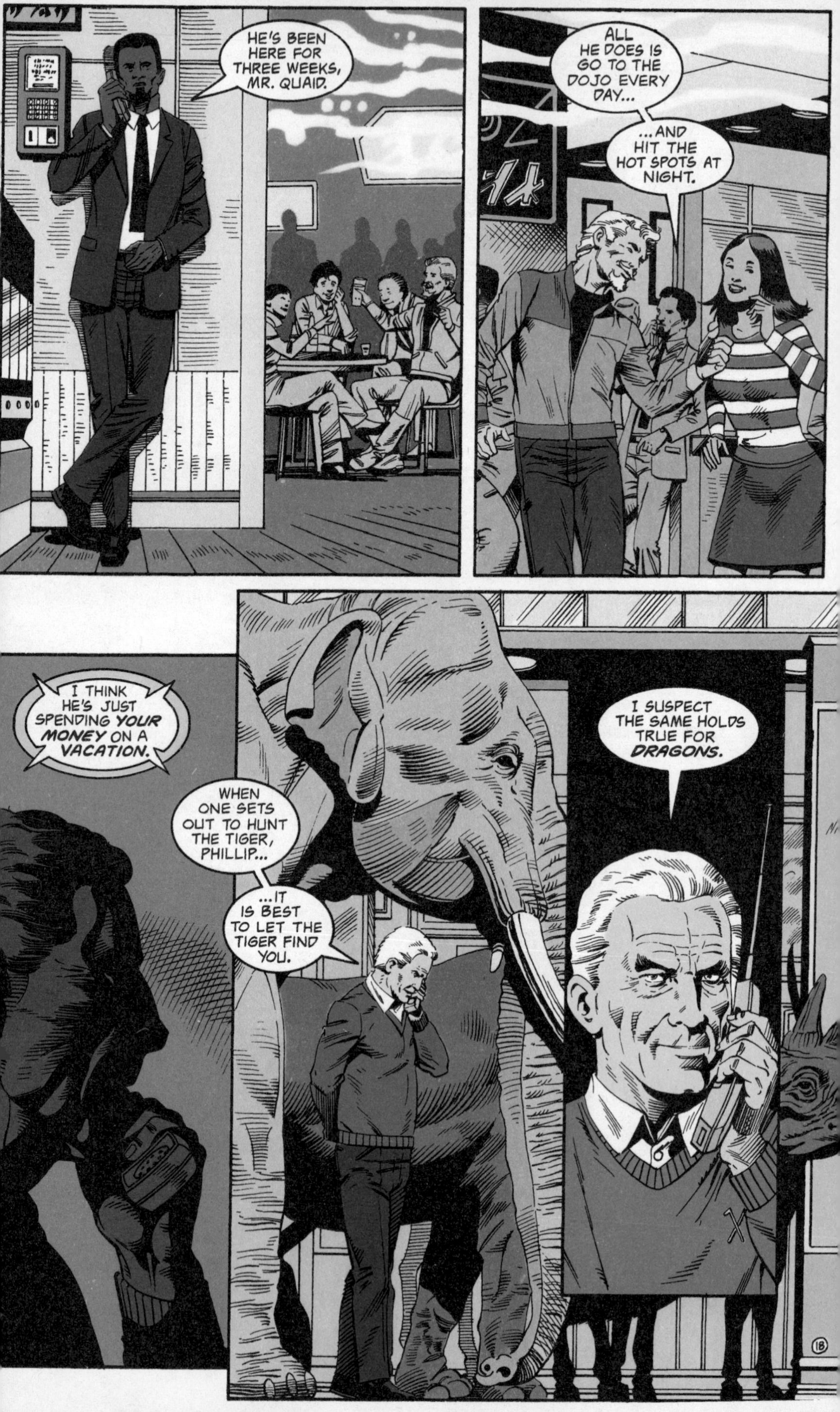

HE'S BEEN HERE FOR THREE WEEKS, MR. QUAID.
ALL HE DOES IS GO TO THE DOJO EVERY DAY...
...AND HIT THE HOT SPOTS AT NIGHT.
I THINK HE'S JUST SPENDING YOUR MONEY ON A VACATION.
WHEN ONE SETS OUT TO HUNT THE TIGER, PHILLIP...
...IT IS BEST TO LET THE TIGER FIND YOU.
I SUSPECT THE SAME HOLDS TRUE FOR DRAGONS.

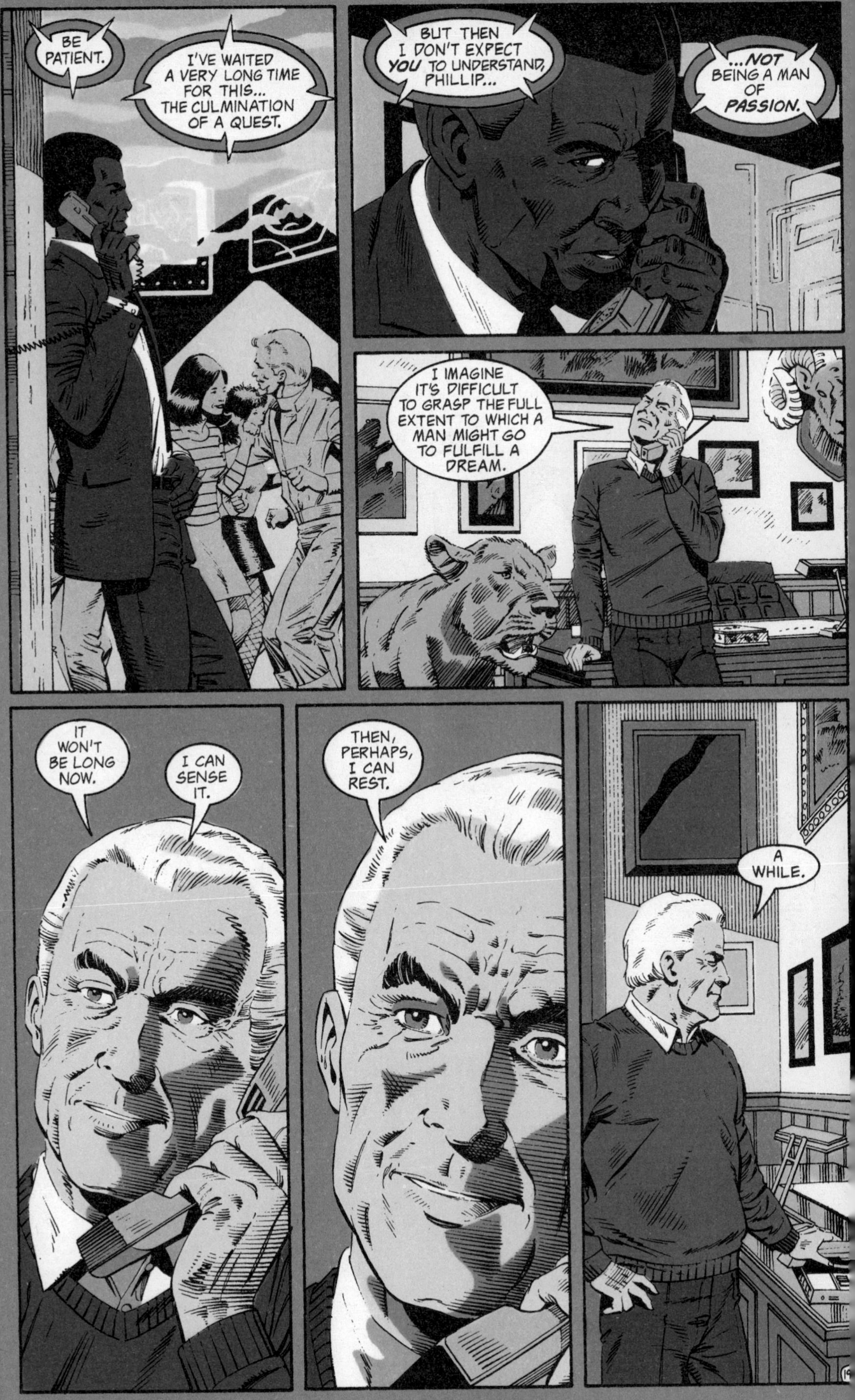
BE PATIENT.
I'VE WAITED A VERY LONG TIME FOR THIS... THE CULMINATION OF A QUEST.
BUT THEN I DON'T EXPECT YOU TO UNDERSTAND, PHILLIP...
...NOT BEING A MAN OF PASSION.
I IMAGINE IT'S DIFFICULT TO GRASP THE FULL EXTENT TO WHICH A MAN MIGHT GO TO FULFILL A DREAM.
IT WON'T BE LONG NOW.
I CAN SENSE IT.
THEN, PERHAPS, I CAN REST.
A WHILE.
19

LET ME SEE HOW YOU SHOOT THIS.

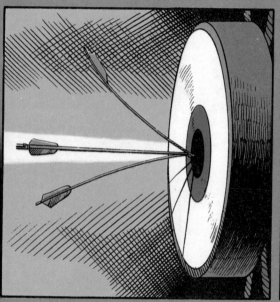

FOOLISH TO WASTE A GOOD ARROW.

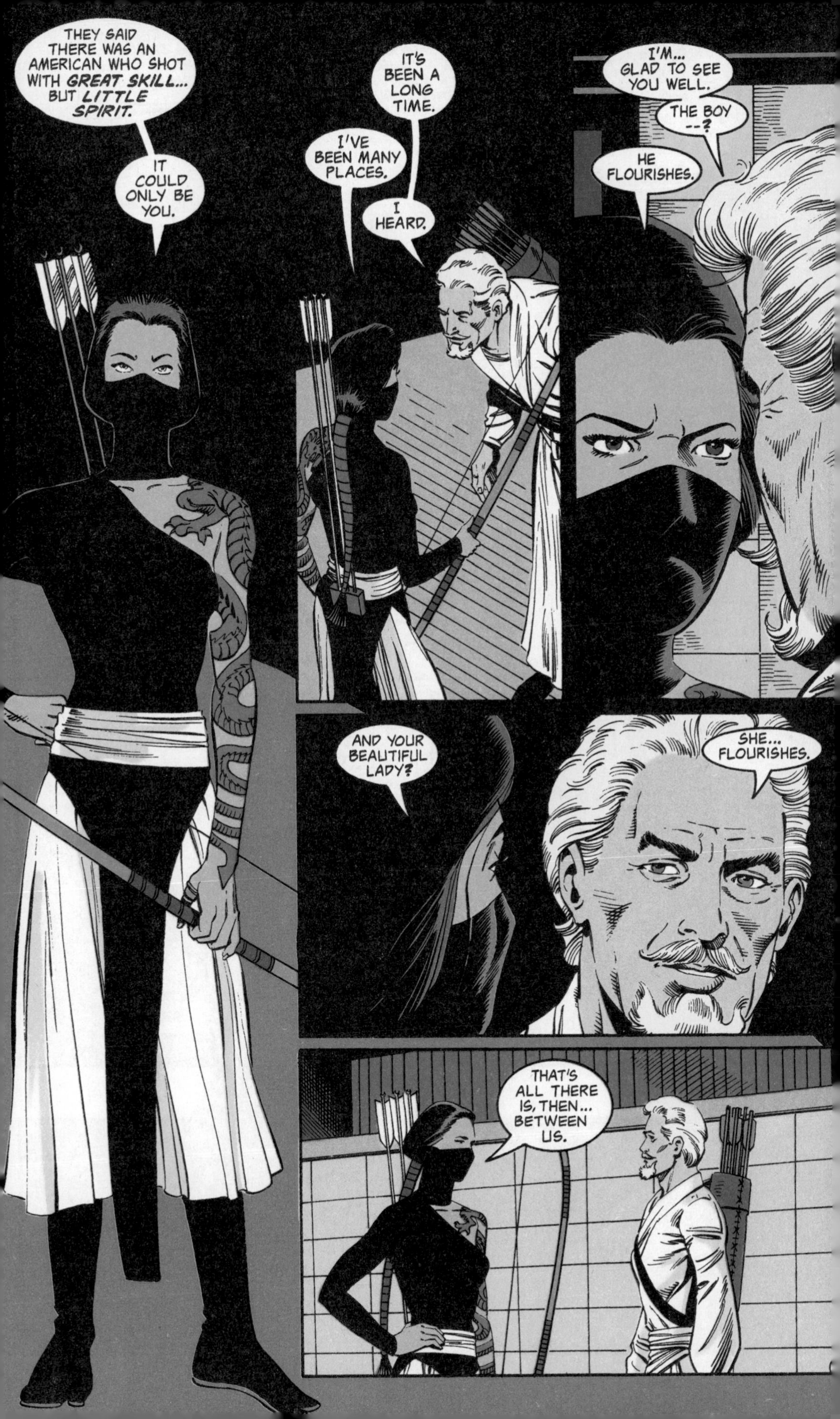
THEY SAID THERE WAS AN AMERICAN WHO SHOT WITH GREAT SKILL... BUT LITTLE SPIRIT.
IT COULD ONLY BE YOU.
I'VE BEEN MANY PLACES.
IT'S BEEN A LONG TIME.
I HEARD.
I'M... GLAD TO SEE YOU WELL.
THE BOY --?
HE FLOURISHES.
AND YOUR BEAUTIFUL LADY?
SHE... FLOURISHES.
THAT'S ALL THERE IS, THEN... BETWEEN US.

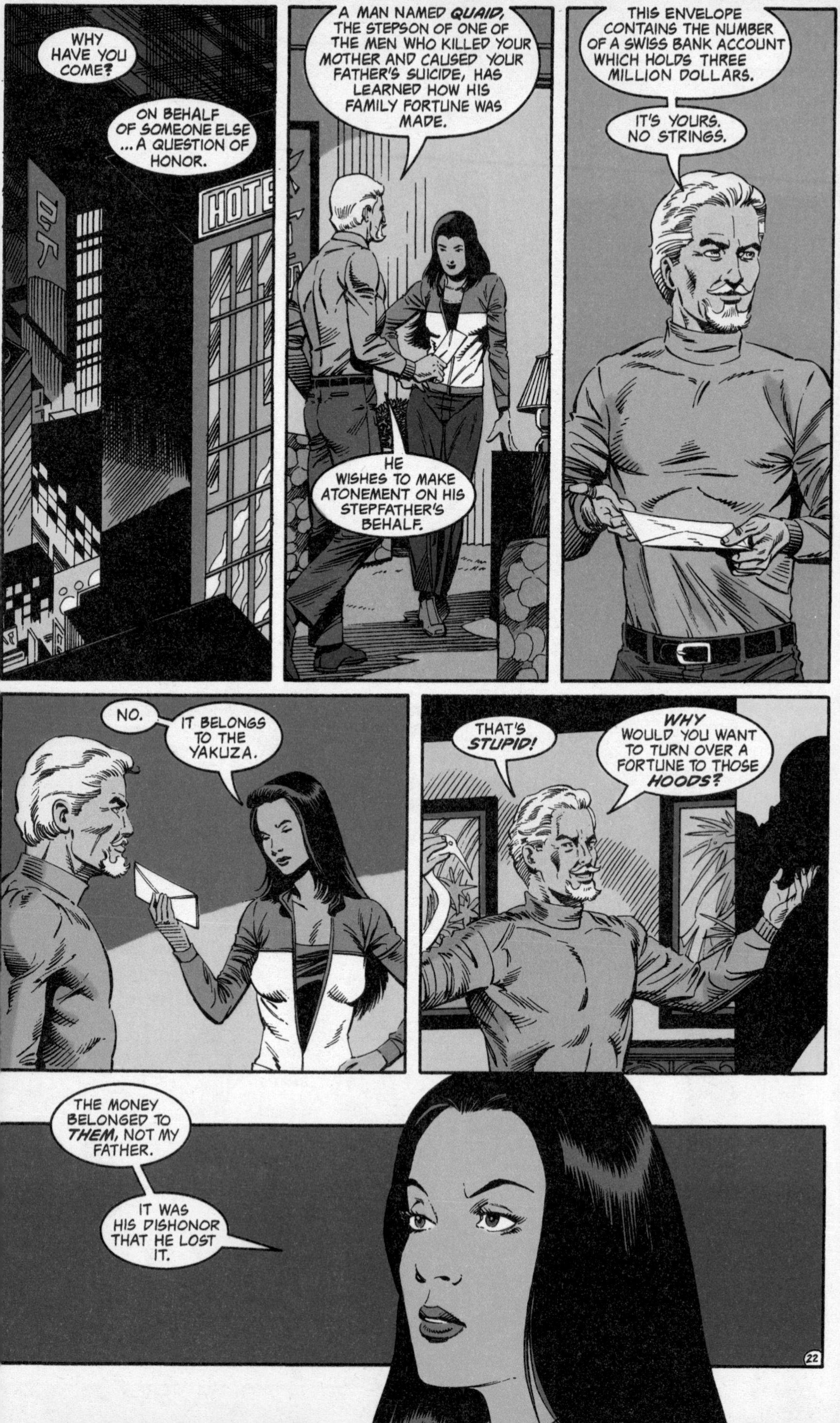
WHY HAVE YOU COME?
ON BEHALF OF SOMEONE ELSE ...A QUESTION OF HONOR.
HOTE
A MAN NAMED QUAID, THE STEPSON OF ONE OF THE MEN WHO KILLED YOUR MOTHER AND CAUSED YOUR FATHER'S SUICIDE, HAS LEARNED HOW HIS FAMILY FORTUNE WAS MADE.
HE WISHES TO MAKE ATONEMENT ON HIS STEPFATHER'S BEHALF.
THIS ENVELOPE CONTAINS THE NUMBER OF A SWISS BANK ACCOUNT WHICH HOLDS THREE MILLION DOLLARS.
IT'S YOURS. NO STRINGS.
NO.
IT BELONGS TO THE YAKUZA.
THAT'S STUPID!
WHY WOULD YOU WANT TO TURN OVER A FORTUNE TO THOSE HOODS?
THE MONEY BELONGED TO THEM, NOT MY FATHER.
IT WAS HIS DISHONOR THAT HE LOST IT.

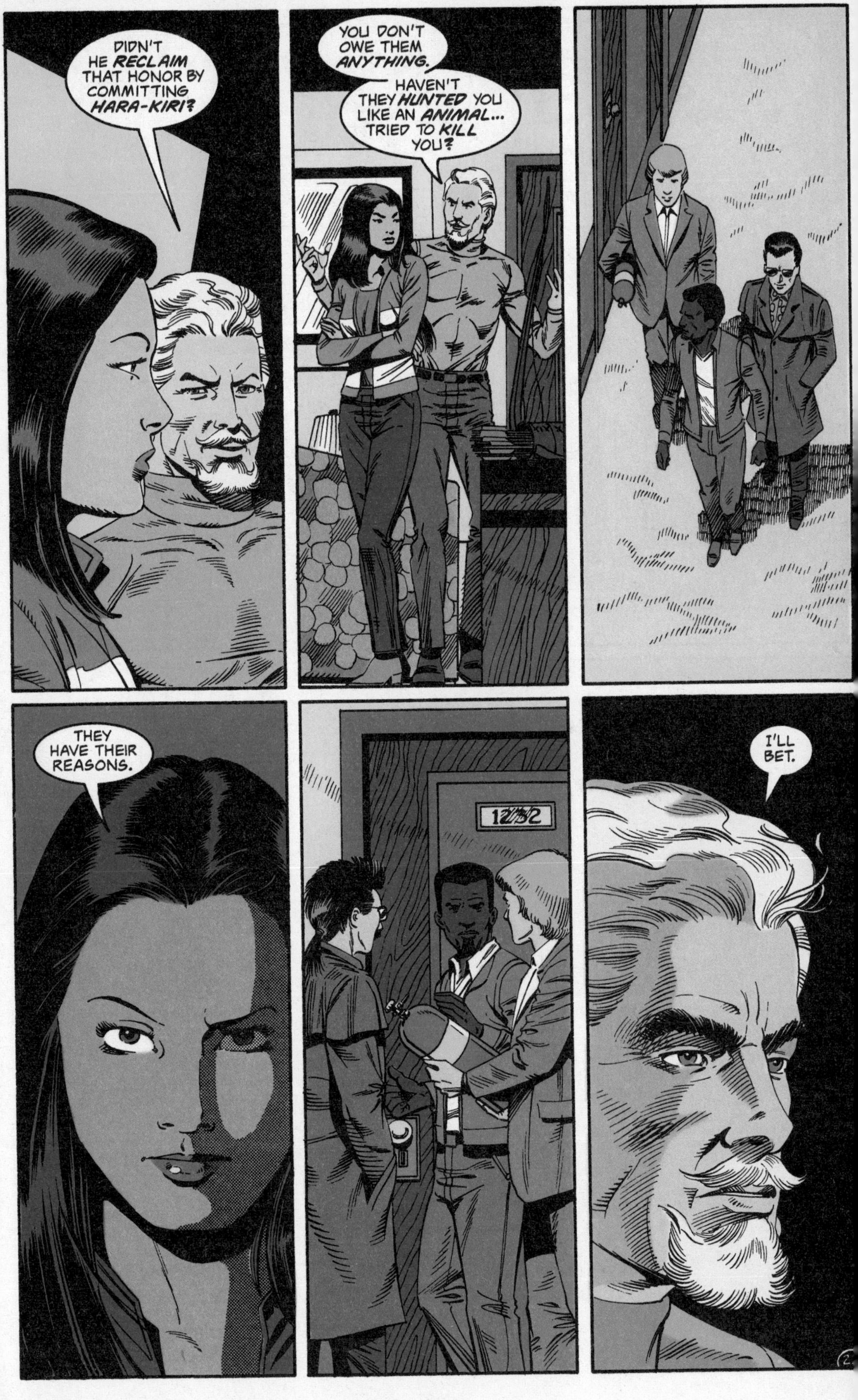

DIDN'T HE RECLAIM THAT HONOR BY COMMITTING HARA-KIRI?
YOU DON'T OWE THEM ANYTHING.
HAVEN'T THEY HUNTED YOU LIKE AN ANIMAL... TRIED TO KILL YOU?
THEY HAVE THEIR REASONS.
1232
I'LL BET.

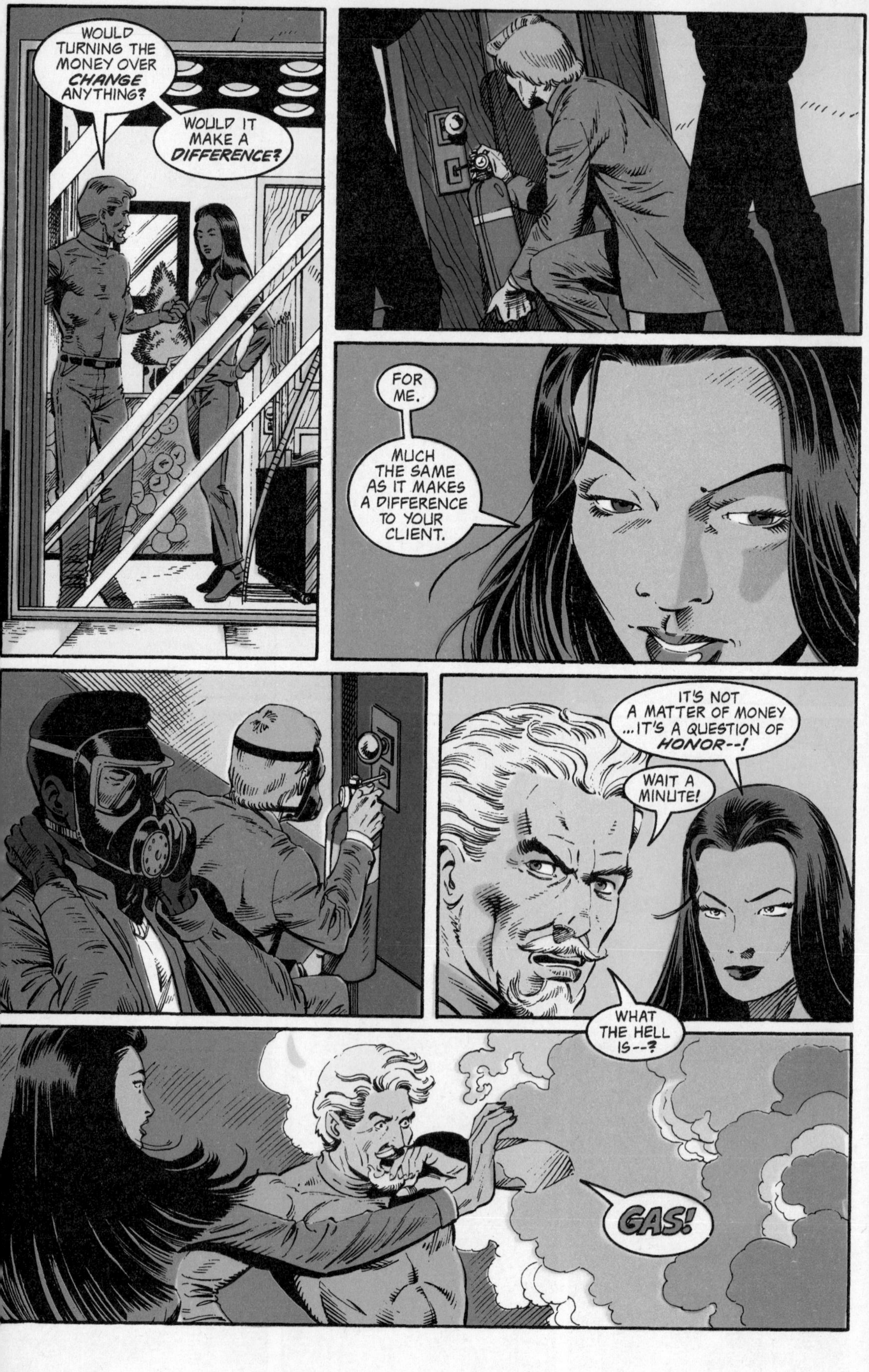
WOULD TURNING THE MONEY OVER CHANGE ANYTHING?
WOULD IT MAKE A DIFFERENCE?
FOR ME.
MUCH THE SAME AS IT MAKES A DIFFERENCE TO YOUR CLIENT.
IT'S NOT A MATTER OF MONEY ...IT'S A QUESTION OF HONOR--!
WAIT A MINUTE!
WHAT THE HELL IS--?
GAS!

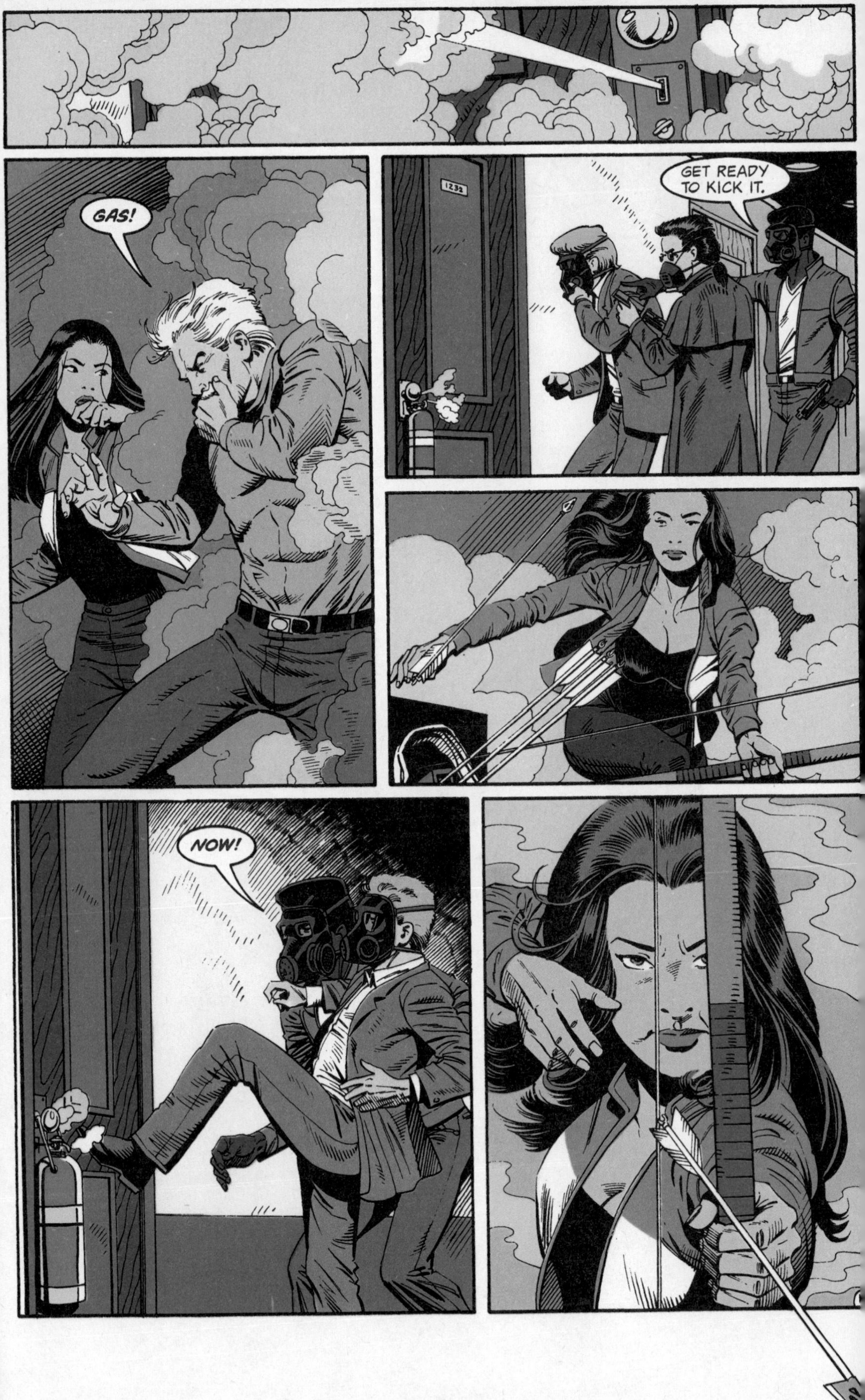
GAS!
GET READY TO KICK IT.
NOW!

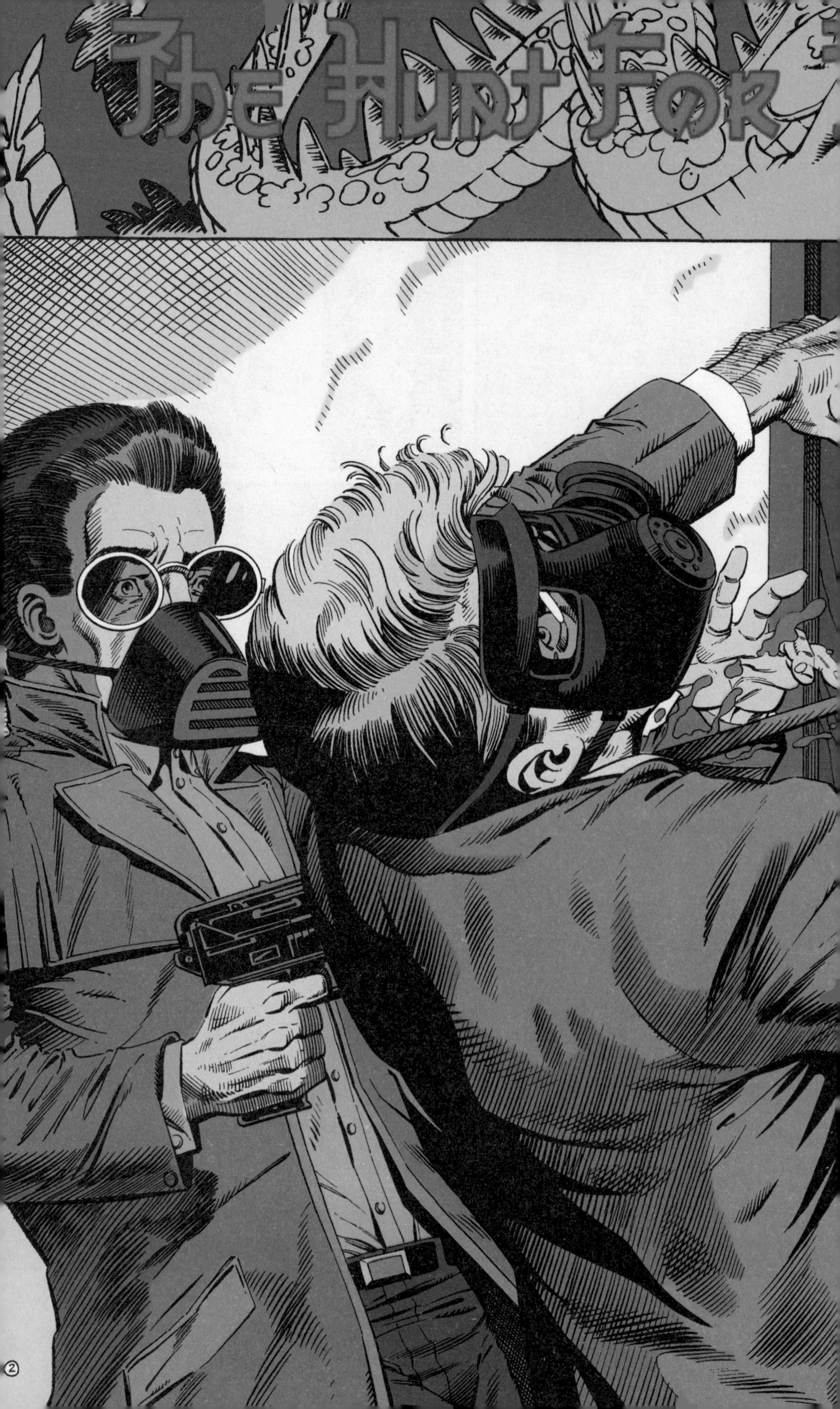
The Hunt For

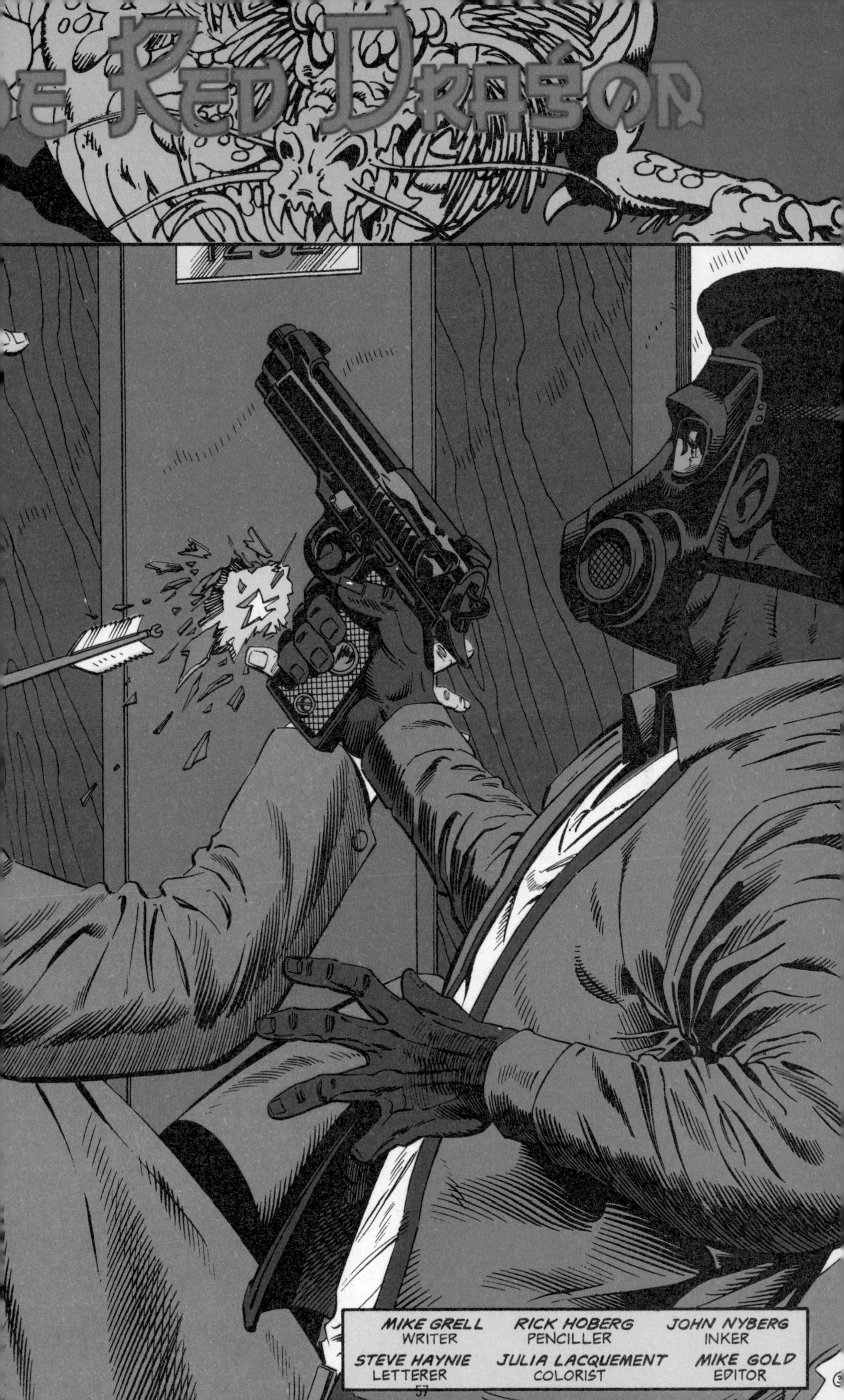
RED DRAGON
MIKE GRELL WRITER
RICK HOBERG PENCILLER
JOHN NYBERG INKER
STEVE HAYNIE LETTERER
JULIA LACQUEMENT COLORIST
MIKE GOLD EDITOR

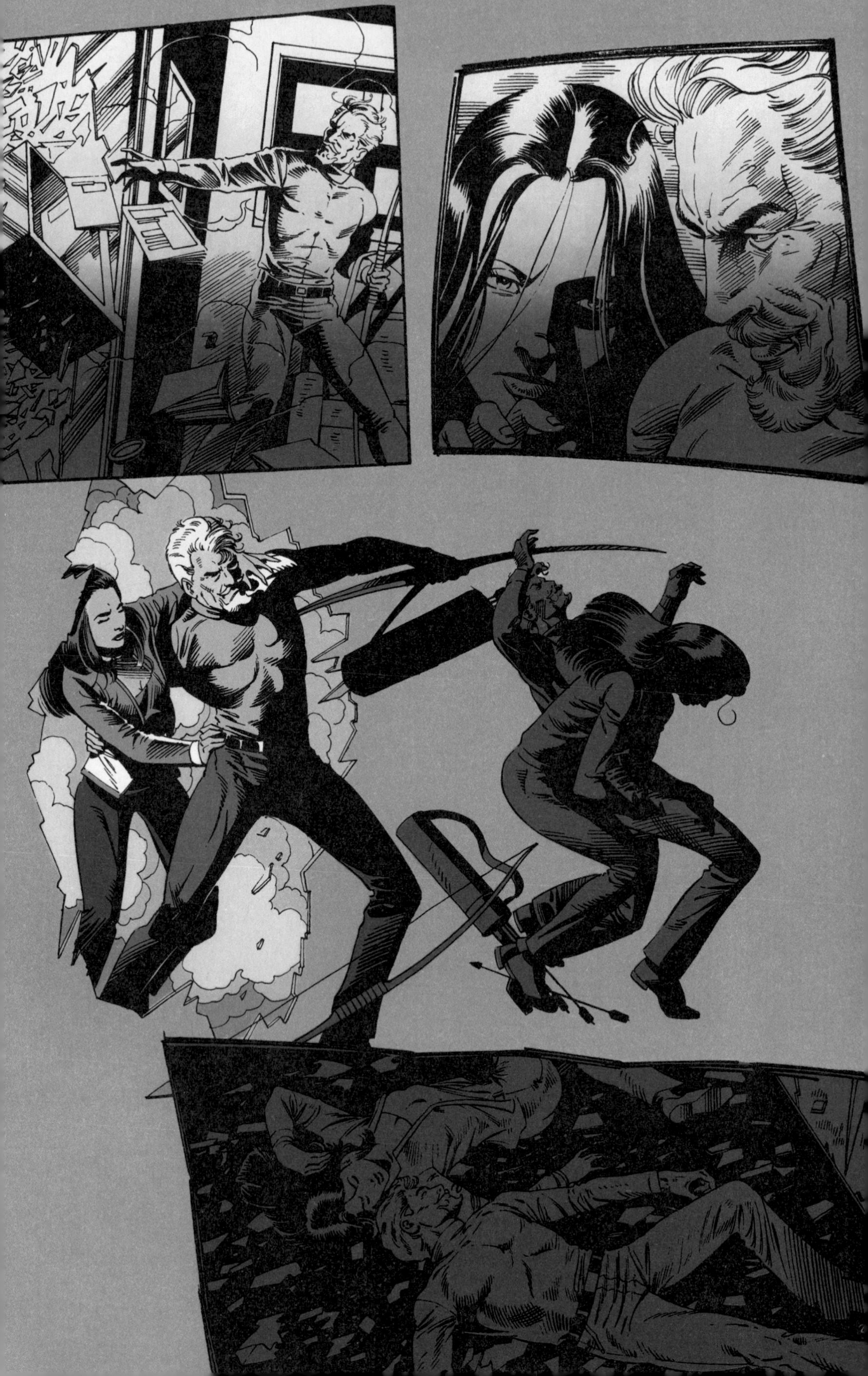

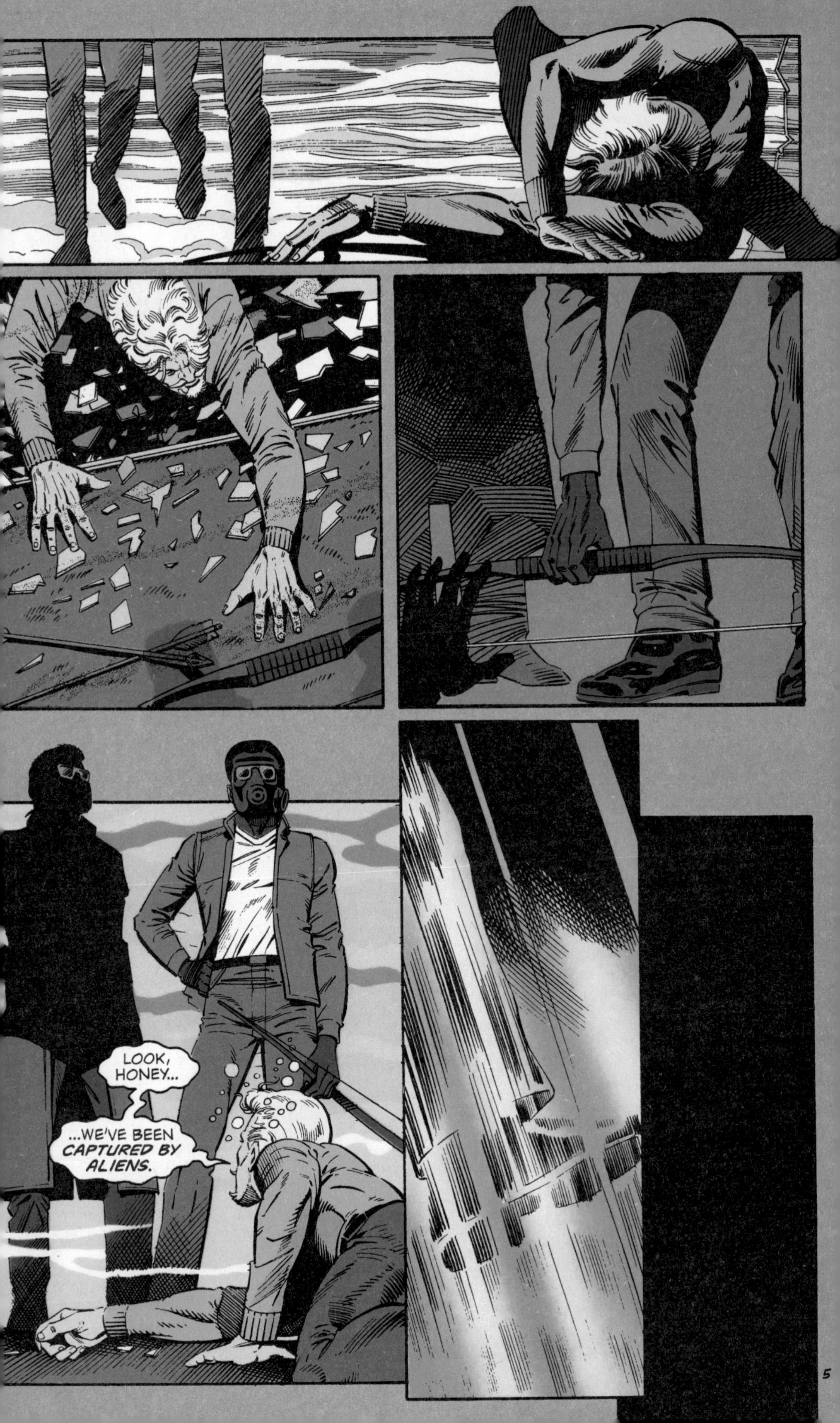
LOOK, HONEY...
...WE'VE BEEN CAPTURED BY ALIENS.

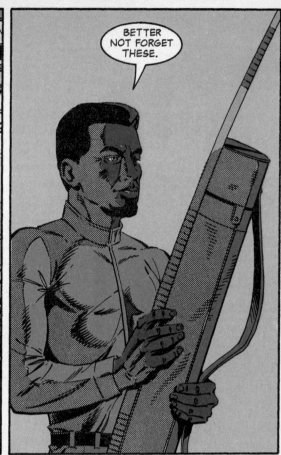

BETTER NOT FORGET THESE.

THESE ARE THE *TRANSPLANT* DONORS.

AS YOU CAN SEE, WE'RE KEEPING THEM ALIVE ON LIFE-SUPPORT UNTIL WE CAN REMOVE AND DISTRIBUTE THE ORGANS PROPERLY.

EVERYTHING SEEMS IN ORDER. GOOD LUCK.

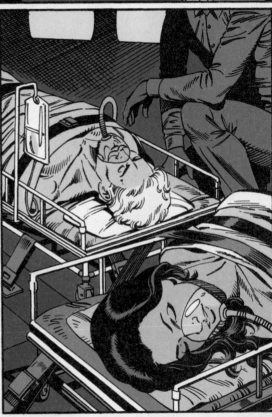

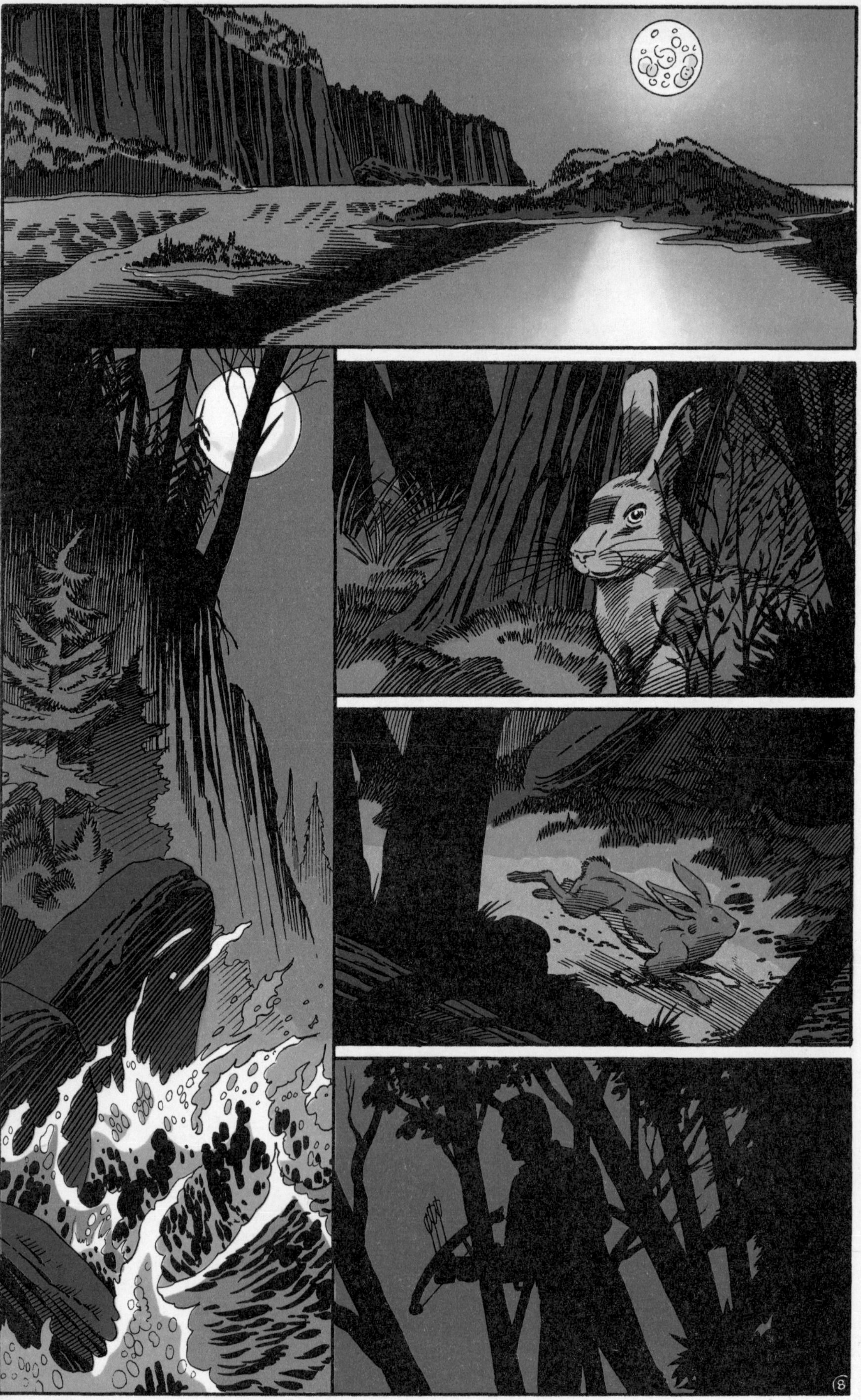

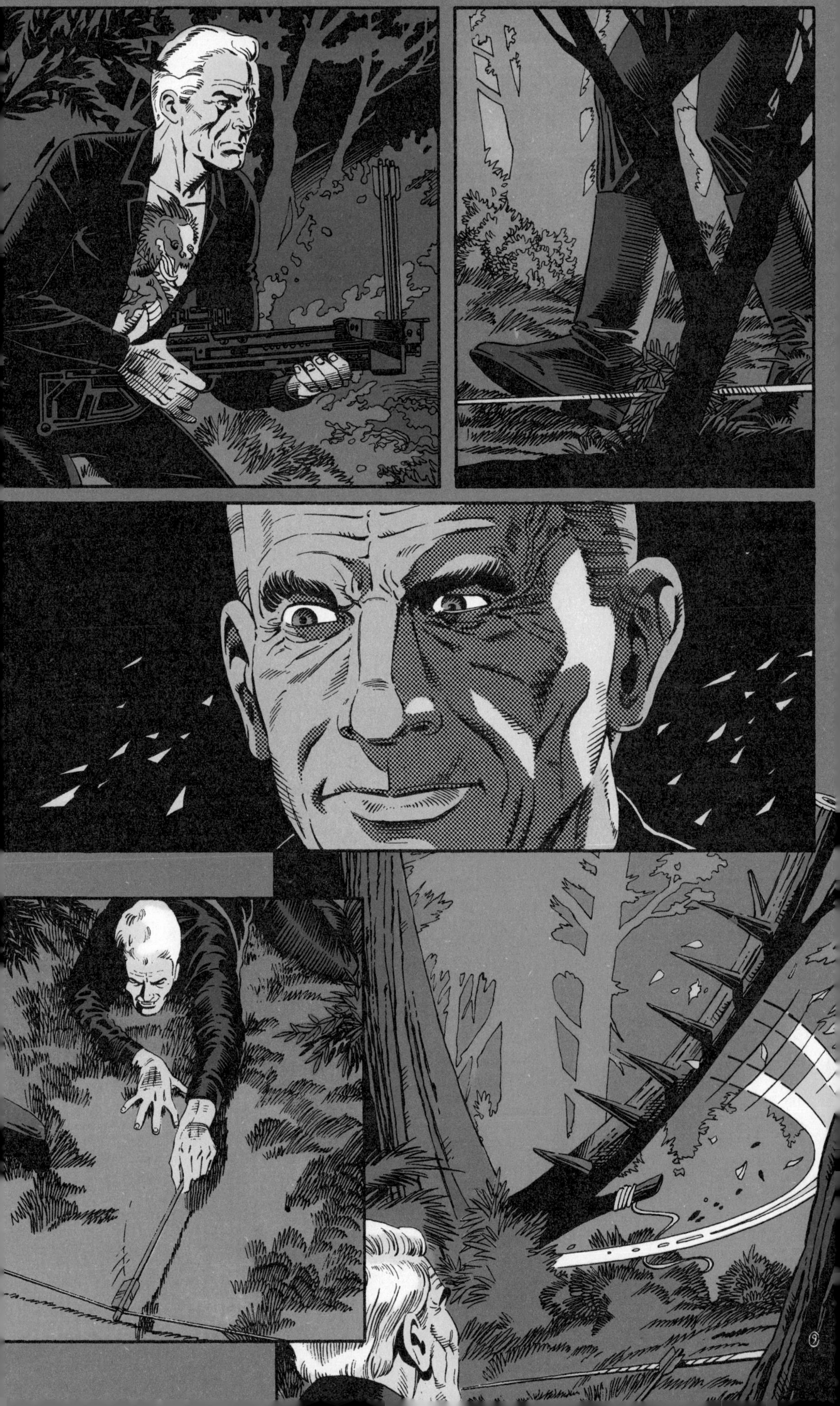

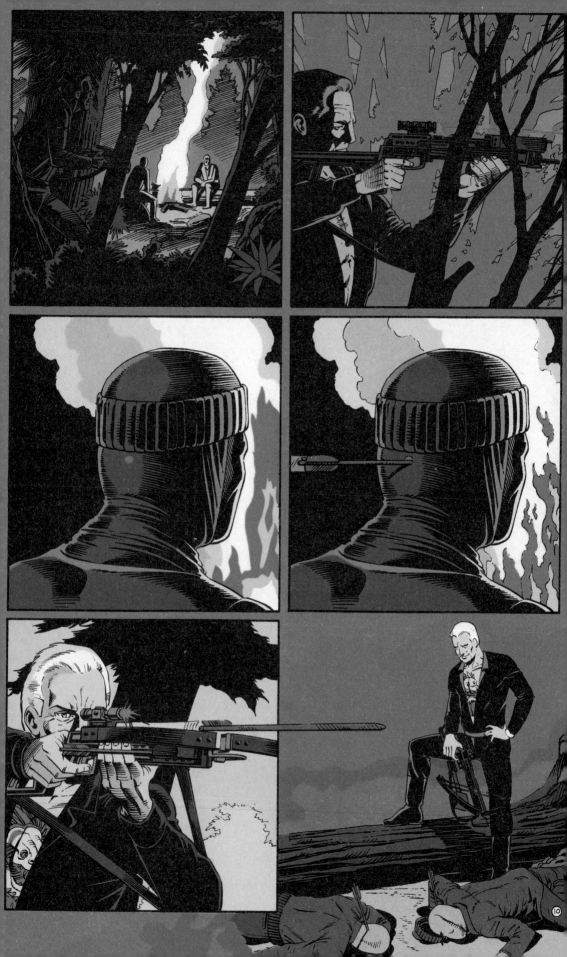

10

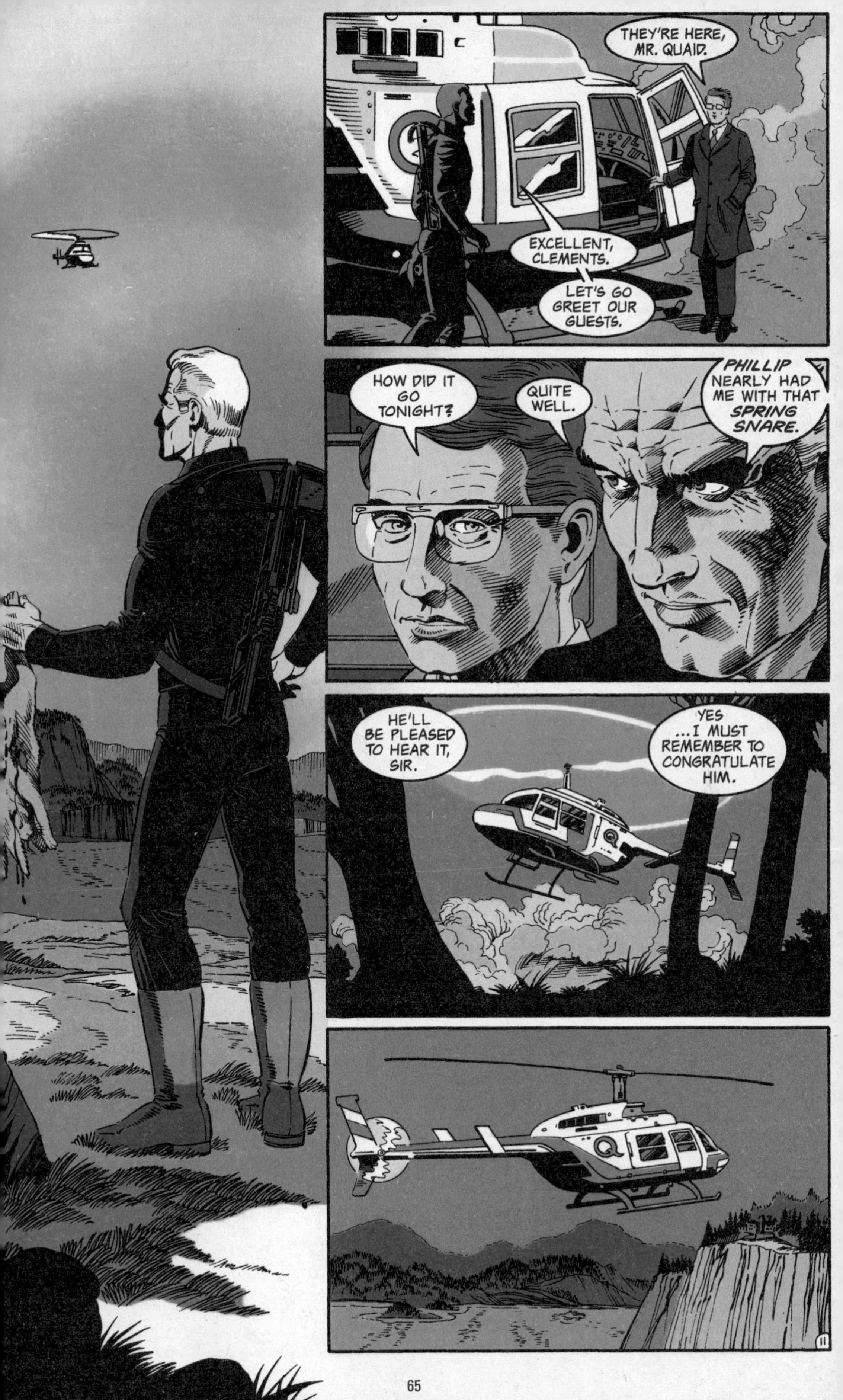
THEY'RE HERE, MR. QUAID.
EXCELLENT, CLEMENTS.
LET'S GO GREET OUR GUESTS.
HOW DID IT GO TONIGHT?
QUITE WELL.
PHILLIP NEARLY HAD ME WITH THAT SPRING SNARE.
HE'LL BE PLEASED TO HEAR IT, SIR.
YES ...I MUST REMEMBER TO CONGRATULATE HIM.
11

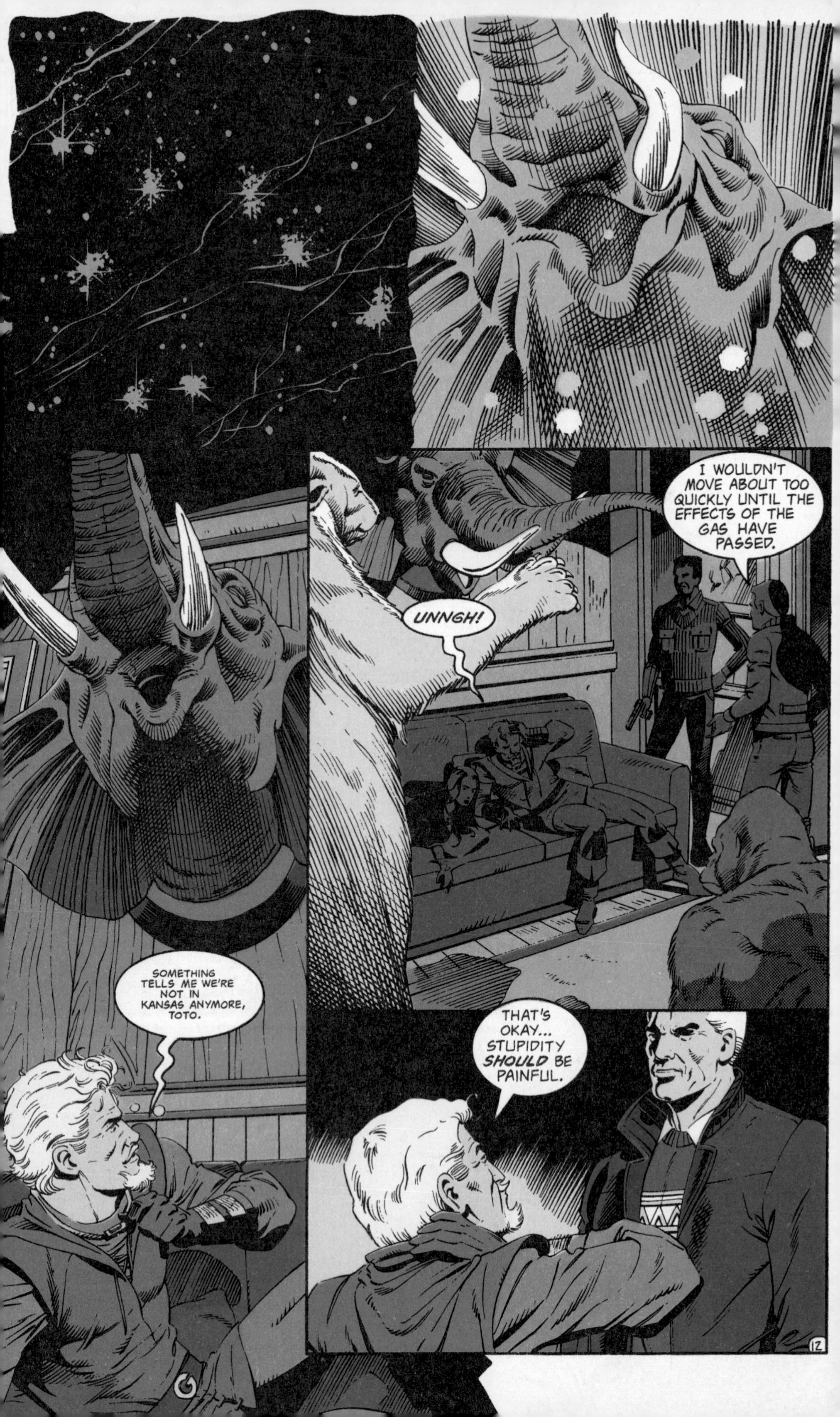
I WOULDN'T MOVE ABOUT TOO QUICKLY UNTIL THE EFFECTS OF THE GAS HAVE PASSED.
UNNGH!
SOMETHING TELLS ME WE'RE NOT IN KANSAS ANYMORE, TOTO.
THAT'S OKAY... STUPIDITY SHOULD BE PAINFUL.
12

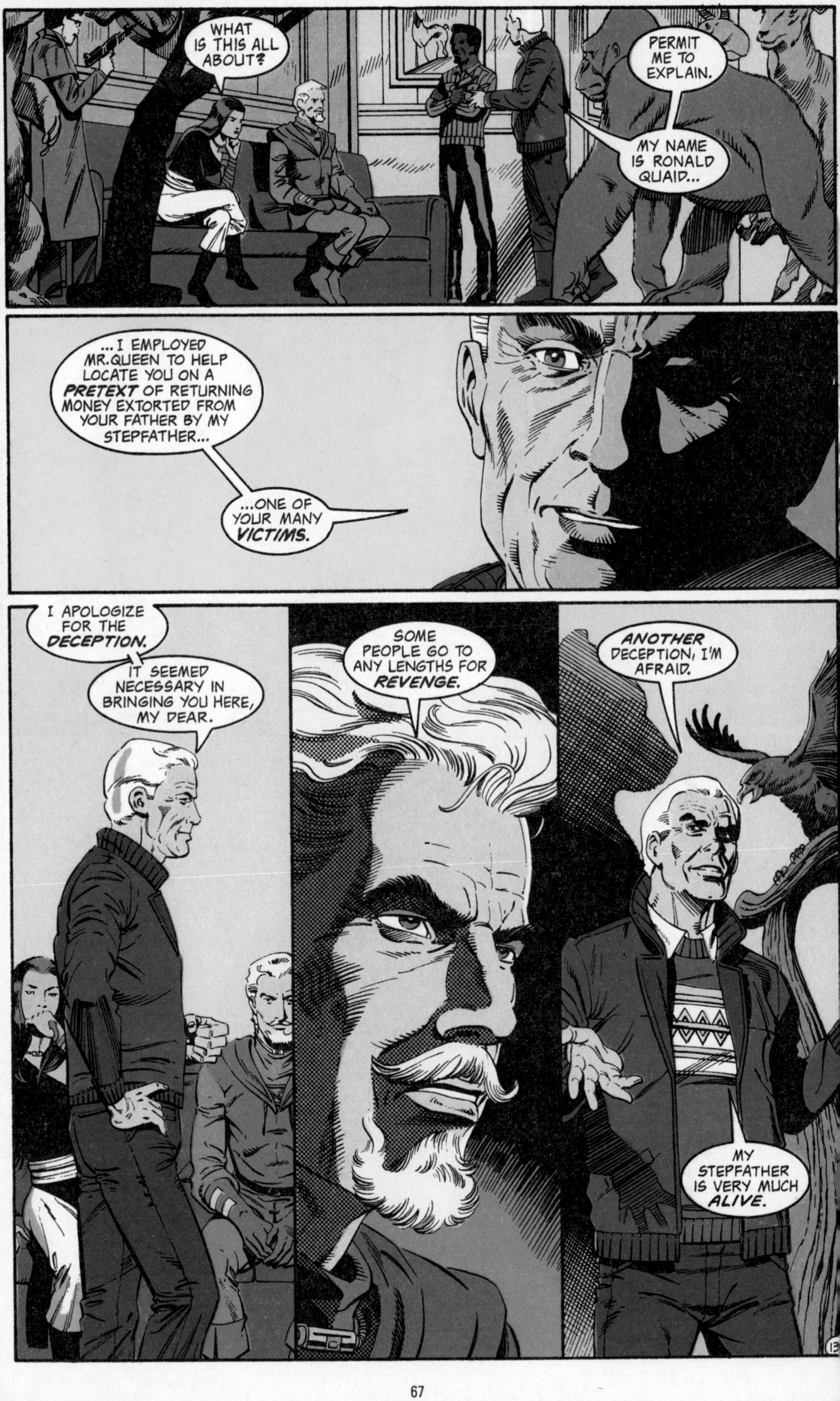
WHAT IS THIS ALL ABOUT?
PERMIT ME TO EXPLAIN.
MY NAME IS RONALD QUAID...
...I EMPLOYED MR.QUEEN TO HELP LOCATE YOU ON A PRETEXT OF RETURNING MONEY EXTORTED FROM YOUR FATHER BY MY STEPFATHER...
...ONE OF YOUR MANY VICTIMS.
I APOLOGIZE FOR THE DECEPTION.
IT SEEMED NECESSARY IN BRINGING YOU HERE, MY DEAR.
SOME PEOPLE GO TO ANY LENGTHS FOR REVENGE.
ANOTHER DECEPTION, I'M AFRAID.
MY STEPFATHER IS VERY MUCH ALIVE.
13

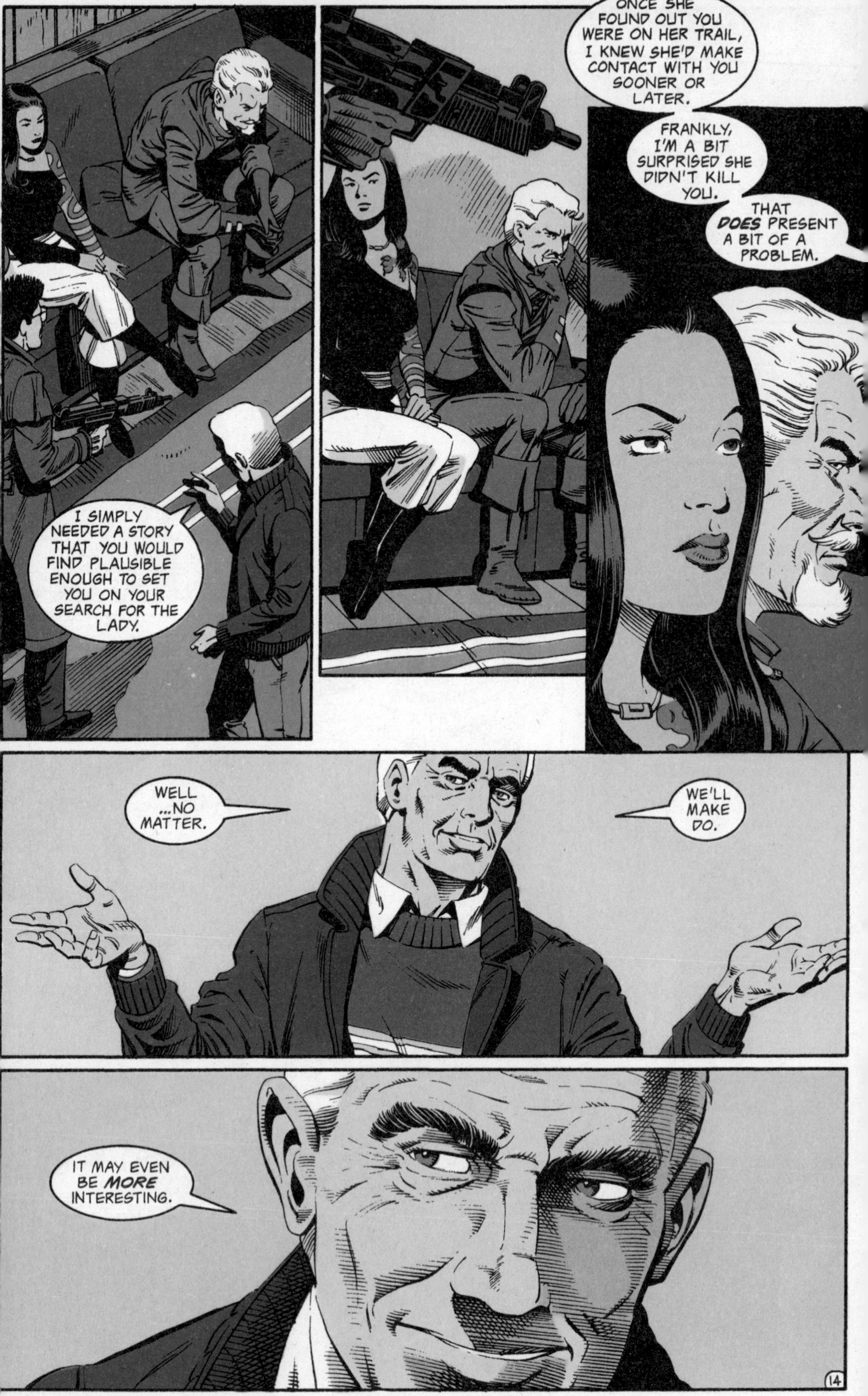
I SIMPLY NEEDED A STORY THAT YOU WOULD FIND PLAUSIBLE ENOUGH TO SET YOU ON YOUR SEARCH FOR THE LADY.
ONCE SHE FOUND OUT YOU WERE ON HER TRAIL, I KNEW SHE'D MAKE CONTACT WITH YOU SOONER OR LATER.
FRANKLY, I'M A BIT SURPRISED SHE DIDN'T KILL YOU.
THAT DOES PRESENT A BIT OF A PROBLEM.
WELL ...NO MATTER.
WE'LL MAKE DO.
IT MAY EVEN BE MORE INTERESTING.
14

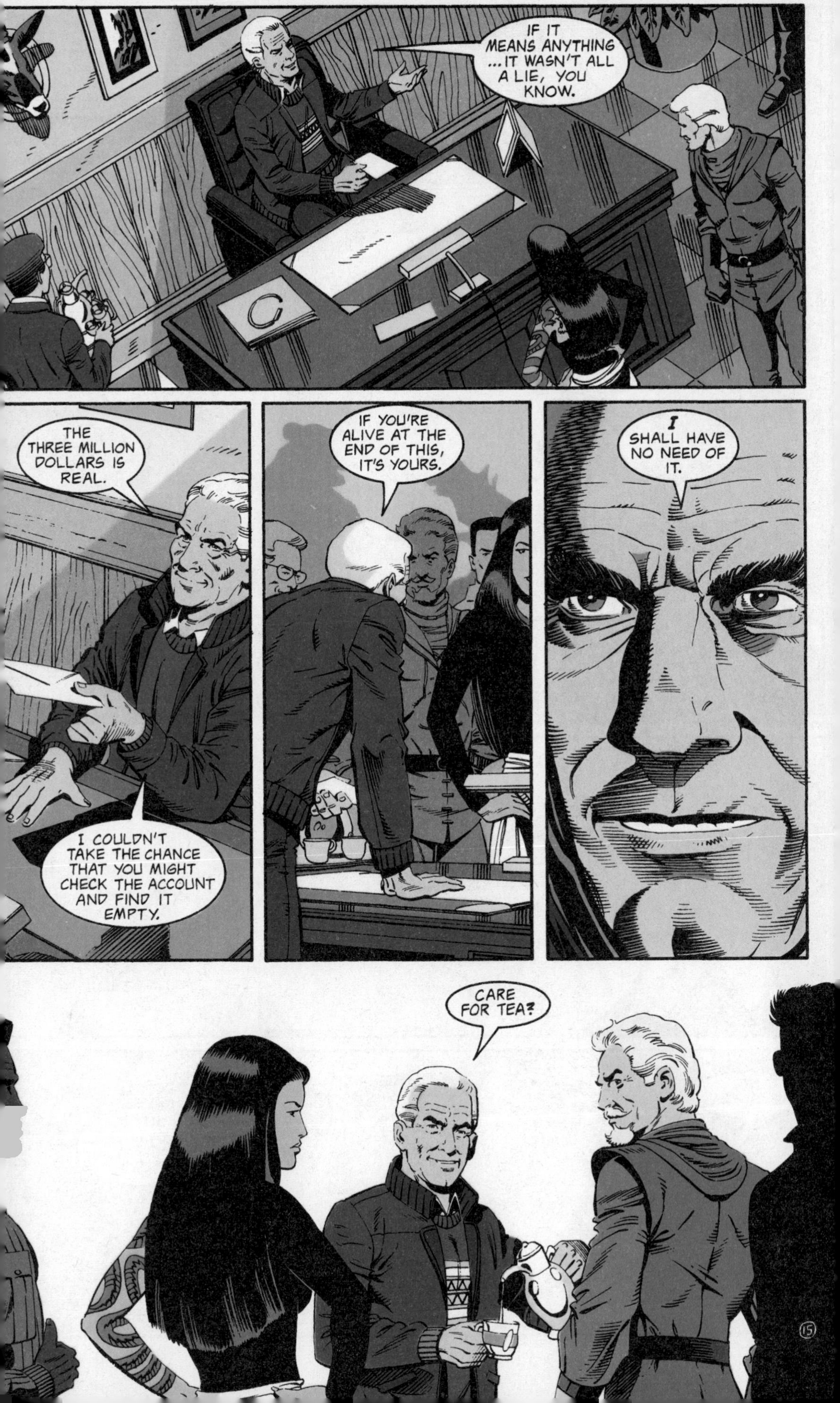
IF IT MEANS ANYTHING ...IT WASN'T ALL A LIE, YOU KNOW.
THE THREE MILLION DOLLARS IS REAL.
I COULDN'T TAKE THE CHANCE THAT YOU MIGHT CHECK THE ACCOUNT AND FIND IT EMPTY.
IF YOU'RE ALIVE AT THE END OF THIS, IT'S YOURS.
I SHALL HAVE NO NEED OF IT.
CARE FOR TEA?

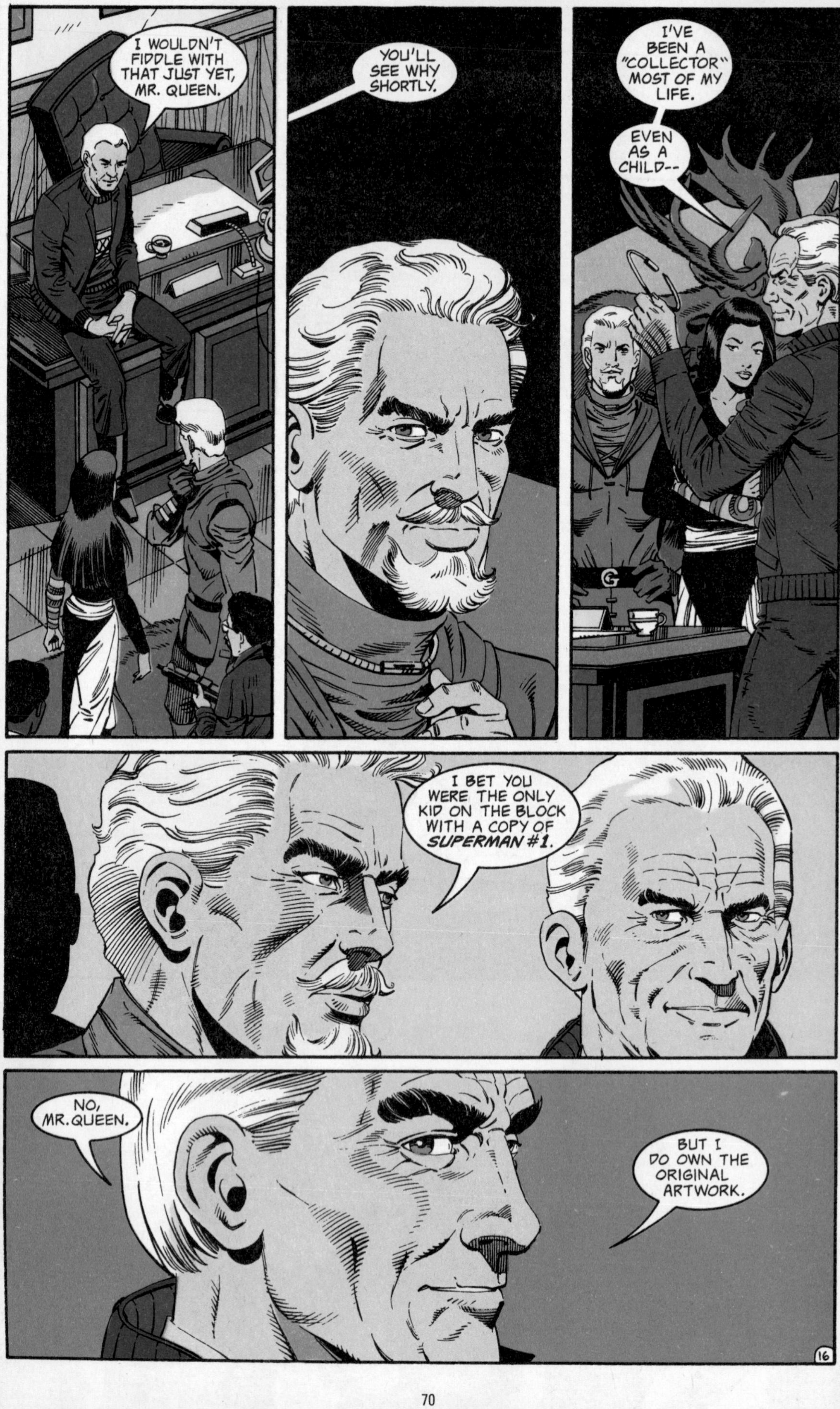
I WOULDN'T FIDDLE WITH THAT JUST YET, MR. QUEEN.
YOU'LL SEE WHY SHORTLY.
I'VE BEEN A "COLLECTOR" MOST OF MY LIFE.
EVEN AS A CHILD--
I BET YOU WERE THE ONLY KID ON THE BLOCK WITH A COPY OF *SUPERMAN #1*.
NO, MR. QUEEN.
BUT I DO OWN THE ORIGINAL ARTWORK.
16

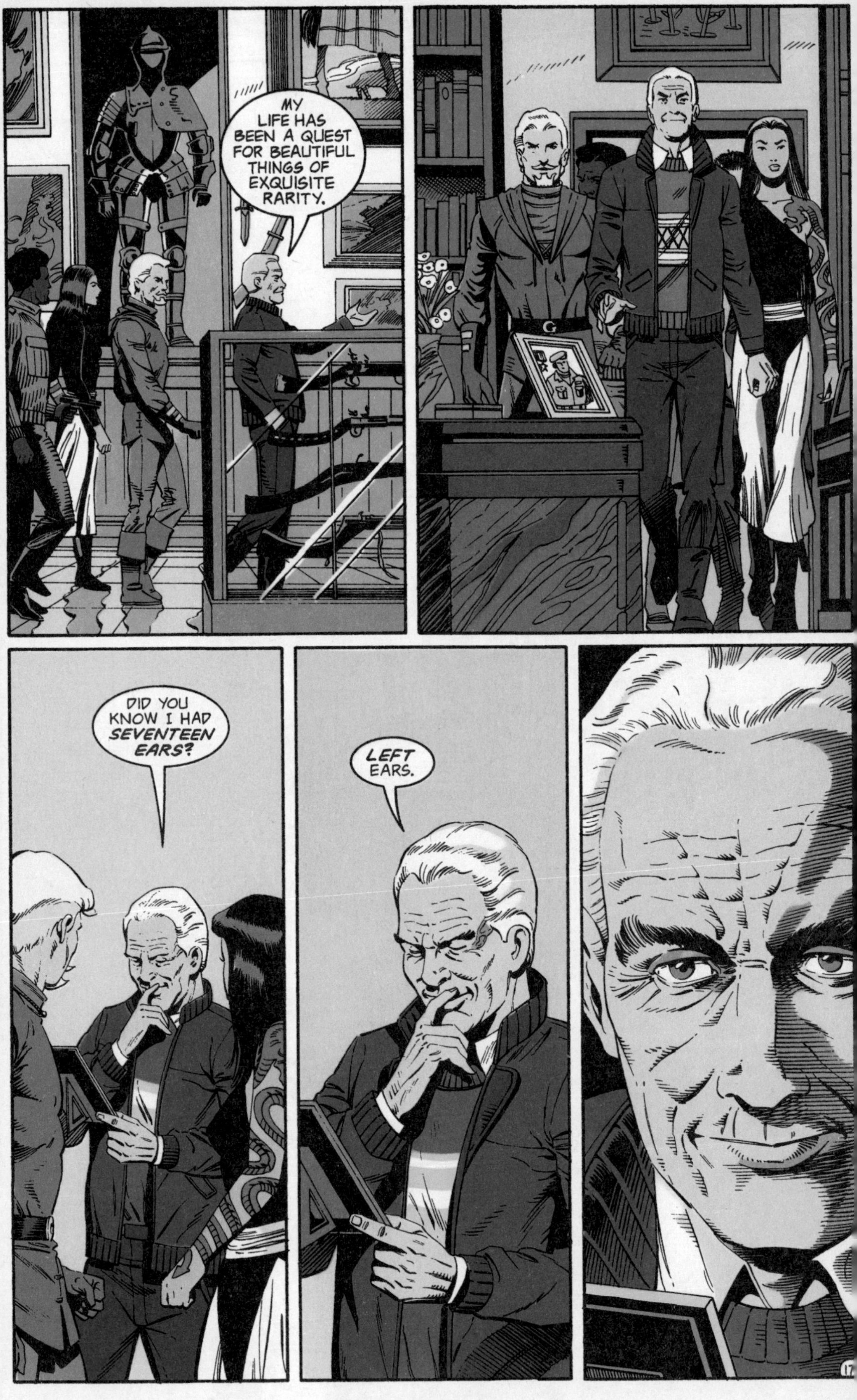
MY LIFE HAS BEEN A QUEST FOR BEAUTIFUL THINGS OF EXQUISITE RARITY.
DID YOU KNOW I HAD *SEVENTEEN EARS?*
LEFT EARS.

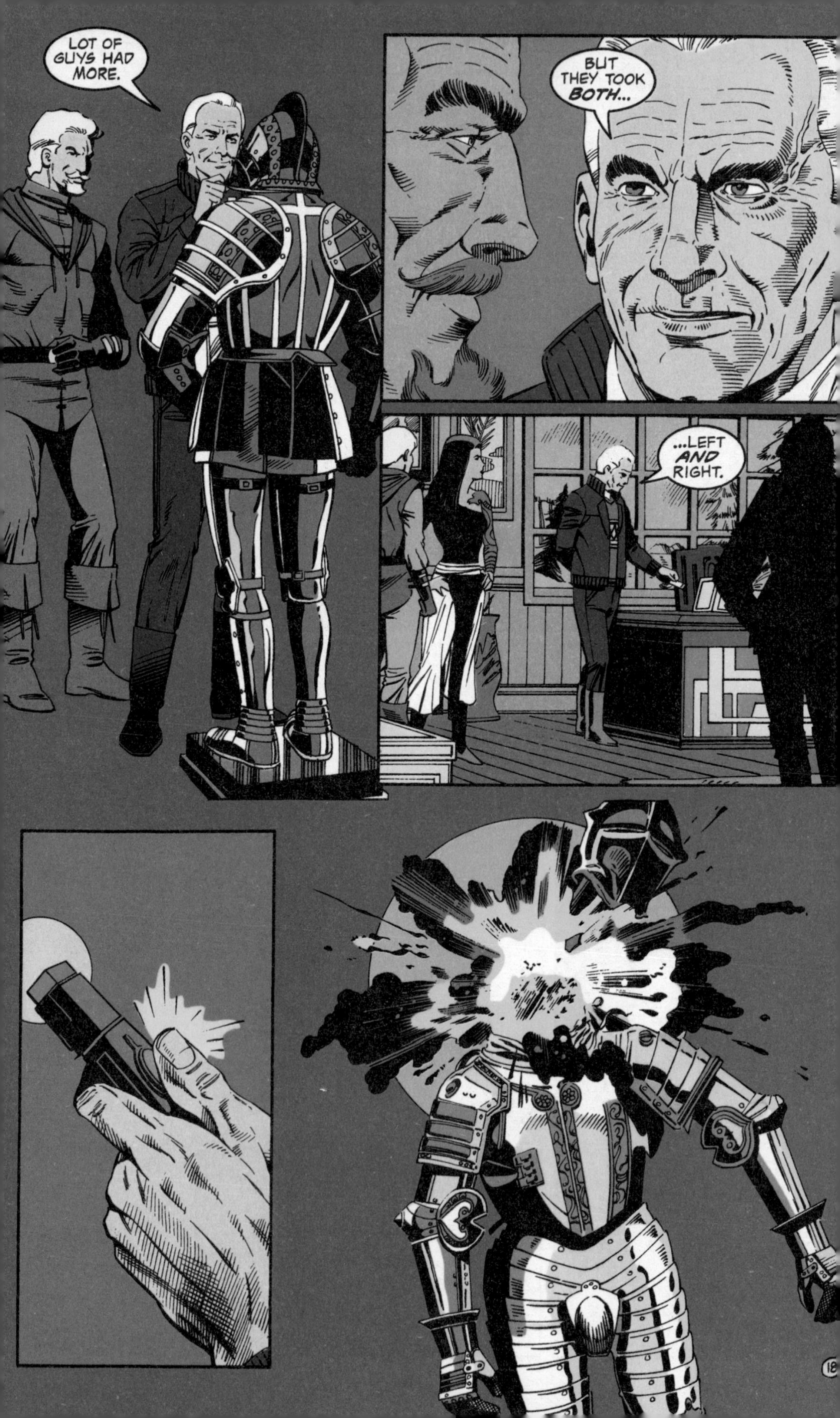
LOT OF GUYS HAD MORE.
BUT THEY TOOK BOTH...
...LEFT AND RIGHT.

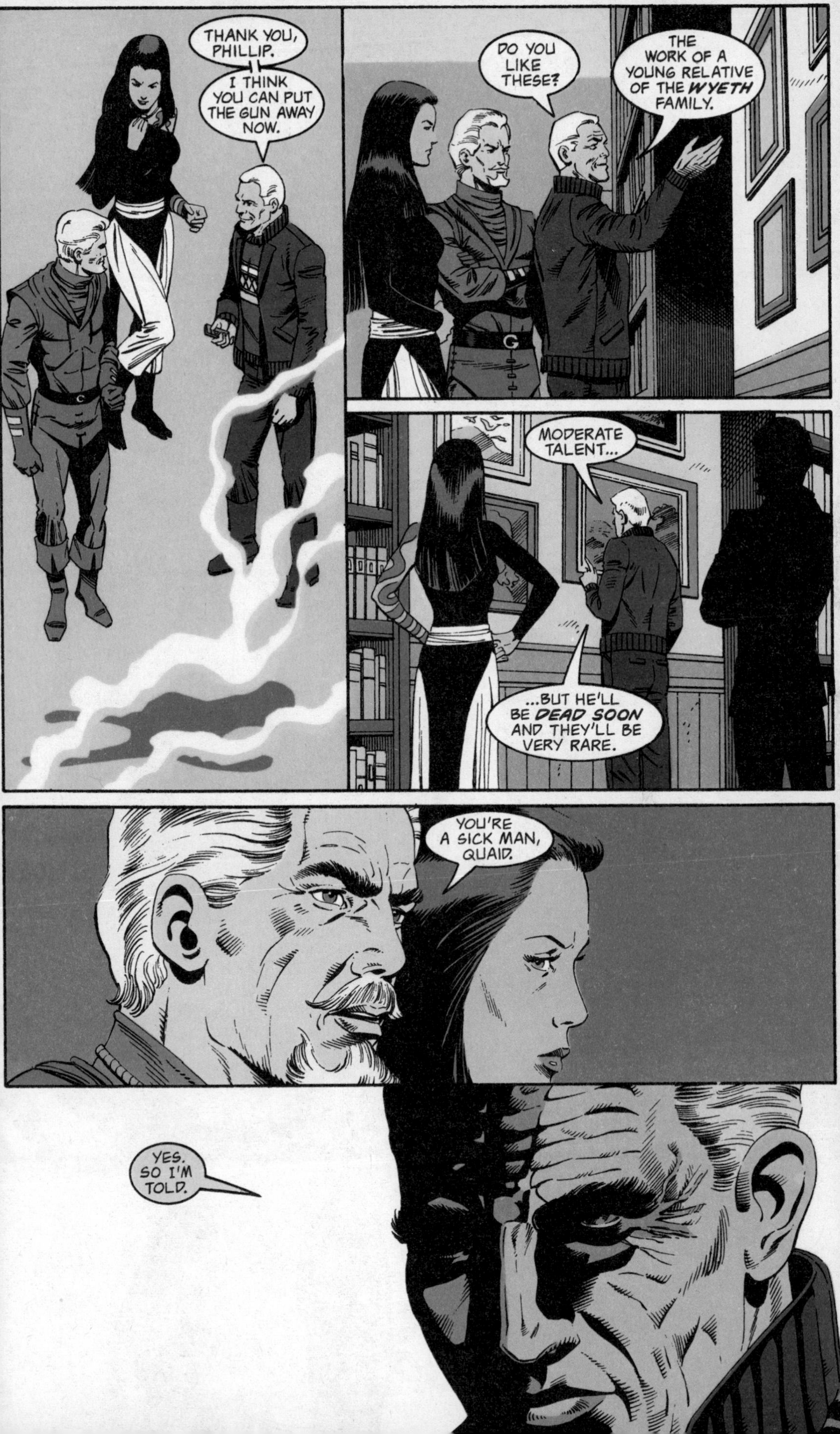

THANK YOU, PHILLIP.
I THINK YOU CAN PUT THE GUN AWAY NOW.
DO YOU LIKE THESE?
THE WORK OF A YOUNG RELATIVE OF THE WYETH FAMILY.
MODERATE TALENT...
...BUT HE'LL BE DEAD SOON AND THEY'LL BE VERY RARE.
YOU'RE A SICK MAN, QUAID.
YES. SO I'M TOLD.

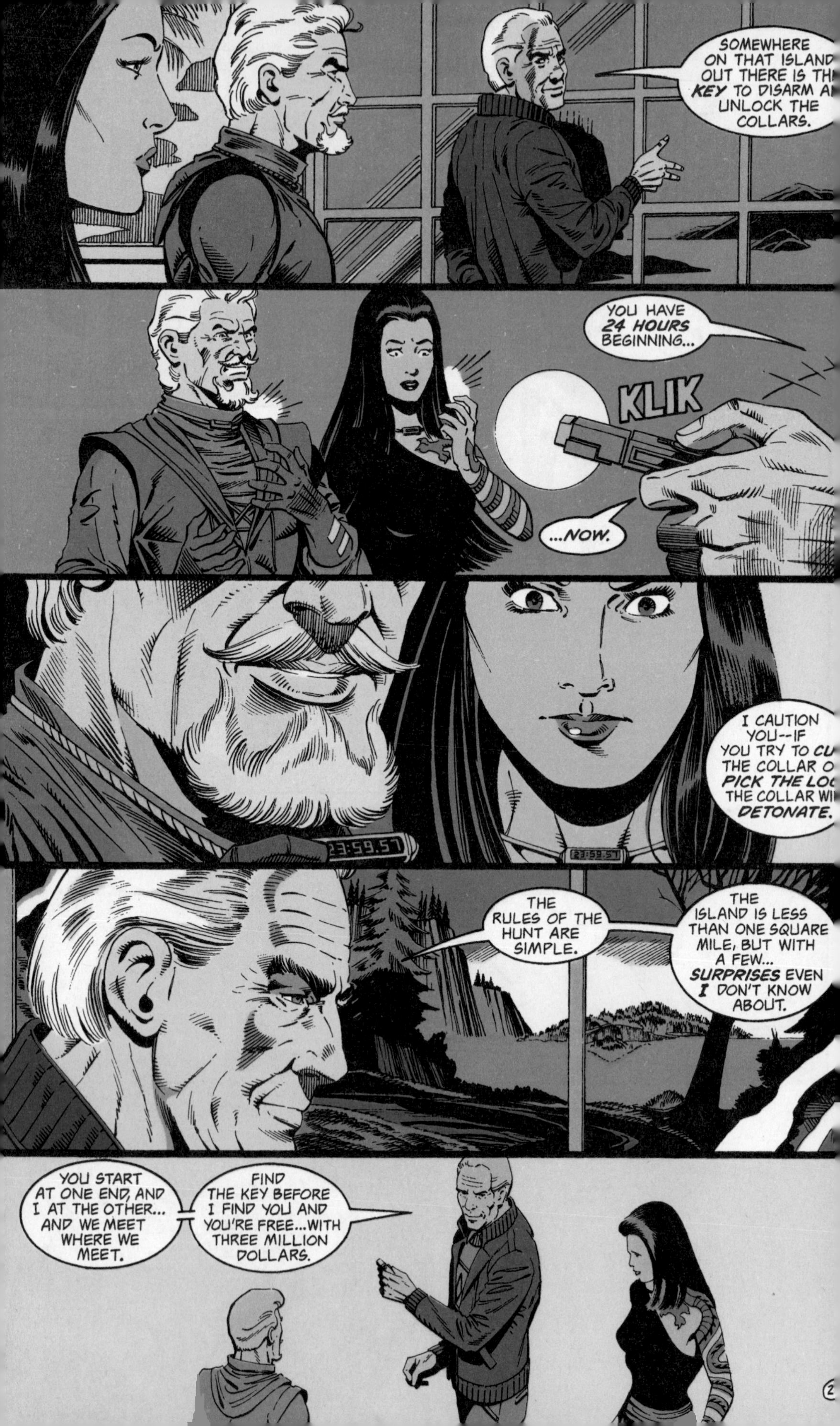
SOMEWHERE ON THAT ISLAND OUT THERE IS TH KEY TO DISARM A UNLOCK THE COLLARS.
YOU HAVE 24 HOURS BEGINNING...
KLIK
...NOW.
23:59.57
23:59.57
I CAUTION YOU--IF YOU TRY TO CU THE COLLAR O PICK THE LO THE COLLAR WI DETONATE.
THE RULES OF THE HUNT ARE SIMPLE.
THE ISLAND IS LESS THAN ONE SQUARE MILE, BUT WITH A FEW... SURPRISES EVEN I DON'T KNOW ABOUT.
YOU START AT ONE END, AND I AT THE OTHER... AND WE MEET WHERE WE MEET.
FIND THE KEY BEFORE I FIND YOU AND YOU'RE FREE...WITH THREE MILLION DOLLARS.

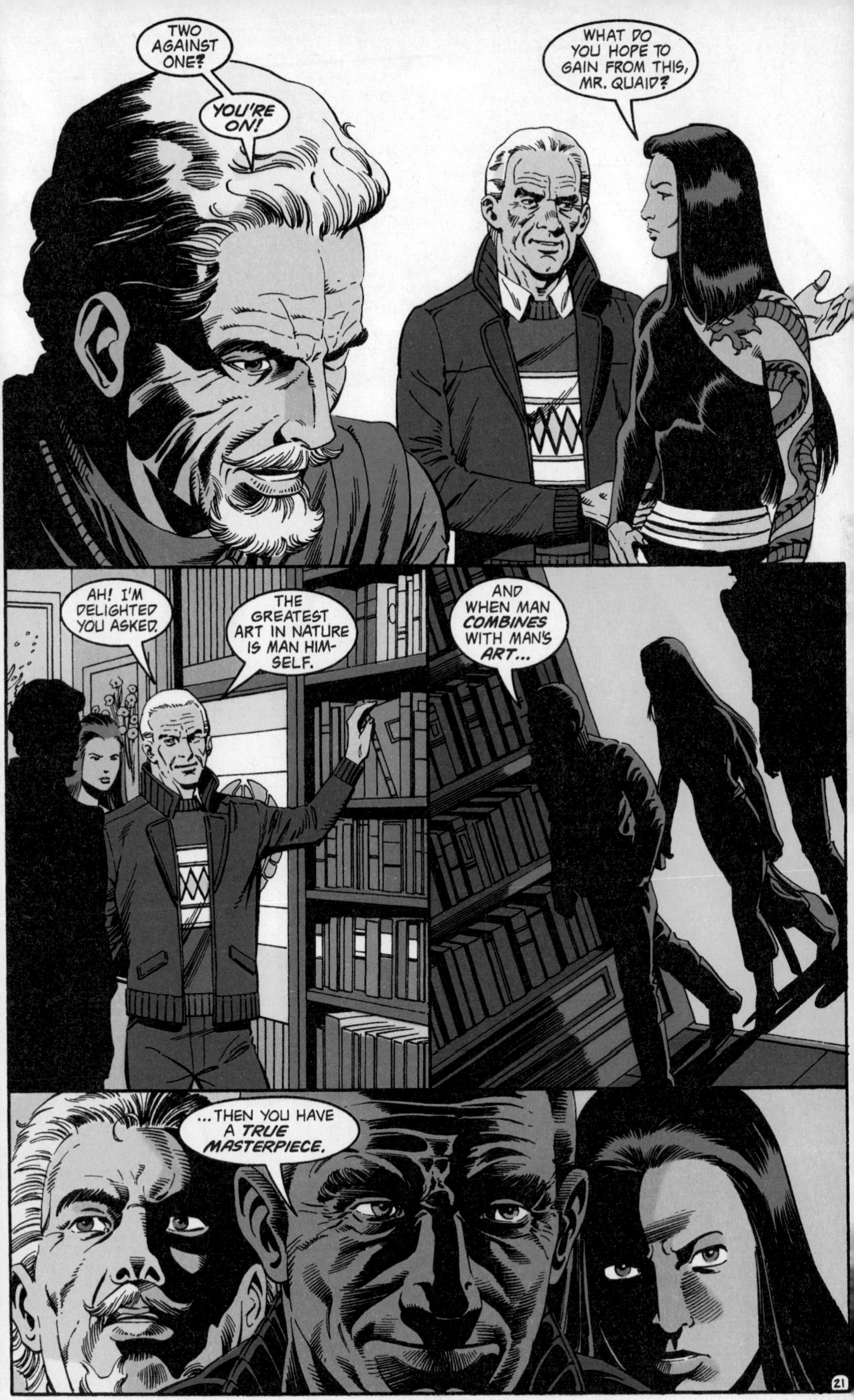
TWO AGAINST ONE?
YOU'RE ON!
WHAT DO YOU HOPE TO GAIN FROM THIS, MR. QUAID?
AH! I'M DELIGHTED YOU ASKED.
THE GREATEST ART IN NATURE IS MAN HIM-SELF.
AND WHEN MAN COMBINES WITH MAN'S ART...
...THEN YOU HAVE A TRUE MASTERPIECE.
21

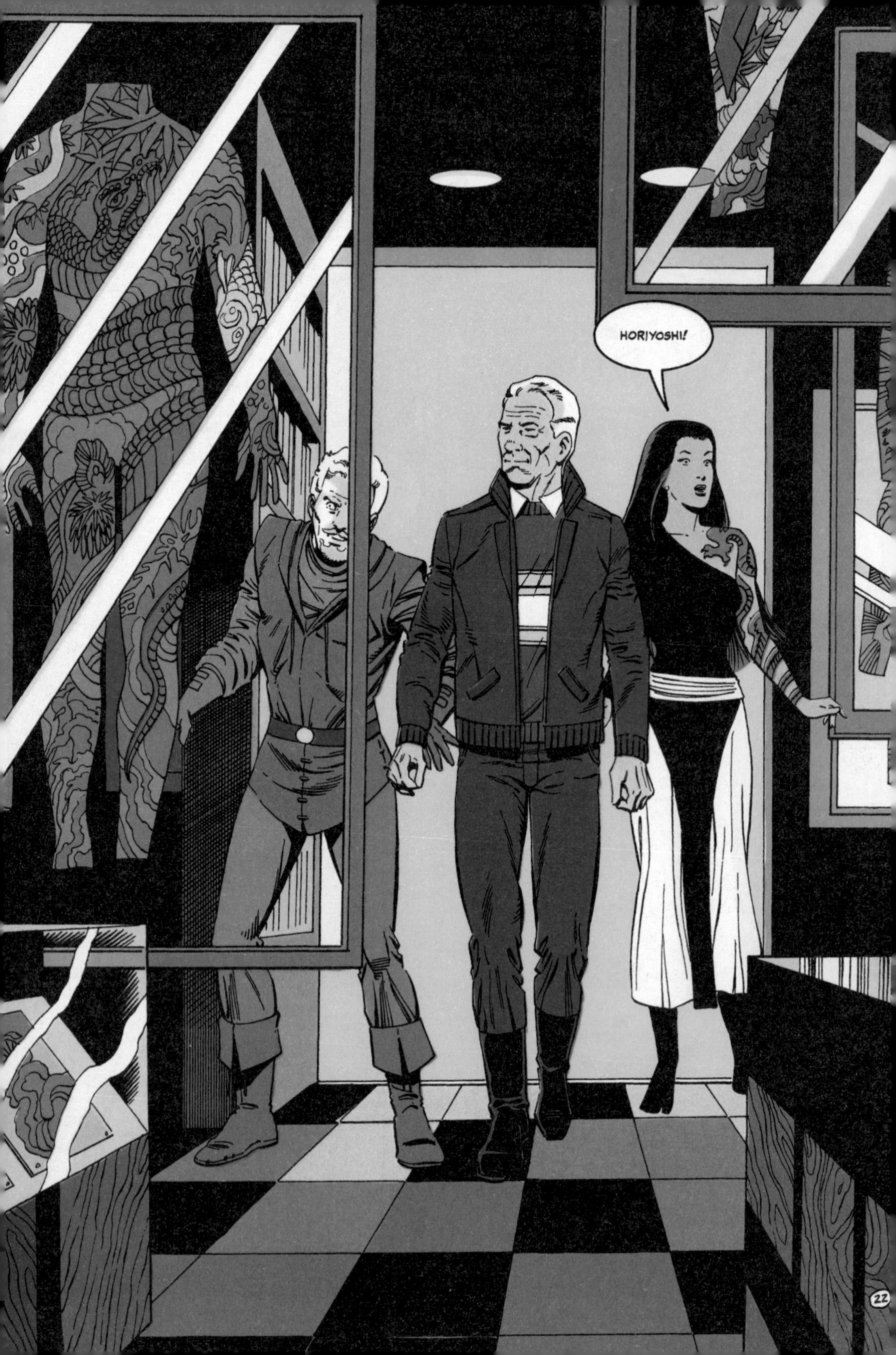
HORIYOSHI!

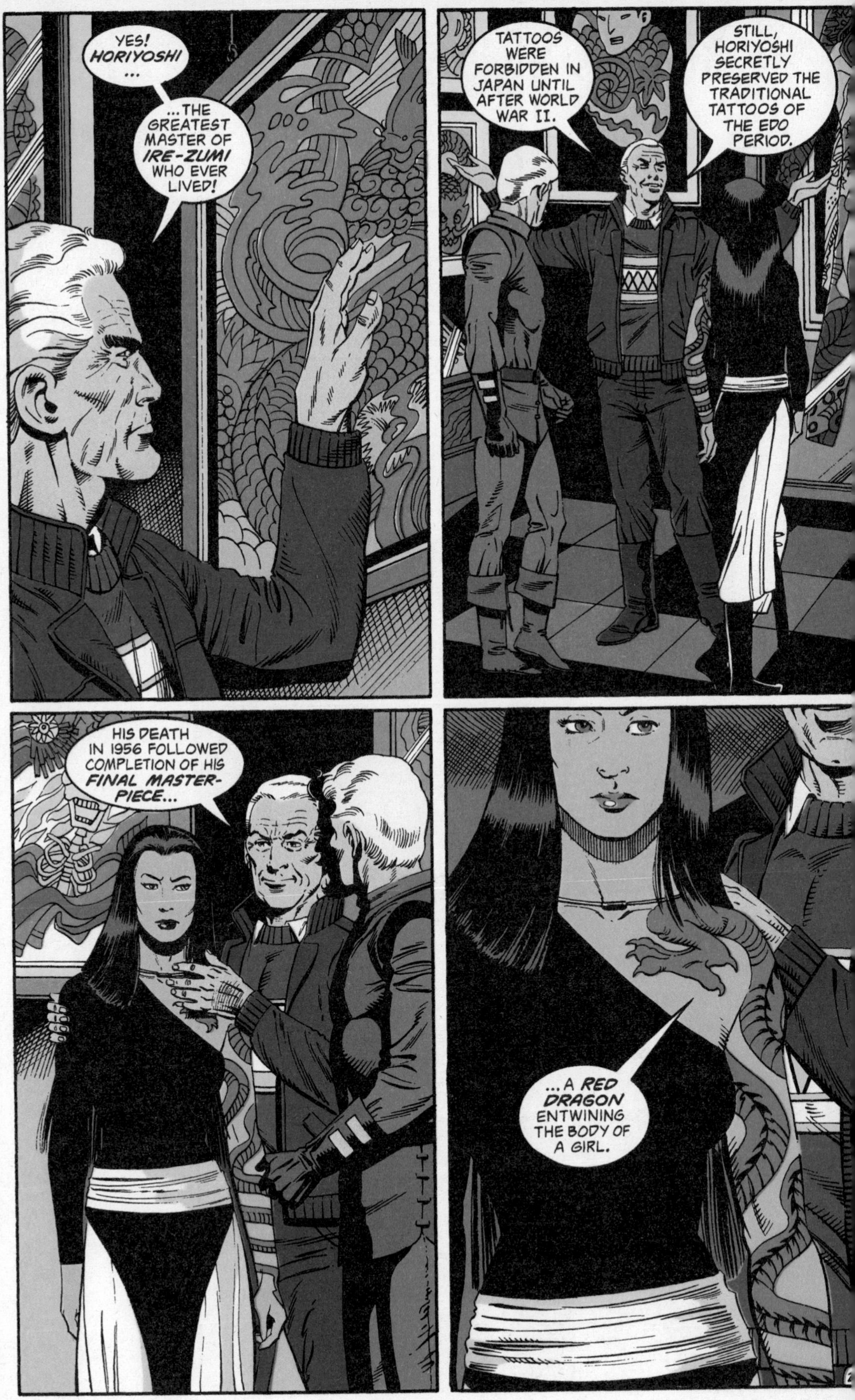
YES! HORIYOSHI ...
...THE GREATEST MASTER OF IRE-ZUMI WHO EVER LIVED!
TATTOOS WERE FORBIDDEN IN JAPAN UNTIL AFTER WORLD WAR II.
STILL, HORIYOSHI SECRETLY PRESERVED THE TRADITIONAL TATTOOS OF THE EDO PERIOD.
HIS DEATH IN 1956 FOLLOWED COMPLETION OF HIS FINAL MASTER-PIECE...
...A RED DRAGON ENTWINING THE BODY OF A GIRL.

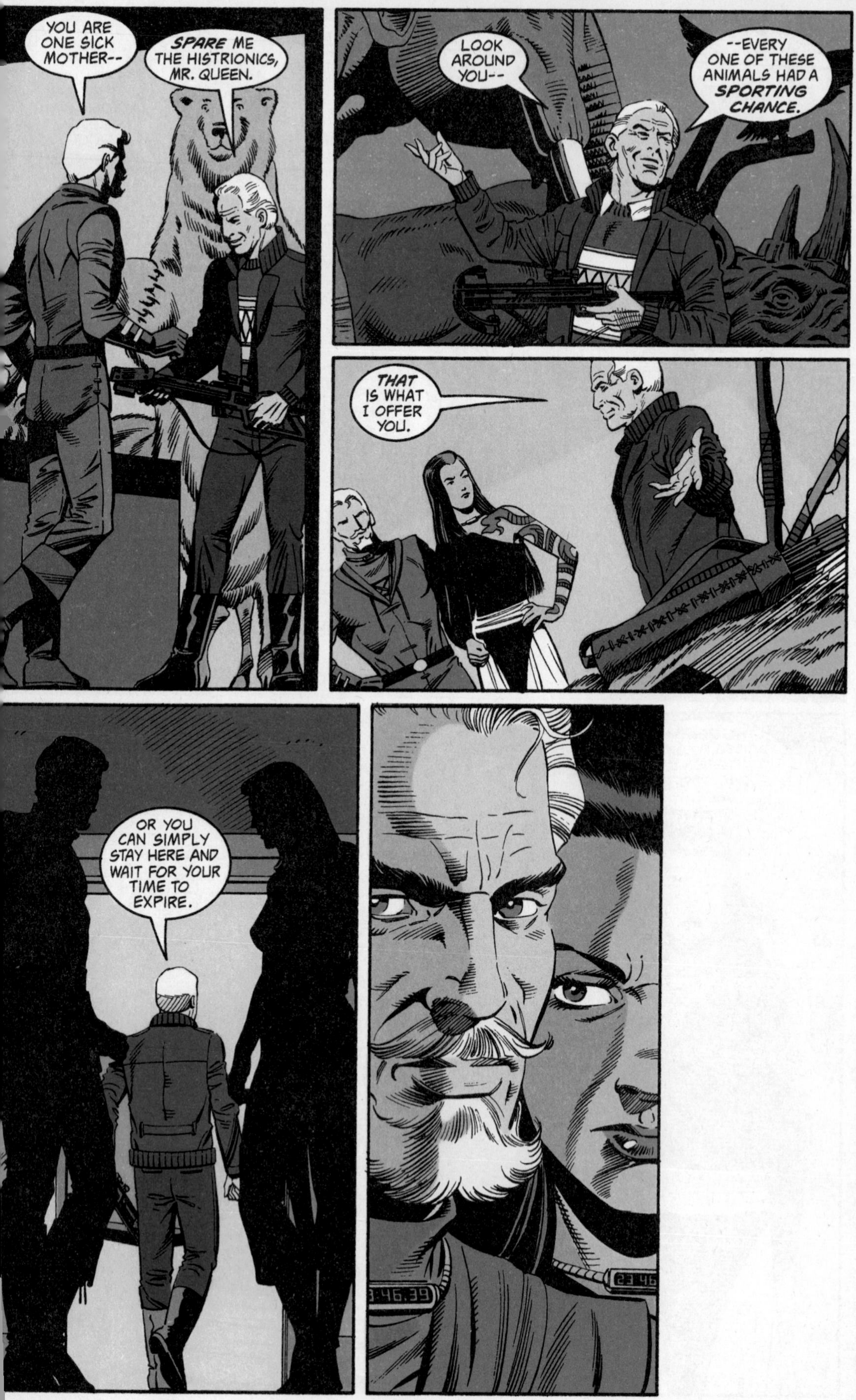
YOU ARE ONE SICK MOTHER--
SPARE ME THE HISTRIONICS, MR. QUEEN.
LOOK AROUND YOU--
--EVERY ONE OF THESE ANIMALS HAD A SPORTING CHANCE.
THAT IS WHAT I OFFER YOU.
OR YOU CAN SIMPLY STAY HERE AND WAIT FOR YOUR TIME TO EXPIRE.

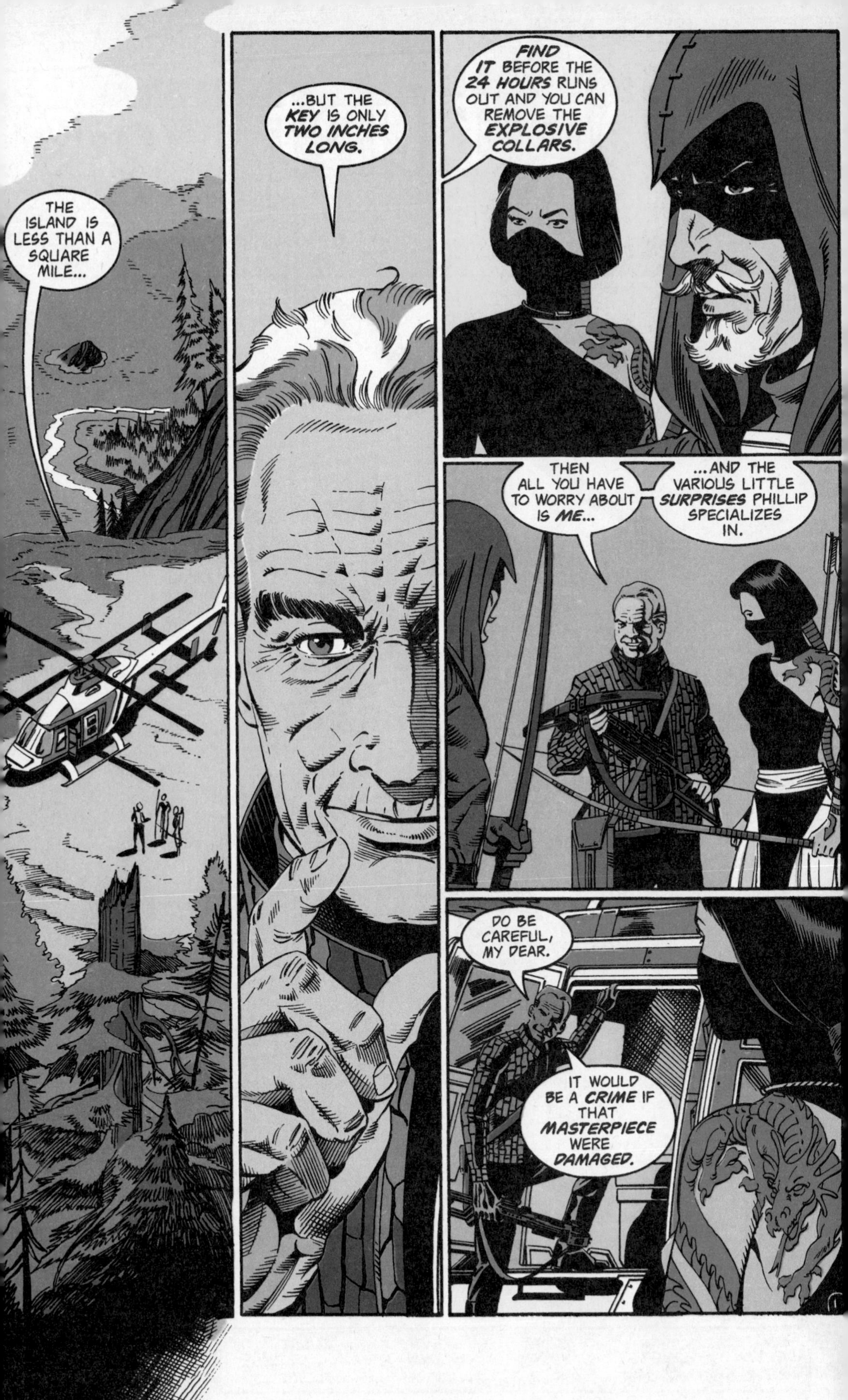
THE ISLAND IS LESS THAN A SQUARE MILE...
...BUT THE KEY IS ONLY TWO INCHES LONG.
FIND IT BEFORE THE 24 HOURS RUNS OUT AND YOU CAN REMOVE THE EXPLOSIVE COLLARS.
THEN ALL YOU HAVE TO WORRY ABOUT IS ME...
...AND THE VARIOUS LITTLE SURPRISES PHILLIP SPECIALIZES IN.
DO BE CAREFUL, MY DEAR.
IT WOULD BE A CRIME IF THAT MASTERPIECE WERE DAMAGED.

The Hunt For

MIKE GRELL	RICK HOBERG	JOHN NYBERG	STEVE HAYNIE	JULIA LACQUEMENT	MIKE GOLD
WRITER	PENCILLER	INKER	LETTERER	COLORIST	EDITOR

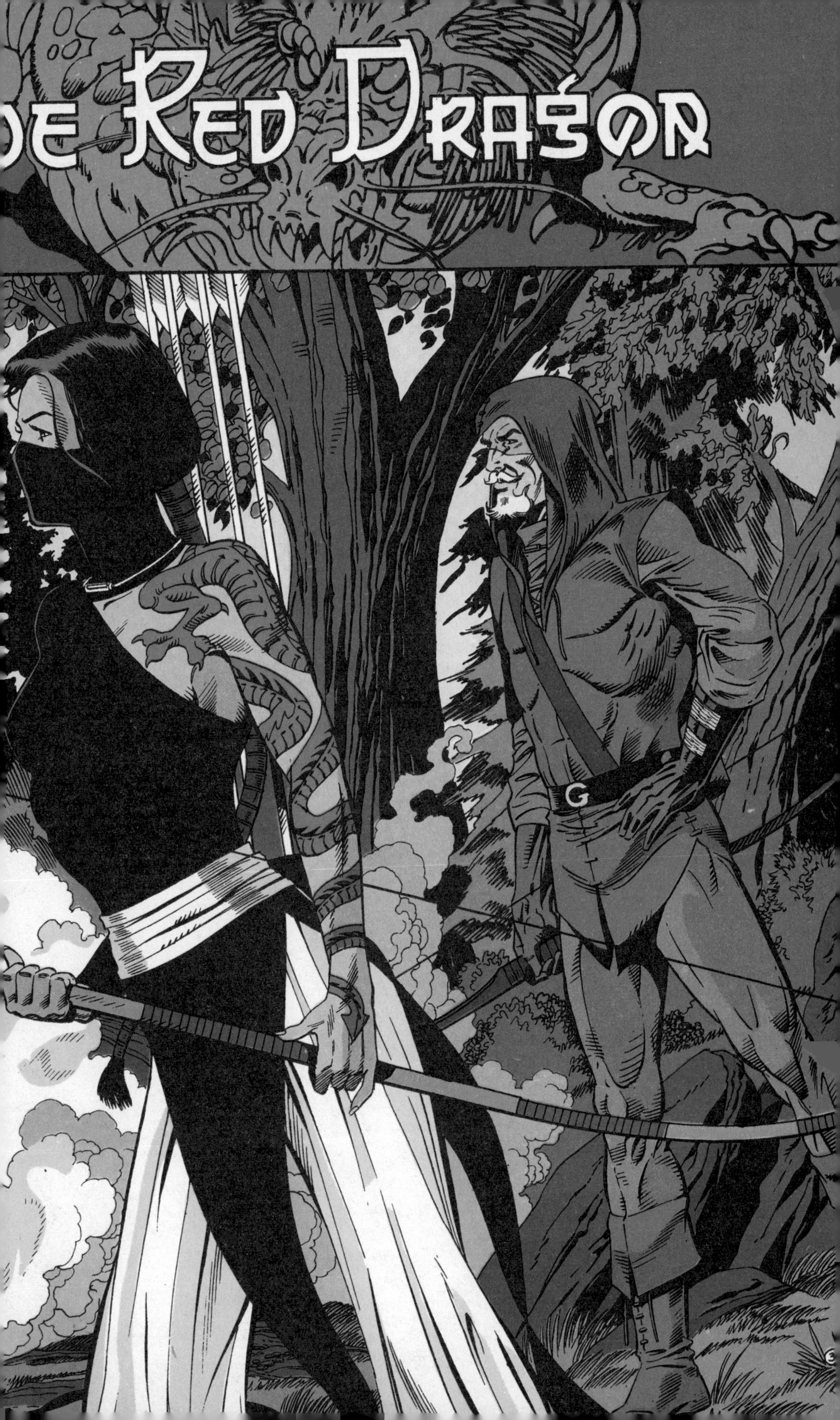
Red Dragon

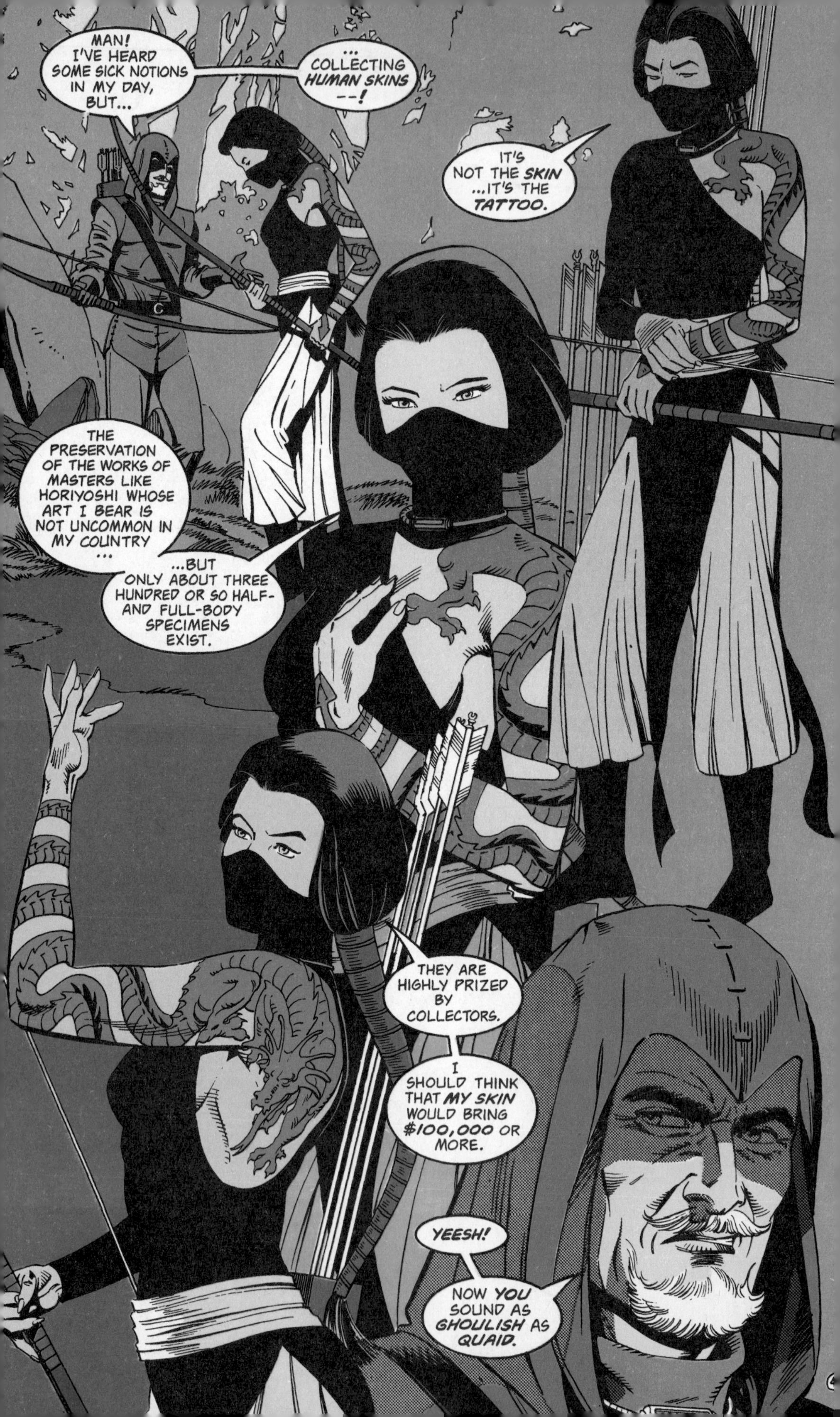
MAN! I'VE HEARD SOME SICK NOTIONS IN MY DAY, BUT...
... COLLECTING HUMAN SKINS --!
IT'S NOT THE SKIN ...IT'S THE TATTOO.
THE PRESERVATION OF THE WORKS OF MASTERS LIKE HORIYOSHI WHOSE ART I BEAR IS NOT UNCOMMON IN MY COUNTRY ...
...BUT ONLY ABOUT THREE HUNDRED OR SO HALF- AND FULL-BODY SPECIMENS EXIST.
THEY ARE HIGHLY PRIZED BY COLLECTORS.
I SHOULD THINK THAT MY SKIN WOULD BRING $100,000 OR MORE.
YEESH!
NOW YOU SOUND AS GHOULISH AS QUAID.

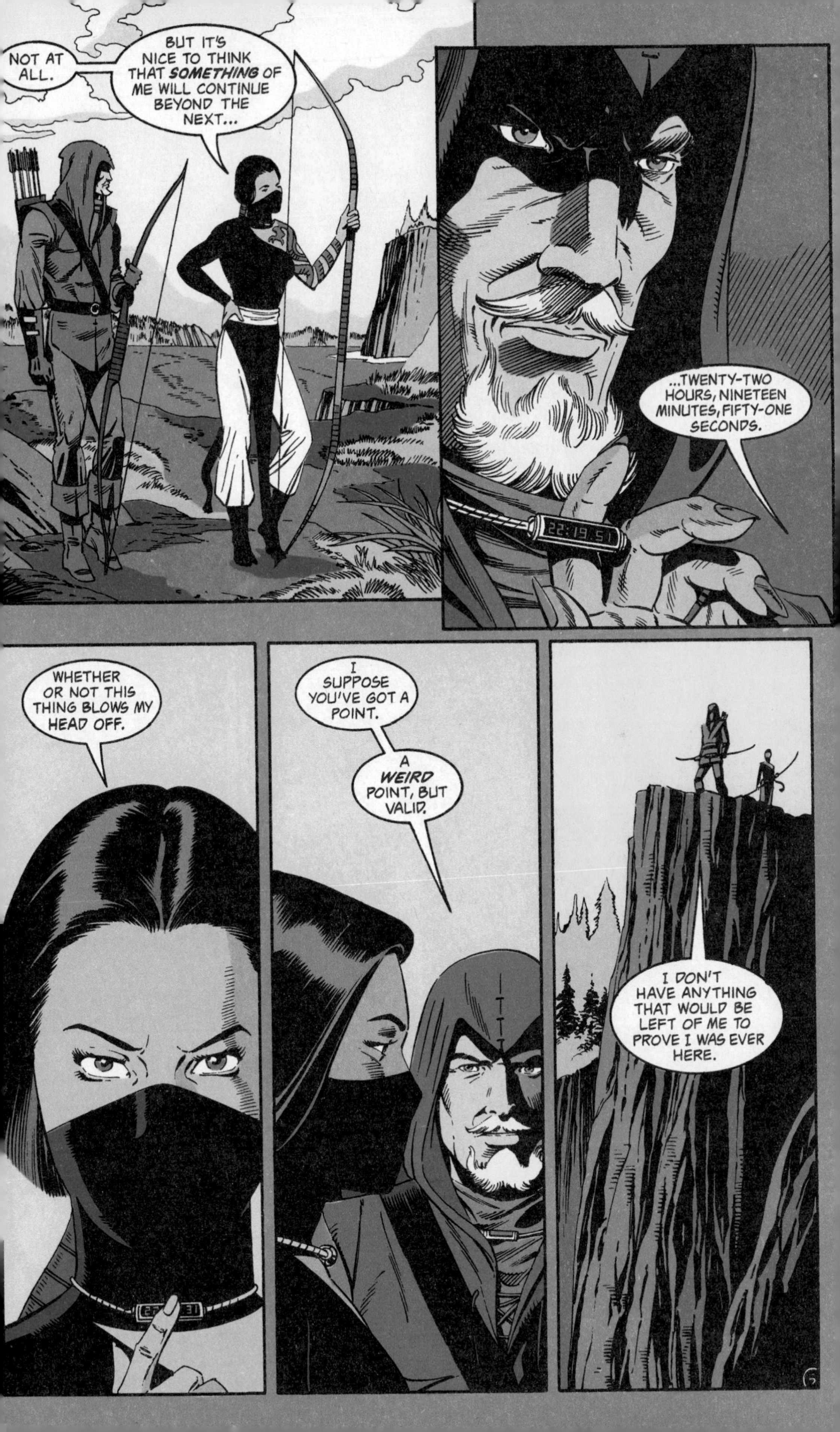
NOT AT ALL.
BUT IT'S NICE TO THINK THAT SOMETHING OF ME WILL CONTINUE BEYOND THE NEXT...
...TWENTY-TWO HOURS, NINETEEN MINUTES, FIFTY-ONE SECONDS.
22:19.51
WHETHER OR NOT THIS THING BLOWS MY HEAD OFF.
I SUPPOSE YOU'VE GOT A POINT.
A WEIRD POINT, BUT VALID.
I DON'T HAVE ANYTHING THAT WOULD BE LEFT OF ME TO PROVE I WAS EVER HERE.
6

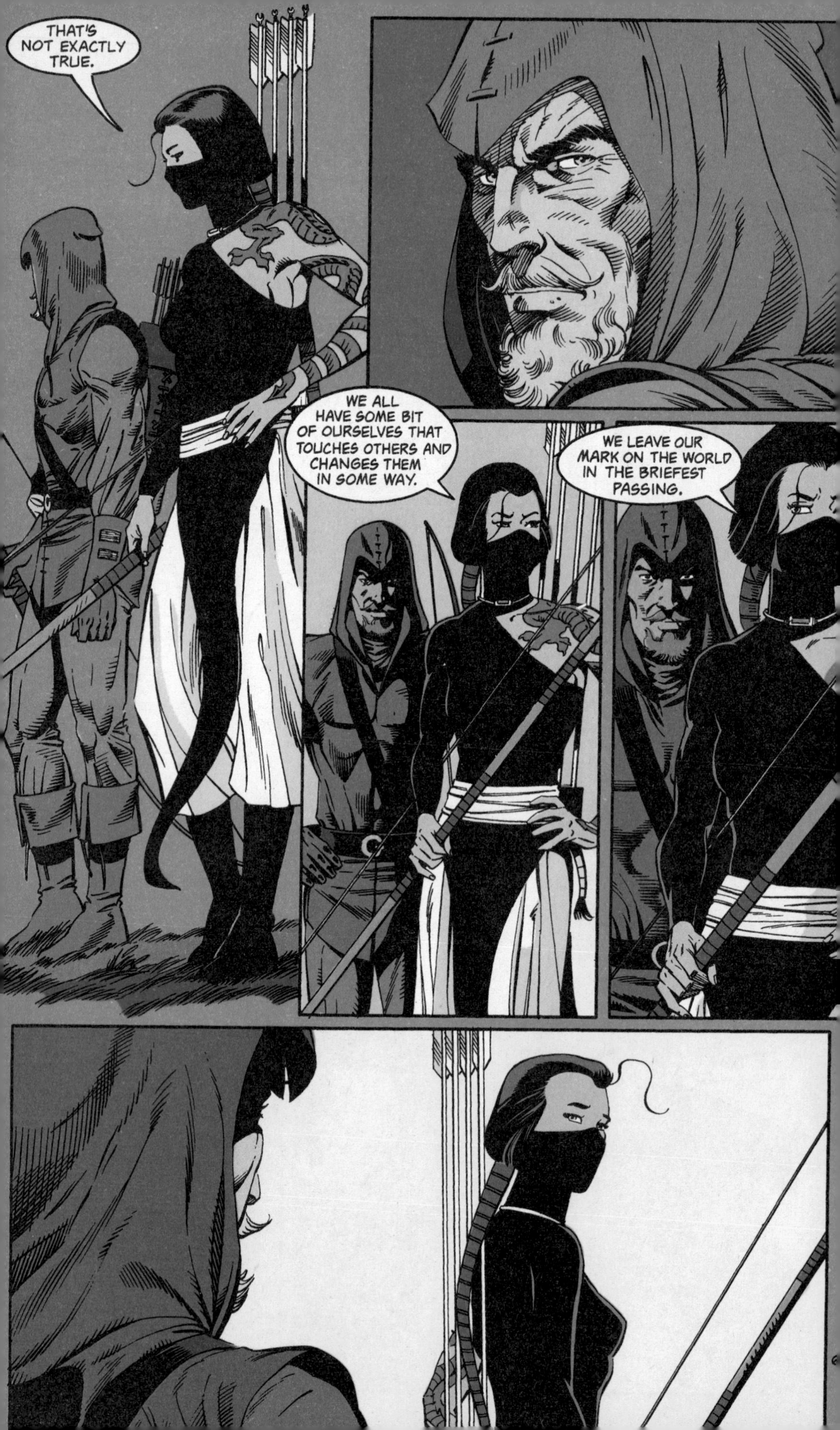
THAT'S NOT EXACTLY TRUE.
WE ALL HAVE SOME BIT OF OURSELVES THAT TOUCHES OTHERS AND CHANGES THEM IN SOME WAY.
WE LEAVE OUR MARK ON THE WORLD IN THE BRIEFEST PASSING.

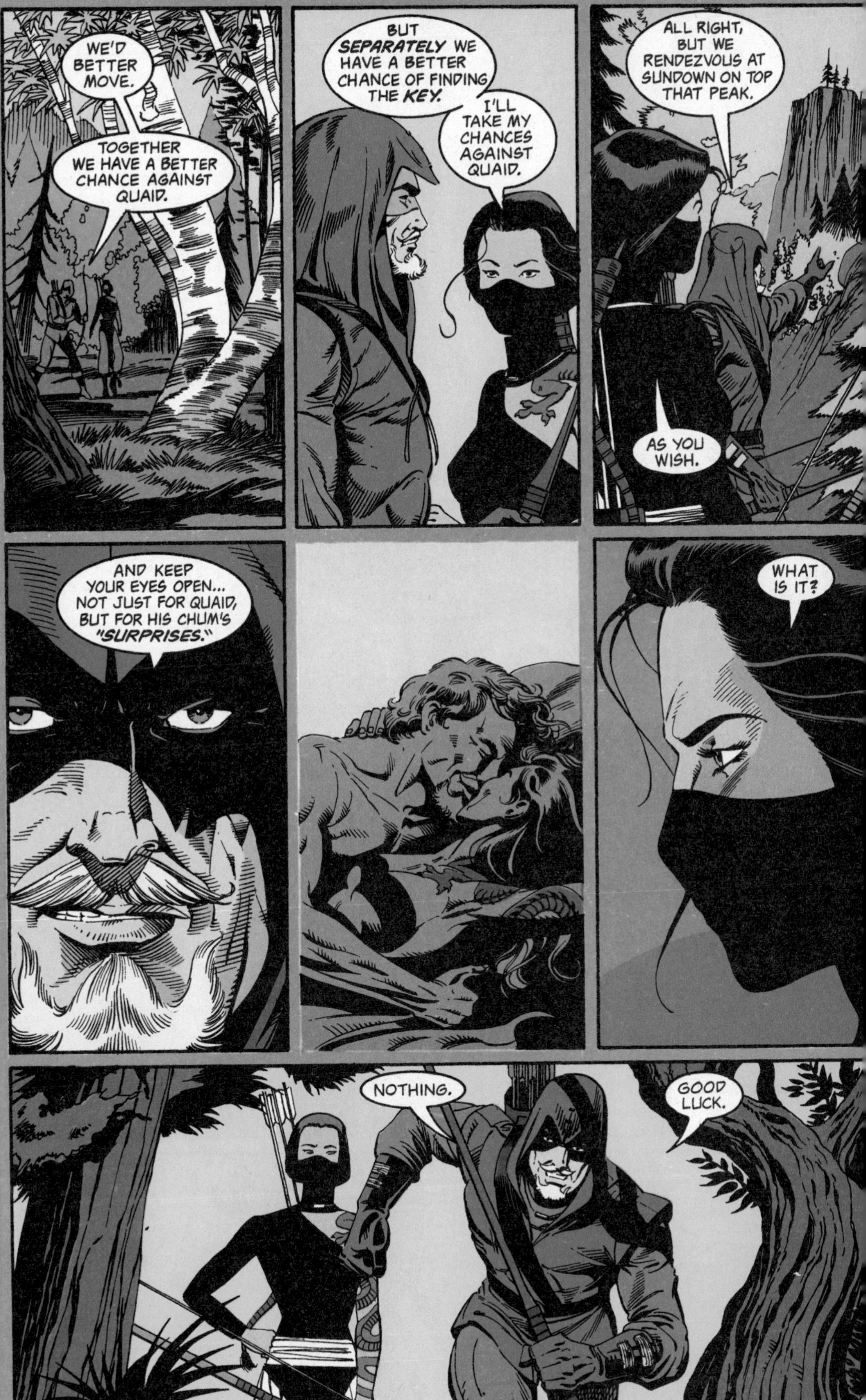
WE'D BETTER MOVE.
TOGETHER WE HAVE A BETTER CHANCE AGAINST QUAID.
BUT SEPARATELY WE HAVE A BETTER CHANCE OF FINDING THE KEY.
I'LL TAKE MY CHANCES AGAINST QUAID.
ALL RIGHT, BUT WE RENDEZVOUS AT SUNDOWN ON TOP THAT PEAK.
AS YOU WISH.
AND KEEP YOUR EYES OPEN... NOT JUST FOR QUAID, BUT FOR HIS CHUM'S "SURPRISES."
WHAT IS IT?
NOTHING.
GOOD LUCK.

THIS IS YOUR LUCKY DAY.

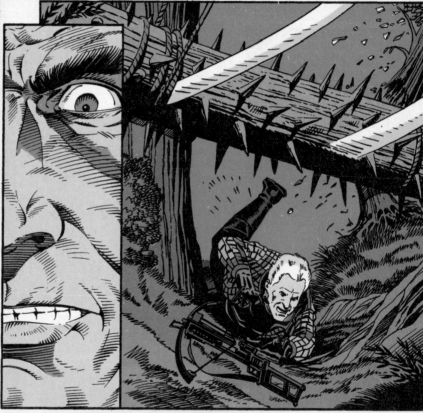

VERY GOOD, PHILLIP. PERHAPS YOU HAVE A PASSION AFTER ALL...

FOR *KILLING.*

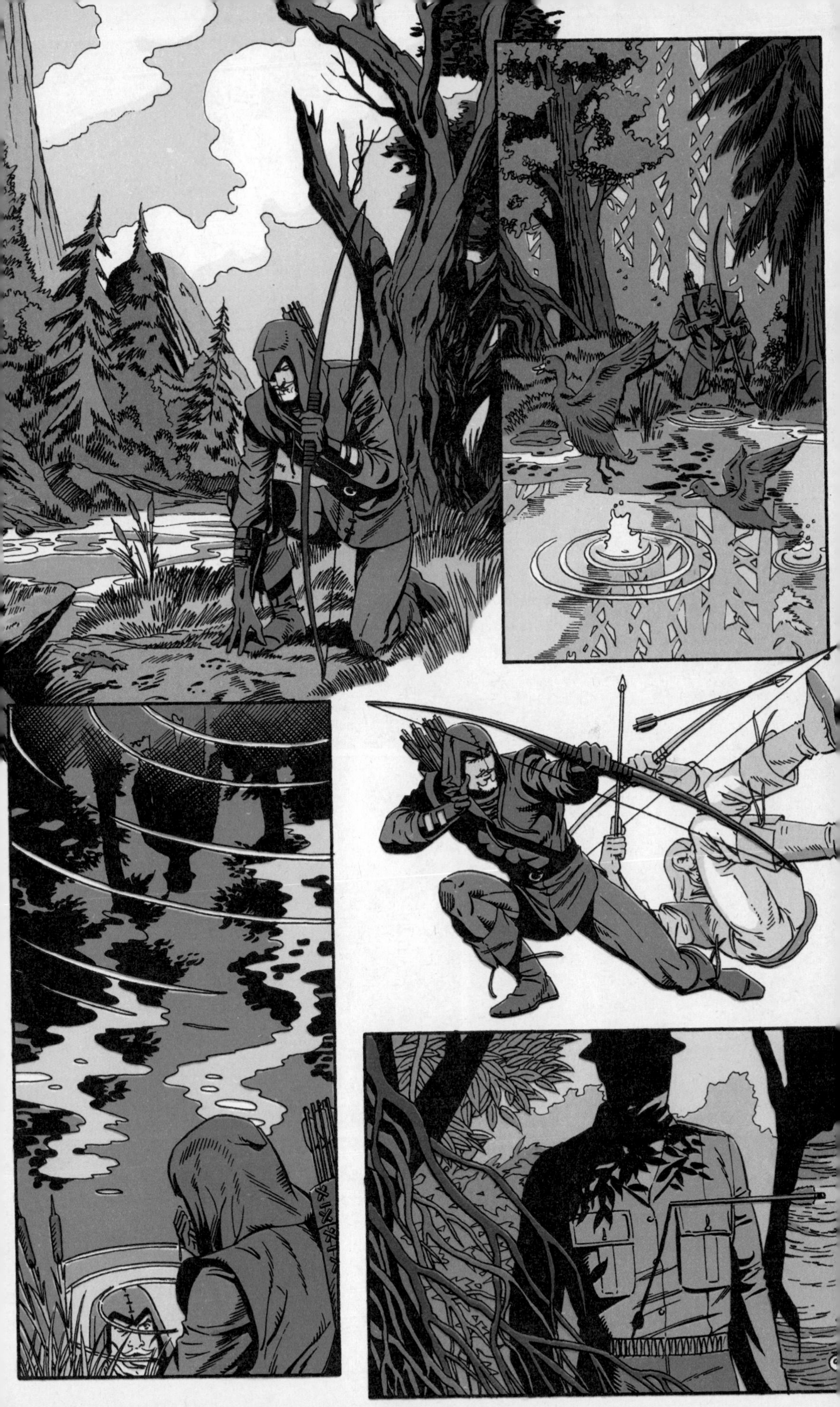

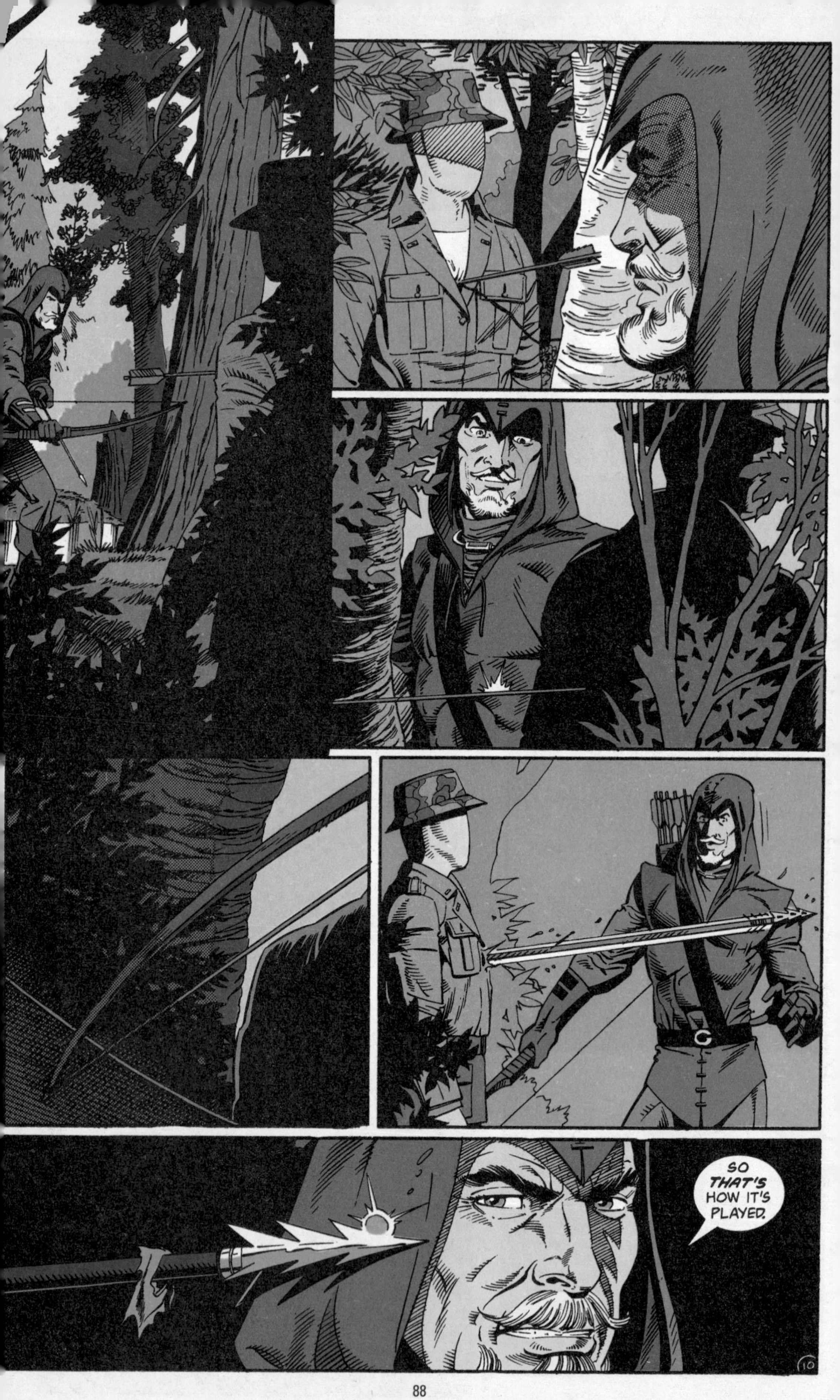
SO *THAT'S* HOW IT'S PLAYED.
10

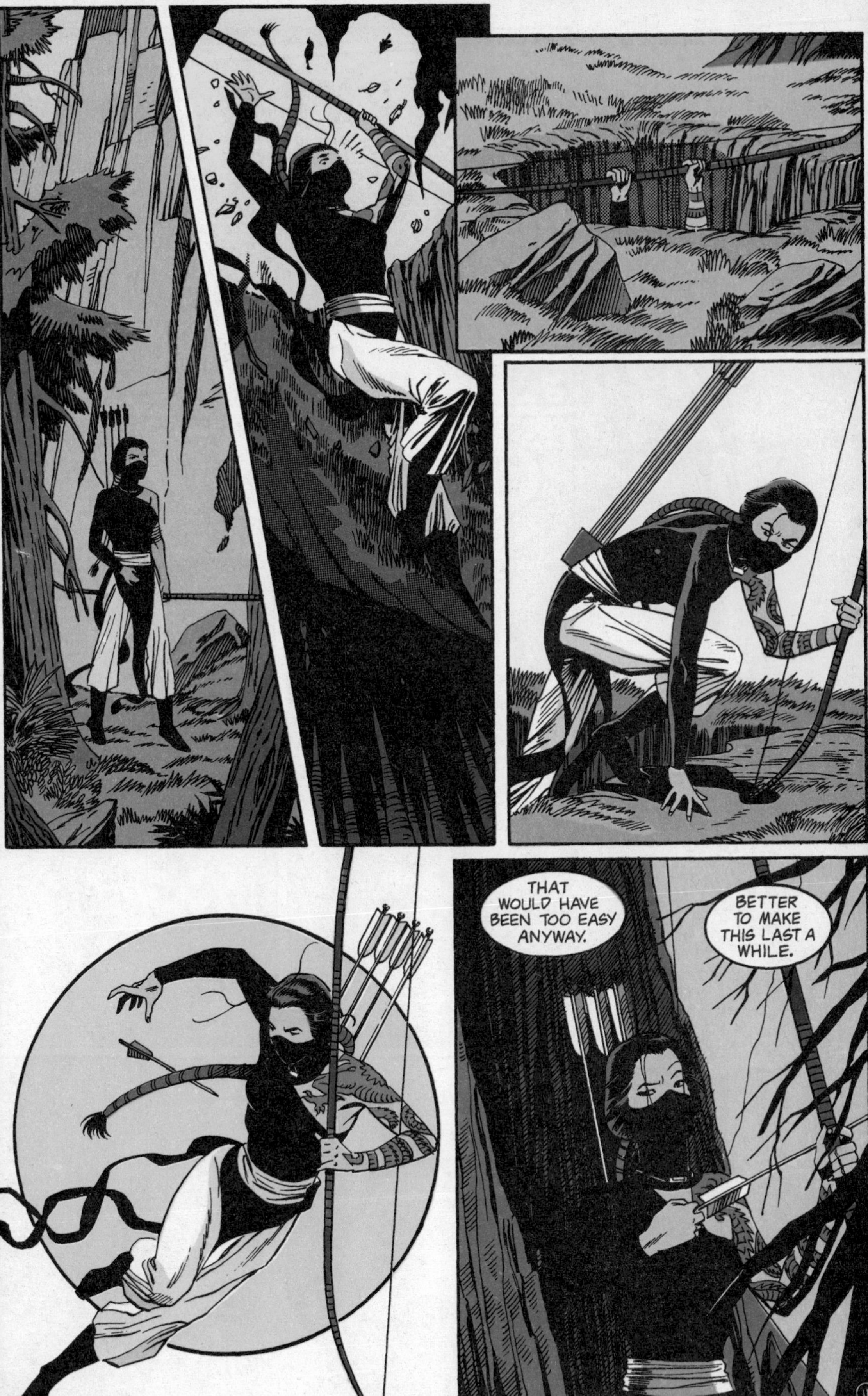
THAT WOULD HAVE BEEN TOO EASY ANYWAY.
BETTER TO MAKE THIS LAST A WHILE.

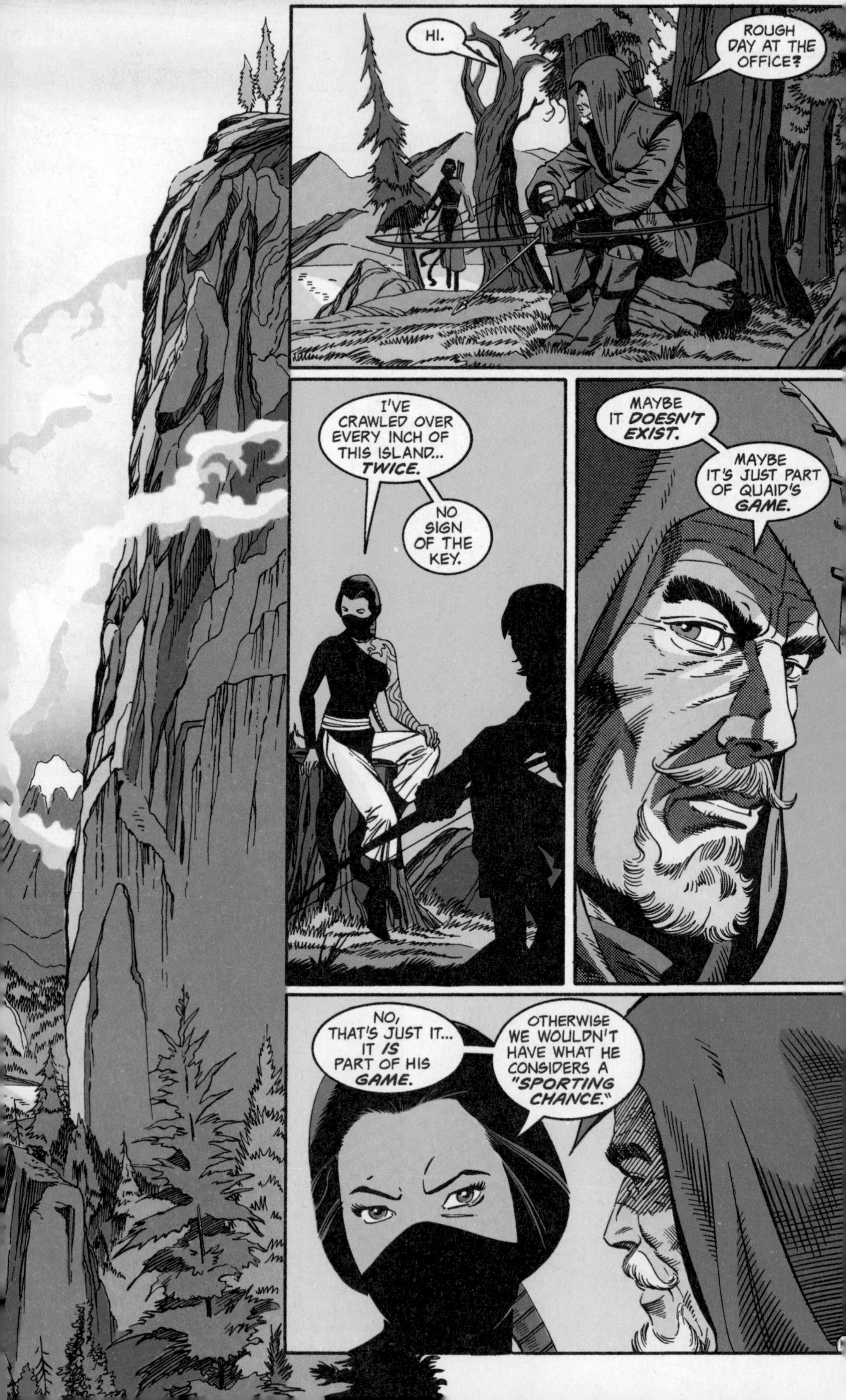
HI.
ROUGH DAY AT THE OFFICE?
I'VE CRAWLED OVER EVERY INCH OF THIS ISLAND... TWICE.
NO SIGN OF THE KEY.
MAYBE IT DOESN'T EXIST.
MAYBE IT'S JUST PART OF QUAID'S GAME.
NO, THAT'S JUST IT... IT IS PART OF HIS GAME.
OTHERWISE WE WOULDN'T HAVE WHAT HE CONSIDERS A "SPORTING CHANCE."

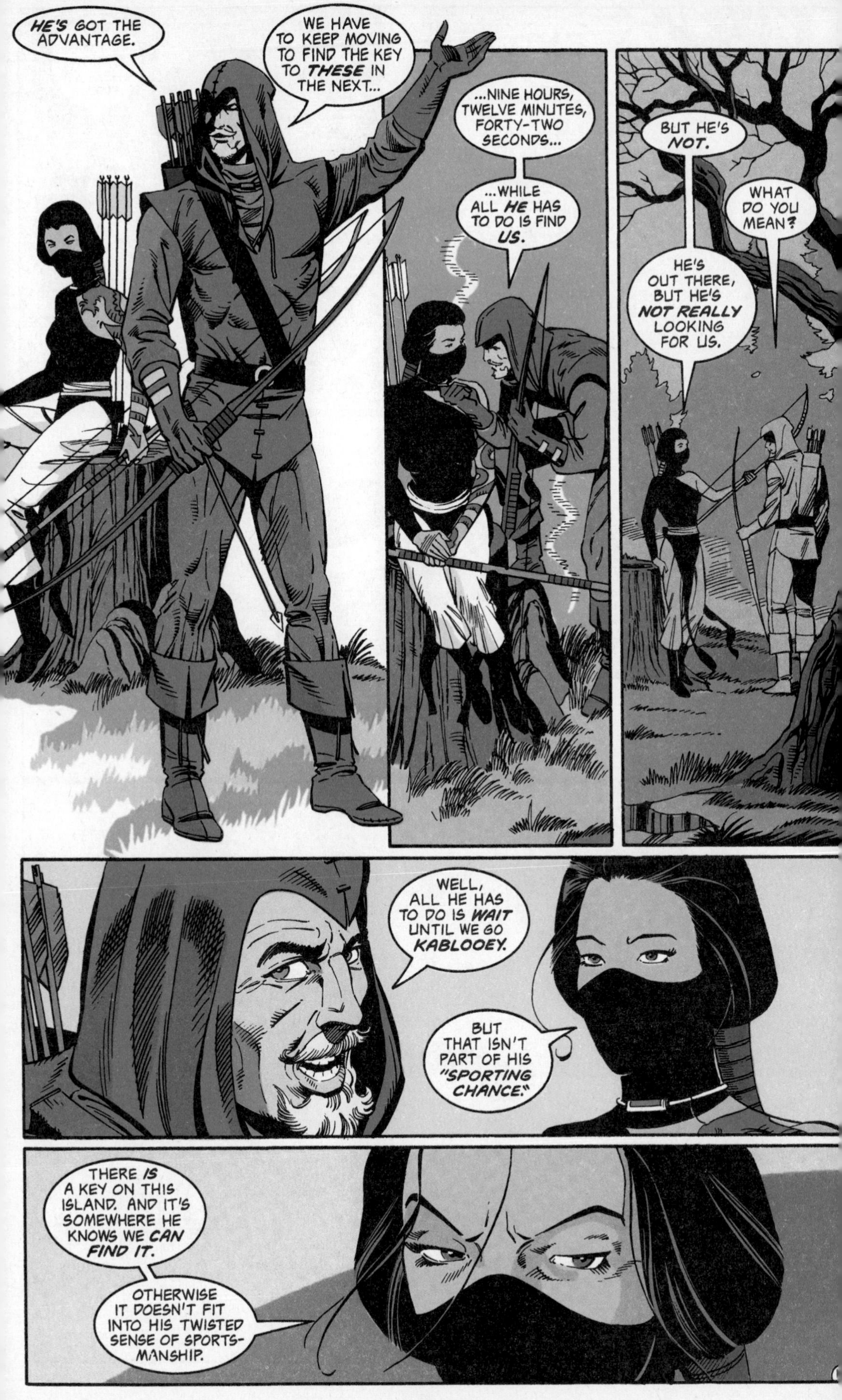
HE'S GOT THE ADVANTAGE.
WE HAVE TO KEEP MOVING TO FIND THE KEY TO THESE IN THE NEXT...
...NINE HOURS, TWELVE MINUTES, FORTY-TWO SECONDS...
...WHILE ALL HE HAS TO DO IS FIND US.
BUT HE'S NOT.
WHAT DO YOU MEAN?
HE'S OUT THERE, BUT HE'S NOT REALLY LOOKING FOR US.
WELL, ALL HE HAS TO DO IS WAIT UNTIL WE GO KABLOOEY.
BUT THAT ISN'T PART OF HIS "SPORTING CHANCE."
THERE IS A KEY ON THIS ISLAND. AND IT'S SOMEWHERE HE KNOWS WE CAN FIND IT.
OTHERWISE IT DOESN'T FIT INTO HIS TWISTED SENSE OF SPORTS-MANSHIP.

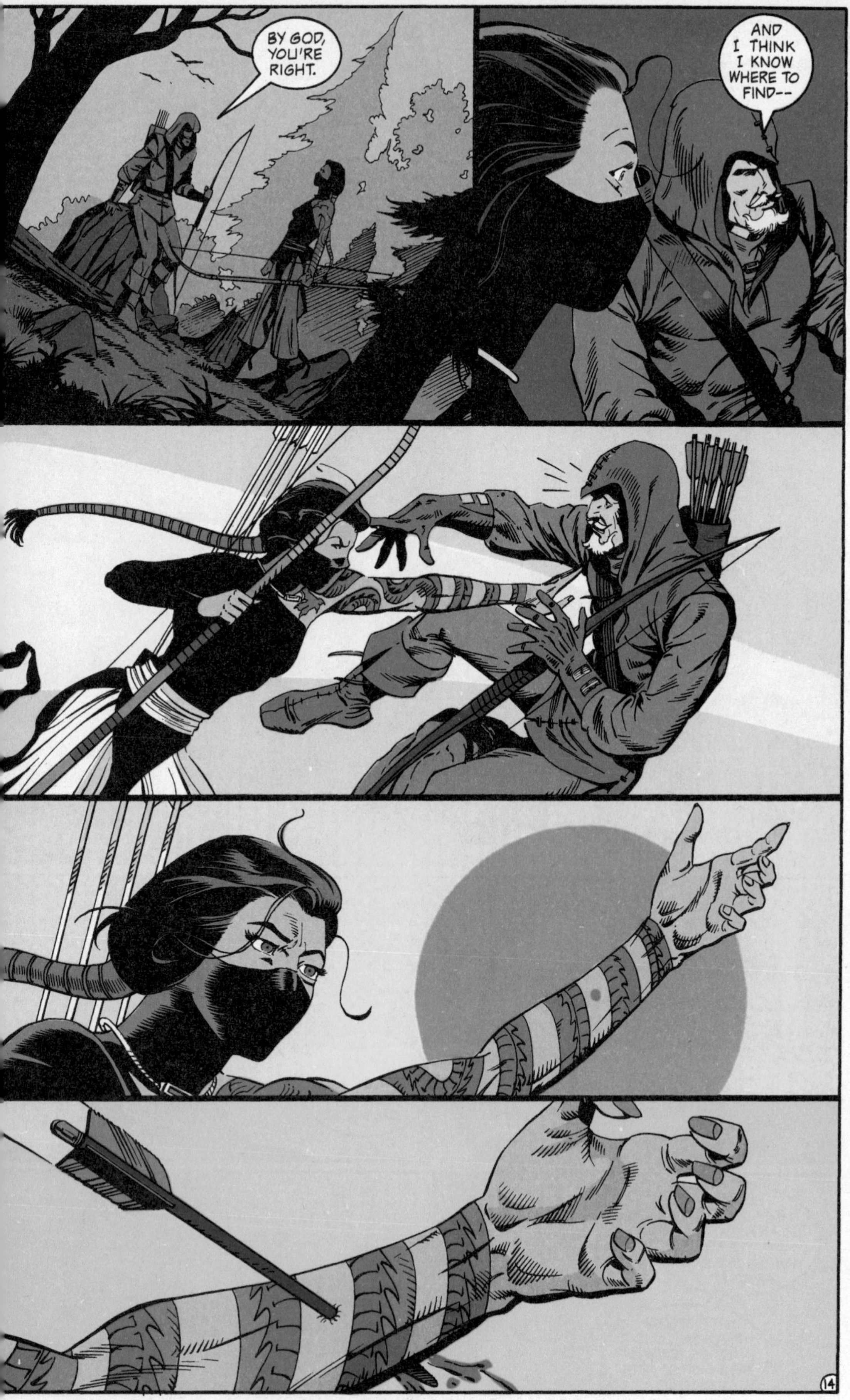
BY GOD, YOU'RE RIGHT.
AND I THINK I KNOW WHERE TO FIND--
14

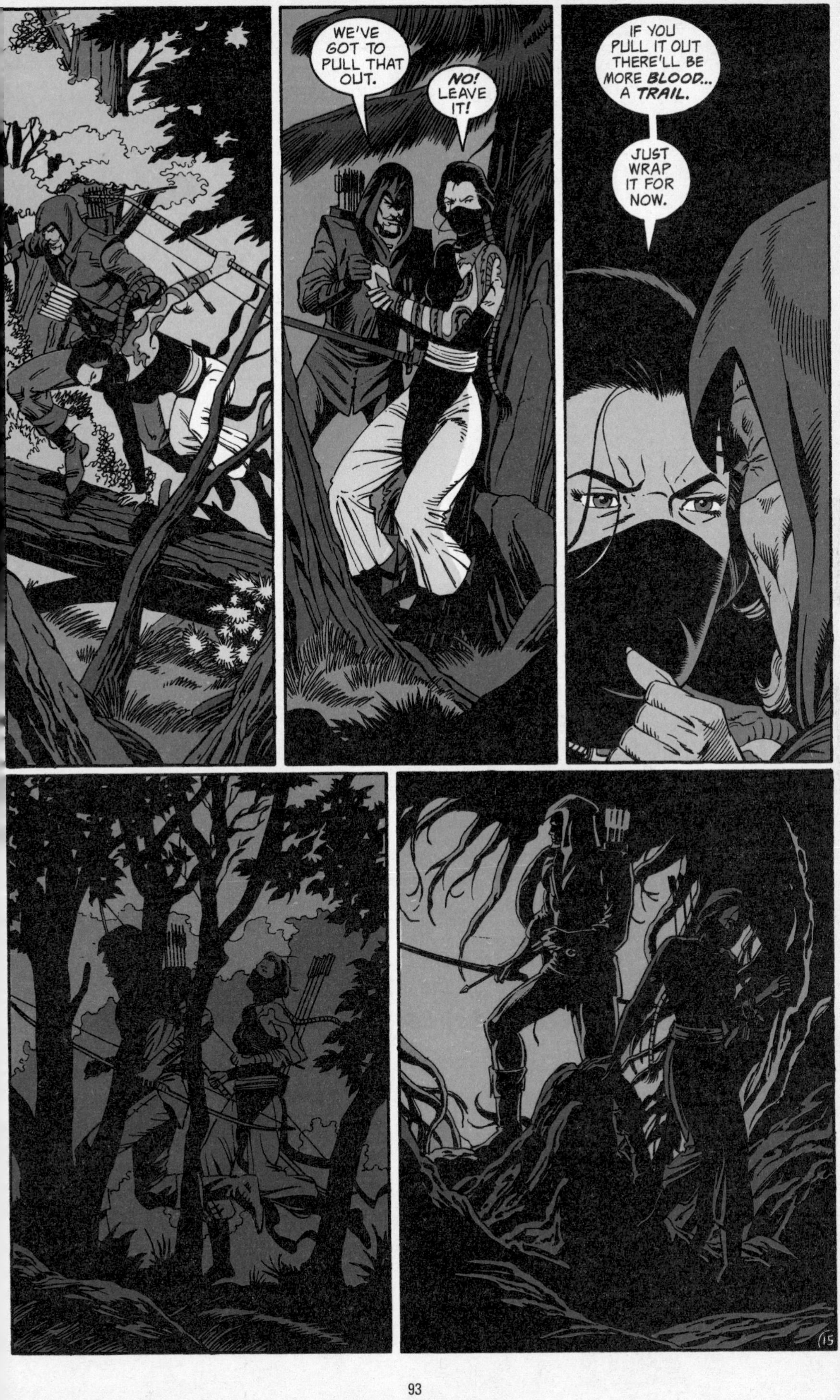
WE'VE GOT TO PULL THAT OUT.
NO! LEAVE IT!
IF YOU PULL IT OUT THERE'LL BE MORE BLOOD... A TRAIL.
JUST WRAP IT FOR NOW.
15

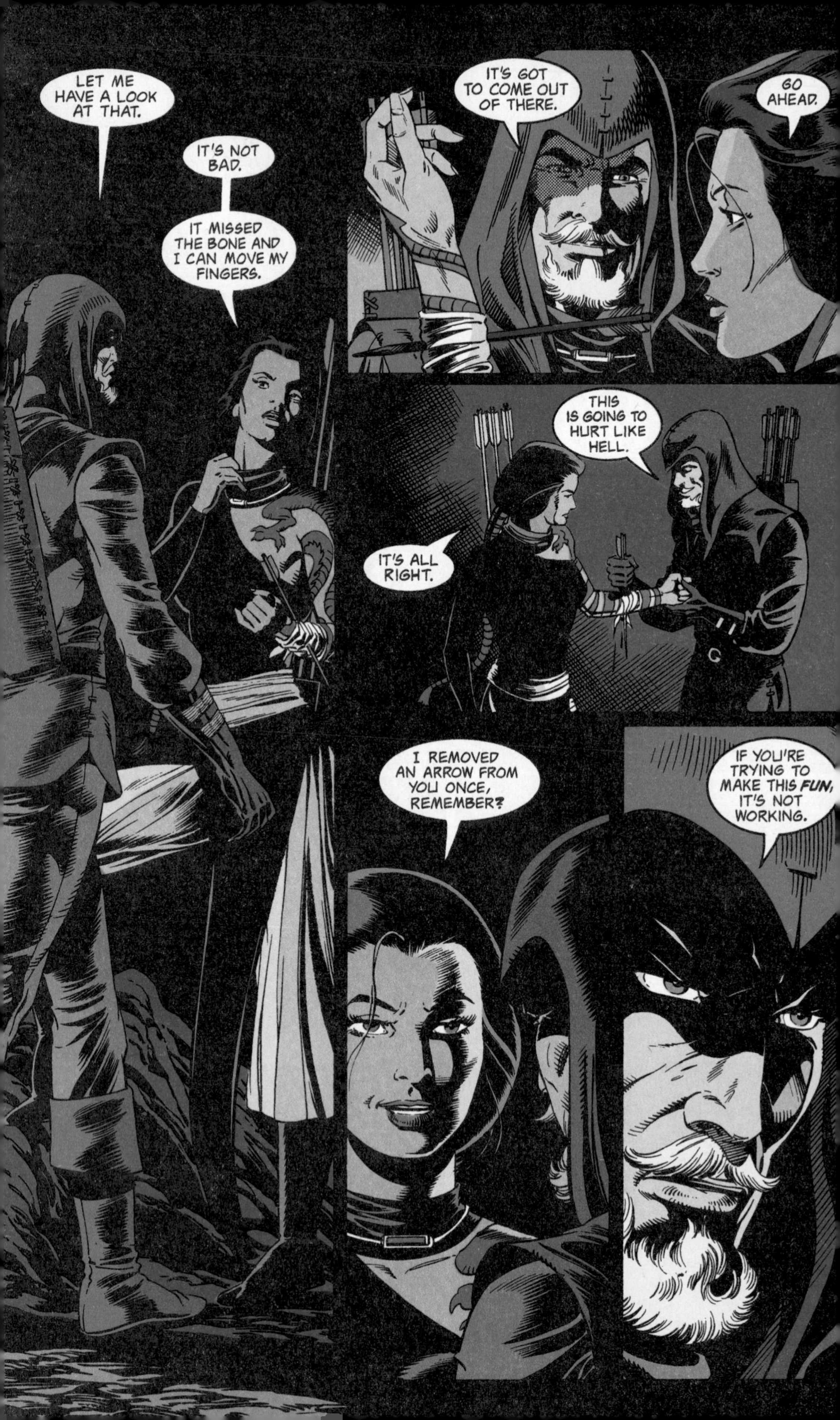
LET ME HAVE A LOOK AT THAT.
IT'S NOT BAD.
IT MISSED THE BONE AND I CAN MOVE MY FINGERS.
IT'S GOT TO COME OUT OF THERE.
GO AHEAD.
THIS IS GOING TO HURT LIKE HELL.
IT'S ALL RIGHT.
I REMOVED AN ARROW FROM YOU ONCE, REMEMBER?
IF YOU'RE TRYING TO MAKE THIS FUN, IT'S NOT WORKING.

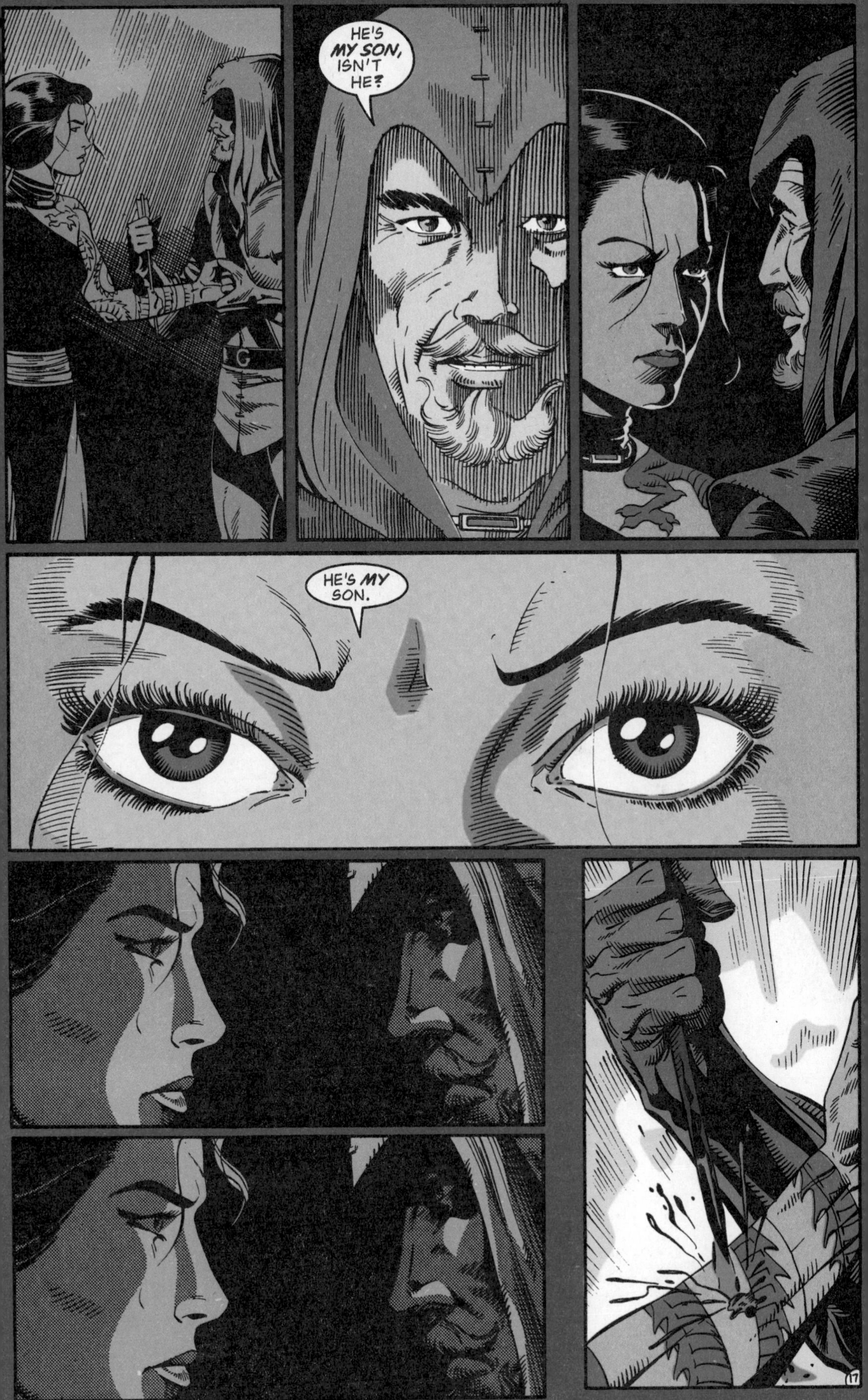
HE'S *MY SON,* ISN'T HE?
HE'S *MY* SON.
17

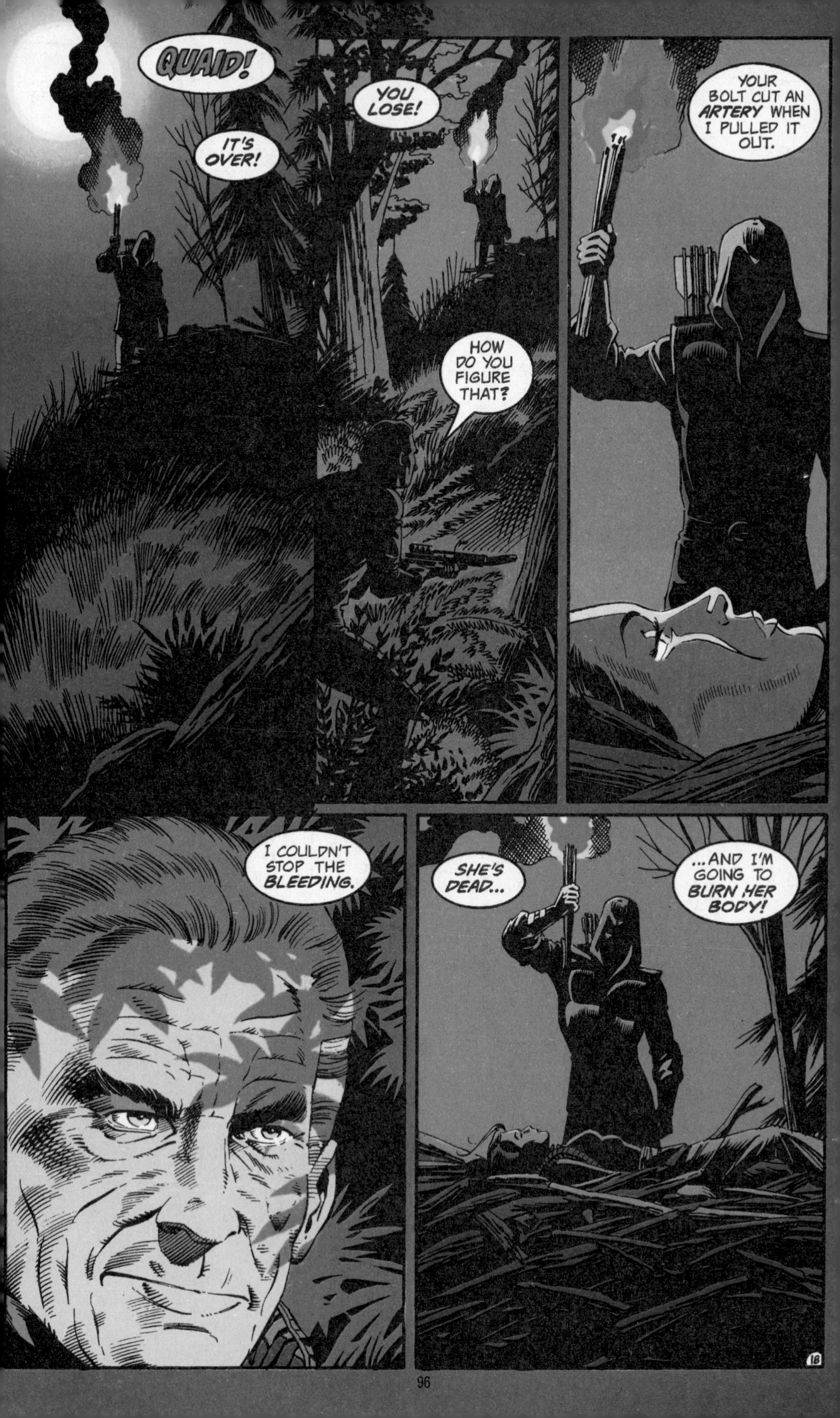
QUAID!
IT'S OVER!
YOU LOSE!
HOW DO YOU FIGURE THAT?
YOUR BOLT CUT AN ARTERY WHEN I PULLED IT OUT.
I COULDN'T STOP THE BLEEDING.
SHE'S DEAD...
...AND I'M GOING TO BURN HER BODY!
18

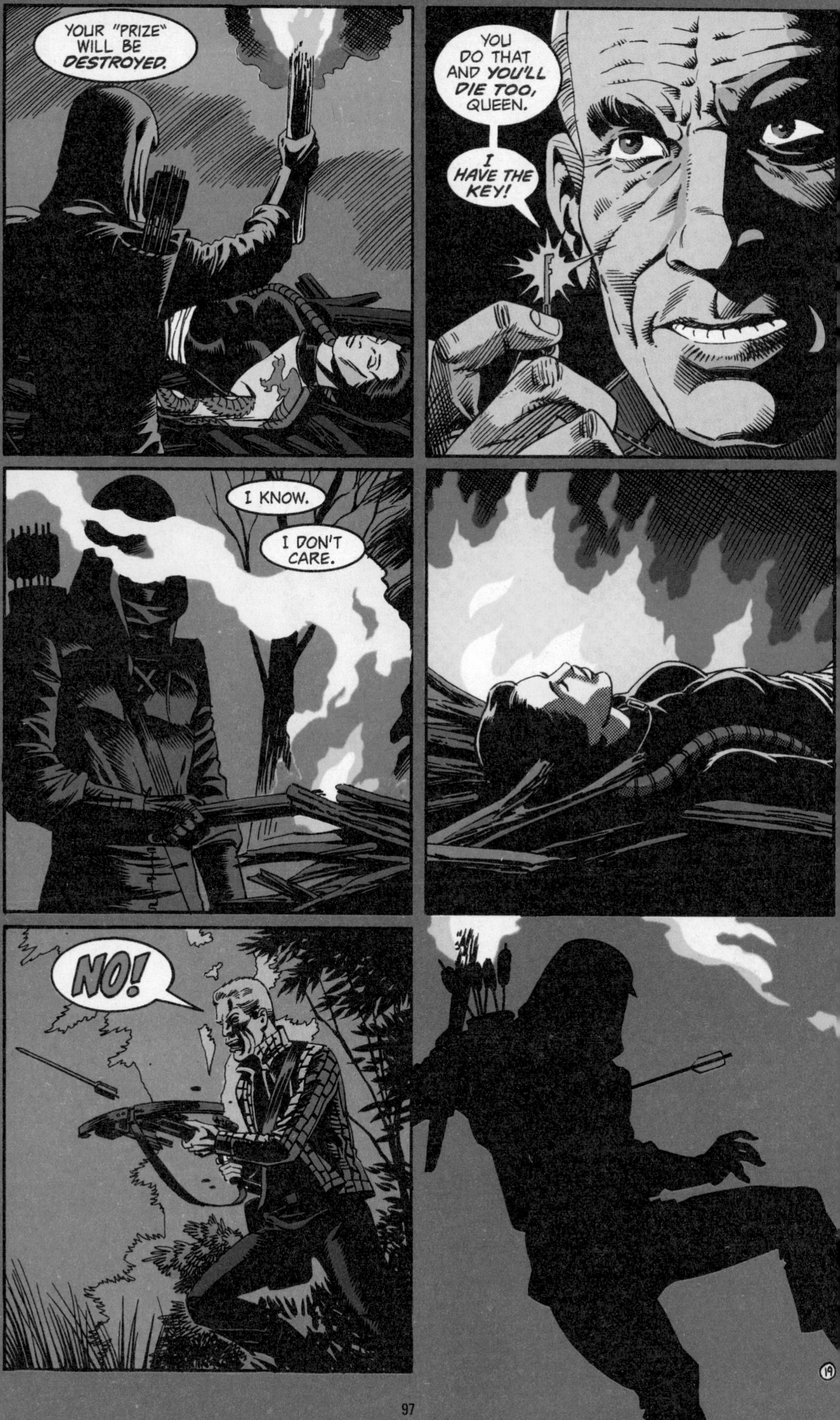

YOUR "PRIZE" WILL BE DESTROYED.
YOU DO THAT AND YOU'LL DIE TOO, QUEEN.
I HAVE THE KEY!
I KNOW.
I DON'T CARE.
NO!
19

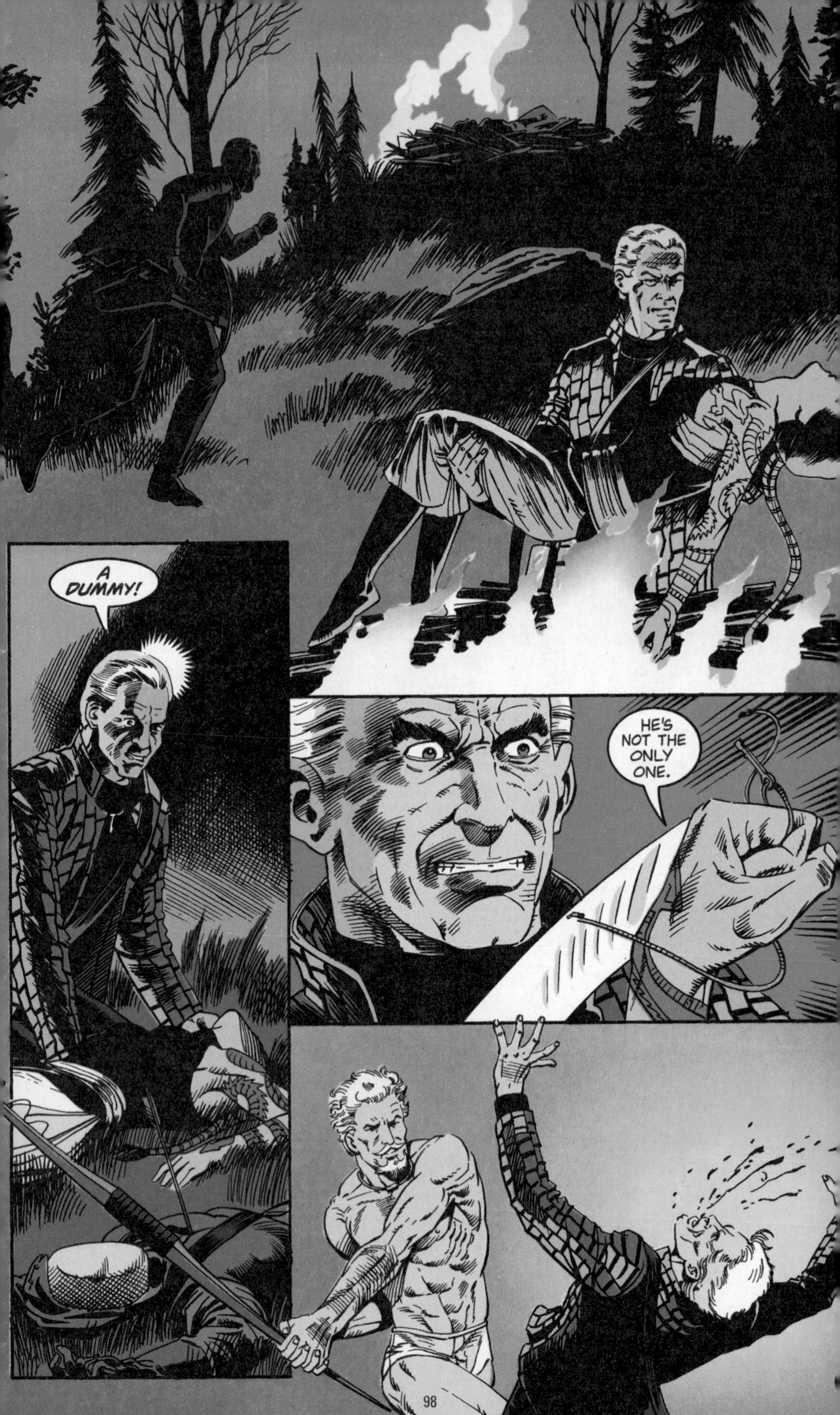
A DUMMY!
HE'S NOT THE ONLY ONE.

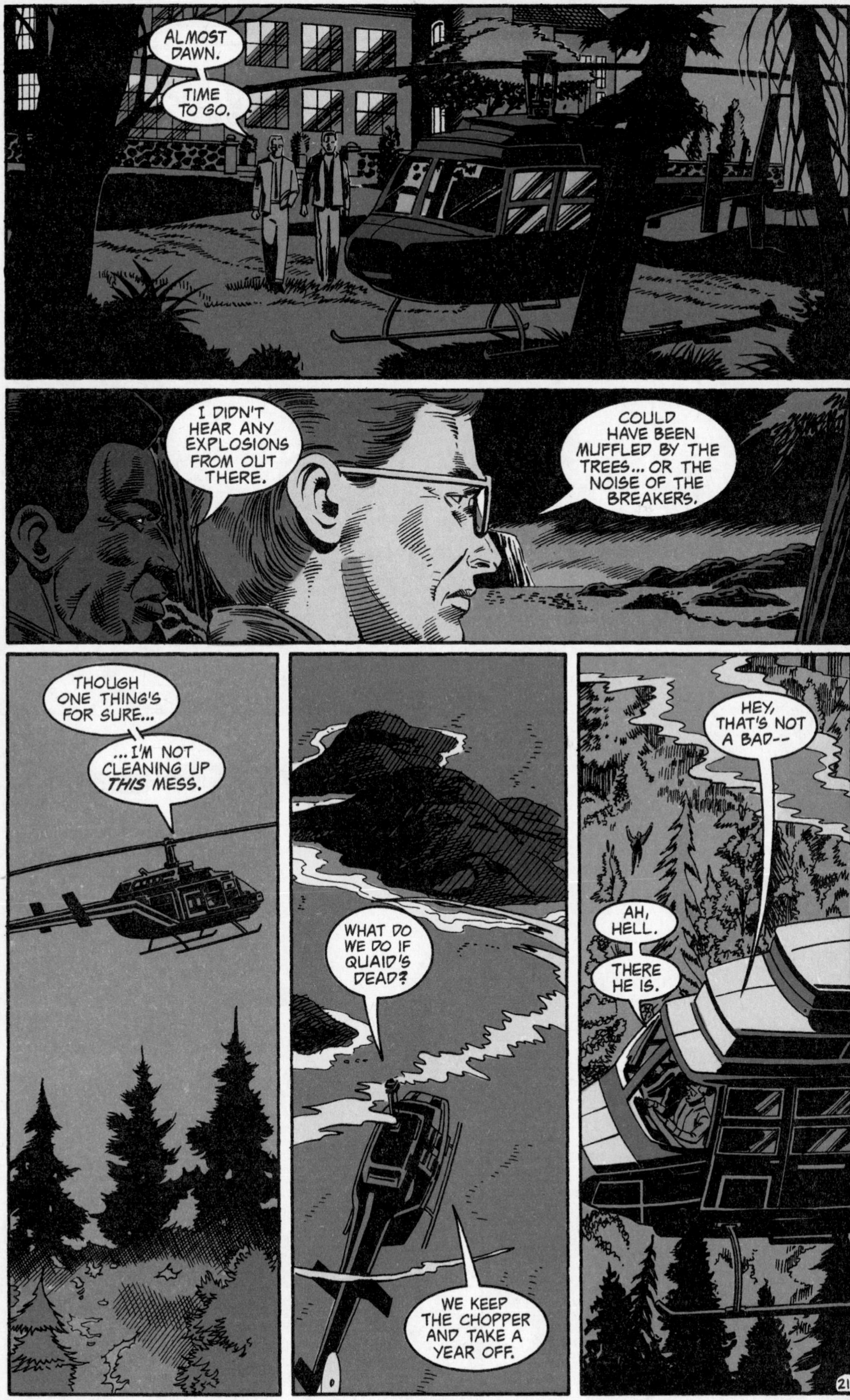
ALMOST DAWN.
TIME TO GO.
I DIDN'T HEAR ANY EXPLOSIONS FROM OUT THERE.
COULD HAVE BEEN MUFFLED BY THE TREES... OR THE NOISE OF THE BREAKERS.
THOUGH ONE THING'S FOR SURE...
...I'M NOT CLEANING UP *THIS* MESS.
WHAT DO WE DO IF QUAID'S DEAD?
WE KEEP THE CHOPPER AND TAKE A YEAR OFF.
HEY, THAT'S NOT A BAD--
AH, HELL.
THERE HE IS.
21

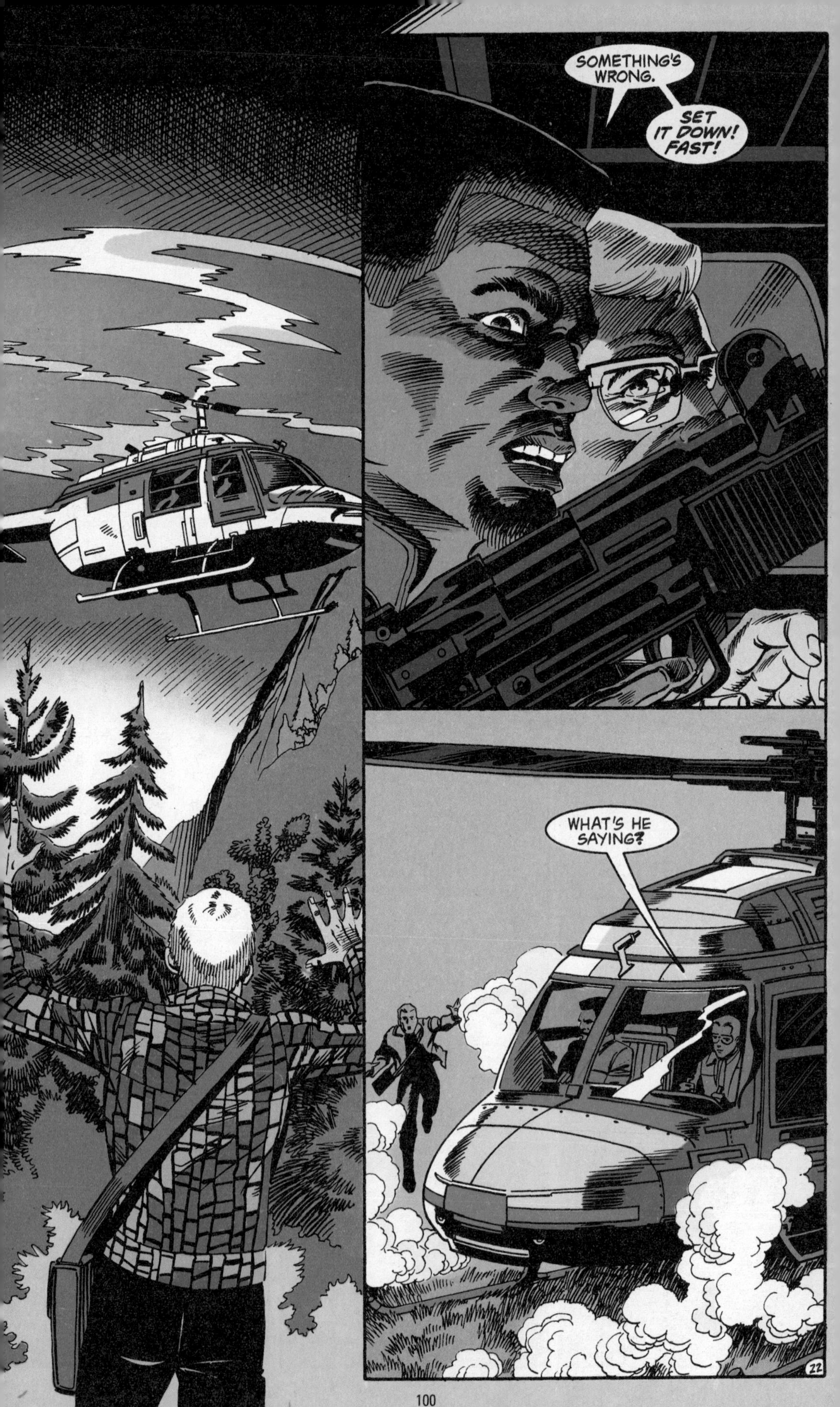
SOMETHING'S WRONG.
SET IT DOWN! FAST!
WHAT'S HE SAYING?
22

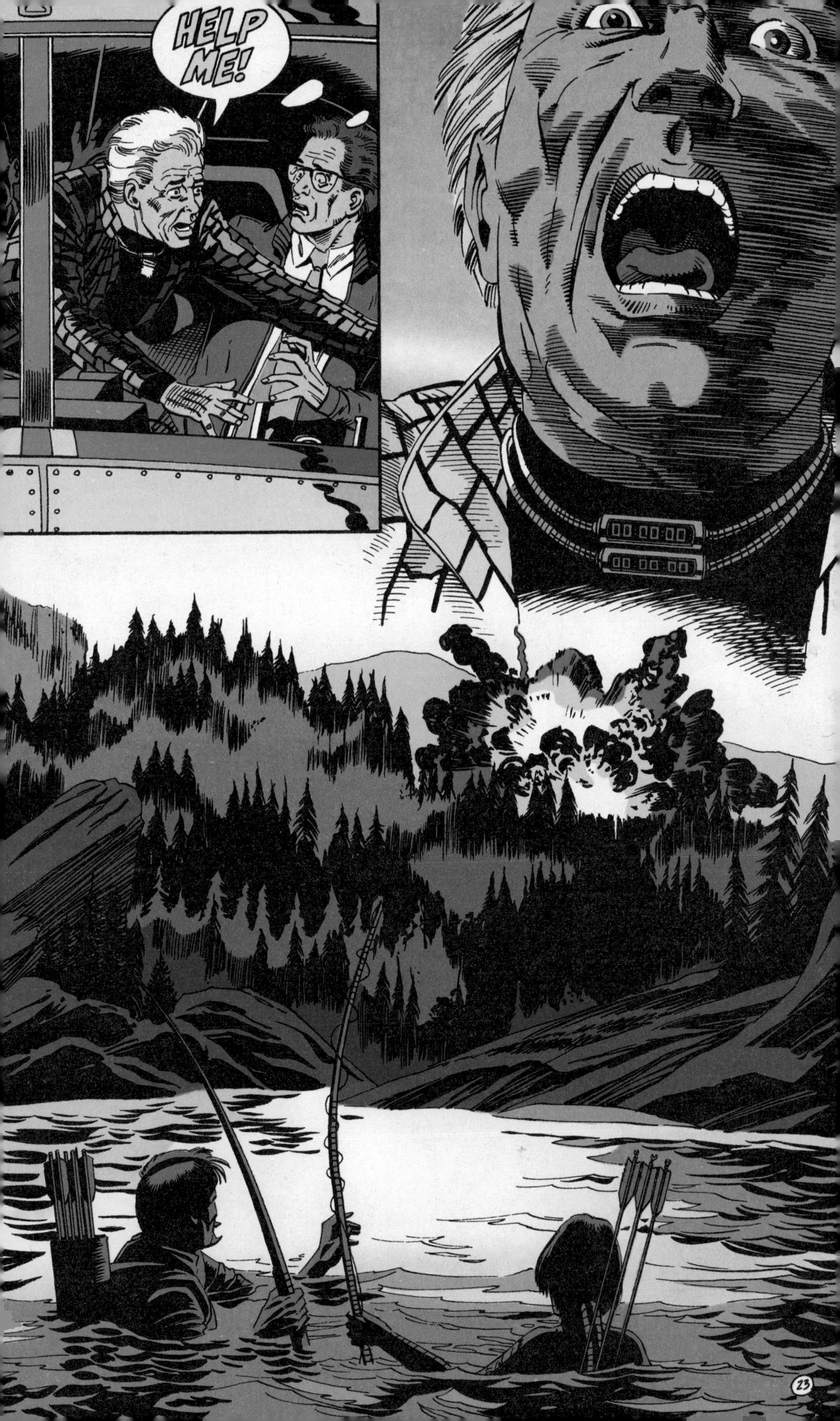
HELP ME!

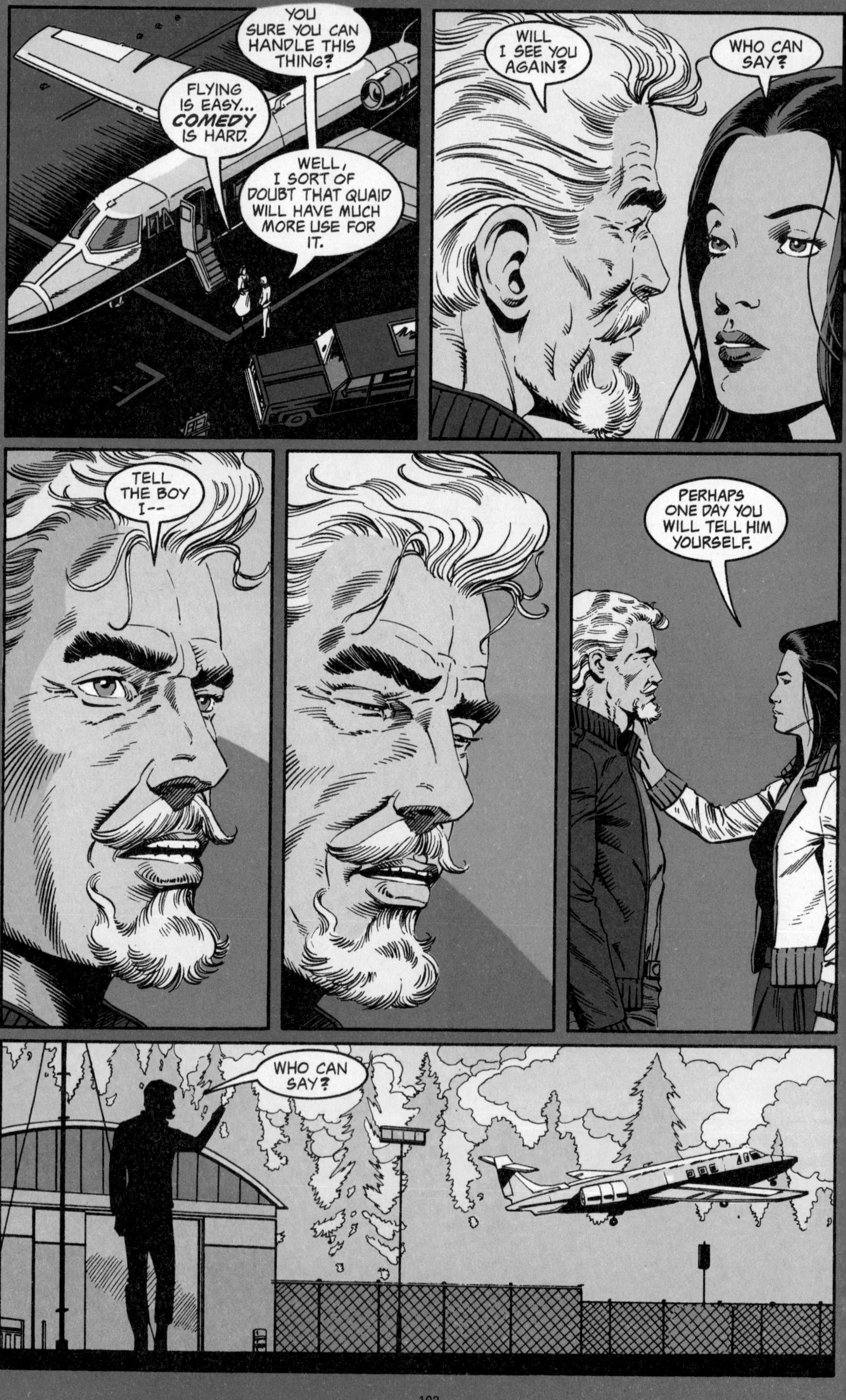
YOU SURE YOU CAN HANDLE THIS THING?
FLYING IS EASY... COMEDY IS HARD.
WELL, I SORT OF DOUBT THAT QUAID WILL HAVE MUCH MORE USE FOR IT.
WILL I SEE YOU AGAIN?
WHO CAN SAY?
TELL THE BOY I--
PERHAPS ONE DAY YOU WILL TELL HIM YOURSELF.
WHO CAN SAY?

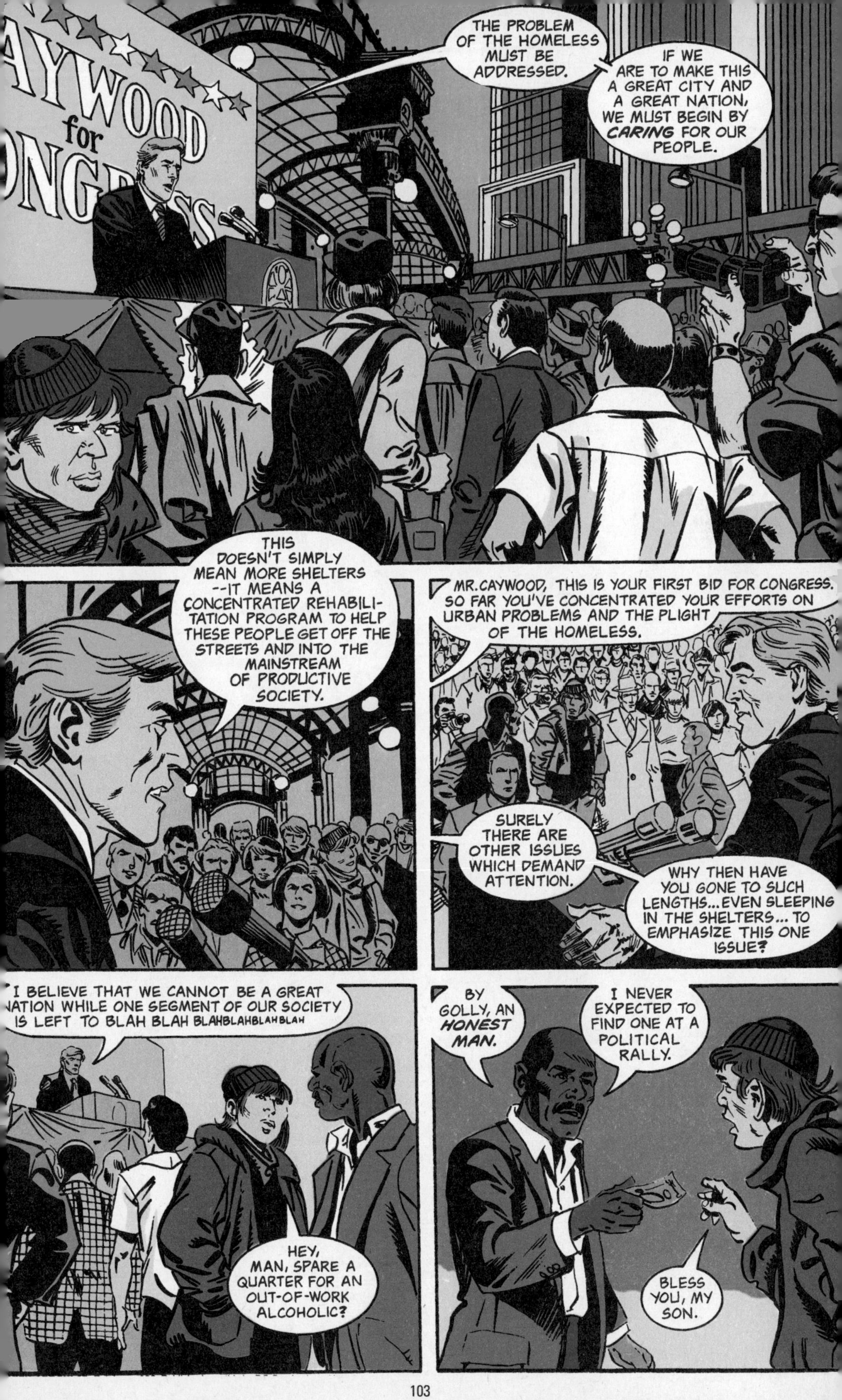
AYWOOD for ONGR SS
THE PROBLEM OF THE HOMELESS MUST BE ADDRESSED.
IF WE ARE TO MAKE THIS A GREAT CITY AND A GREAT NATION, WE MUST BEGIN BY CARING FOR OUR PEOPLE.
THIS DOESN'T SIMPLY MEAN MORE SHELTERS --IT MEANS A CONCENTRATED REHABILITATION PROGRAM TO HELP THESE PEOPLE GET OFF THE STREETS AND INTO THE MAINSTREAM OF PRODUCTIVE SOCIETY.
MR. CAYWOOD, THIS IS YOUR FIRST BID FOR CONGRESS. SO FAR YOU'VE CONCENTRATED YOUR EFFORTS ON URBAN PROBLEMS AND THE PLIGHT OF THE HOMELESS.
SURELY THERE ARE OTHER ISSUES WHICH DEMAND ATTENTION.
WHY THEN HAVE YOU GONE TO SUCH LENGTHS... EVEN SLEEPING IN THE SHELTERS... TO EMPHASIZE THIS ONE ISSUE?
I BELIEVE THAT WE CANNOT BE A GREAT NATION WHILE ONE SEGMENT OF OUR SOCIETY IS LEFT TO BLAH BLAH BLAHBLAHBLAHBLAH
HEY, MAN, SPARE A QUARTER FOR AN OUT-OF-WORK ALCOHOLIC?
BY GOLLY, AN HONEST MAN.
I NEVER EXPECTED TO FIND ONE AT A POLITICAL RALLY.
BLESS YOU, MY SON.

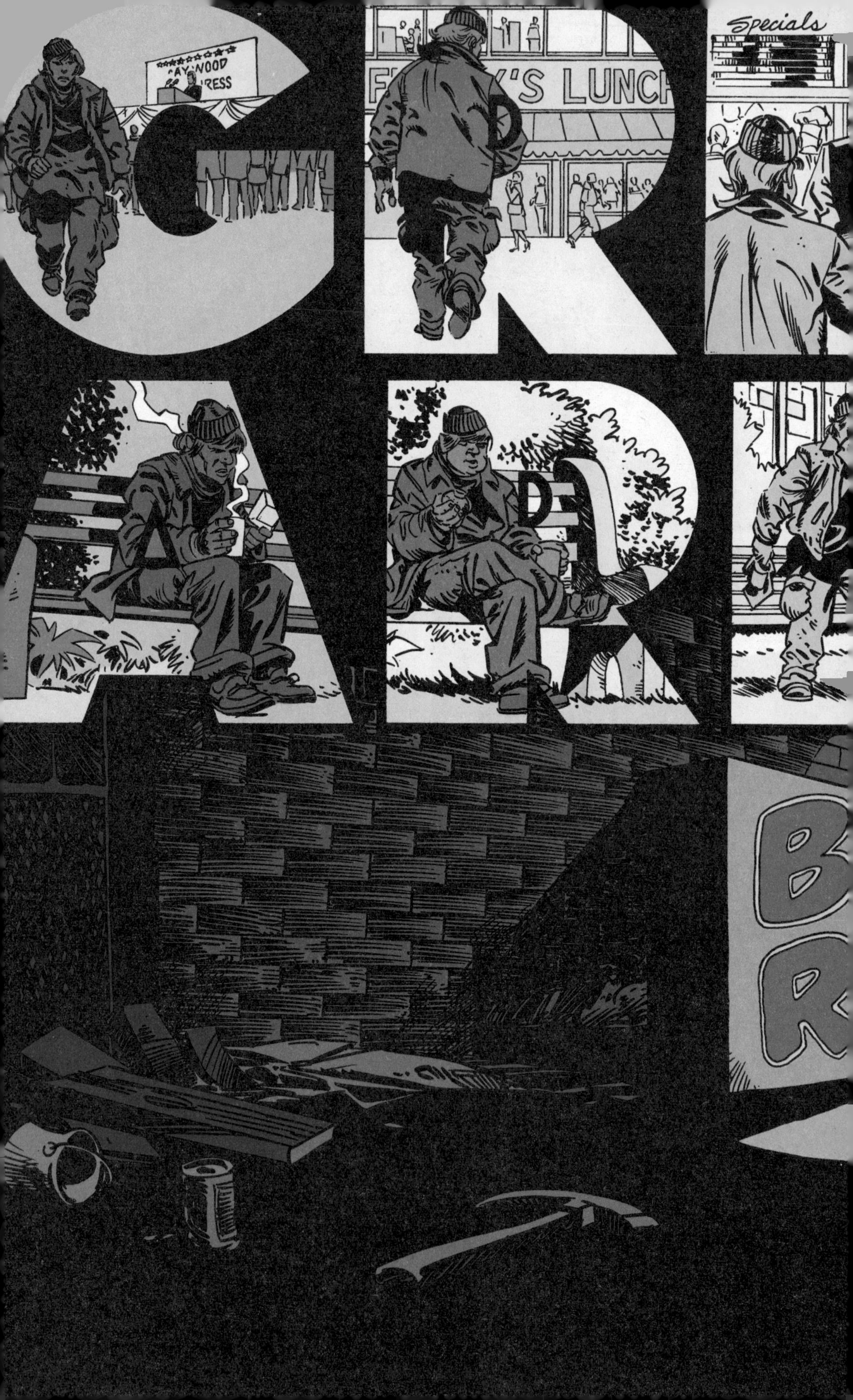
Specials

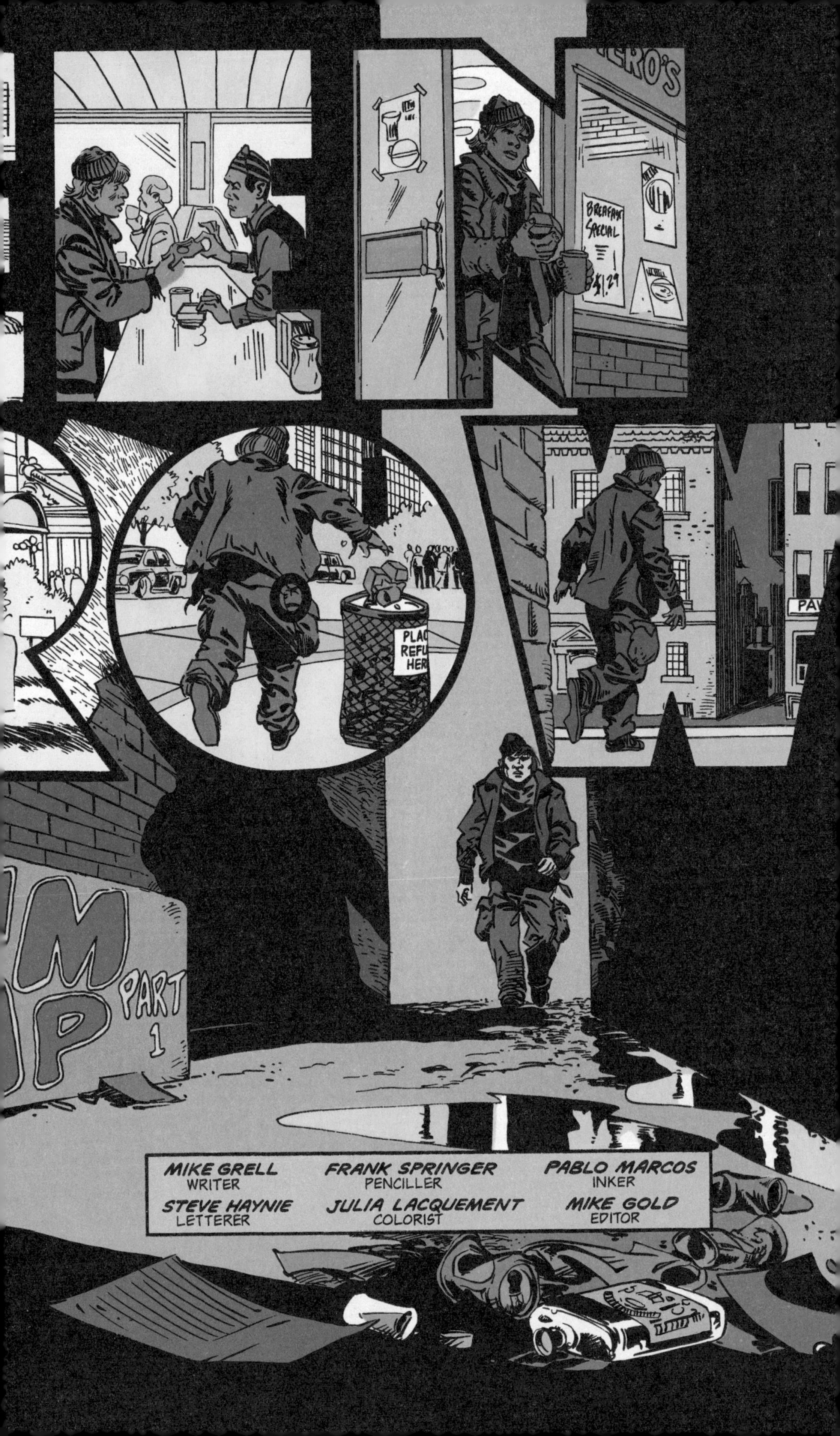

ERO'S
BREAKFAST SPECIAL
$1.29
PLACE REFU HER
PAW
PART 1
MIKE GRELL WRITER
FRANK SPRINGER PENCILLER
PABLO MARCOS INKER
STEVE HAYNIE LETTERER
JULIA LACQUEMENT COLORIST
MIKE GOLD EDITOR

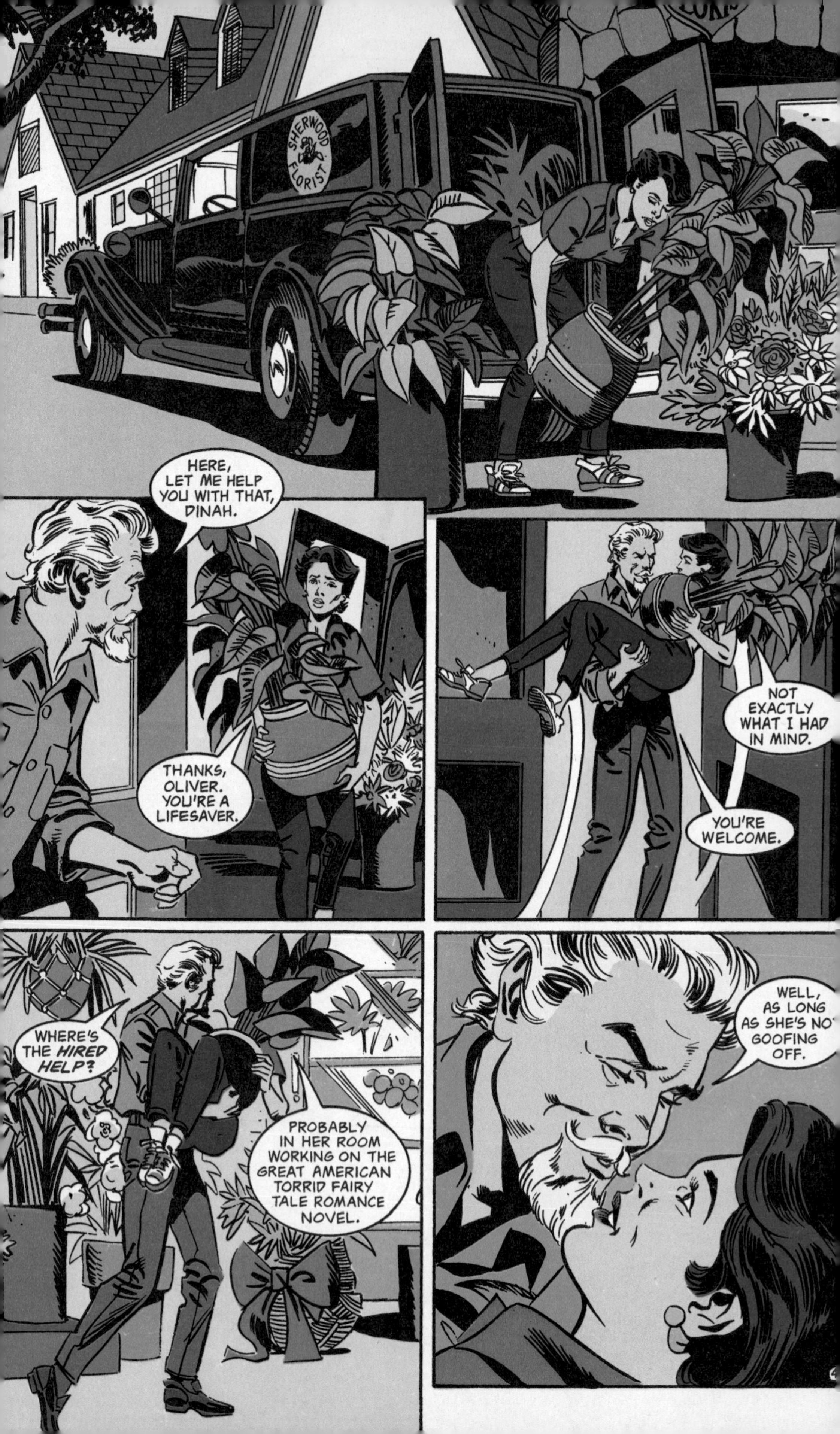
HERE, LET ME HELP YOU WITH THAT, DINAH.
THANKS, OLIVER. YOU'RE A LIFESAVER.
NOT EXACTLY WHAT I HAD IN MIND.
YOU'RE WELCOME.
WHERE'S THE *HIRED HELP?*
PROBABLY IN HER ROOM WORKING ON THE GREAT AMERICAN TORRID FAIRY TALE ROMANCE NOVEL.
WELL, AS LONG AS SHE'S NOT GOOFING OFF.
SHERWOOD FLORIST

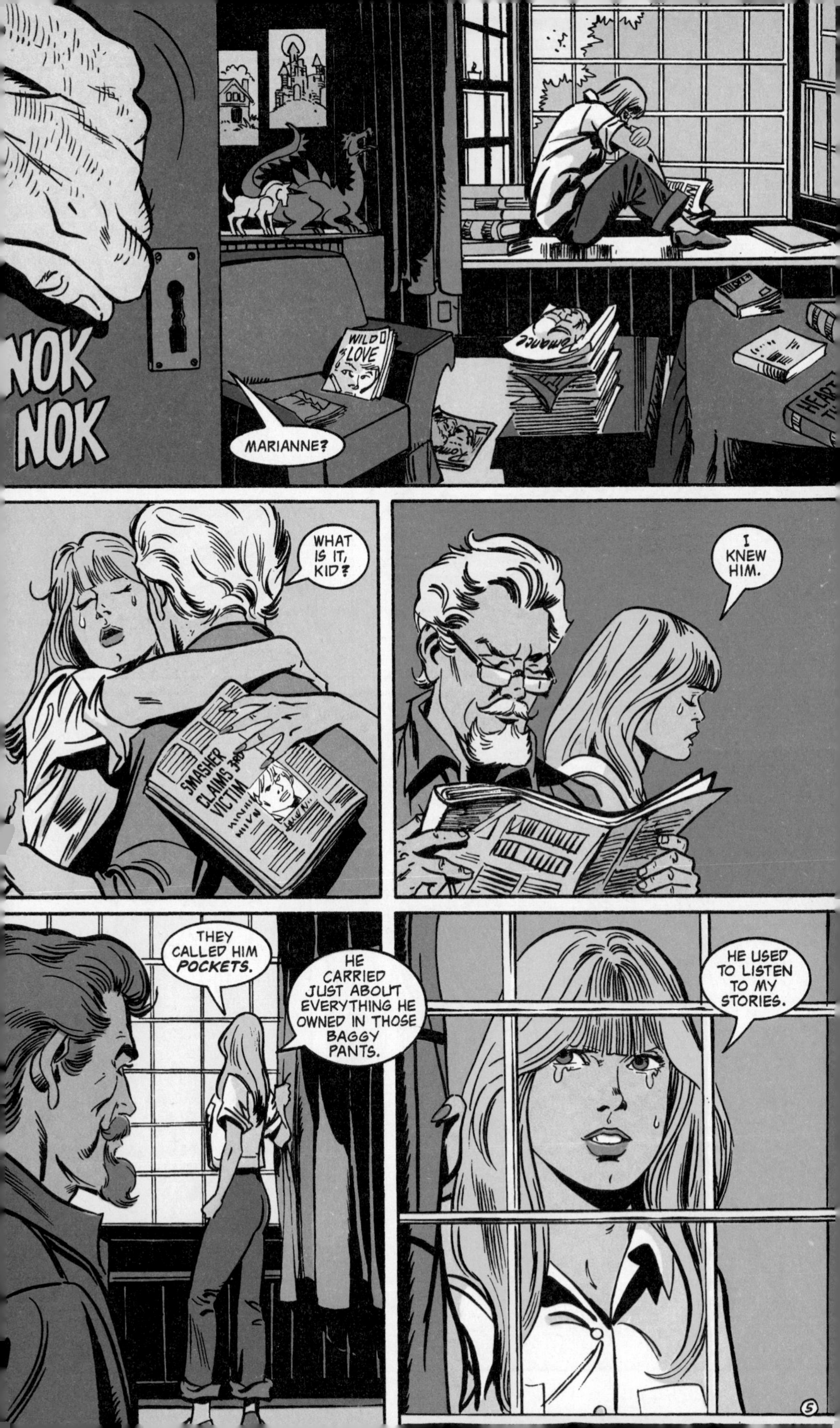
NOK NOK
MARIANNE?
WILD LOVE
Romance
WHAT IS IT, KID?
SMASHER CLAIMS 3RD VICTIM
I KNEW HIM.
THEY CALLED HIM *POCKETS.*
HE CARRIED JUST ABOUT EVERYTHING HE OWNED IN THOSE BAGGY PANTS.
HE USED TO LISTEN TO MY STORIES.

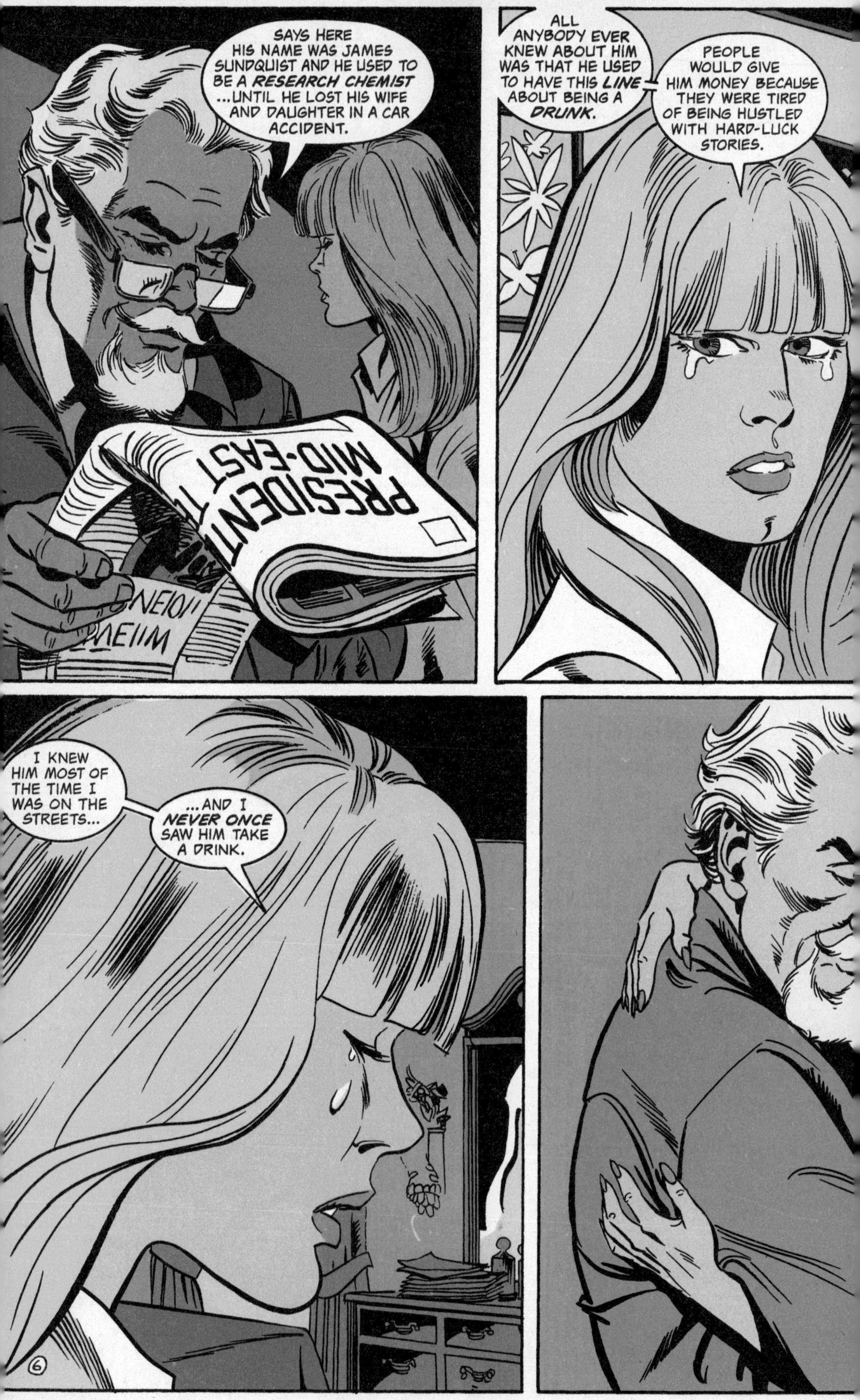
SAYS HERE HIS NAME WAS JAMES SUNDQUIST AND HE USED TO BE A *RESEARCH CHEMIST* ...UNTIL HE LOST HIS WIFE AND DAUGHTER IN A CAR ACCIDENT.
PRESIDENT
MID-EAST
ALL ANYBODY EVER KNEW ABOUT HIM WAS THAT HE USED TO HAVE THIS *LINE* ABOUT BEING A *DRUNK.*
PEOPLE WOULD GIVE HIM MONEY BECAUSE THEY WERE TIRED OF BEING HUSTLED WITH HARD-LUCK STORIES.
I KNEW HIM MOST OF THE TIME I WAS ON THE STREETS...
...AND I *NEVER ONCE* SAW HIM TAKE A DRINK.

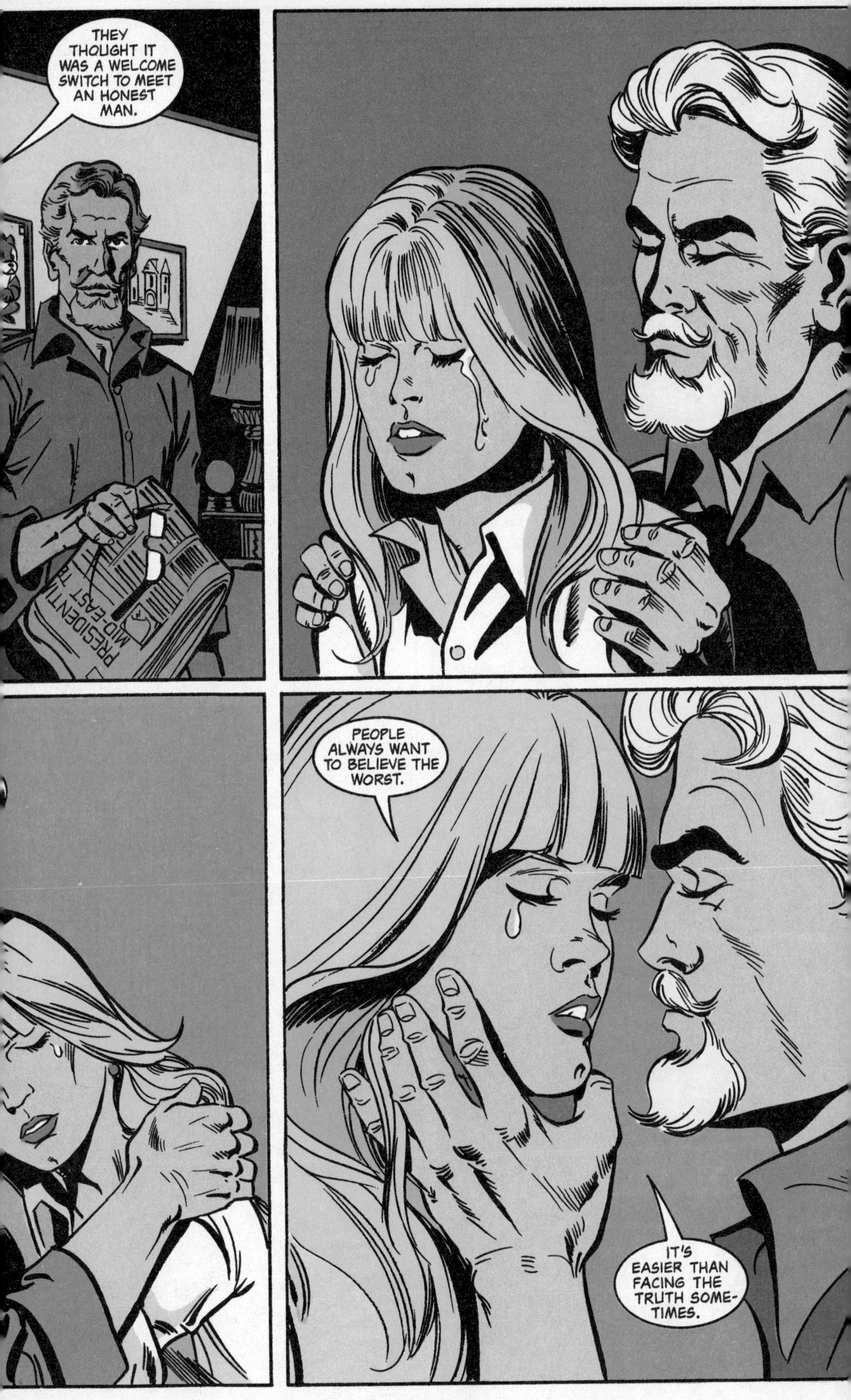

THEY THOUGHT IT WAS A WELCOME SWITCH TO MEET AN HONEST MAN.
PRESIDENT
MID-EAST
PEOPLE ALWAYS WANT TO BELIEVE THE WORST.
IT'S EASIER THAN FACING THE TRUTH SOME-TIMES.

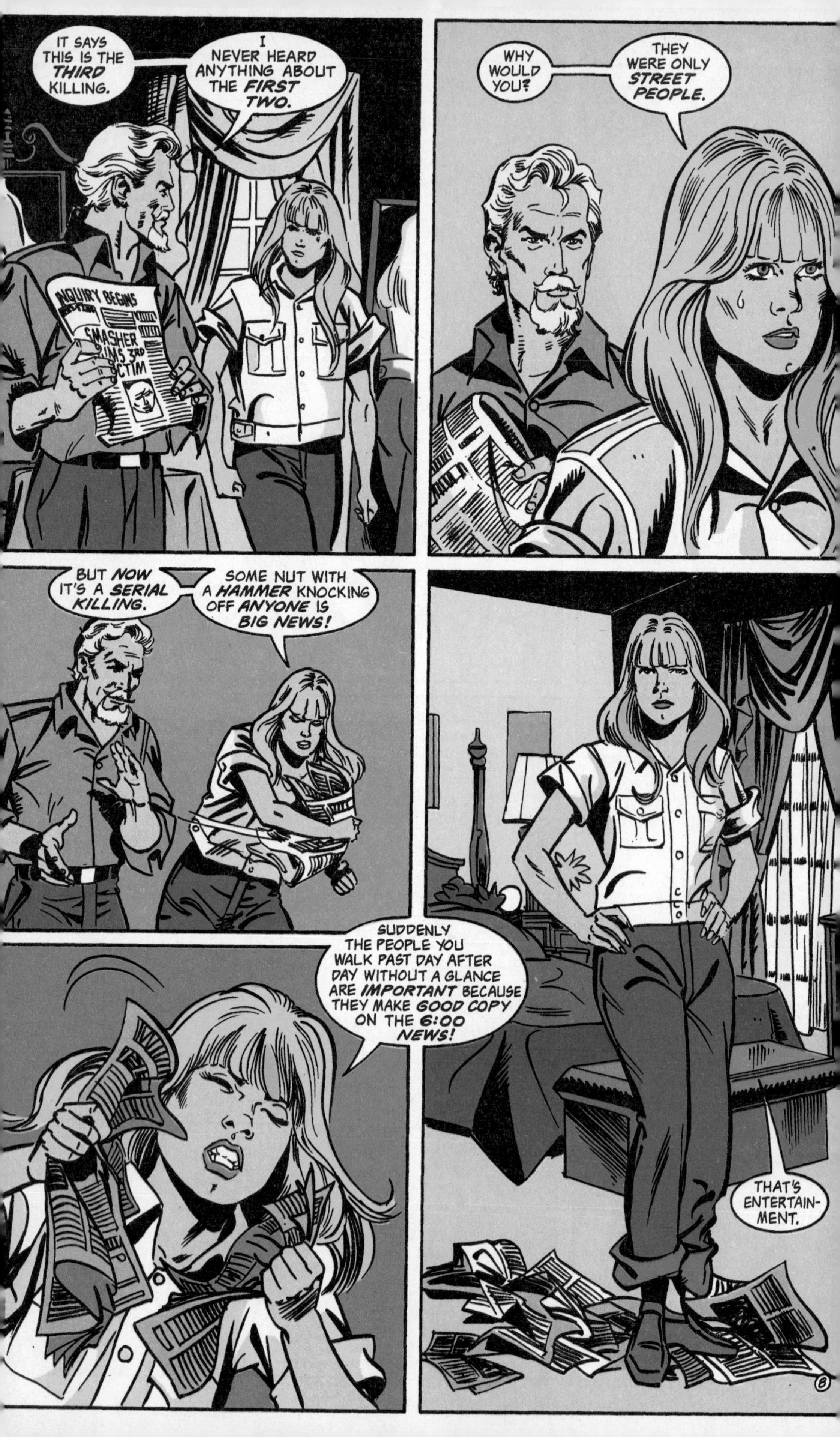
IT SAYS THIS IS THE THIRD KILLING.
I NEVER HEARD ANYTHING ABOUT THE FIRST TWO.
INQUIRY BEGINS
SMASHER CLAIMS 3RD VICTIM
WHY WOULD YOU?
THEY WERE ONLY STREET PEOPLE.
BUT NOW IT'S A SERIAL KILLING.
SOME NUT WITH A HAMMER KNOCKING OFF ANYONE IS BIG NEWS!
SUDDENLY THE PEOPLE YOU WALK PAST DAY AFTER DAY WITHOUT A GLANCE ARE IMPORTANT BECAUSE THEY MAKE GOOD COPY ON THE 6:00 NEWS!
THAT'S ENTERTAIN-MENT.
8

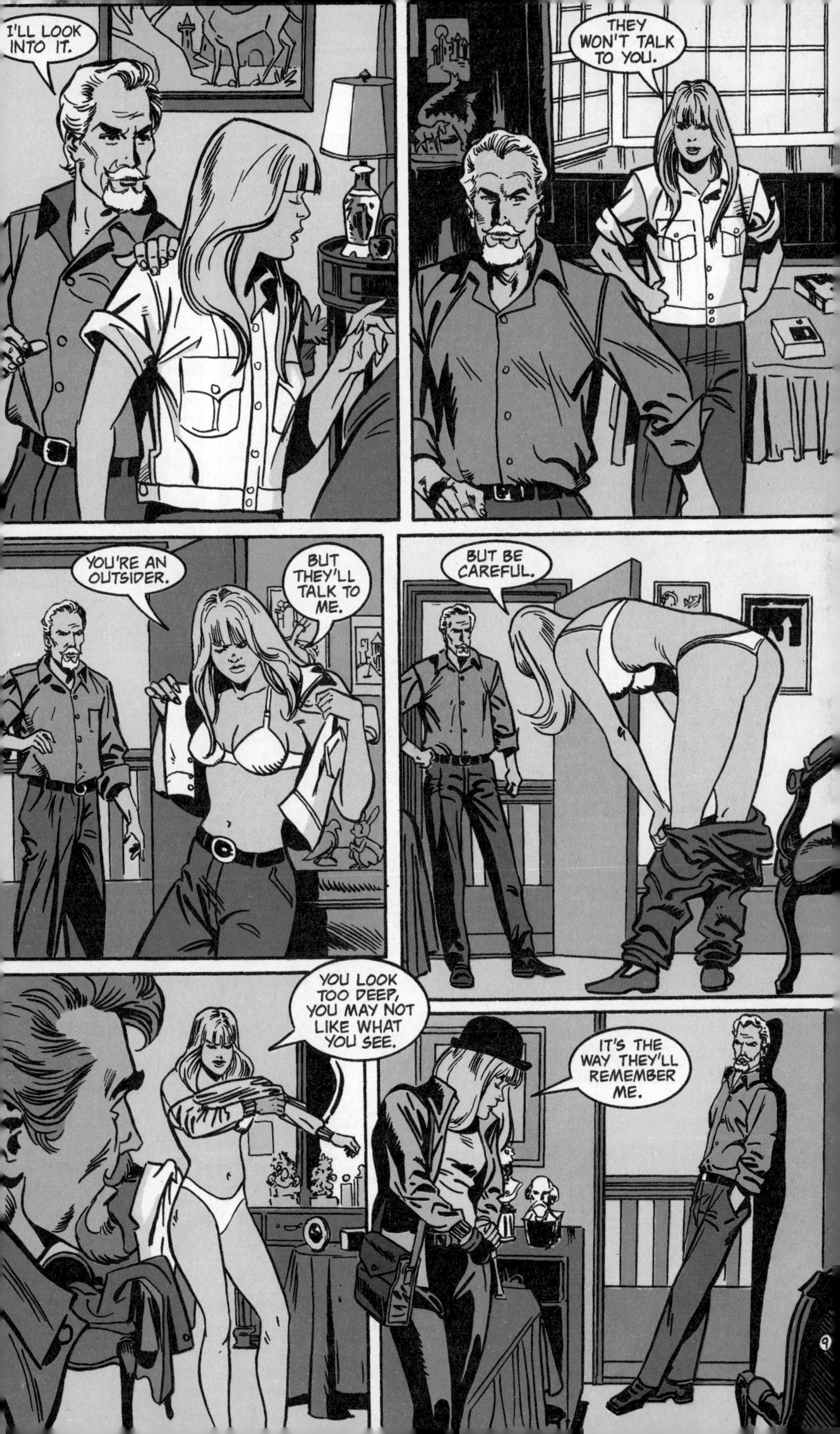
I'LL LOOK INTO IT.
THEY WON'T TALK TO YOU.
YOU'RE AN OUTSIDER.
BUT THEY'LL TALK TO ME.
BUT BE CAREFUL.
YOU LOOK TOO DEEP, YOU MAY NOT LIKE WHAT YOU SEE.
IT'S THE WAY THEY'LL REMEMBER ME.
9

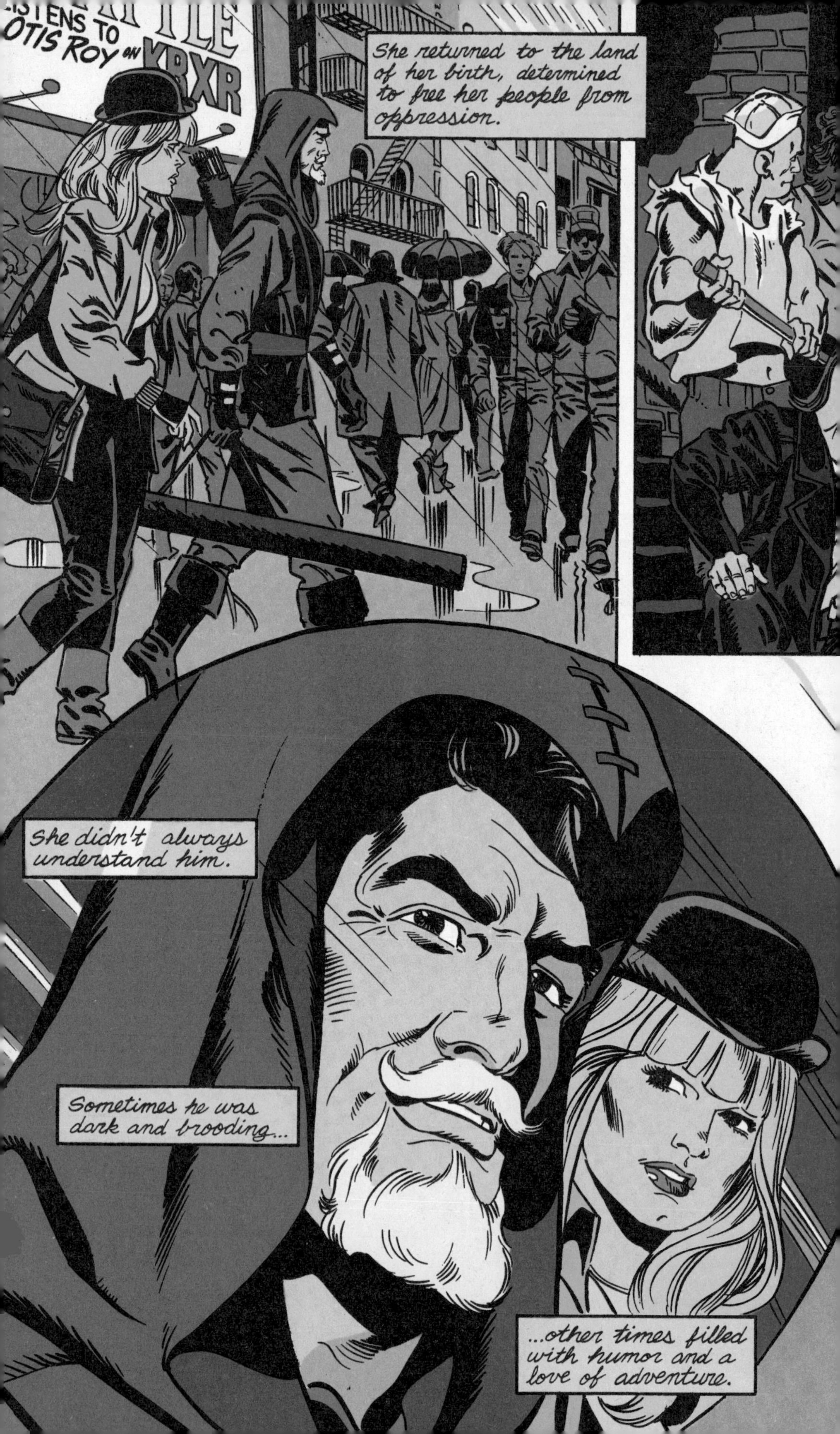
LISTENS TO
OTIS ROY ON KRXR
She returned to the land of her birth, determined to free her people from oppression.
She didn't always understand him.
Sometimes he was dark and brooding...
...other times filled with humor and a love of adventure.

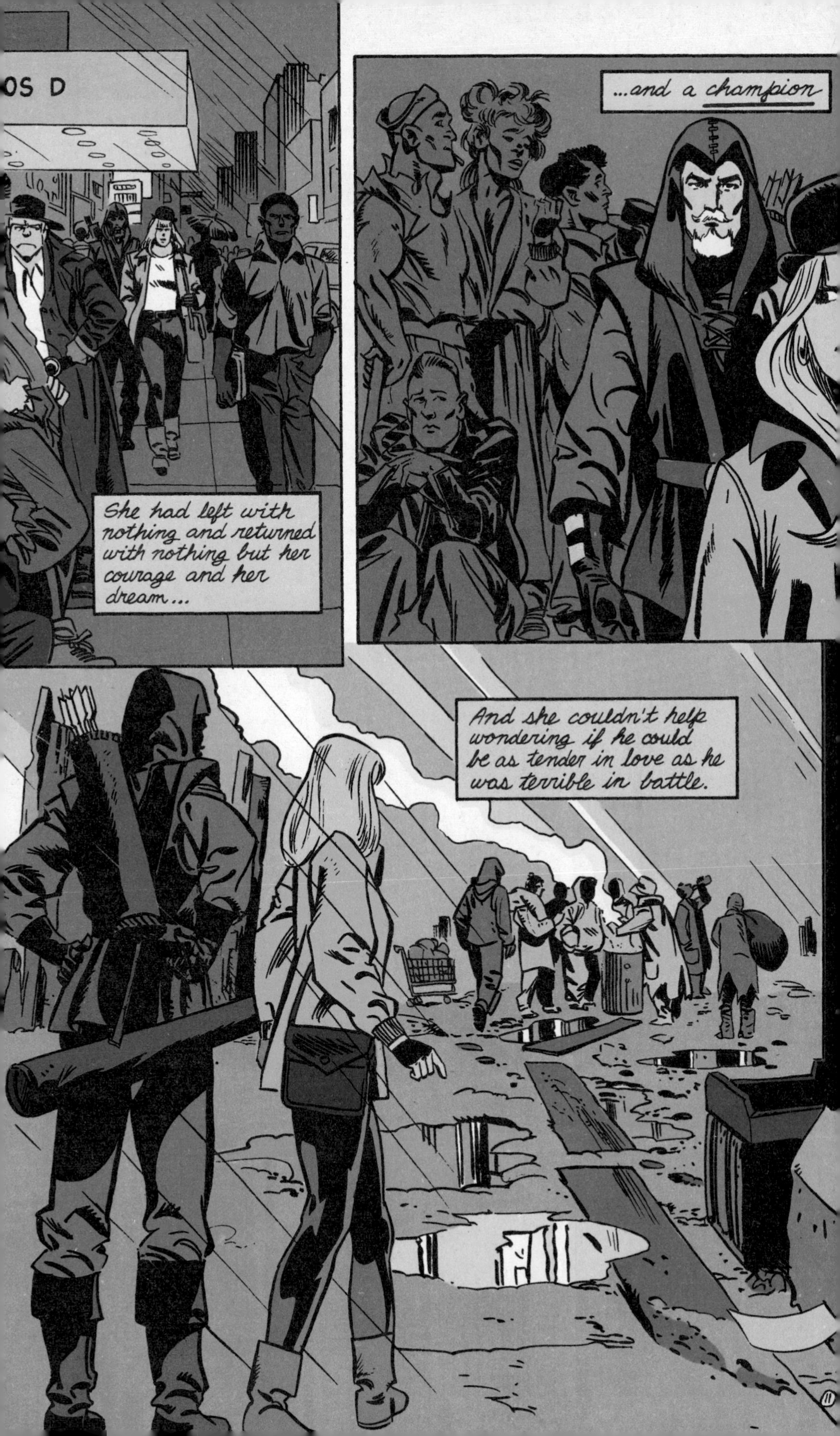
OS D
She had left with nothing and returned with nothing but her courage and her dream...
...and a champion
And she couldn't help wondering if he could be as tender in love as he was terrible in battle.

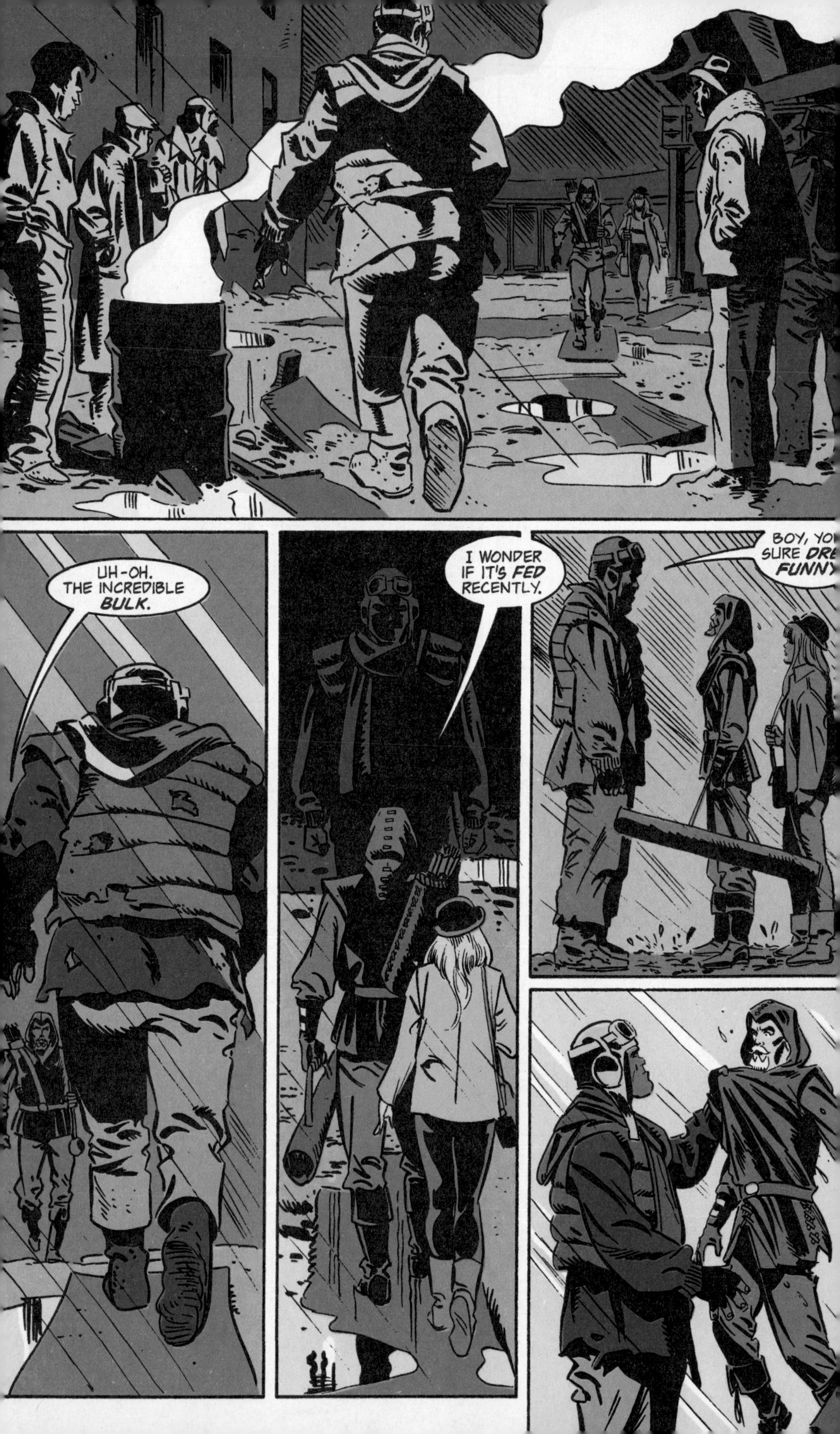

UH-OH. THE INCREDIBLE *BULK.*
I WONDER IF IT'S *FED* RECENTLY.
BOY, YO SURE *DRE FUNNY*

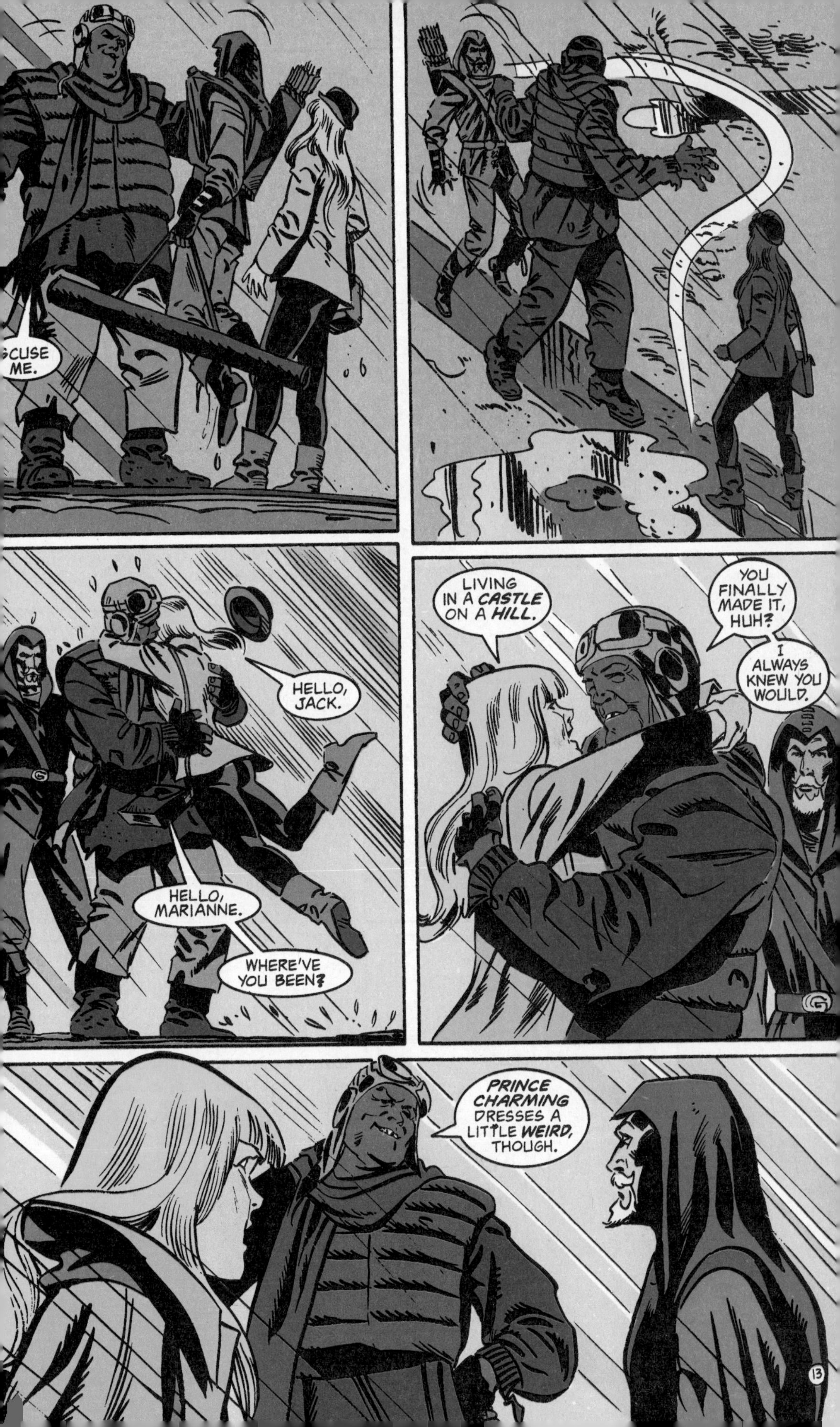

'SCUSE ME.
HELLO, JACK.
HELLO, MARIANNE.
WHERE'VE YOU BEEN?
LIVING IN A *CASTLE* ON A *HILL*.
YOU FINALLY MADE IT, HUH?
I ALWAYS KNEW YOU WOULD.
PRINCE CHARMING DRESSES A LITTLE *WEIRD*, THOUGH.

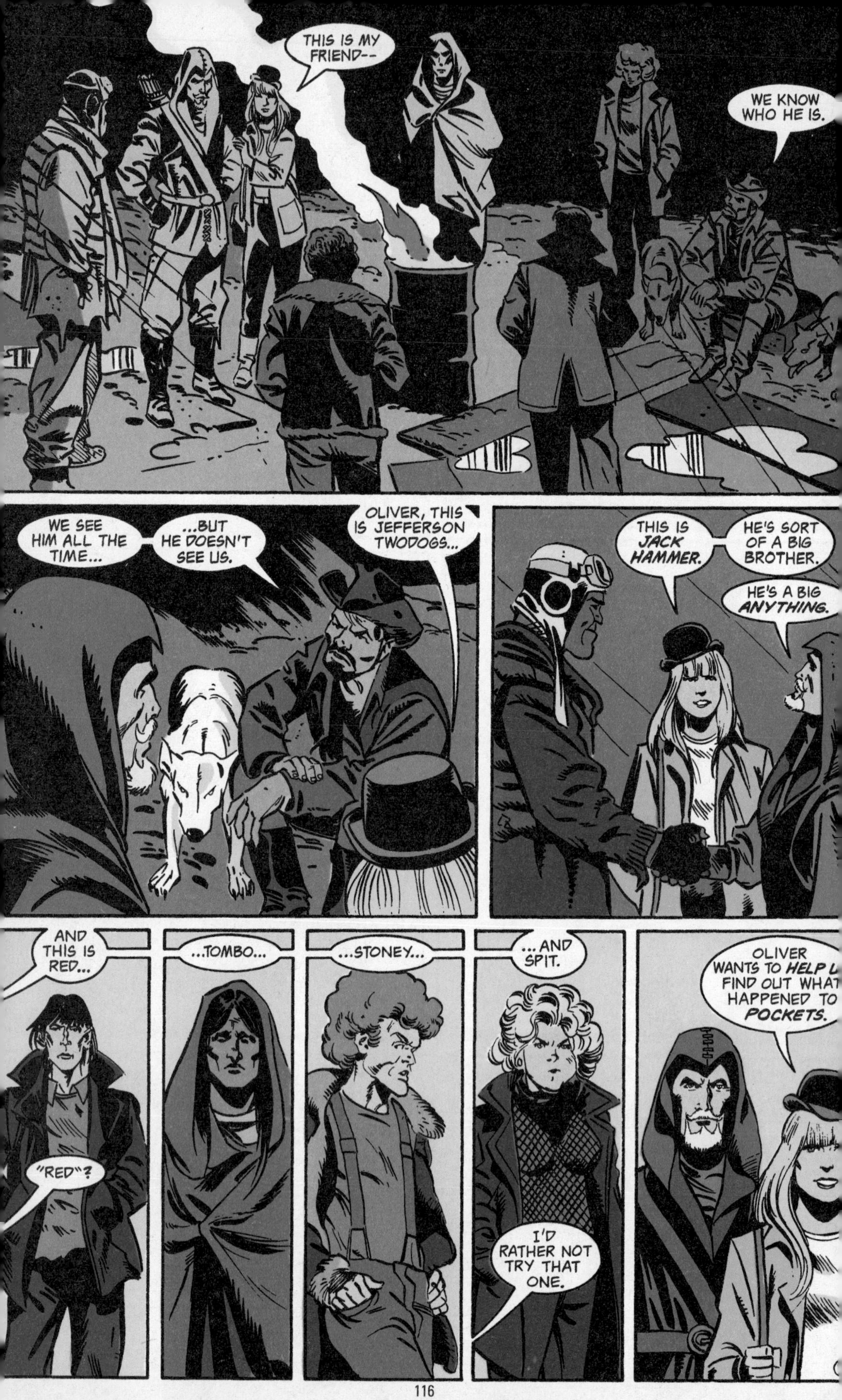
THIS IS MY FRIEND--
WE KNOW WHO HE IS.
WE SEE HIM ALL THE TIME...
...BUT HE DOESN'T SEE US.
OLIVER, THIS IS JEFFERSON TWODOGS...
THIS IS JACK HAMMER.
HE'S SORT OF A BIG BROTHER.
HE'S A BIG ANYTHING.
AND THIS IS RED...
"RED"?
...TOMBO...
...STONEY...
...AND SPIT.
I'D RATHER NOT TRY THAT ONE.
OLIVER WANTS TO HELP U
FIND OUT WHAT HAPPENED TO POCKETS.

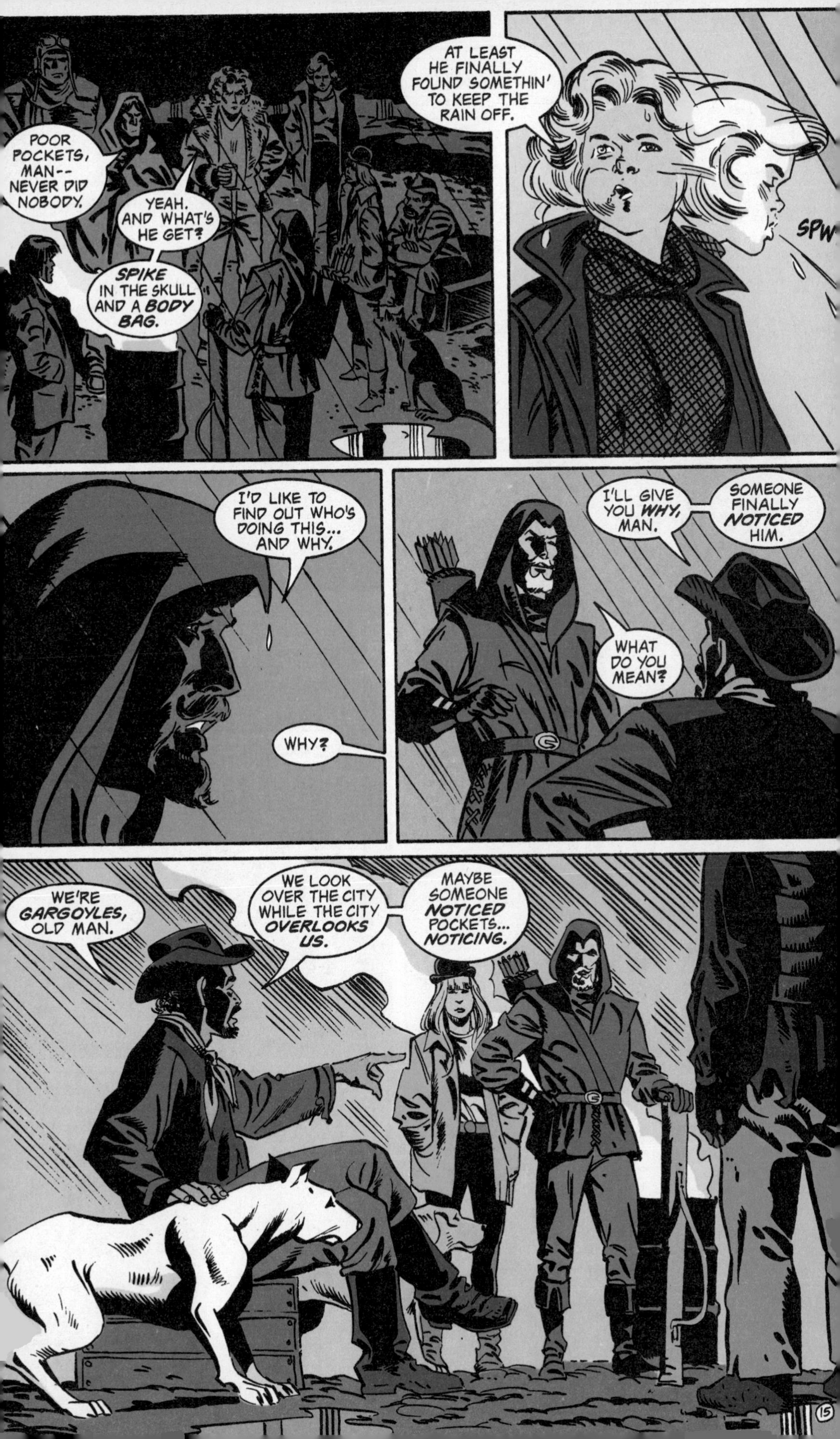
POOR POCKETS, MAN-- NEVER DID NOBODY.
YEAH. AND WHAT'S HE GET?
SPIKE IN THE SKULL AND A BODY BAG.
AT LEAST HE FINALLY FOUND SOMETHIN' TO KEEP THE RAIN OFF.
SPW
I'D LIKE TO FIND OUT WHO'S DOING THIS... AND WHY.
WHY?
I'LL GIVE YOU WHY, MAN.
SOMEONE FINALLY NOTICED HIM.
WHAT DO YOU MEAN?
WE'RE GARGOYLES, OLD MAN.
WE LOOK OVER THE CITY WHILE THE CITY OVERLOOKS US.
MAYBE SOMEONE NOTICED POCKETS... NOTICING.
15

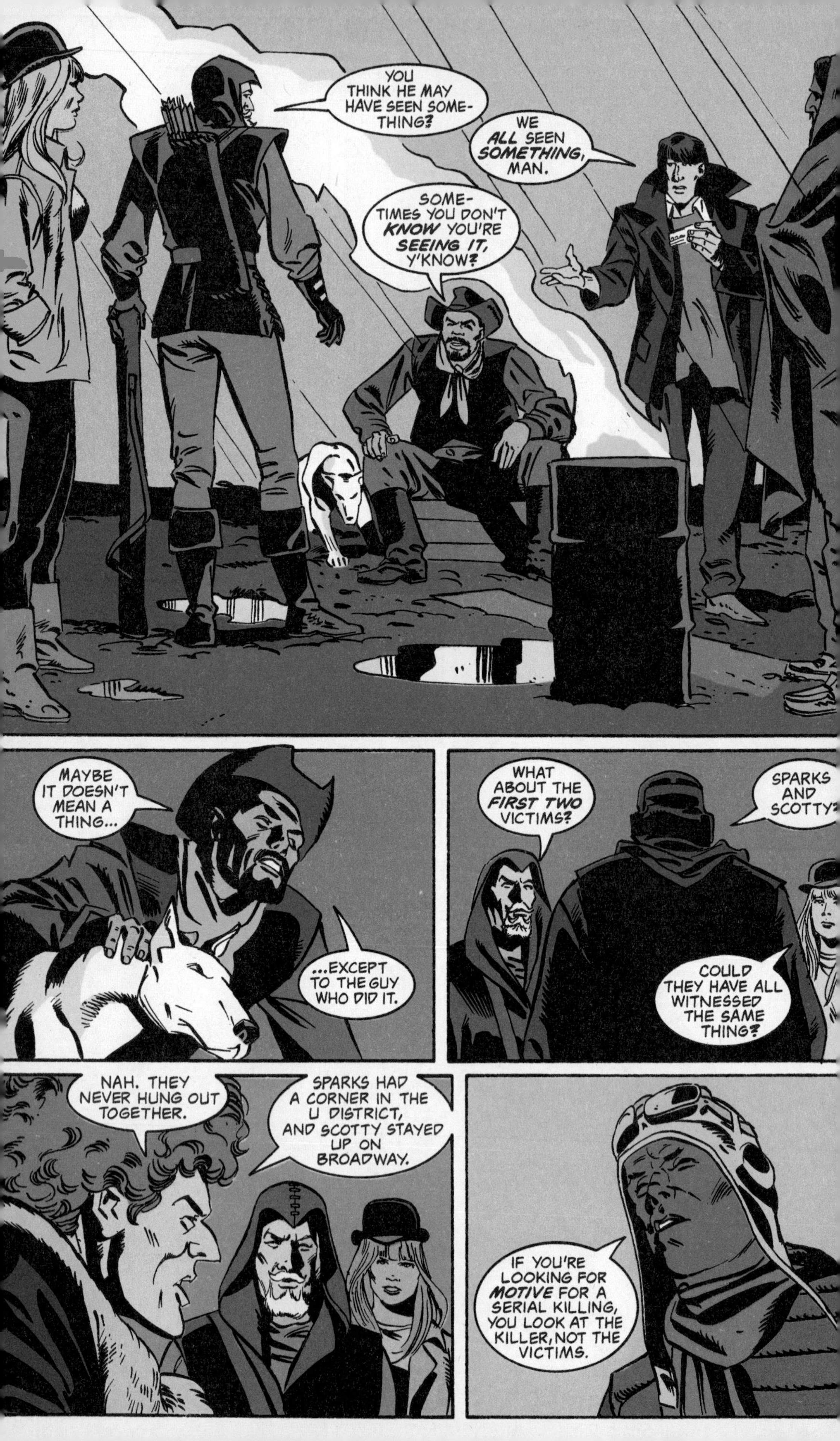
YOU THINK HE MAY HAVE SEEN SOME-THING?
WE ALL SEEN SOMETHING, MAN.
SOME-TIMES YOU DON'T KNOW YOU'RE SEEING IT, Y'KNOW?
MAYBE IT DOESN'T MEAN A THING...
...EXCEPT TO THE GUY WHO DID IT.
WHAT ABOUT THE FIRST TWO VICTIMS?
SPARKS AND SCOTTY?
COULD THEY HAVE ALL WITNESSED THE SAME THING?
NAH. THEY NEVER HUNG OUT TOGETHER.
SPARKS HAD A CORNER IN THE U DISTRICT, AND SCOTTY STAYED UP ON BROADWAY.
IF YOU'RE LOOKING FOR MOTIVE FOR A SERIAL KILLING, YOU LOOK AT THE KILLER, NOT THE VICTIMS.

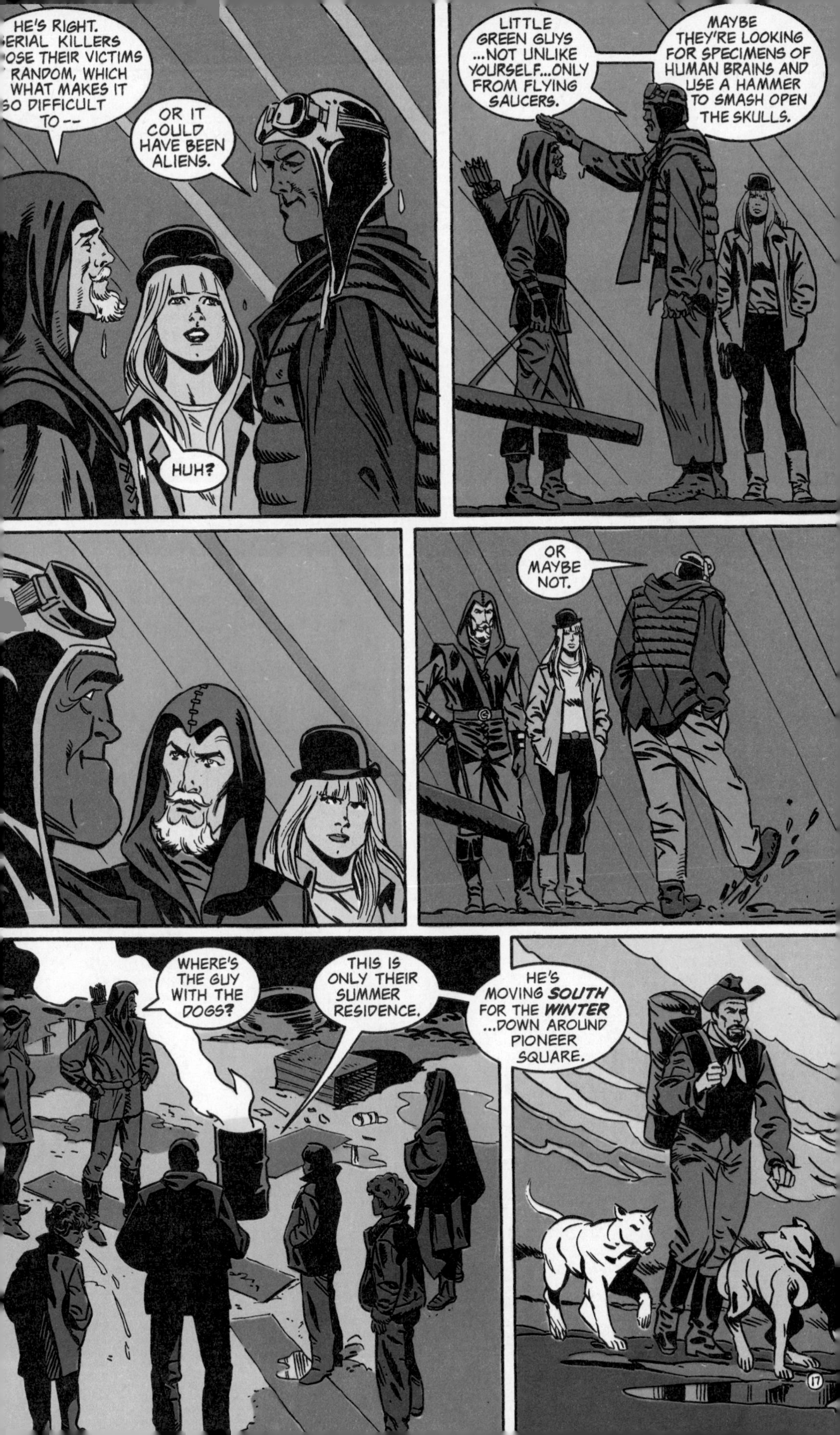
HE'S RIGHT. ERIAL KILLERS OSE THEIR VICTIMS RANDOM, WHICH WHAT MAKES IT SO DIFFICULT TO --
OR IT COULD HAVE BEEN ALIENS.
HUH?
LITTLE GREEN GUYS ...NOT UNLIKE YOURSELF...ONLY FROM FLYING SAUCERS.
MAYBE THEY'RE LOOKING FOR SPECIMENS OF HUMAN BRAINS AND USE A HAMMER TO SMASH OPEN THE SKULLS.
OR MAYBE NOT.
WHERE'S THE GUY WITH THE DOGS?
THIS IS ONLY THEIR SUMMER RESIDENCE.
HE'S MOVING SOUTH FOR THE WINTER ...DOWN AROUND PIONEER SQUARE.
17

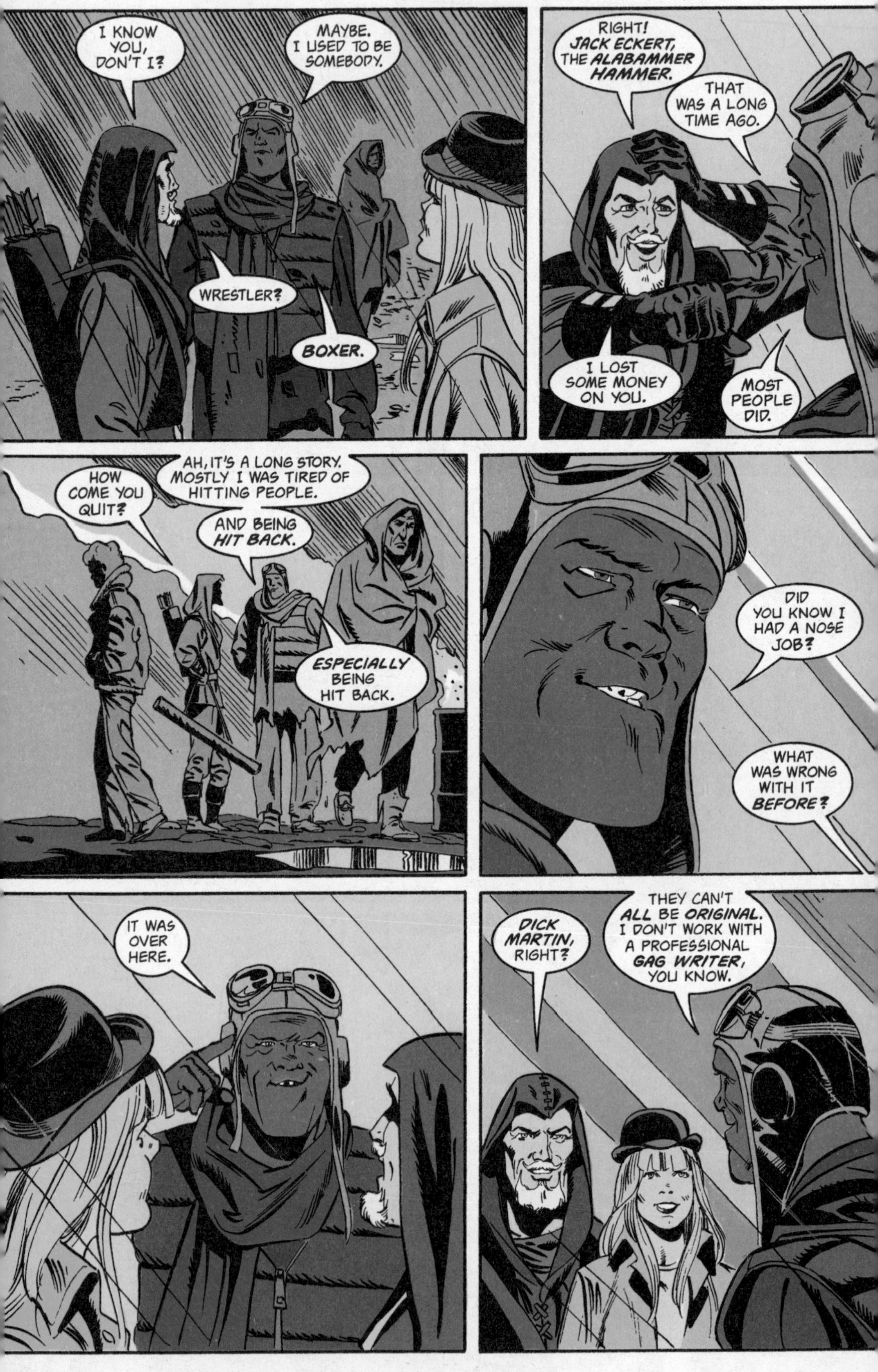

I KNOW YOU, DON'T I?
MAYBE. I USED TO BE SOMEBODY.
WRESTLER?
BOXER.
RIGHT! JACK ECKERT, THE ALABAMMER HAMMER.
THAT WAS A LONG TIME AGO.
I LOST SOME MONEY ON YOU.
MOST PEOPLE DID.
HOW COME YOU QUIT?
AH, IT'S A LONG STORY. MOSTLY I WAS TIRED OF HITTING PEOPLE.
AND BEING HIT BACK.
ESPECIALLY BEING HIT BACK.
DID YOU KNOW I HAD A NOSE JOB?
WHAT WAS WRONG WITH IT BEFORE?
IT WAS OVER HERE.
DICK MARTIN, RIGHT?
THEY CAN'T ALL BE ORIGINAL. I DON'T WORK WITH A PROFESSIONAL GAG WRITER, YOU KNOW.

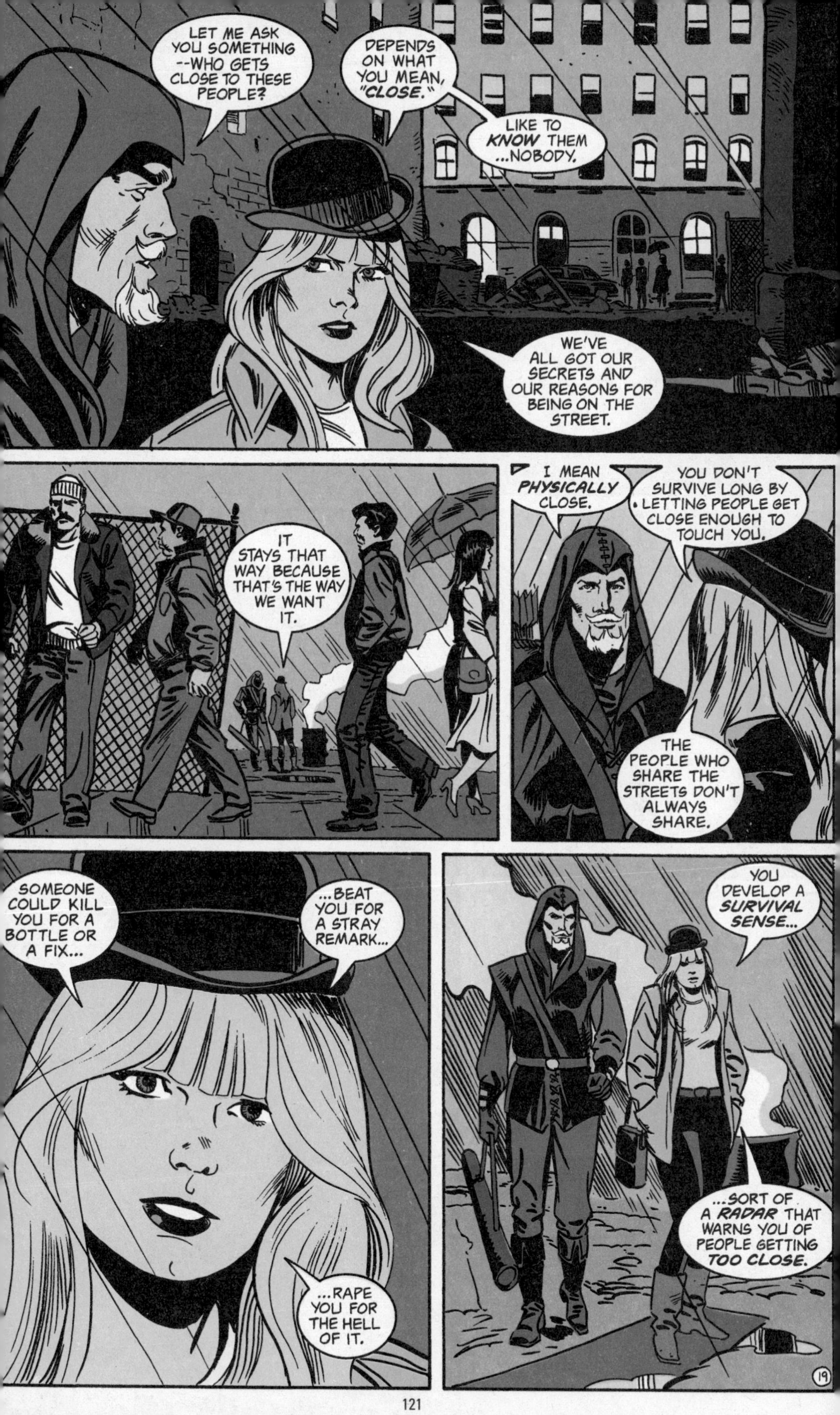
LET ME ASK YOU SOMETHING --WHO GETS CLOSE TO THESE PEOPLE?
DEPENDS ON WHAT YOU MEAN, "CLOSE."
LIKE TO KNOW THEM ...NOBODY.
WE'VE ALL GOT OUR SECRETS AND OUR REASONS FOR BEING ON THE STREET.
IT STAYS THAT WAY BECAUSE THAT'S THE WAY WE WANT IT.
I MEAN PHYSICALLY CLOSE.
YOU DON'T SURVIVE LONG BY LETTING PEOPLE GET CLOSE ENOUGH TO TOUCH YOU.
THE PEOPLE WHO SHARE THE STREETS DON'T ALWAYS SHARE.
SOMEONE COULD KILL YOU FOR A BOTTLE OR A FIX...
...BEAT YOU FOR A STRAY REMARK...
...RAPE YOU FOR THE HELL OF IT.
YOU DEVELOP A SURVIVAL SENSE...
...SORT OF A RADAR THAT WARNS YOU OF PEOPLE GETTING TOO CLOSE.
19

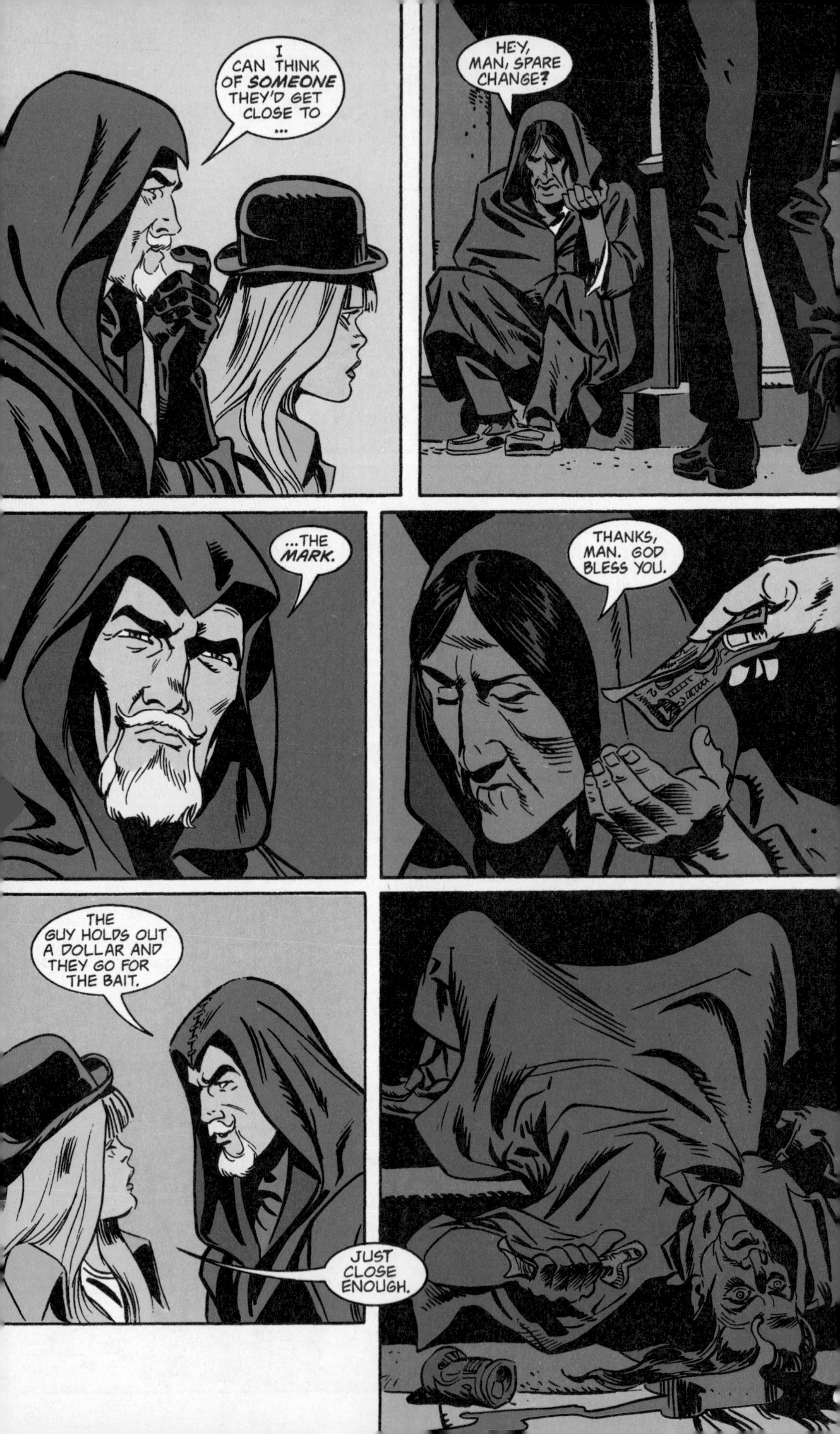
I CAN THINK OF SOMEONE THEY'D GET CLOSE TO ...
HEY, MAN, SPARE CHANGE?
...THE MARK.
THANKS, MAN. GOD BLESS YOU.
THE GUY HOLDS OUT A DOLLAR AND THEY GO FOR THE BAIT.
JUST CLOSE ENOUGH.

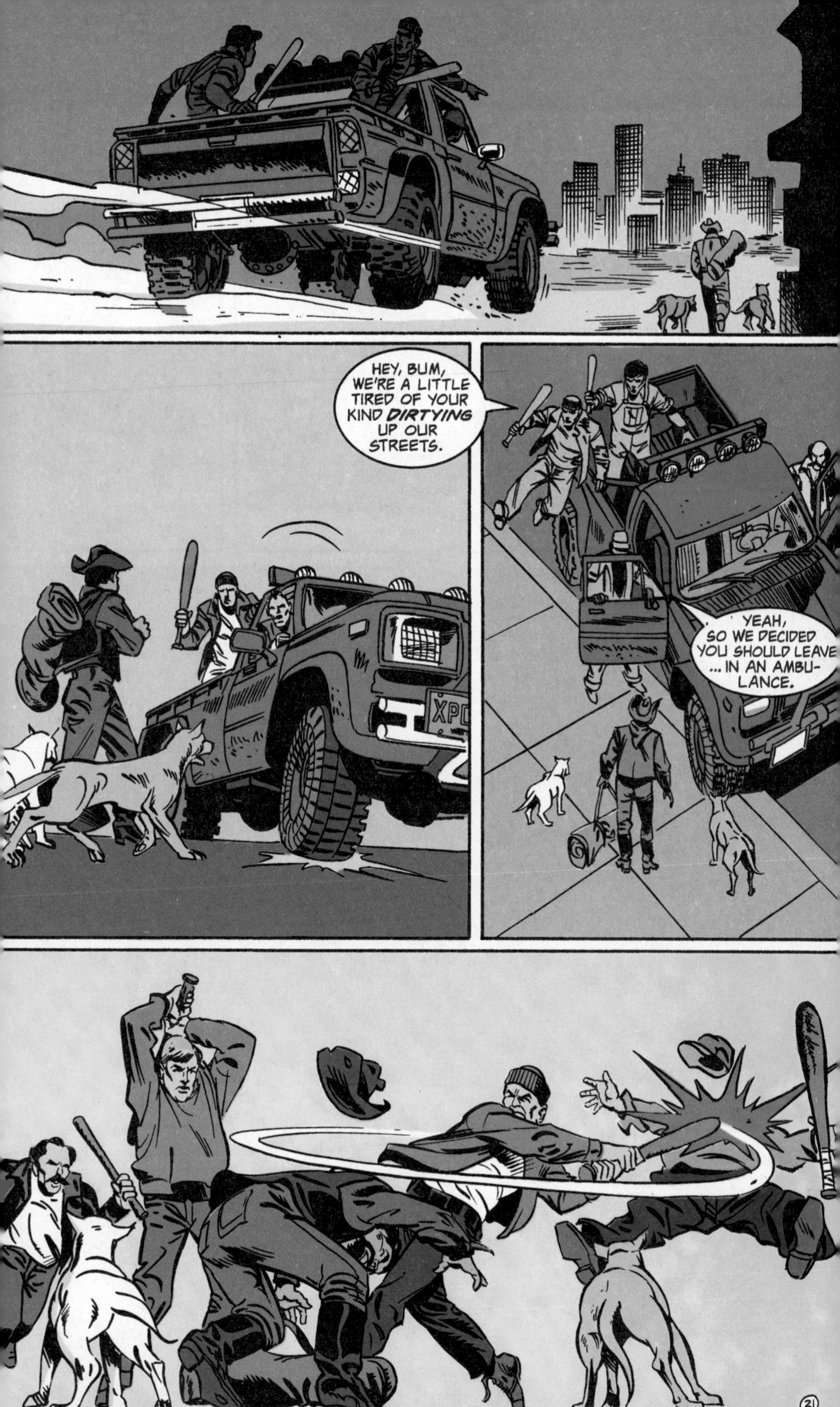
HEY, BUM, WE'RE A LITTLE TIRED OF YOUR KIND DIRTYING UP OUR STREETS.
YEAH, SO WE DECIDED YOU SHOULD LEAVE ...IN AN AMBU-LANCE.

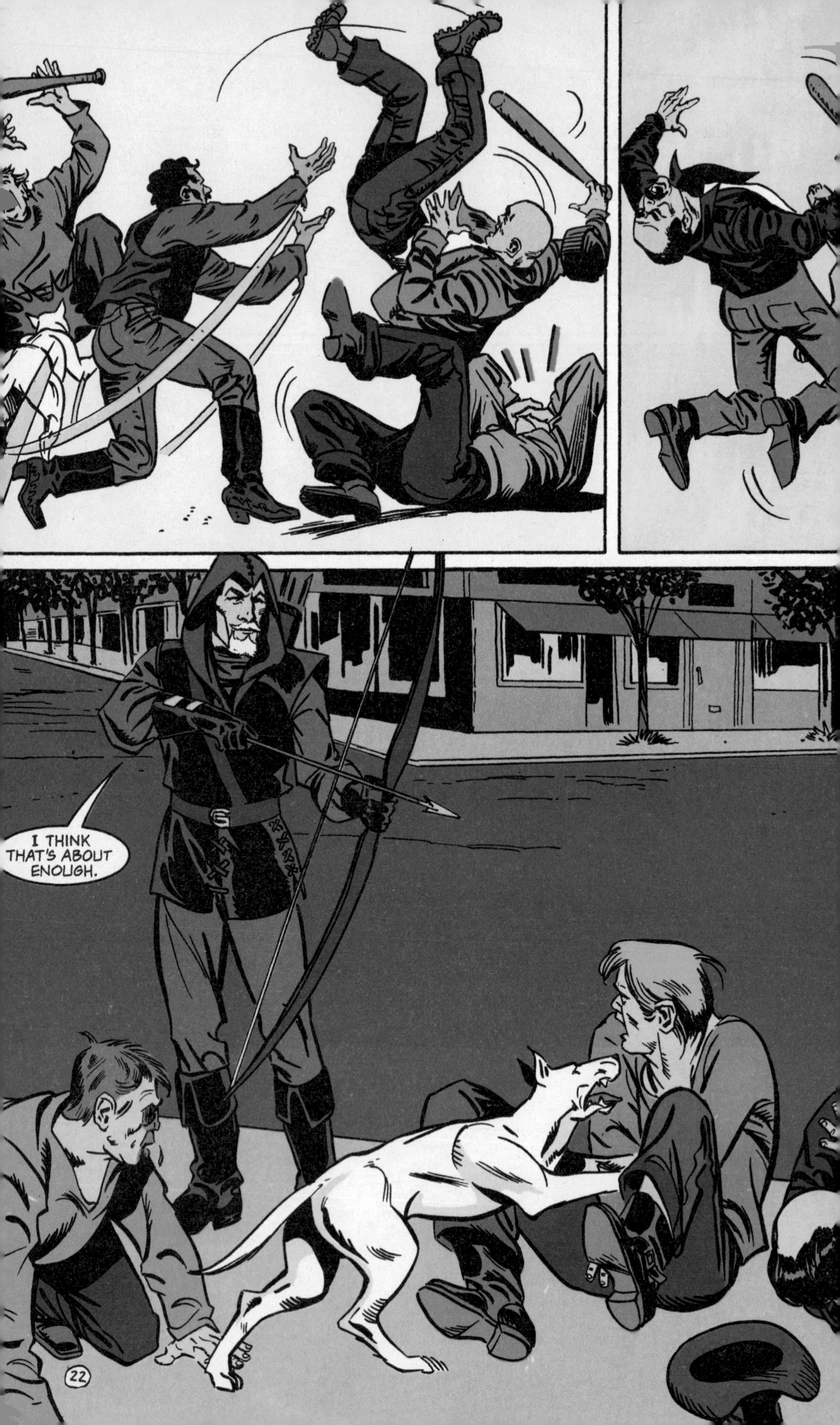
I THINK THAT'S ABOUT ENOUGH.

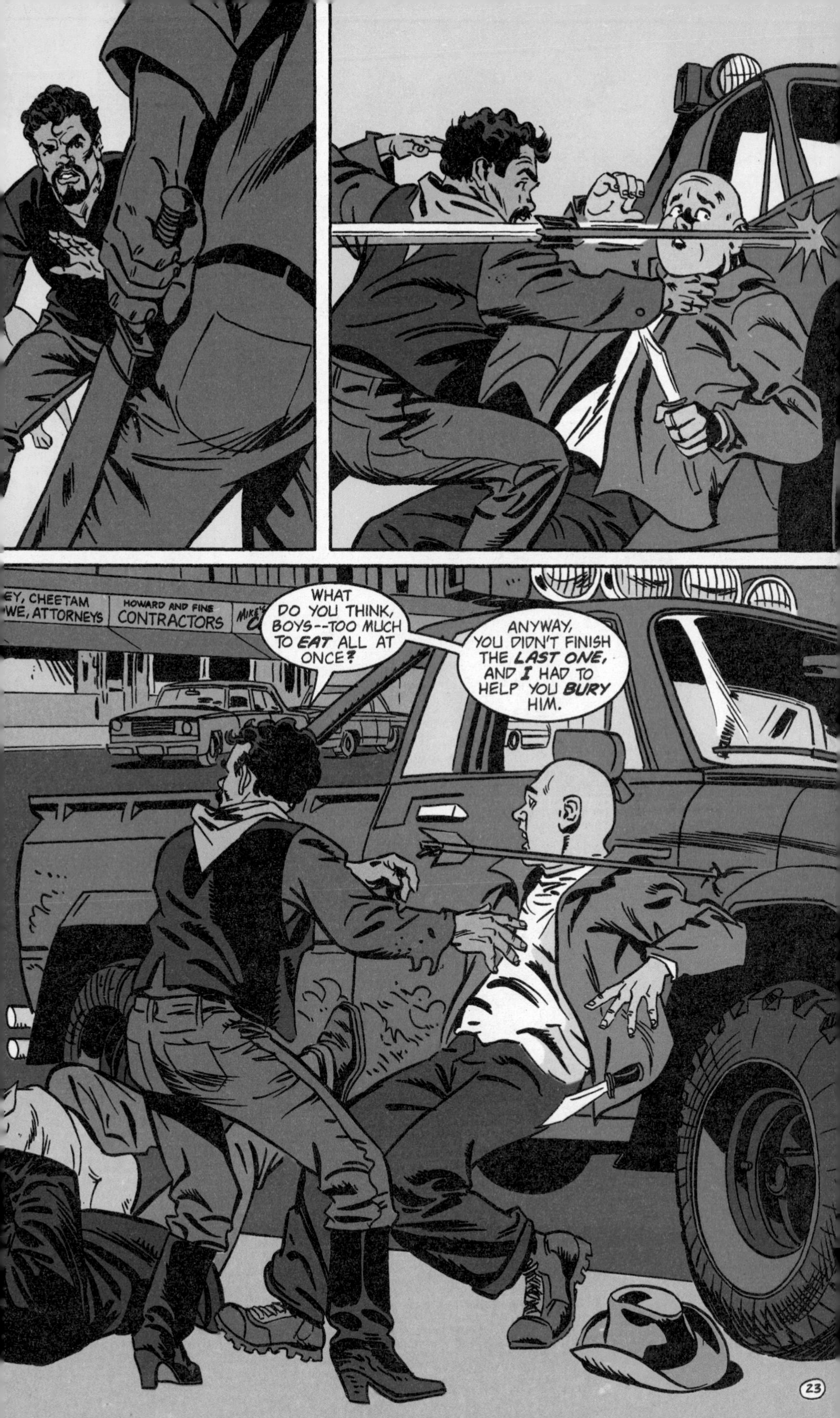

EY, CHEETAM
WE, ATTORNEYS
HOWARD AND FINE
CONTRACTORS
WHAT DO YOU THINK, BOYS--TOO MUCH TO EAT ALL AT ONCE?
ANYWAY, YOU DIDN'T FINISH THE LAST ONE, AND I HAD TO HELP YOU BURY HIM.

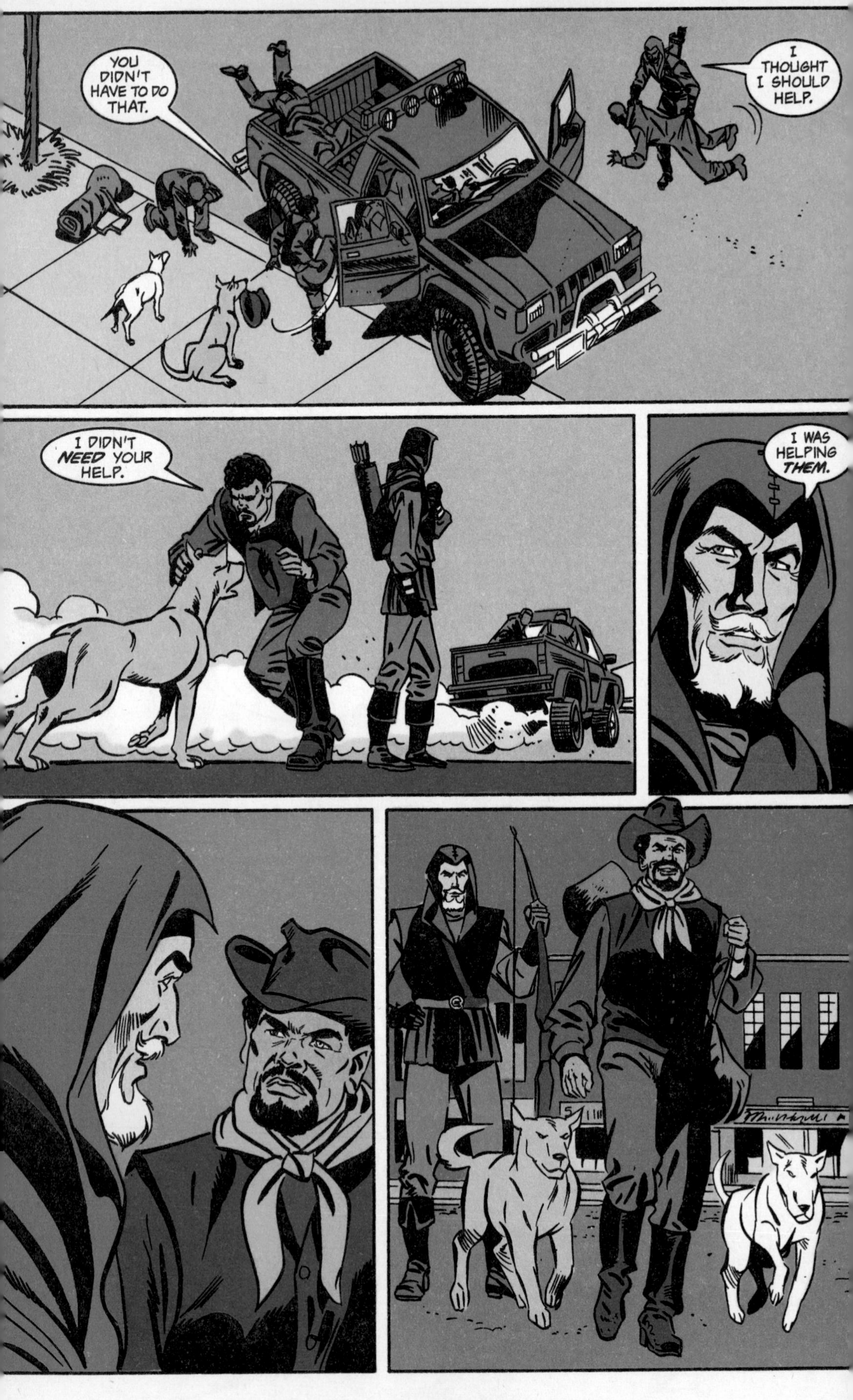
YOU DIDN'T HAVE TO DO THAT.
I THOUGHT I SHOULD HELP.
I DIDN'T NEED YOUR HELP.
I WAS HELPING THEM.

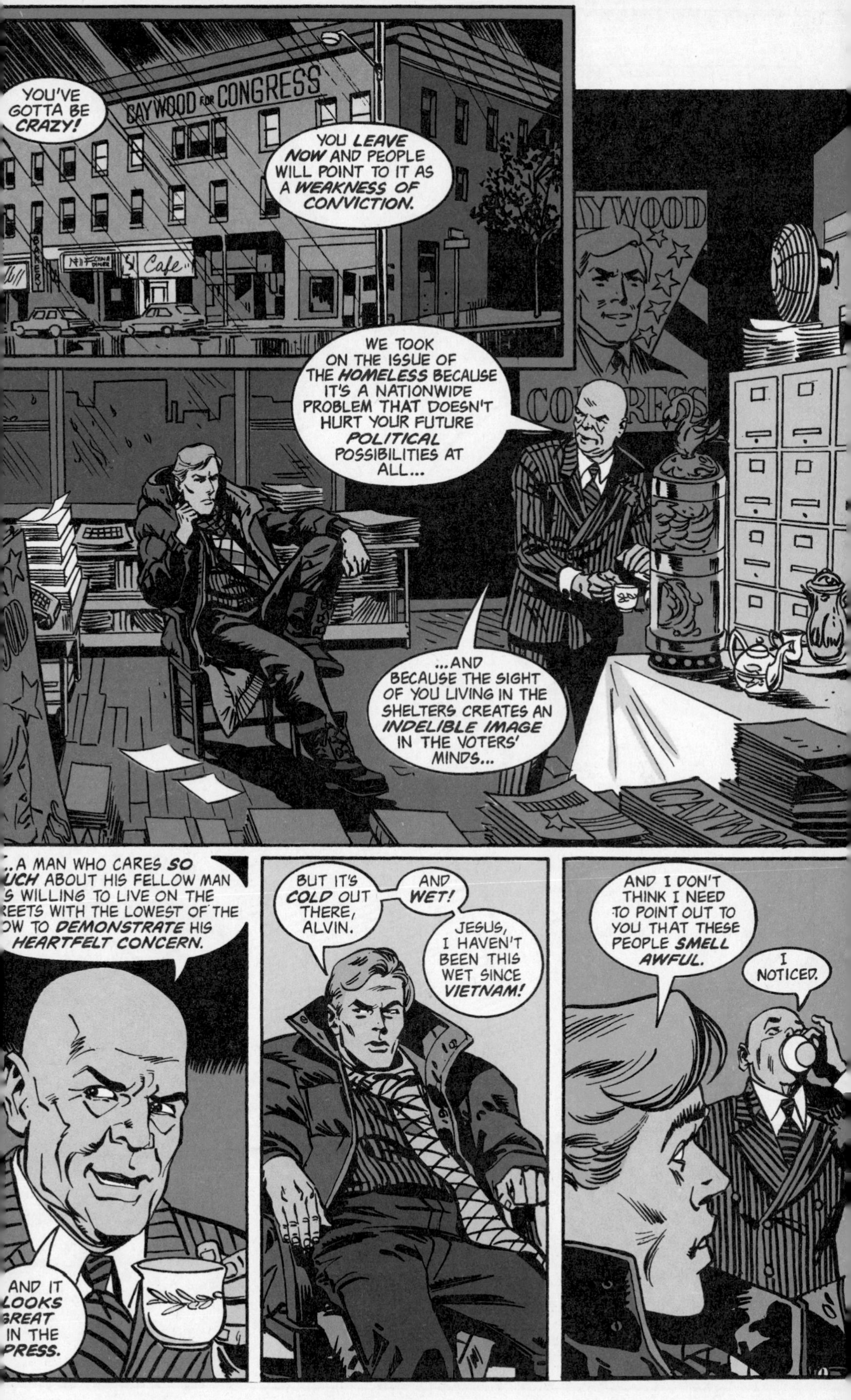
YOU'VE GOTTA BE CRAZY!
CAYWOOD FOR CONGRESS
YOU LEAVE NOW AND PEOPLE WILL POINT TO IT AS A WEAKNESS OF CONVICTION.
WE TOOK ON THE ISSUE OF THE HOMELESS BECAUSE IT'S A NATIONWIDE PROBLEM THAT DOESN'T HURT YOUR FUTURE POLITICAL POSSIBILITIES AT ALL...
...AND BECAUSE THE SIGHT OF YOU LIVING IN THE SHELTERS CREATES AN INDELIBLE IMAGE IN THE VOTERS' MINDS...
..A MAN WHO CARES SO UCH ABOUT HIS FELLOW MAN S WILLING TO LIVE ON THE REETS WITH THE LOWEST OF THE OW TO DEMONSTRATE HIS HEARTFELT CONCERN.
AND IT LOOKS GREAT IN THE PRESS.
BUT IT'S COLD OUT THERE, ALVIN.
AND WET!
JESUS, I HAVEN'T BEEN THIS WET SINCE VIETNAM!
AND I DON'T THINK I NEED TO POINT OUT TO YOU THAT THESE PEOPLE SMELL AWFUL.
I NOTICED.

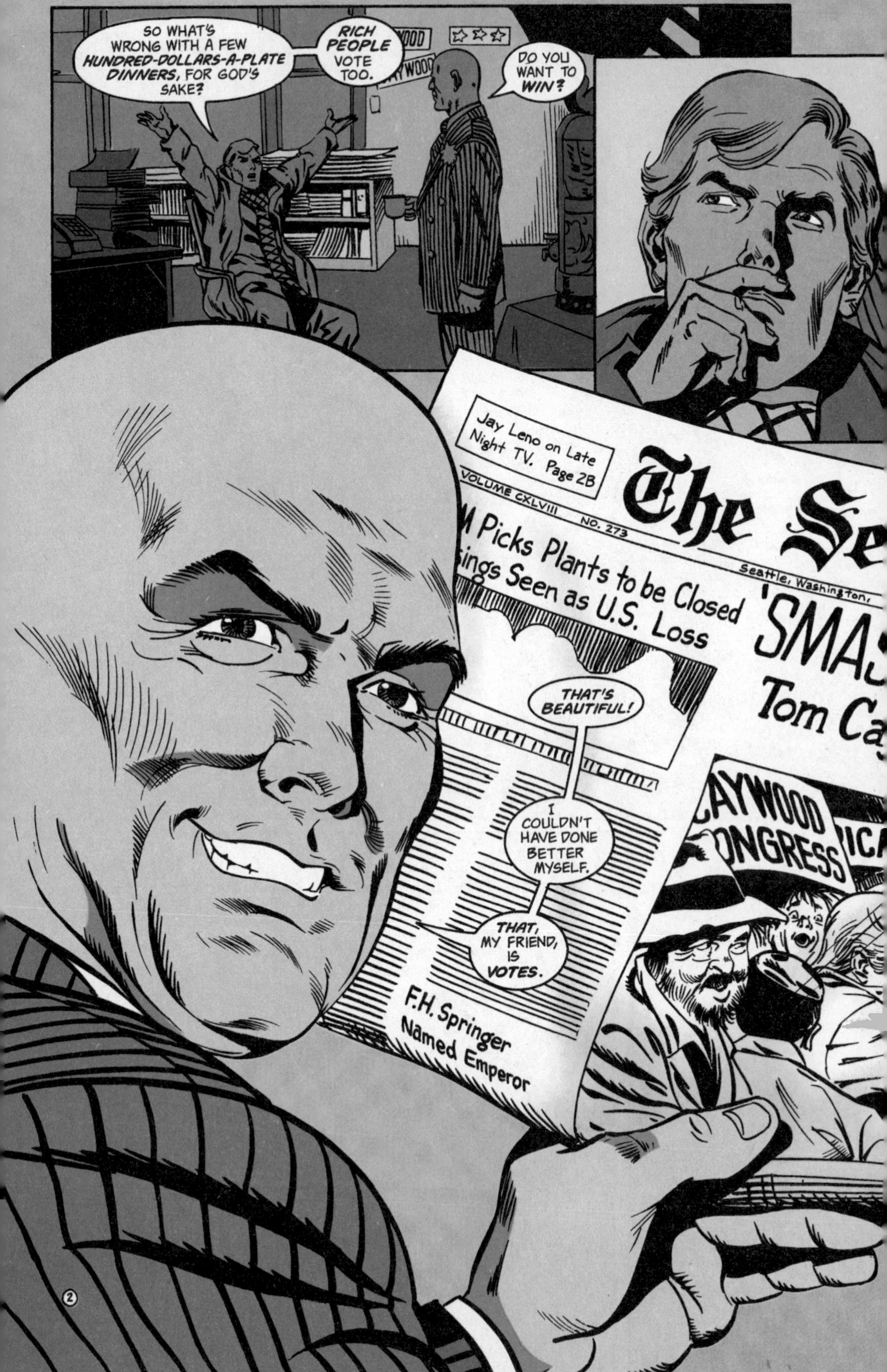

SO WHAT'S WRONG WITH A FEW HUNDRED-DOLLARS-A-PLATE DINNERS, FOR GOD'S SAKE?
RICH PEOPLE VOTE TOO.
DO YOU WANT TO WIN?
Jay Leno on Late Night TV. Page 2B
VOLUME CXLVIII NO. 273
Seattle, Washington,
M Picks Plants to be Closed
ings Seen as U.S. Loss
'SMAS
Tom Ca
AYWOOD
ONGRESS
THAT'S BEAUTIFUL!
I COULDN'T HAVE DONE BETTER MYSELF.
THAT, MY FRIEND, IS VOTES.
F.H. Springer Named Emperor

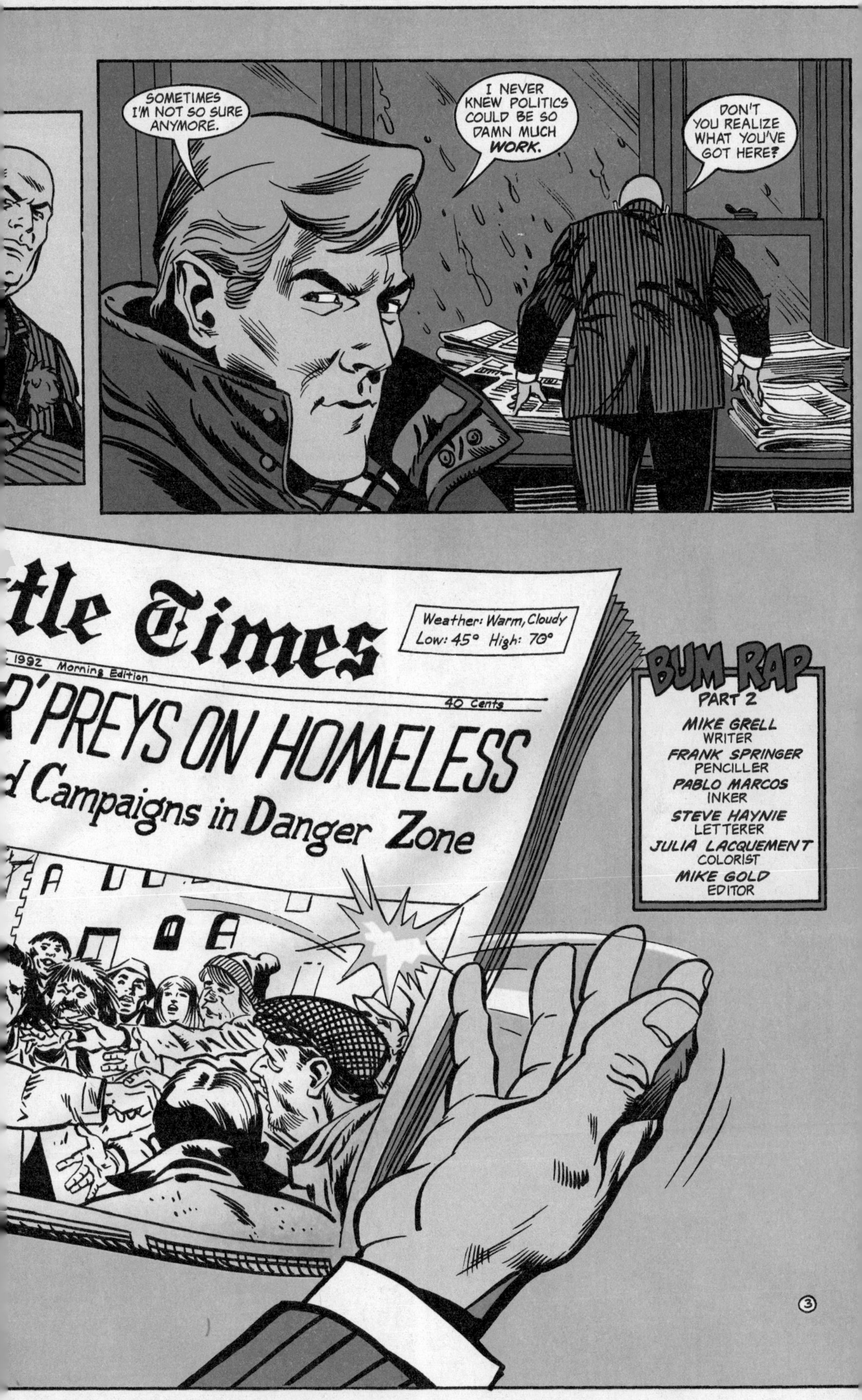
SOMETIMES I'M NOT SO SURE ANYMORE.
I NEVER KNEW POLITICS COULD BE SO DAMN MUCH WORK.
DON'T YOU REALIZE WHAT YOU'VE GOT HERE?
tle Times
Weather: Warm, Cloudy Low: 45° High: 70°
1992 Morning Edition
40 Cents
R' PREYS ON HOMELESS
d Campaigns in Danger Zone
BUM RAP
PART 2
MIKE GRELL WRITER
FRANK SPRINGER PENCILLER
PABLO MARCOS INKER
STEVE HAYNIE LETTERER
JULIA LACQUEMENT COLORIST
MIKE GOLD EDITOR
3

DO YOU HAVE ANY IDEA HOW MUCH IT WOULD COST TO *BUY* THIS KIND OF PRESS?

AND WE GET IT *FREE* JUST BECAUSE SOME NUTCASE IS OUT THERE KNOCKING OFF YOUR CONSTITUENTS.

IF ONLY THEY *CATCH HIM* IN THE NEXT MONT IT WOULD BE *PERFECT--*

YOU CAN GIVE YOUR WHOLEHEARTED SUPPORT TO THE POLICE DEPARTMENT FOR THEIR *HEROIC EFFORTS* TO BRING THIS *MANIAC* TO *JUSTICE...*

...AND *THEN* COME OUT WITH YOUR STAND ON *CAPITAL PUNISHMENT.*

WHAT *IS* MY STAND? I FORGET.

I *HAVEN'T DECIDED* YET WHETHER YOU'RE A *STERN BELIEV* IN *JUSTICE* AND *RETRIBUTION...*

...OR A *COMPASSIONATE HUMANITARIAN* IN FAVOR OF *REHABILITATION* OF THE SOCIALLY *DISENFRANCHISED* RESIDENTS OF OUR *PENAL FACILITIES.*

CAY WOO FOR CONGRES

CAY FOR CONG

HORSE HOCKEY.

POLITICS.

SAME THING.

YEAH. I *LOVE* THIS BUSINESS.

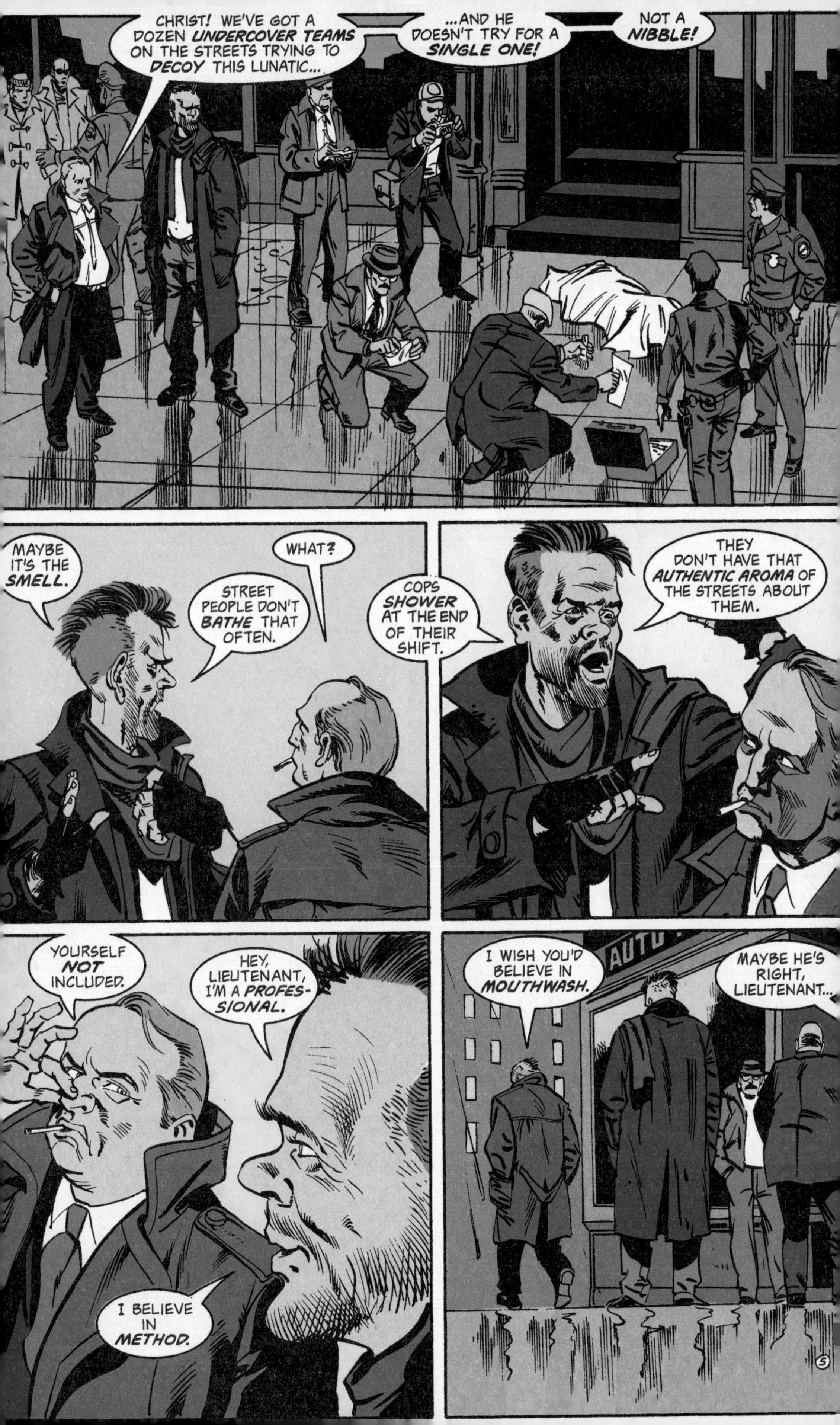

CHRIST! WE'VE GOT A DOZEN UNDERCOVER TEAMS ON THE STREETS TRYING TO DECOY THIS LUNATIC...
...AND HE DOESN'T TRY FOR A SINGLE ONE!
NOT A NIBBLE!
MAYBE IT'S THE SMELL.
STREET PEOPLE DON'T BATHE THAT OFTEN.
WHAT?
COPS SHOWER AT THE END OF THEIR SHIFT.
THEY DON'T HAVE THAT AUTHENTIC AROMA OF THE STREETS ABOUT THEM.
YOURSELF NOT INCLUDED.
HEY, LIEUTENANT, I'M A PROFESSIONAL.
I BELIEVE IN METHOD.
I WISH YOU'D BELIEVE IN MOUTHWASH.
MAYBE HE'S RIGHT, LIEUTENANT...
5

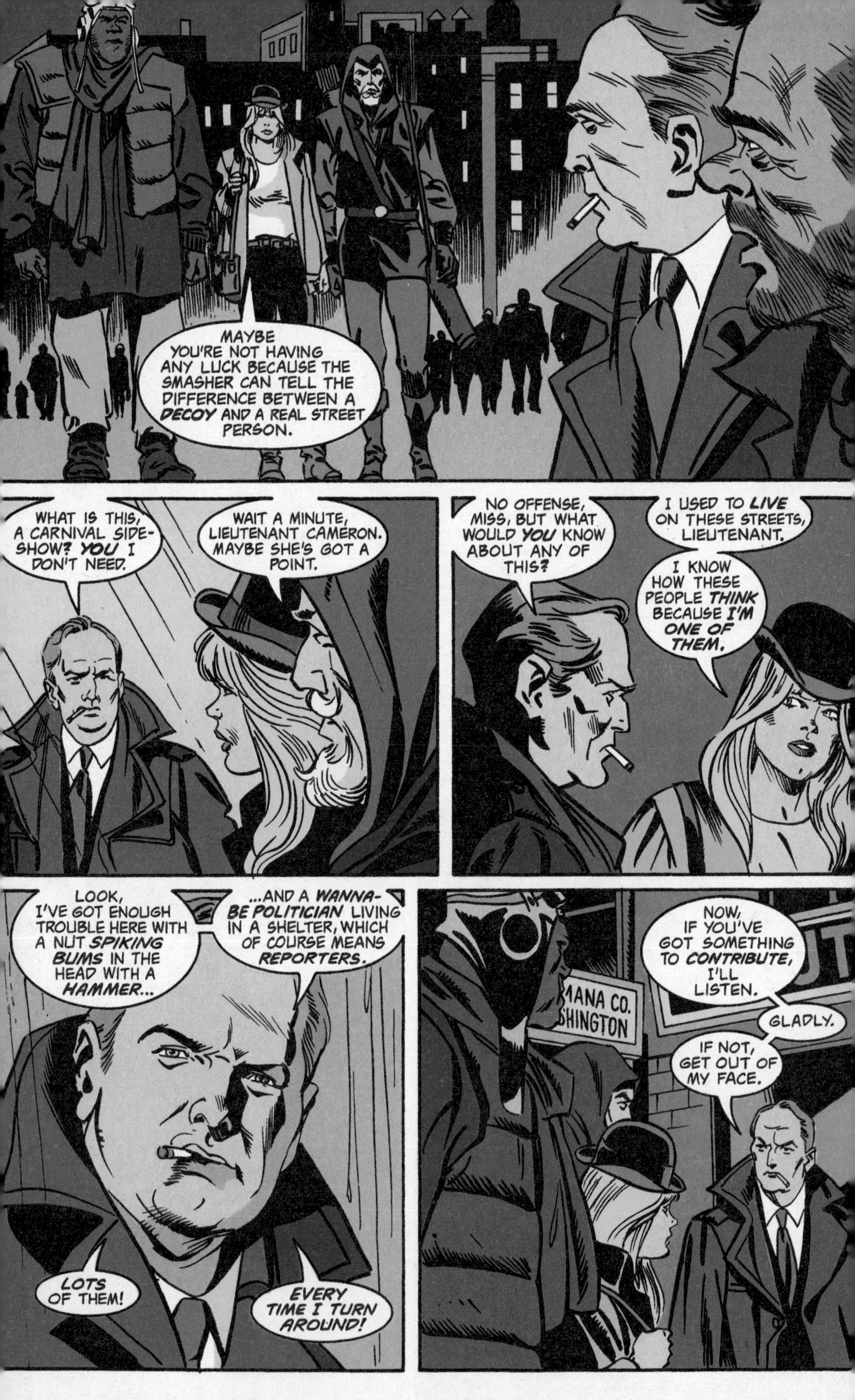
MAYBE YOU'RE NOT HAVING ANY LUCK BECAUSE THE SMASHER CAN TELL THE DIFFERENCE BETWEEN A DECOY AND A REAL STREET PERSON.
WHAT IS THIS, A CARNIVAL SIDE-SHOW? YOU I DON'T NEED.
WAIT A MINUTE, LIEUTENANT CAMERON. MAYBE SHE'S GOT A POINT.
NO OFFENSE, MISS, BUT WHAT WOULD YOU KNOW ABOUT ANY OF THIS?
I USED TO LIVE ON THESE STREETS, LIEUTENANT.
I KNOW HOW THESE PEOPLE THINK BECAUSE I'M ONE OF THEM.
LOOK, I'VE GOT ENOUGH TROUBLE HERE WITH A NUT SPIKING BUMS IN THE HEAD WITH A HAMMER...
...AND A WANNA-BE POLITICIAN LIVING IN A SHELTER, WHICH OF COURSE MEANS REPORTERS.
LOTS OF THEM!
EVERY TIME I TURN AROUND!
MANA CO.
SHINGTON
NOW, IF YOU'VE GOT SOMETHING TO CONTRIBUTE, I'LL LISTEN.
GLADLY.
IF NOT, GET OUT OF MY FACE.

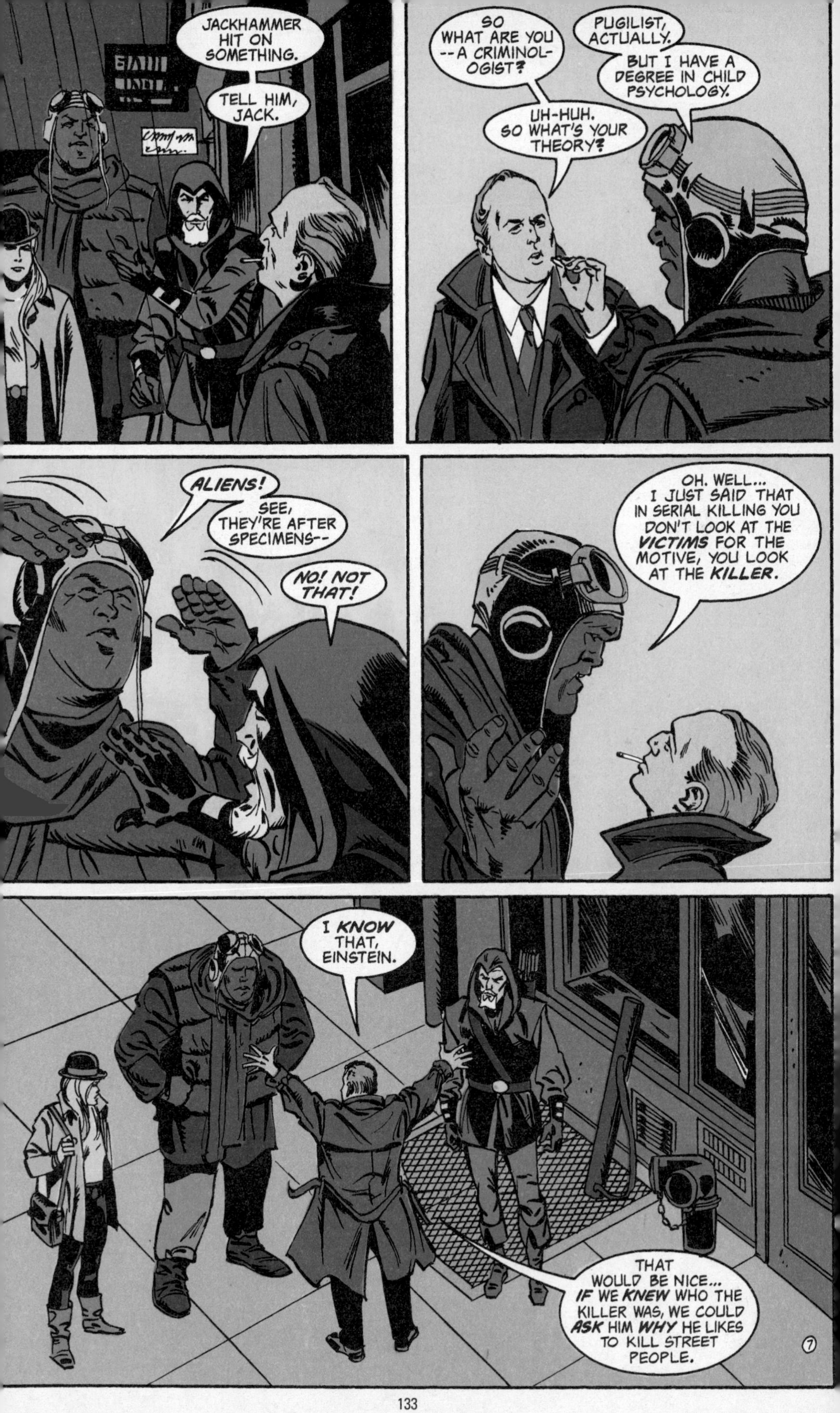
JACKHAMMER HIT ON SOMETHING.
TELL HIM, JACK.
SO WHAT ARE YOU --A CRIMINOLOGIST?
PUGILIST, ACTUALLY.
BUT I HAVE A DEGREE IN CHILD PSYCHOLOGY.
UH-HUH. SO WHAT'S YOUR THEORY?
ALIENS!
SEE, THEY'RE AFTER SPECIMENS--
NO! NOT THAT!
OH. WELL... I JUST SAID THAT IN SERIAL KILLING YOU DON'T LOOK AT THE VICTIMS FOR THE MOTIVE, YOU LOOK AT THE KILLER.
I KNOW THAT, EINSTEIN.
THAT WOULD BE NICE... IF WE KNEW WHO THE KILLER WAS, WE COULD ASK HIM WHY HE LIKES TO KILL STREET PEOPLE.
7

WAIT A MINUTE, LIEUTENANT. DON'T YOU SEE? THAT'S THE WAY YOU'VE *BEEN* THINKING.

YOU'VE BEEN LOOKING AT THE VICTIMS AS *JUST THAT*...STREET PEOPLE.

BUT THEY'RE *NOT* ALL THE SAME.

THEY'RE *DIFFERENT*, EVERY ONE OF THEM, WITH DIFFERENT *BACK-GROUNDS*.

THEY'RE *INDIVIDU*

SOME OF THEM ARE OBVIOUSL* MORE "INDIVIDUAL" THAN OTHERS.

SO WHAT ARE YOU GETTING AT?

MAYBE IT'S *NOT STREET PEOPLE* THE SMASHER'S AFTER...

...MAYBE IT'S *ONE* PERSON.

THEN WHY KILL *ALL* OF THEM TO GET TO ONE GUY?

MAYBE JUST TO BE SURE.

OR MAYBE THE KILLER *DOESN'T KNOW* EXACTLY *WHICH* STREET PERSON HE'S AFTER.

OR MAYBE HE KNOWS *EXACTLY* WHICH ONE...

...AND T* OTHERS AR* TO *COVER TRAIL*

OH, SWELL.

THAT LEAVES EVERY BUM... EXCUSE ME ...*PERSON* ON THE STREETS A POTENTIAL VICTIM.

AND STILL NO WAY TO TELL WHO OR WHY, EXCEPT TO CATCH HIM IN THE ACT.

JUST TRYING TO HELP, LIEUTENANT.

THANKS A BUNCH.

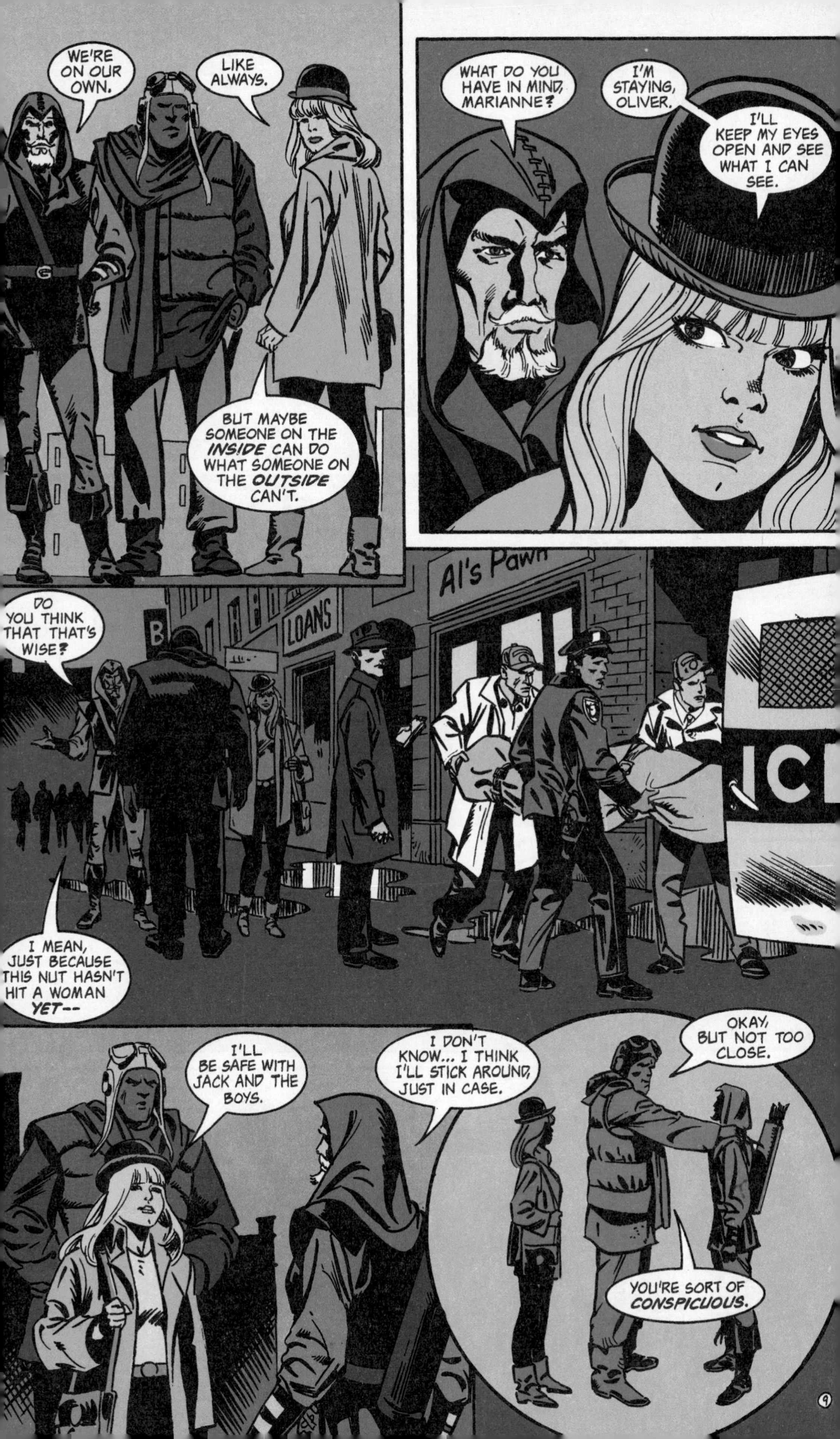

WE'RE ON OUR OWN.
LIKE ALWAYS.
BUT MAYBE SOMEONE ON THE *INSIDE* CAN DO WHAT SOMEONE ON THE *OUTSIDE* CAN'T.
WHAT DO YOU HAVE IN MIND, MARIANNE?
I'M STAYING, OLIVER.
I'LL KEEP MY EYES OPEN AND SEE WHAT I CAN SEE.
Al's Pawn
LOANS
DO YOU THINK THAT THAT'S WISE?
I MEAN, JUST BECAUSE THIS NUT HASN'T HIT A WOMAN *YET--*
I'LL BE SAFE WITH JACK AND THE BOYS.
I DON'T KNOW... I THINK I'LL STICK AROUND, JUST IN CASE.
OKAY, BUT NOT TOO CLOSE.
YOU'RE SORT OF *CONSPICUOUS.*

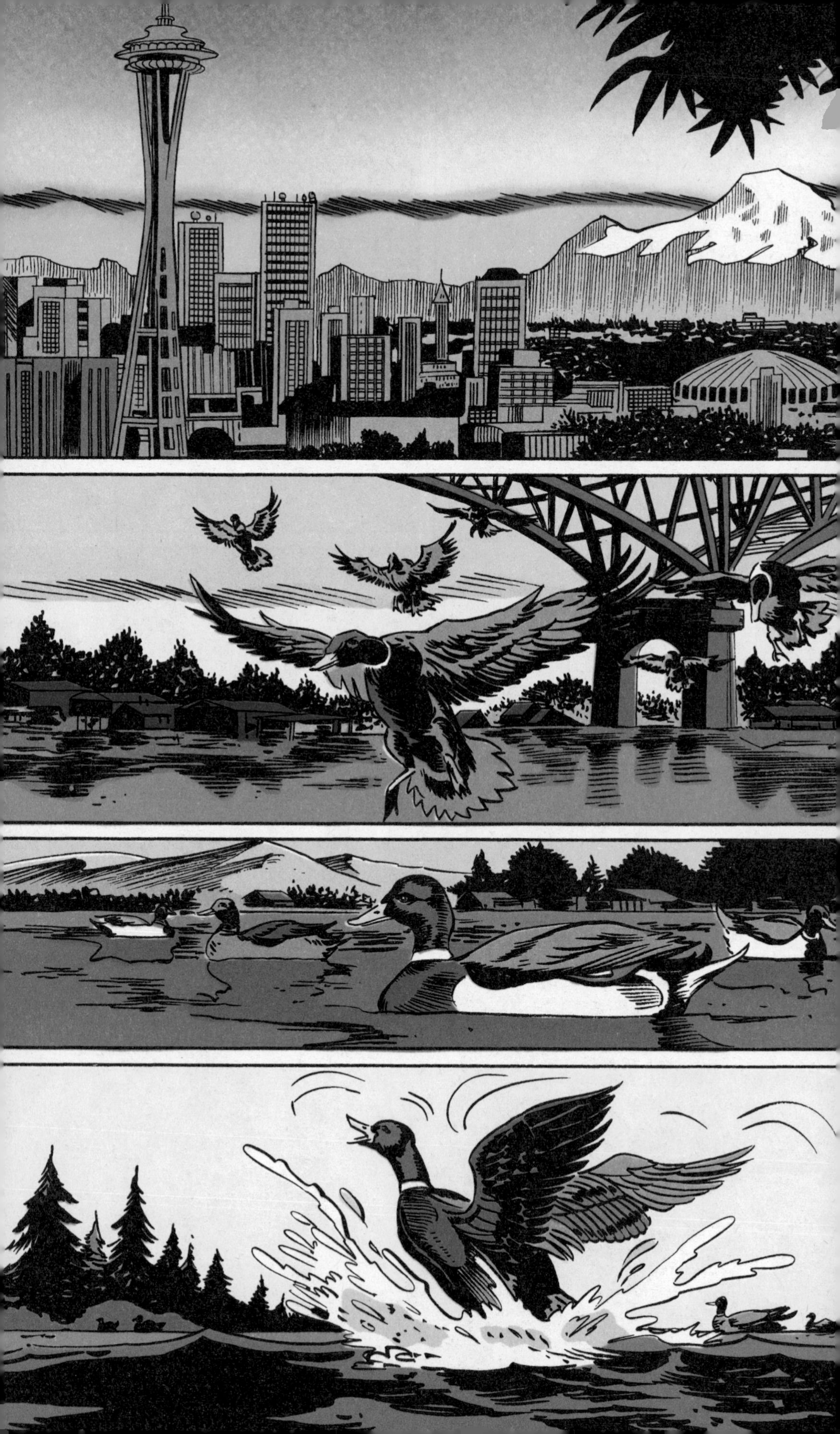

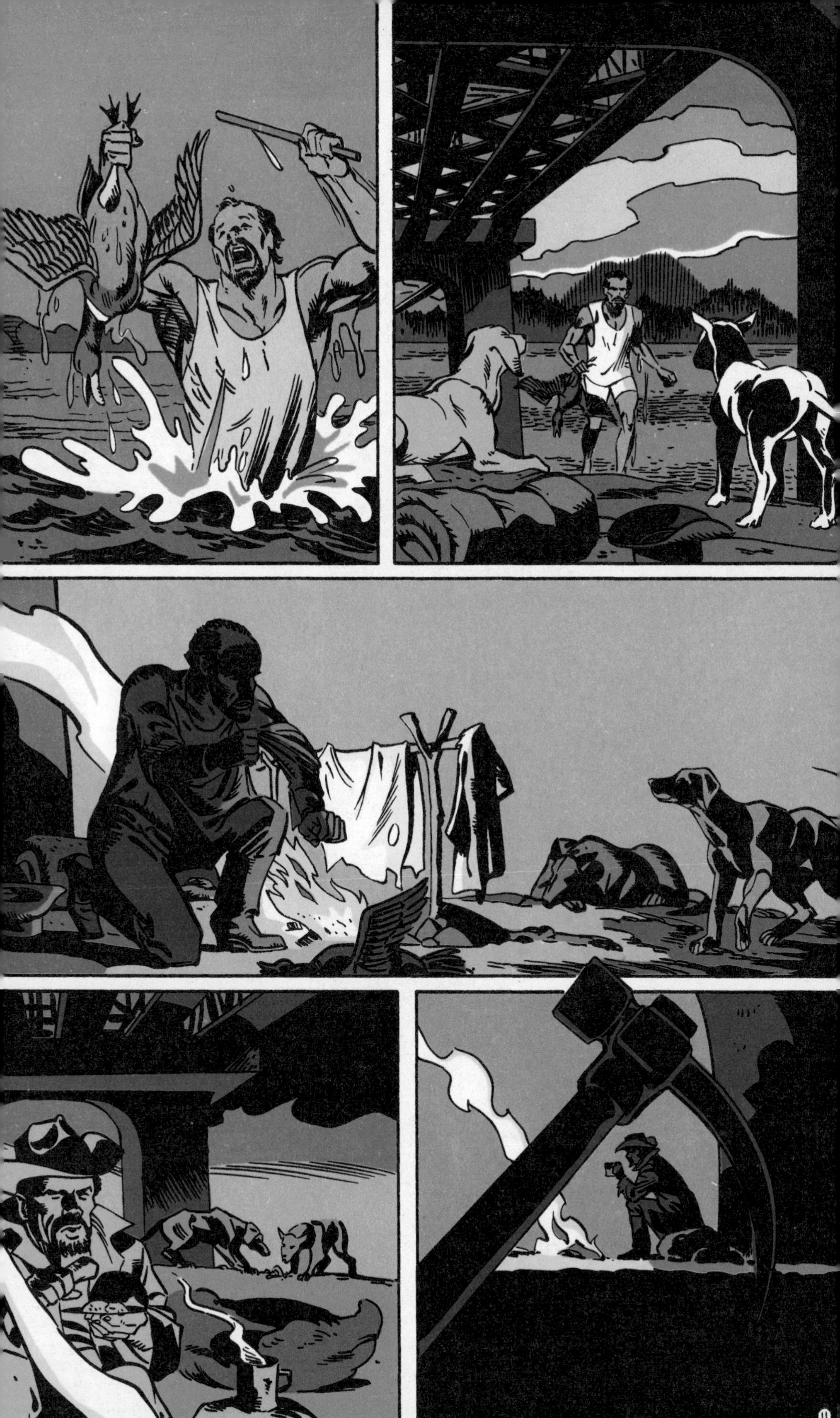

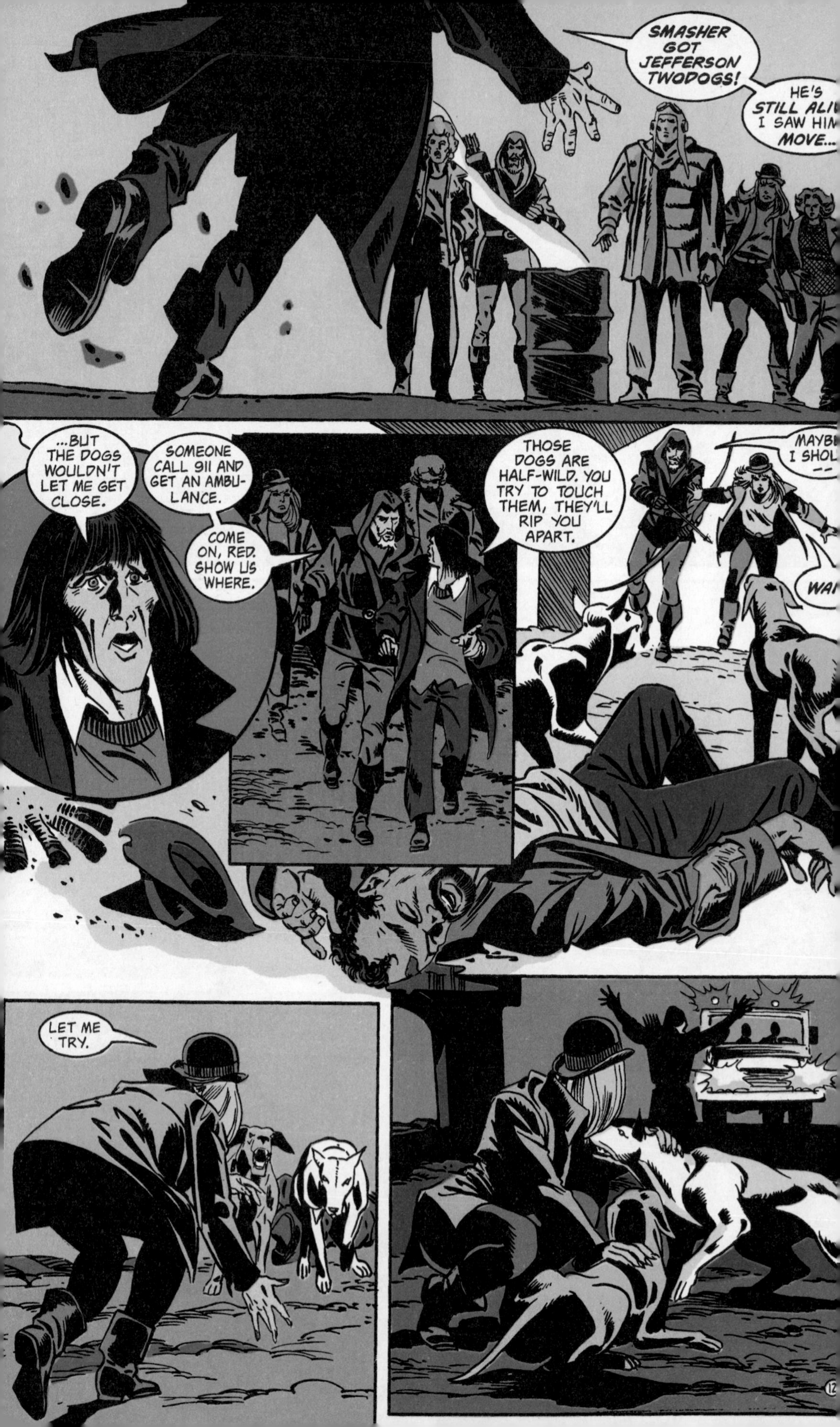
SMASHER GOT JEFFERSON TWODOGS!
HE'S STILL ALI I SAW HIM MOVE...
...BUT THE DOGS WOULDN'T LET ME GET CLOSE.
SOMEONE CALL 911 AND GET AN AMBU-LANCE.
COME ON, RED. SHOW US WHERE.
THOSE DOGS ARE HALF-WILD. YOU TRY TO TOUCH THEM, THEY'LL RIP YOU APART.
MAYB I SHOU --
WA
LET ME TRY.
12

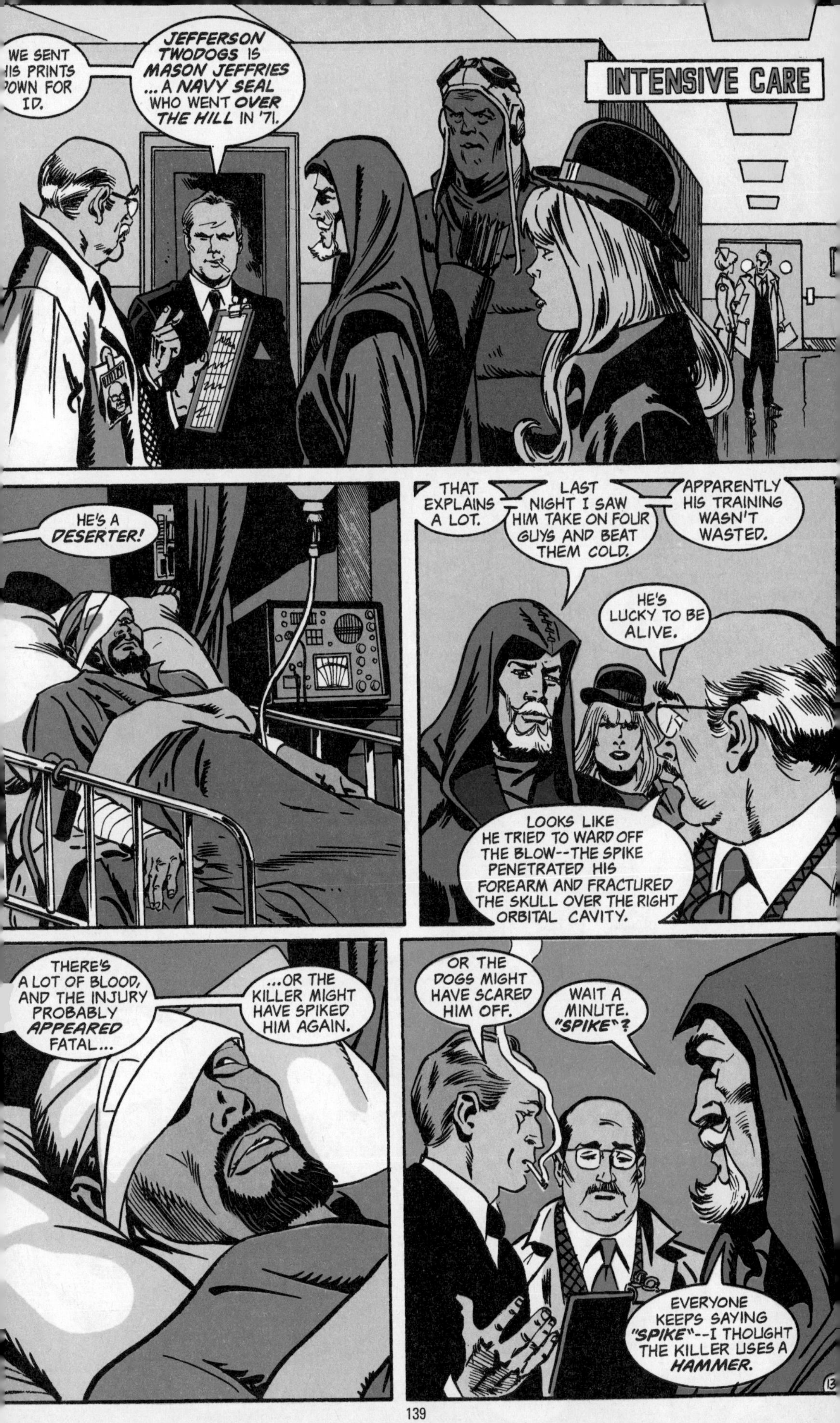
INTENSIVE CARE
WE SENT HIS PRINTS DOWN FOR ID.
JEFFERSON TWODOGS IS MASON JEFFRIES ...A NAVY SEAL WHO WENT OVER THE HILL IN '71.
HE'S A DESERTER!
THAT EXPLAINS A LOT.
LAST NIGHT I SAW HIM TAKE ON FOUR GUYS AND BEAT THEM COLD.
APPARENTLY HIS TRAINING WASN'T WASTED.
HE'S LUCKY TO BE ALIVE.
LOOKS LIKE HE TRIED TO WARD OFF THE BLOW--THE SPIKE PENETRATED HIS FOREARM AND FRACTURED THE SKULL OVER THE RIGHT ORBITAL CAVITY.
THERE'S A LOT OF BLOOD, AND THE INJURY PROBABLY APPEARED FATAL...
...OR THE KILLER MIGHT HAVE SPIKED HIM AGAIN.
OR THE DOGS MIGHT HAVE SCARED HIM OFF.
WAIT A MINUTE. "SPIKE"?
EVERYONE KEEPS SAYING "SPIKE"--I THOUGHT THE KILLER USES A HAMMER.
13

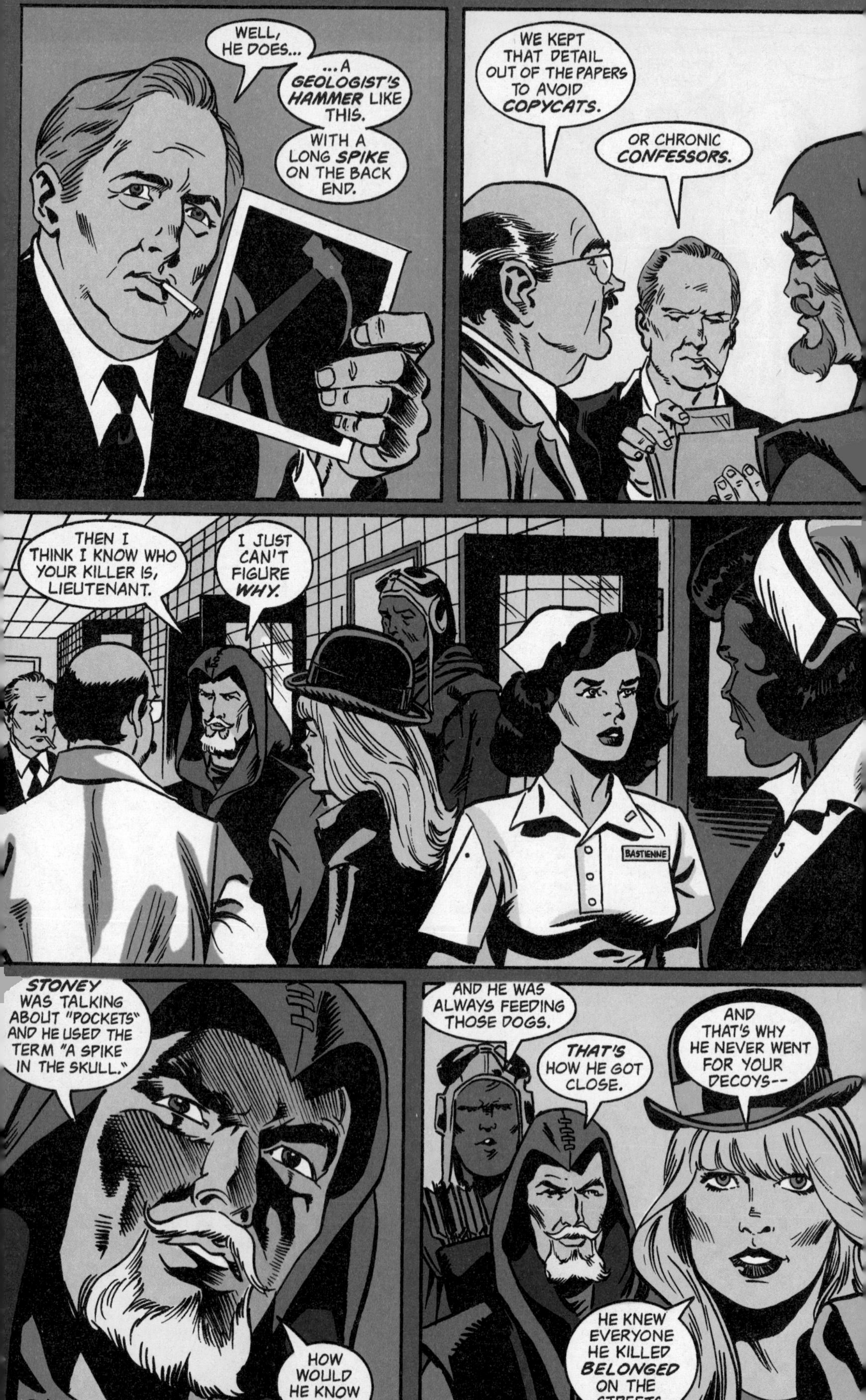
WELL, HE DOES...
...A GEOLOGIST'S HAMMER LIKE THIS.
WITH A LONG SPIKE ON THE BACK END.
WE KEPT THAT DETAIL OUT OF THE PAPERS TO AVOID COPYCATS.
OR CHRONIC CONFESSORS.
THEN I THINK I KNOW WHO YOUR KILLER IS, LIEUTENANT.
I JUST CAN'T FIGURE WHY.
BASTIENNE
STONEY WAS TALKING ABOUT "POCKETS" AND HE USED THE TERM "A SPIKE IN THE SKULL."
HOW WOULD HE KNOW THAT?
AND HE WAS ALWAYS FEEDING THOSE DOGS.
THAT'S HOW HE GOT CLOSE.
AND THAT'S WHY HE NEVER WENT FOR YOUR DECOYS--
HE KNEW EVERYONE HE KILLED BELONGED ON THE STREETS.

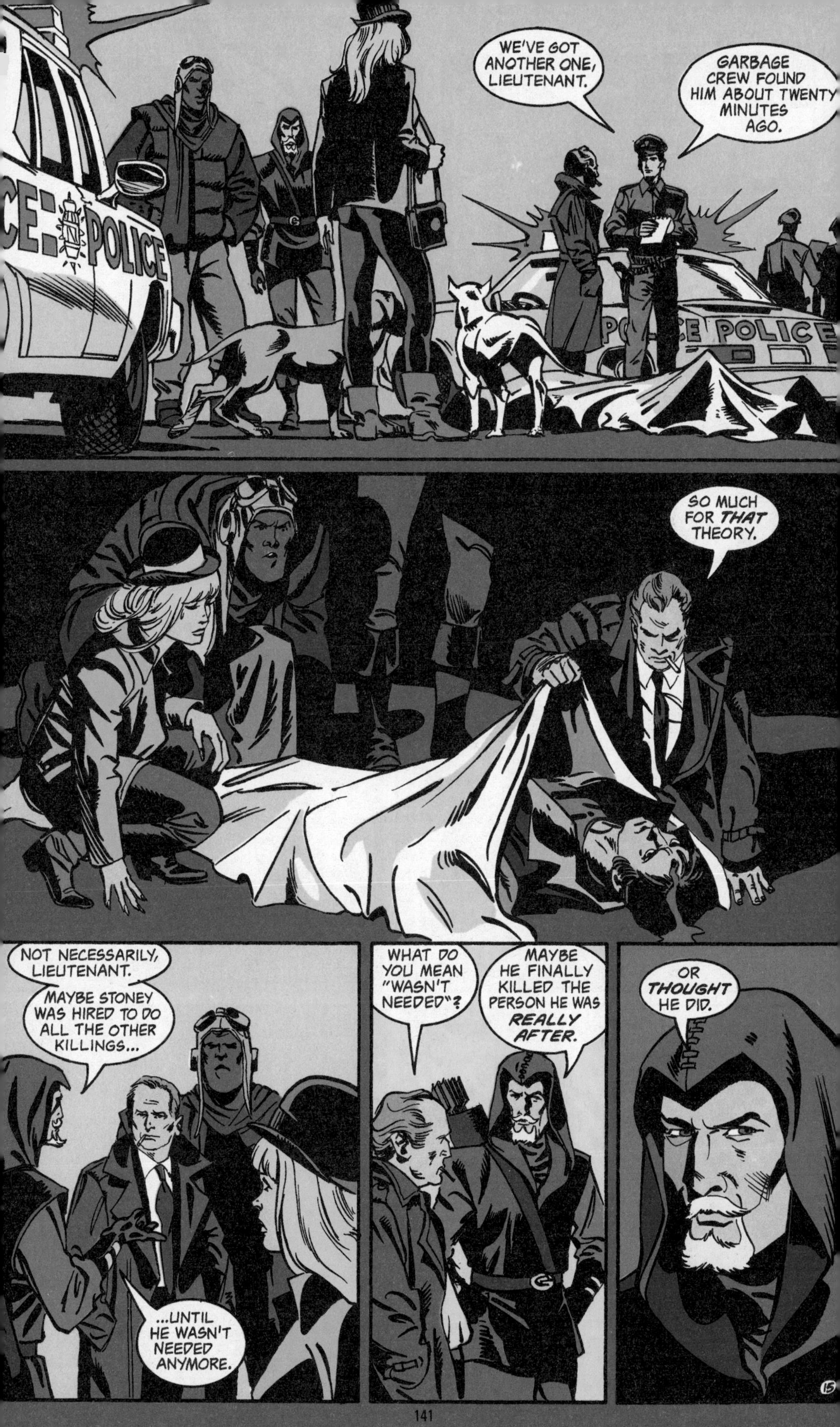
WE'VE GOT ANOTHER ONE, LIEUTENANT.
GARBAGE CREW FOUND HIM ABOUT TWENTY MINUTES AGO.
POLICE
POLICE
SO MUCH FOR THAT THEORY.
NOT NECESSARILY, LIEUTENANT.
MAYBE STONEY WAS HIRED TO DO ALL THE OTHER KILLINGS...
...UNTIL HE WASN'T NEEDED ANYMORE.
WHAT DO YOU MEAN "WASN'T NEEDED"?
MAYBE HE FINALLY KILLED THE PERSON HE WAS REALLY AFTER.
OR THOUGHT HE DID.
15

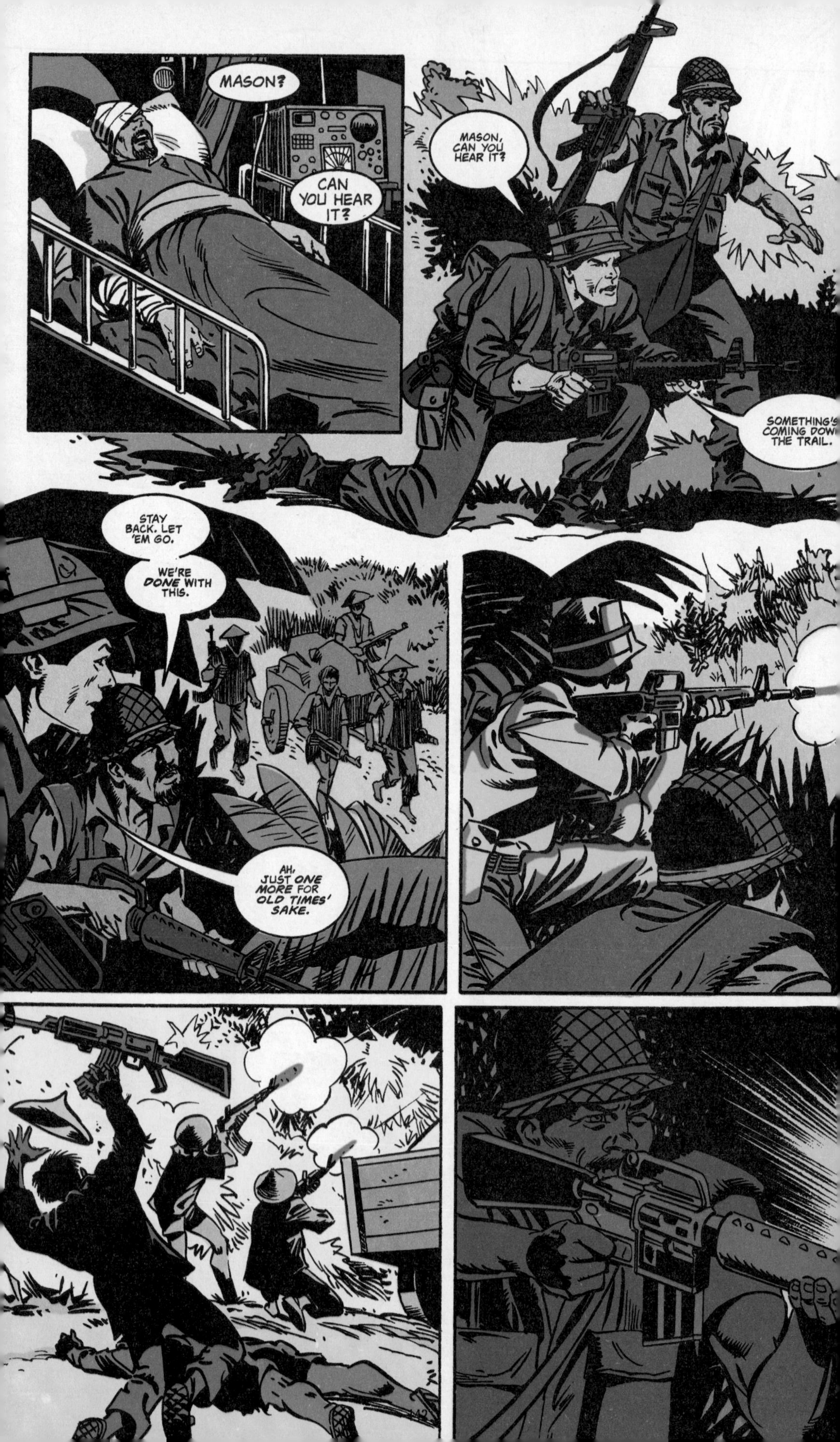
MASON?
CAN YOU HEAR IT?
MASON, CAN YOU HEAR IT?
SOMETHING'S COMING DOW THE TRAIL.
STAY BACK. LET 'EM GO.
WE'RE DONE WITH THIS.
AH, JUST ONE MORE FOR OLD TIMES' SAKE.

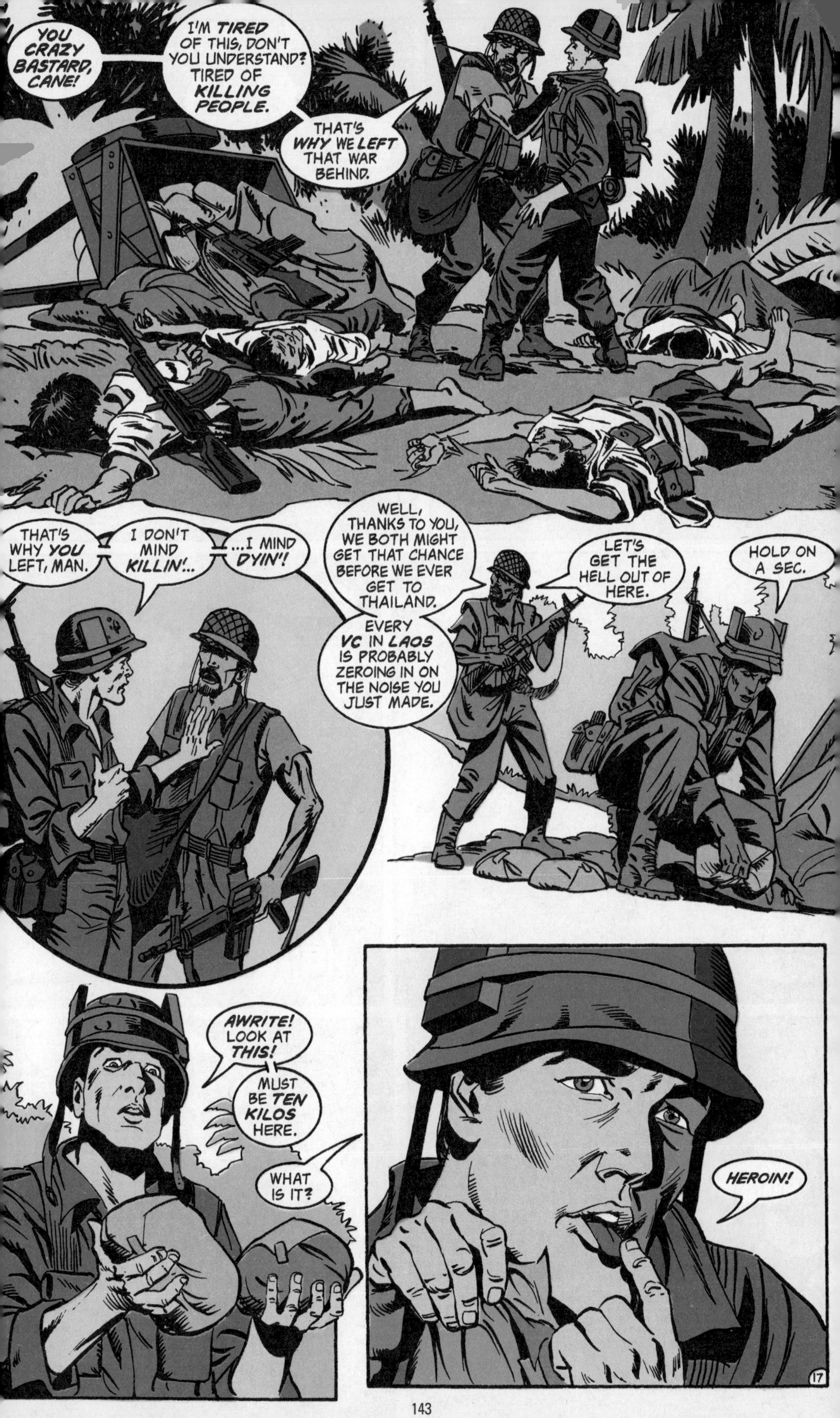

YOU CRAZY BASTARD, CANE!
I'M TIRED OF THIS, DON'T YOU UNDERSTAND? TIRED OF KILLING PEOPLE.
THAT'S WHY WE LEFT THAT WAR BEHIND.
THAT'S WHY YOU LEFT, MAN.
I DON'T MIND KILLIN'...
...I MIND DYIN'!
WELL, THANKS TO YOU, WE BOTH MIGHT GET THAT CHANCE BEFORE WE EVER GET TO THAILAND.
EVERY VC IN LAOS IS PROBABLY ZEROING IN ON THE NOISE YOU JUST MADE.
LET'S GET THE HELL OUT OF HERE.
HOLD ON A SEC.
AWRITE! LOOK AT THIS!
MUST BE TEN KILOS HERE.
WHAT IS IT?
HEROIN!
17

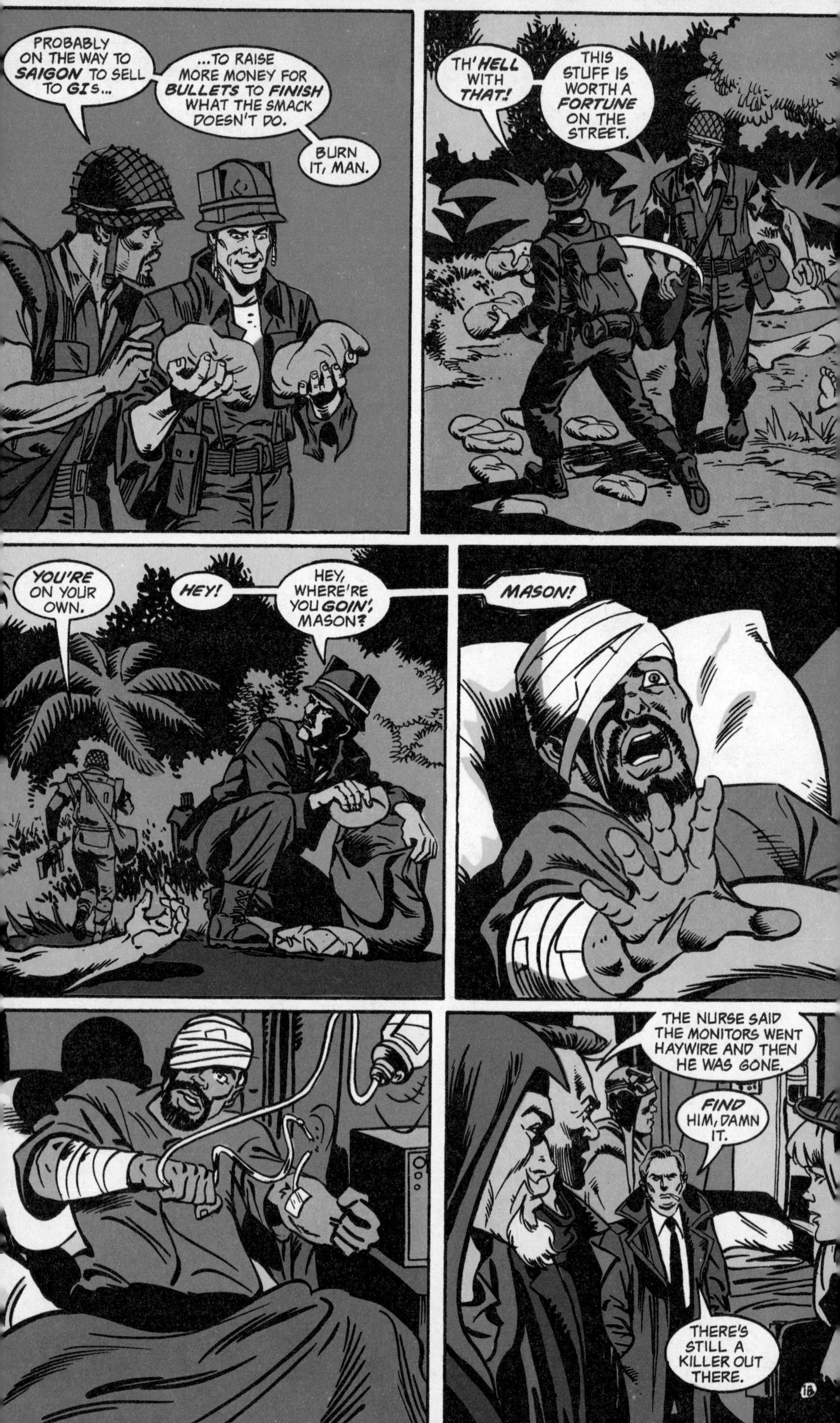
PROBABLY ON THE WAY TO SAIGON TO SELL TO GIs...
...TO RAISE MORE MONEY FOR BULLETS TO FINISH WHAT THE SMACK DOESN'T DO.
BURN IT, MAN.
TH' HELL WITH THAT!
THIS STUFF IS WORTH A FORTUNE ON THE STREET.
YOU'RE ON YOUR OWN.
HEY!
HEY, WHERE'RE YOU GOIN', MASON?
MASON!
THE NURSE SAID THE MONITORS WENT HAYWIRE AND THEN HE WAS GONE.
FIND HIM, DAMN IT.
THERE'S STILL A KILLER OUT THERE.

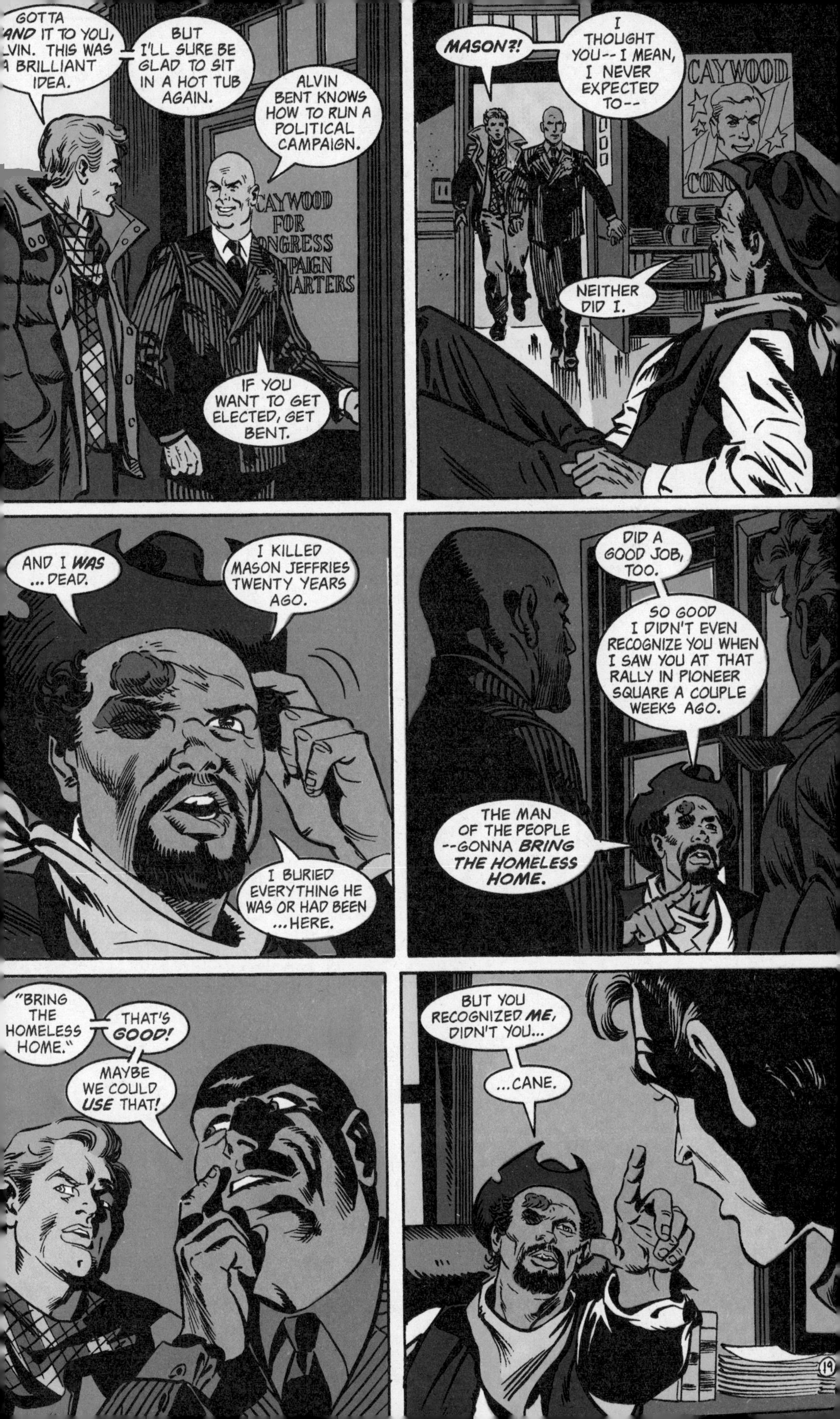
GOTTA HAND IT TO YOU, ALVIN. THIS WAS A BRILLIANT IDEA.
BUT I'LL SURE BE GLAD TO SIT IN A HOT TUB AGAIN.
ALVIN BENT KNOWS HOW TO RUN A POLITICAL CAMPAIGN.
CAYWOOD FOR CONGRESS CAMPAIGN HEADQUARTERS
IF YOU WANT TO GET ELECTED, GET BENT.
MASON?!
I THOUGHT YOU-- I MEAN, I NEVER EXPECTED TO--
CAYWOOD
NEITHER DID I.
AND I WAS ...DEAD.
I KILLED MASON JEFFRIES TWENTY YEARS AGO.
I BURIED EVERYTHING HE WAS OR HAD BEEN ...HERE.
DID A GOOD JOB, TOO.
SO GOOD I DIDN'T EVEN RECOGNIZE YOU WHEN I SAW YOU AT THAT RALLY IN PIONEER SQUARE A COUPLE WEEKS AGO.
THE MAN OF THE PEOPLE --GONNA BRING THE HOMELESS HOME.
"BRING THE HOMELESS HOME."
THAT'S GOOD!
MAYBE WE COULD USE THAT!
BUT YOU RECOGNIZED ME, DIDN'T YOU...
...CANE.

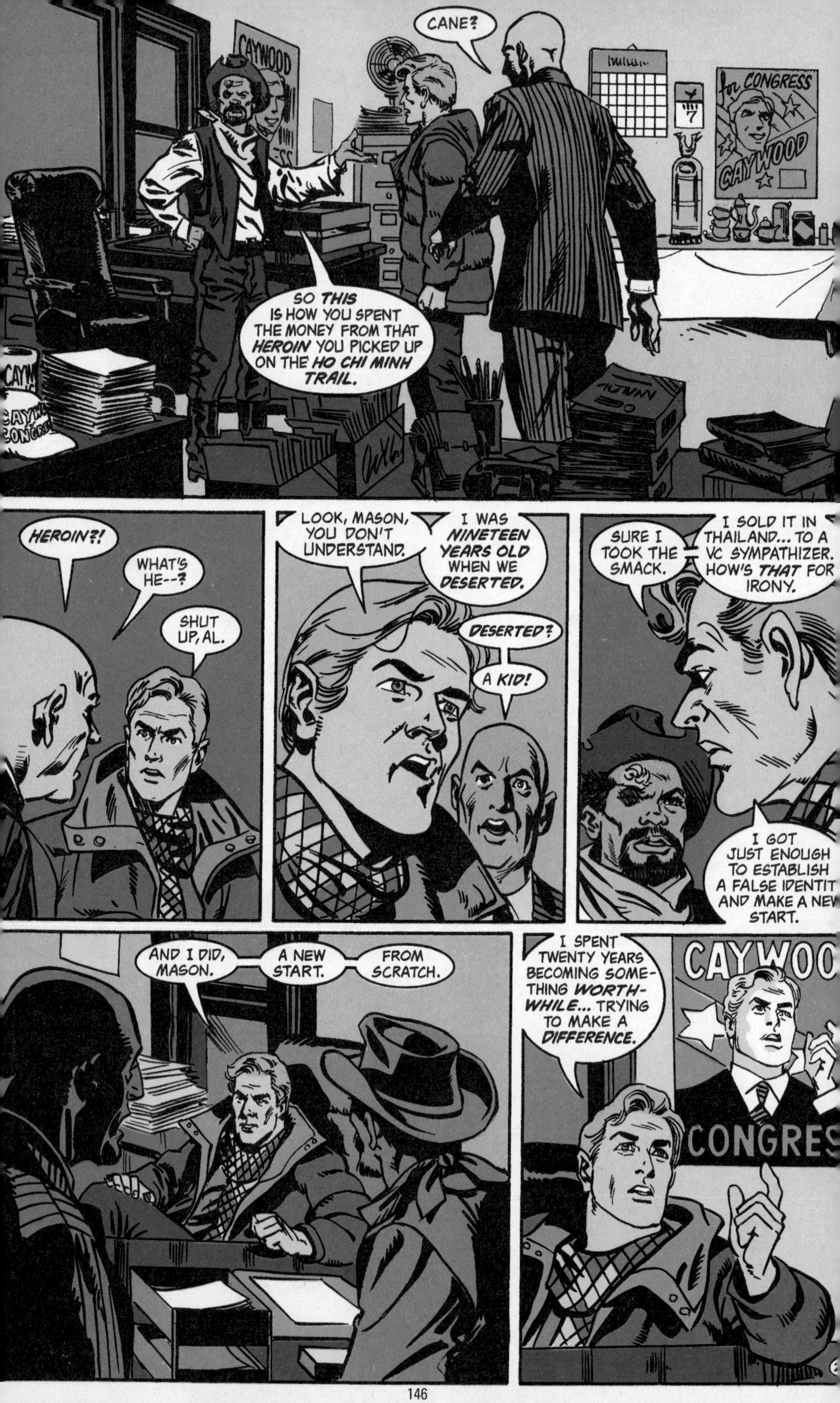
CAYWOOD
CANE?
for CONGRESS
CAYWOOD
SO THIS IS HOW YOU SPENT THE MONEY FROM THAT HEROIN YOU PICKED UP ON THE HO CHI MINH TRAIL.
HEROIN?!
WHAT'S HE--?
SHUT UP, AL.
LOOK, MASON, YOU DON'T UNDERSTAND.
I WAS NINETEEN YEARS OLD WHEN WE DESERTED.
DESERTED?
A KID!
SURE I TOOK THE SMACK.
I SOLD IT IN THAILAND... TO A VC SYMPATHIZER. HOW'S THAT FOR IRONY.
I GOT JUST ENOUGH TO ESTABLISH A FALSE IDENTIT AND MAKE A NEV START.
AND I DID, MASON.
A NEW START.
FROM SCRATCH.
I SPENT TWENTY YEARS BECOMING SOMETHING WORTHWHILE... TRYING TO MAKE A DIFFERENCE.
CAYWOO
CONGRES

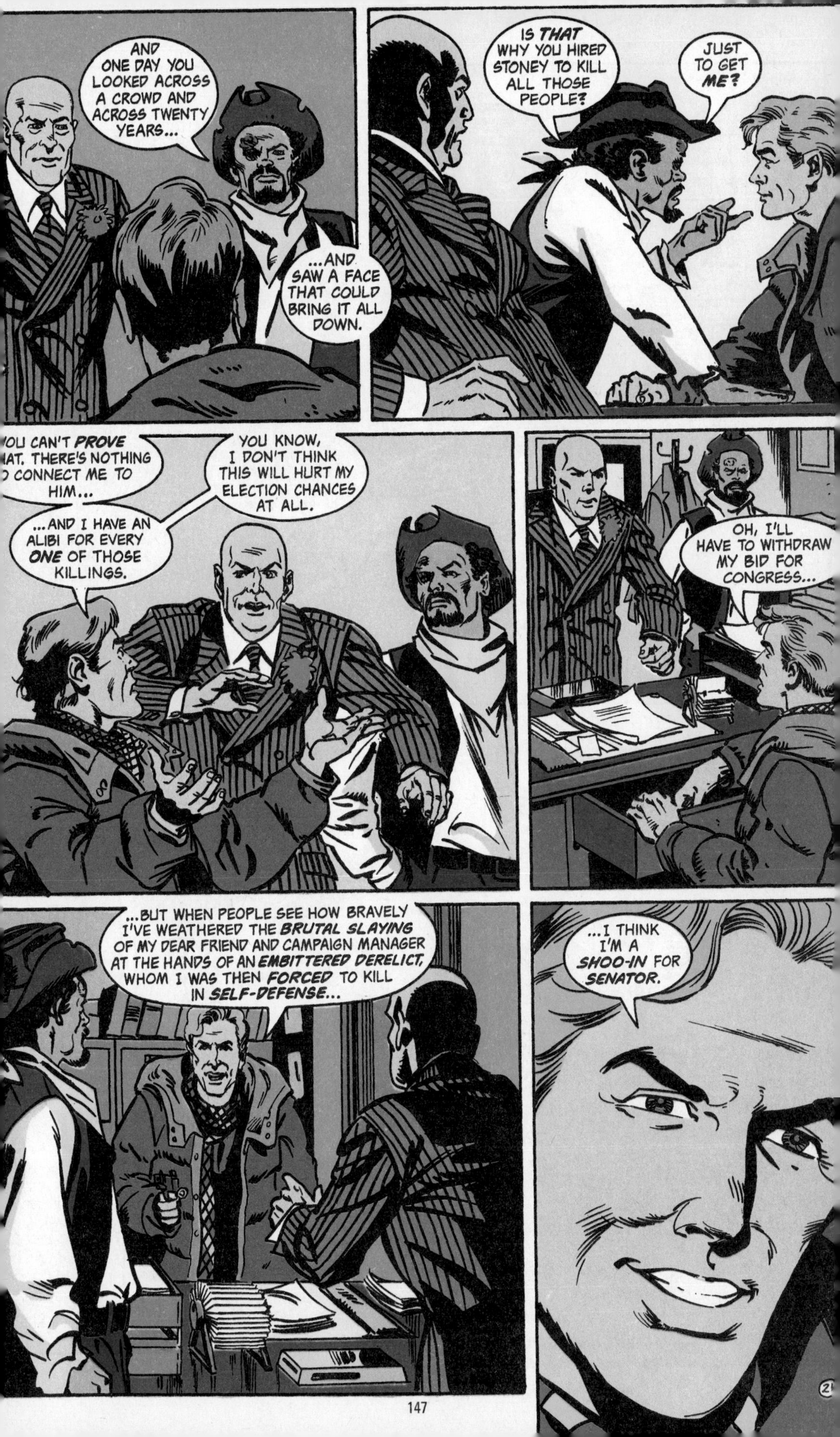
AND ONE DAY YOU LOOKED ACROSS A CROWD AND ACROSS TWENTY YEARS...
...AND SAW A FACE THAT COULD BRING IT ALL DOWN.
IS THAT WHY YOU HIRED STONEY TO KILL ALL THOSE PEOPLE?
JUST TO GET ME?
OU CAN'T PROVE AT. THERE'S NOTHING O CONNECT ME TO HIM...
...AND I HAVE AN ALIBI FOR EVERY ONE OF THOSE KILLINGS.
YOU KNOW, I DON'T THINK THIS WILL HURT MY ELECTION CHANCES AT ALL.
OH, I'LL HAVE TO WITHDRAW MY BID FOR CONGRESS...
...BUT WHEN PEOPLE SEE HOW BRAVELY I'VE WEATHERED THE BRUTAL SLAYING OF MY DEAR FRIEND AND CAMPAIGN MANAGER AT THE HANDS OF AN EMBITTERED DERELICT, WHOM I WAS THEN FORCED TO KILL IN SELF-DEFENSE...
...I THINK I'M A SHOO-IN FOR SENATOR.

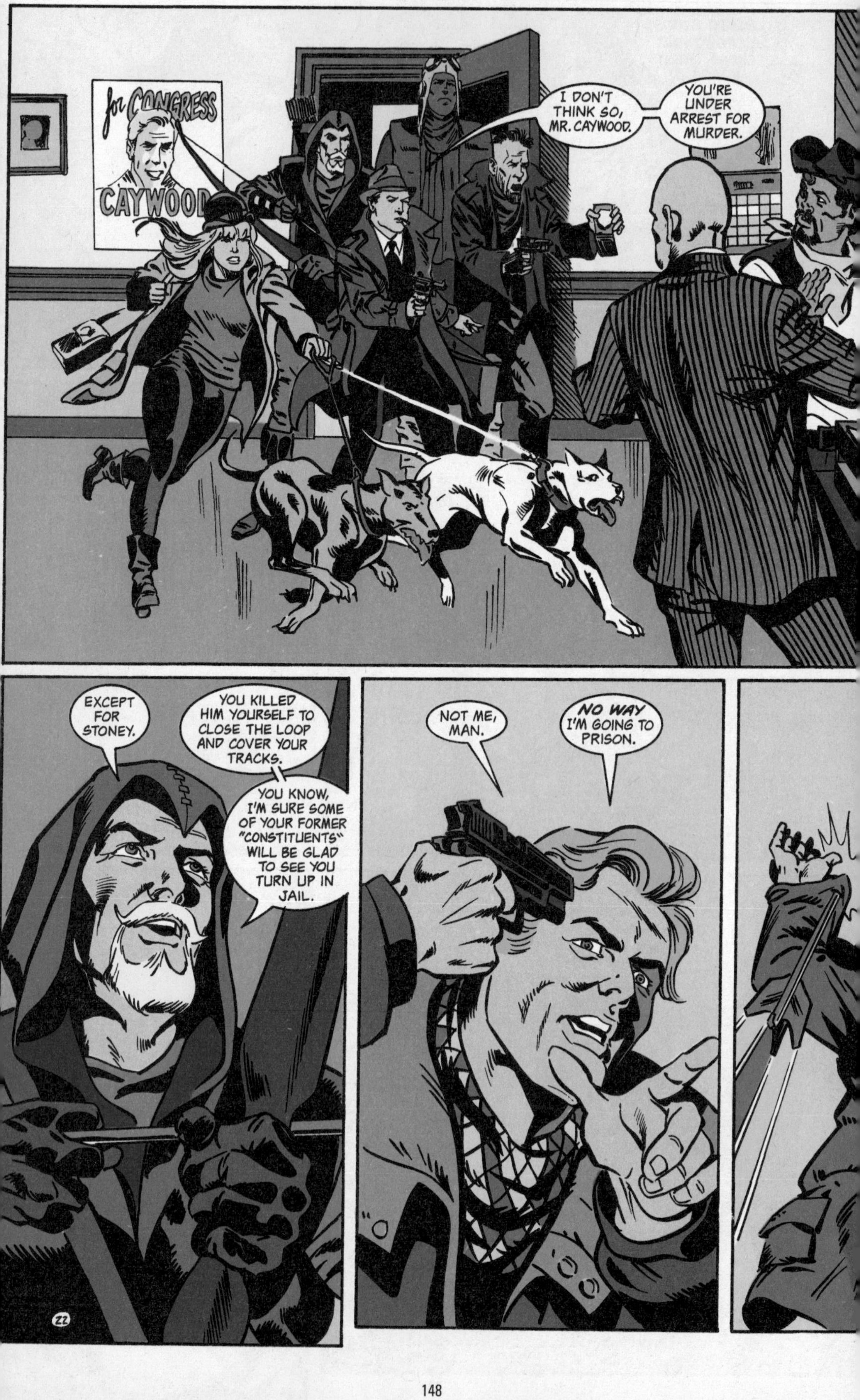
for CONGRESS
CAYWOOD
I DON'T THINK SO, MR. CAYWOOD.
YOU'RE UNDER ARREST FOR MURDER.
EXCEPT FOR STONEY.
YOU KILLED HIM YOURSELF TO CLOSE THE LOOP AND COVER YOUR TRACKS.
YOU KNOW, I'M SURE SOME OF YOUR FORMER "CONSTITUENTS" WILL BE GLAD TO SEE YOU TURN UP IN JAIL.
NOT ME, MAN.
NO WAY I'M GOING TO PRISON.

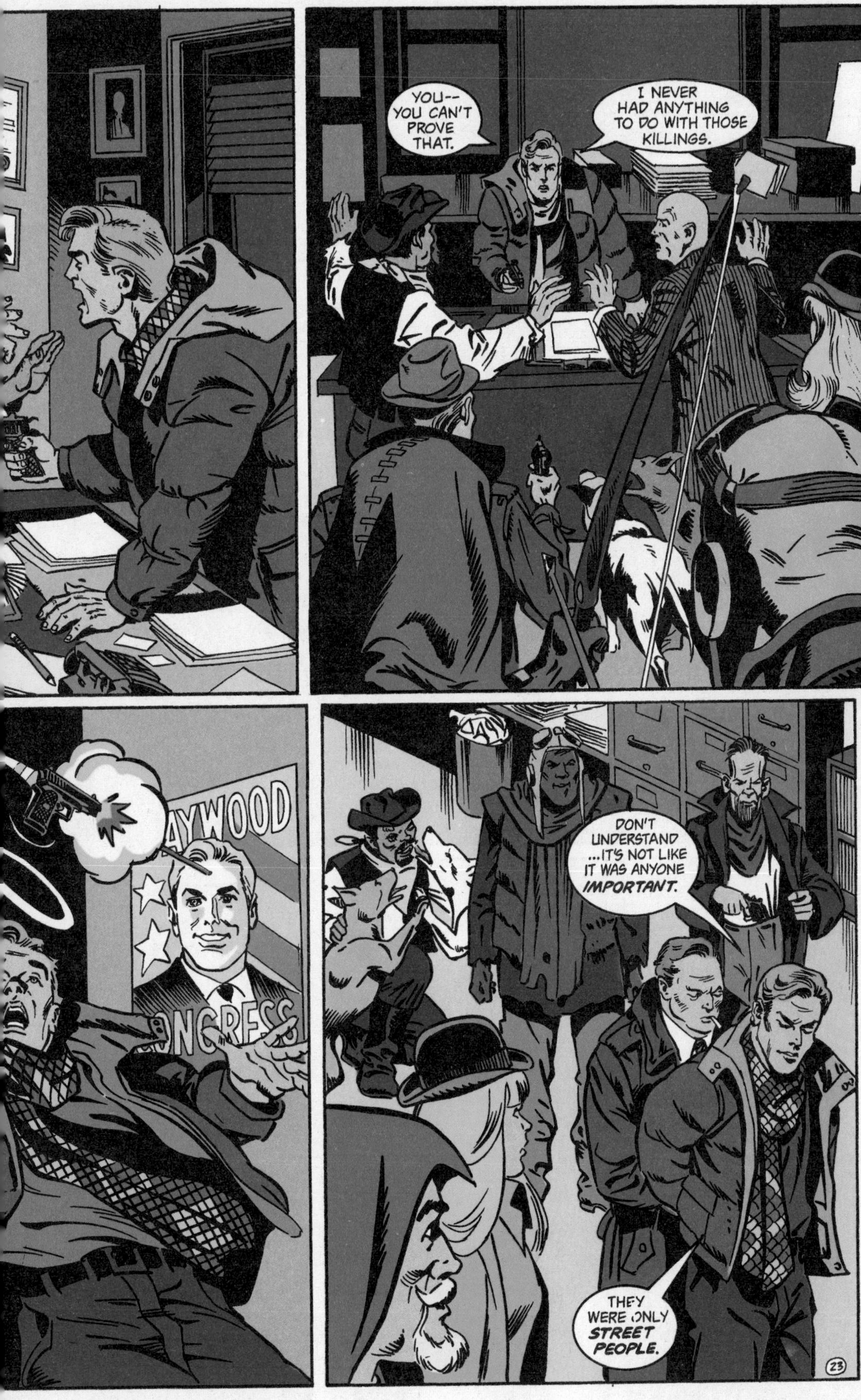
YOU-- YOU CAN'T PROVE THAT.
I NEVER HAD ANYTHING TO DO WITH THOSE KILLINGS.
AYWOOD
ONGRESS
DON'T UNDERSTAND ...IT'S NOT LIKE IT WAS ANYONE IMPORTANT.
THEY WERE ONLY STREET PEOPLE.
23

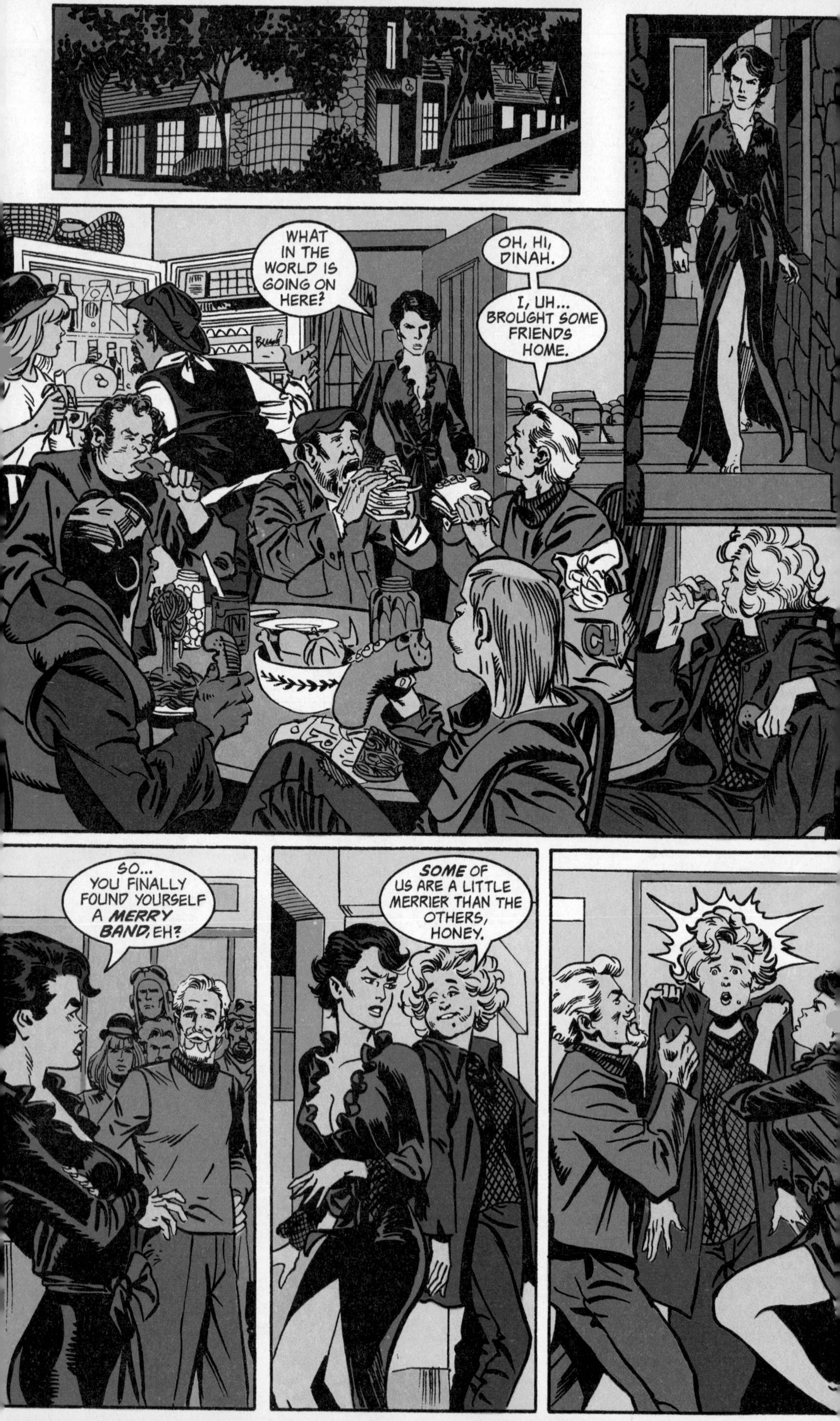
WHAT IN THE WORLD IS GOING ON HERE?
OH, HI, DINAH.
I, UH... BROUGHT SOME FRIENDS HOME.
SO... YOU FINALLY FOUND YOURSELF A MERRY BAND, EH?
SOME OF US ARE A LITTLE MERRIER THAN THE OTHERS, HONEY.

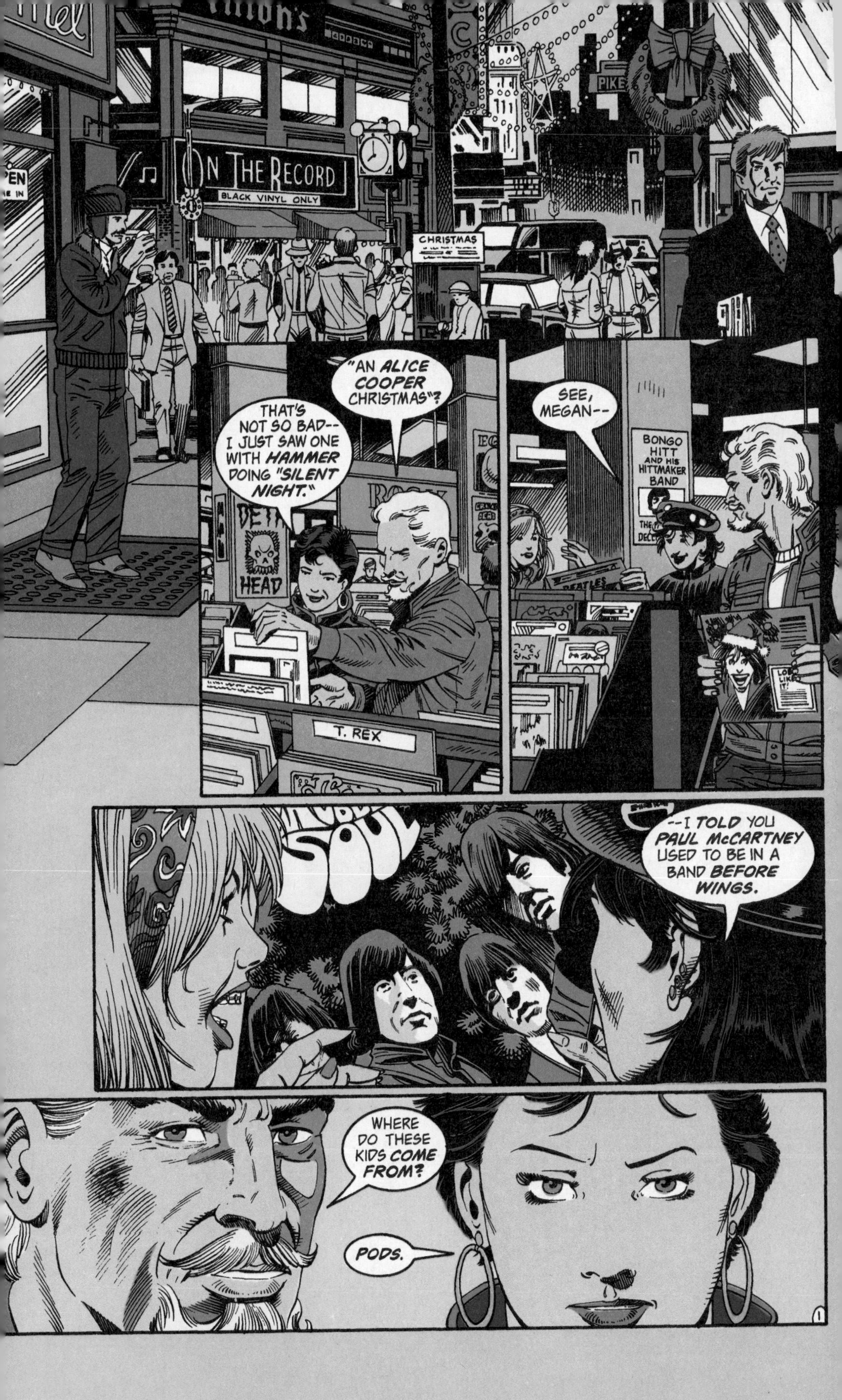
ON THE RECORD
BLACK VINYL ONLY
CHRISTMAS
PIKE
"AN ALICE COOPER CHRISTMAS"?
THAT'S NOT SO BAD-- I JUST SAW ONE WITH HAMMER DOING "SILENT NIGHT."
T. REX
SEE, MEGAN--
BONGO HITT AND HIS HITTMAKER BAND
--I TOLD YOU PAUL McCARTNEY USED TO BE IN A BAND BEFORE WINGS.
WHERE DO THESE KIDS COME FROM?
PODS.
1

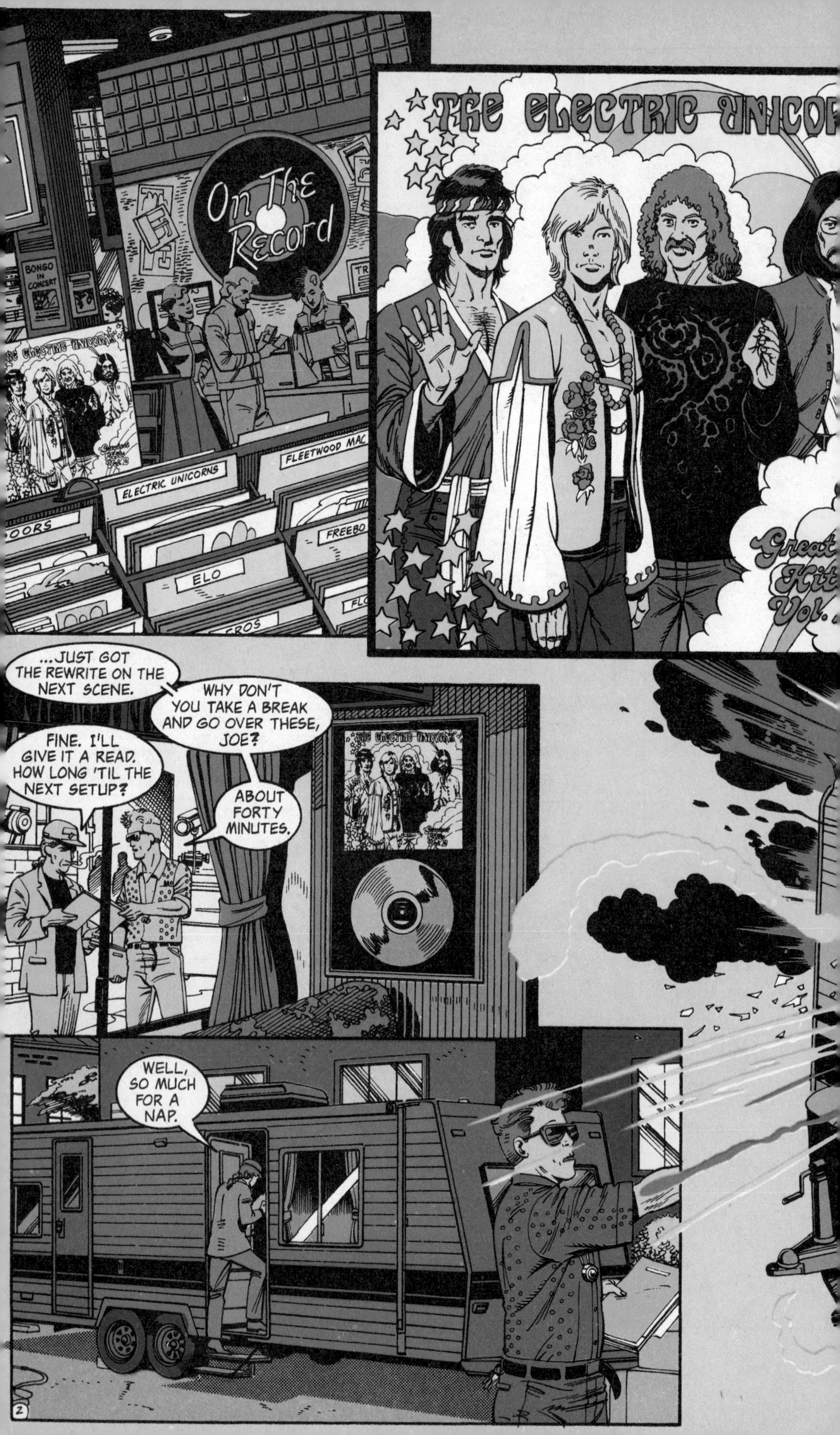

ON THE RECORD
BONGO IN CONCERT
THE ELECTRIC UNICORNS
FLEETWOOD MAC
ELECTRIC UNICORNS
ELO
FREEBO
THE ELECTRIC UNICOR
...JUST GOT THE REWRITE ON THE NEXT SCENE.
WHY DON'T YOU TAKE A BREAK AND GO OVER THESE, JOE?
FINE. I'LL GIVE IT A READ. HOW LONG 'TIL THE NEXT SETUP?
ABOUT FORTY MINUTES.
WELL, SO MUCH FOR A NAP.

REUNION TOUR
PART 1

MIKE GRELL	RICK HOBERG	JOHN NYBERG
WRITER	PENCILLER	INKER
STEVE HAYNIE	JULIA LACQUEMENT	MIKE GOLD
LETTERER	COLORIST	EDITOR

③

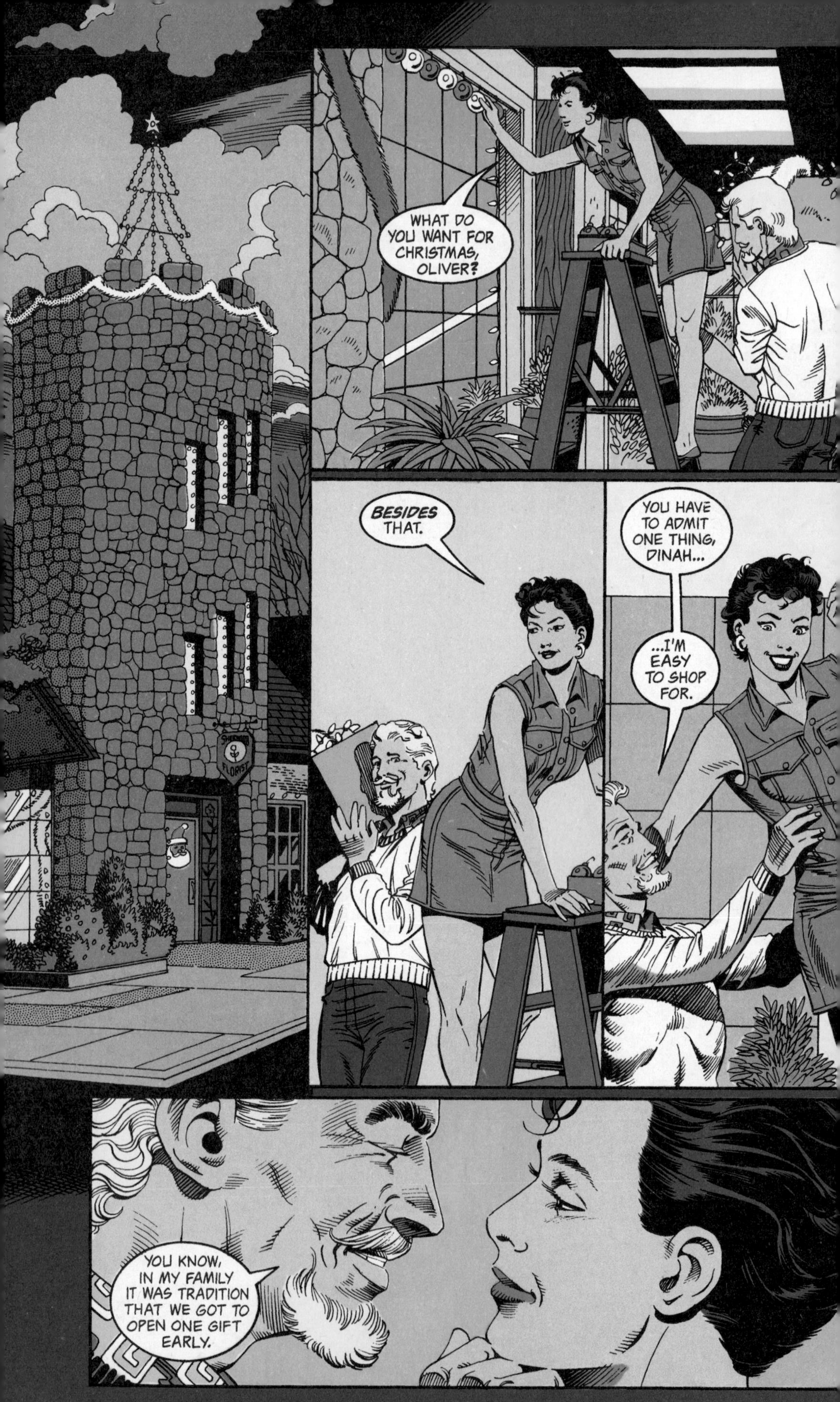

WHAT DO YOU WANT FOR CHRISTMAS, OLIVER?
BESIDES THAT.
YOU HAVE TO ADMIT ONE THING, DINAH...
...I'M EASY TO SHOP FOR.
YOU KNOW, IN MY FAMILY IT WAS TRADITION THAT WE GOT TO OPEN ONE GIFT EARLY.

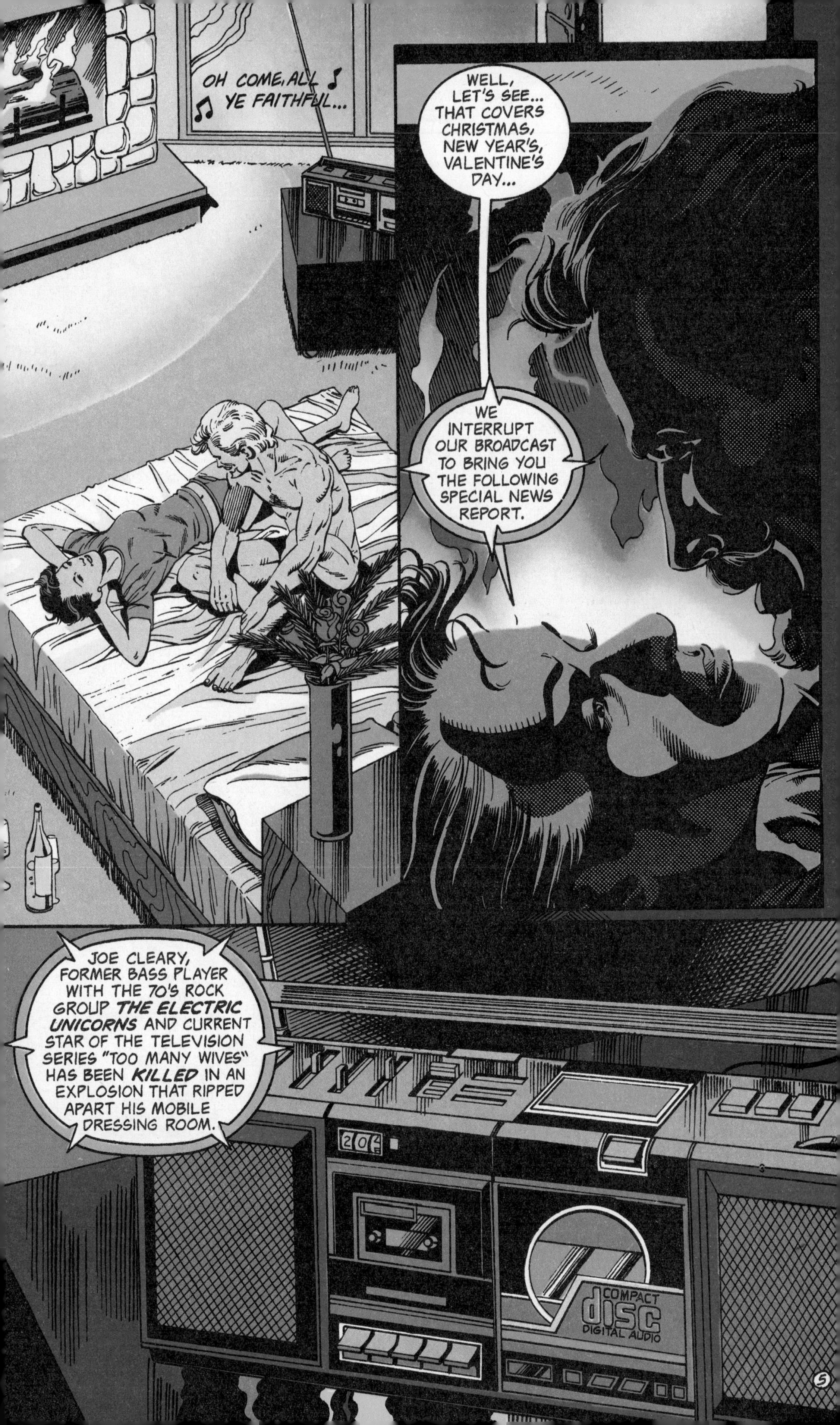

OH COME, ALL ♪ ♫ YE FAITHFUL...
WELL, LET'S SEE... THAT COVERS CHRISTMAS, NEW YEAR'S, VALENTINE'S DAY...
WE INTERRUPT OUR BROADCAST TO BRING YOU THE FOLLOWING SPECIAL NEWS REPORT.
JOE CLEARY, FORMER BASS PLAYER WITH THE 70'S ROCK GROUP ***THE ELECTRIC UNICORNS*** AND CURRENT STAR OF THE TELEVISION SERIES "TOO MANY WIVES" HAS BEEN ***KILLED*** IN AN EXPLOSION THAT RIPPED APART HIS MOBILE DRESSING ROOM.
COMPACT disc DIGITAL AUDIO

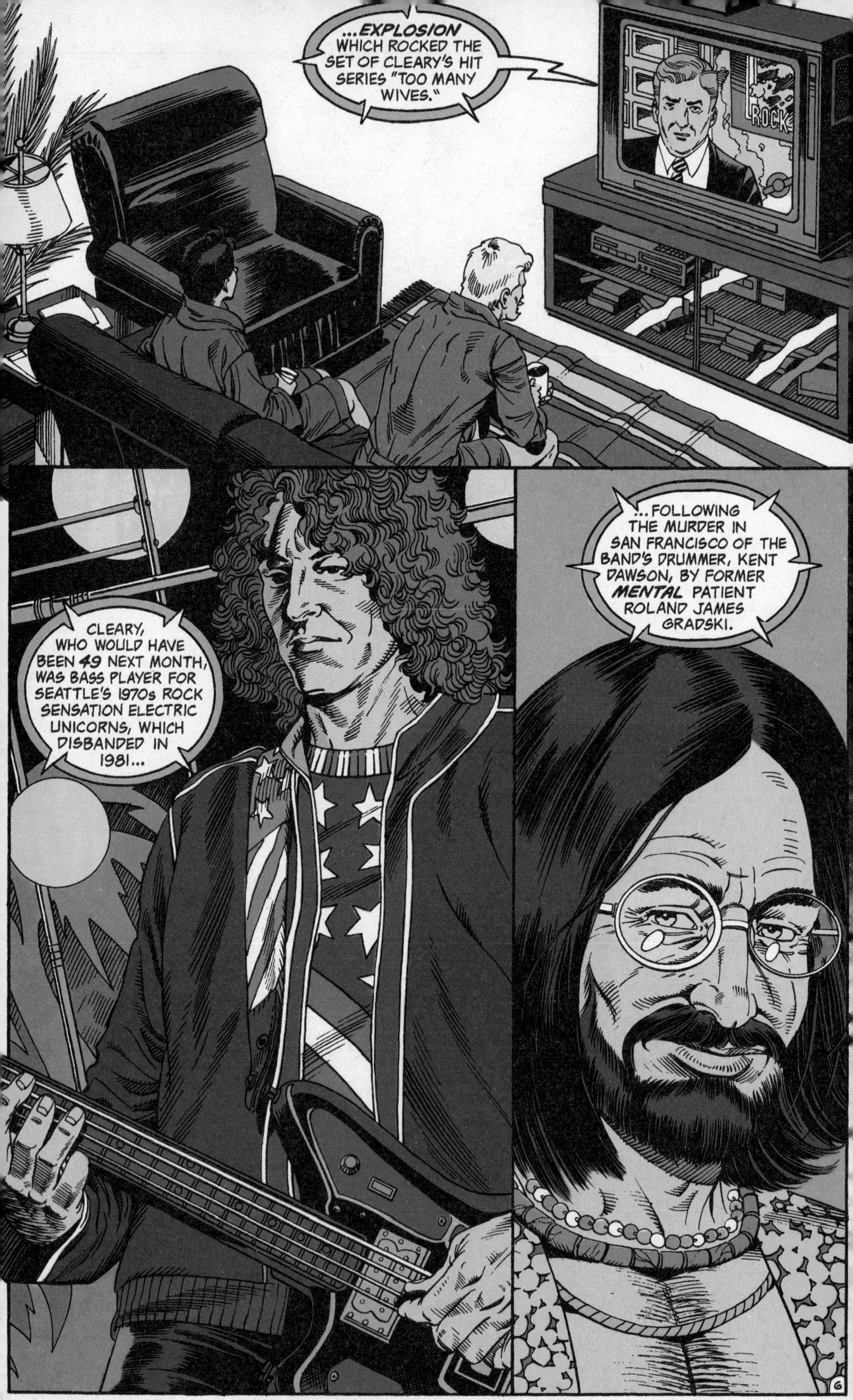
...EXPLOSION WHICH ROCKED THE SET OF CLEARY'S HIT SERIES "TOO MANY WIVES."
ROCK
CLEARY, WHO WOULD HAVE BEEN 49 NEXT MONTH, WAS BASS PLAYER FOR SEATTLE'S 1970s ROCK SENSATION ELECTRIC UNICORNS, WHICH DISBANDED IN 1981...
...FOLLOWING THE MURDER IN SAN FRANCISCO OF THE BAND'S DRUMMER, KENT DAWSON, BY FORMER MENTAL PATIENT ROLAND JAMES GRADSKI.
6

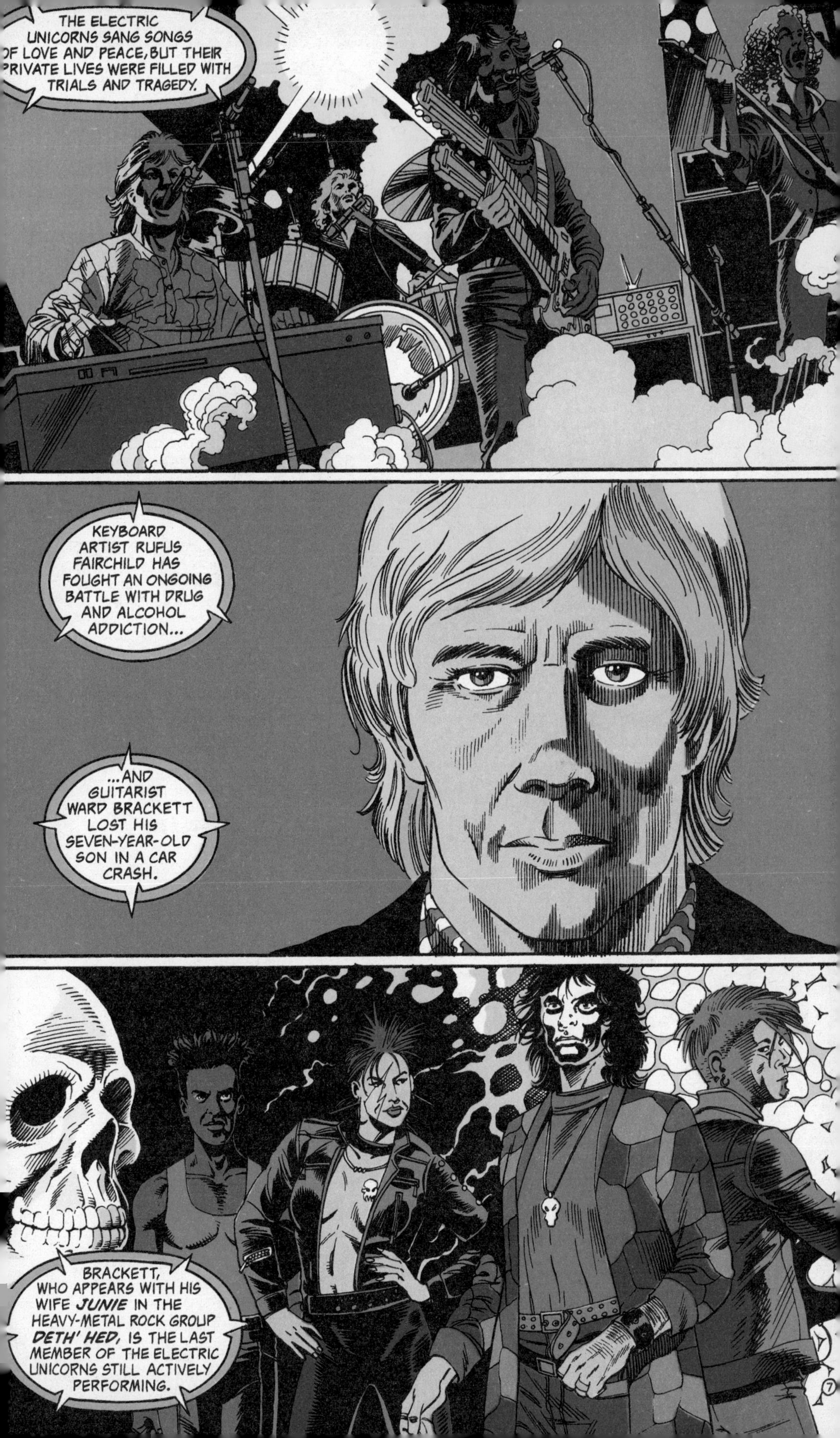
THE ELECTRIC UNICORNS SANG SONGS OF LOVE AND PEACE, BUT THEIR PRIVATE LIVES WERE FILLED WITH TRIALS AND TRAGEDY.
KEYBOARD ARTIST RUFUS FAIRCHILD HAS FOUGHT AN ONGOING BATTLE WITH DRUG AND ALCOHOL ADDICTION...
...AND GUITARIST WARD BRACKETT LOST HIS SEVEN-YEAR-OLD SON IN A CAR CRASH.
BRACKETT, WHO APPEARS WITH HIS WIFE *JUNIE* IN THE HEAVY-METAL ROCK GROUP *DETH' HED,* IS THE LAST MEMBER OF THE ELECTRIC UNICORNS STILL ACTIVELY PERFORMING.
7

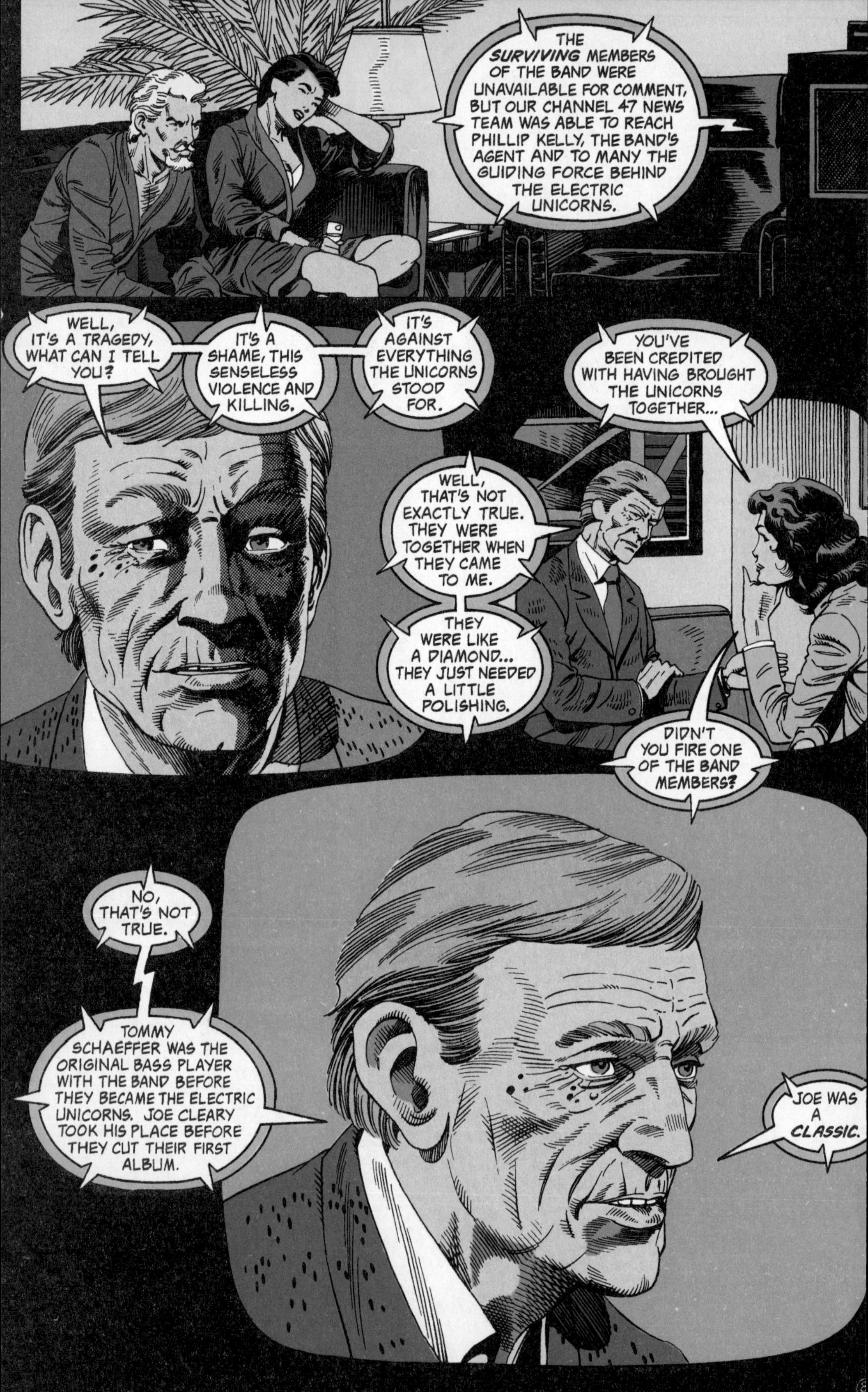
THE SURVIVING MEMBERS OF THE BAND WERE UNAVAILABLE FOR COMMENT, BUT OUR CHANNEL 47 NEWS TEAM WAS ABLE TO REACH PHILLIP KELLY, THE BAND'S AGENT AND TO MANY THE GUIDING FORCE BEHIND THE ELECTRIC UNICORNS.
WELL, IT'S A TRAGEDY, WHAT CAN I TELL YOU?
IT'S A SHAME, THIS SENSELESS VIOLENCE AND KILLING.
IT'S AGAINST EVERYTHING THE UNICORNS STOOD FOR.
YOU'VE BEEN CREDITED WITH HAVING BROUGHT THE UNICORNS TOGETHER...
WELL, THAT'S NOT EXACTLY TRUE. THEY WERE TOGETHER WHEN THEY CAME TO ME.
THEY WERE LIKE A DIAMOND... THEY JUST NEEDED A LITTLE POLISHING.
DIDN'T YOU FIRE ONE OF THE BAND MEMBERS?
NO, THAT'S NOT TRUE.
TOMMY SCHAEFFER WAS THE ORIGINAL BASS PLAYER WITH THE BAND BEFORE THEY BECAME THE ELECTRIC UNICORNS. JOE CLEARY TOOK HIS PLACE BEFORE THEY CUT THEIR FIRST ALBUM.
JOE WAS A CLASSIC.

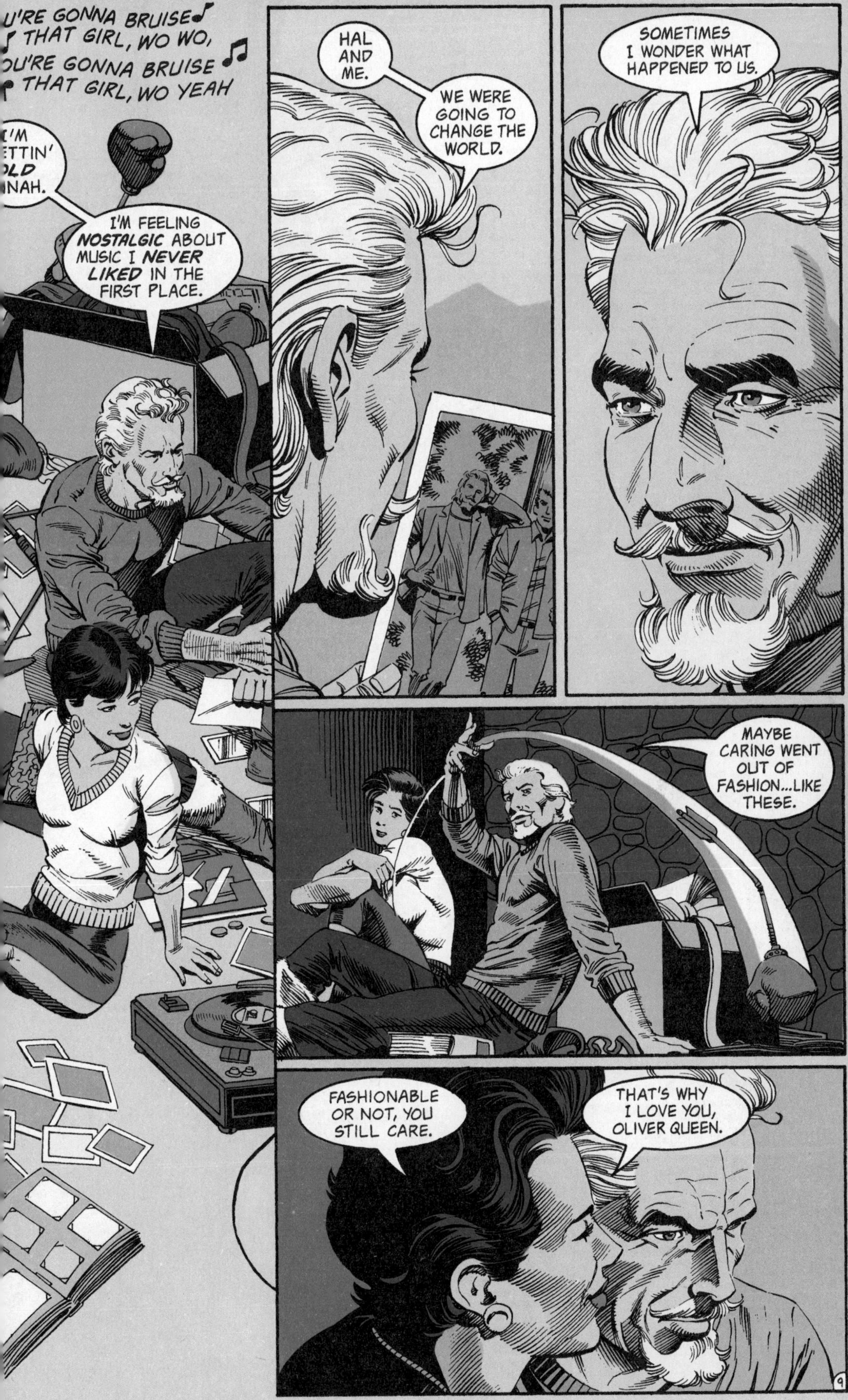
U'RE GONNA BRUISE THAT GIRL, WO WO, OU'RE GONNA BRUISE THAT GIRL, WO YEAH
I'M ETTIN' OLD NAH.
I'M FEELING NOSTALGIC ABOUT MUSIC I NEVER LIKED IN THE FIRST PLACE.
HAL AND ME.
WE WERE GOING TO CHANGE THE WORLD.
SOMETIMES I WONDER WHAT HAPPENED TO US.
MAYBE CARING WENT OUT OF FASHION...LIKE THESE.
FASHIONABLE OR NOT, YOU STILL CARE.
THAT'S WHY I LOVE YOU, OLIVER QUEEN.
9

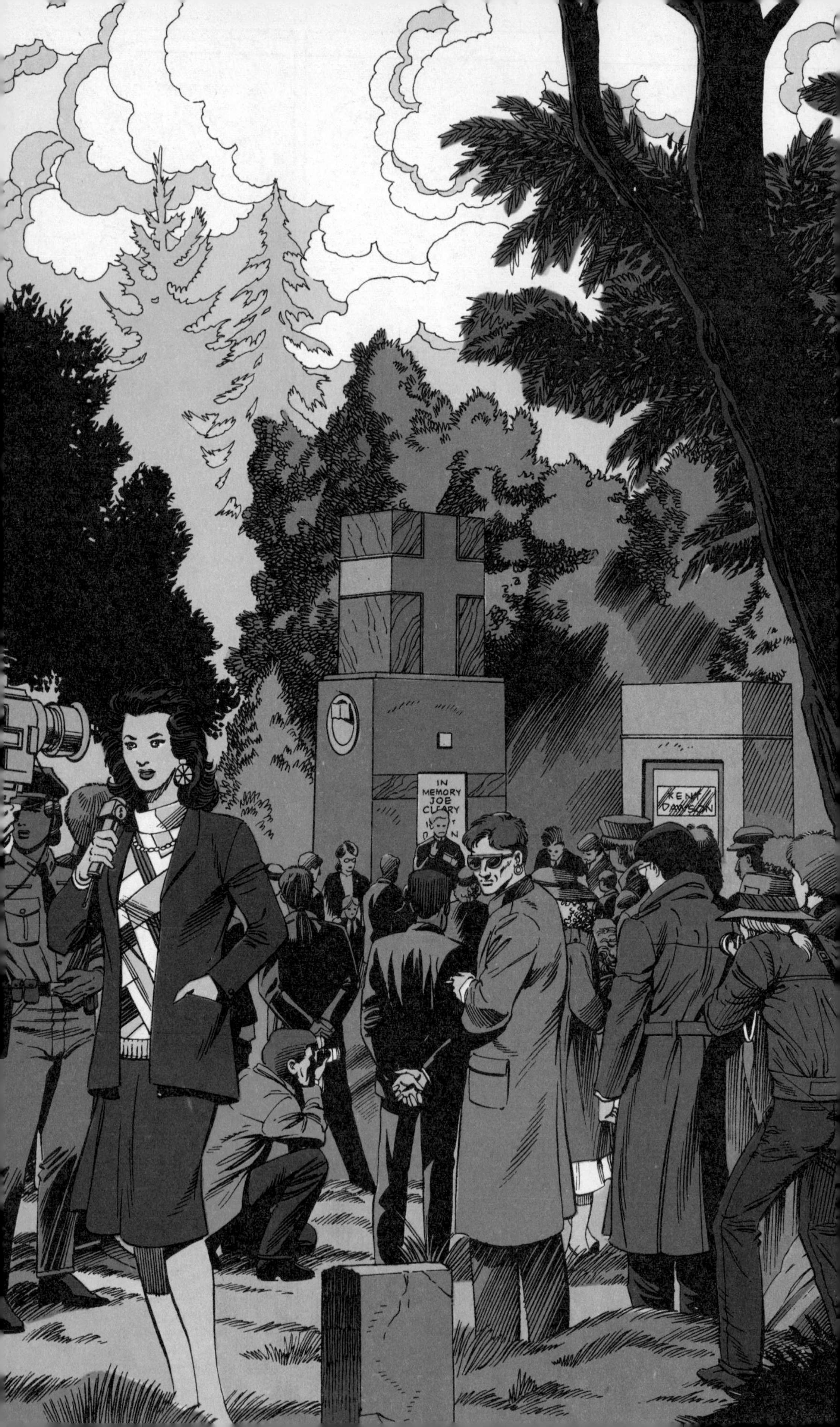
IN
MEMORY
JOE
CLEARY

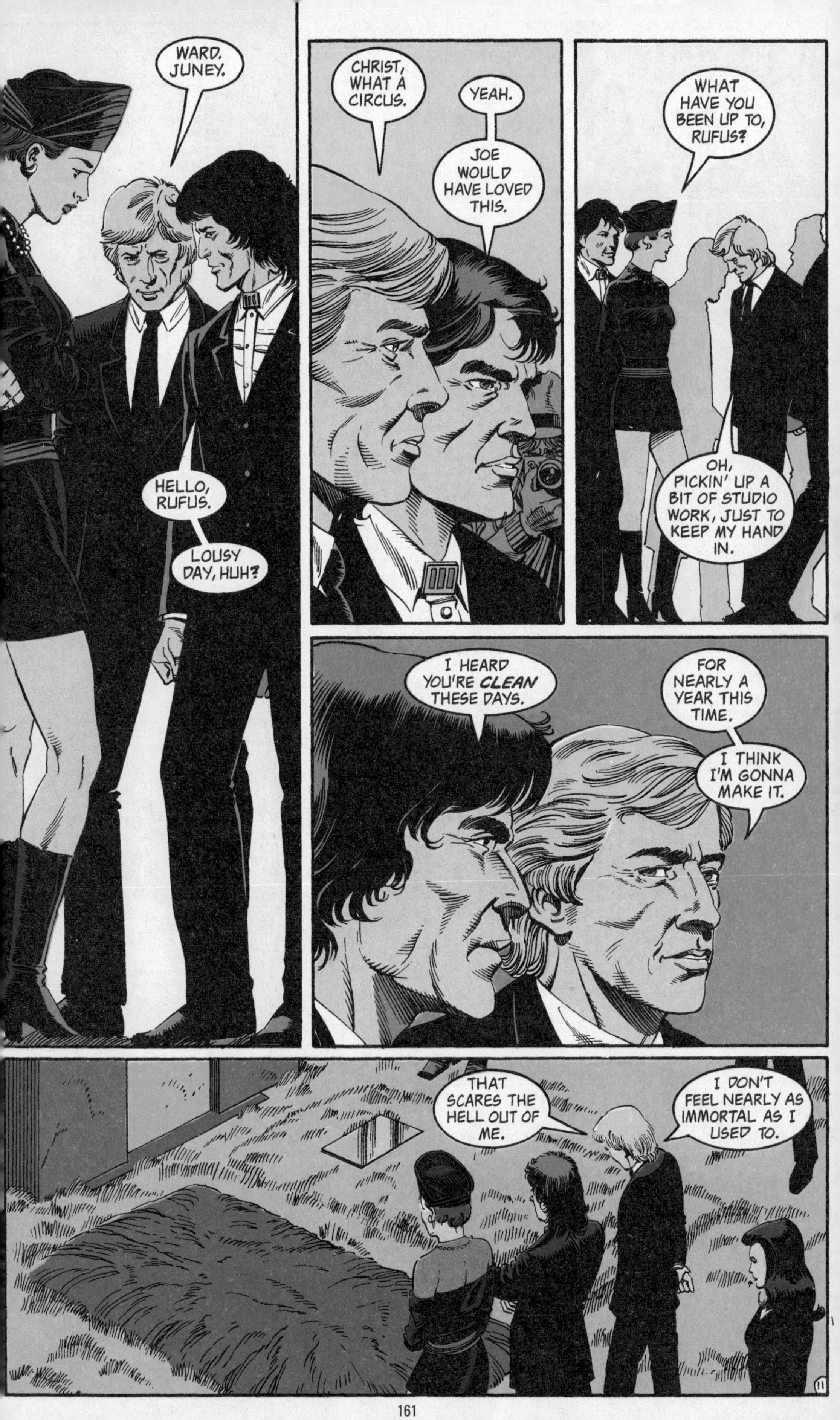
WARD. JUNEY.
HELLO, RUFUS.
LOUSY DAY, HUH?
CHRIST, WHAT A CIRCUS.
YEAH.
JOE WOULD HAVE LOVED THIS.
WHAT HAVE YOU BEEN UP TO, RUFUS?
OH, PICKIN' UP A BIT OF STUDIO WORK, JUST TO KEEP MY HAND IN.
I HEARD YOU'RE CLEAN THESE DAYS.
FOR NEARLY A YEAR THIS TIME.
I THINK I'M GONNA MAKE IT.
THAT SCARES THE HELL OUT OF ME.
I DON'T FEEL NEARLY AS IMMORTAL AS I USED TO.
11

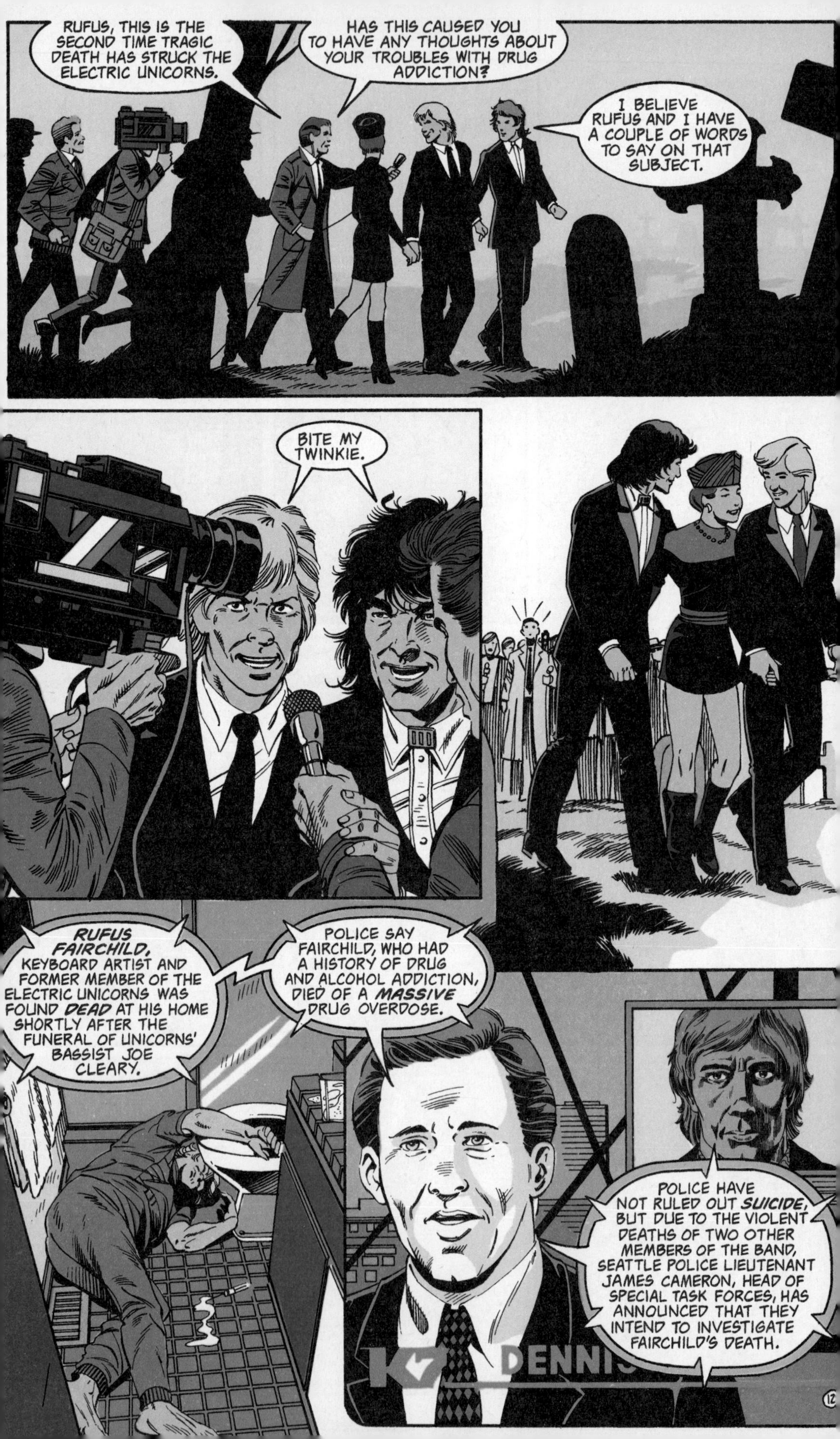
RUFUS, THIS IS THE SECOND TIME TRAGIC DEATH HAS STRUCK THE ELECTRIC UNICORNS.
HAS THIS CAUSED YOU TO HAVE ANY THOUGHTS ABOUT YOUR TROUBLES WITH DRUG ADDICTION?
I BELIEVE RUFUS AND I HAVE A COUPLE OF WORDS TO SAY ON THAT SUBJECT.
BITE MY TWINKIE.
RUFUS FAIRCHILD, KEYBOARD ARTIST AND FORMER MEMBER OF THE ELECTRIC UNICORNS WAS FOUND DEAD AT HIS HOME SHORTLY AFTER THE FUNERAL OF UNICORNS' BASSIST JOE CLEARY.
POLICE SAY FAIRCHILD, WHO HAD A HISTORY OF DRUG AND ALCOHOL ADDICTION, DIED OF A MASSIVE DRUG OVERDOSE.
POLICE HAVE NOT RULED OUT SUICIDE, BUT DUE TO THE VIOLENT DEATHS OF TWO OTHER MEMBERS OF THE BAND, SEATTLE POLICE LIEUTENANT JAMES CAMERON, HEAD OF SPECIAL TASK FORCES, HAS ANNOUNCED THAT THEY INTEND TO INVESTIGATE FAIRCHILD'S DEATH.
K7 DENNIS

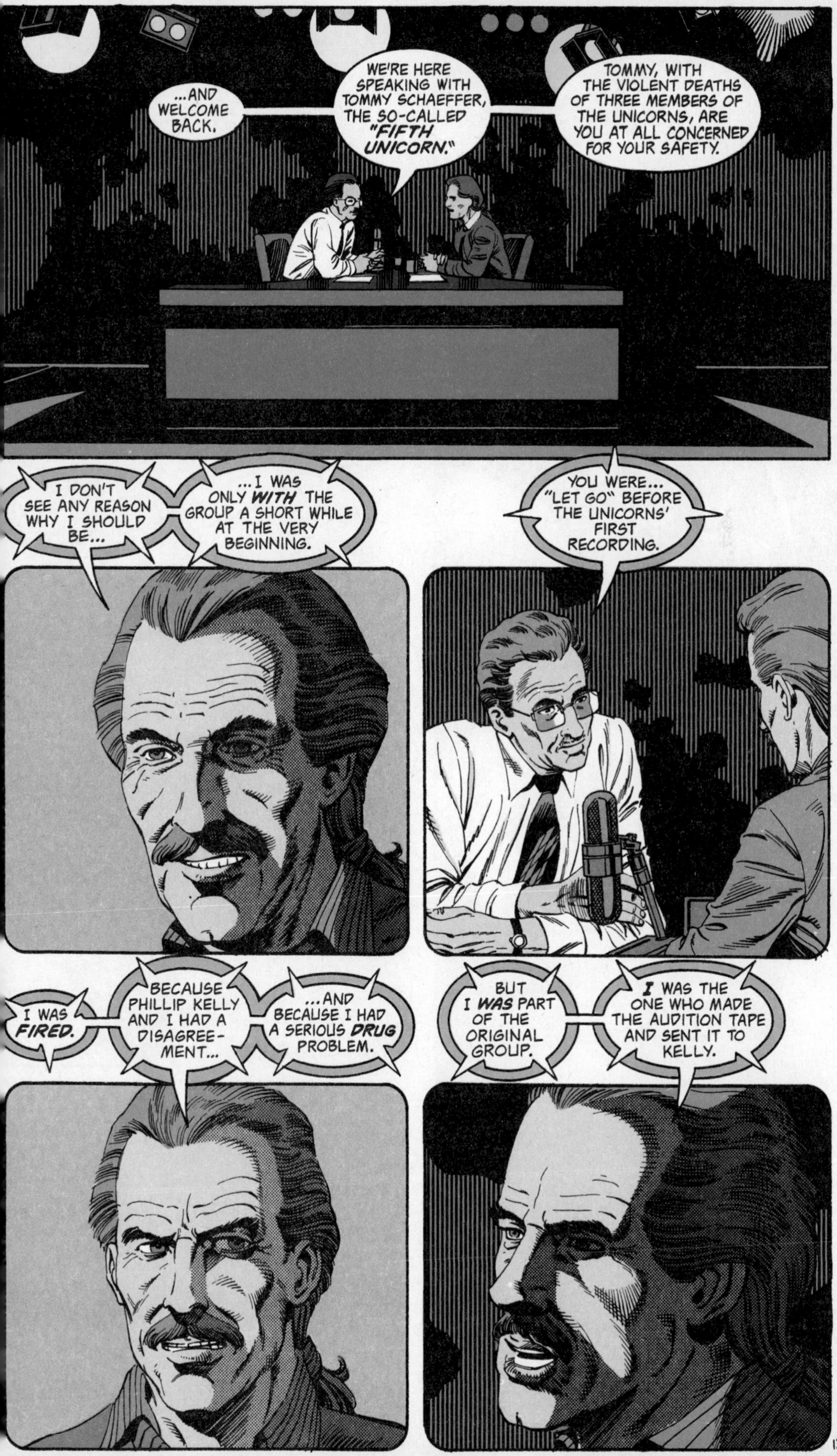
...AND WELCOME BACK.
WE'RE HERE SPEAKING WITH TOMMY SCHAEFFER, THE SO-CALLED "FIFTH UNICORN."
TOMMY, WITH THE VIOLENT DEATHS OF THREE MEMBERS OF THE UNICORNS, ARE YOU AT ALL CONCERNED FOR YOUR SAFETY.
I DON'T SEE ANY REASON WHY I SHOULD BE...
...I WAS ONLY WITH THE GROUP A SHORT WHILE AT THE VERY BEGINNING.
YOU WERE... "LET GO" BEFORE THE UNICORNS' FIRST RECORDING.
I WAS FIRED.
BECAUSE PHILLIP KELLY AND I HAD A DISAGREE-MENT...
...AND BECAUSE I HAD A SERIOUS DRUG PROBLEM.
BUT I WAS PART OF THE ORIGINAL GROUP.
I WAS THE ONE WHO MADE THE AUDITION TAPE AND SENT IT TO KELLY.

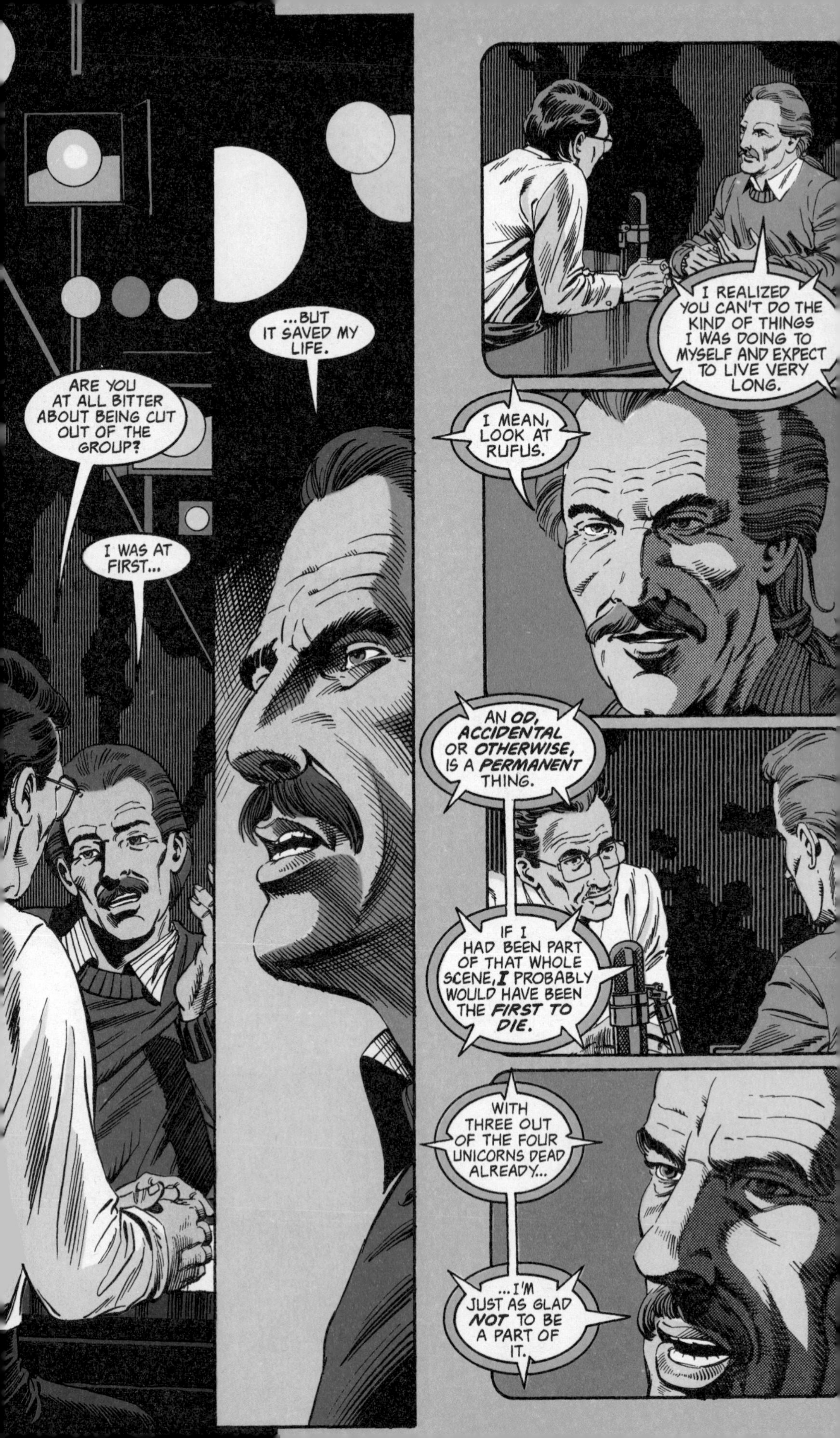
ARE YOU AT ALL BITTER ABOUT BEING CUT OUT OF THE GROUP?
I WAS AT FIRST...
...BUT IT SAVED MY LIFE.
I REALIZED YOU CAN'T DO THE KIND OF THINGS I WAS DOING TO MYSELF AND EXPECT TO LIVE VERY LONG.
I MEAN, LOOK AT RUFUS.
AN *OD*, *ACCIDENTAL* OR *OTHERWISE*, IS A *PERMANENT* THING.
IF I HAD BEEN PART OF THAT WHOLE SCENE, *I* PROBABLY WOULD HAVE BEEN THE *FIRST TO DIE*.
WITH THREE OUT OF THE FOUR UNICORNS DEAD ALREADY...
...I'M JUST AS GLAD *NOT* TO BE A PART OF IT.

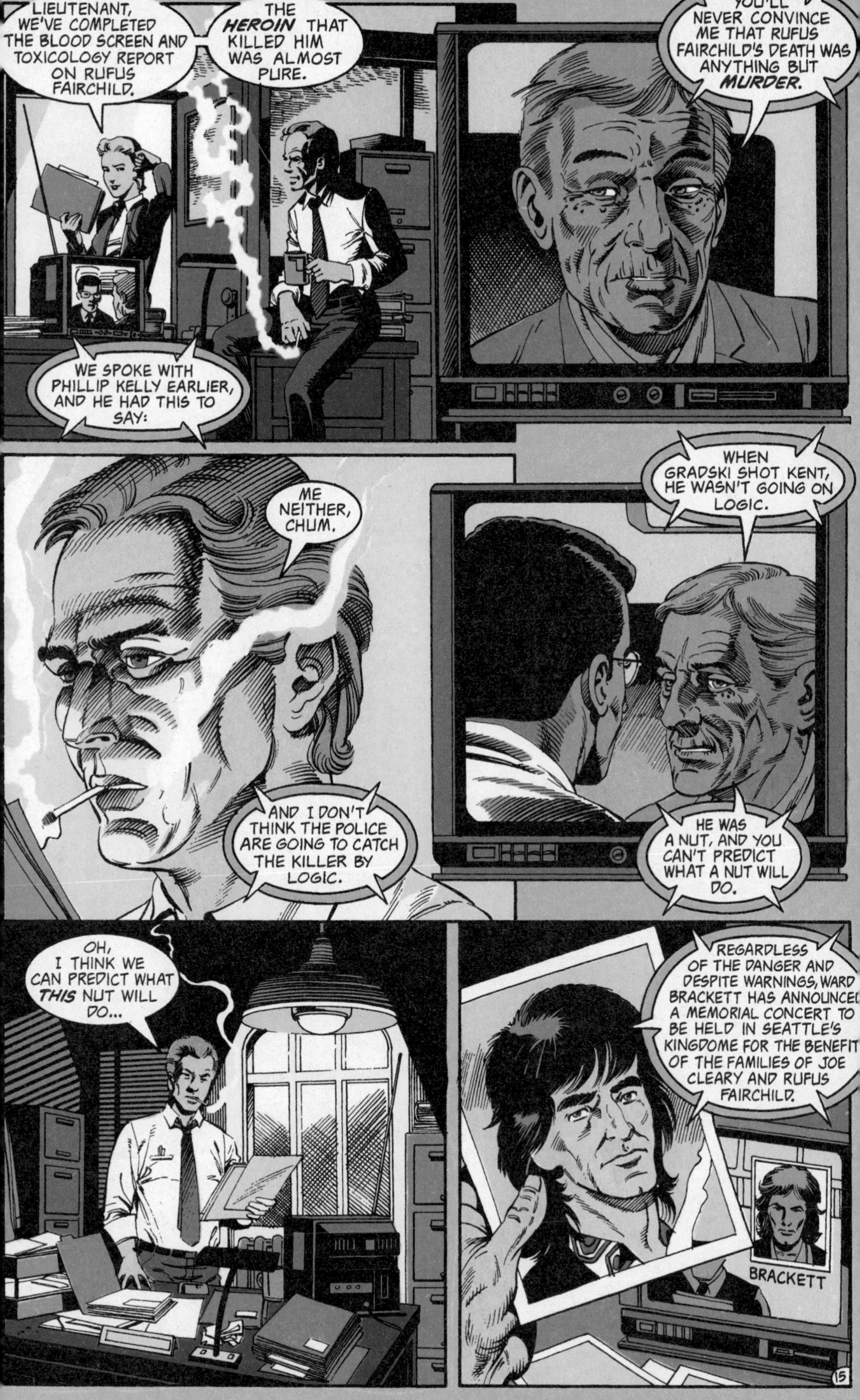

LIEUTENANT, WE'VE COMPLETED THE BLOOD SCREEN AND TOXICOLOGY REPORT ON RUFUS FAIRCHILD.
THE HEROIN THAT KILLED HIM WAS ALMOST PURE.
WE SPOKE WITH PHILLIP KELLY EARLIER, AND HE HAD THIS TO SAY:
YOU'LL NEVER CONVINCE ME THAT RUFUS FAIRCHILD'S DEATH WAS ANYTHING BUT MURDER.
ME NEITHER, CHUM.
AND I DON'T THINK THE POLICE ARE GOING TO CATCH THE KILLER BY LOGIC.
WHEN GRADSKI SHOT KENT, HE WASN'T GOING ON LOGIC.
HE WAS A NUT, AND YOU CAN'T PREDICT WHAT A NUT WILL DO.
OH, I THINK WE CAN PREDICT WHAT THIS NUT WILL DO...
REGARDLESS OF THE DANGER AND DESPITE WARNINGS, WARD BRACKETT HAS ANNOUNCED A MEMORIAL CONCERT TO BE HELD IN SEATTLE'S KINGDOME FOR THE BENEFIT OF THE FAMILIES OF JOE CLEARY AND RUFUS FAIRCHILD.
BRACKETT

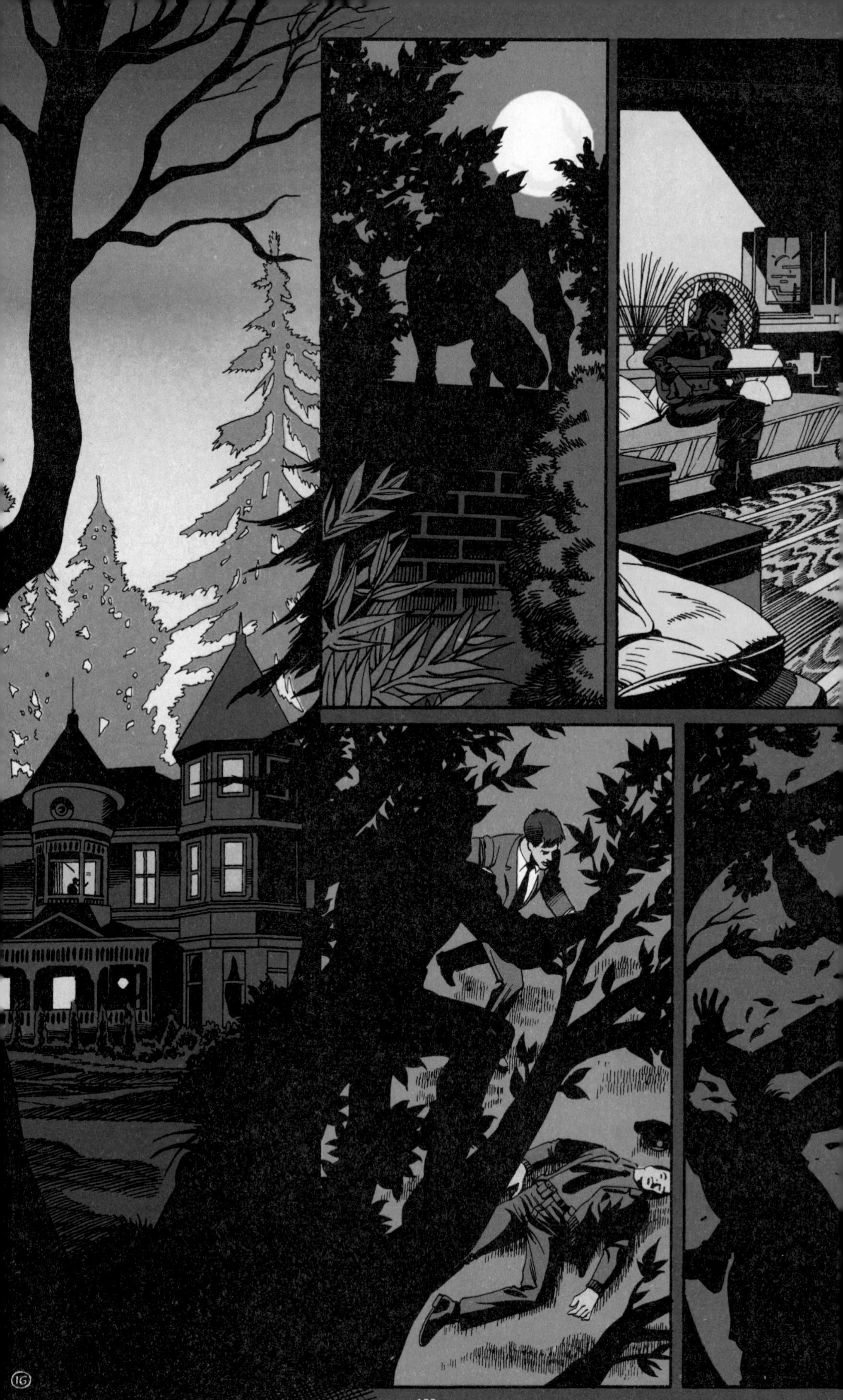
16

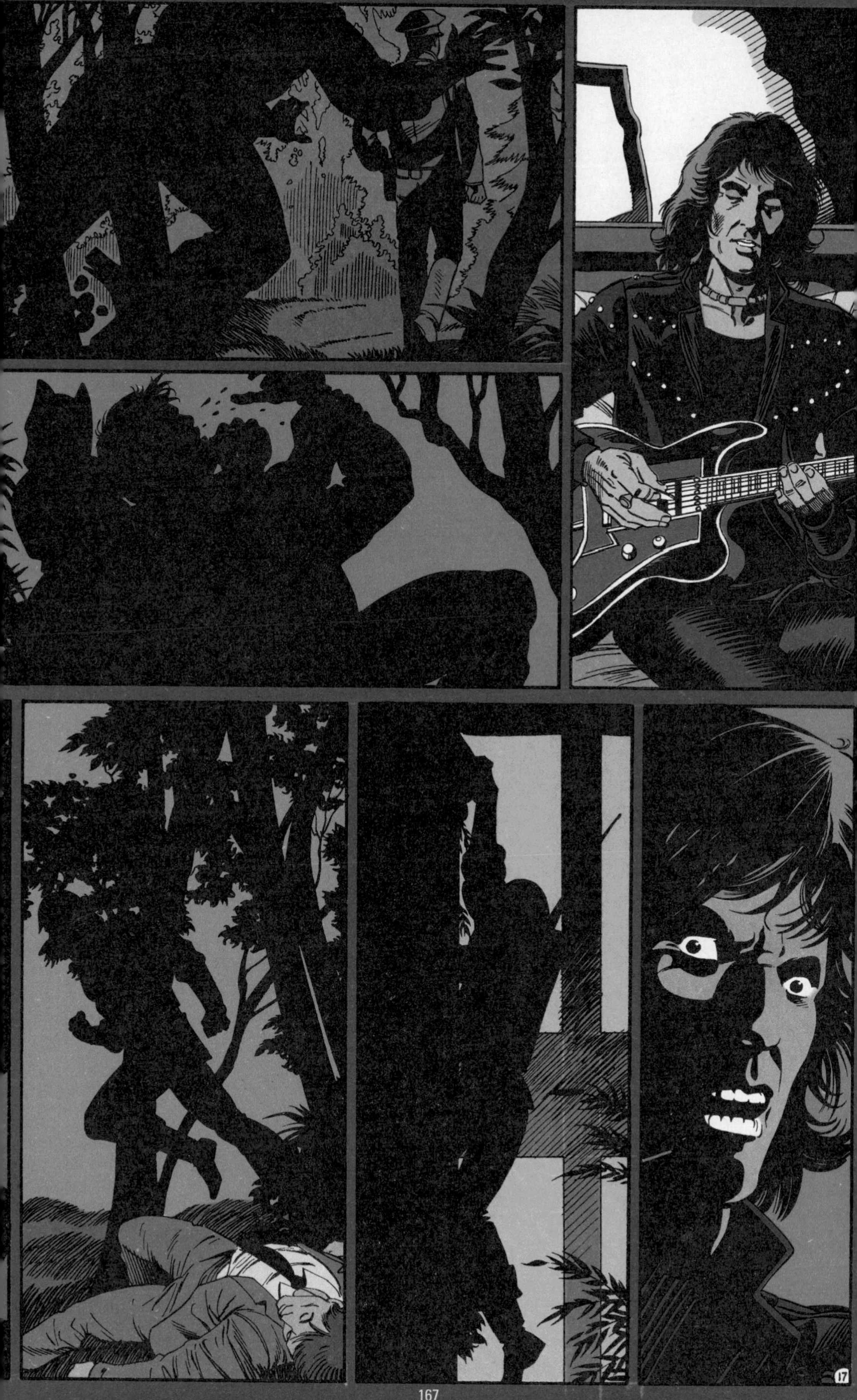

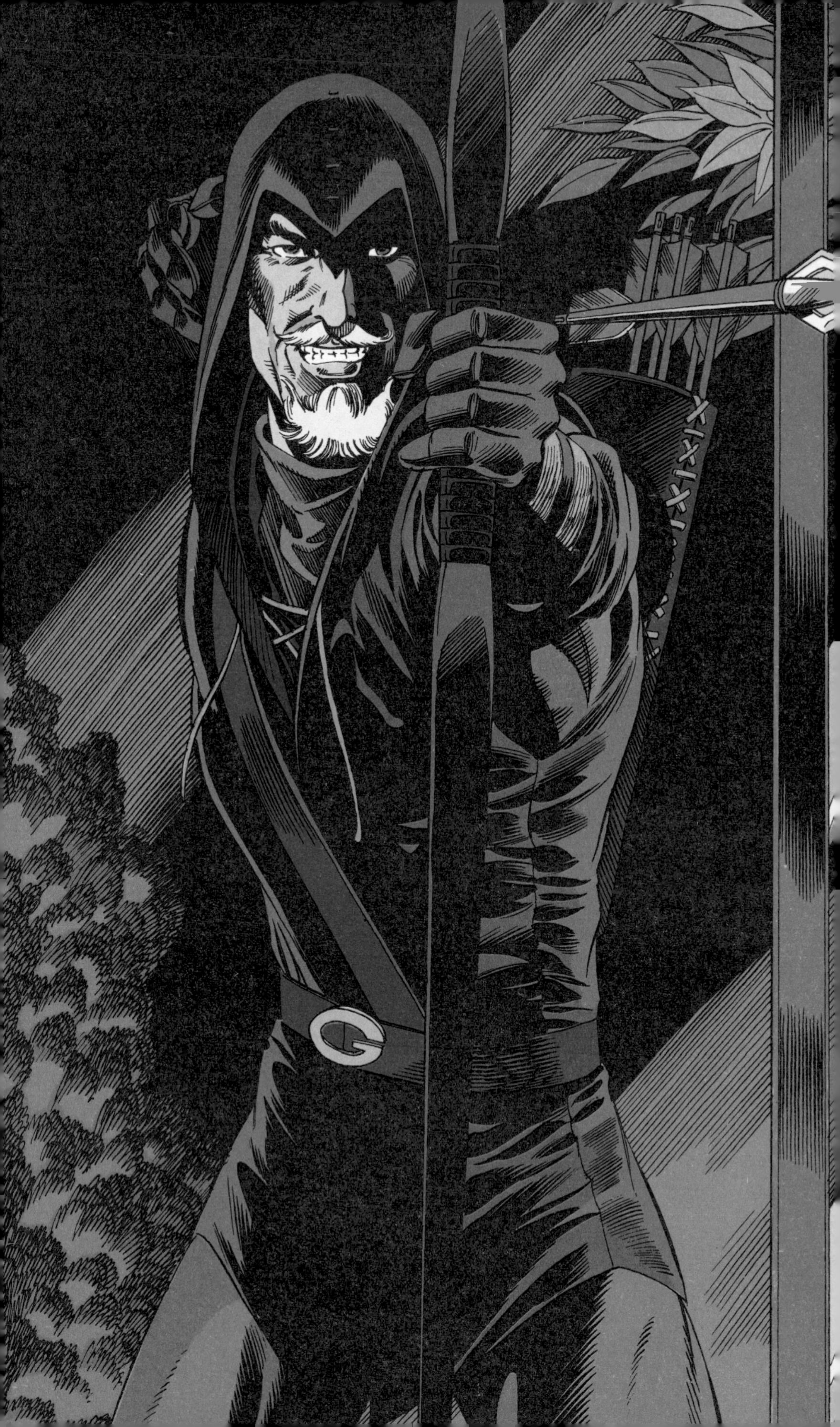

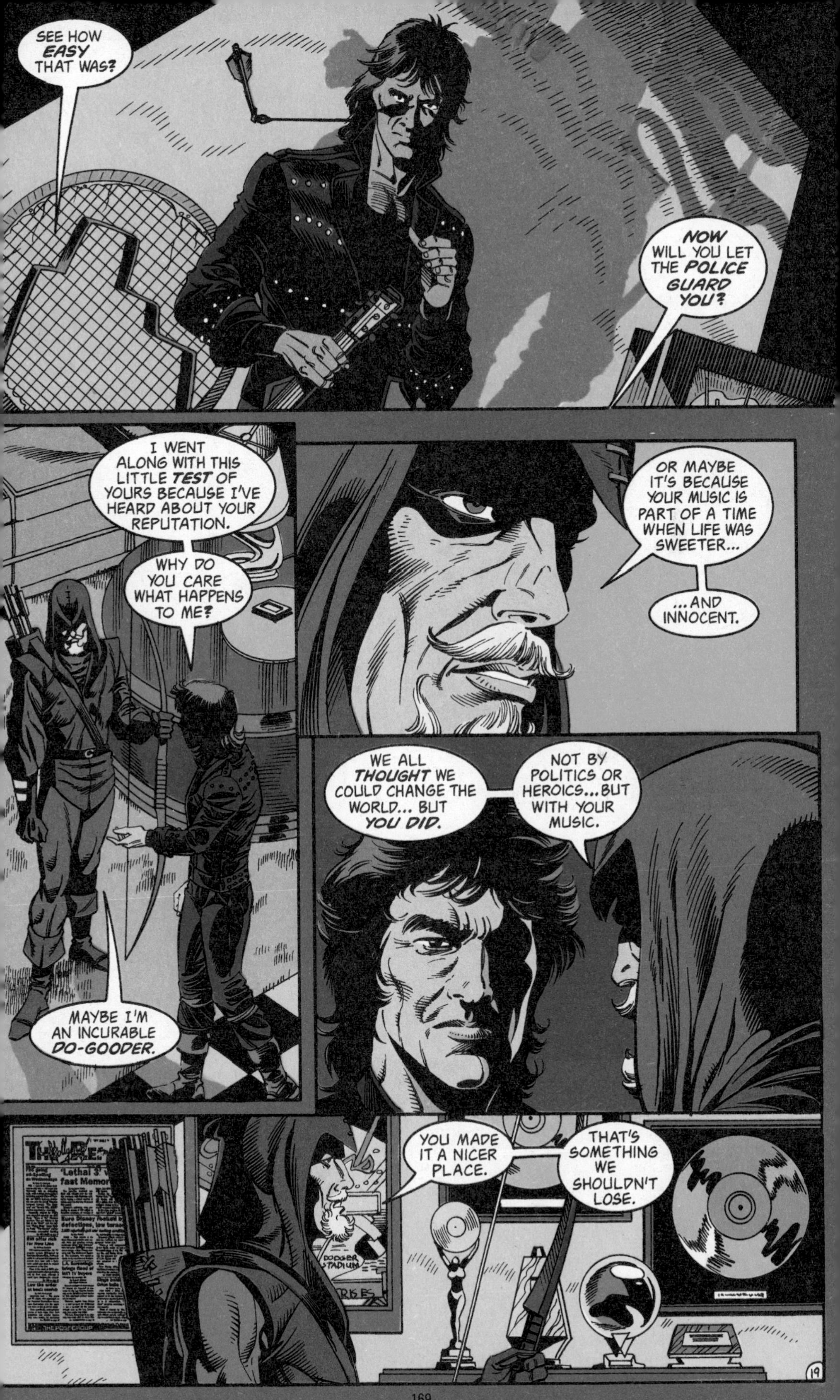
SEE HOW EASY THAT WAS?
NOW WILL YOU LET THE POLICE GUARD YOU?
I WENT ALONG WITH THIS LITTLE TEST OF YOURS BECAUSE I'VE HEARD ABOUT YOUR REPUTATION.
WHY DO YOU CARE WHAT HAPPENS TO ME?
MAYBE I'M AN INCURABLE DO-GOODER.
OR MAYBE IT'S BECAUSE YOUR MUSIC IS PART OF A TIME WHEN LIFE WAS SWEETER...
...AND INNOCENT.
WE ALL THOUGHT WE COULD CHANGE THE WORLD... BUT YOU DID.
NOT BY POLITICS OR HEROICS... BUT WITH YOUR MUSIC.
'Lethal 3'
fast Memor
DODGER STADIUM
YOU MADE IT A NICER PLACE.
THAT'S SOMETHING WE SHOULDN'T LOSE.
19

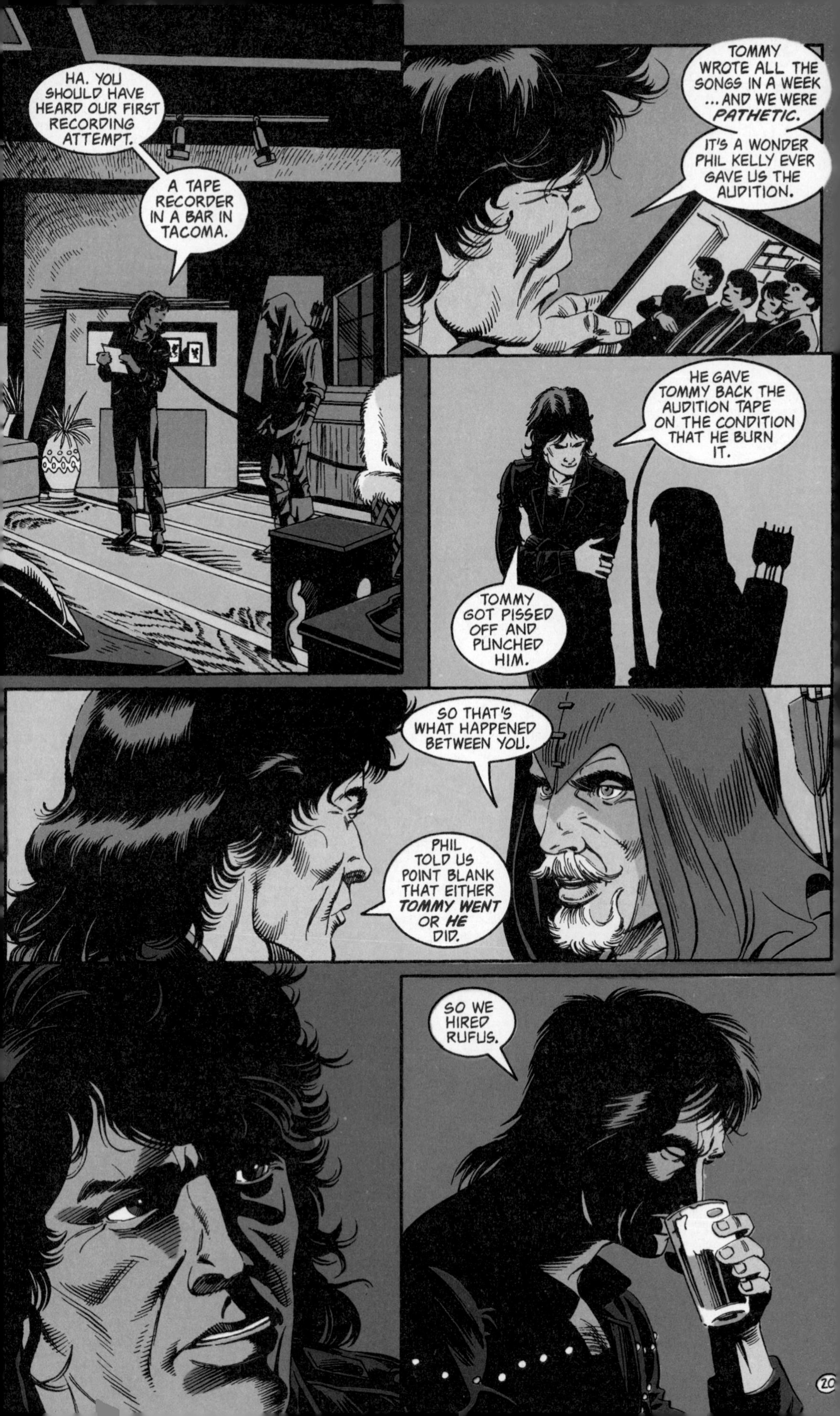
HA. YOU SHOULD HAVE HEARD OUR FIRST RECORDING ATTEMPT.
A TAPE RECORDER IN A BAR IN TACOMA.
TOMMY WROTE ALL THE SONGS IN A WEEK ...AND WE WERE PATHETIC.
IT'S A WONDER PHIL KELLY EVER GAVE US THE AUDITION.
HE GAVE TOMMY BACK THE AUDITION TAPE ON THE CONDITION THAT HE BURN IT.
TOMMY GOT PISSED OFF AND PUNCHED HIM.
SO THAT'S WHAT HAPPENED BETWEEN YOU.
PHIL TOLD US POINT BLANK THAT EITHER TOMMY WENT OR HE DID.
SO WE HIRED RUFUS.
20

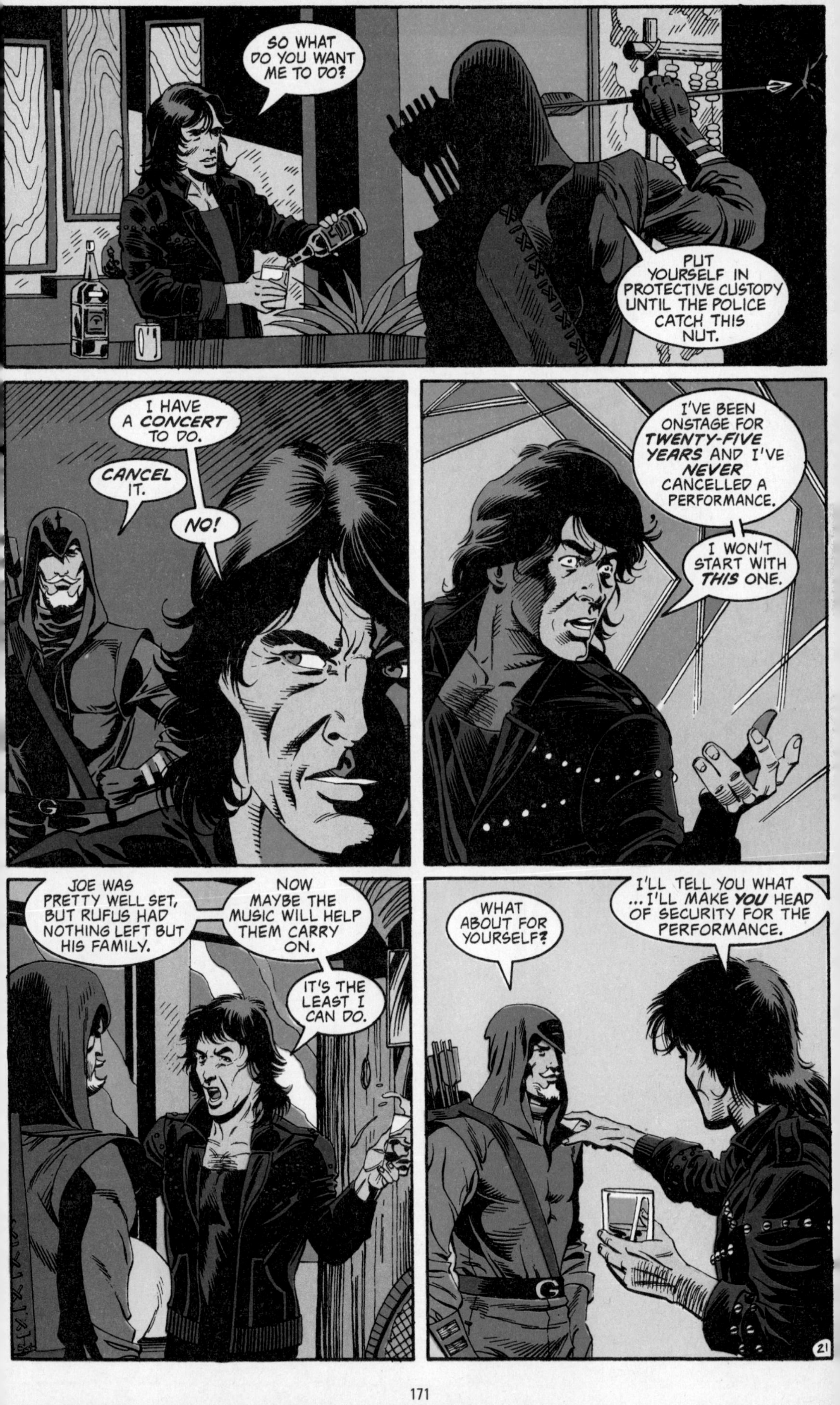
SO WHAT DO YOU WANT ME TO DO?
PUT YOURSELF IN PROTECTIVE CUSTODY UNTIL THE POLICE CATCH THIS NUT.
I HAVE A CONCERT TO DO.
CANCEL IT.
NO!
I'VE BEEN ONSTAGE FOR TWENTY-FIVE YEARS AND I'VE NEVER CANCELLED A PERFORMANCE.
I WON'T START WITH THIS ONE.
JOE WAS PRETTY WELL SET, BUT RUFUS HAD NOTHING LEFT BUT HIS FAMILY.
NOW MAYBE THE MUSIC WILL HELP THEM CARRY ON.
IT'S THE LEAST I CAN DO.
WHAT ABOUT FOR YOURSELF?
I'LL TELL YOU WHAT ...I'LL MAKE YOU HEAD OF SECURITY FOR THE PERFORMANCE.
21

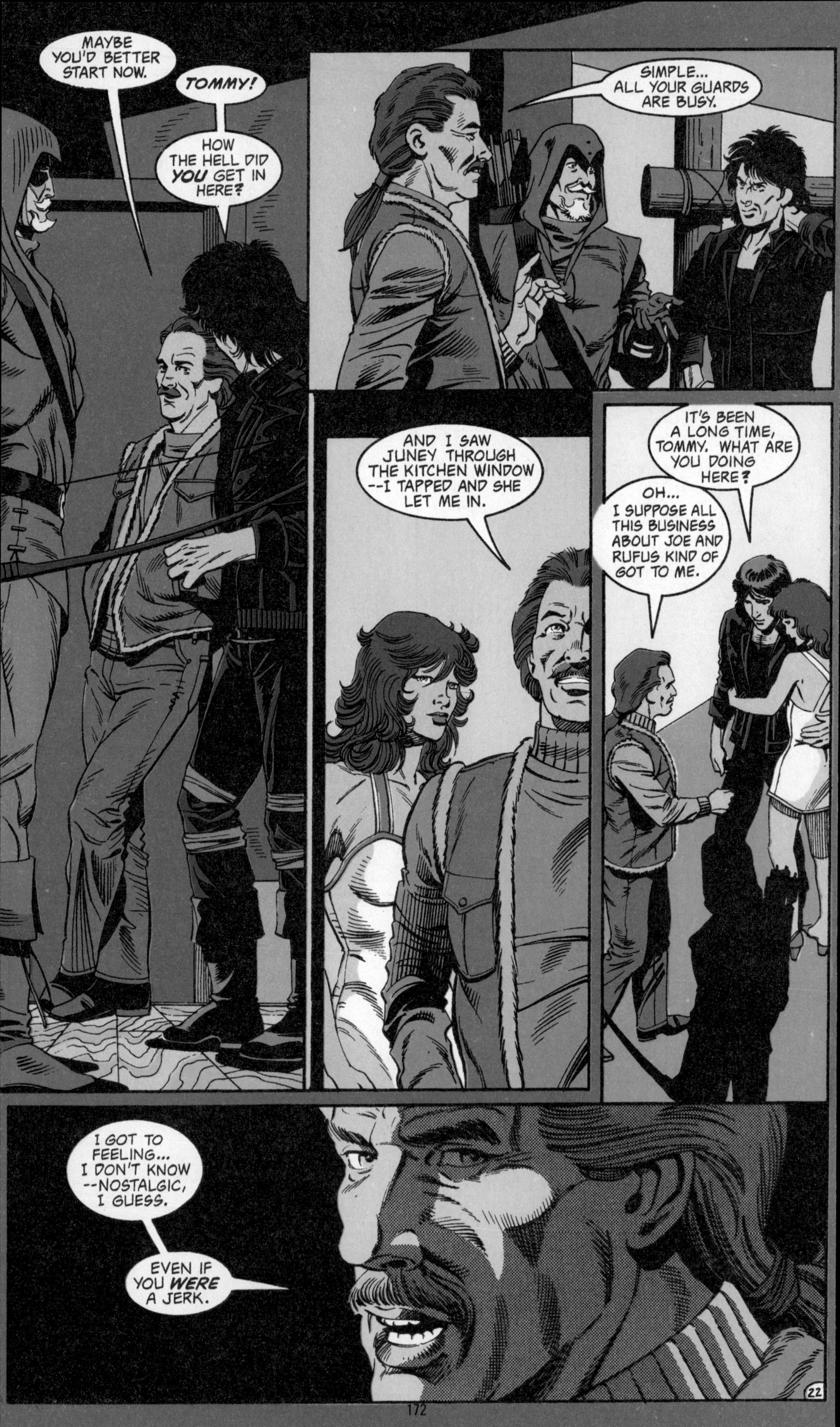
MAYBE YOU'D BETTER START NOW.
TOMMY!
HOW THE HELL DID YOU GET IN HERE?
SIMPLE... ALL YOUR GUARDS ARE BUSY.
AND I SAW JUNEY THROUGH THE KITCHEN WINDOW --I TAPPED AND SHE LET ME IN.
IT'S BEEN A LONG TIME, TOMMY. WHAT ARE YOU DOING HERE?
OH... I SUPPOSE ALL THIS BUSINESS ABOUT JOE AND RUFUS KIND OF GOT TO ME.
I GOT TO FEELING... I DON'T KNOW --NOSTALGIC, I GUESS.
EVEN IF YOU WERE A JERK.
22

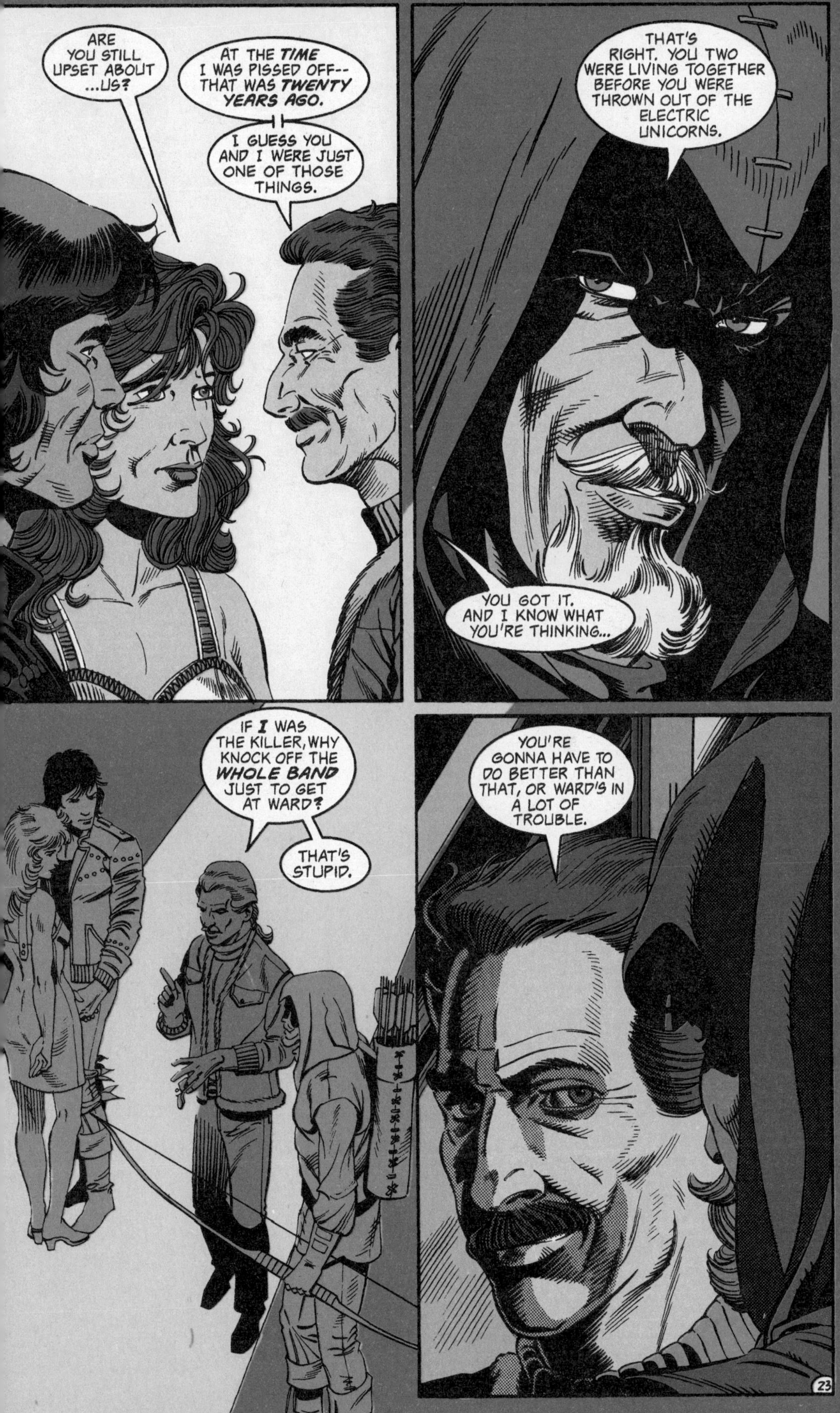
ARE YOU STILL UPSET ABOUT ...US?
AT THE TIME I WAS PISSED OFF-- THAT WAS TWENTY YEARS AGO.
I GUESS YOU AND I WERE JUST ONE OF THOSE THINGS.
THAT'S RIGHT. YOU TWO WERE LIVING TOGETHER BEFORE YOU WERE THROWN OUT OF THE ELECTRIC UNICORNS.
YOU GOT IT. AND I KNOW WHAT YOU'RE THINKING...
IF I WAS THE KILLER, WHY KNOCK OFF THE WHOLE BAND JUST TO GET AT WARD?
THAT'S STUPID.
YOU'RE GONNA HAVE TO DO BETTER THAN THAT, OR WARD'S IN A LOT OF TROUBLE.
23

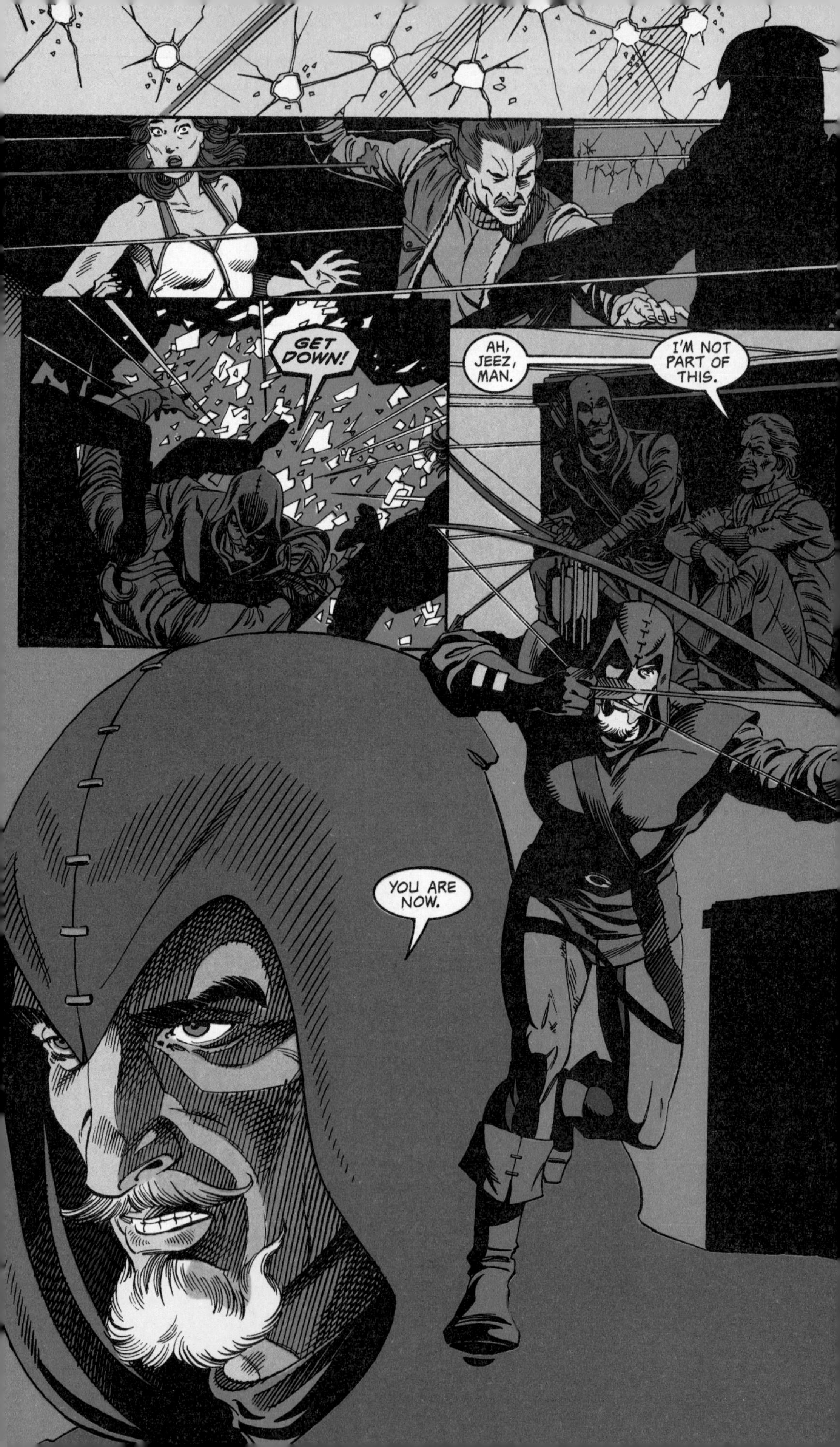
GET DOWN!
AH, JEEZ, MAN.
I'M NOT PART OF THIS.
YOU ARE NOW.

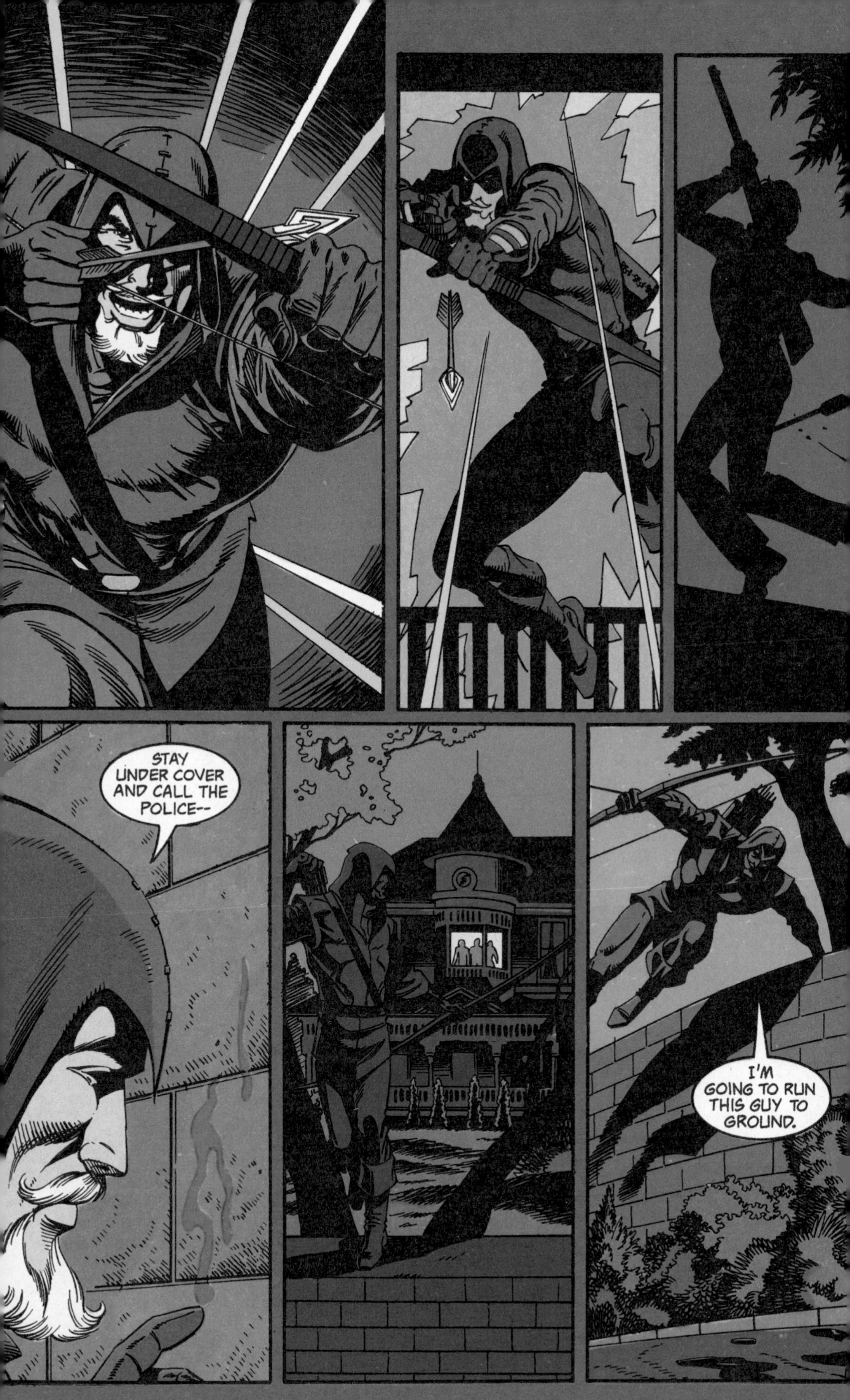
STAY UNDER COVER AND CALL THE POLICE--
I'M GOING TO RUN THIS GUY TO GROUND.

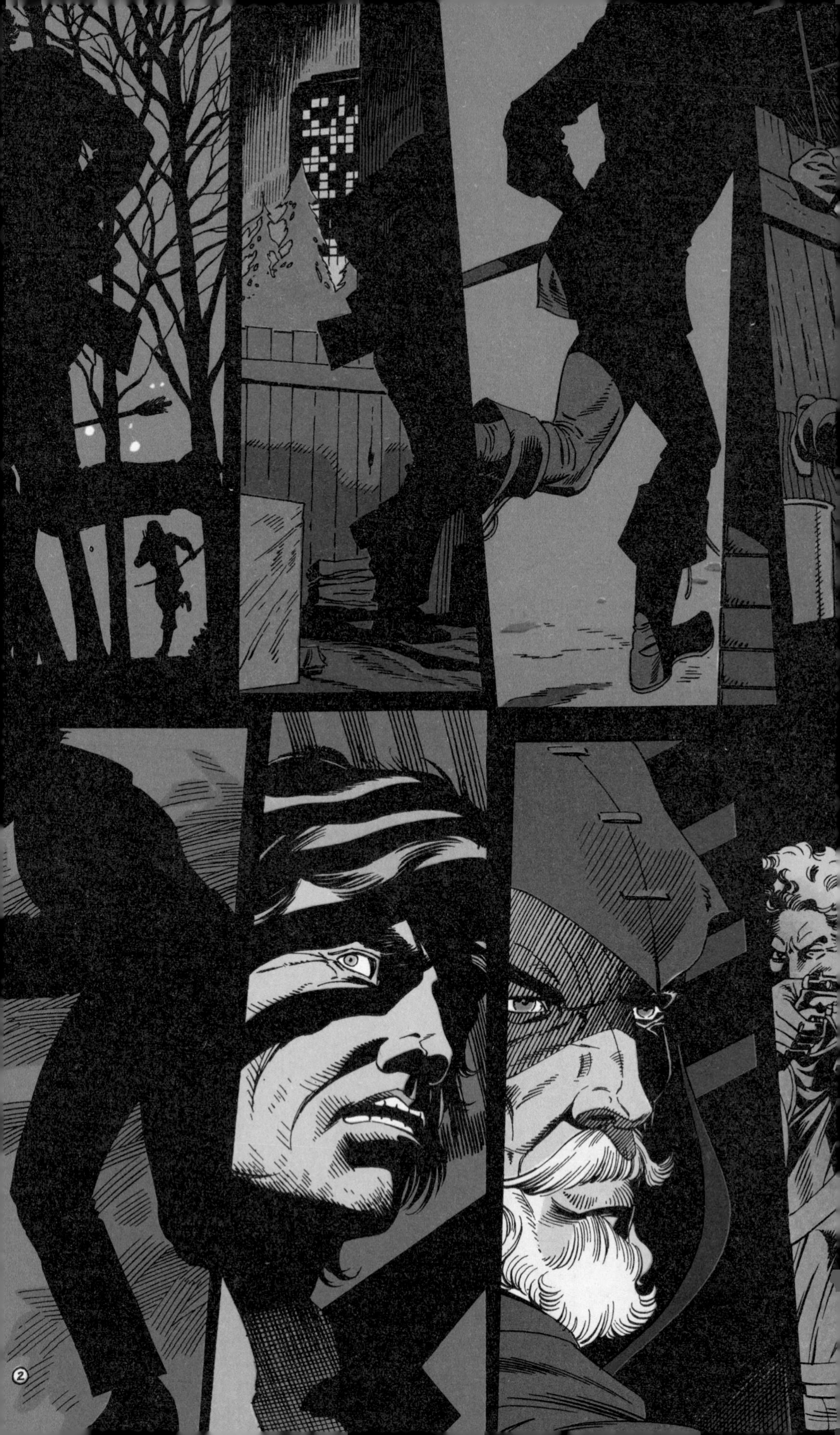

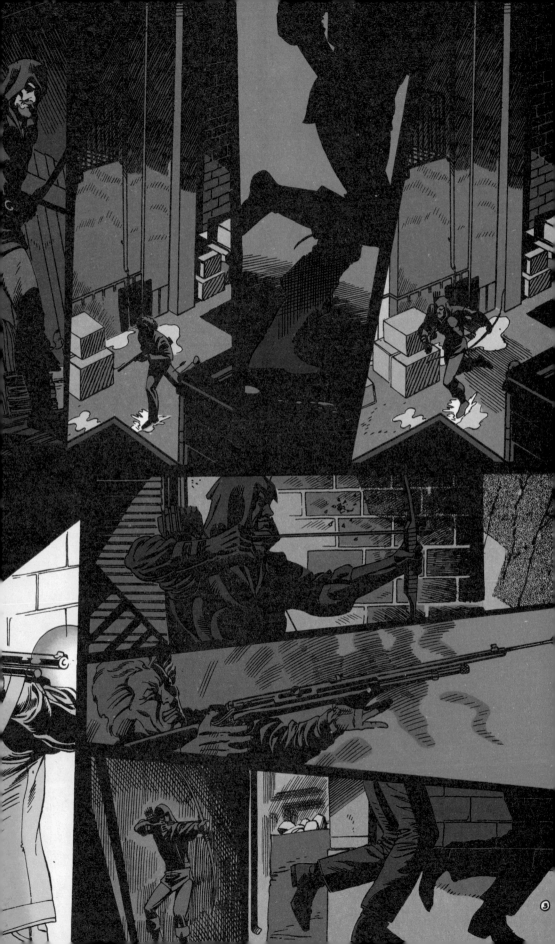

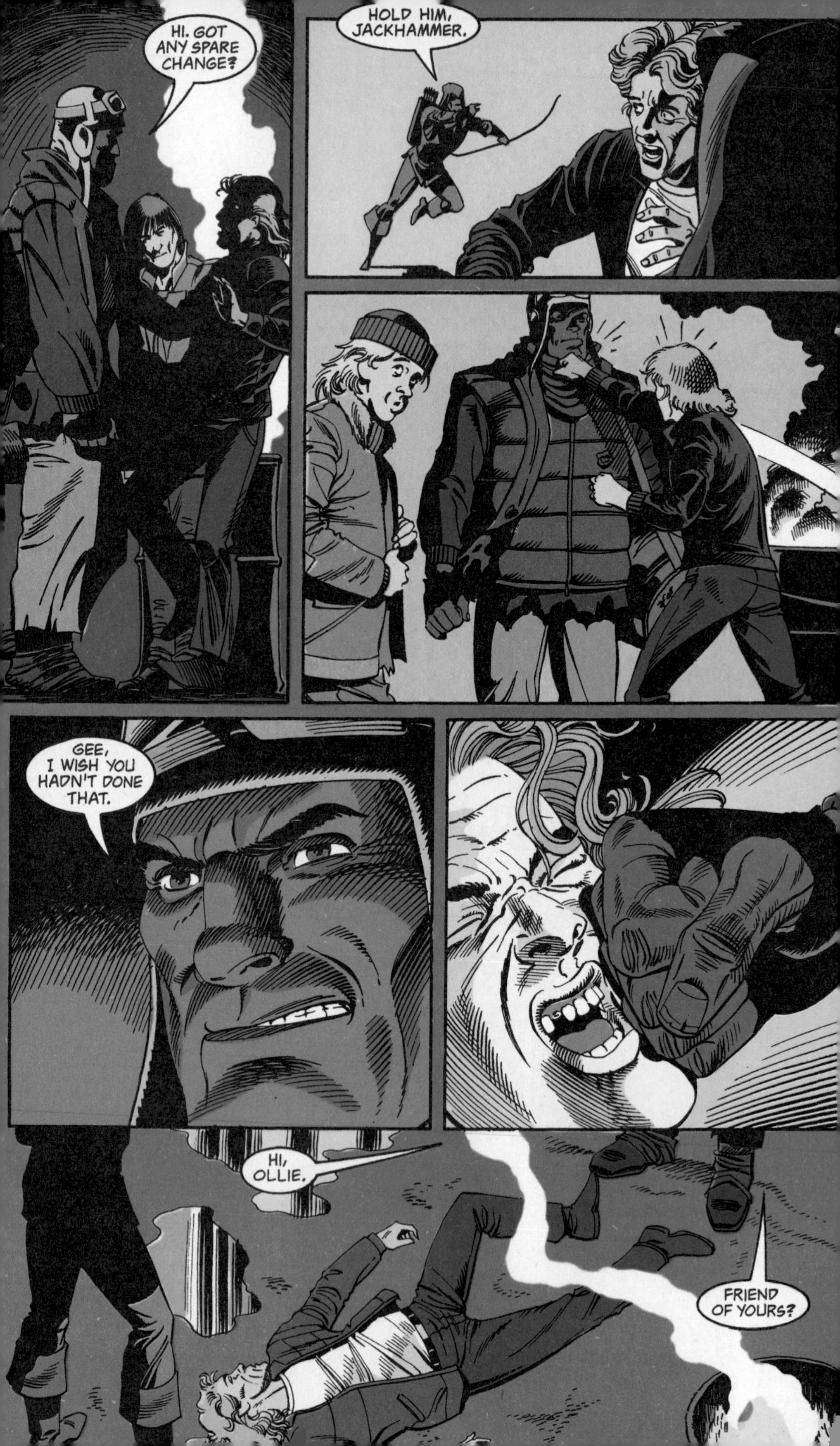
HI. GOT ANY SPARE CHANGE?
HOLD HIM, JACKHAMMER.
GEE, I WISH YOU HADN'T DONE THAT.
HI, OLLIE.
FRIEND OF YOURS?

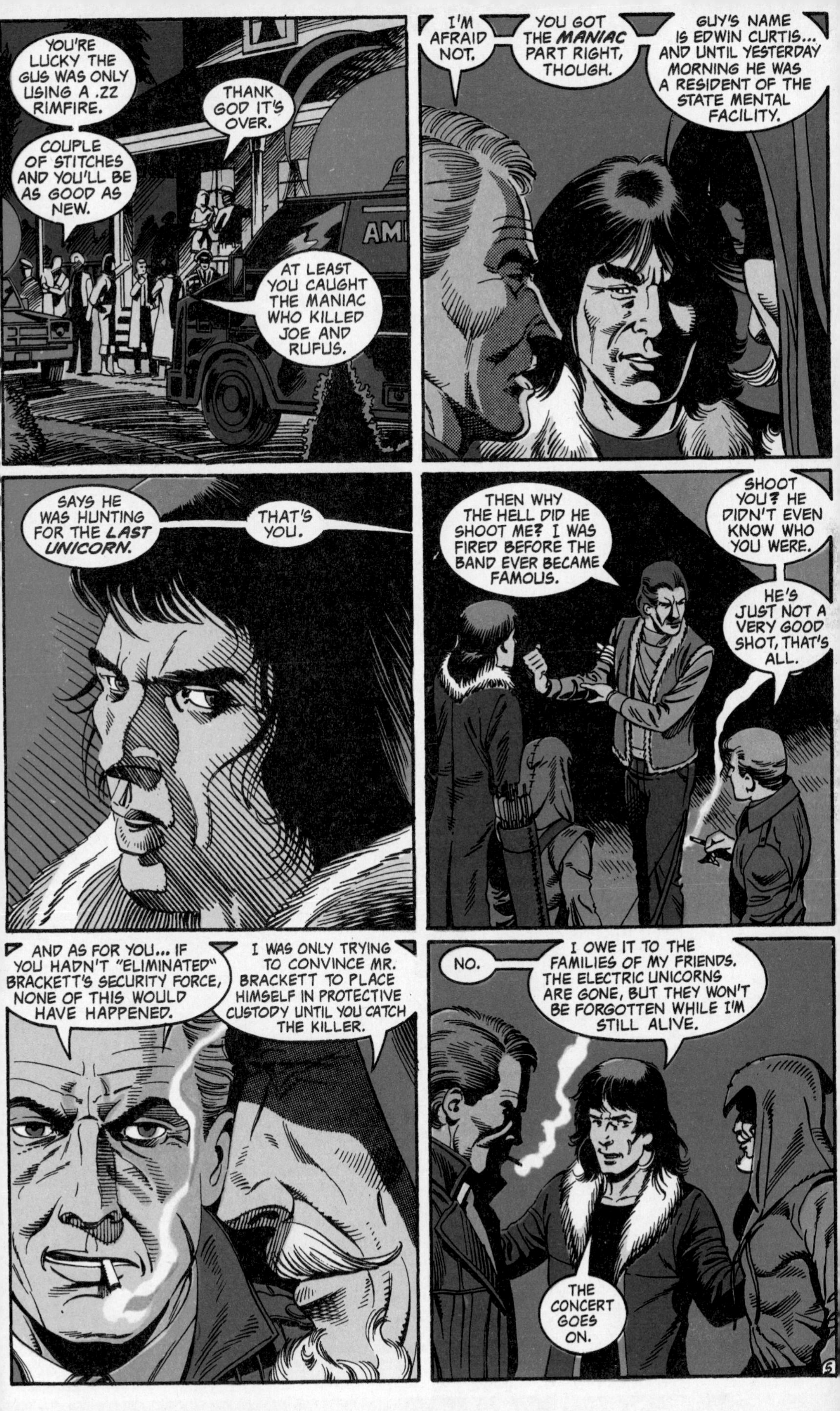
YOU'RE LUCKY THE GUS WAS ONLY USING A .22 RIMFIRE.
COUPLE OF STITCHES AND YOU'LL BE AS GOOD AS NEW.
THANK GOD IT'S OVER.
AMB
AT LEAST YOU CAUGHT THE MANIAC WHO KILLED JOE AND RUFUS.
I'M AFRAID NOT.
YOU GOT THE MANIAC PART RIGHT, THOUGH.
GUY'S NAME IS EDWIN CURTIS... AND UNTIL YESTERDAY MORNING HE WAS A RESIDENT OF THE STATE MENTAL FACILITY.
SAYS HE WAS HUNTING FOR THE LAST UNICORN.
THAT'S YOU.
THEN WHY THE HELL DID HE SHOOT ME? I WAS FIRED BEFORE THE BAND EVER BECAME FAMOUS.
SHOOT YOU? HE DIDN'T EVEN KNOW WHO YOU WERE.
HE'S JUST NOT A VERY GOOD SHOT, THAT'S ALL.
AND AS FOR YOU... IF YOU HADN'T "ELIMINATED" BRACKETT'S SECURITY FORCE, NONE OF THIS WOULD HAVE HAPPENED.
I WAS ONLY TRYING TO CONVINCE MR. BRACKETT TO PLACE HIMSELF IN PROTECTIVE CUSTODY UNTIL YOU CATCH THE KILLER.
NO.
I OWE IT TO THE FAMILIES OF MY FRIENDS. THE ELECTRIC UNICORNS ARE GONE, BUT THEY WON'T BE FORGOTTEN WHILE I'M STILL ALIVE.
THE CONCERT GOES ON.
5

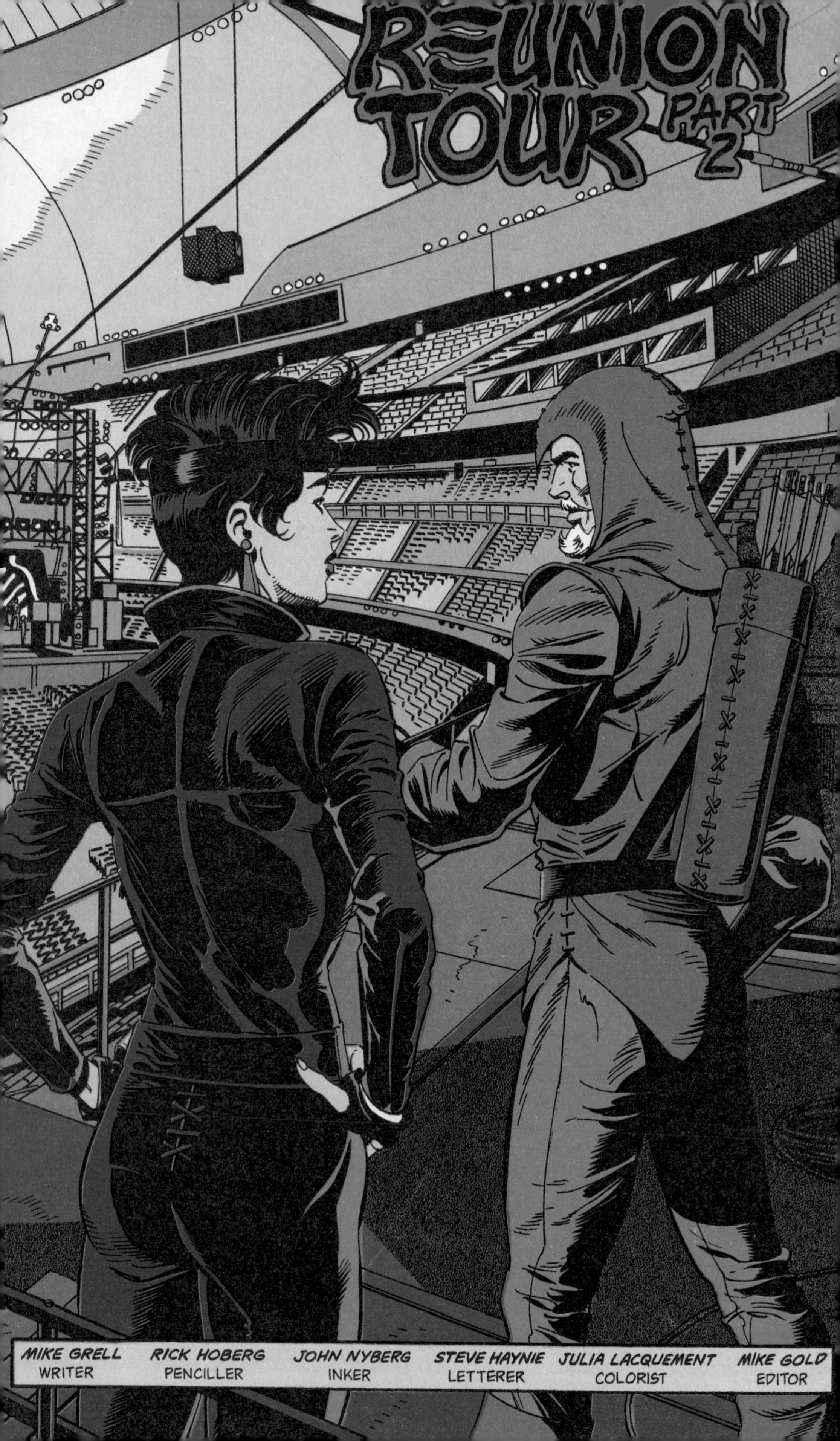
REUNION TOUR PART 2
MIKE GRELL WRITER
RICK HOBERG PENCILLER
JOHN NYBERG INKER
STEVE HAYNIE LETTERER
JULIA LACQUEMENT COLORIST
MIKE GOLD EDITOR

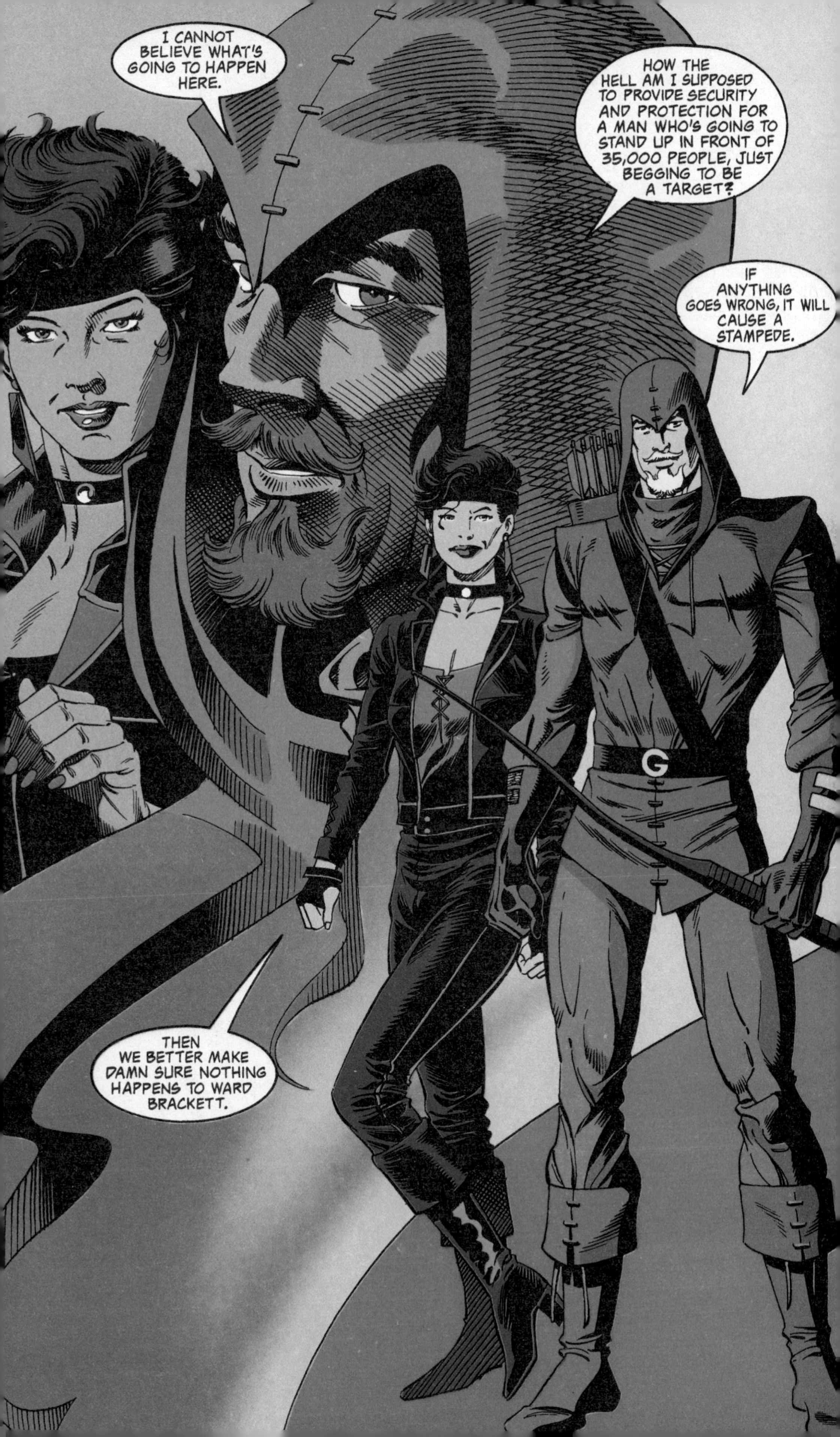
I CANNOT BELIEVE WHAT'S GOING TO HAPPEN HERE.
HOW THE HELL AM I SUPPOSED TO PROVIDE SECURITY AND PROTECTION FOR A MAN WHO'S GOING TO STAND UP IN FRONT OF 35,000 PEOPLE, JUST BEGGING TO BE A TARGET?
IF ANYTHING GOES WRONG, IT WILL CAUSE A STAMPEDE.
THEN WE BETTER MAKE DAMN SURE NOTHING HAPPENS TO WARD BRACKETT.

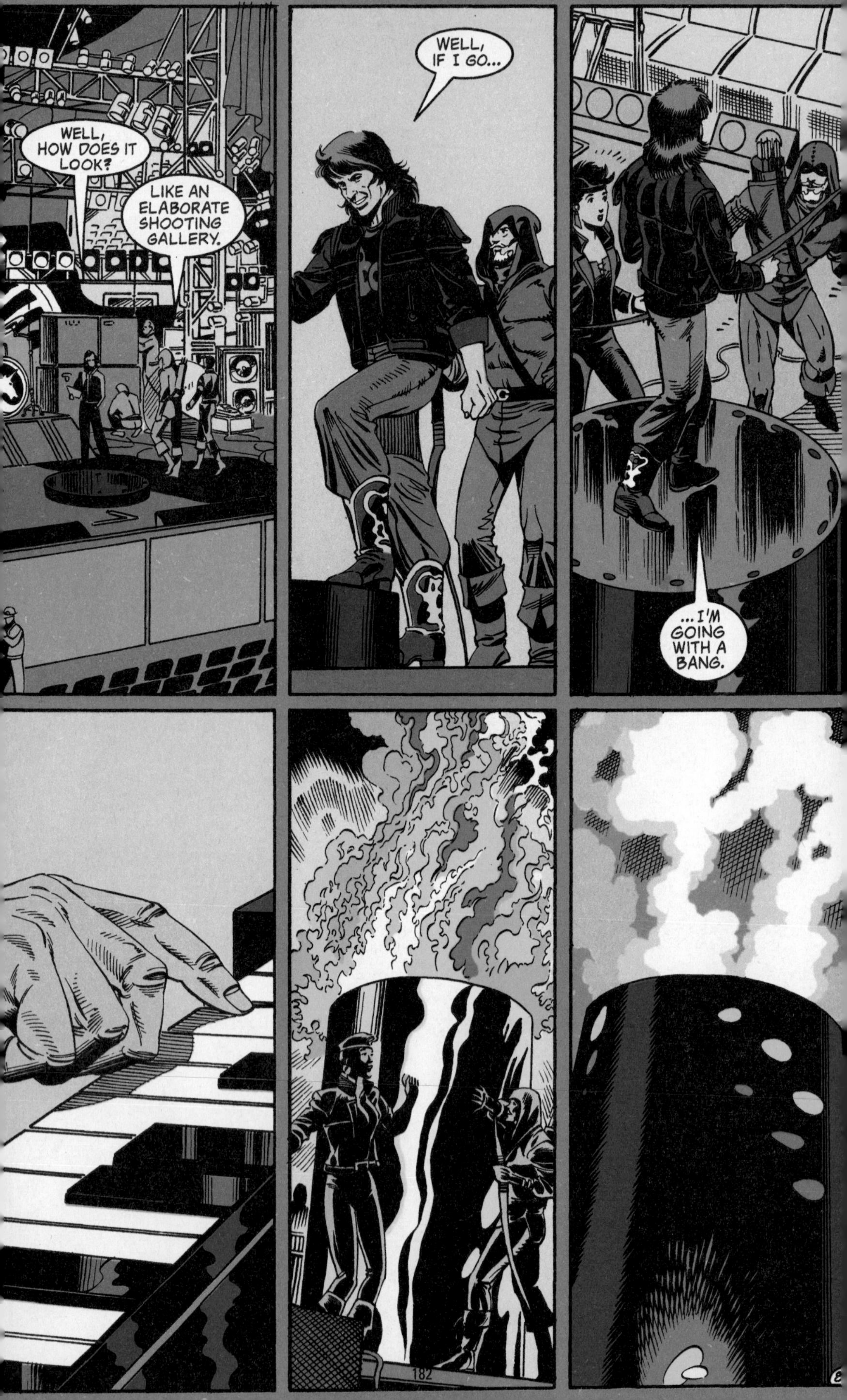
WELL, HOW DOES IT LOOK?
LIKE AN ELABORATE SHOOTING GALLERY.
WELL, IF I GO...
...I'M GOING WITH A BANG.

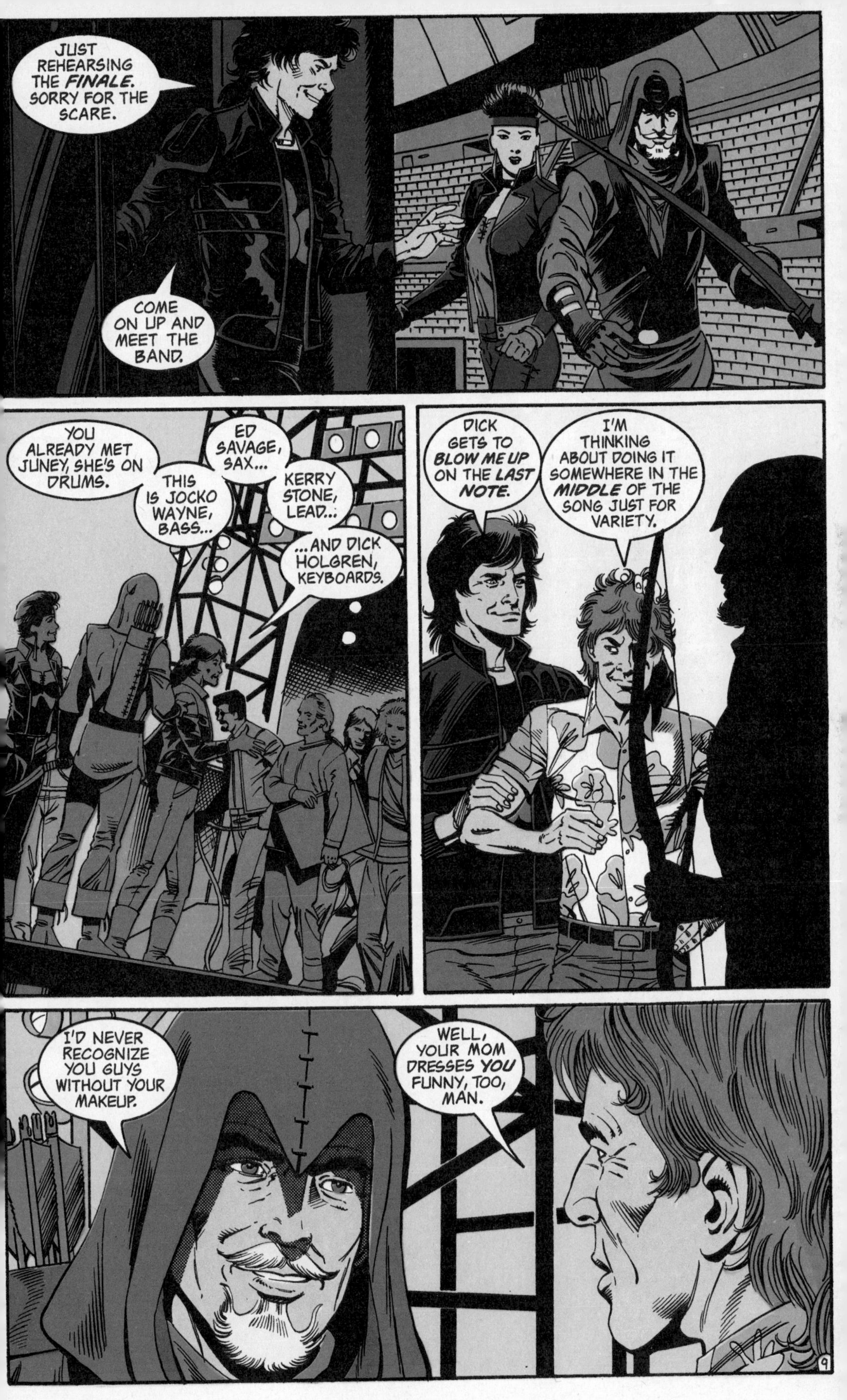
JUST REHEARSING THE *FINALE*. SORRY FOR THE SCARE.
COME ON UP AND MEET THE BAND.
YOU ALREADY MET JUNEY, SHE'S ON DRUMS.
THIS IS JOCKO WAYNE, BASS...
ED SAVAGE, SAX...
KERRY STONE, LEAD...
...AND DICK HOLGREN, KEYBOARDS.
DICK GETS TO *BLOW ME UP* ON THE *LAST NOTE*.
I'M THINKING ABOUT DOING IT SOMEWHERE IN THE *MIDDLE* OF THE SONG JUST FOR VARIETY.
I'D NEVER RECOGNIZE YOU GUYS WITHOUT YOUR MAKEUP.
WELL, YOUR MOM DRESSES *YOU* FUNNY, TOO, MAN.
9

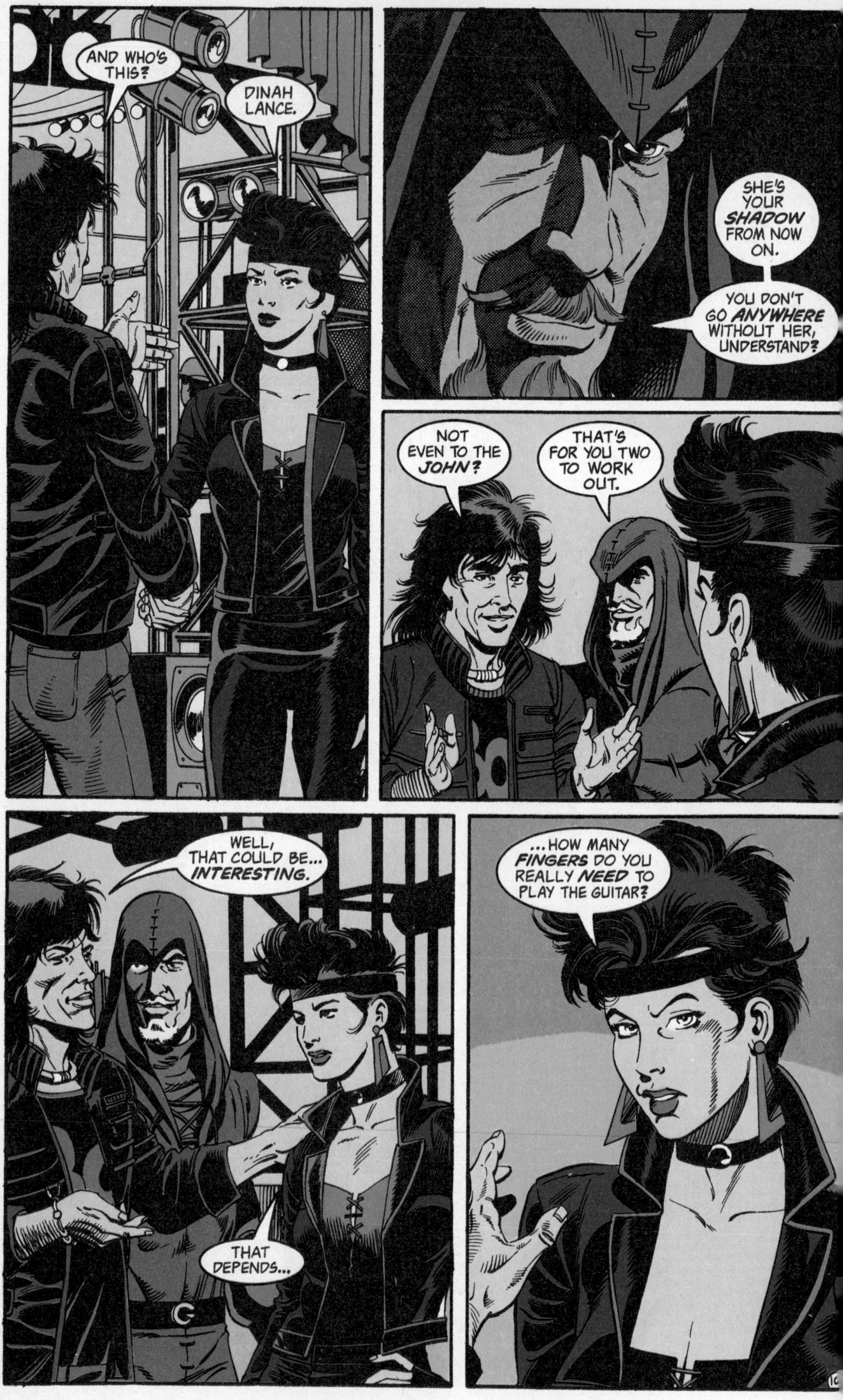
AND WHO'S THIS?
DINAH LANCE.
SHE'S YOUR SHADOW FROM NOW ON.
YOU DON'T GO ANYWHERE WITHOUT HER, UNDERSTAND?
NOT EVEN TO THE JOHN?
THAT'S FOR YOU TWO TO WORK OUT.
WELL, THAT COULD BE... INTERESTING.
THAT DEPENDS...
...HOW MANY FINGERS DO YOU REALLY NEED TO PLAY THE GUITAR?

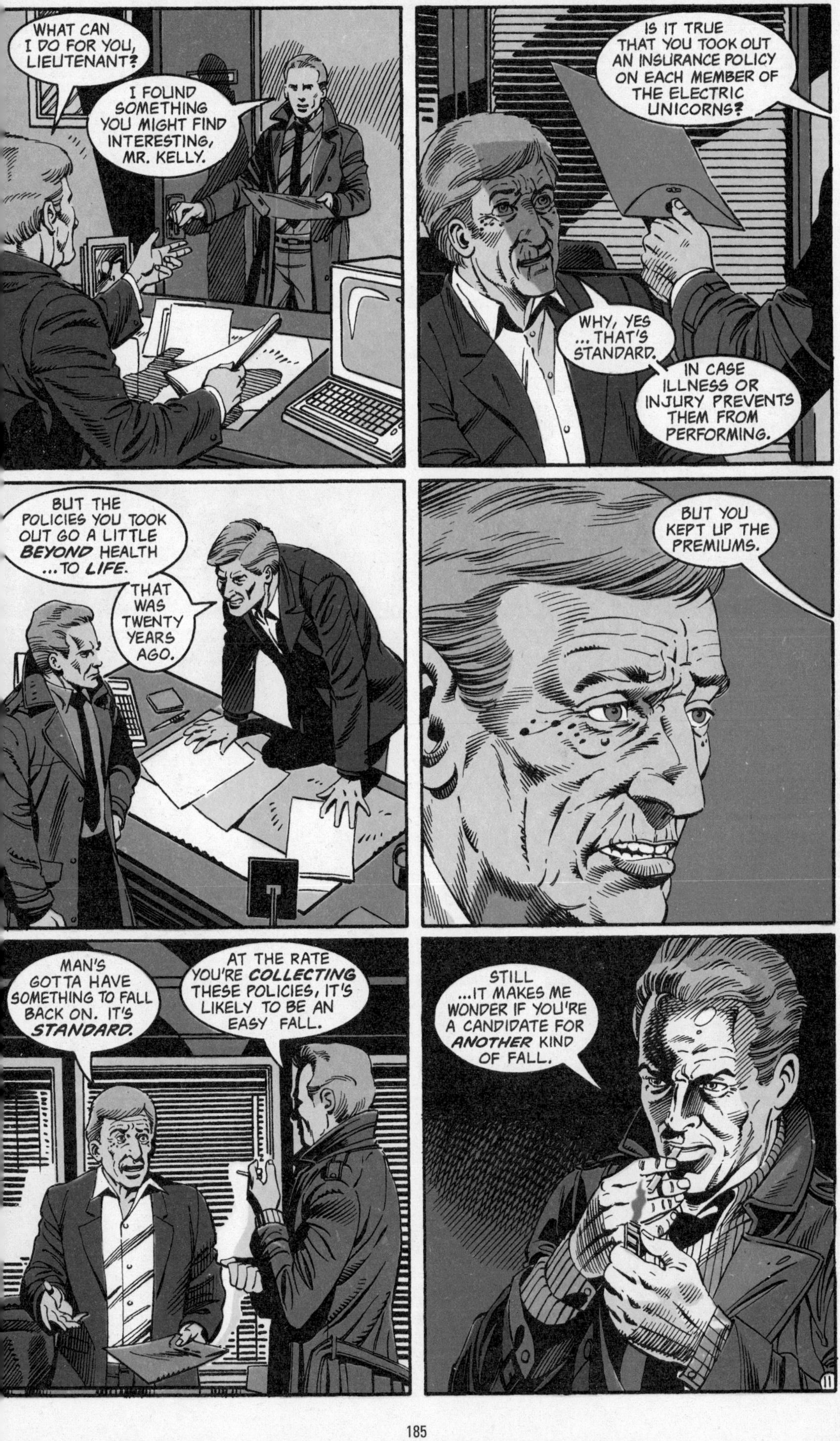
WHAT CAN I DO FOR YOU, LIEUTENANT?
I FOUND SOMETHING YOU MIGHT FIND INTERESTING, MR. KELLY.
IS IT TRUE THAT YOU TOOK OUT AN INSURANCE POLICY ON EACH MEMBER OF THE ELECTRIC UNICORNS?
WHY, YES ...THAT'S STANDARD.
IN CASE ILLNESS OR INJURY PREVENTS THEM FROM PERFORMING.
BUT THE POLICIES YOU TOOK OUT GO A LITTLE BEYOND HEALTH ...TO LIFE.
THAT WAS TWENTY YEARS AGO.
BUT YOU KEPT UP THE PREMIUMS.
MAN'S GOTTA HAVE SOMETHING TO FALL BACK ON. IT'S STANDARD.
AT THE RATE YOU'RE COLLECTING THESE POLICIES, IT'S LIKELY TO BE AN EASY FALL.
STILL ...IT MAKES ME WONDER IF YOU'RE A CANDIDATE FOR ANOTHER KIND OF FALL.
11

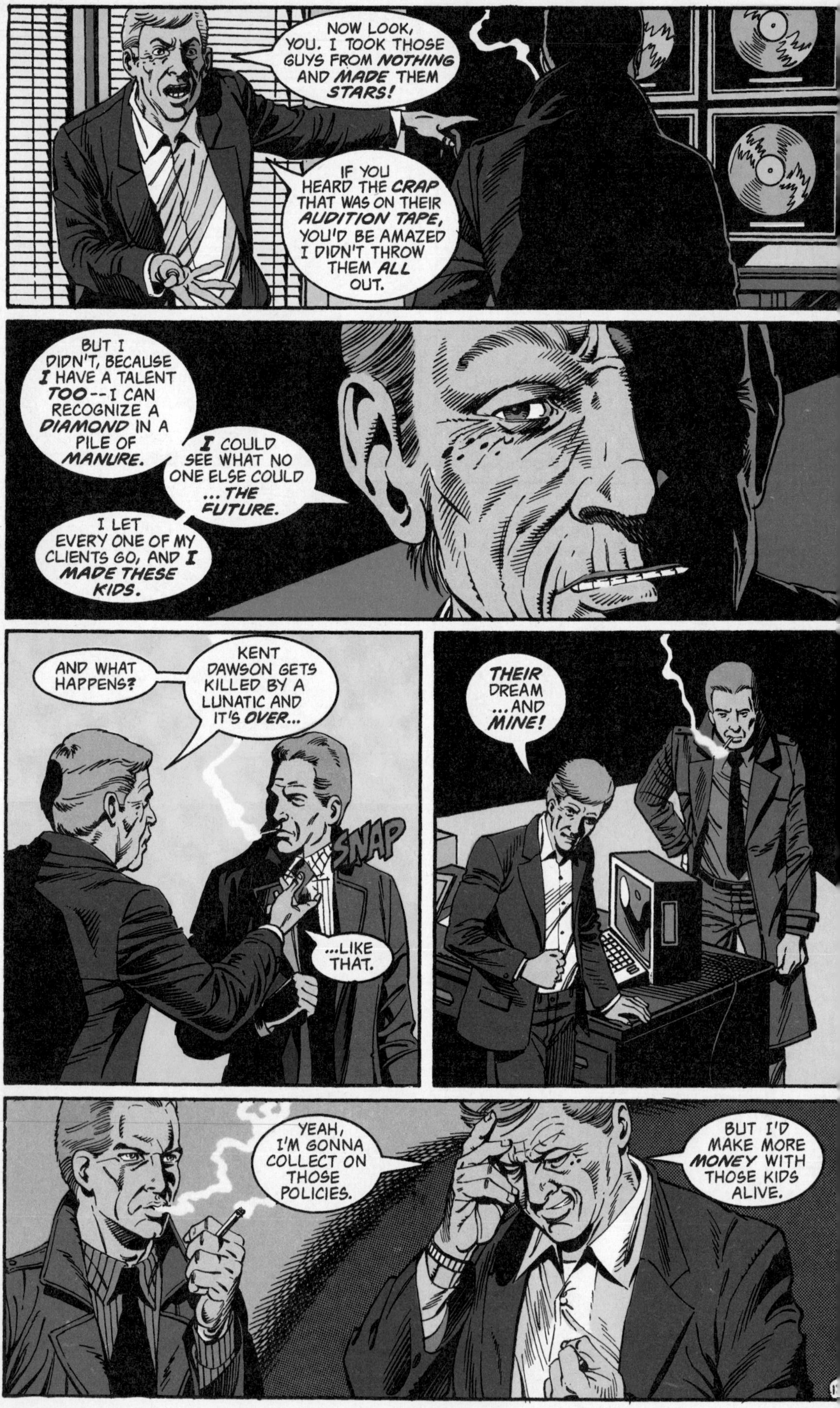
NOW LOOK, YOU. I TOOK THOSE GUYS FROM NOTHING AND MADE THEM STARS!
IF YOU HEARD THE CRAP THAT WAS ON THEIR AUDITION TAPE, YOU'D BE AMAZED I DIDN'T THROW THEM ALL OUT.
BUT I DIDN'T, BECAUSE I HAVE A TALENT TOO--I CAN RECOGNIZE A DIAMOND IN A PILE OF MANURE.
I COULD SEE WHAT NO ONE ELSE COULD ...THE FUTURE.
I LET EVERY ONE OF MY CLIENTS GO, AND I MADE THESE KIDS.
AND WHAT HAPPENS?
KENT DAWSON GETS KILLED BY A LUNATIC AND IT'S OVER...
SNAP
...LIKE THAT.
THEIR DREAM ...AND MINE!
YEAH, I'M GONNA COLLECT ON THOSE POLICIES.
BUT I'D MAKE MORE MONEY WITH THOSE KIDS ALIVE.

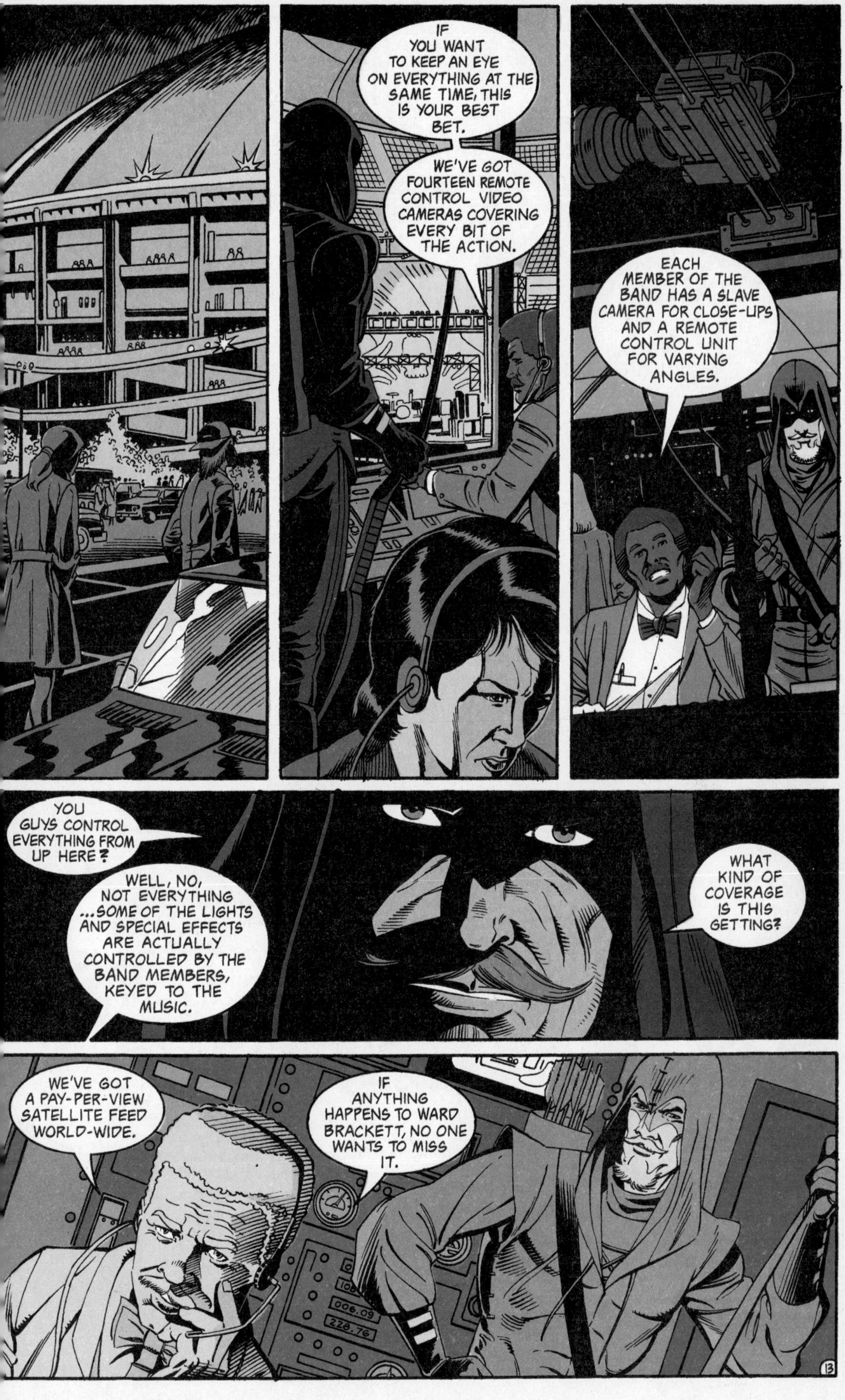
IF YOU WANT TO KEEP AN EYE ON EVERYTHING AT THE SAME TIME, THIS IS YOUR BEST BET.
WE'VE GOT FOURTEEN REMOTE CONTROL VIDEO CAMERAS COVERING EVERY BIT OF THE ACTION.
EACH MEMBER OF THE BAND HAS A SLAVE CAMERA FOR CLOSE-UPS AND A REMOTE CONTROL UNIT FOR VARYING ANGLES.
YOU GUYS CONTROL EVERYTHING FROM UP HERE?
WELL, NO, NOT EVERYTHING ...SOME OF THE LIGHTS AND SPECIAL EFFECTS ARE ACTUALLY CONTROLLED BY THE BAND MEMBERS, KEYED TO THE MUSIC.
WHAT KIND OF COVERAGE IS THIS GETTING?
WE'VE GOT A PAY-PER-VIEW SATELLITE FEED WORLD-WIDE.
IF ANYTHING HAPPENS TO WARD BRACKETT, NO ONE WANTS TO MISS IT.
13

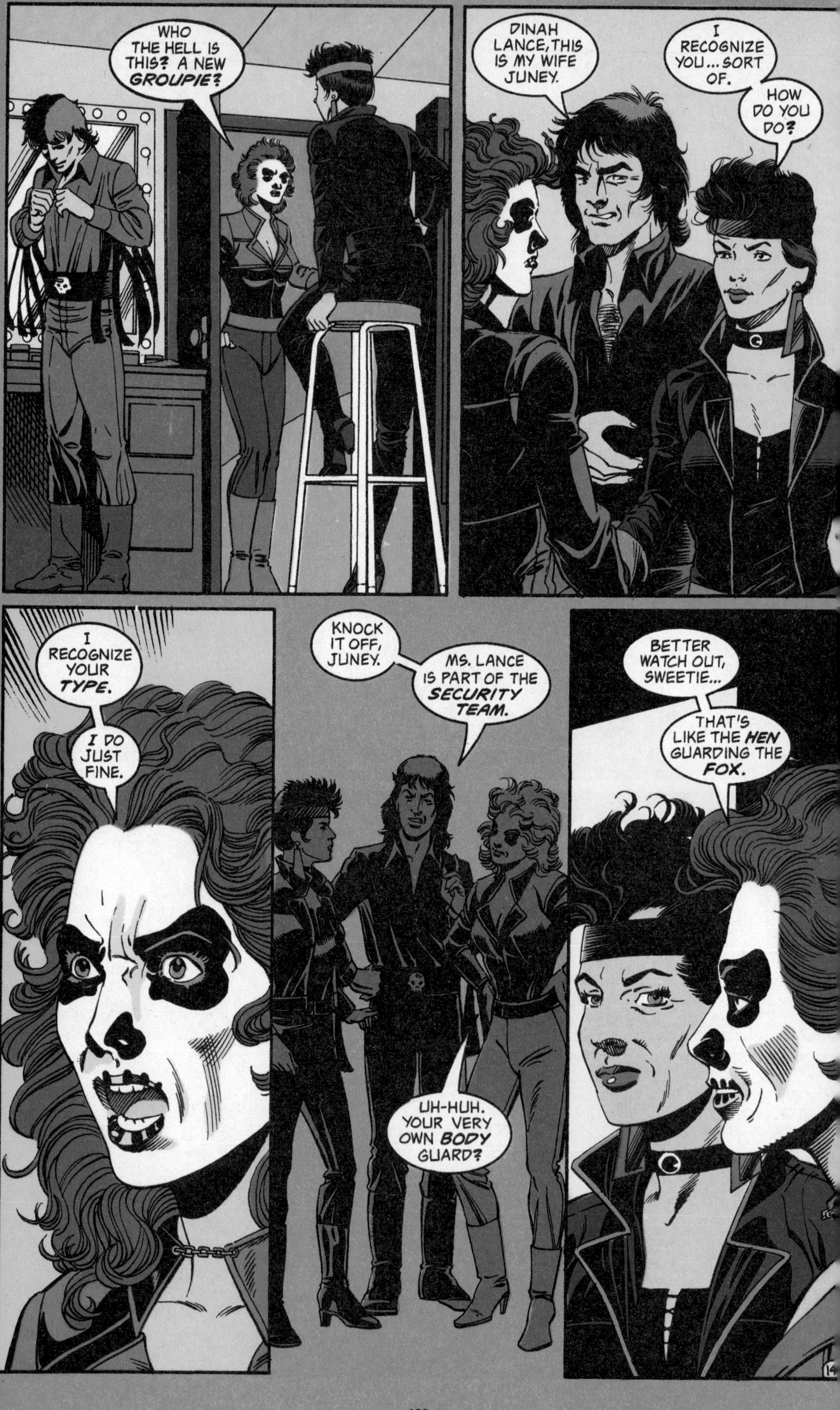
WHO THE HELL IS THIS? A NEW GROUPIE?
DINAH LANCE, THIS IS MY WIFE JUNEY.
I RECOGNIZE YOU... SORT OF.
HOW DO YOU DO?
I RECOGNIZE YOUR TYPE.
I DO JUST FINE.
KNOCK IT OFF, JUNEY.
MS. LANCE IS PART OF THE SECURITY TEAM.
UH-HUH. YOUR VERY OWN BODY GUARD?
BETTER WATCH OUT, SWEETIE...
THAT'S LIKE THE HEN GUARDING THE FOX.
14

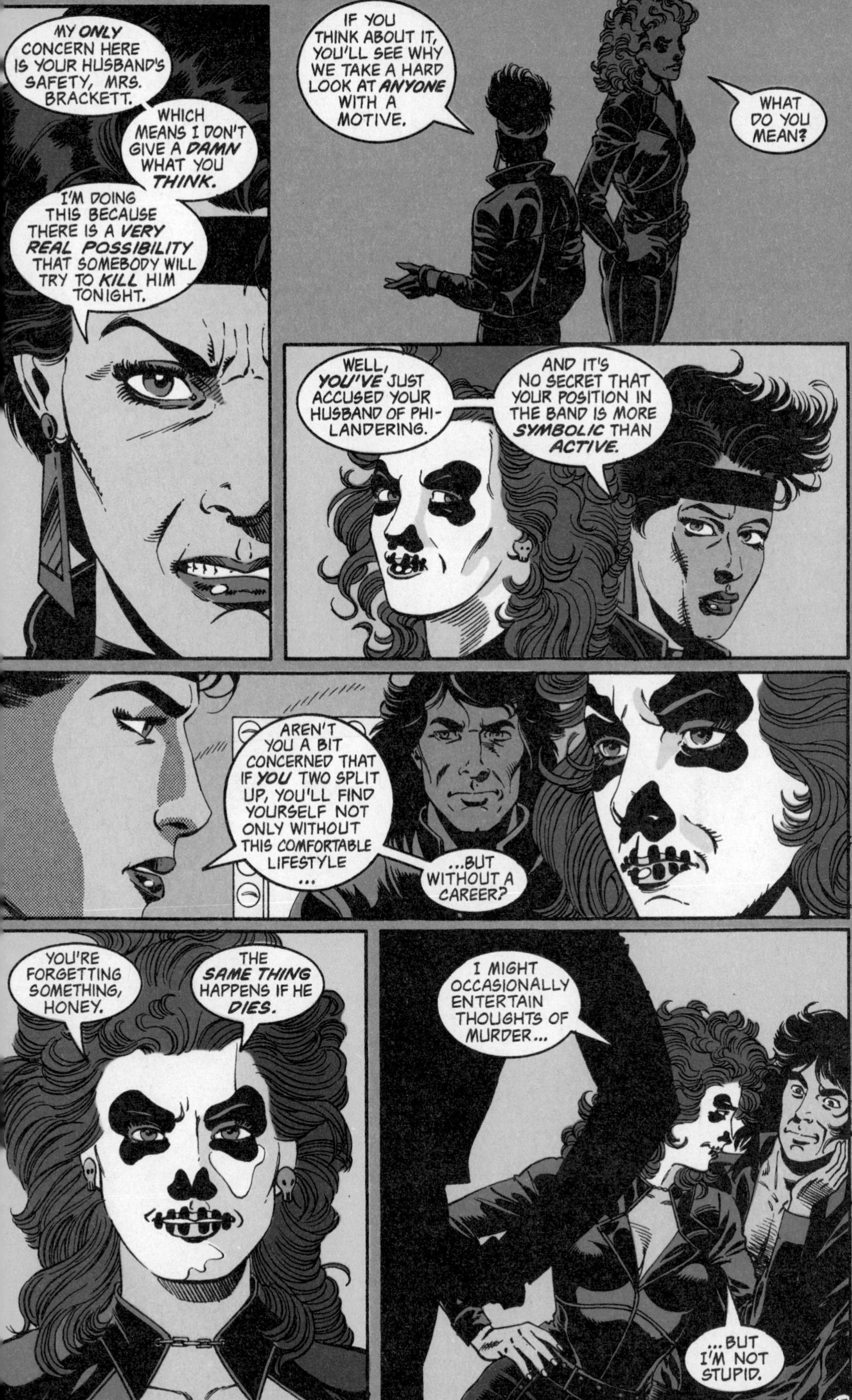
MY ONLY CONCERN HERE IS YOUR HUSBAND'S SAFETY, MRS. BRACKETT.
WHICH MEANS I DON'T GIVE A DAMN WHAT YOU THINK.
I'M DOING THIS BECAUSE THERE IS A VERY REAL POSSIBILITY THAT SOMEBODY WILL TRY TO KILL HIM TONIGHT.
IF YOU THINK ABOUT IT, YOU'LL SEE WHY WE TAKE A HARD LOOK AT ANYONE WITH A MOTIVE.
WHAT DO YOU MEAN?
WELL, YOU'VE JUST ACCUSED YOUR HUSBAND OF PHI-LANDERING.
AND IT'S NO SECRET THAT YOUR POSITION IN THE BAND IS MORE SYMBOLIC THAN ACTIVE.
AREN'T YOU A BIT CONCERNED THAT IF YOU TWO SPLIT UP, YOU'LL FIND YOURSELF NOT ONLY WITHOUT THIS COMFORTABLE LIFESTYLE ...
...BUT WITHOUT A CAREER?
YOU'RE FORGETTING SOMETHING, HONEY.
THE SAME THING HAPPENS IF HE DIES.
I MIGHT OCCASIONALLY ENTERTAIN THOUGHTS OF MURDER...
...BUT I'M NOT STUPID.
15

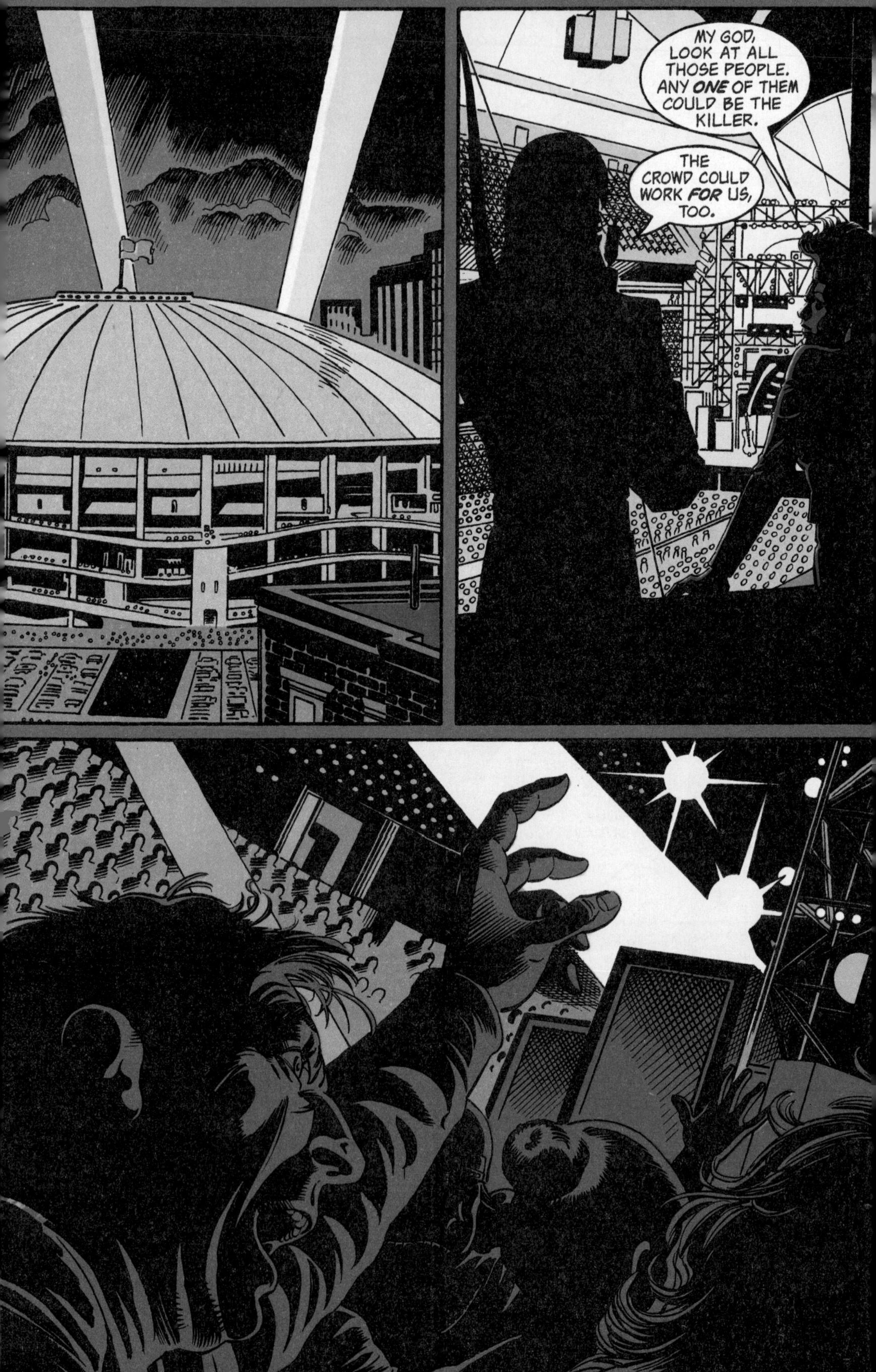
MY GOD, LOOK AT ALL THOSE PEOPLE. ANY ONE OF THEM COULD BE THE KILLER.
THE CROWD COULD WORK FOR US, TOO.

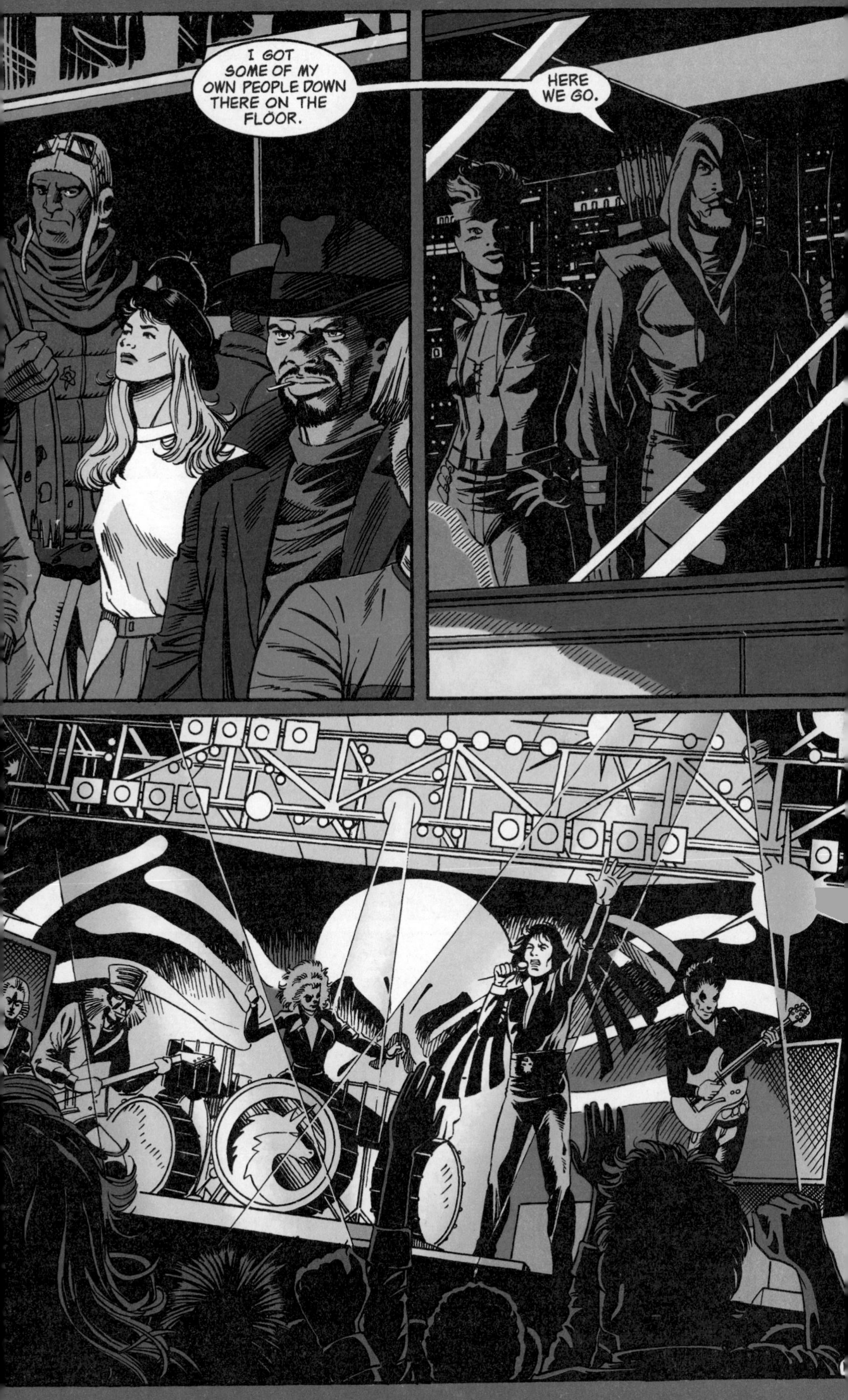
I GOT SOME OF MY OWN PEOPLE DOWN THERE ON THE FLOOR.
HERE WE GO.

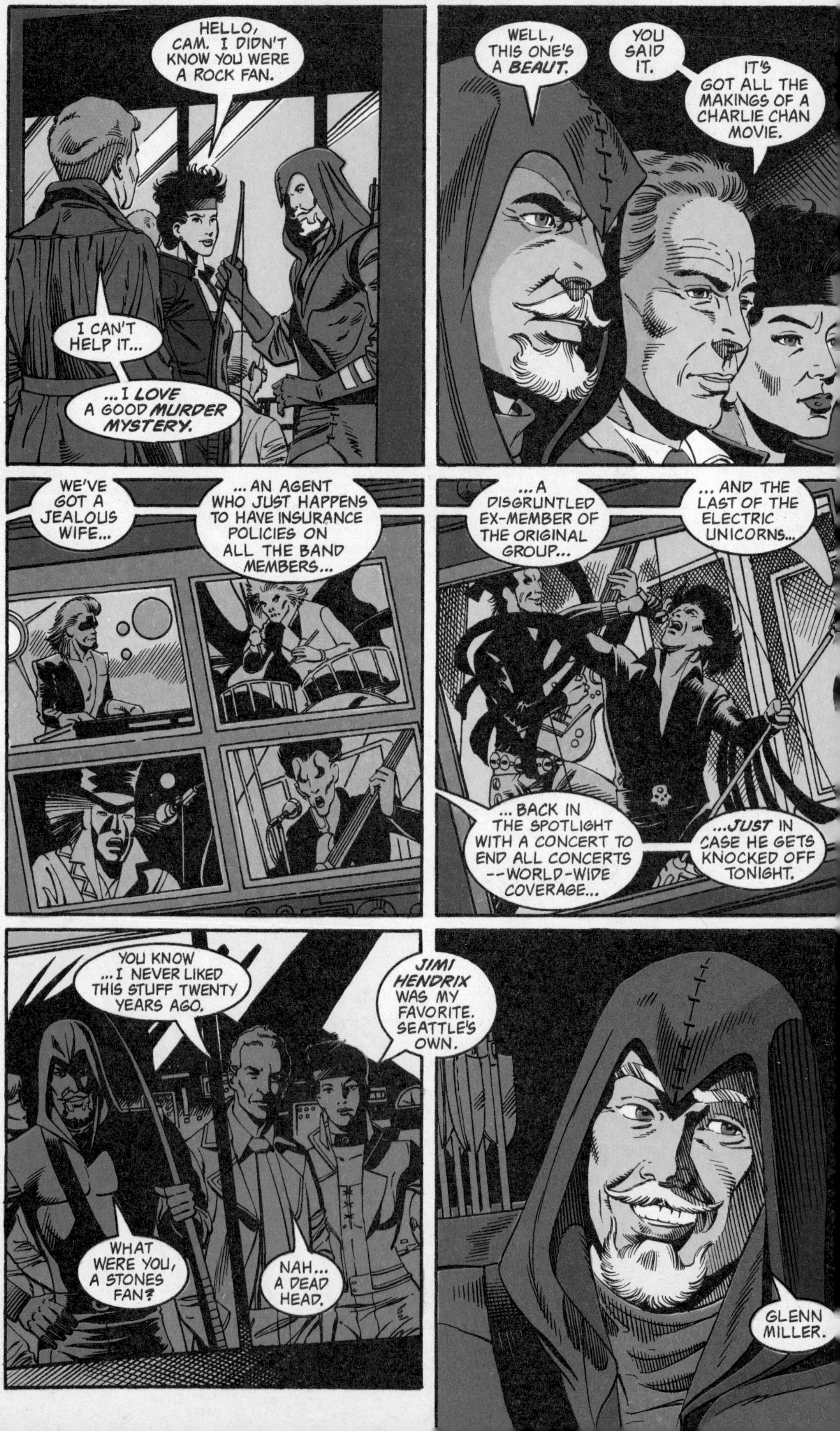
HELLO, CAM. I DIDN'T KNOW YOU WERE A ROCK FAN.
I CAN'T HELP IT...
...I LOVE A GOOD MURDER MYSTERY.
WELL, THIS ONE'S A BEAUT.
YOU SAID IT.
IT'S GOT ALL THE MAKINGS OF A CHARLIE CHAN MOVIE.
WE'VE GOT A JEALOUS WIFE...
...AN AGENT WHO JUST HAPPENS TO HAVE INSURANCE POLICIES ON ALL THE BAND MEMBERS...
...A DISGRUNTLED EX-MEMBER OF THE ORIGINAL GROUP...
...AND THE LAST OF THE ELECTRIC UNICORNS...
...BACK IN THE SPOTLIGHT WITH A CONCERT TO END ALL CONCERTS --WORLD-WIDE COVERAGE...
...JUST IN CASE HE GETS KNOCKED OFF TONIGHT.
YOU KNOW ...I NEVER LIKED THIS STUFF TWENTY YEARS AGO.
JIMI HENDRIX WAS MY FAVORITE. SEATTLE'S OWN.
WHAT WERE YOU, A STONES FAN?
NAH... A DEAD HEAD.
GLENN MILLER.

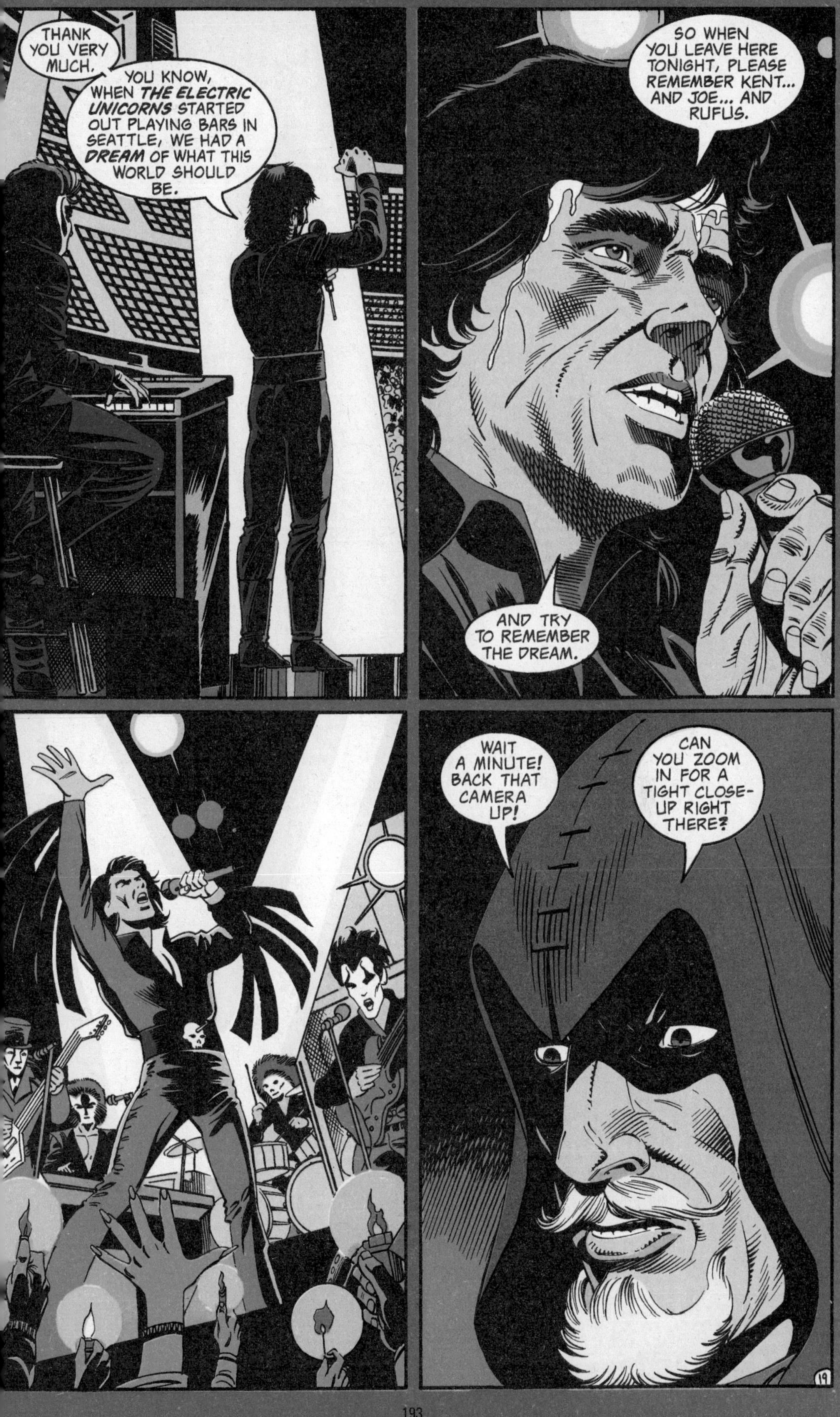
THANK YOU VERY MUCH.
YOU KNOW, WHEN THE ELECTRIC UNICORNS STARTED OUT PLAYING BARS IN SEATTLE, WE HAD A DREAM OF WHAT THIS WORLD SHOULD BE.
SO WHEN YOU LEAVE HERE TONIGHT, PLEASE REMEMBER KENT... AND JOE... AND RUFUS.
AND TRY TO REMEMBER THE DREAM.
WAIT A MINUTE! BACK THAT CAMERA UP!
CAN YOU ZOOM IN FOR A TIGHT CLOSE-UP RIGHT THERE?
19

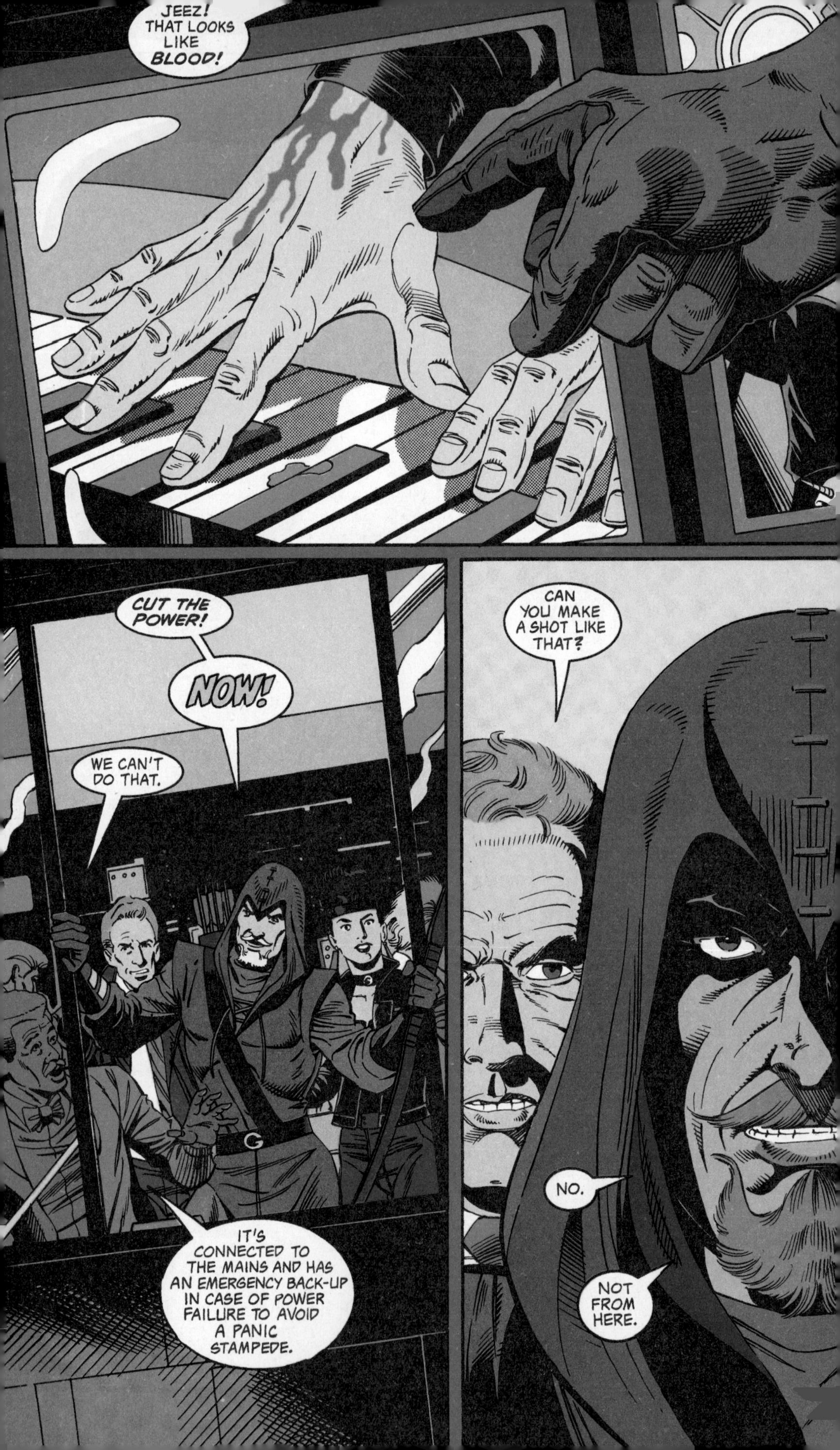
JEEZ! THAT LOOKS LIKE BLOOD!
CUT THE POWER!
NOW!
WE CAN'T DO THAT.
IT'S CONNECTED TO THE MAINS AND HAS AN EMERGENCY BACK-UP IN CASE OF POWER FAILURE TO AVOID A PANIC STAMPEDE.
CAN YOU MAKE A SHOT LIKE THAT?
NO.
NOT FROM HERE.

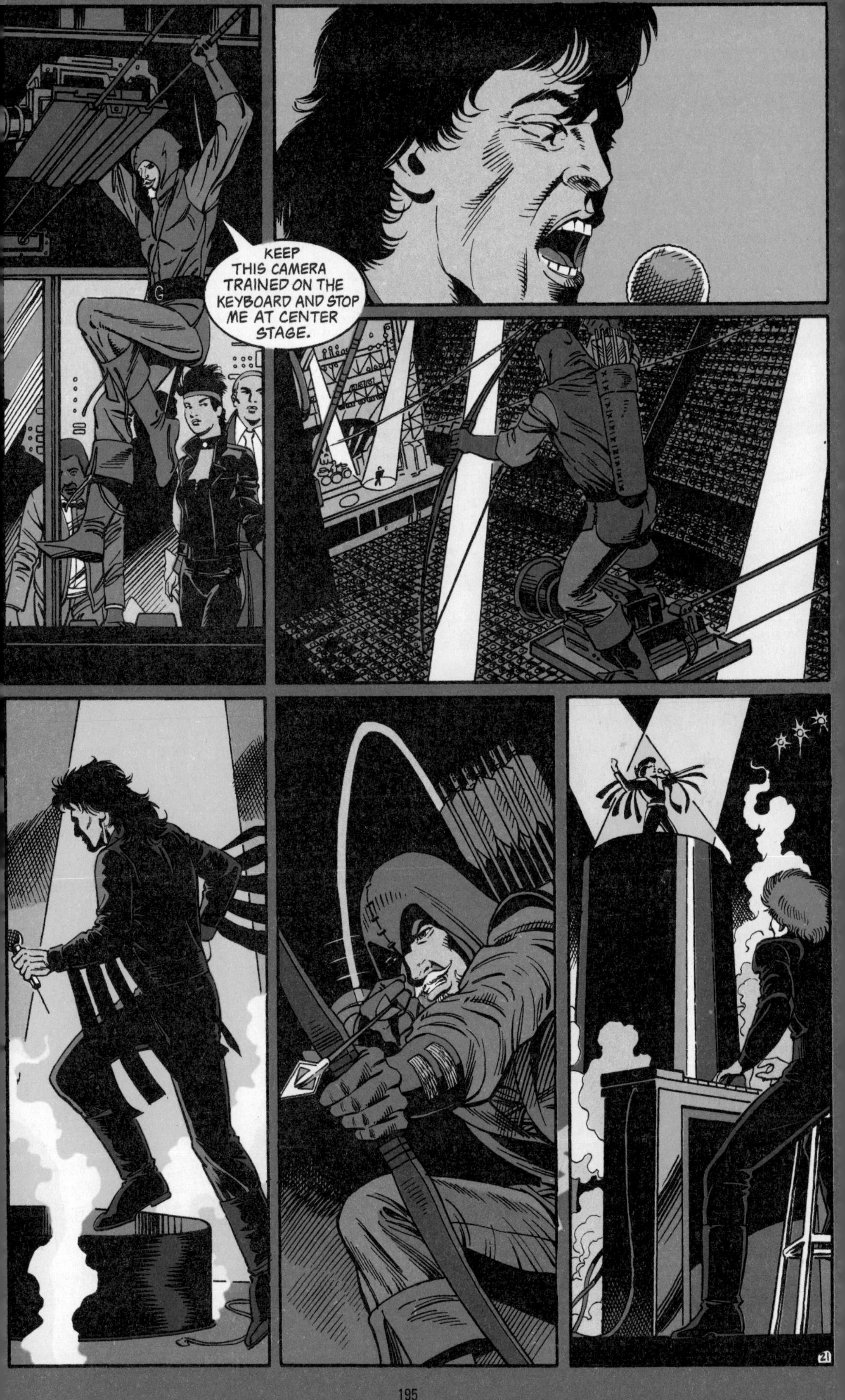
KEEP THIS CAMERA TRAINED ON THE KEYBOARD AND STOP ME AT CENTER STAGE.
21

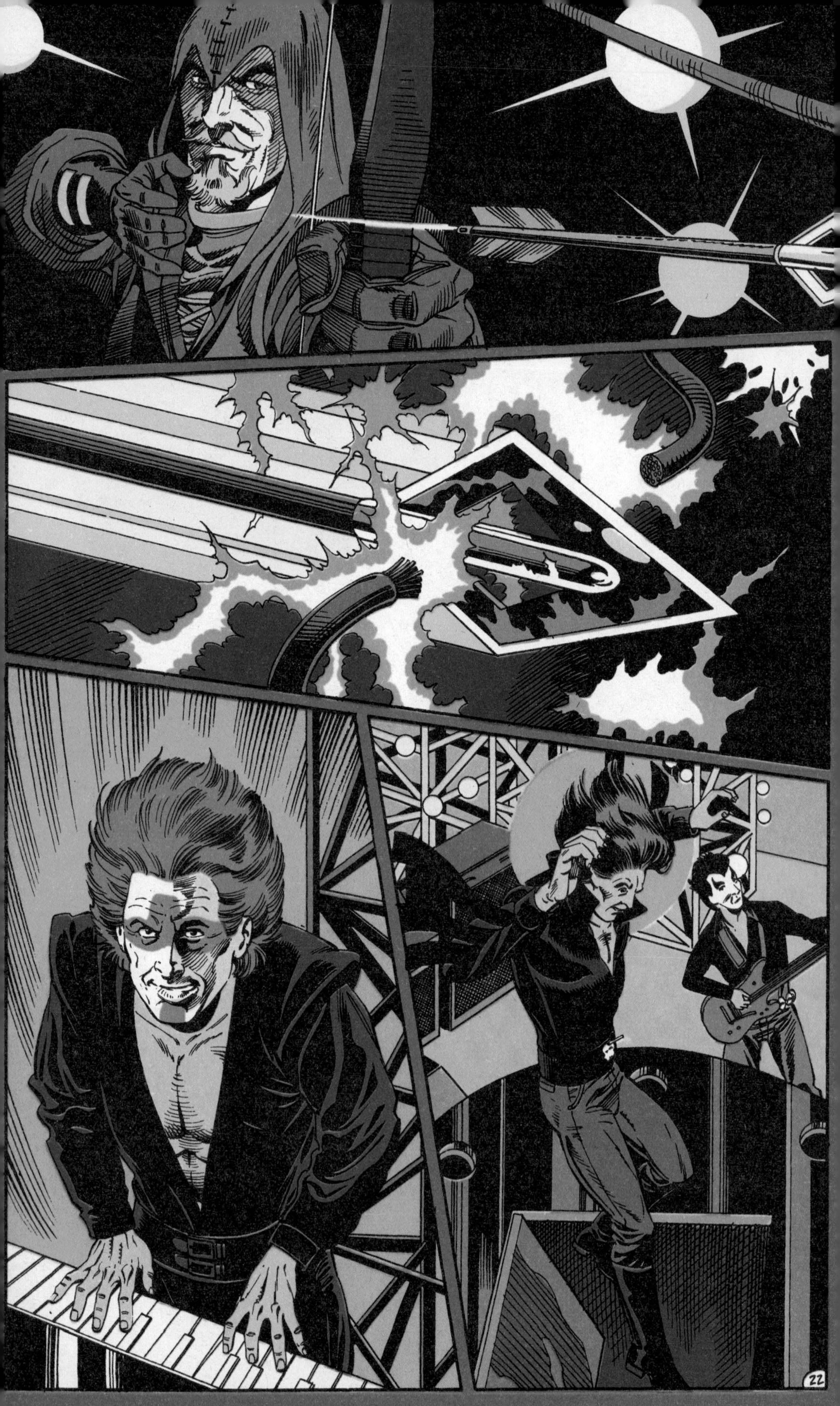
22

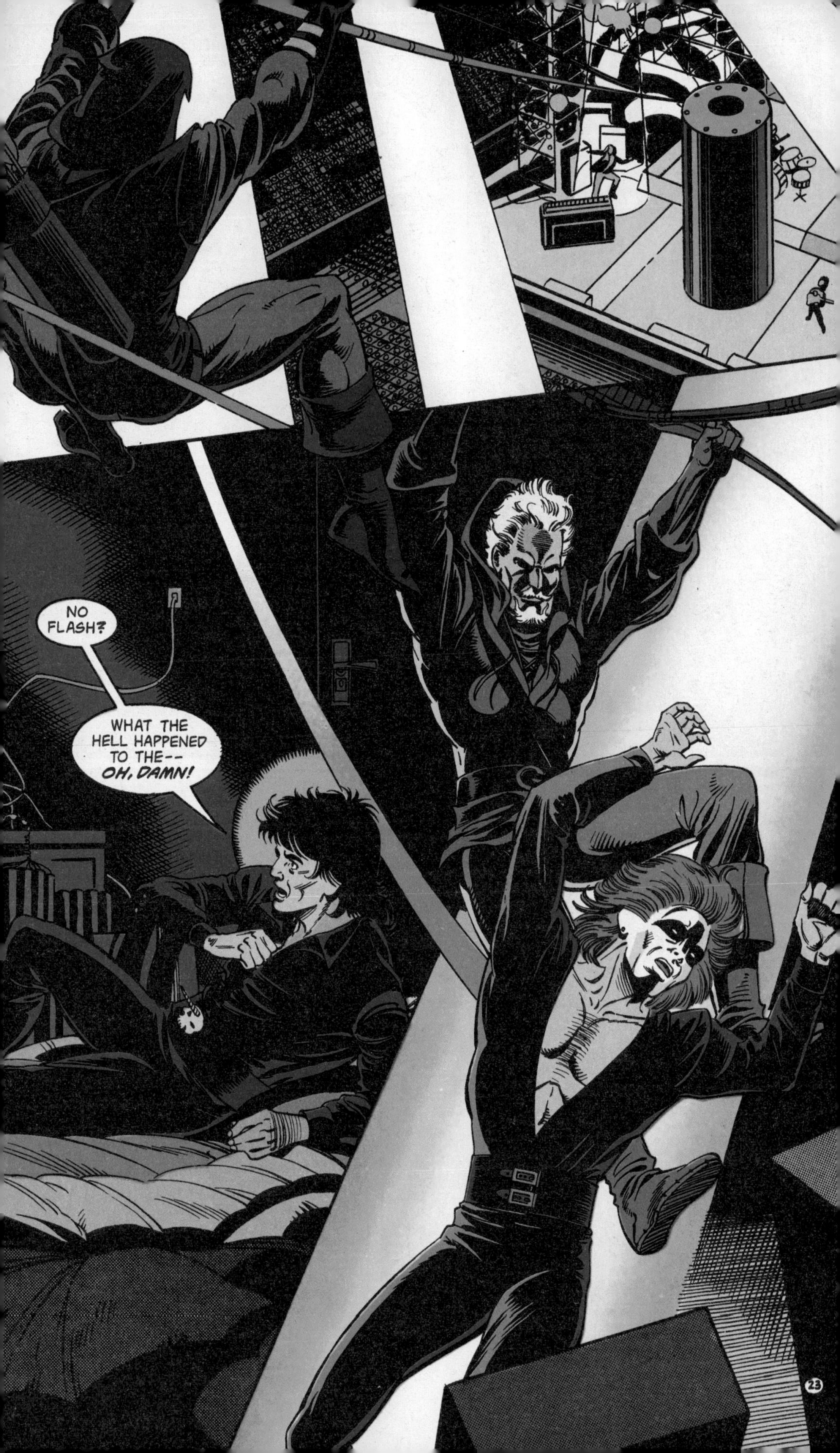
NO FLASH?
WHAT THE HELL HAPPENED TO THE-- OH, DAMN!
23

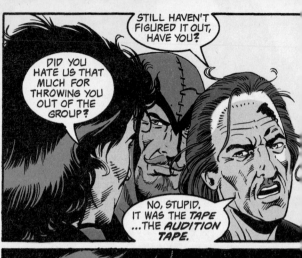

TOMMY! YOU?

WE ALL WROTE HIM OFF AS A SUSPECT WHEN HE GOT SHOT...

...BUT THAT HAD NOTHING TO DO WITH THE *OTHER* KILLINGS.

STILL HAVEN'T FIGURED IT OUT, HAVE YOU?

DID YOU HATE US THAT MUCH FOR THROWING YOU OUT OF THE GROUP?

NO, STUPID, IT WAS THE *TAPE* ...THE *AUDITION* TAPE.

YOU STILL GOT THAT THING?

BUT... IT'S A PIECE OF CRAP. NO ONE WOULD EVER BUY IT.

NOT WHILE YOU'RE *ALIVE*, THAT'S FOR SURE.

REMEMBER JOHN LENNON'S "LOST SESSION" TAPES?

WHEN YOU'RE *DEAD*, THEY'LL BUY *ANYTHING*.

THEN IT LOOKS LIKE YOU MIGHT GET TO BE A STAR AFTER ALL...

...RIGHT AFTER THE *EXECUTION*.

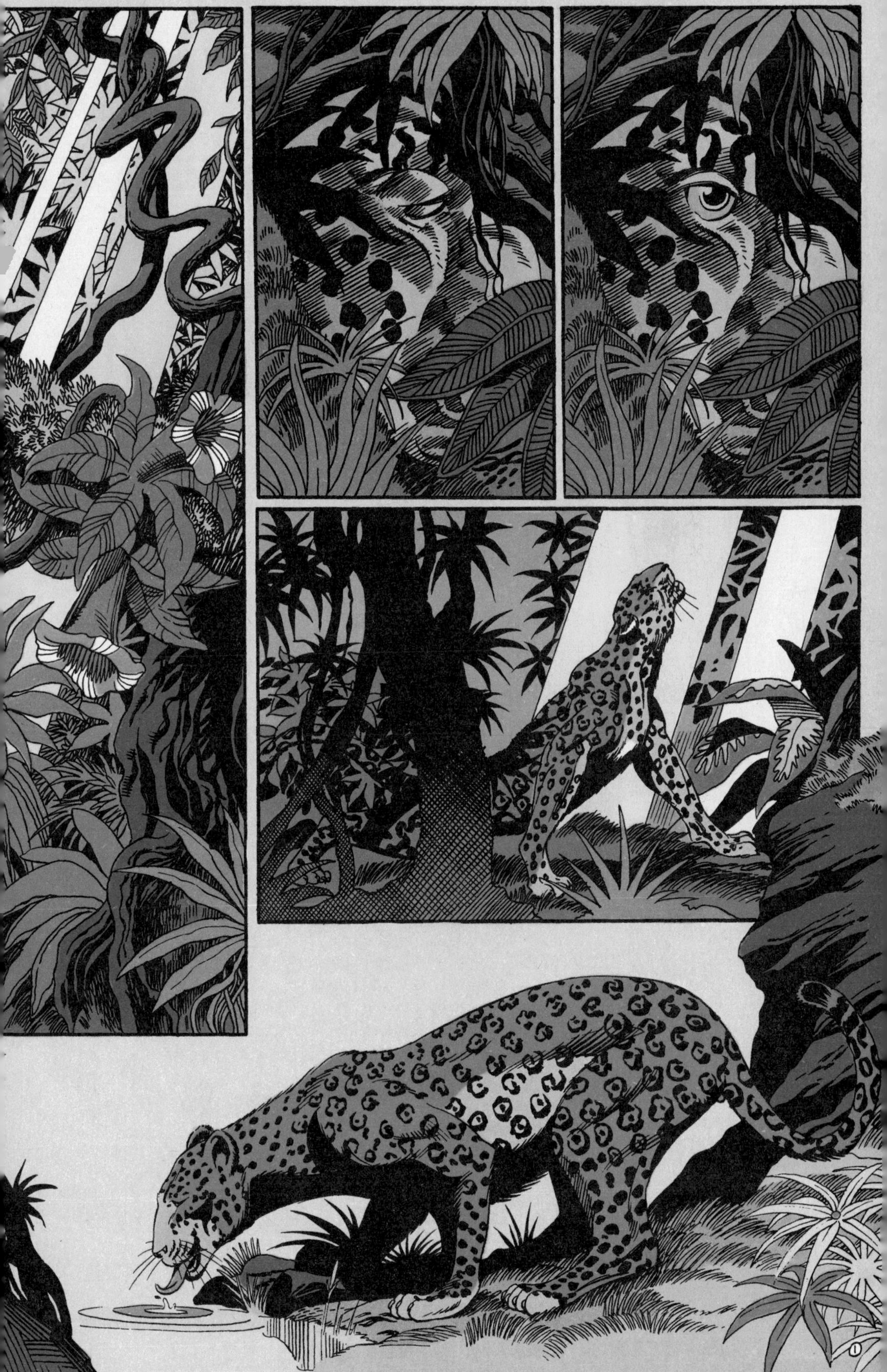

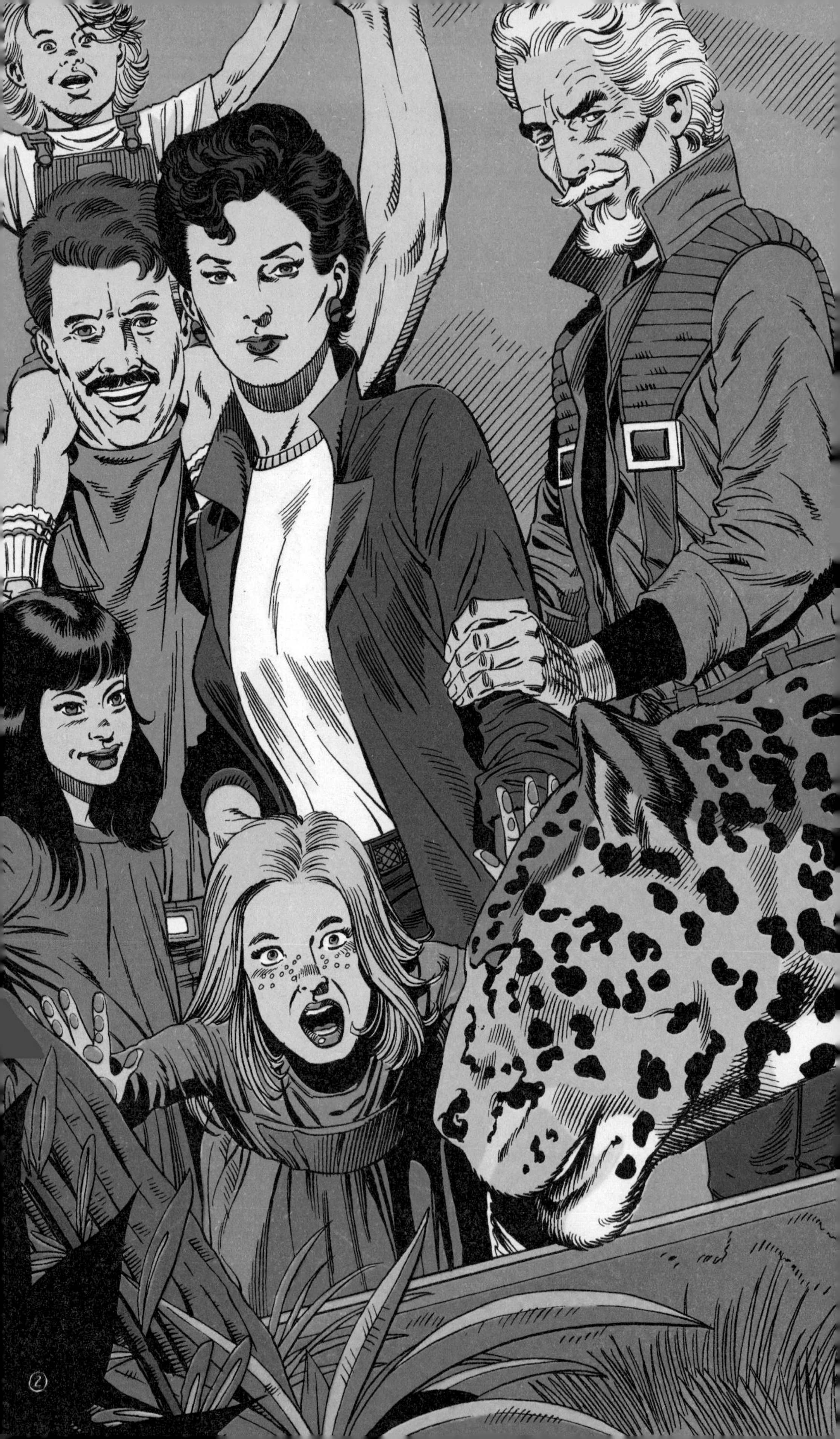

WILD IN THE STREETS

MIKE GRELL	RICK HOBERG	JOHN NYBERG
WRITER	PENCILLER	INKER
STEVE HAYNIE	JULIA LACQUEMENT	MIKE GOLD
LETTERER	COLORIST	EDITOR

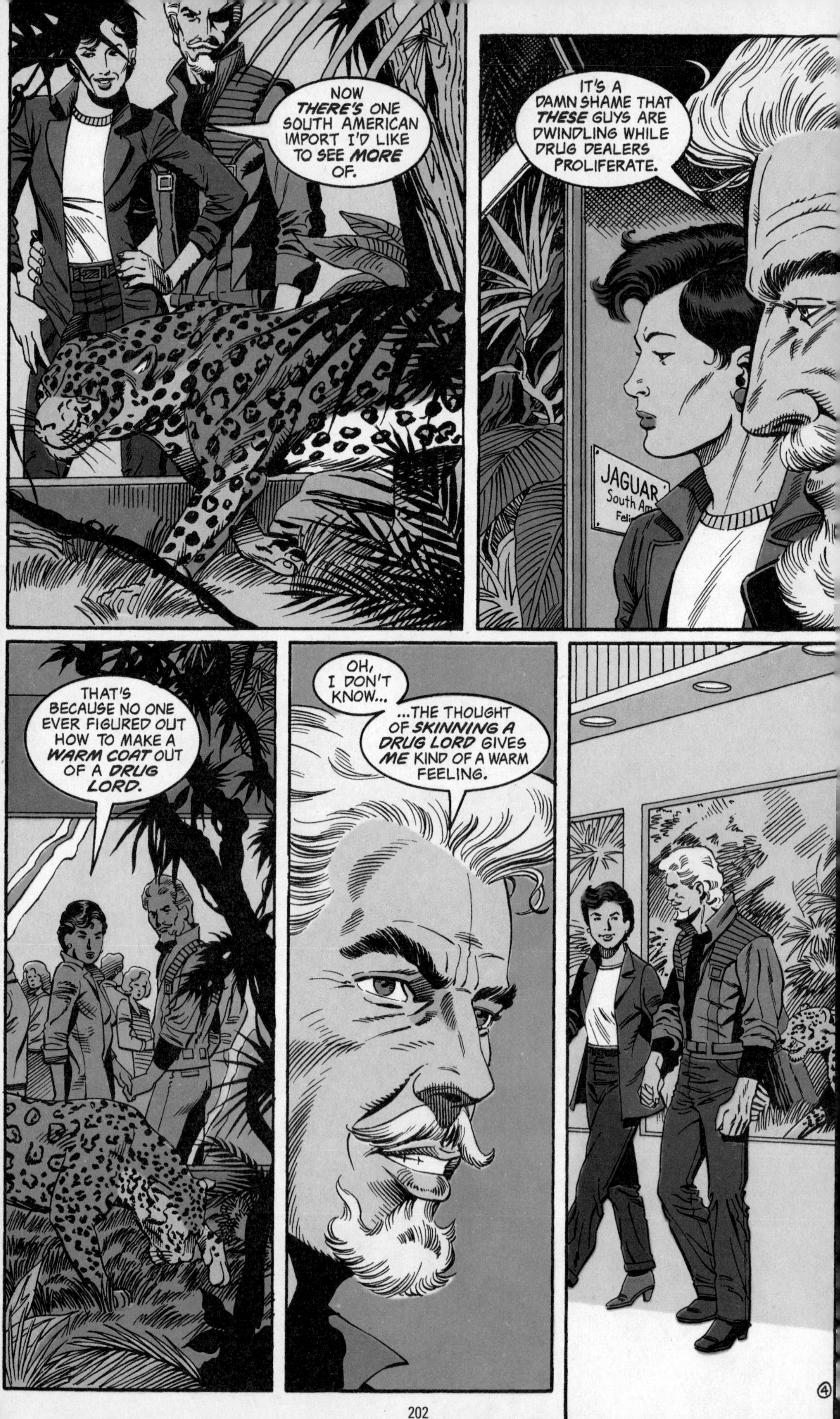
NOW THERE'S ONE SOUTH AMERICAN IMPORT I'D LIKE TO SEE MORE OF.
IT'S A DAMN SHAME THAT THESE GUYS ARE DWINDLING WHILE DRUG DEALERS PROLIFERATE.
JAGUAR
THAT'S BECAUSE NO ONE EVER FIGURED OUT HOW TO MAKE A WARM COAT OUT OF A DRUG LORD.
OH, I DON'T KNOW...
...THE THOUGHT OF SKINNING A DRUG LORD GIVES ME KIND OF A WARM FEELING.
4

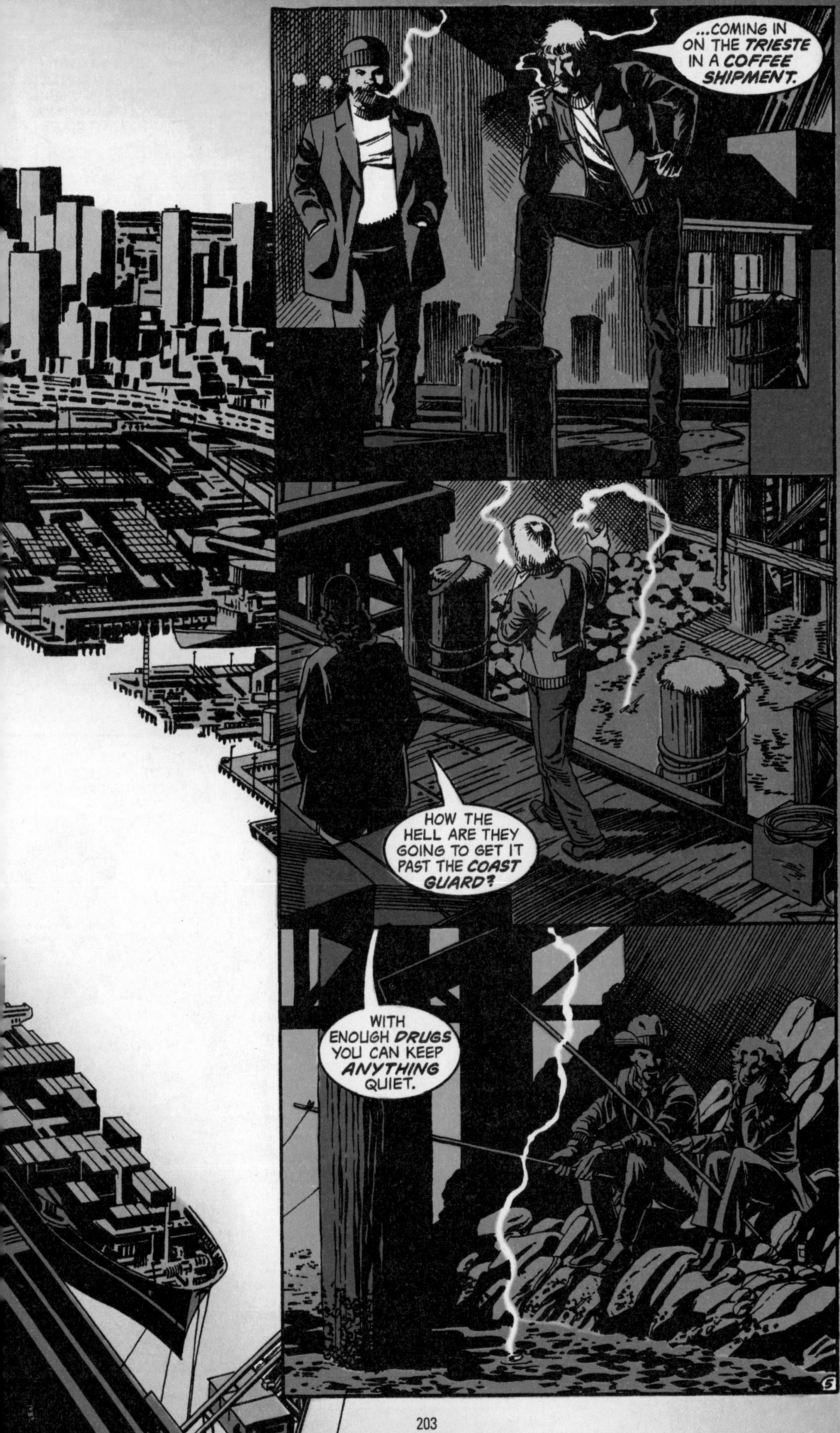

...COMING IN ON THE *TRIESTE* IN A *COFFEE SHIPMENT.*
HOW THE HELL ARE THEY GOING TO GET IT PAST THE *COAST GUARD?*
WITH ENOUGH *DRUGS* YOU CAN KEEP *ANYTHING* QUIET.
5

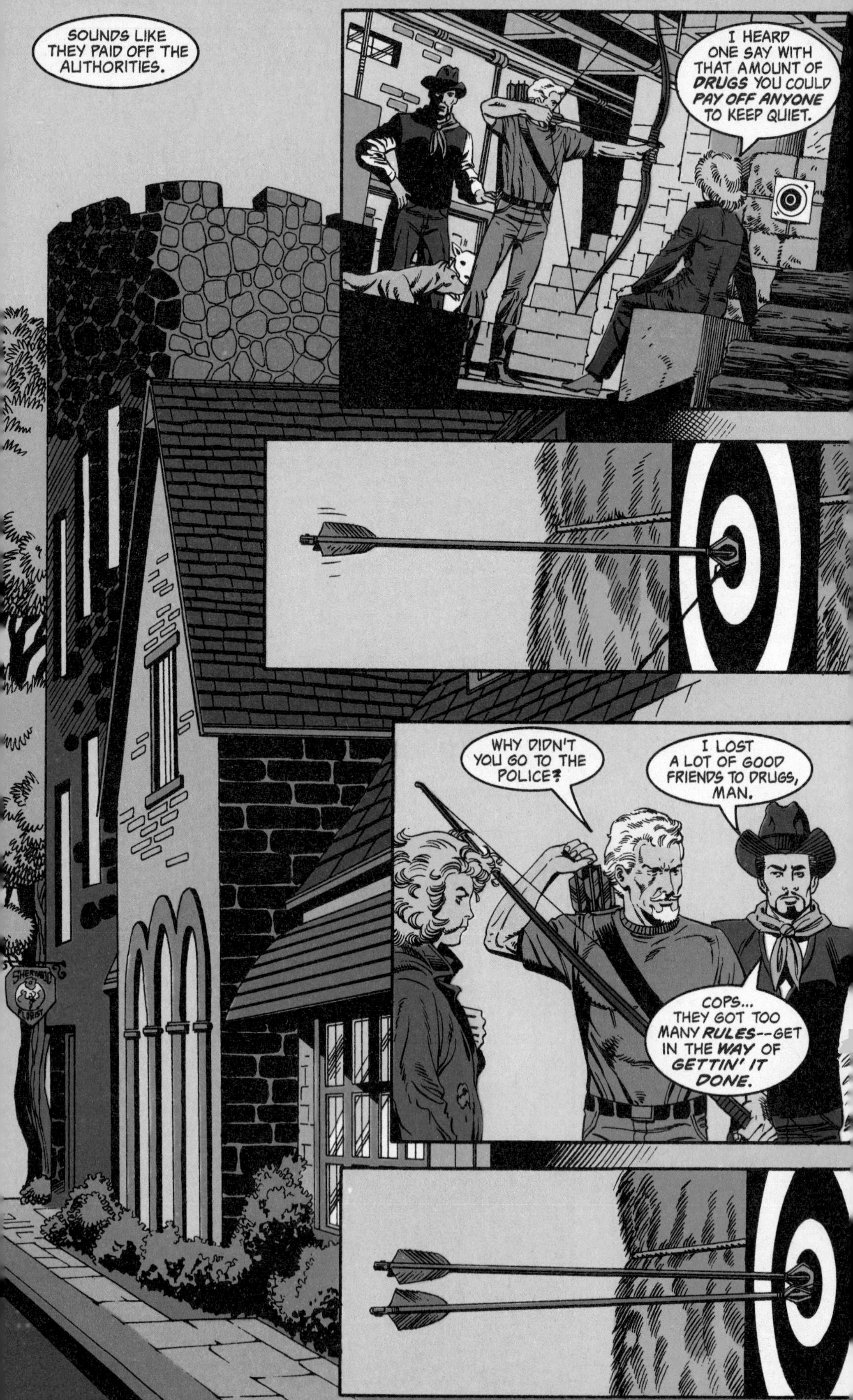
SOUNDS LIKE THEY PAID OFF THE AUTHORITIES.
I HEARD ONE SAY WITH THAT AMOUNT OF DRUGS YOU COULD PAY OFF ANYONE TO KEEP QUIET.
WHY DIDN'T YOU GO TO THE POLICE?
I LOST A LOT OF GOOD FRIENDS TO DRUGS, MAN.
COPS... THEY GOT TOO MANY RULES--GET IN THE WAY OF GETTIN' IT DONE.
SHERWOOD FLORIST

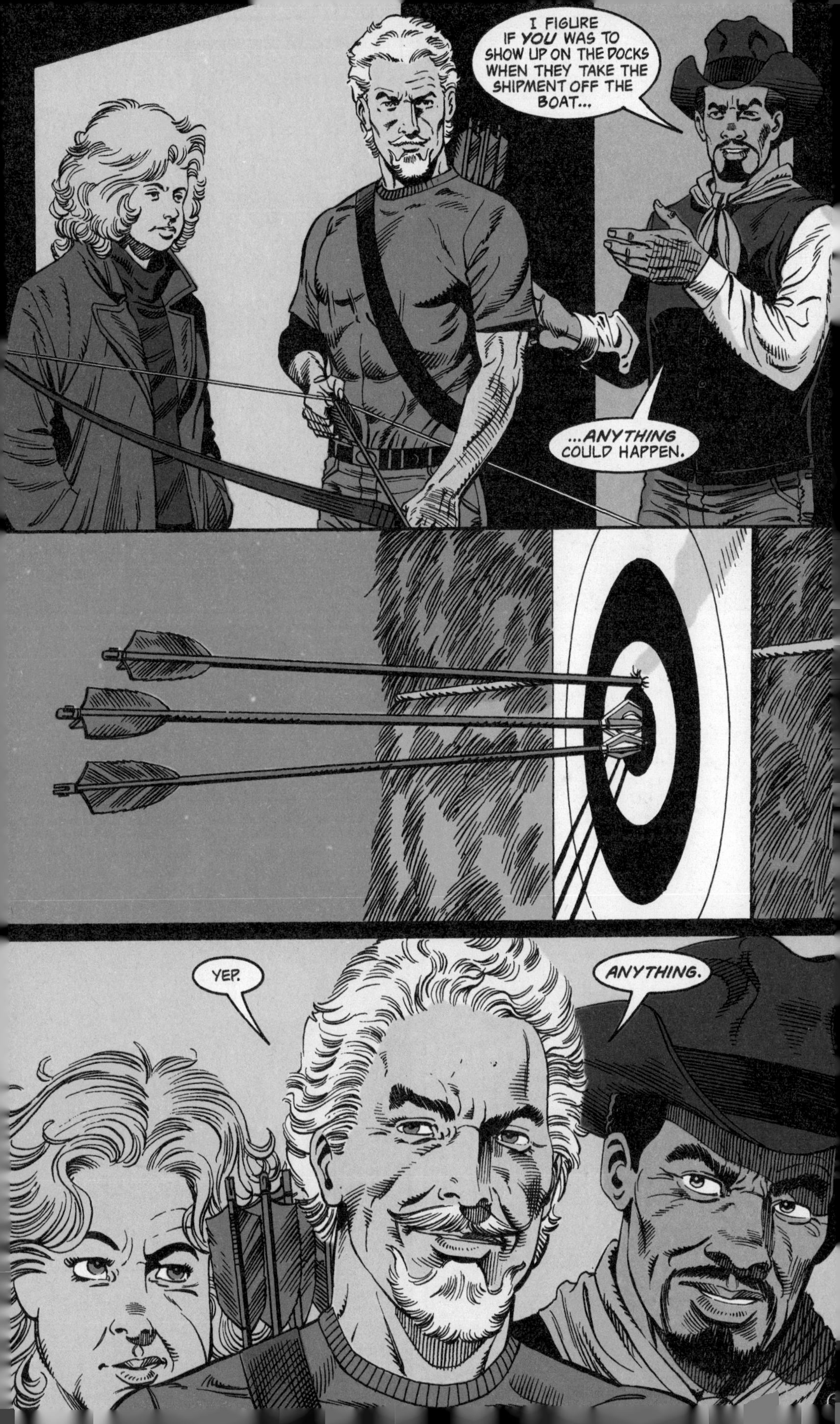
I FIGURE IF YOU WAS TO SHOW UP ON THE DOCKS WHEN THEY TAKE THE SHIPMENT OFF THE BOAT...
...ANYTHING COULD HAPPEN.
YEP.
ANYTHING.

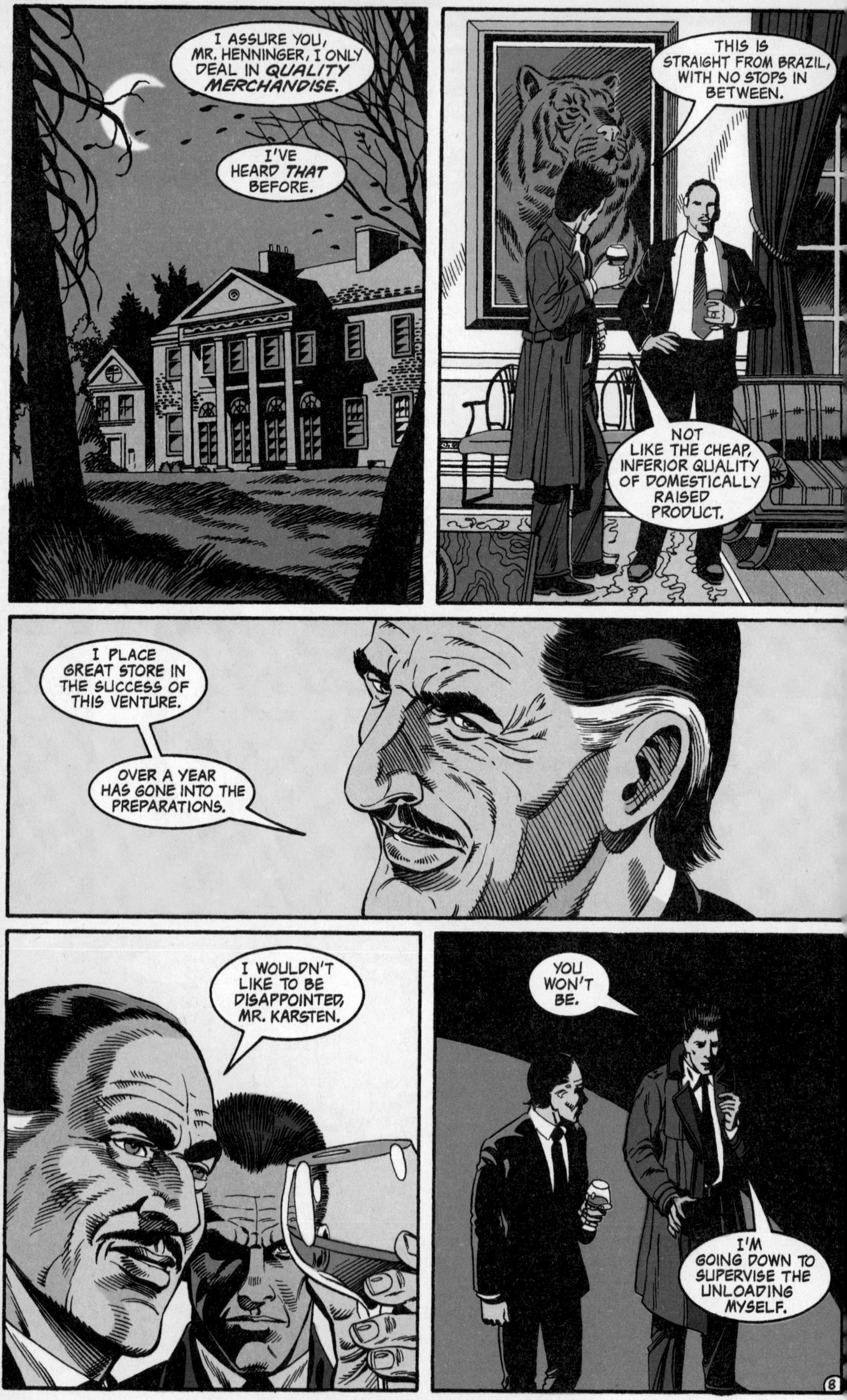
I ASSURE YOU, MR. HENNINGER, I ONLY DEAL IN *QUALITY MERCHANDISE.*
I'VE HEARD *THAT* BEFORE.
THIS IS STRAIGHT FROM BRAZIL, WITH NO STOPS IN BETWEEN.
NOT LIKE THE CHEAP, INFERIOR QUALITY OF DOMESTICALLY RAISED PRODUCT.
I PLACE GREAT STORE IN THE SUCCESS OF THIS VENTURE.
OVER A YEAR HAS GONE INTO THE PREPARATIONS.
I WOULDN'T LIKE TO BE DISAPPOINTED, MR. KARSTEN.
YOU WON'T BE.
I'M GOING DOWN TO SUPERVISE THE UNLOADING MYSELF.
8

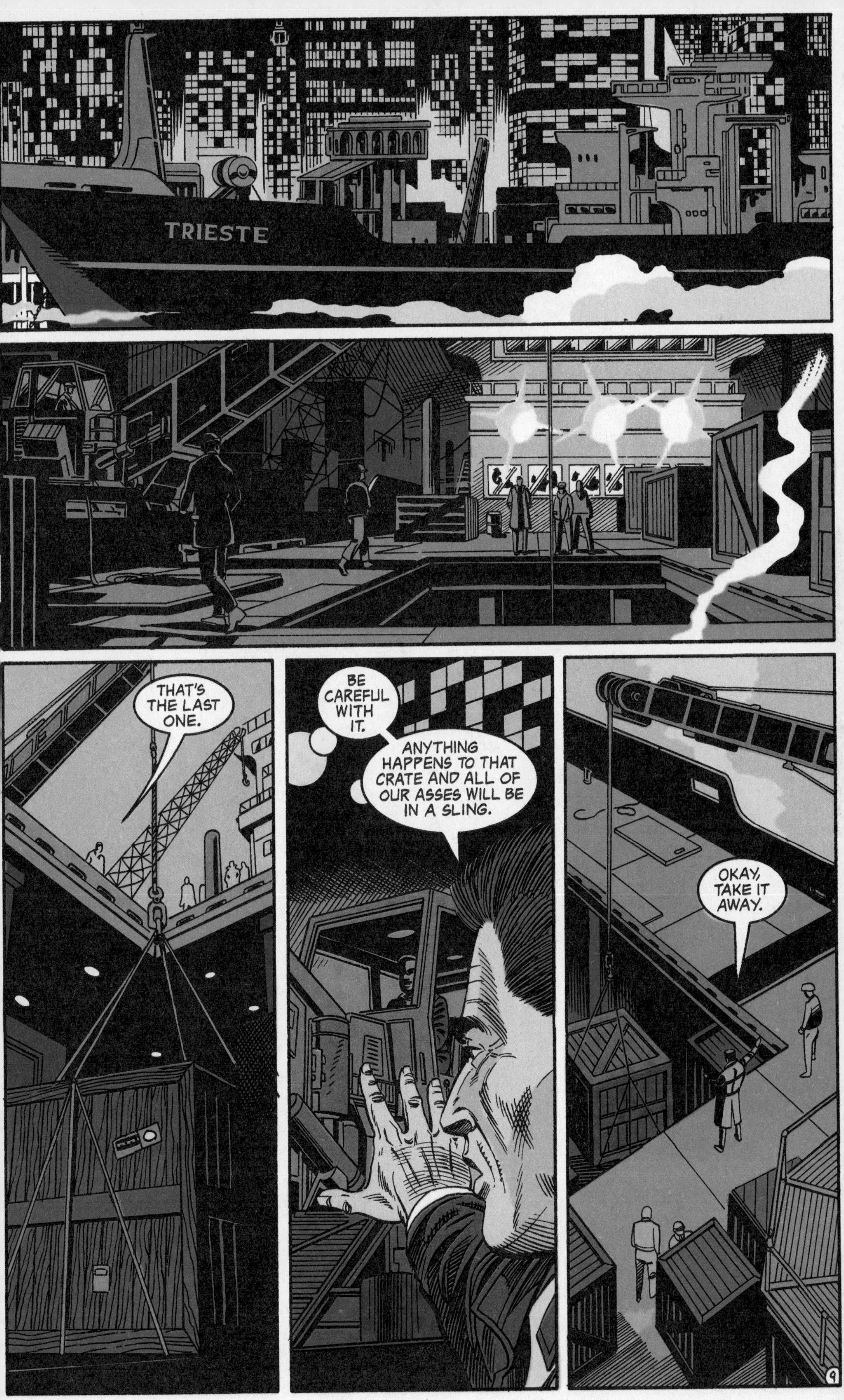
TRIESTE
THAT'S THE LAST ONE.
BE CAREFUL WITH IT.
ANYTHING HAPPENS TO THAT CRATE AND ALL OF OUR ASSES WILL BE IN A SLING.
OKAY, TAKE IT AWAY.
9

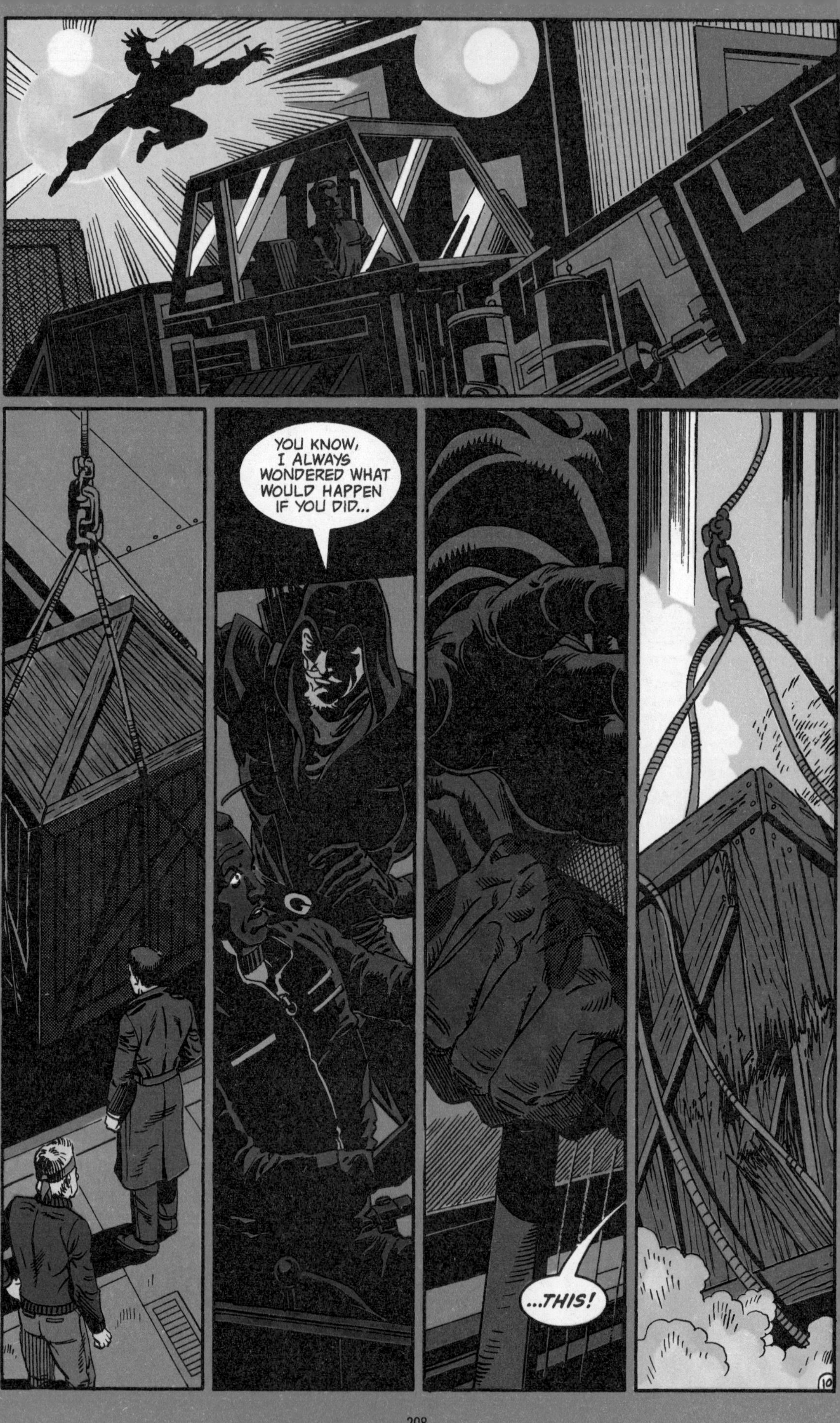
YOU KNOW, I ALWAYS WONDERED WHAT WOULD HAPPEN IF YOU DID...
...THIS!
10

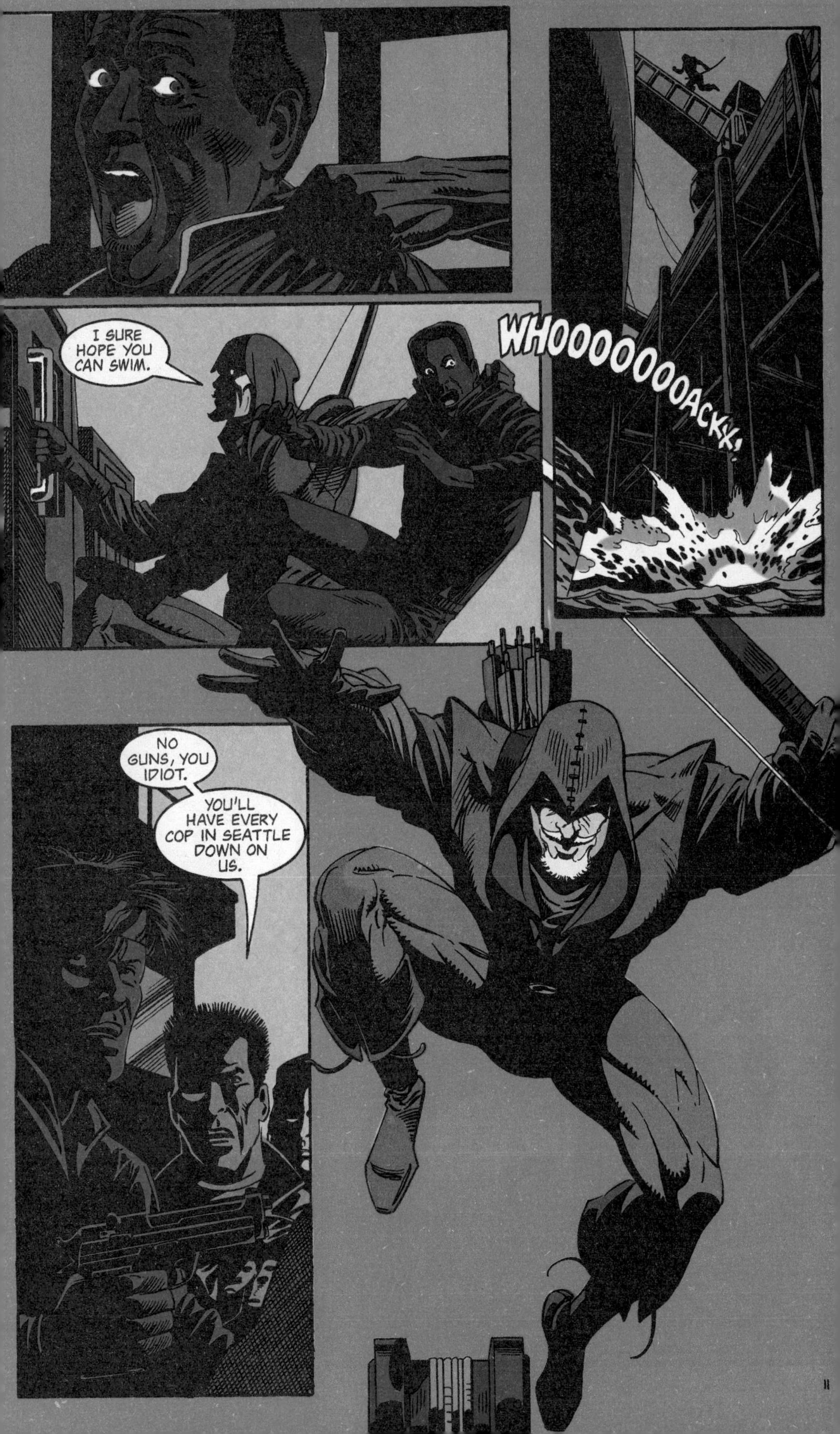
I SURE HOPE YOU CAN SWIM.
WHOOOOOOOOACKX!
NO GUNS, YOU IDIOT.
YOU'LL HAVE EVERY COP IN SEATTLE DOWN ON US.

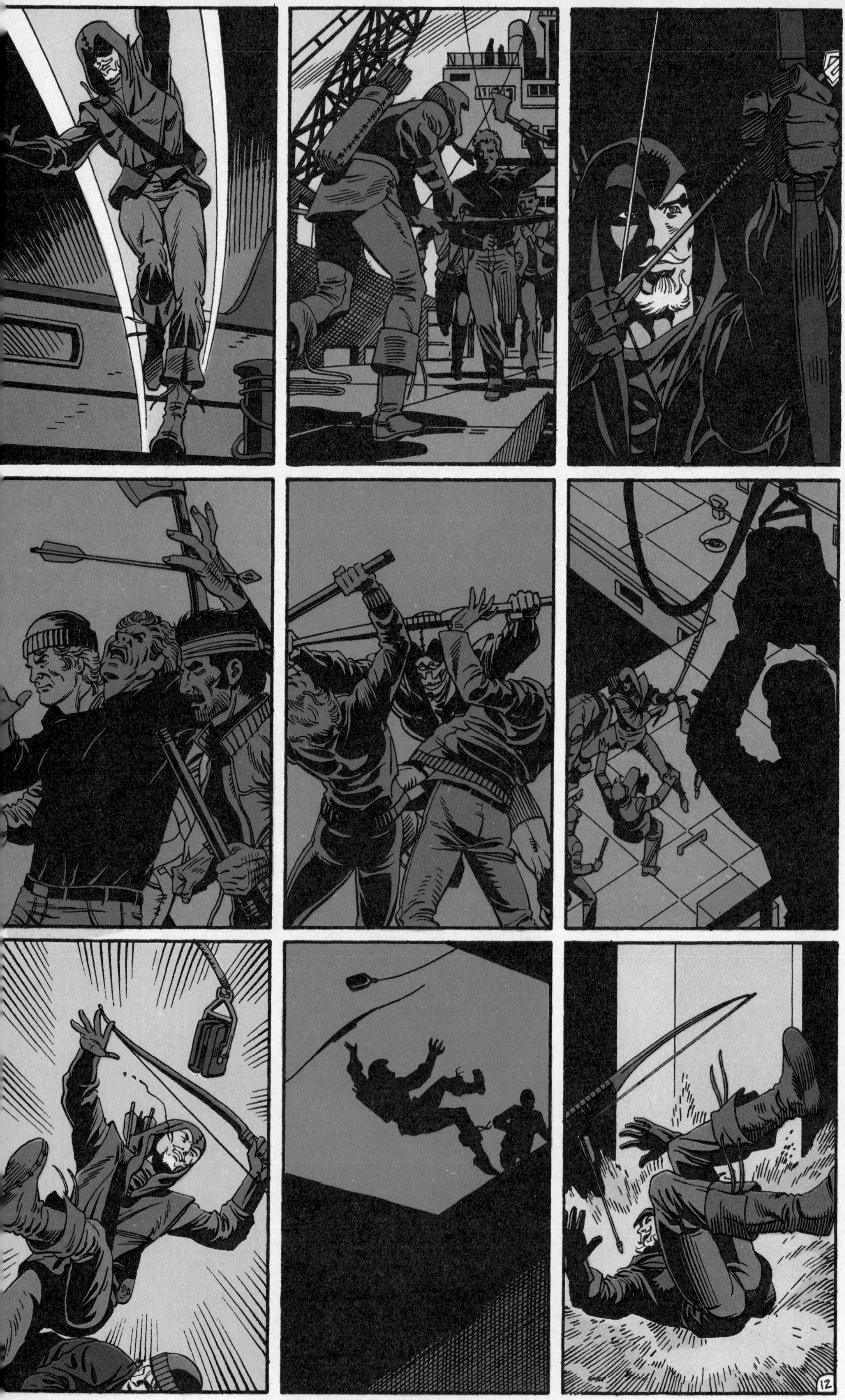
12

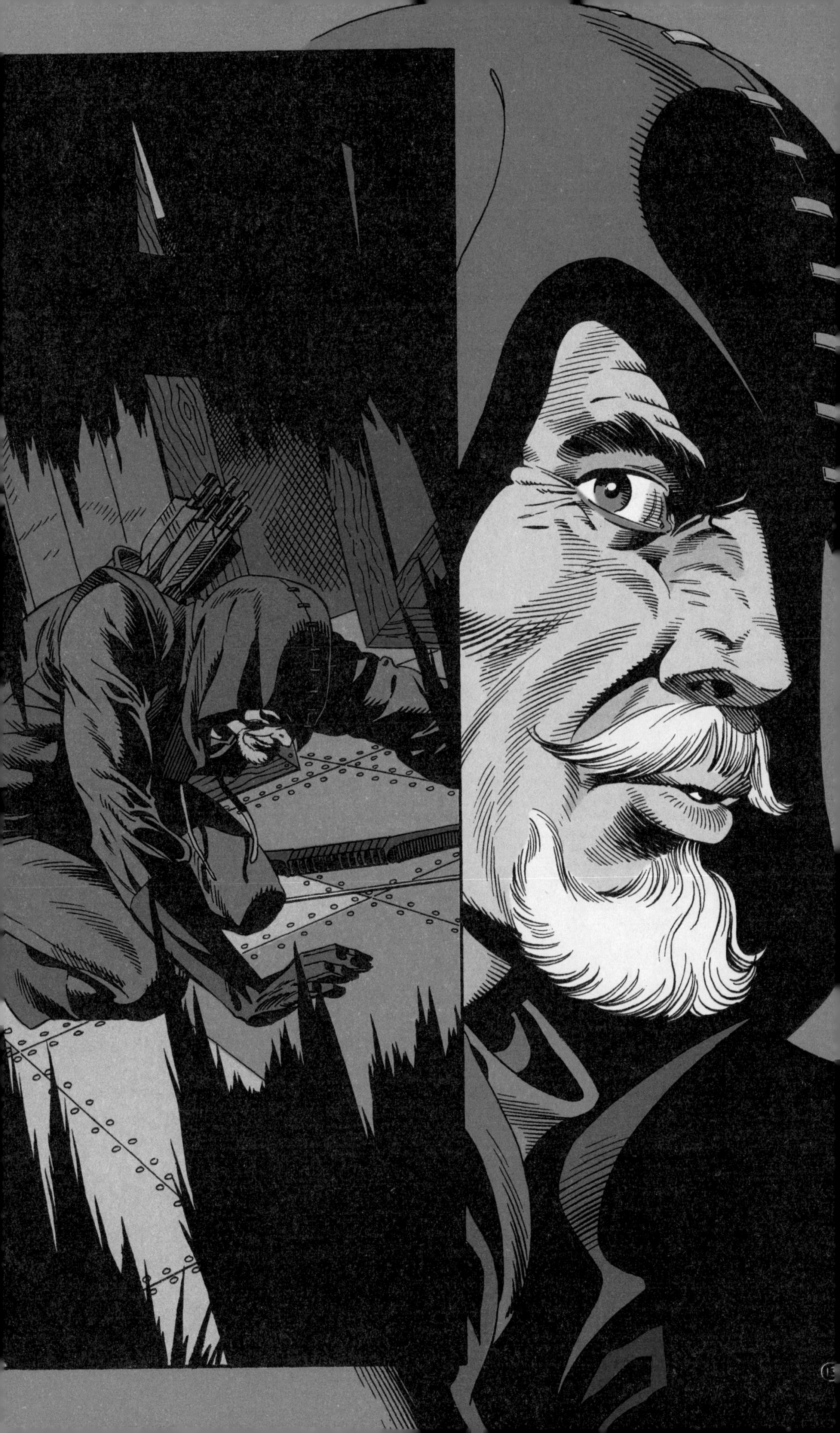

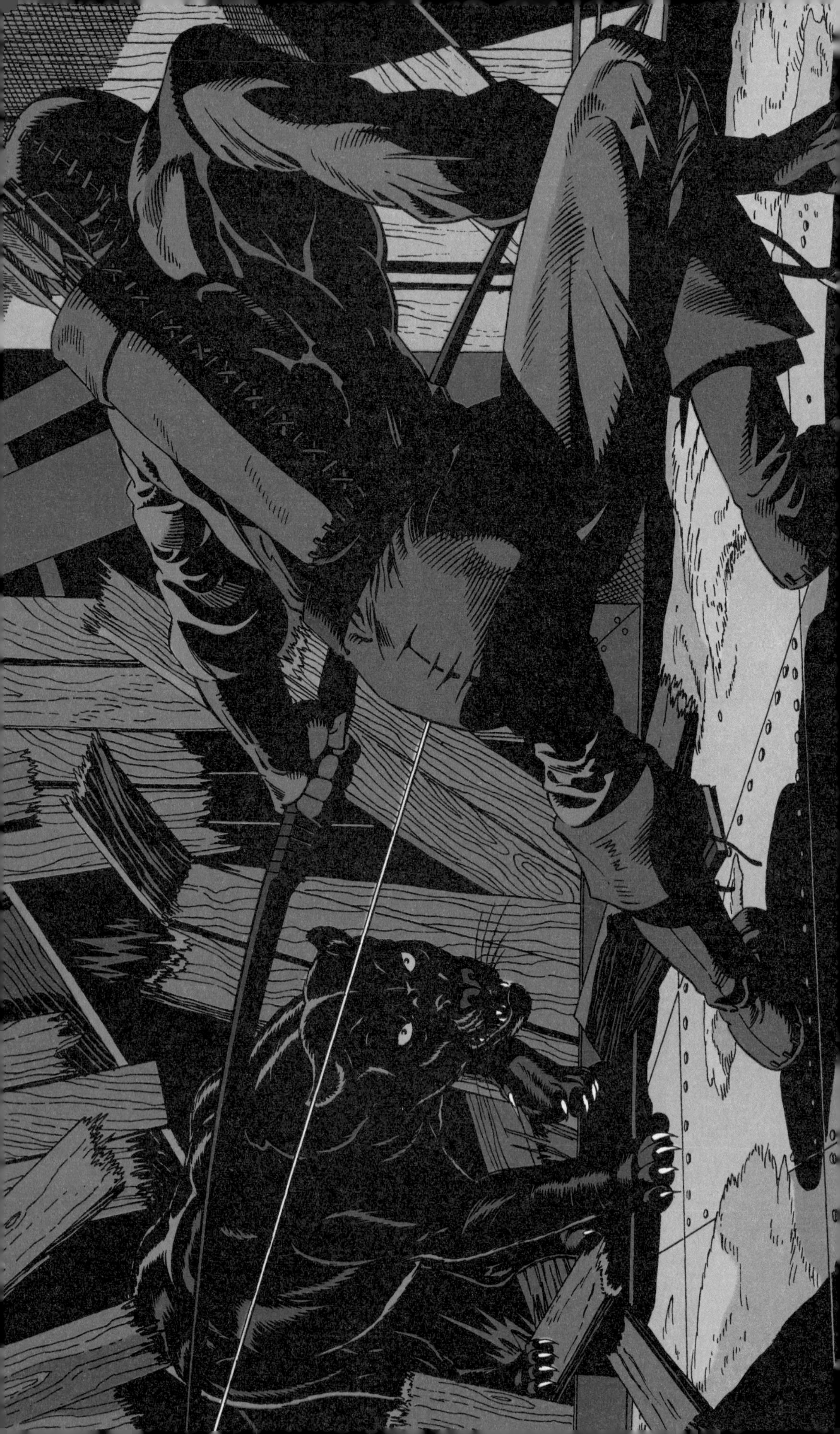

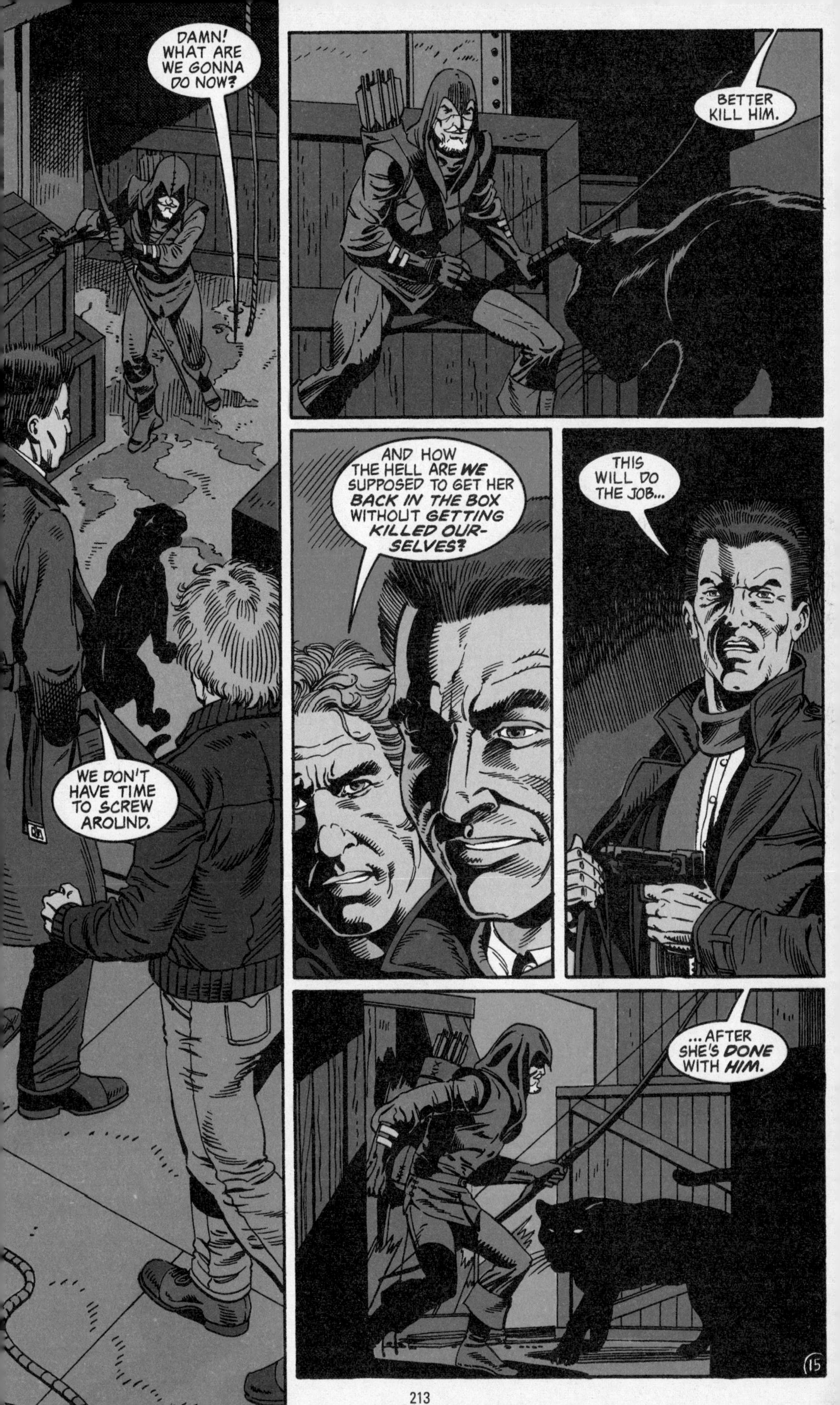
DAMN! WHAT ARE WE GONNA DO NOW?
WE DON'T HAVE TIME TO SCREW AROUND.
BETTER KILL HIM.
AND HOW THE HELL ARE *WE* SUPPOSED TO GET HER *BACK IN THE BOX* WITHOUT *GETTING KILLED OUR-SELVES?*
THIS WILL DO THE JOB...
...AFTER SHE'S *DONE* WITH *HIM*.
15

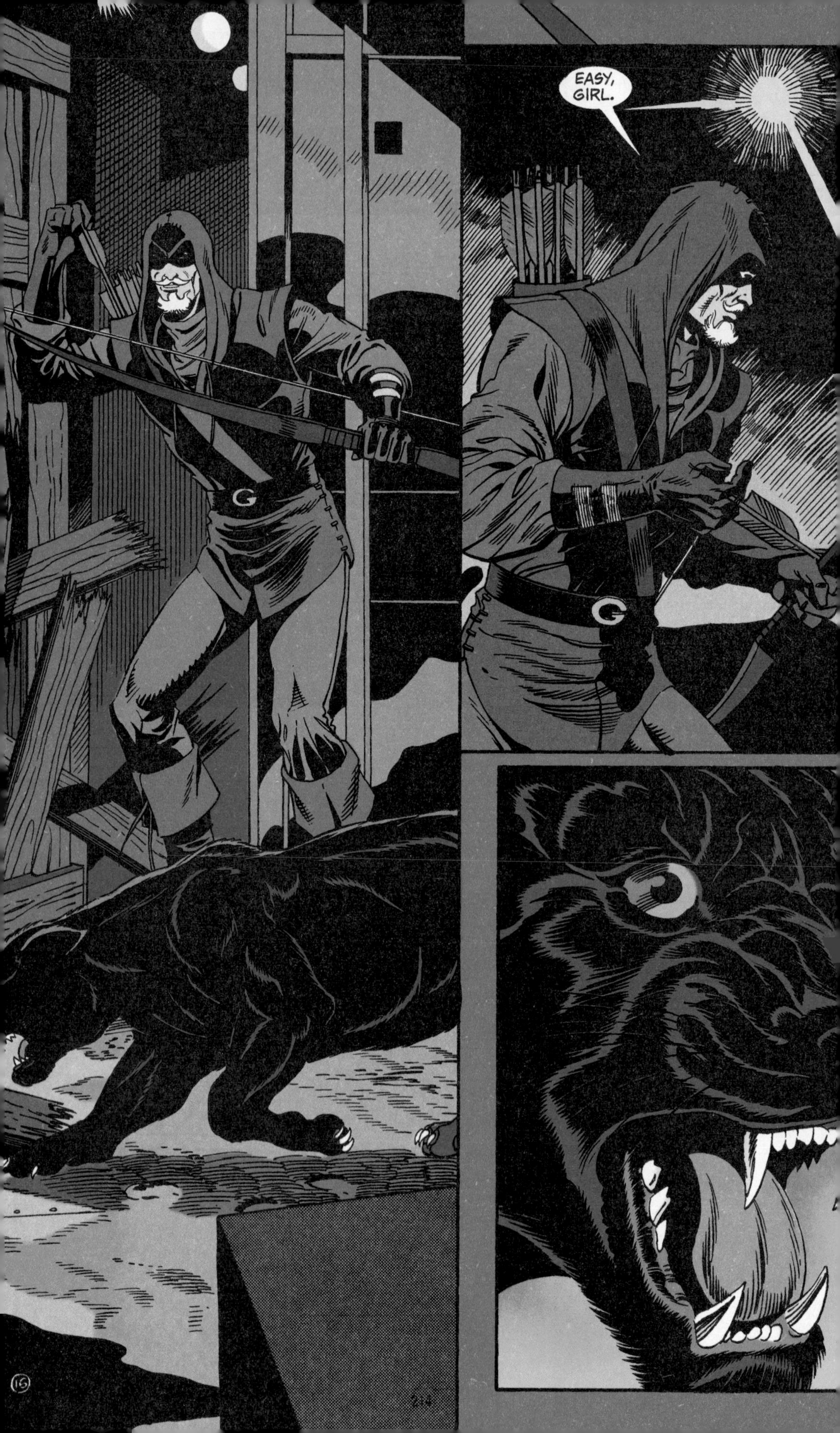
EASY,
GIRL.

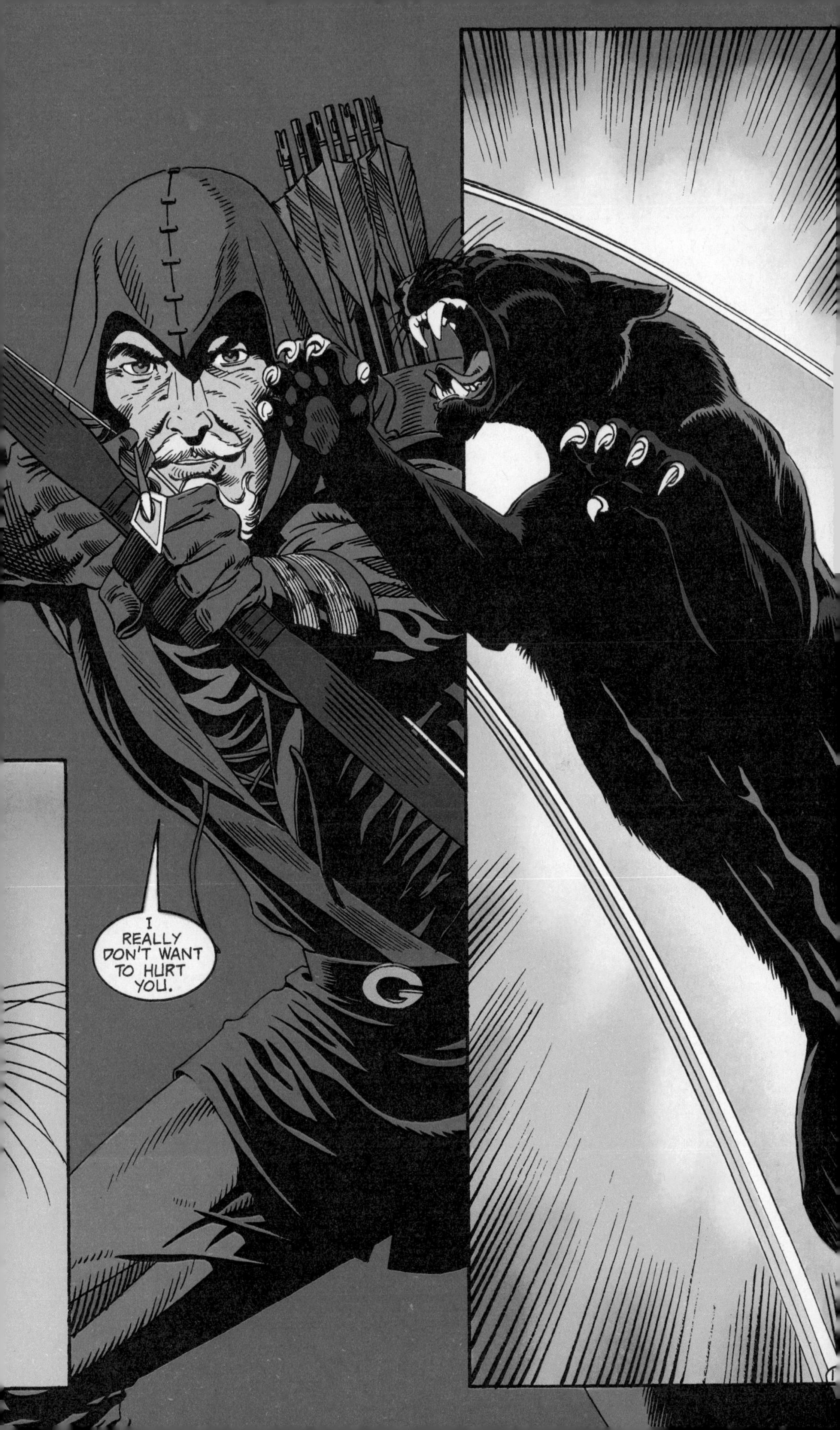
I REALLY DON'T WANT TO HURT YOU.

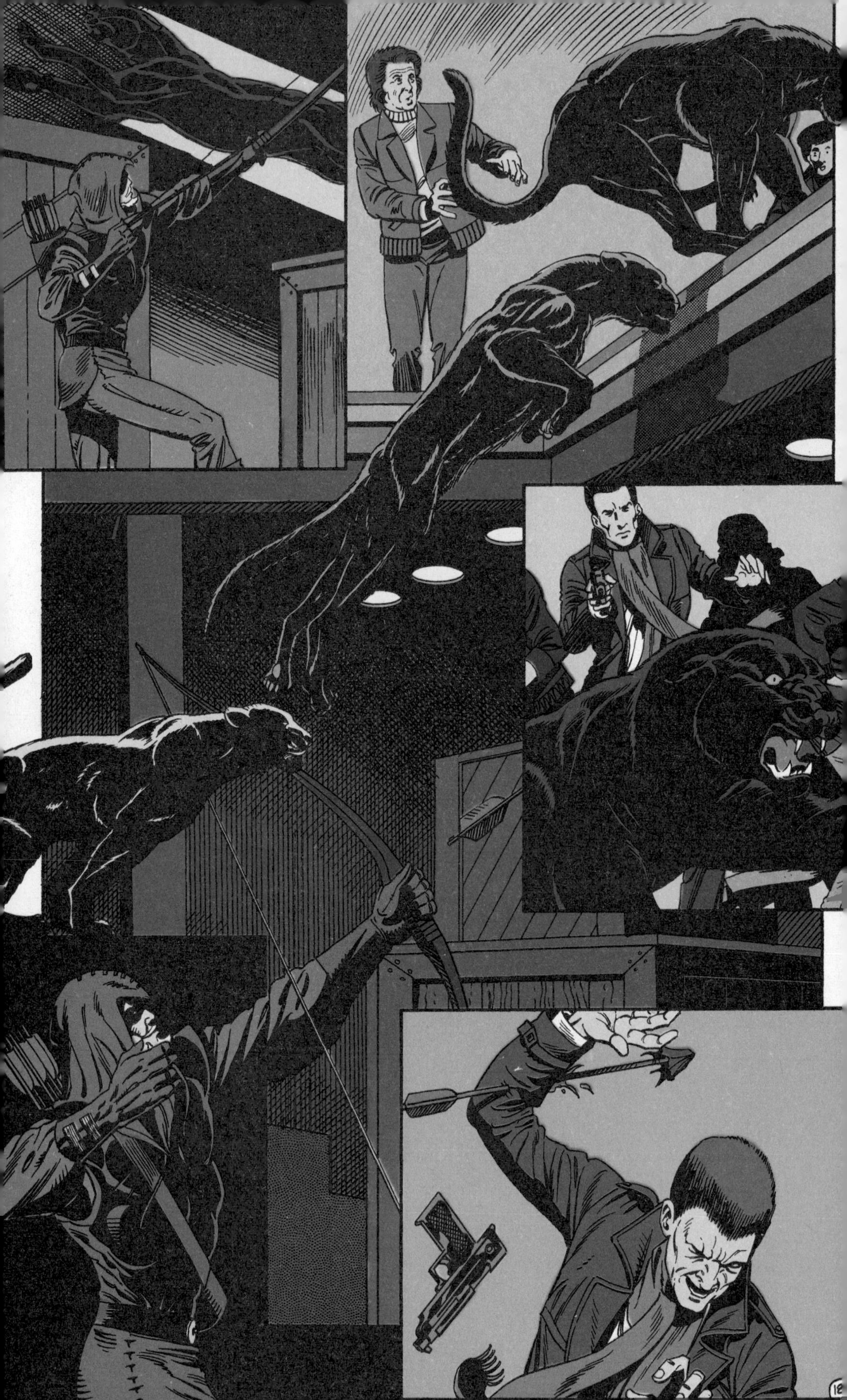

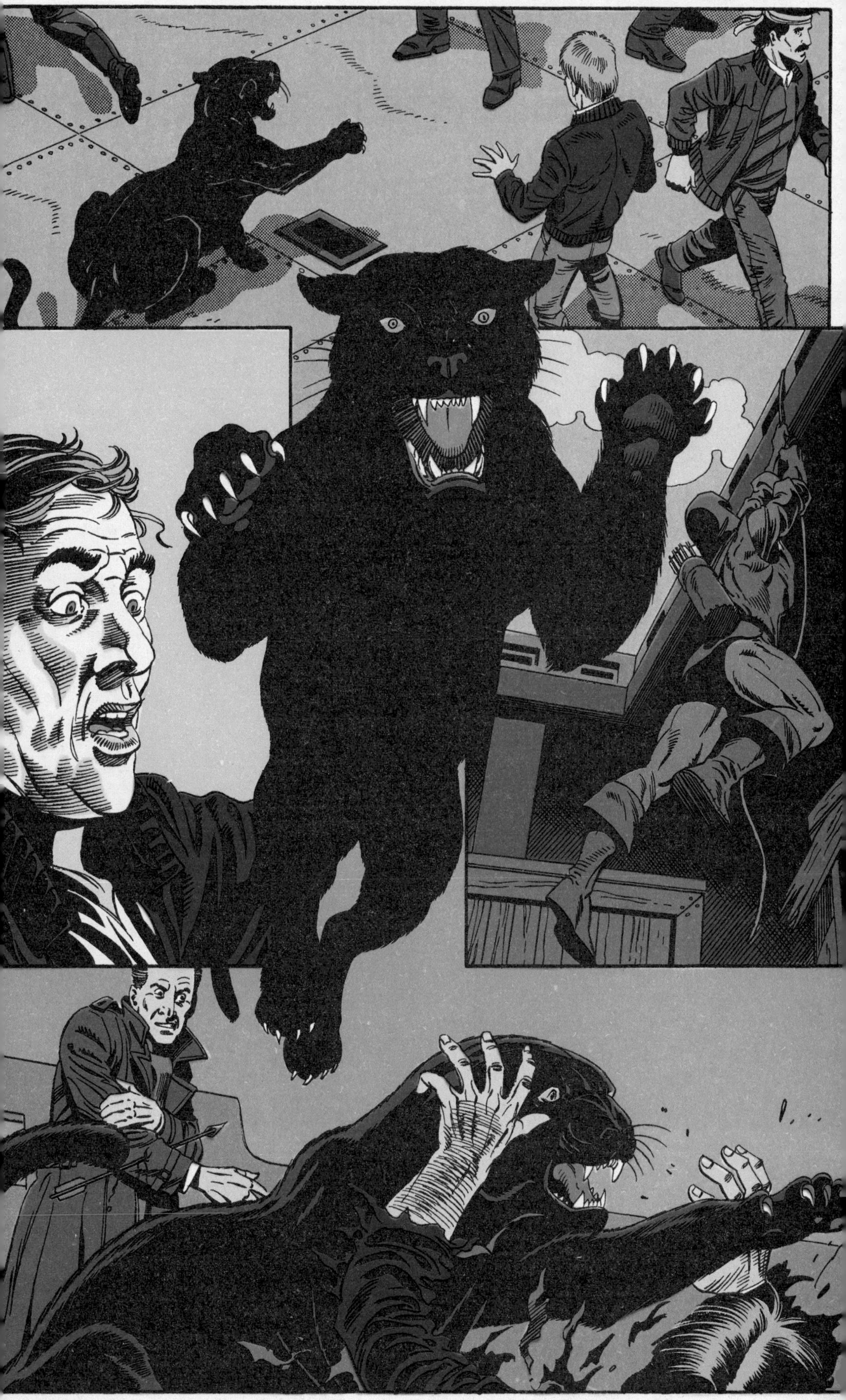

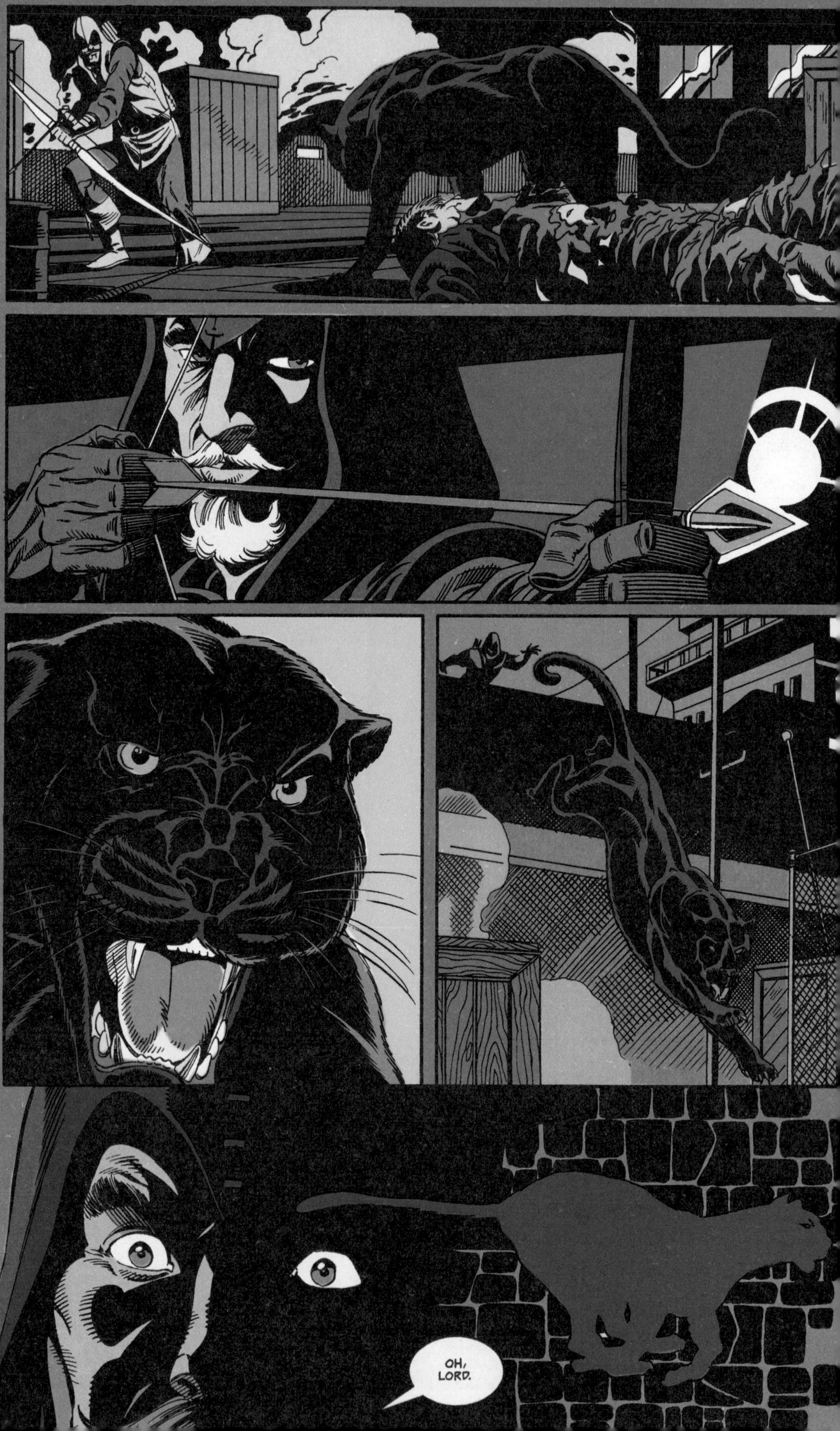
OH, LORD.

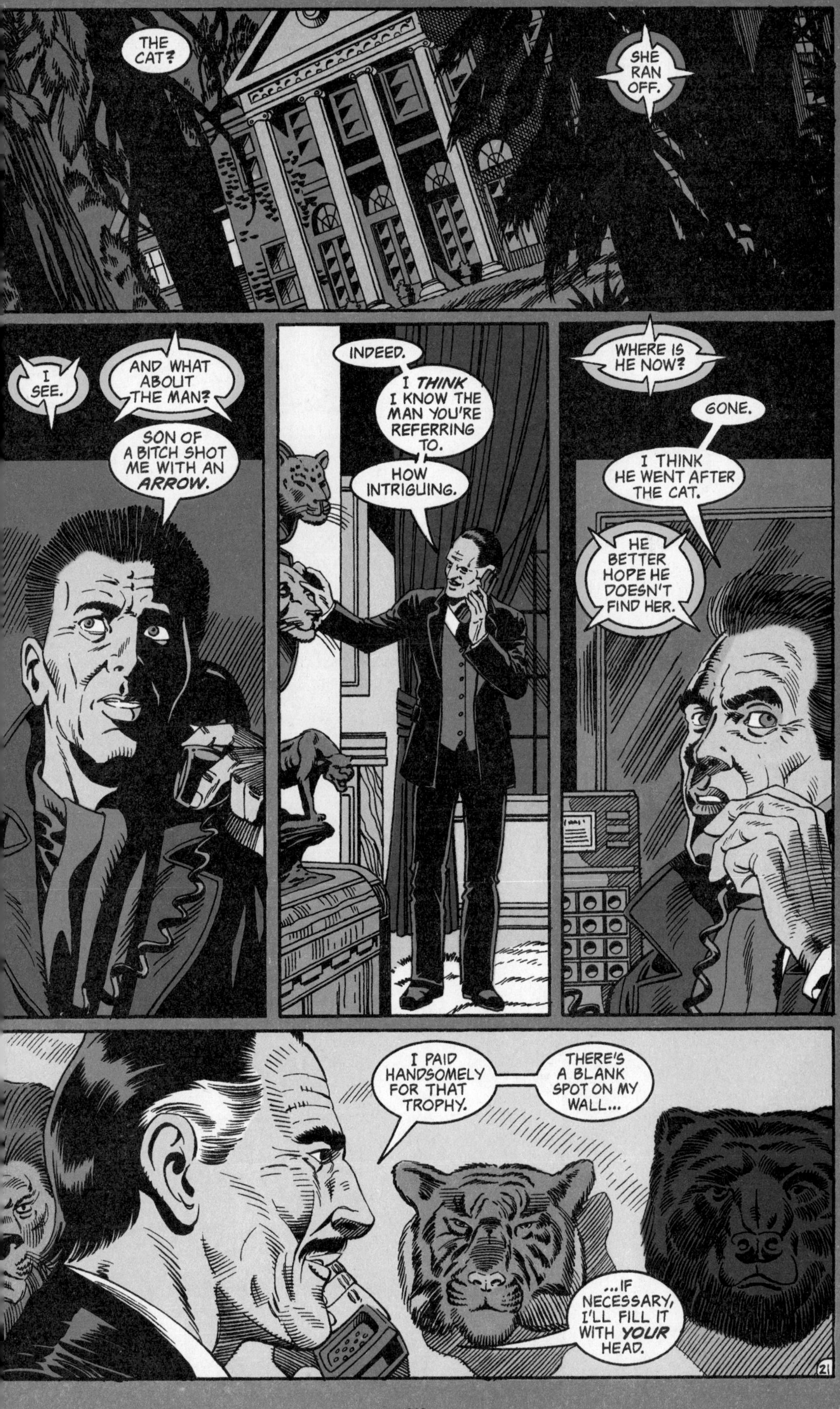
THE CAT?
SHE RAN OFF.
I SEE.
AND WHAT ABOUT THE MAN?
SON OF A BITCH SHOT ME WITH AN ARROW.
INDEED.
I THINK I KNOW THE MAN YOU'RE REFERRING TO.
HOW INTRIGUING.
WHERE IS HE NOW?
GONE.
I THINK HE WENT AFTER THE CAT.
HE BETTER HOPE HE DOESN'T FIND HER.
I PAID HANDSOMELY FOR THAT TROPHY.
THERE'S A BLANK SPOT ON MY WALL...
...IF NECESSARY, I'LL FILL IT WITH YOUR HEAD.
21

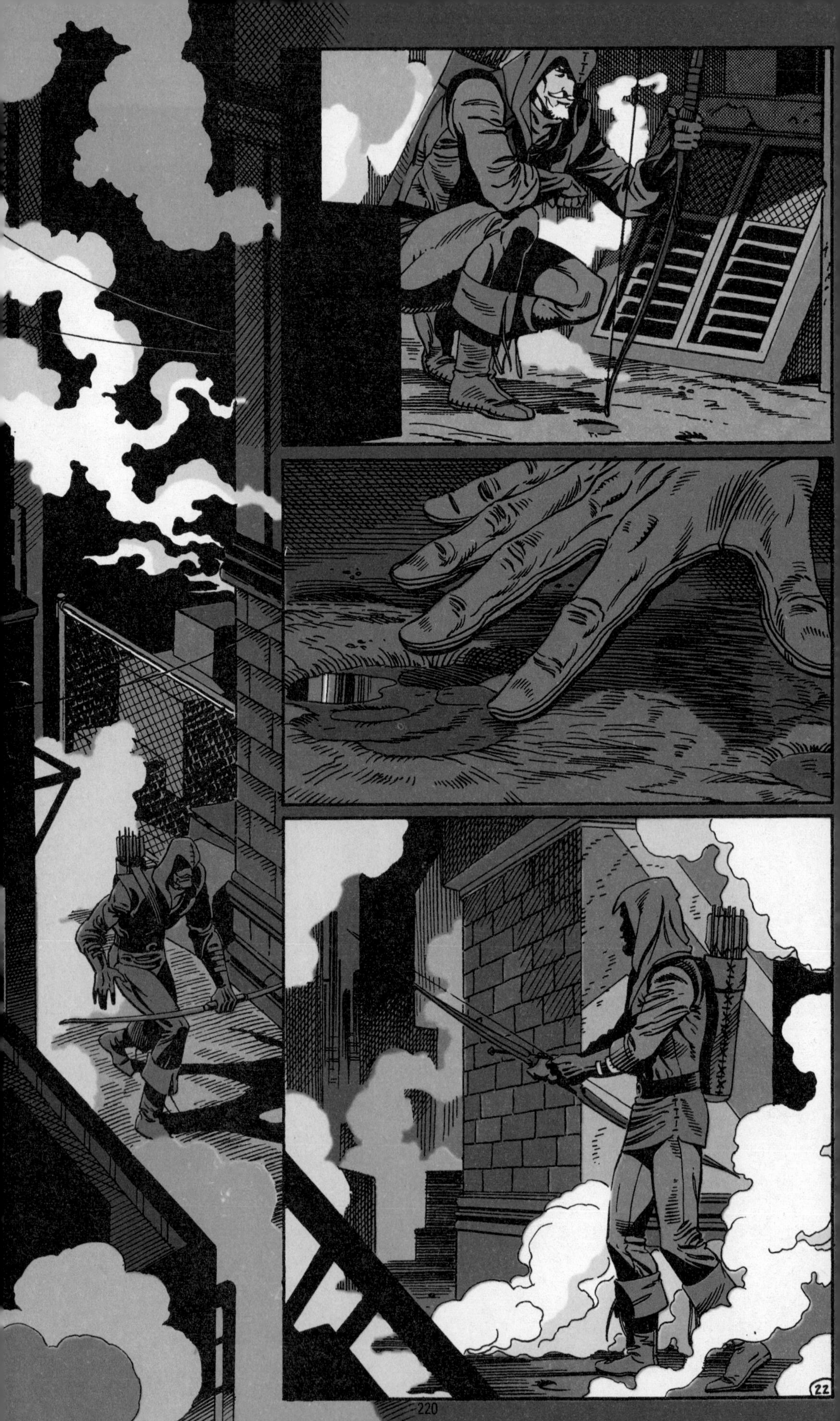
22

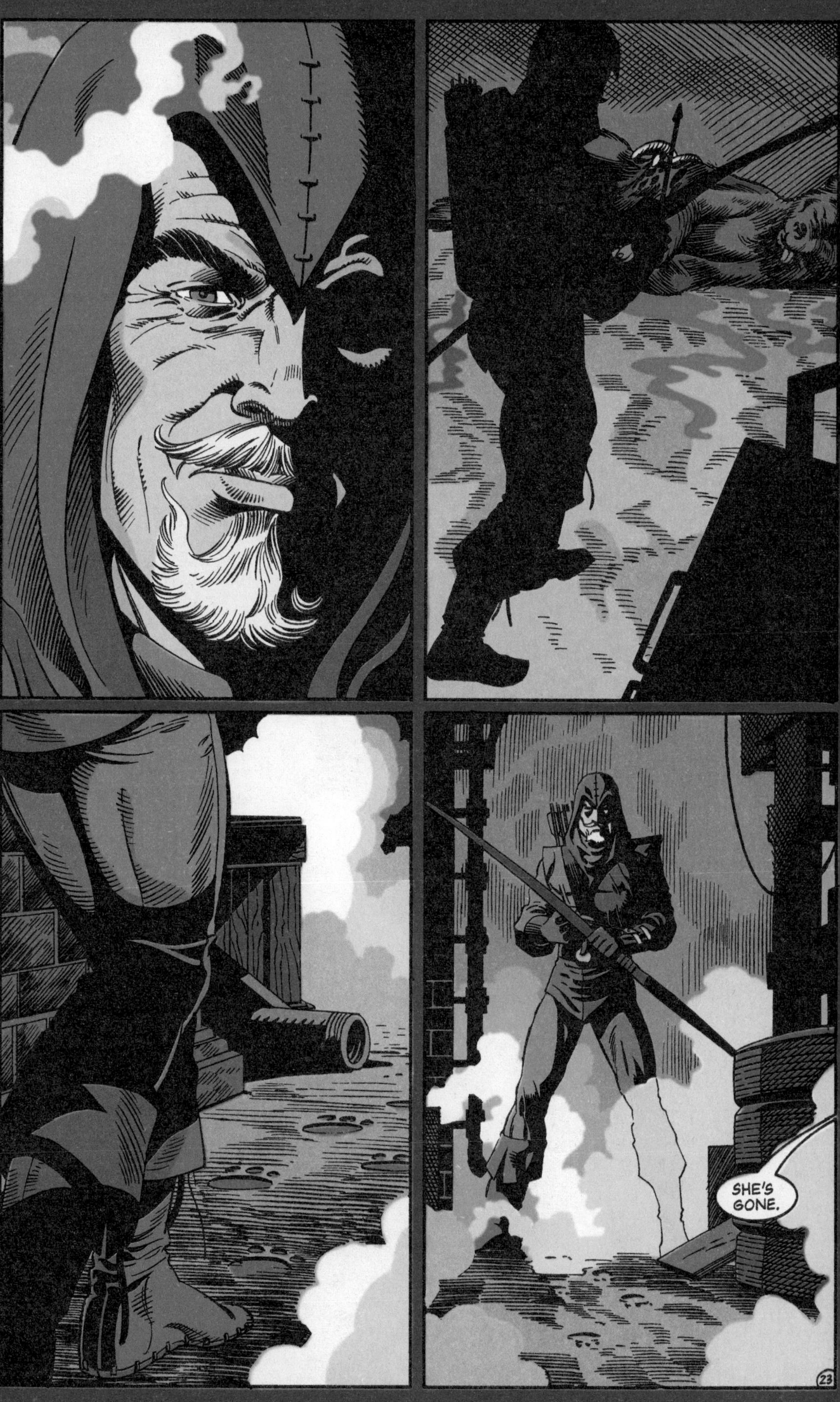
SHE'S GONE.
23

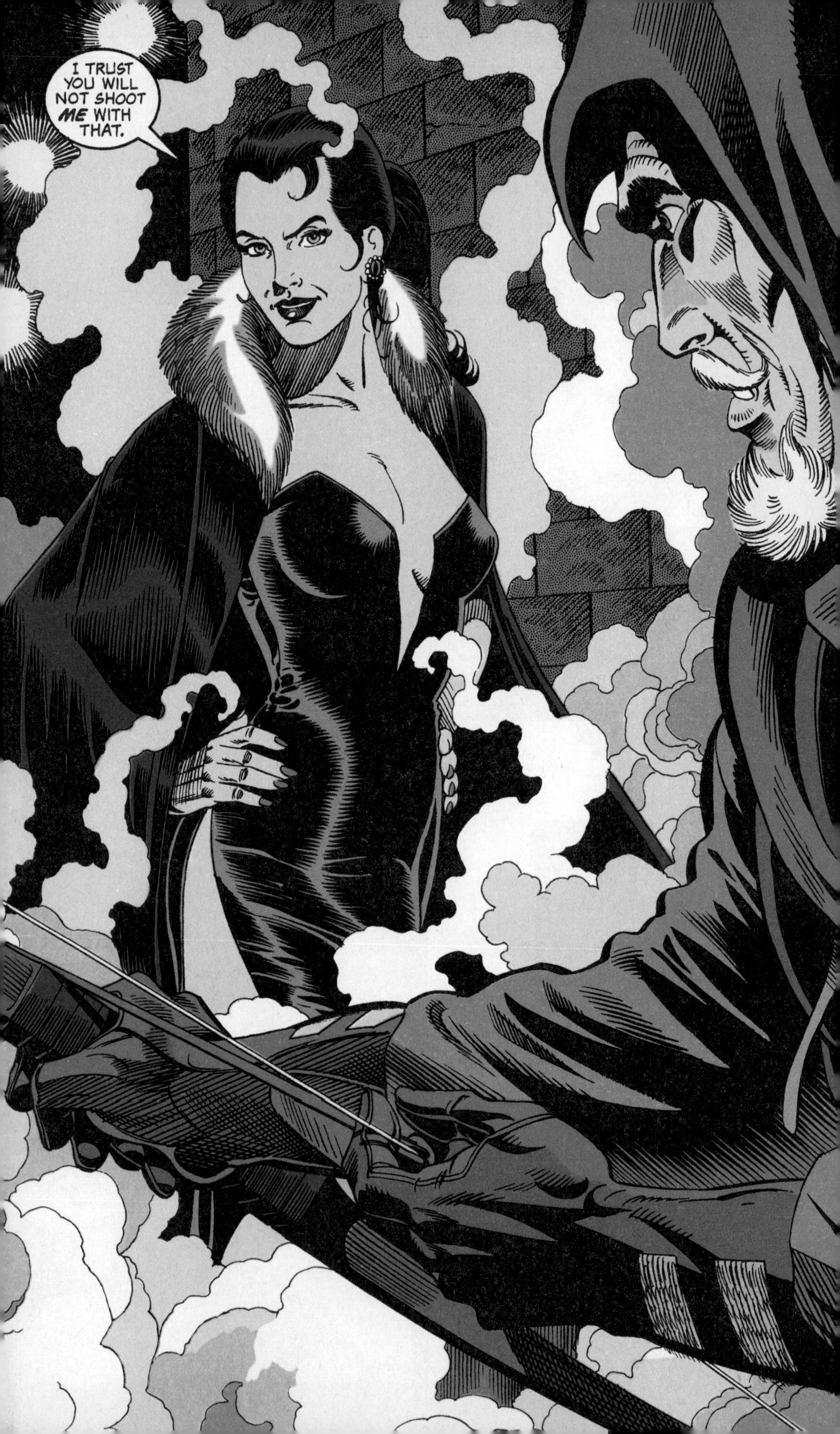
I TRUST YOU WILL NOT SHOOT *ME* WITH THAT.

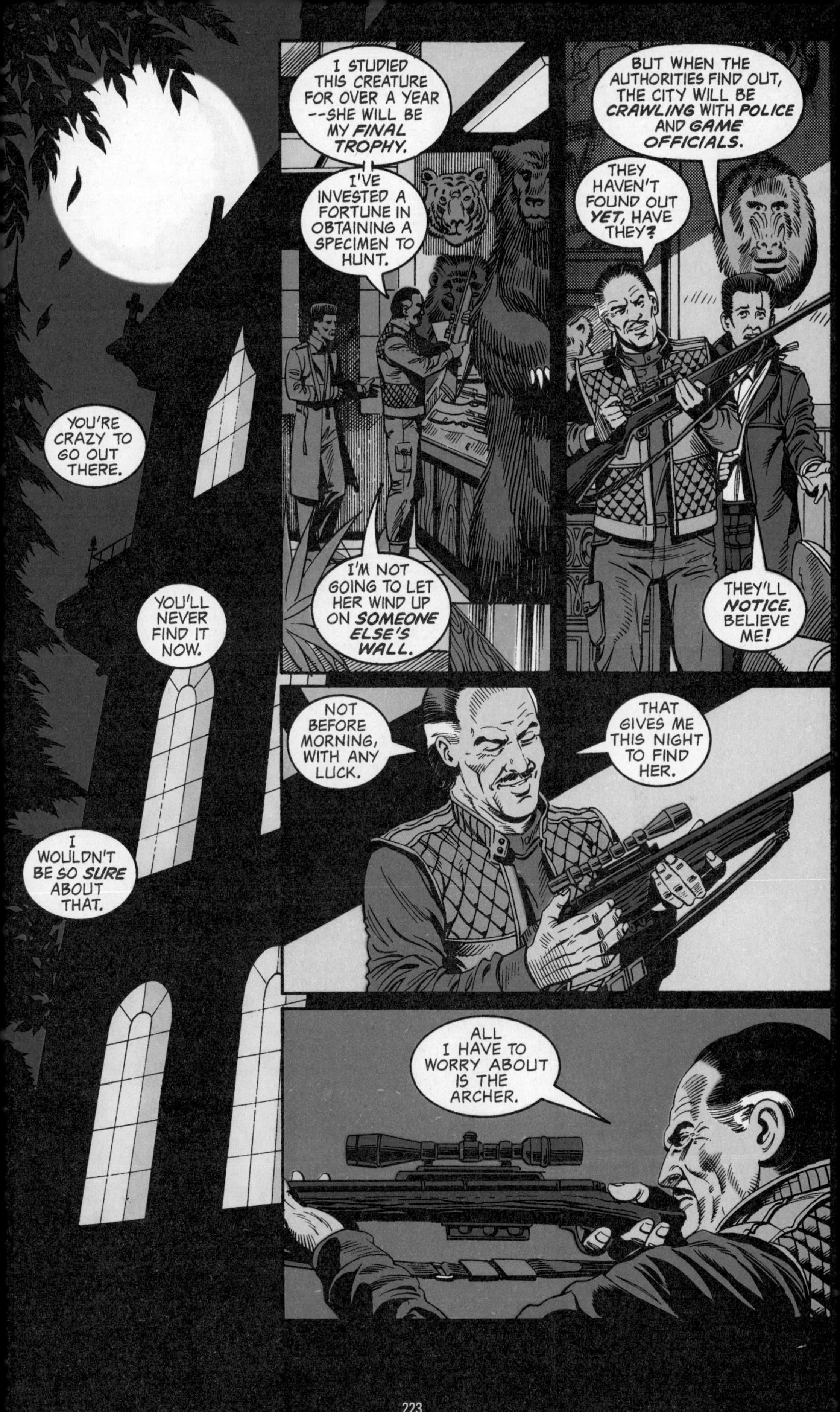

I STUDIED THIS CREATURE FOR OVER A YEAR --SHE WILL BE MY FINAL TROPHY.
I'VE INVESTED A FORTUNE IN OBTAINING A SPECIMEN TO HUNT.
I'M NOT GOING TO LET HER WIND UP ON SOMEONE ELSE'S WALL.
BUT WHEN THE AUTHORITIES FIND OUT, THE CITY WILL BE CRAWLING WITH POLICE AND GAME OFFICIALS.
THEY HAVEN'T FOUND OUT YET, HAVE THEY?
THEY'LL NOTICE. BELIEVE ME!
YOU'RE CRAZY TO GO OUT THERE.
NOT BEFORE MORNING, WITH ANY LUCK.
THAT GIVES ME THIS NIGHT TO FIND HER.
YOU'LL NEVER FIND IT NOW.
I WOULDN'T BE SO SURE ABOUT THAT.
ALL I HAVE TO WORRY ABOUT IS THE ARCHER.

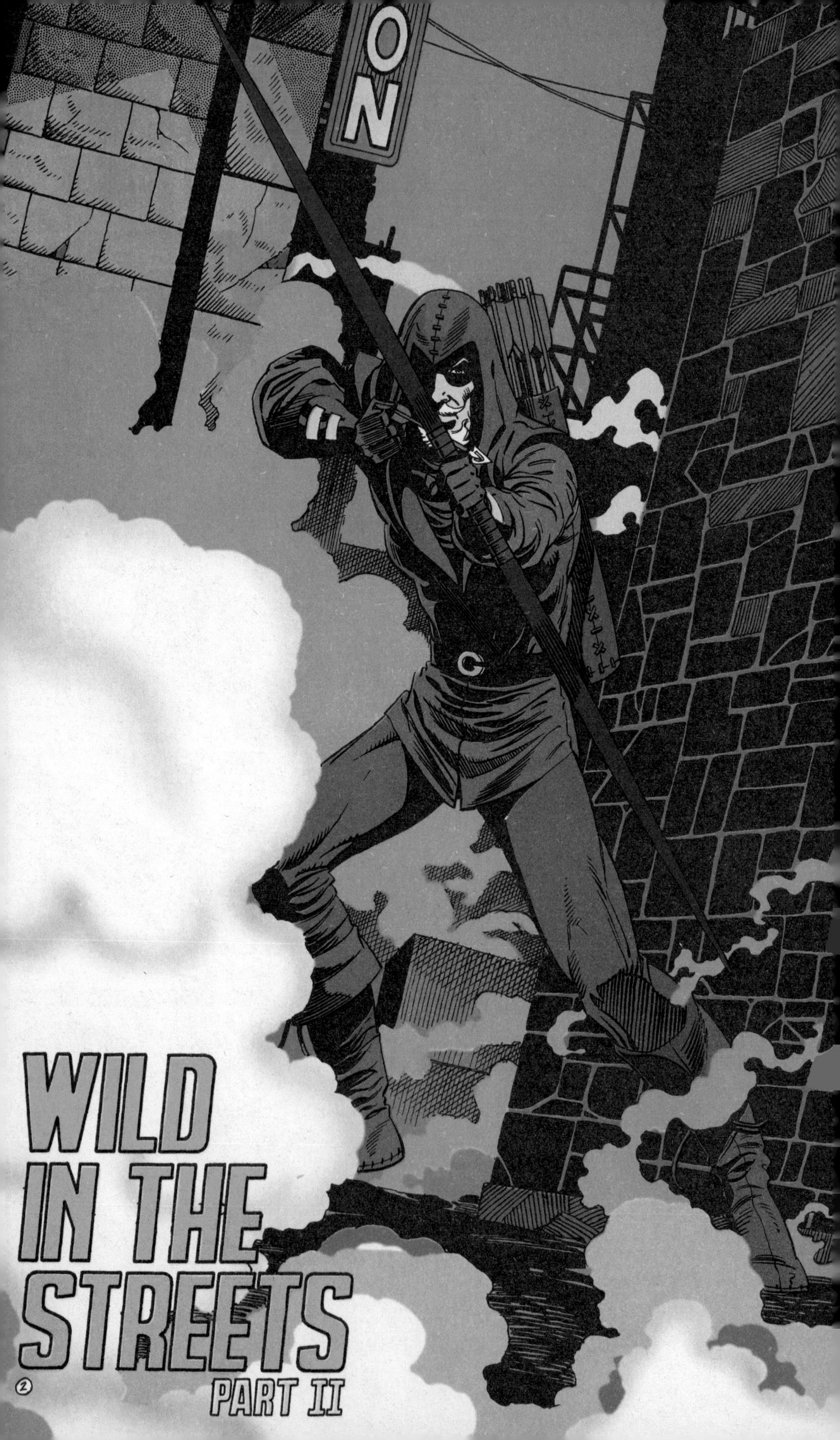
ON
WILD IN THE STREETS
PART II
2

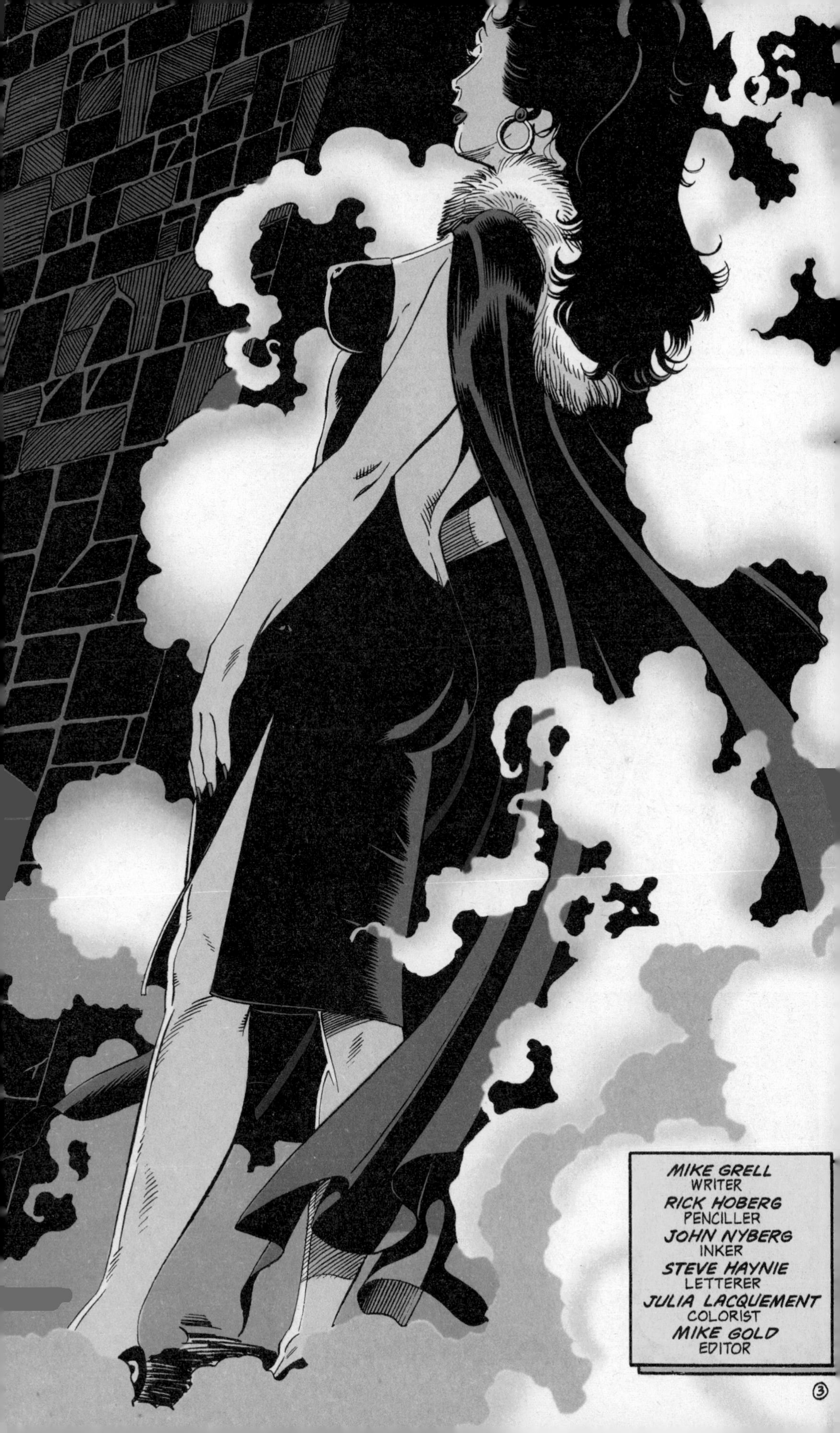
MIKE GRELL
WRITER
RICK HOBERG
PENCILLER
JOHN NYBERG
INKER
STEVE HAYNIE
LETTERER
JULIA LACQUEMENT
COLORIST
MIKE GOLD
EDITOR

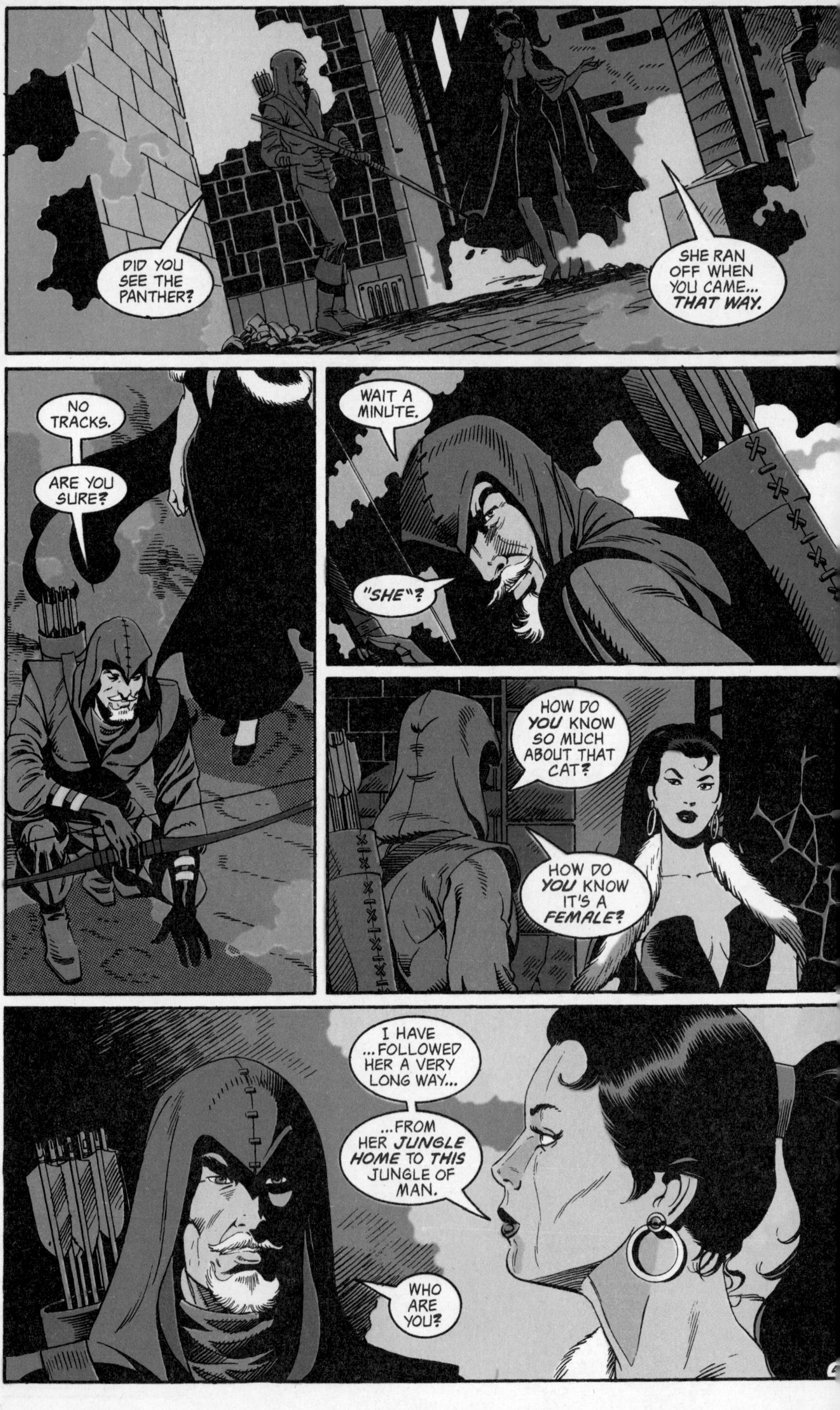
DID YOU SEE THE PANTHER?
SHE RAN OFF WHEN YOU CAME... **THAT WAY.**
NO TRACKS.
ARE YOU SURE?
WAIT A MINUTE.
"*SHE*"?
HOW DO *YOU* KNOW SO MUCH ABOUT THAT CAT?
HOW DO *YOU* KNOW IT'S A *FEMALE*?
I HAVE ...FOLLOWED HER A VERY LONG WAY...
...FROM HER *JUNGLE HOME* TO *THIS* JUNGLE OF MAN.
WHO ARE YOU?

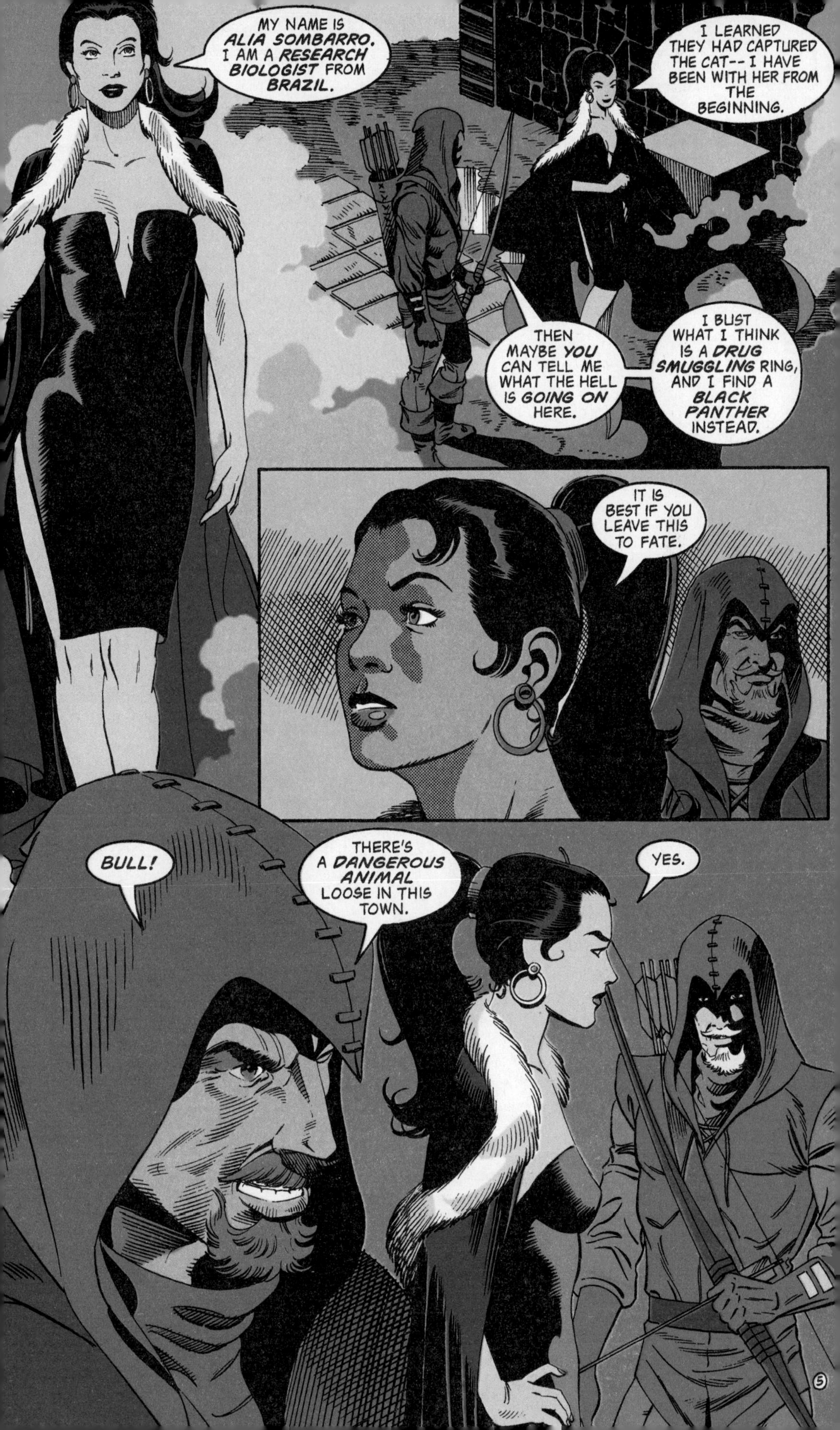
MY NAME IS ALIA SOMBARRO. I AM A RESEARCH BIOLOGIST FROM BRAZIL.
I LEARNED THEY HAD CAPTURED THE CAT-- I HAVE BEEN WITH HER FROM THE BEGINNING.
THEN MAYBE YOU CAN TELL ME WHAT THE HELL IS GOING ON HERE.
I BUST WHAT I THINK IS A DRUG SMUGGLING RING, AND I FIND A BLACK PANTHER INSTEAD.
IT IS BEST IF YOU LEAVE THIS TO FATE.
BULL!
THERE'S A DANGEROUS ANIMAL LOOSE IN THIS TOWN.
YES.
5

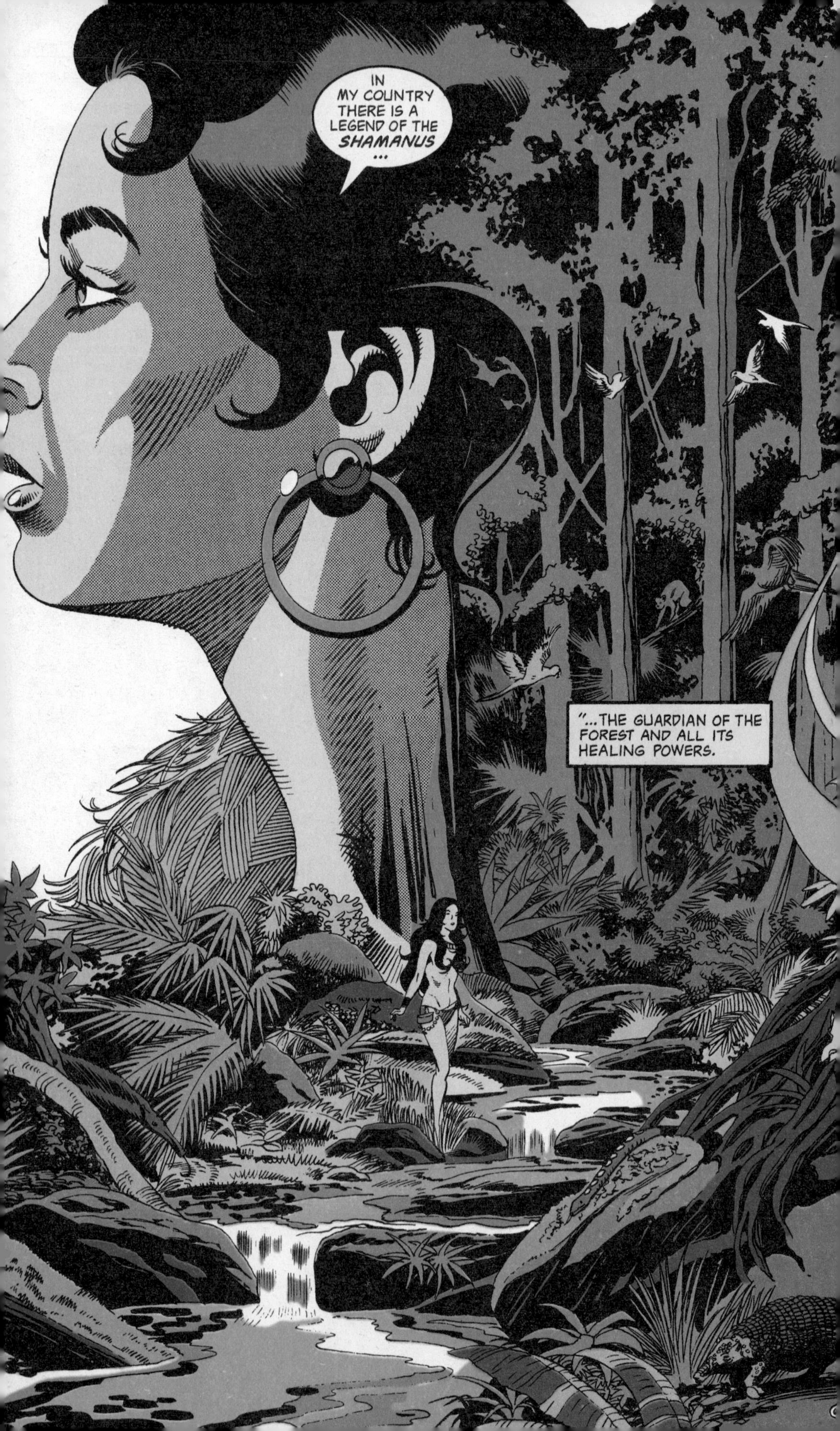
IN MY COUNTRY THERE IS A LEGEND OF THE SHAMANUS ...
"...THE GUARDIAN OF THE FOREST AND ALL ITS HEALING POWERS.

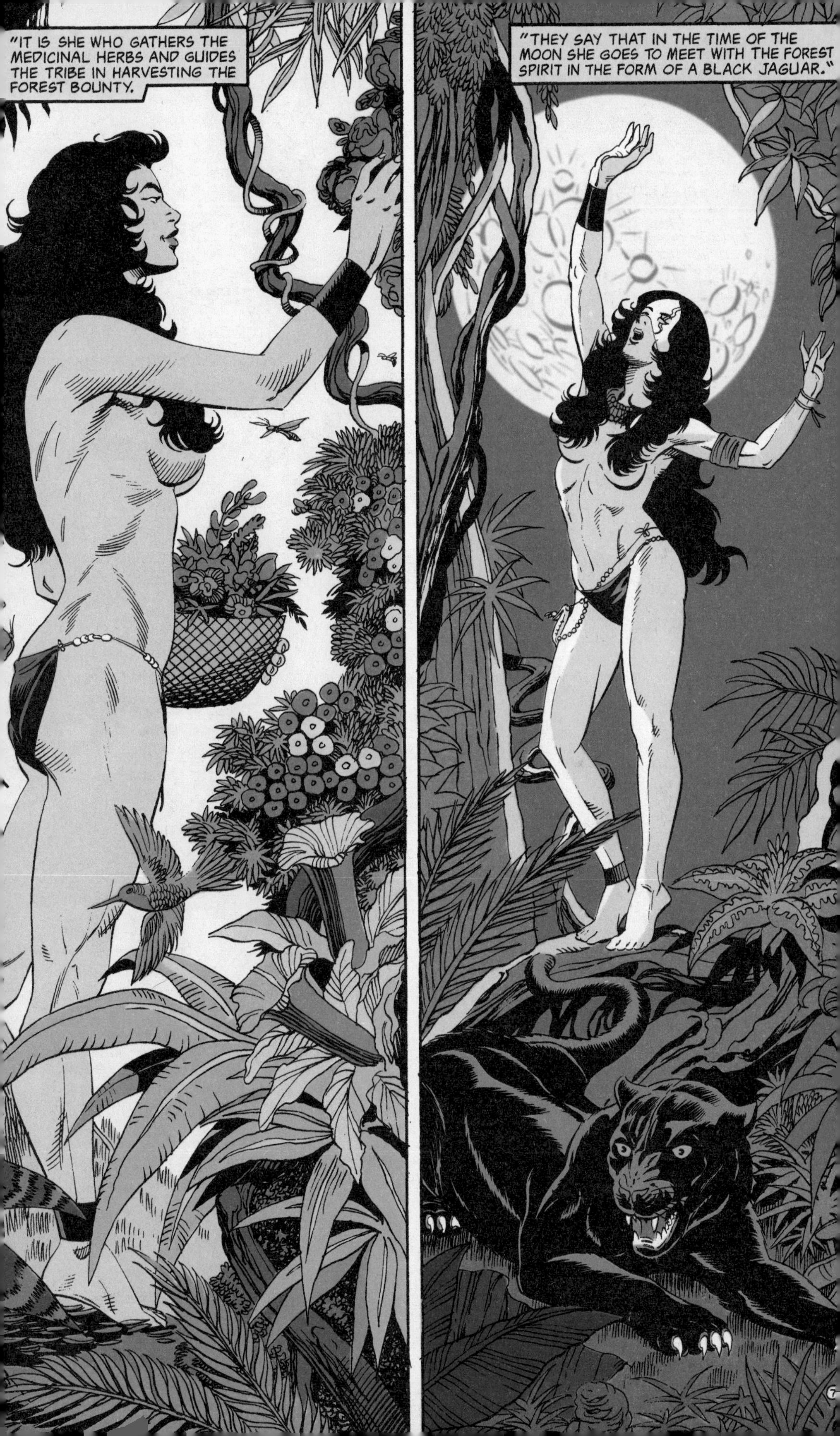
"IT IS SHE WHO GATHERS THE MEDICINAL HERBS AND GUIDES THE TRIBE IN HARVESTING THE FOREST BOUNTY.
"THEY SAY THAT IN THE TIME OF THE MOON SHE GOES TO MEET WITH THE FOREST SPIRIT IN THE FORM OF A BLACK JAGUAR."

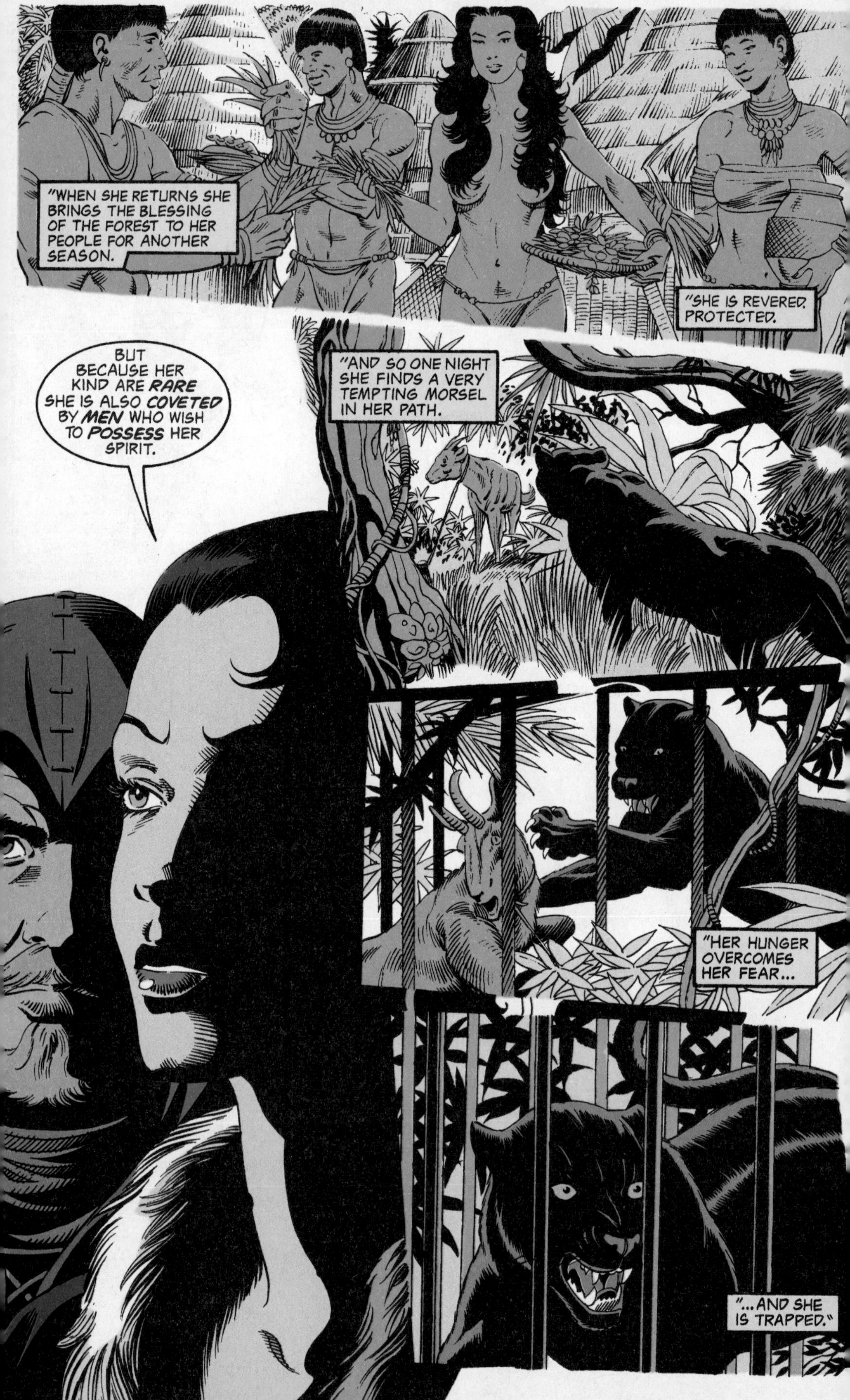
"WHEN SHE RETURNS SHE BRINGS THE BLESSING OF THE FOREST TO HER PEOPLE FOR ANOTHER SEASON.
"SHE IS REVERED. PROTECTED.
BUT BECAUSE HER KIND ARE RARE SHE IS ALSO COVETED BY MEN WHO WISH TO POSSESS HER SPIRIT.
"AND SO ONE NIGHT SHE FINDS A VERY TEMPTING MORSEL IN HER PATH.
"HER HUNGER OVERCOMES HER FEAR...
"...AND SHE IS TRAPPED."

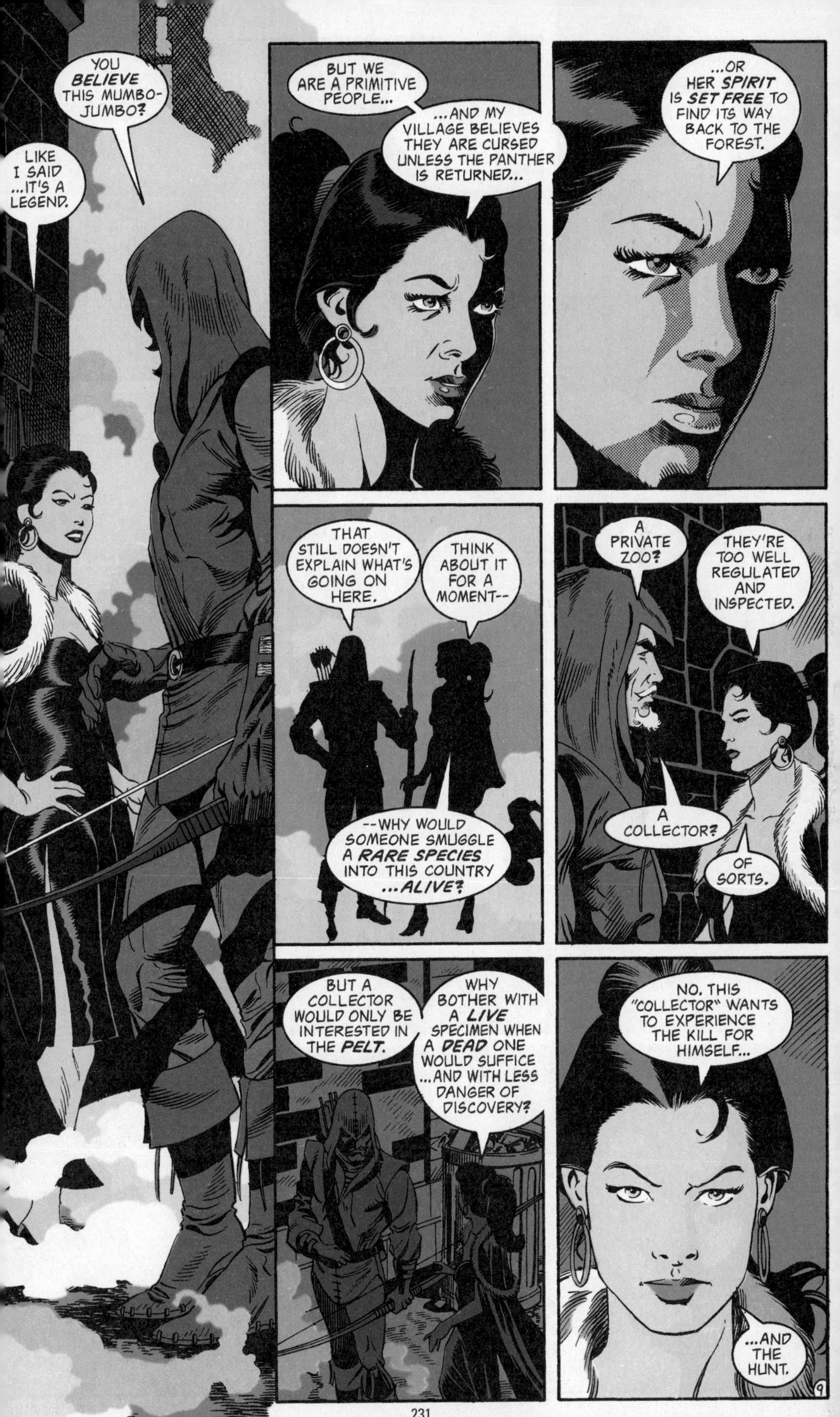

YOU BELIEVE THIS MUMBO-JUMBO?
LIKE I SAID ...IT'S A LEGEND.
BUT WE ARE A PRIMITIVE PEOPLE...
...AND MY VILLAGE BELIEVES THEY ARE CURSED UNLESS THE PANTHER IS RETURNED...
...OR HER SPIRIT IS SET FREE TO FIND ITS WAY BACK TO THE FOREST.
THAT STILL DOESN'T EXPLAIN WHAT'S GOING ON HERE.
THINK ABOUT IT FOR A MOMENT--
--WHY WOULD SOMEONE SMUGGLE A RARE SPECIES INTO THIS COUNTRY ...ALIVE?
A PRIVATE ZOO?
THEY'RE TOO WELL REGULATED AND INSPECTED.
A COLLECTOR?
OF SORTS.
BUT A COLLECTOR WOULD ONLY BE INTERESTED IN THE PELT.
WHY BOTHER WITH A LIVE SPECIMEN WHEN A DEAD ONE WOULD SUFFICE ...AND WITH LESS DANGER OF DISCOVERY?
NO. THIS "COLLECTOR" WANTS TO EXPERIENCE THE KILL FOR HIMSELF...
...AND THE HUNT.
9

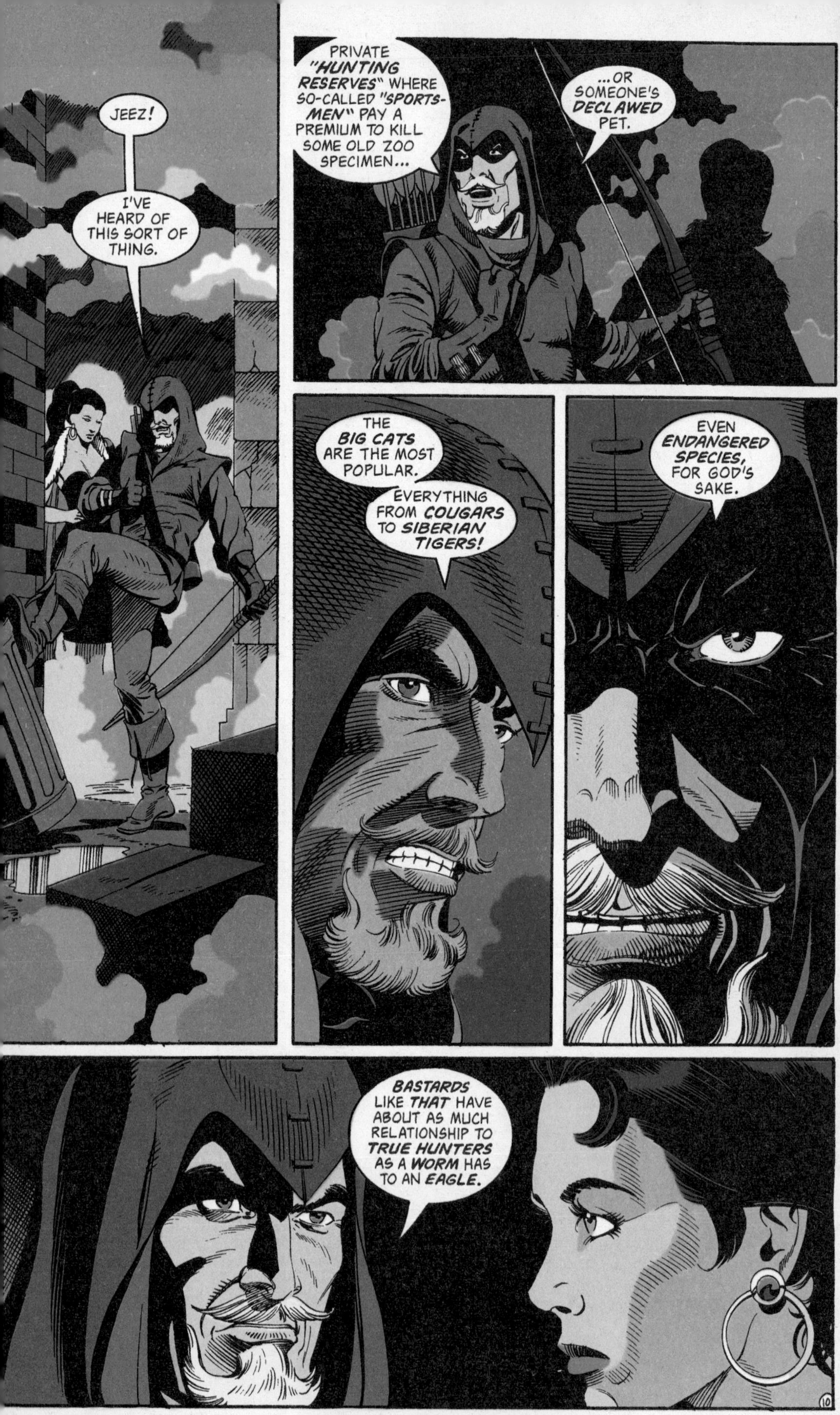
JEEZ!
I'VE HEARD OF THIS SORT OF THING.
PRIVATE "HUNTING RESERVES" WHERE SO-CALLED "SPORTS-MEN" PAY A PREMIUM TO KILL SOME OLD ZOO SPECIMEN...
...OR SOMEONE'S DECLAWED PET.
THE BIG CATS ARE THE MOST POPULAR.
EVERYTHING FROM COUGARS TO SIBERIAN TIGERS!
EVEN ENDANGERED SPECIES, FOR GOD'S SAKE.
BASTARDS LIKE THAT HAVE ABOUT AS MUCH RELATIONSHIP TO TRUE HUNTERS AS A WORM HAS TO AN EAGLE.
10

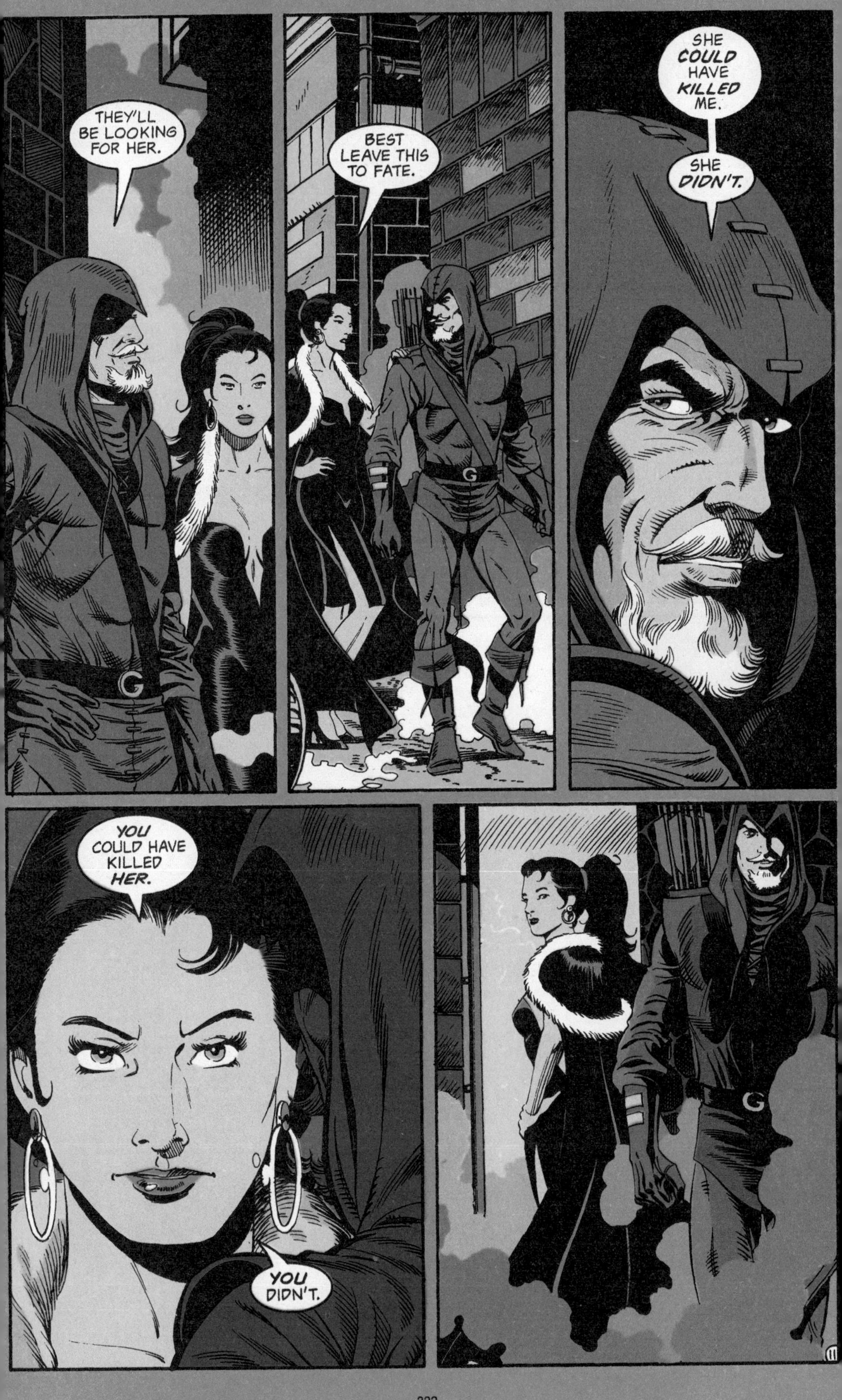
THEY'LL BE LOOKING FOR HER.
BEST LEAVE THIS TO FATE.
SHE COULD HAVE KILLED ME.
SHE DIDN'T.
YOU COULD HAVE KILLED HER.
YOU DIDN'T.
11

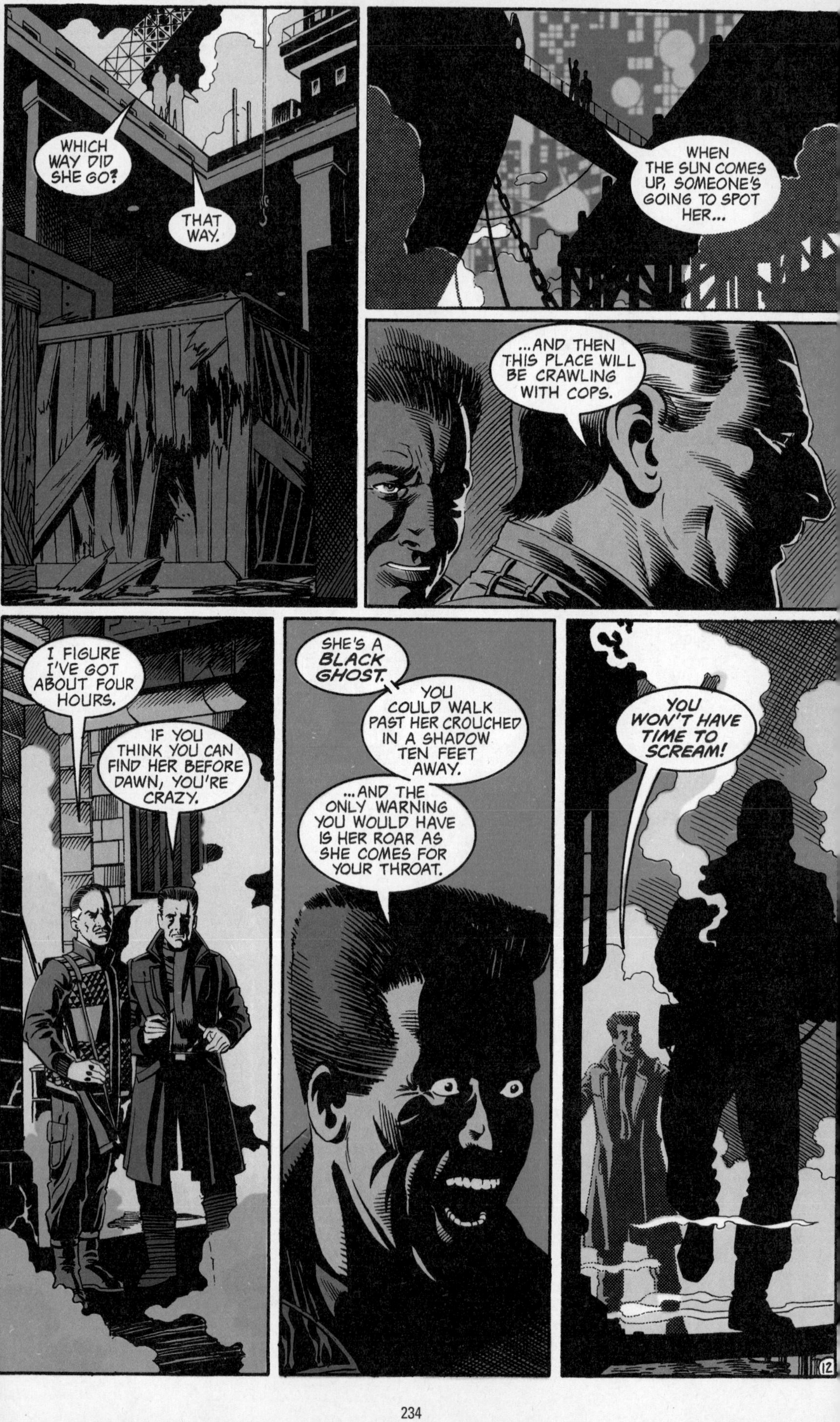
WHICH WAY DID SHE GO?
THAT WAY.
WHEN THE SUN COMES UP, SOMEONE'S GOING TO SPOT HER...
...AND THEN THIS PLACE WILL BE CRAWLING WITH COPS.
I FIGURE I'VE GOT ABOUT FOUR HOURS.
IF YOU THINK YOU CAN FIND HER BEFORE DAWN, YOU'RE CRAZY.
SHE'S A BLACK GHOST.
YOU COULD WALK PAST HER CROUCHED IN A SHADOW TEN FEET AWAY.
...AND THE ONLY WARNING YOU WOULD HAVE IS HER ROAR AS SHE COMES FOR YOUR THROAT.
YOU WON'T HAVE TIME TO SCREAM!
12

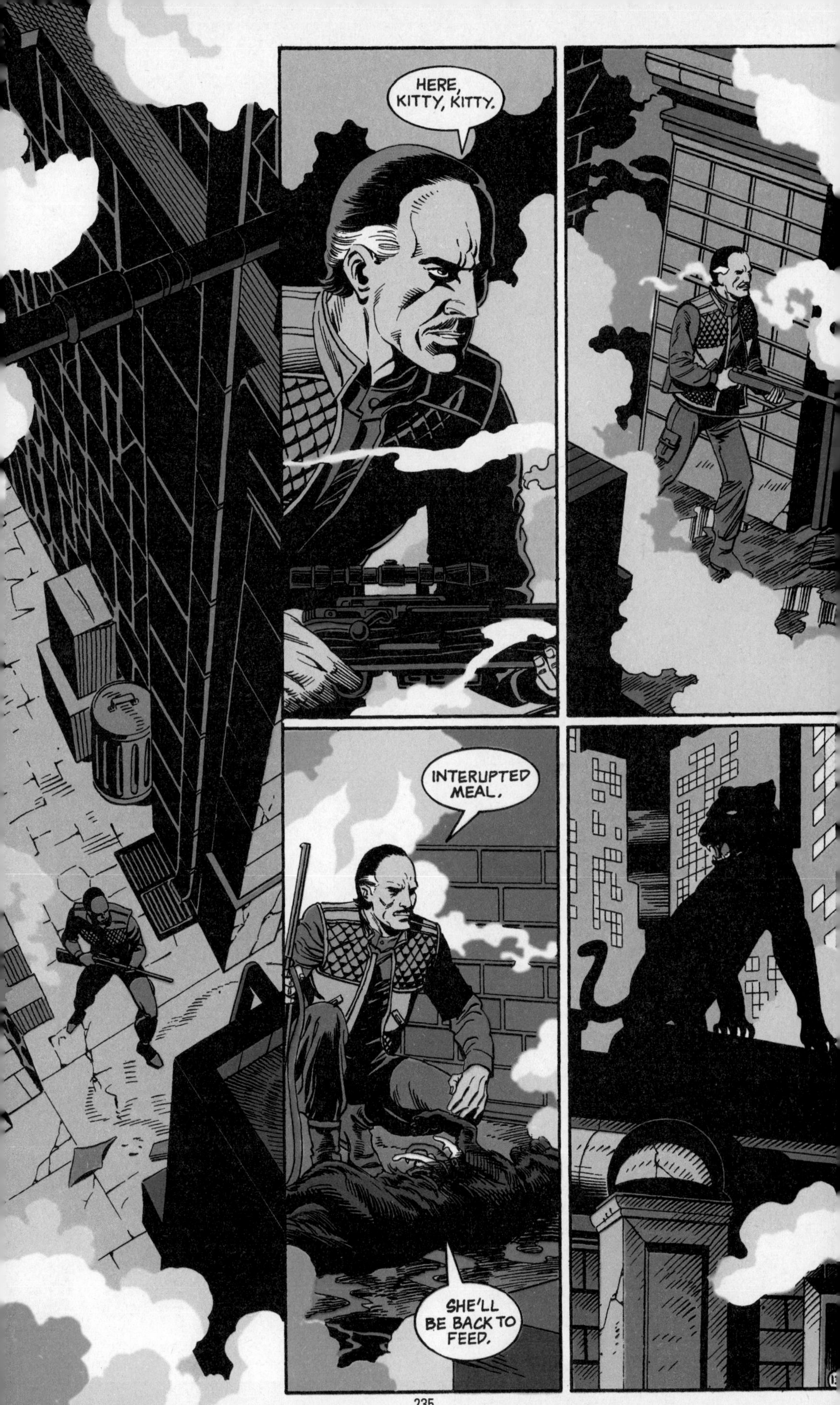
HERE, KITTY, KITTY.
INTERUPTED MEAL.
SHE'LL BE BACK TO FEED.

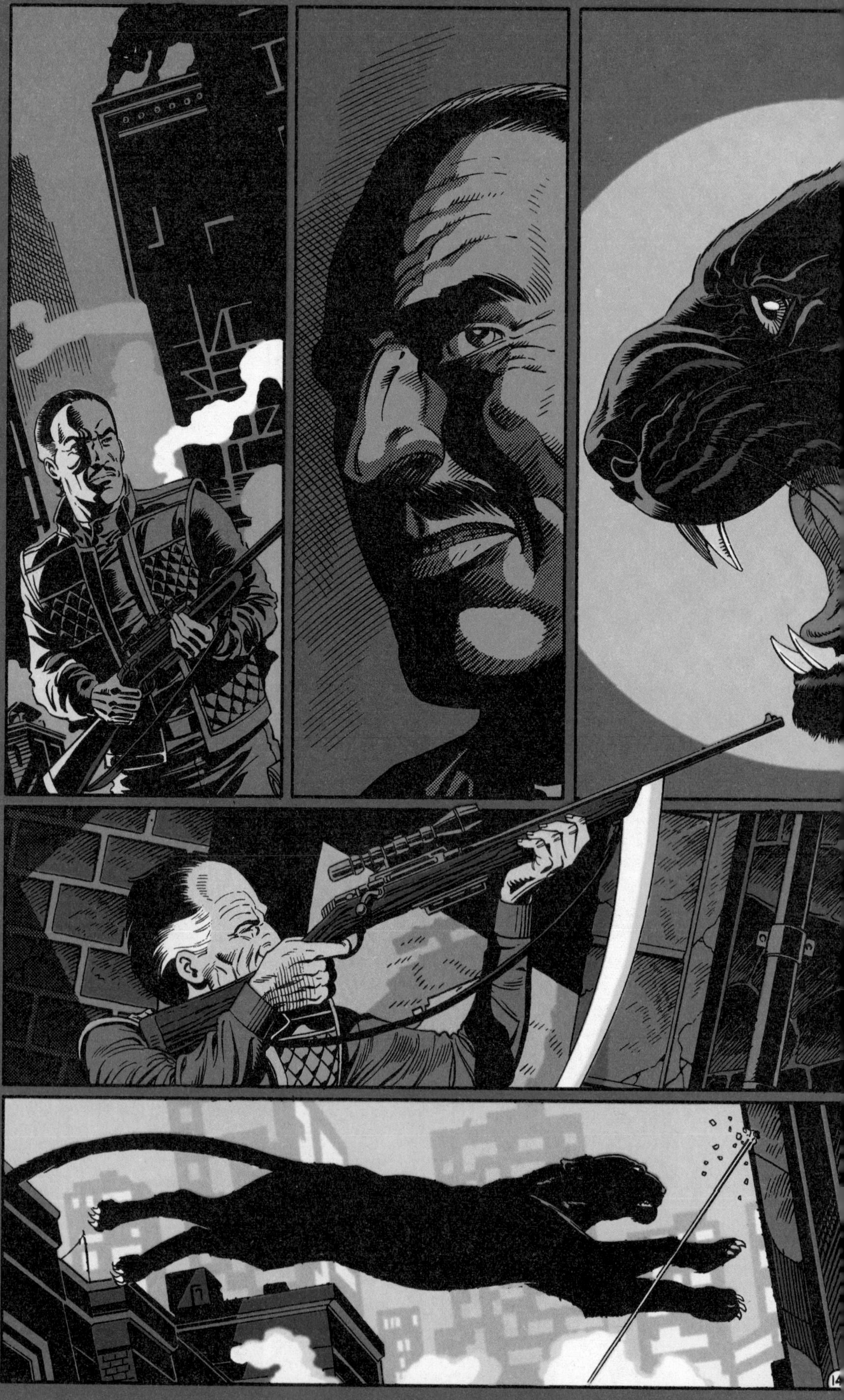
14

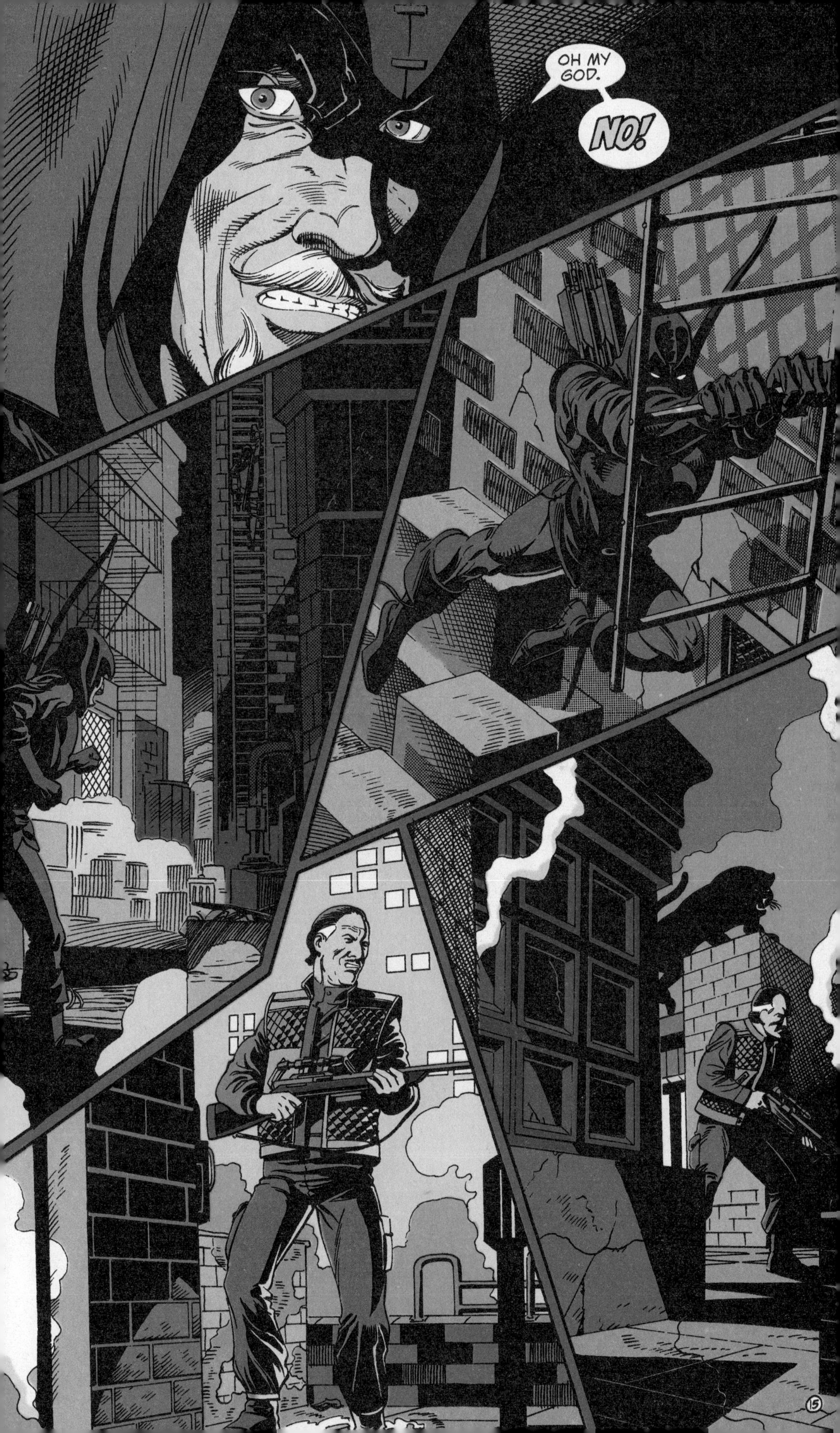
OH MY GOD.
NO!

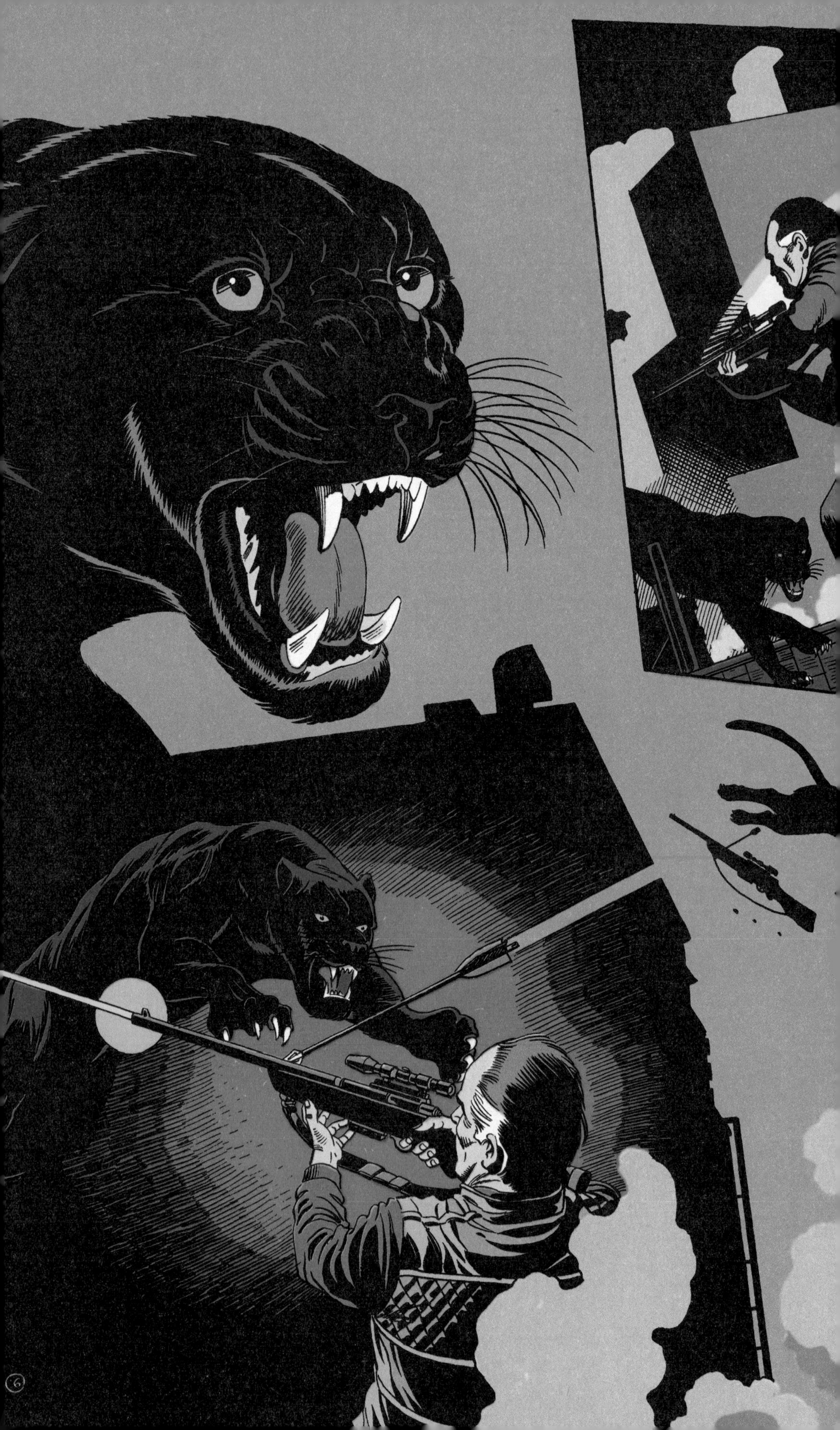

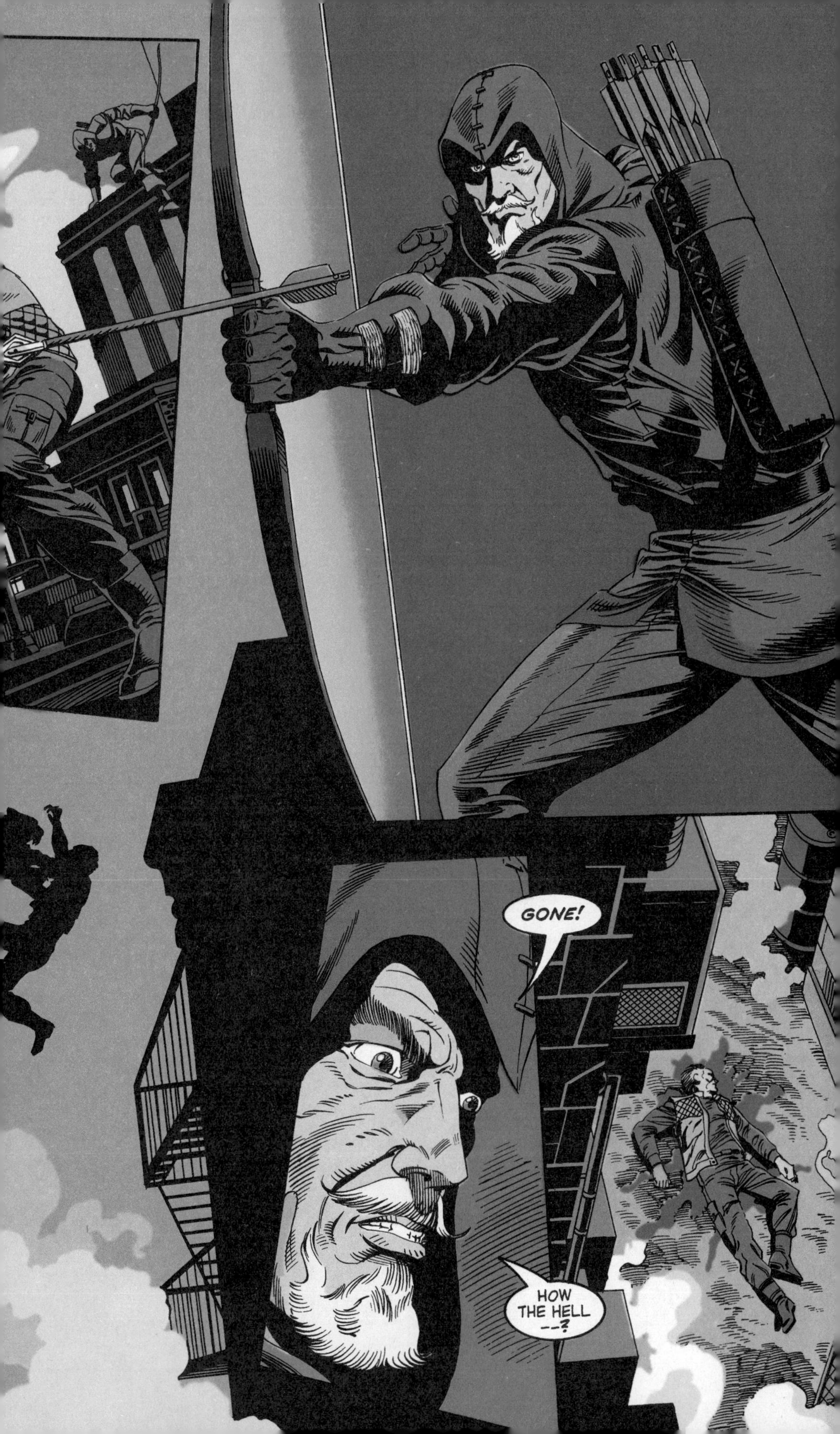
GONE!
HOW THE HELL --?

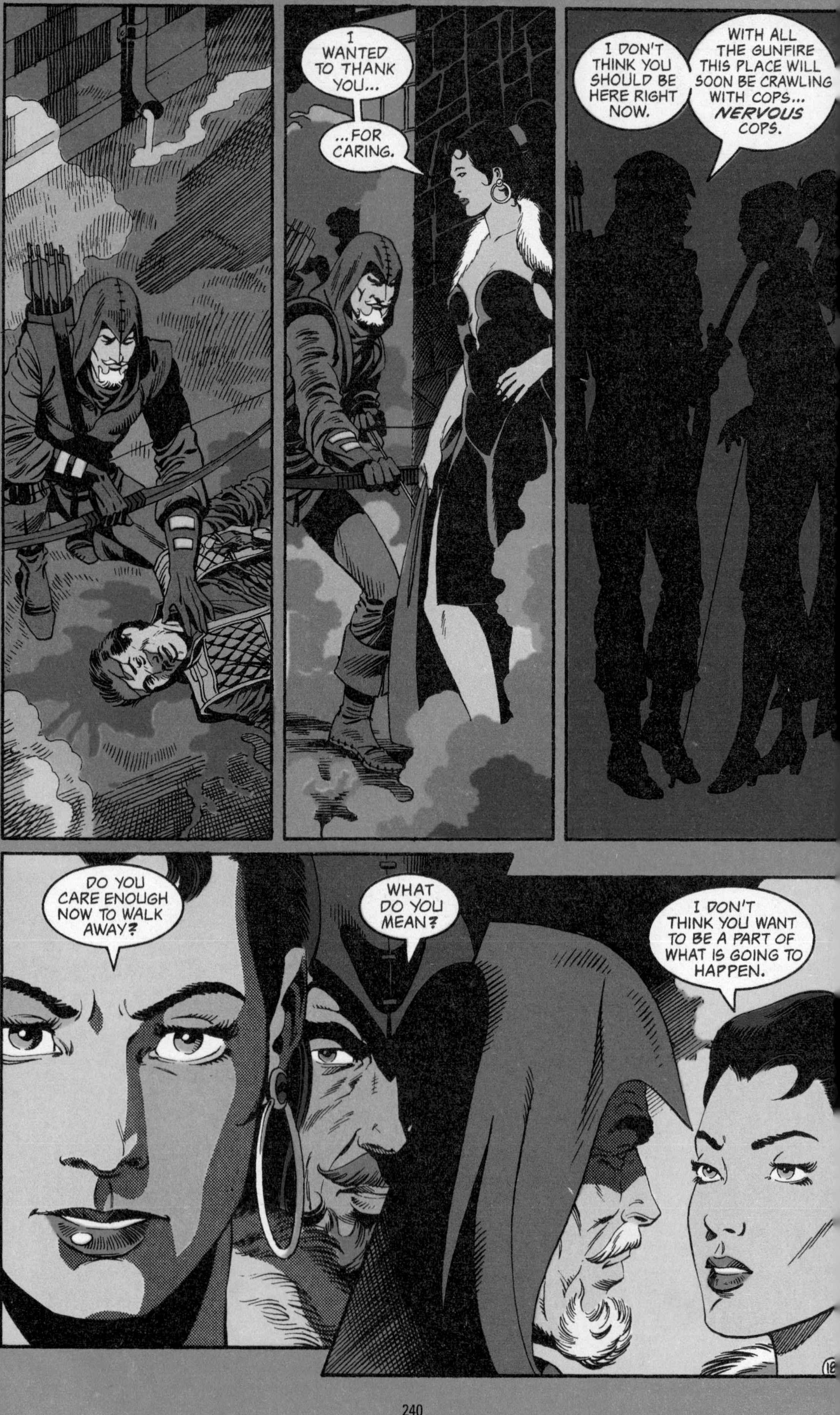
I WANTED TO THANK YOU...
...FOR CARING.
I DON'T THINK YOU SHOULD BE HERE RIGHT NOW.
WITH ALL THE GUNFIRE THIS PLACE WILL SOON BE CRAWLING WITH COPS... *NERVOUS* COPS.
DO YOU CARE ENOUGH NOW TO WALK AWAY?
WHAT DO YOU MEAN?
I DON'T THINK YOU WANT TO BE A PART OF WHAT IS GOING TO HAPPEN.
18

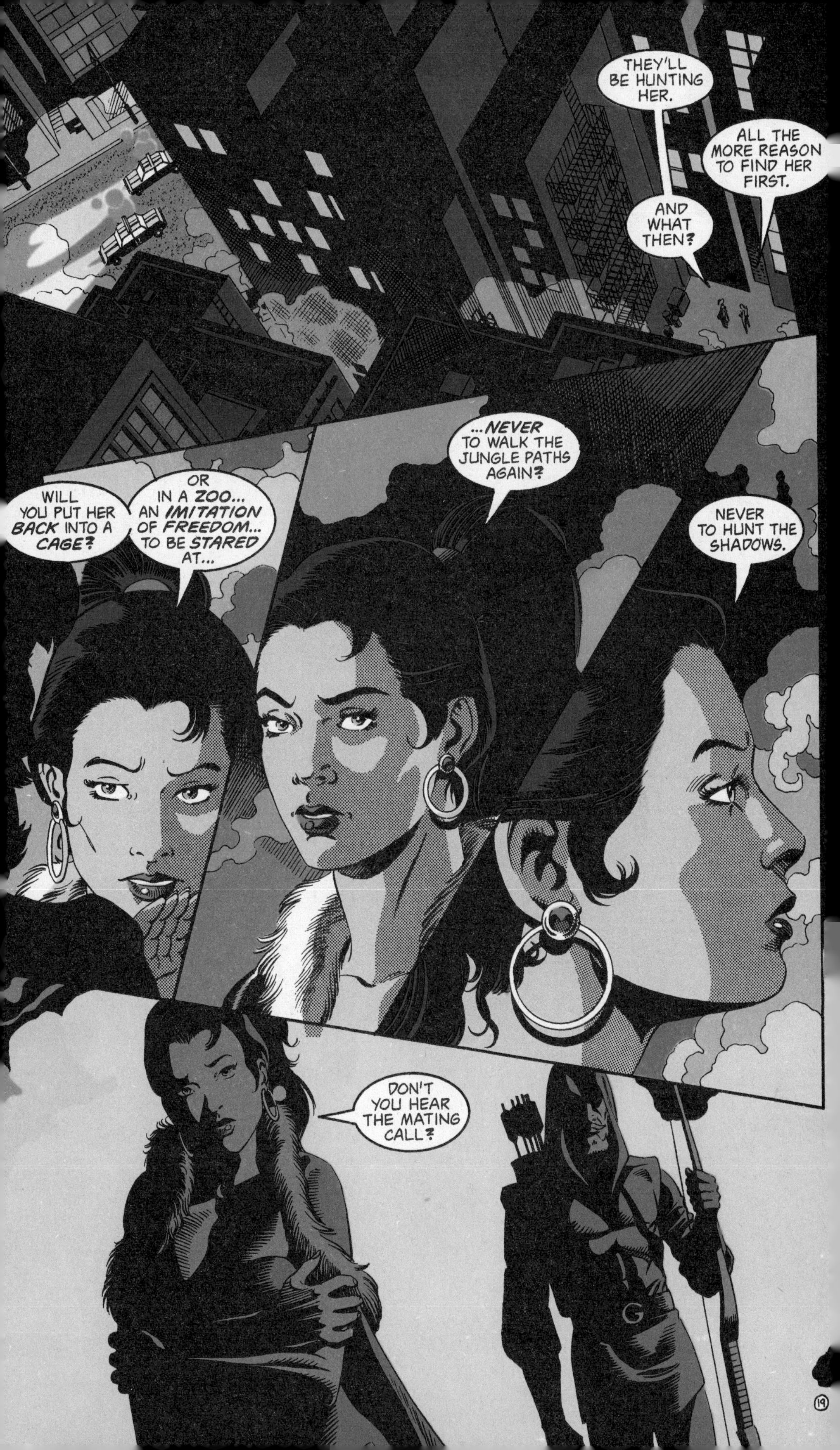

THEY'LL BE HUNTING HER.
ALL THE MORE REASON TO FIND HER FIRST.
AND WHAT THEN?
WILL YOU PUT HER BACK INTO A CAGE?
OR IN A ZOO... AN IMITATION OF FREEDOM... TO BE STARED AT...
...NEVER TO WALK THE JUNGLE PATHS AGAIN?
NEVER TO HUNT THE SHADOWS.
DON'T YOU HEAR THE MATING CALL?

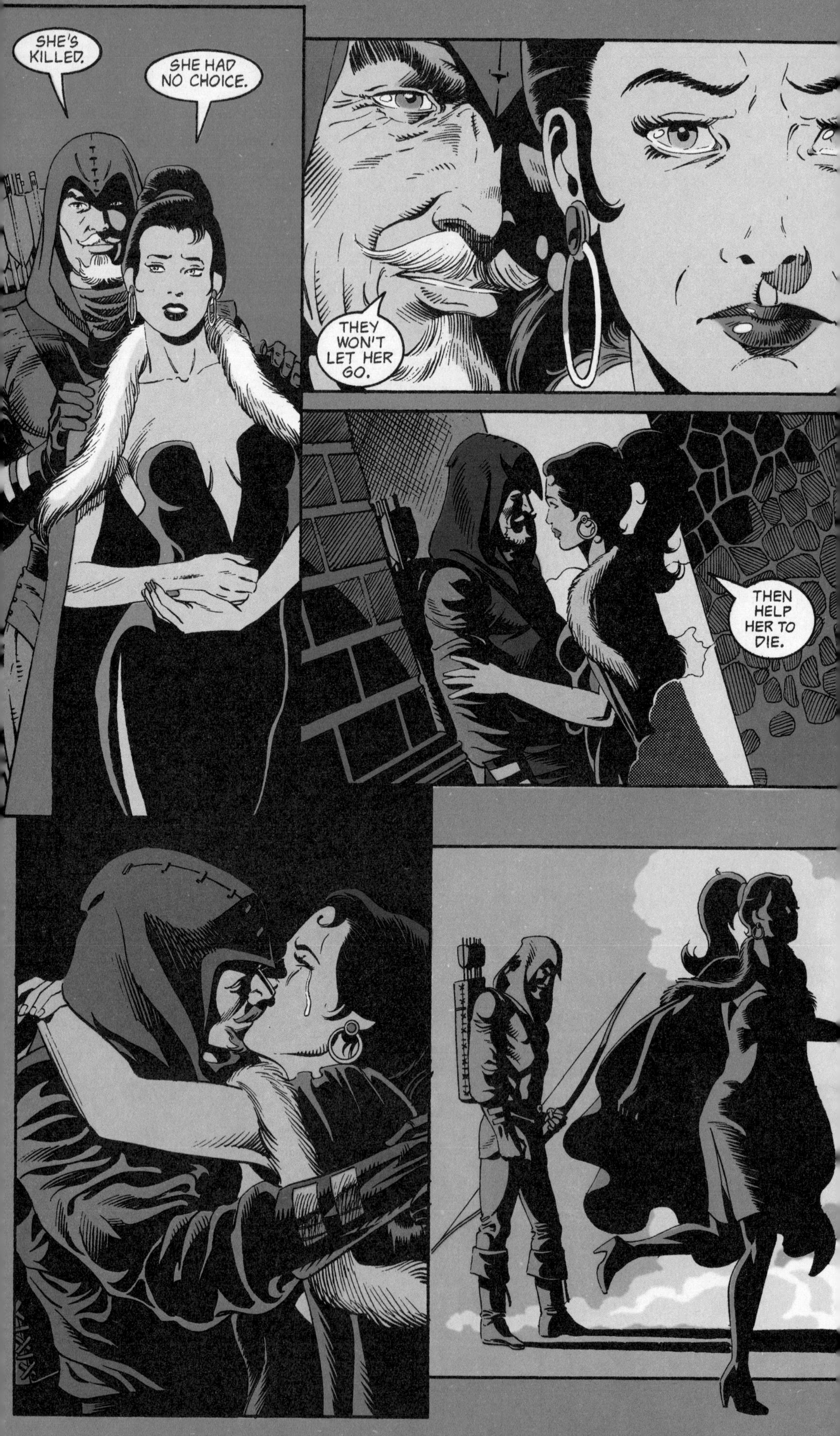
SHE'S KILLED.
SHE HAD NO CHOICE.
THEY WON'T LET HER GO.
THEN HELP HER TO DIE.

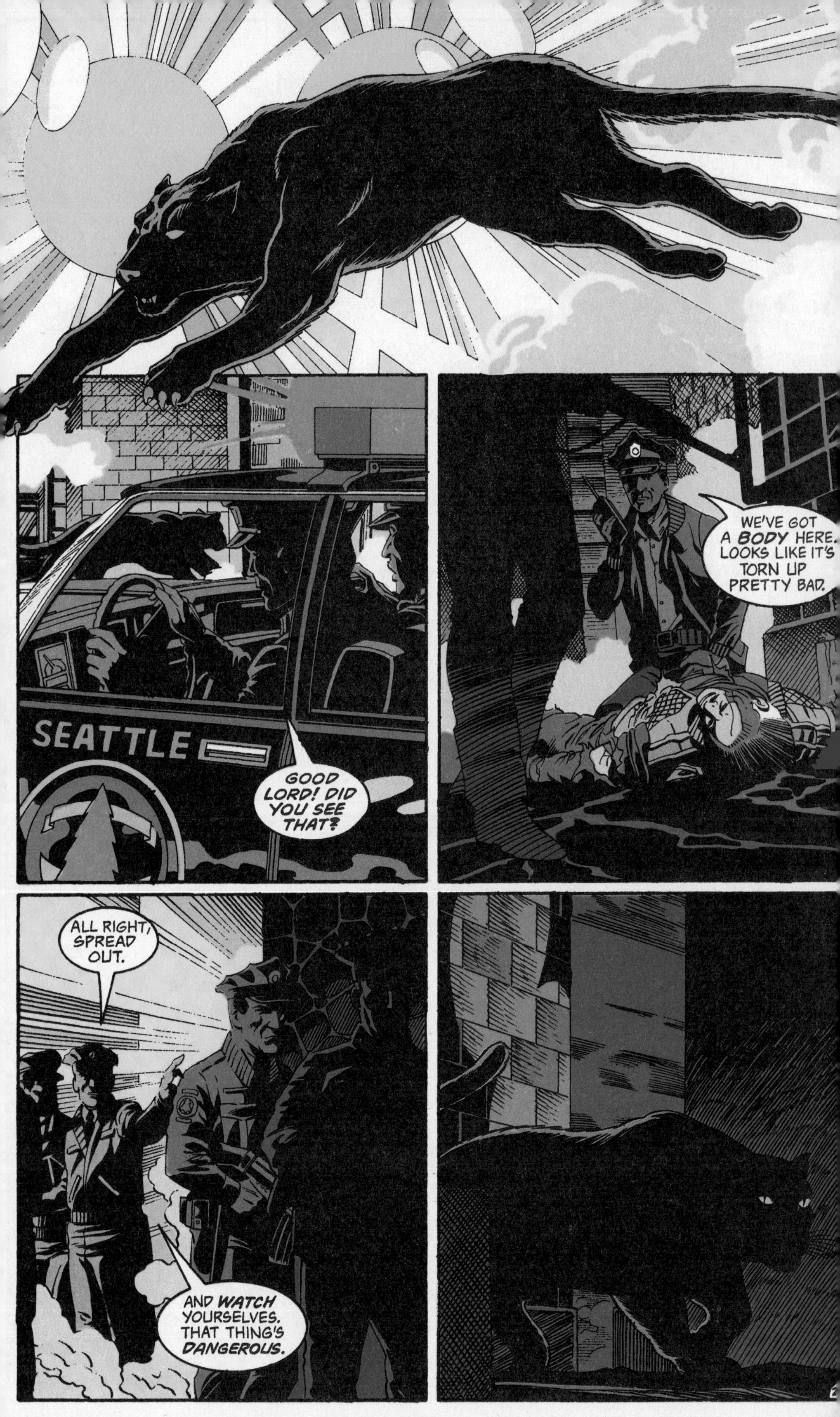
SEATTLE
GOOD LORD! DID YOU SEE THAT?
WE'VE GOT A BODY HERE. LOOKS LIKE IT'S TORN UP PRETTY BAD.
ALL RIGHT, SPREAD OUT.
AND WATCH YOURSELVES. THAT THING'S DANGEROUS.

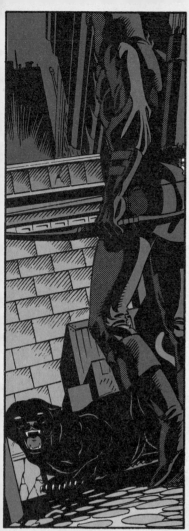
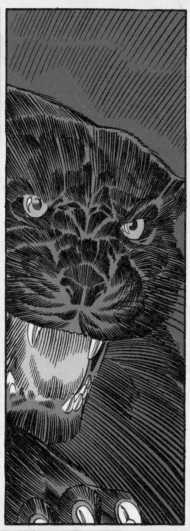
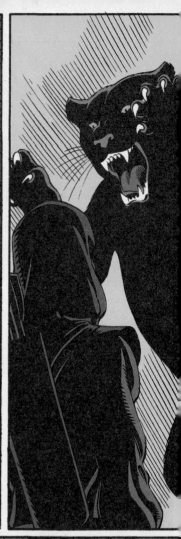
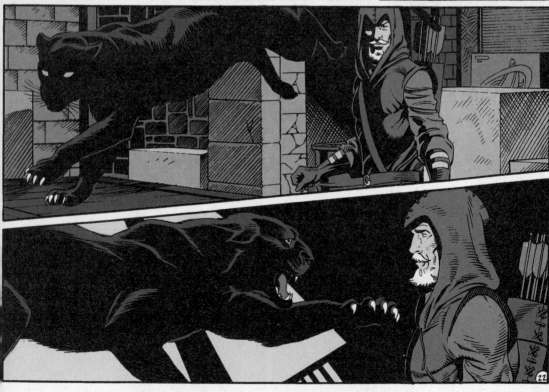

22

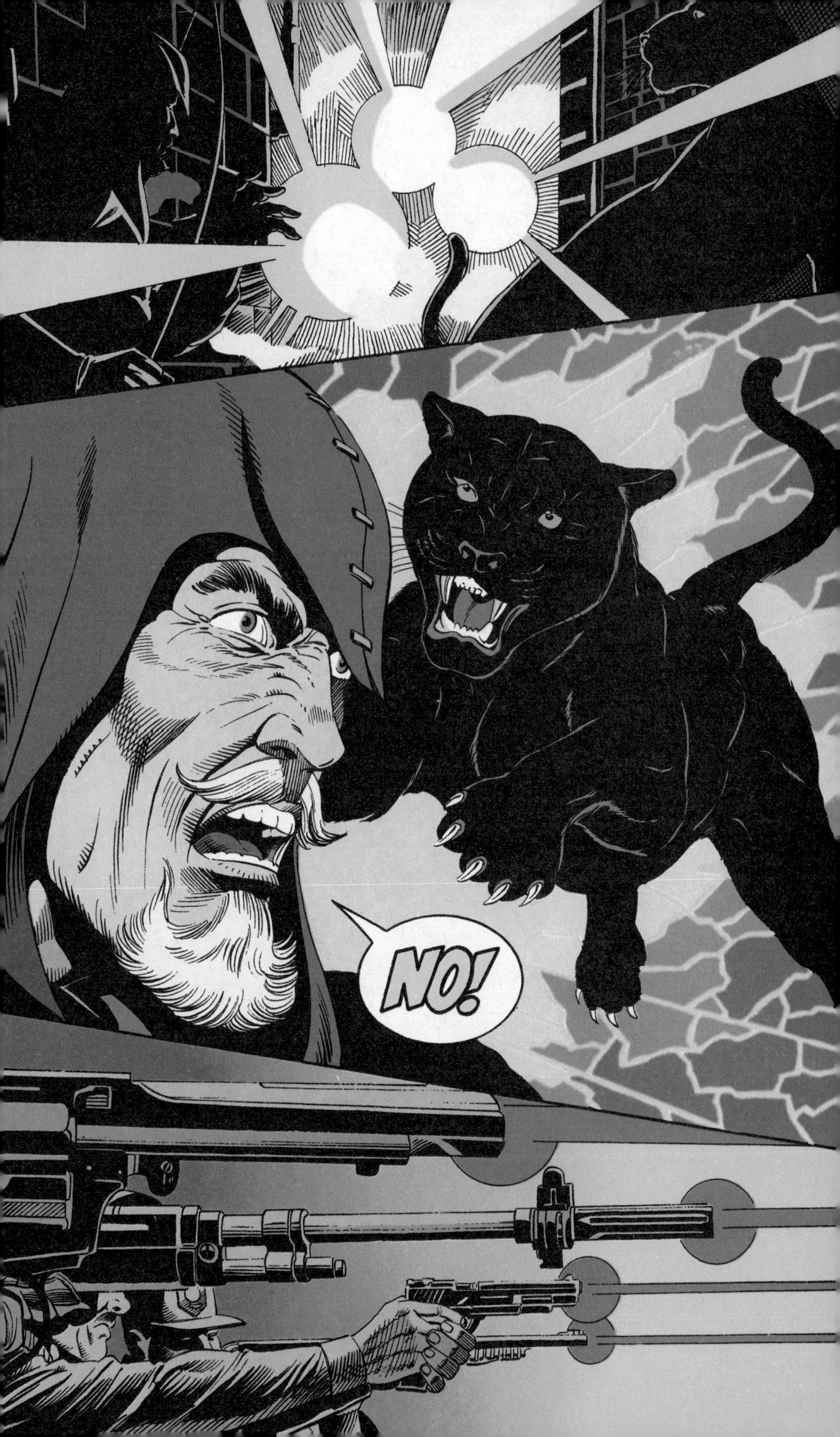
NO!

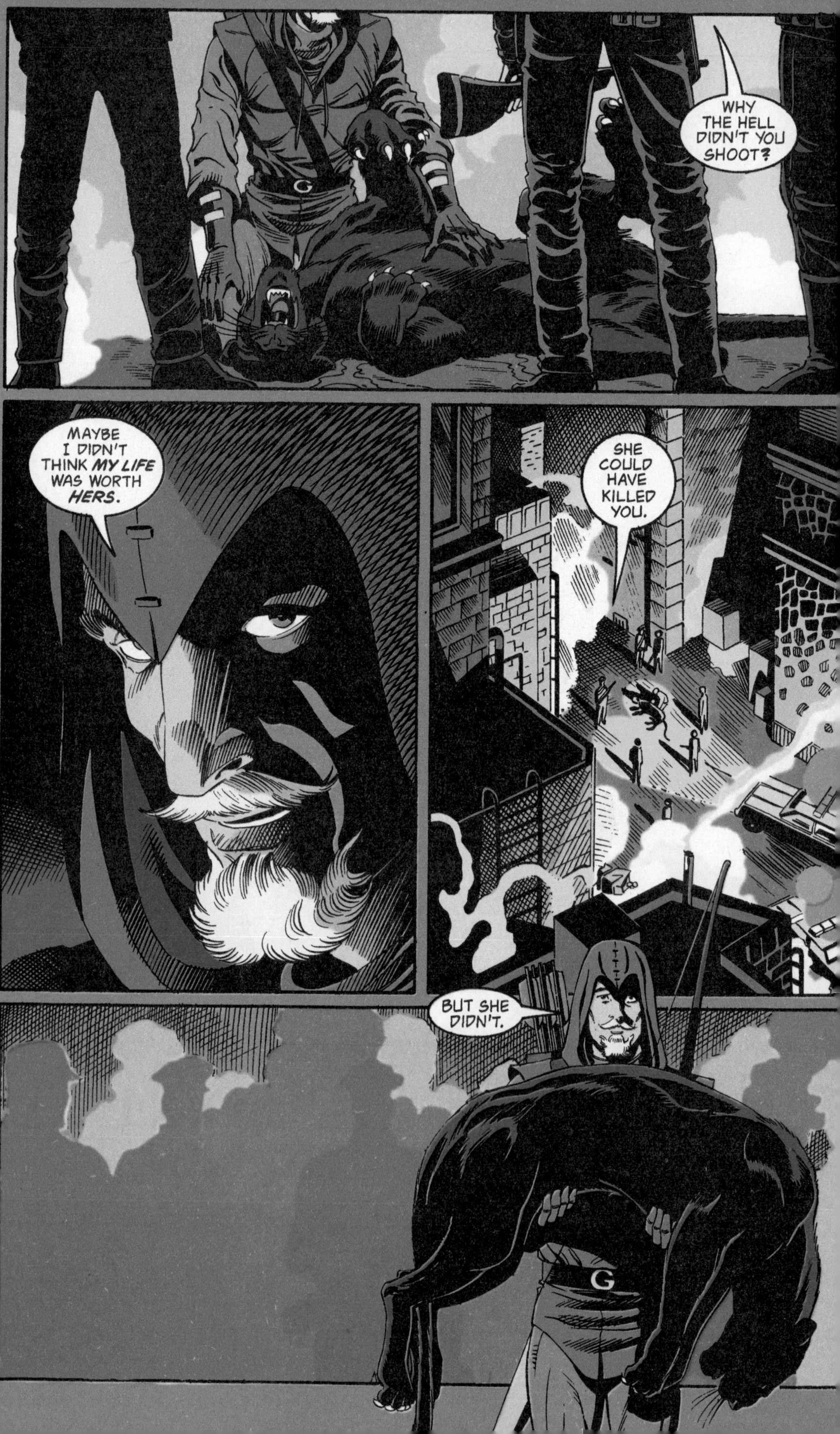
WHY THE HELL DIDN'T YOU SHOOT?
MAYBE I DIDN'T THINK MY LIFE WAS WORTH HERS.
SHE COULD HAVE KILLED YOU.
BUT SHE DIDN'T.

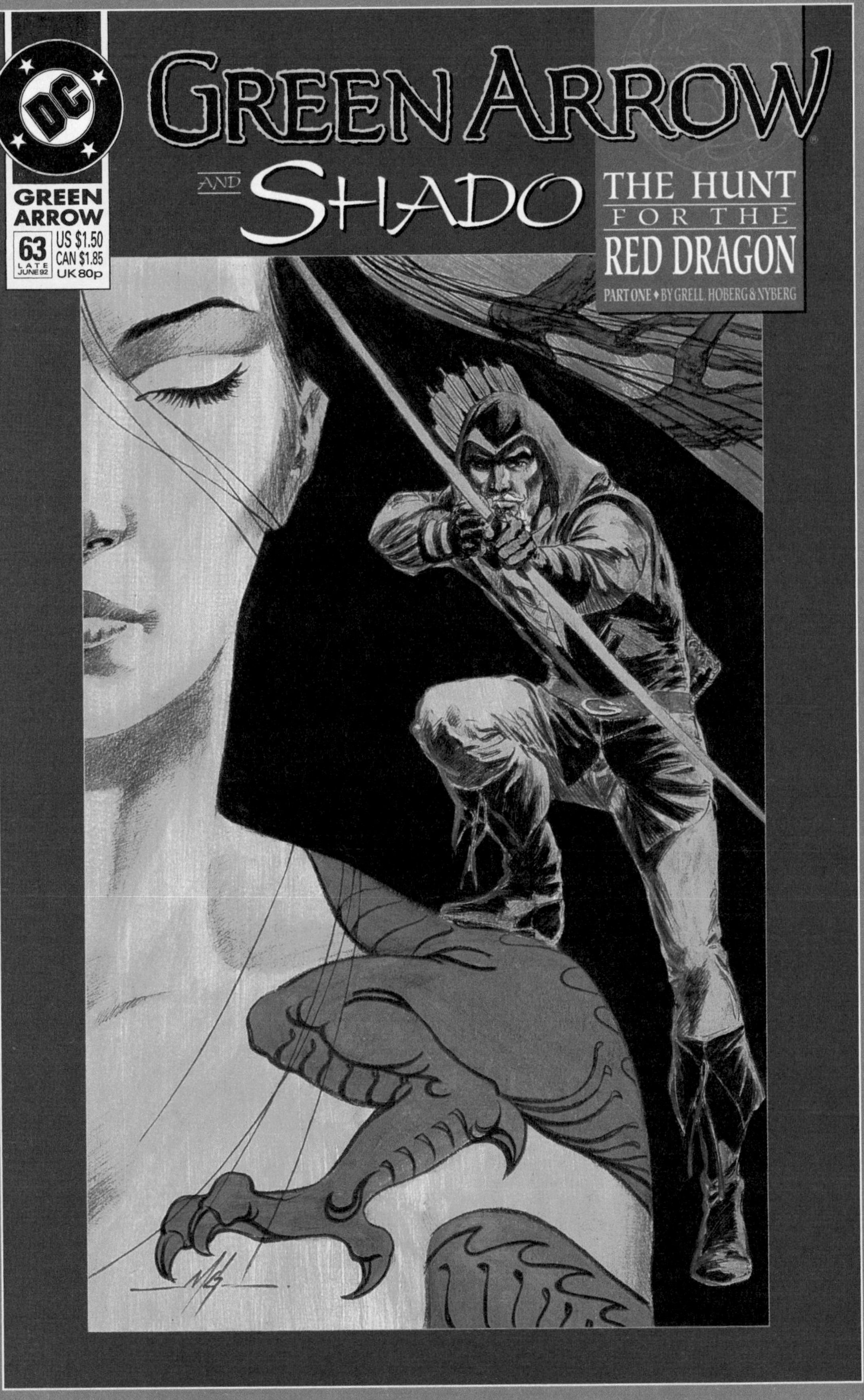
GREEN ARROW
AND SHADO
THE HUNT FOR THE RED DRAGON
PART ONE ♦ BY GRELL, HOBERG & NYBERG
GREEN ARROW
63
LATE JUNE 92
US $1.50
CAN $1.85
UK 80p

Cover art by Mike Grell

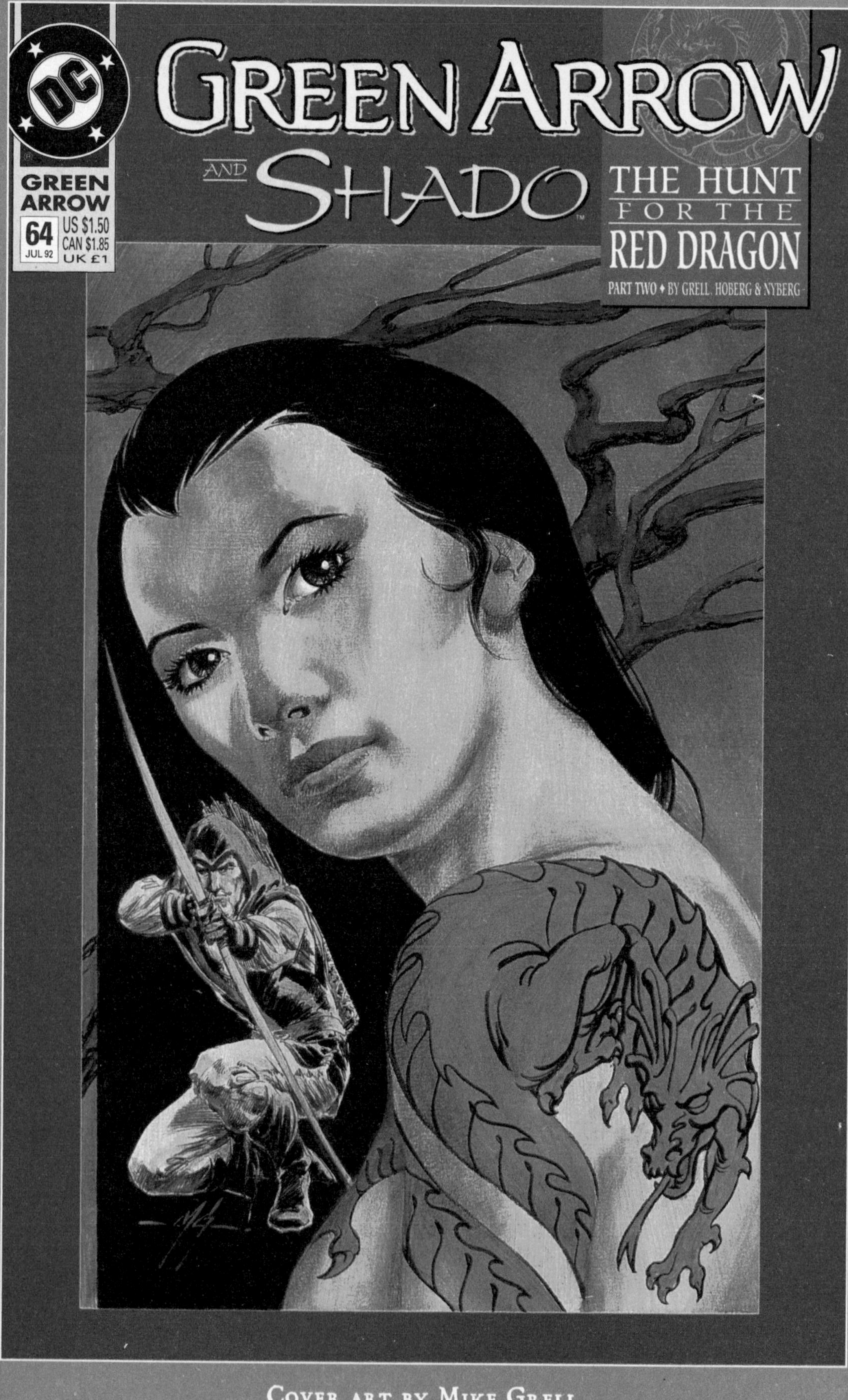
GREEN ARROW
AND SHADO
THE HUNT FOR THE RED DRAGON
PART TWO ♦ BY GRELL, HOBERG & NYBERG
GREEN ARROW
64
JUL 92
US $1.50
CAN $1.85
UK £1

Cover art by Mike Grell

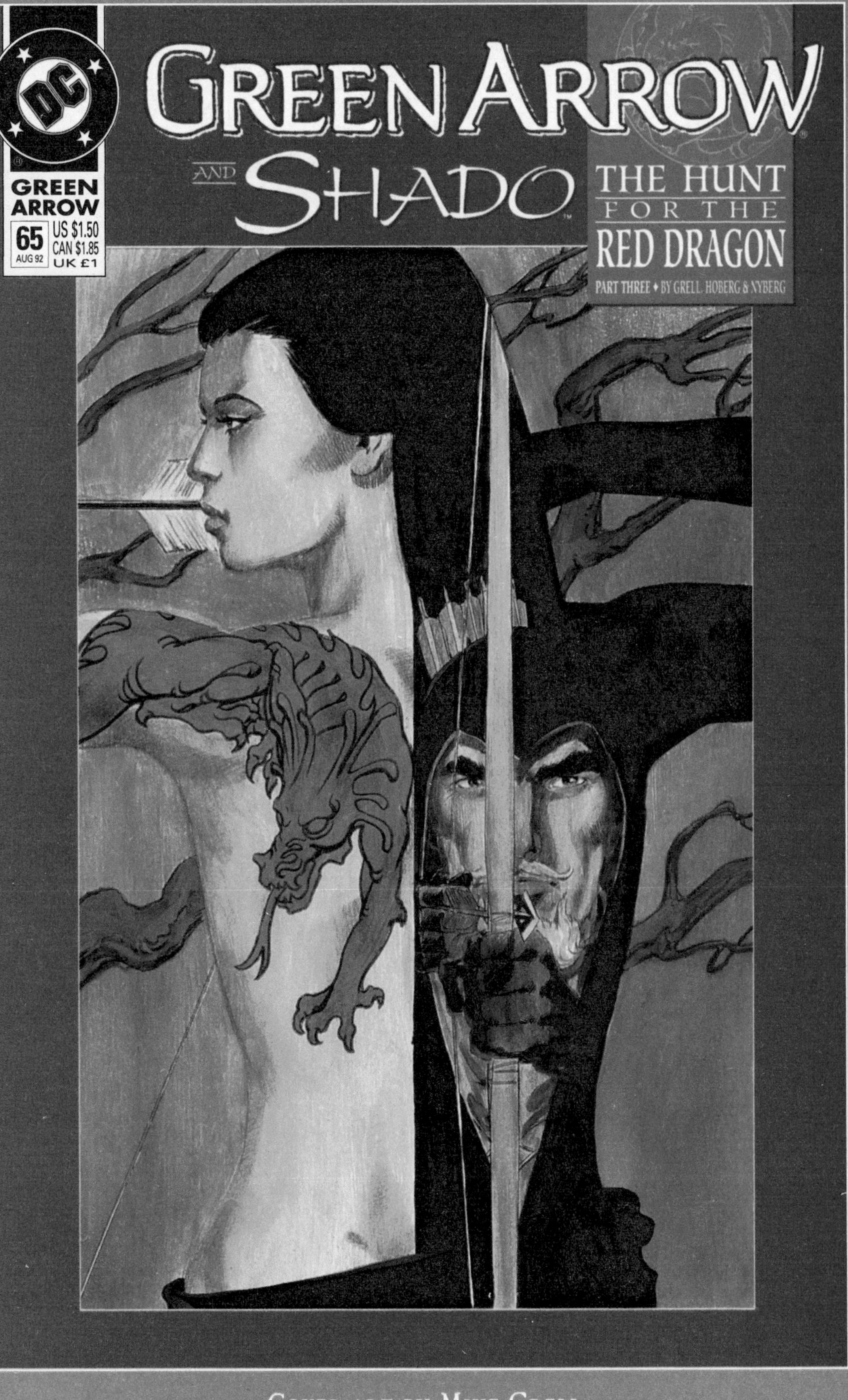
GREEN ARROW
AND SHADO
THE HUNT FOR THE RED DRAGON
PART THREE • BY GRELL, HOBERG & NYBERG
DC
GREEN ARROW
65
AUG 92
US $1.50
CAN $1.85
UK £1

Cover art by Mike Grell

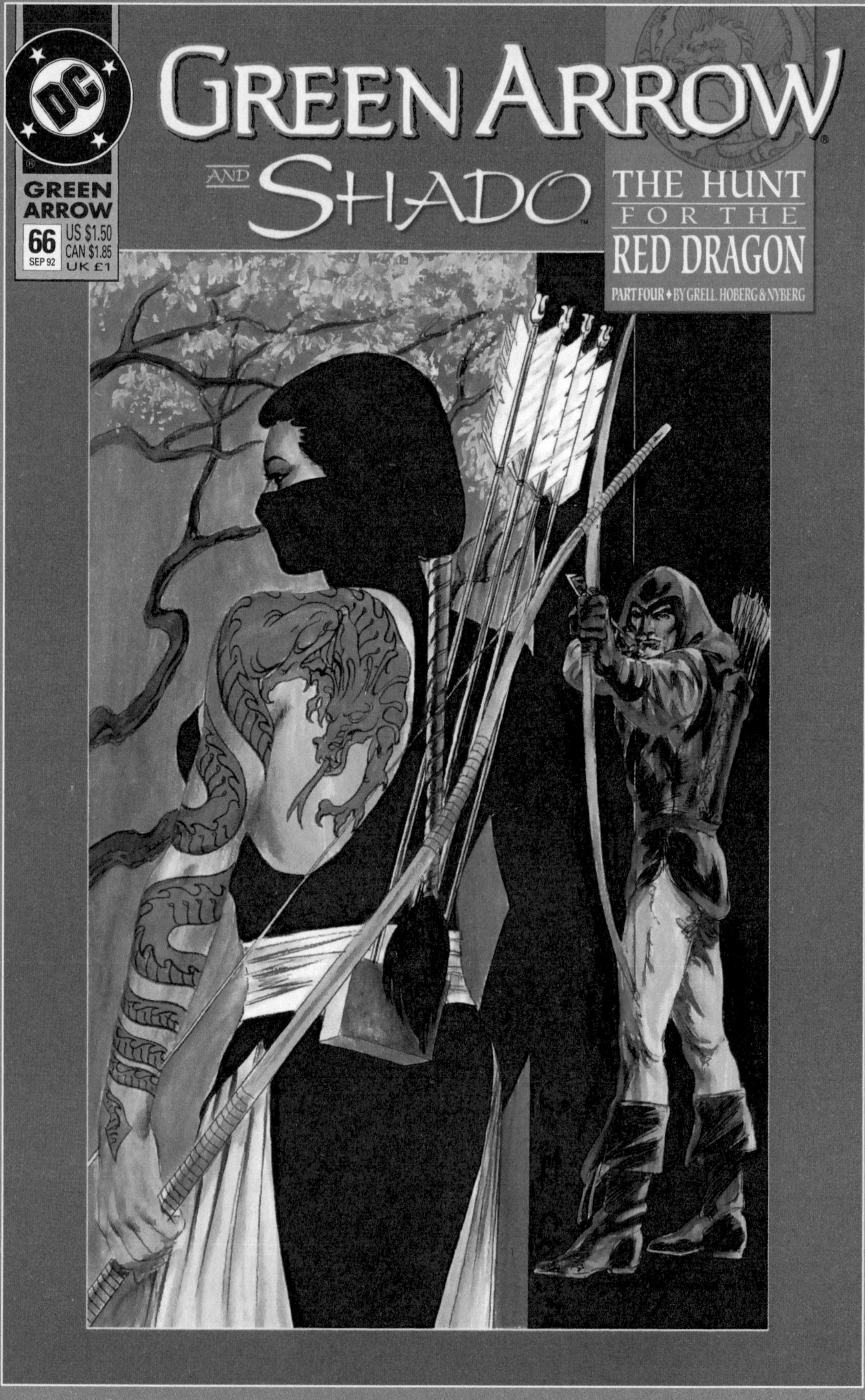
DC
GREEN ARROW
66
SEP 92
US $1.50
CAN $1.85
UK £1
GREEN ARROW
AND SHADO
THE HUNT FOR THE RED DRAGON
PART FOUR ♦ BY GRELL, HOBERG & NYBERG

Cover art by Mike Grell

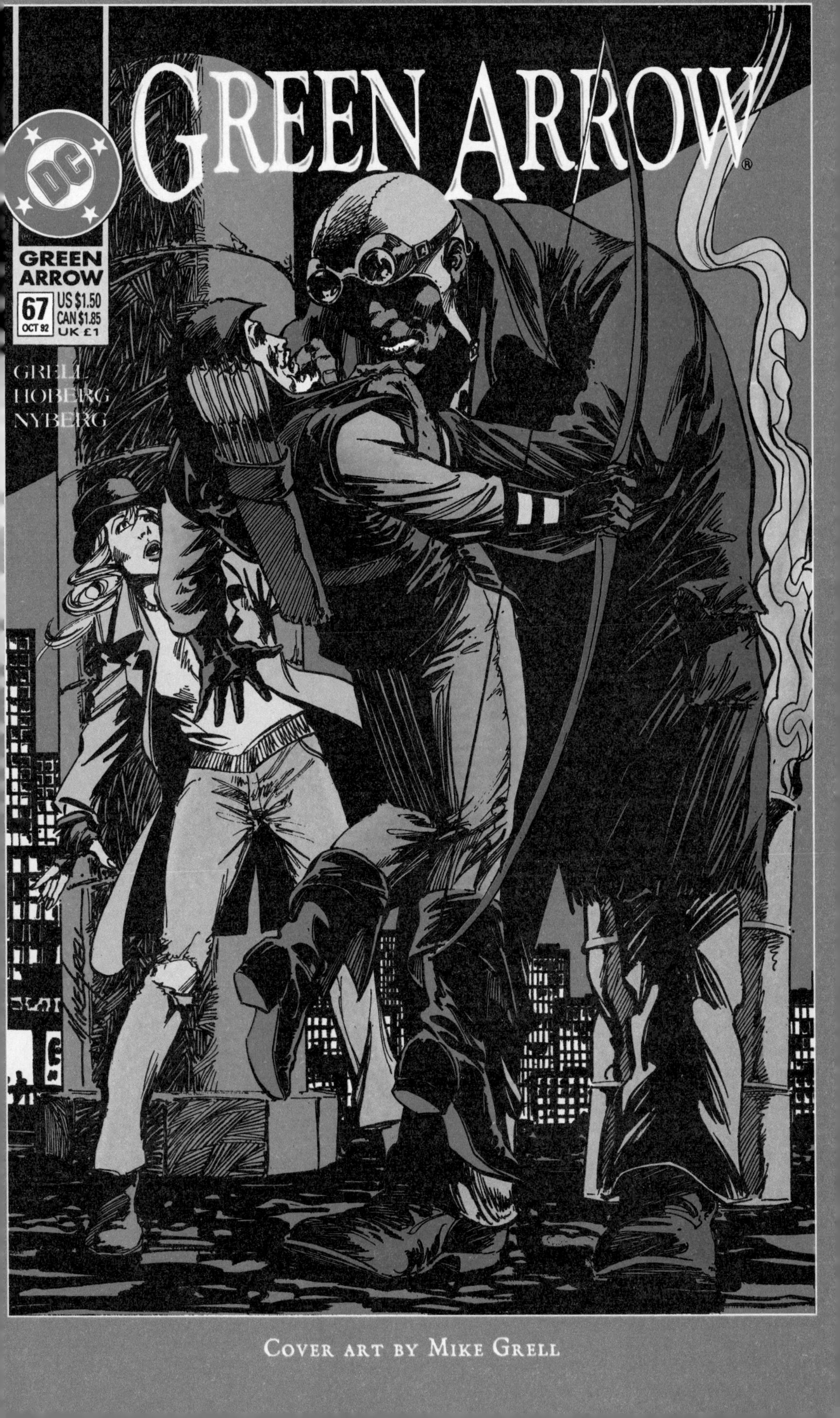
GREEN ARROW
DC
GREEN ARROW
67
OCT 92
US $1.50
CAN $1.85
UK £1
GRELL
HOBERG
NYBERG

Cover art by Mike Grell

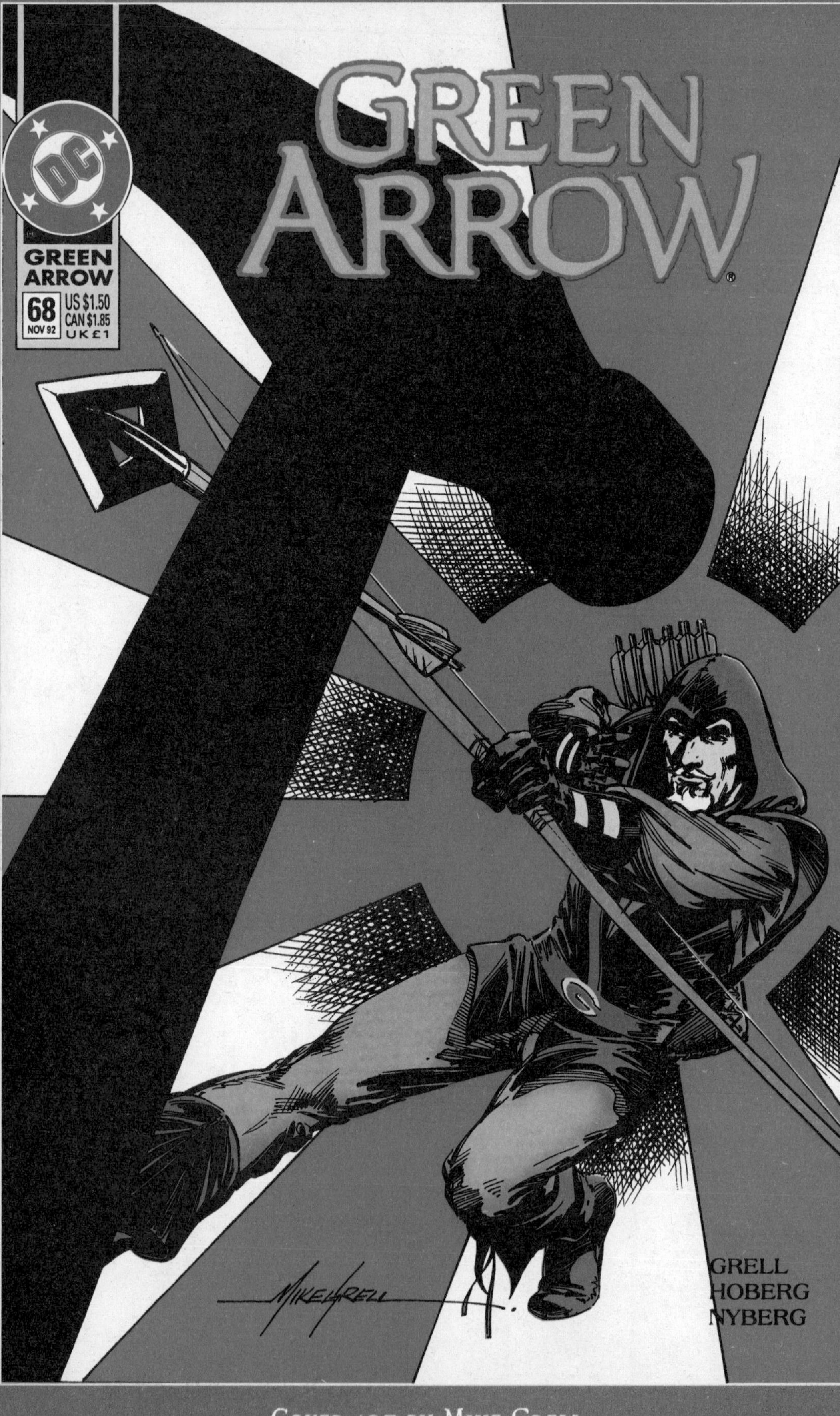
GREEN ARROW
GREEN ARROW
68
NOV 92
US $1.50
CAN $1.85
UK £1
GRELL
HOBERG
NYBERG

Cover art by Mike Grell

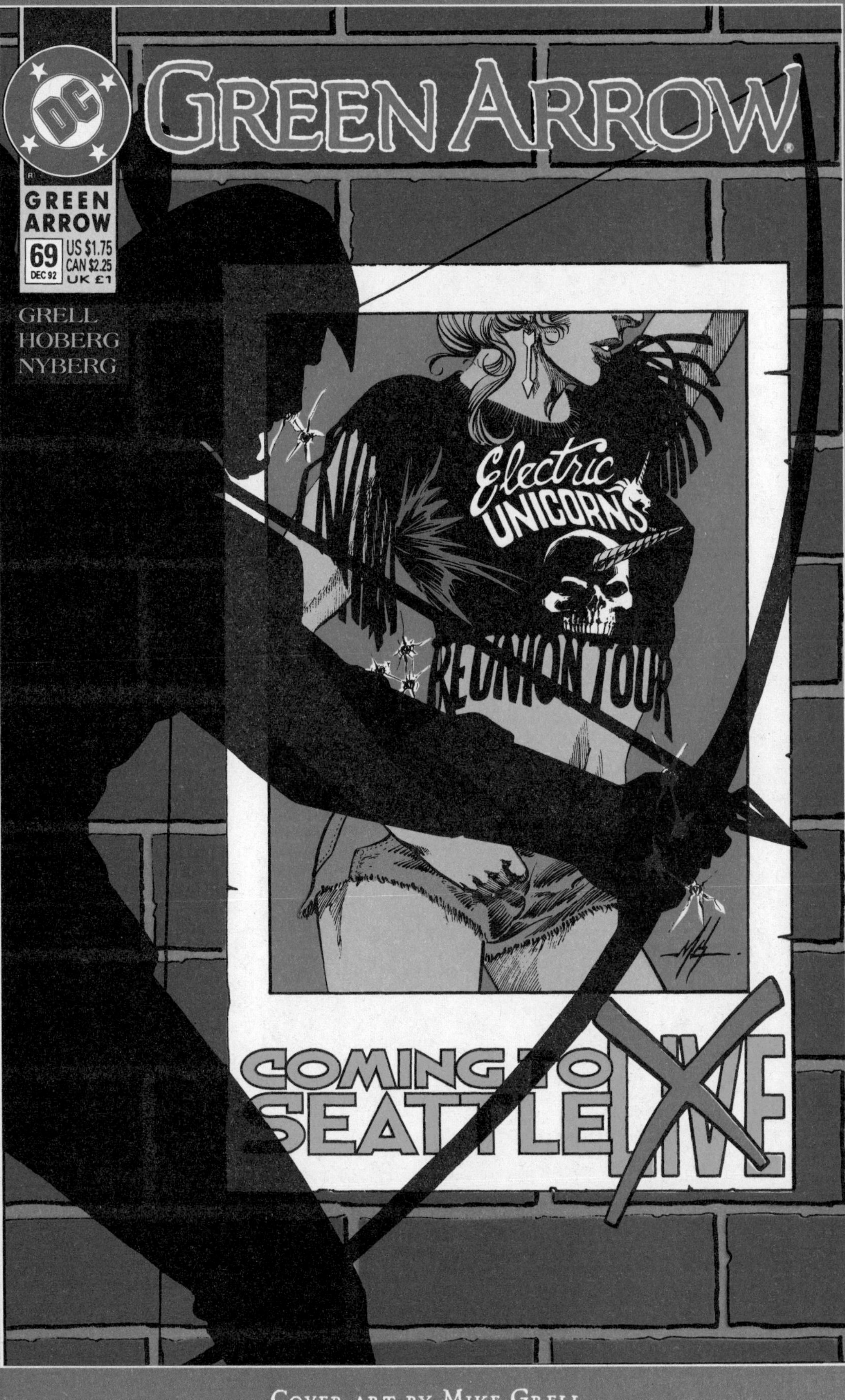
GREEN ARROW
DC
GREEN ARROW
69
DEC 92
US $1.75
CAN $2.25
UK £1
GRELL
HOBERG
NYBERG
Electric
UNICORNS
REUNION TOUR
COMING TO
SEATTLE
LIVE

Cover art by Mike Grell

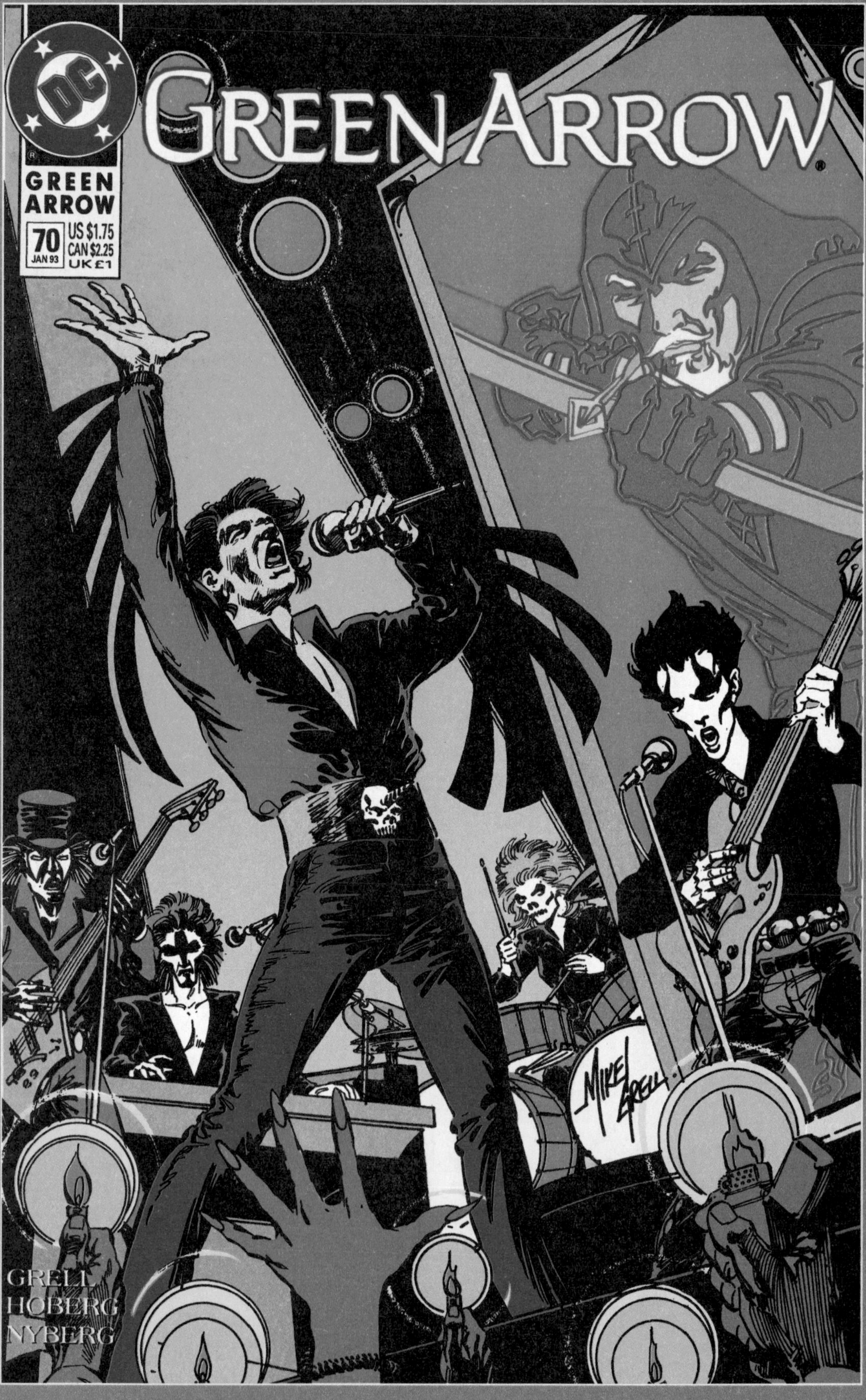
GREEN ARROW
GREEN
ARROW
70
JAN 93
US $1.75
CAN $2.25
UK £1
MIKE GRELL
GRELL
HOBERG
NYBERG

Cover art by Mike Grell

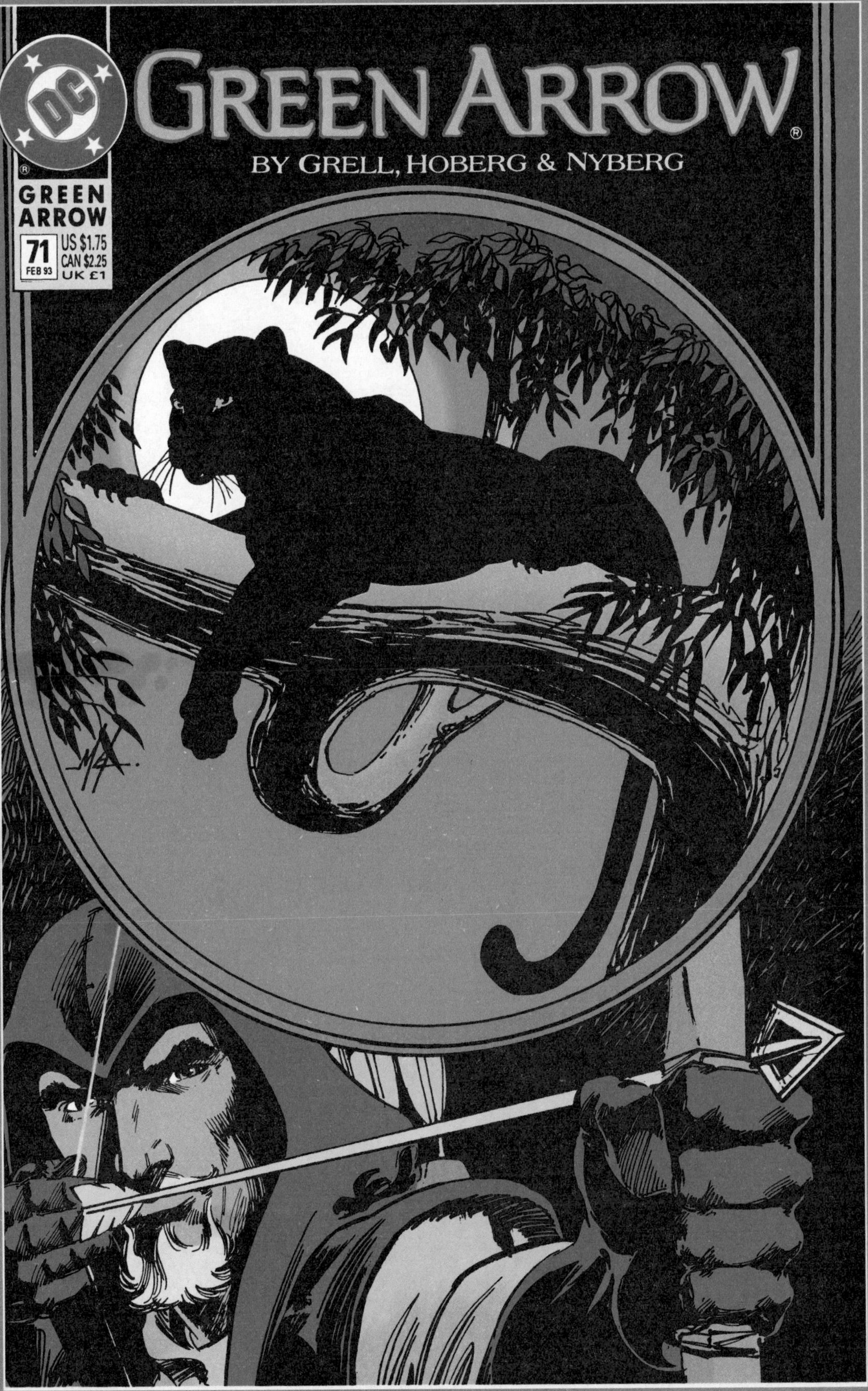
GREEN ARROW
BY GRELL, HOBERG & NYBERG
DC
GREEN ARROW
71
FEB 93
US $1.75
CAN $2.25
UK £1

Cover art by Mike Grell

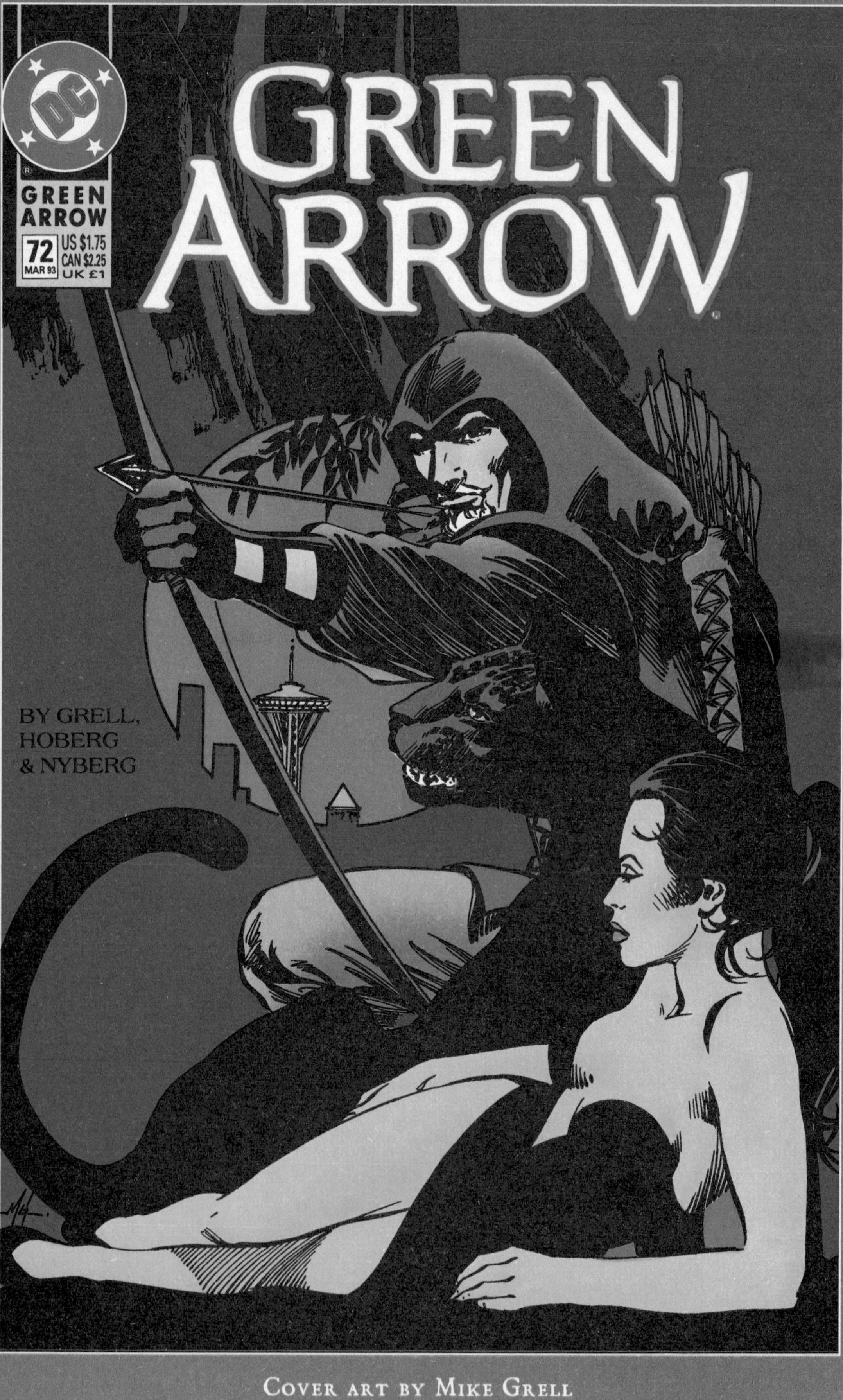
GREEN ARROW
GREEN ARROW
72
MAR 93
US $1.75
CAN $2.25
UK £1
BY GRELL,
HOBERG
& NYBERG

Cover art by Mike Grell